EX LEBRES

HE THAT COMETH

HE THAT COMETH

S. MOWINCKEL

Translated by
G. W. ANDERSON

Lecturer in Old Testament Literature and Theology,
St. Mary's College, University of St. Andrews

ABINGDON PRESS
NEW YORK . NASHVILLE

PRINTED IN GREAT BRITAIN
BY WESTERN PRINTING SERVICES LTD. BRISTOL

THIS VOLUME IS DEDICATED
TO THE
REVEREND G. W. ANDERSON
IN FRIENDSHIP AND
GRATITUDE

Author's Preface to the American Edition

This book originated in a series of lectures delivered in the early years of the Second World War to theological students at the University of Oslo. After the War, when normal communications with other countries were restored, and the most recent literature on the subject became accessible, it seemed desirable to discuss various theories which had been advanced by other scholars. This explains the extensive notes, which are carried at the bottom of the page in order not to cumber the actual text of the book with the details of technical discussion. The translation has been made from a partly revised Norwegian text.

I am very glad to know that arrangements have been made for an American edition. Before the Second World War, it was already evident that the English-speaking countries, and not least the United States of America, had gained a leading position in oriental and Biblical scholarship, especially in the philological and archaeological fields. In the post-war years, it has been still more evident. It is also a matter for satisfaction that these advances in scholarship have been made by fruitful interconfessional co-operation, and are thus a real element in the ecumenical enterprise.

But scholarly co-operation between generations is also both rewarding and necessary. Here the European exegetical tradition, with its all-round continuity, has a value alongside the recent, fresh viewpoints and the advances which have been made in the new world. We know that we have much to learn from our collaborators across the sea. We also believe that we have something to give in return. If this book can help to promote further fruitful interchange of ideas and viewpoints, it will give me great satisfaction.

I wish to repeat here the thanks expressed in the preface to the English edition to the translator, the Rev. G. W. Anderson, for his careful and devoted work, not least for his help in checking and often correcting the many hundreds of references. As an expression of my gratitude, I dedicate this American edition to him.

SIGMUND MOWINCKEL

Translator's Preface

The present work is an examination of some of the central themes of biblical religion by one of the most influential of living Old Testament scholars. As such, it needs no commendation. It has a further interest, in that many of the theories advanced in recent years by the younger generation of Scandinavian scholars are here discussed by one who is himself a Scandinavian.

In this edition, the Old Testament is cited according to the chapter and verse divisions of the Hebrew (BH^3). Quotations from the Old and New Testaments, and from most other ancient documents, are based on the author's own Norwegian renderings. The renderings in *The Apocrypha and Pseudepigrapha of the Old Testament* I–II, edited by R. H. Charles, have been followed (with minor exceptions, which are indicated in the notes) in all quotations from these books. For permission to use them, I am indebted to the Delegates of the Clarendon Press.

It is hoped that the system of transliteration of Hebrew and other Semitic languages will be found to be both clear and consistent. But no attempt has been made to modify the familiar forms of names in the interest of consistency.

I am deeply grateful to the author for the patience and care with which he has answered my many questions. He has also read the translation. The reader may therefore be assured of its general accuracy; but for all defects in expression, the responsibility is mine.

Wherever practicable, references have been checked, and foreign works cited according to their English editions. Through the kindness of Canon E. W. Heaton, I have been able to include references to *King and Messiah* (the English edition of Bentzen's *Messias—Moses redivivus—Menschensohn*), which was still in proof when the present translation went to the printer.

I wish to thank the publisher for unfailing courtesy and patience, Professors G. R. Driver, C. R. North, and H. H. Rowley for information and advice readily given and for the loan of books, the Rev. A. W. Wainwright for undertaking a considerable part of the indexing, Mrs. M. Noble for typing a substantial part of the translation, and my wife for unstinted help in typing and checking.

Advent, 1954   G. W. ANDERSON

NOTE. The Norwegian edition of this work was published in 1951, under the title *Han som kommer*, by G. E. C. Gad of Copenhagen.

Contents

PART I

THE FUTURE KING IN EARLY JEWISH ESCHATOLOGY

xiii

CONTENTS

CONTENTS

PART II

THE MESSIAH IN LATER JUDAISM

CONTENTS

PART I

The Future King in Early Jewish Eschatology

CHAPTER I

The Term 'Messiah' and its Content

1. The Messiah an Eschatological Figure

'MESSIAH' (Greek, *Messias*) represents the Aramaic *mᵉšîḥâ*, Hebrew *ham-māšîᵃḥ*, 'the Anointed One'. The word expresses an idea characteristic of later Judaism and early Christianity. In the time of Jesus the Jews were awaiting a Messiah; and it was part of the message of Jesus, and later the central point in the teaching of His disciples, that He was this Messiah, 'He that cometh'.[1]

'Jesus Messiah', or in Greek 'Jesus Christ', were His name and His title in the speech of the community, until the term 'Christ' also came to be regarded as a personal name. In order, therefore, to understand the consciousness and the message of Jesus it is necessary to have as a background some idea of the Messianic conceptions of His time.

In later Judaism the term 'Messiah' denotes an *eschatological* figure. He belongs to 'the last time'; his advent lies in the future. To use the word 'Messiah' is to imply eschatology, the last things. It is, therefore, a misuse of the words 'Messiah' and 'Messianic' to apply them, for instance, to those ideas which were associated in Israel or in the ancient east with kings who were actually reigning, even if, as we shall see, these ideas were expressed in exalted and mythical terms. The word 'Messiah' by itself, as a title and a name, originated in later Judaism as the designation of an eschatological figure; and it is therefore only to such a figure that it may be applied.[2]

In Christian eschatology, too, the Messiah (Christ) became the central figure in the expectation of the last time. The expected day of judgement became 'the day of our Lord Jesus Christ'. That is why theologians have sometimes used the expressions 'Messianic prophecies' or 'Messianic expectations' as synonymous with 'eschatological expectations'. This is done by F. Delitzsch

---

[1] Matt. xi, 3; Luke vii, 20.   [2] See Additional Note 1.

and F. Buhl in their books which bear this title.[1] But the use of the term is incorrect.[2] The Messiah is not the central and dominating figure in the future hope of later Judaism, and even less so in that of the Old Testament. The fact is that the Messiah as a concrete eschatological figure, the king of the final age, the founder of the glorious kingdom, is far less prominent in the Old Testament than in the New.[3] The title 'Messiah', 'the Anointed One', as a title or technical term for the king of the final age, does not even occur in the Old Testament.

Nevertheless it was above all to the Old Testament that the early Church turned for evidence in support of its belief that Jesus was the Messiah. In the thought and theology of the early Church (if it is legitimate to speak of a theology at that period) the Old Testament was the ground and source of the conception of the Messiah. A survey of Messianic conceptions in later Judaism, in the teaching of Jesus, and in the early Church must therefore of necessity begin with the Old Testament.

2. *The Messiah Originally a Political Figure*

The expression *ham-māšiaḥ* is really a shortened form of *mešiaḥ YHWH*, 'Yahweh's Anointed', i.e., the reigning king of Israel. In the ancient east both persons and things were anointed by having sweet-smelling oil poured or smeared over them.[4] For instance, the cultic stone (*maṣṣēḇâh*) was anointed; and thereby worship was offered to the deity who inhabited it or was represented by it.[5] The first anointing of the stone was regarded as the power-conferring act in virtue of which it was set apart as a holy stone; to anoint a stone meant simply to make it a holy stone. When a temple was consecrated, the building, its several parts, and the holy vessels were anointed. There are accounts of the same practice in Babylonia. Anointing was also used in cultic purification from sickness and defilement. Thus the act had a sacral

---

[1] Delitzsch, *Messianische Weissagungen*; Buhl, *De messianske Forjaettelser i det gamle Testamente*.

[2] Cf. also Gressmann, *Ursprung*, p. 7. In his *Der Messias* Gressmann does not seem to adhere so strictly to this manifestly correct terminology.

[3] See below, pp. 138ff., 210ff.   [4] See Gressmann, *Der Messias*, pp. 2ff.

[5] The *maṣṣēḇâh*, or sacred stone pillar, formed part of the sanctuary in both the Canaanite and early Israelite periods. Cf. Isa. xix, 9; see *G.T.M.M.M.* III, ad loc.; Stade, *Biblische Theologie des Alten Testaments* I, pp. 114ff., and Index, s.v.; Cook, *The Religion of Ancient Palestine in the Light of Archaeology*, pp. 8off., 96, 100, 140, 160; Albright, *Archaeology and the Religion of Israel*, pp. 42, 78, 106, 144. It symbolized the presence of the deity at the cultic site; and it is perhaps connected with the ancient stone-cult; cf. Robertson Smith, *The Religion of the Semites*[3], pp. 203ff., 456f., 568ff.; Beer, *Steinverehrung bei den Israeliten*, pp. 8ff., 12ff.

significance. The original idea was, no doubt, that the oil possessed an abnormal, 'holy' power, or 'mana', to use the familiar term from the phenomenology of religion. In the act of anointing, this power and holiness were transmitted to the person anointed, or the holiness and supernatural power with which he was already endowed were renewed and strengthened. Practical experience of the power and usefulness of oil, both as a food and as a medicine, readily explains this belief in its sacral, mana-like character.

Among all the persons and objects which may be anointed there is one who is 'Yahweh's Anointed' in a special sense, one who is 'the Anointed', namely the king. In the Old Testament the primary and proper sense of the expression 'Yahweh's Anointed' is the king, the earthly king who at any given time is reigning over Yahweh's people. The expression implies his close relationship to Yahweh, the sacral character of his office and his person (as priest-king), and the abnormal endowment of holy power which is his because he has been anointed king. The essential characteristic of a king is that he has been anointed. The Israelite speaks not of crowning a man, but of anointing him in the sense of making him king (himlîk).

The custom of anointing the king in order to install him in his sacred office was taken over by the Israelites from the inhabitants of Canaan.[1] It is presupposed in the Amarna Letters (the correspondence from the vassal princes in Canaan to their overlord, the king of Egypt, dating from the fifteenth and fourteenth centuries B.C.);[2] and there is also some evidence that it was practised in Egypt and Assyria. The references to anointing in connexion with Melchizedek, king of Jerusalem,[3] and with Phoenician kings, show that it was primarily as a priest-king that a king was anointed, that is, as a sacral king who represented his people before the deity, and thus also took a leading and active part in the cult. Anointing made him a 'holy' person, similar to the priest in character and function. In practically every passage in the Old Testament where the expressions 'Yahweh's Anointed', or 'the Anointed One', occur, the reference is to the reigning king of David's line, the king in Jerusalem, designated, installed, and anointed by Yahweh through His cultic representative the priest. For a prophet to perform the anointing seems to have been

[1] References to sources and literature in Gressmann, Der Messias, pp. 5f.
[2] The best edition of the Amarna Letters is still the one by Knudtzon in V.A.B.
[3] Gen. xiv, 18; Ps. cx, 4.

irregular and exceptional; and, in the main, only usurpers were so anointed. Samuel is regarded as a priestly seer, not as a *nābī'* (prophet).[1]

Yahweh's Anointed is, of course, king of Yahweh's people Israel, or of Judah, which is also called Israel in religious usage.[2] It is quite exceptional for a prophet like Deutero-Isaiah, in the exuberant enthusiasm of his faith, to call a heathen king like Cyrus 'Yahweh's Anointed',[3] because Yahweh has made him king in order to fulfil His plan for Israel. This use does not help to define the meaning of the term.

In the post-exilic age the High-priests became in many respects the heirs of the kings. As early as the period of the monarchy there is evidence that the authentic professional priesthood tried to exclude the king from the exercise of cultic functions. This was a stage in the struggle of the Levitical or Leviticized priesthood[4] to monopolize the cult. Both in the legend about King Uzziah's leprosy[5] and in Ps. cx we have echoes of rivalry of this kind between the king and the priesthood. In the post-exilic age it was established that the cult was the exclusive privilege of the priesthood; and the High-priest claimed kingly status through his anointing and the wearing of the diadem.[6] In time it became customary to anoint all priests when they were installed in their office.[7] Thus the original sacral significance of the custom survived and prevailed, when the political monarchy had disappeared, and the High-priest's claim to political power remained little more than theory. 'The Anointed One', or the indefinite form of the term, 'an anointed one', could also be applied in the later period to the High-priest or to any priest. Usually, however, we find the explicit designation, 'the anointed priest', i.e., the High-priest.[8]

It appears that on occasion prophets also were anointed when they were consecrated and admitted to the prophetic guild.[9] It is

[1] 1 Sam. ix; see *Ps.St.* V, pp. 20f., 24f.
[2] See Rost, *Israel bei den Propheten*, p. 115; Danell, *Studies in the Name Israel in the Old Testament*, p. 291 and passim. [3] Isa. xlv, 1.
[4] On the spread of Levitical ideas and ideals among the Israelite priesthood see Meyer, *Die Israeliten und ihre Nachbarstämme*, pp. 85, 90f., 138, 167; Hölscher, *Die Profeten*, pp. 166ff.
[5] 2 Chron. xxvi, 16ff. [6] Exod. xxviii, 36ff.; xxxix, 30ff.; Lev. viii, 9.
[7] Exod. xxix, 21; Lev. viii, 30. We find among the Mandeans an interesting parallel to the transference to the priest or the High-priest of the ideology and ritual of priesthood; see Engnell, *Divine Kingship*, p. 17 n. 6, with references.
[8] Dan. ix, 25ff.; Lev. iv, 3, 5, 16; xvi, 15.
[9] 1 Kings xix, 16. On the organization of 'temple prophets', see Mowinckel in *N.T.T.* x, 1909, pp. 198ff.; *Ps.St.* III; Johnson, *The Cultic Prophet in Ancient Israel*; Haldar, *Associations*.

to this custom that the prophet alludes in Isa. lxi, 1: 'Yahweh has anointed me.' Consequently we find one incidental example in late linguistic usage, and in the idiom of religious poetry, of Yahweh's calling the patriarchs 'Mine anointed ones':[1] in the later Old Testament period and subsequently, all the great religious figures of the past, 'the patriarchs', were regarded as prophets.

At one time many scholars maintained that the term 'Yahweh's Anointed' could denote the Israelite people.[2] This view was based on erroneous exegesis, and in part on erroneous assumptions about the date of the sources, particularly of the Psalms.

The expression 'the Anointed One' does not occur in the Old Testament as a technical term for the Messiah. On the other hand, 'the Anointed One', or 'His', or 'My Anointed One' does occur as the ceremonial religious title of the reigning king in Israel, king 'by the grace of God'. To the content of this title we shall return below (pp. 56ff.). It is, however, obvious that there must be a historical connexion between the two titles; and there can be no doubt which is the older. As title and name for the eschatological king, Messiah does not occur in the Old Testament, but appears first in the literature of later Judaism; and as we have already seen, the word 'Messiah' is an abbreviation of the fuller expression, 'Yahweh's Anointed'. This shows that the eschatological Messiah derived his name from the sacral title of the ancient kings of Israel.

This historical association of ideas is further corroborated by the fact that the Messiah was not only an eschatological figure, but always had a measure of political significance. The Messiah is he who shall restore Israel as a people, free her from her enemies, rule over her as king, and bring other nations under her political and religious sway. This conception of the future king as a this-worldly political figure is clearly and explicitly present in most if not all of the passages in the Old Testament which refer to him. According to the express testimony of the evangelists it was against this political conception of the Messiah, present in the minds and thoughts of the disciples and of the multitude, that Jesus had to contend. Just as the word 'Messiah' has an eschatological character wherever it has become a clearly defined term, so too it has a political sense from the beginning.

---

[1] Ps. cv, 15 = 1 Chron. xvi, 22.
[2] See, e.g., Gesenius-Buhl[16], s.v., 2; Buhl, Psalmerne[1], on Ps. ii; similarly Wellhausen, Skizzen und Vorarbeiten VI, pp. 163ff.; Baethgen, Die Psalmen[3]; and other older commentaries on the Psalms.

Both the term and its content reveal a clear connexion between the idea of the Messiah and the Old Testament conceptions of 'Yahweh's Anointed', the earthly king of Yahweh's people. What is the character of this connexion; and what is the difference between the two ideas? In other words, in what way did the concept of 'Yahweh's Anointed' develop, so that the earthly, political king became the eschatological figure? Is this an instance of development in religious thought (the word 'development' does not, of course, here imply a purely immanent evolutionary process); or is it possible that in the course of time, and as a result of certain factors in the history of religion, the term 'the Anointed One' was transferred to an eschatological figure, and that this figure existed independently of, or side by side with, the thought of the earthly and political 'Anointed One'?

In either case an examination of the political concept of 'the Anointed One' must precede any investigation and exposition of the idea of the Messiah in the Old Testament and in later Judaism. This means that at the outset we must take account of the ancient Israelite conceptions of the king and of kingship. But Israel took over the monarchy and many of the ideas associated with it from the older civilized nations which were her neighbours. If, then, Israelite conceptions of kingship are to be rightly understood, it is essential to relate them to the general oriental background.

But we must also try to ascertain to what wider religious context the idea of the Messiah belongs. If that idea is eschatological, then it must be seen against the background of the general eschatological conceptions of the Old Testament and later Judaism; and its relation to them must be more precisely defined. Is the connexion of the Messiah with eschatology original or not? Does history show that he is an essential and indispensable element in these concepts?

In the chapters which follow, the content of the Messianic idea will be unfolded in such a way as to make it still more evident that in its strict sense it is bound up with the future hope and eschatology of Israel and Judaism. An eschatology without a Messiah is conceivable, but not a Messiah apart from a future hope. All genuine Messianic prophecies in the Old Testament point forward.

But can it be taken for granted that Jesus simply took over the ideas about the Messiah (in the strict sense) which were to be found in the Old Testament? Clearly He did not. Between them there lies the entire development of intertestamental Judaism.

8

THE TERM 'MESSIAH' AND ITS CONTENT

The Messianic concepts of later Judaism are readily seen to have developed in many ways beyond those of the Old Testament, and indeed to be in a measure different in character. It will become apparent that thoughts derived from many quarters and from many other religious figures were laid under tribute before the conceptions of the Messiah reached the stage at which we find them in the time of Jesus. But it goes without saying that the later Jewish Messianic ideas form the most natural background to those of Jesus Himself. It was to those current Jewish conceptions which His disciples held that He had to relate His own thought of Messiahship, in part positively by confirming them, in part negatively by correcting them. The New Testament documents themselves readily make this clear.

But the very fact that Jesus related His teaching both positively and negatively to the Messianic ideas prevalent in later Judaism shows that He did not adopt them just as they were. The Gospels depict Him as constantly in conflict with certain aspects of the Jewish Messianic ideal which was in the minds of His disciples. This raises a new problem. What was the historical origin of these unusual, and possibly new, elements in Jesus' thought of the Messiah? Is it possible that, in His conflict with the Jewish Messianic ideal, Jesus adopted other biblical or late Jewish ideas which had, perhaps, originally no connexion with the figure of the Messiah, and combined them with the Jewish Messianic ideal, that He might use it to express His own thought of His person and vocation? We shall see that this was so. This is true not only of the thought of 'the Son of Man', which was already associated with the idea of the Messiah in some circles in later Judaism, but above all of the presentation of the suffering and atoning 'Servant of the Lord' in Deutero-Isaiah.

CHAPTER II

Survey of the Material

TO understand the Messianic faith of the Old Testament and of later Judaism we must approach it historically; and every historical inquiry must begin with a critical investigation of the sources: their dates, their relation to each other, and their reliability must first be established. Only in this way is it possible to reconstruct the true historical background of an idea and of its origin, and the historical development through which it has passed. We must therefore devote one chapter to this critical examination of the sources. The reader may skip it if he wishes, or leave it to the end.

The great and decisive line of demarcation in the religious history of Israel and in the development of its religion is the Exile, the destruction of the political life of the nation and the deportation of its spiritual leaders in 598 and 587. Accordingly we speak of the pre-exilic age, the age of the monarchy, the age of the national religion of Israel, and of the post-exilic age, when the monarchy had disappeared and the national state was replaced by the Jewish religious community, which from 520 onwards was gradually consolidated in the province of Judea with Jerusalem as its centre. Besides this Judean, Jewish community in the homeland, a considerable part of the Jewish people continued to live in the Dispersion or Diaspora, the Babylonian Diaspora being the most important and for long the leading one. The spiritual and religious life of Judaism was sustained by the 'Law' and the future hope, the belief that Israel would again be established as an independent nation.

The question, 'Pre-exilic or post-exilic?' is therefore an important one if we are to date the sources which have been transmitted to us, and it provides a useful framework for arranging them. But not all the Old Testament passages which in the past have been regarded as 'Messianic' deal in fact with the Messiah and the Messianic faith. It is therefore necessary first of all to draw attention to a number of passages which have nothing to do with the subject of this book.

1. *Supposed Messianic Prophecies of Early Date*

Without more ado we begin with the passage which from early times has been regarded as the oldest Messianic prophecy, namely Gen. iii, 15, which refers to the offspring of the woman, who will bruise the serpent's head with his heel. It is now generally admitted by those who adopt the historical approach to theology that there is no allusion here to the Devil or to Christ as 'born of woman', but that it is a quite general statement about mankind, and serpents, and the struggle between them which continues as long as the earth exists. The poisonous serpent strikes at man's foot whenever he is unfortunate enough to come too near to it; and always and everywhere man tries to crush the serpent's head when he has the chance.[1]

What needs to be said of the *royal psalms* in this connexion will be reserved for later discussion.[2] They do not speak of a future, much less an eschatological, Messiah, but of the contemporary, earthly king of David's line, who has just been enthroned. The poet-prophet addresses him as 'my lord' (Ps. cx, 1), and proclaims to him Yahweh's oracle about his future as king (Ps. ii). Or the king is present in the temple and takes part in the cultic acts, presenting his offerings (Ps. xx), receiving the blessings and intercessory prayers of the people (Pss. xx; xxi; lxxii), or himself offering his psalms of lamentation and prayers for help (Pss. xxviii; lxiii), his thank-offerings and psalms of thanksgiving (Ps. xviii), or registering his promise or 'charter' before the face of Yahweh (Ps. ci).

In connexion with the royal psalms we may also refer to those *other psalms* in which traditional theology, sometimes even since

[1] See the interpretation in the commentaries on Genesis by Gunkel and Procksch, the former being what is commonly called 'liberal' and the latter 'positive'. Both in fact take the same view of Gen. iii, 15, although Procksch rejects Gunkel's treatment, and in spite of the Christian homiletical application (in itself justifiable) of the theme, which Procksch finally adopts.

[2] See Gunkel, 'Die Königspsalmen' in *Preussische Jahrbücher* clviii, 1914; Gunkel-Begrich, *Einleitung in die Psalmen*, pp. 140ff.; Mowinckel, *Offersang og sangoffer*, ch. III, with further references. The term 'royal psalms' must be taken in a much wider sense than that adopted by Gunkel or by myself in *Kongesalmerne*; see Birkeland, *Die Feinde des Individuums in der israelitischen Psalmenliteratur*. Many of the individual psalms of lamentation and of thanksgiving are in fact royal psalms, even if the worshipper does not expressly refer to himself as king; cf. next note. Engnell, however, goes too far in regarding practically all psalms with the title *leḏāwīḏ* as royal psalms (*Divine Kingship*, p. 176).

the days of the primitive Church, has found prophecies of Christ, for instance Ps. xxii with its description of the suffering of the worshipper. Of this and other similar psalms it must be said that if they may be applied to Christ at all, it is by typological interpretation and not because they are directly Christological or Messianic prophecies. That is to say that in the thought of the poet, the worshipper, and his contemporaries they have an immediate, contemporary reference; they are in fact not prophecies but prayers, issuing from a real, contemporary situation, that of the poet or the worshipper himself; and they express what he then felt, and thought, and said. The fact that the worshipper is in many instances a historical king of Israel does not alter the fundamental fact that the psalms are not prophecies but prayers with contemporary reference.[1] But the words of these psalms have proved to be more enduring and far-reaching. So powerful are they in faith and in realism that in the fullness of time they could give expression to the situation and the achievement of Jesus, His soul's conflict, His trust in God, His cry of distress, His fellowship with His brethren. The early Christian community therefore regarded them as a perfectly valid expression for what they themselves had witnessed in their Lord and Master. The worshippers of ancient times became 'types' prefiguring Christ. The words of the psalms found their true realization and fulfilment in Jesus Himself. In an account of the history of the Messianic concept all these psalms must be considered again in the appropriate context as sources or documents concerning the thoughts about the Messiah which were current in the Christian community. But of the origin and earliest history of the Messianic idea they can tell us nothing; for, in the thought and feeling of the poet and those for whom he wrote, they referred not to the Messiah but to the conditions of their own time.

Nor is any Messianic prophecy intended by the phrase in the lay of Balaam[2] about the 'star' and 'sceptre', or rather 'comet',

---

[1] The fundamentally sound view of this psalm of lamentation dates back to the last century's historical interpretation of the Bible; but it is most clearly demonstrated and worked out by Gunkel in *Die Psalmen* (on Ps. xxii) and *Einleitung in die Psalmen*, pp. 173ff. Note further that the worshipper in Ps. xxii may in fact be a king. Hitherto the most consistent demonstration that many psalms of lamentation were put into the mouths of kings is that of Birkeland in *Die Feinde des Individuums*. See now also my *Offersang og sangoffer*, ch. III, and preceding note.

[2] For the interpretation of the Balaam lays see Gressmann in *S.A.T.A.* I, 2², pp. 113ff., and Mowinckel in *Z.A.W.* xlviii, 1930, pp. 241ff. I am unconvinced by Albright's attempt (*J.B.L.* lxiii, 1944, pp. 207ff.) to date all four Balaam lays in the period between the middle of the thirteenth and the end of the twelfth century B.C.

which 'shall rise out of Israel, and shatter the temples of Moab and the skulls of the children of Sheth' (Num. xxiv, 17). Both this and the other older Balaam lay are intended as poems in honour of Israel, and are put into the mouth of the ancient, legendary Aramean seer and sage, Balaam. They tell of Israel's greatness, good fortune, and power, and of her supremacy over the other Canaanite peoples, among whom are mentioned Amalek, Moab, the children of Ammon, and Edom. It is in keeping with the character and style of this type of poetry that the poems are put into the mouth of a sage of former days, and that they take the form of a blessing (or, sometimes, of a curse) which accounts for the destiny of the people in question, whether it be good fortune or ill. Thus, because of their character, they take the form of prophecy from ancient times; but in fact it is the poet's own time or the immediate past that they thus describe. In this lay there is also an allusion (one might almost say inevitably) to David, who laid the foundation of Israel's supremacy in Canaan, and subjected Edom, Moab, and Ammon to Israel. It is to David that the poet refers when he speaks of the 'star' and 'comet' (E.VV. 'sceptre') which the ancient seer 'sees, but not now; beholds, but not nigh'.

It is in much the same way that we must interpret the expression in the *Blessing of Jacob*[1] about 'Shiloh' or 'the ruler'[2] of Judah (Gen. xlix, 10), who is to make Judah the ruling tribe among the children of Israel, and to whom the sceptre will always belong. The reference is to David, who made Judah the ruling tribe, and whose house thus won an enduring right to the throne in Israel.[3]

---

[1] For a fundamentally sound interpretation of the Blessing of Jacob in Gen. xlix and a classification of its literary type, see Gunkel, *Genesis*[4], ad loc.

[2] The word *šīlōh* does not call for emendation, nor has it anything to do with the name of the town Shiloh, as has often been supposed. It is a poetical word borrowed from Accadian, and means here simply 'his (i.e. Judah's) ruler'; Accadian *šēlu* or *šīlu* = ruler. See Nötscher in *Z.A.W.* xlvii, 1929, pp. 323ff., and Sellin's observations, ibid., lix, 1944, pp. 57f. Independently of Nötscher, Driver gives the same explanation of the word; see *J.T.S.* xxiii, 1922, pp. 69f. Eisler, too, has hit upon this explanation; see *M.G.W.J.* lxix, pp. 444f. For the application to David see the article by Sellin referred to above.

[3] When Wolff in *Z.A.W.* liv, 1936, pp. 107f., though adopting the correct historical interpretation (*vaticinium ex eventu*), nevertheless would regard these passages as 'Messianic', he is assuming a definition of the idea of prophecy which actually leads to a typological interpretation. They are 'Messianic', because they presuppose a 'Messianic' conception of, e.g., the king (see Additional Note 1), and because they

---

The allusions to David and the Israelite monarchy are too clear to be explained away. Albright also fails to notice the theological difference between the first two lays and the last two. That *šēbeṭ*, 'sceptre', in Num. xxiv, 17, must be interpreted as 'comet', has been shown by Gemser in *Z.A.W.* xliii, 1925, p. 301.

All those scholars (such as Gressmann and Sellin) who have sought to maintain that eschatology and the idea of the Messiah were ancient in Israel admit frankly that the royal psalms and the other passages mentioned above must be interpreted in historical terms. But they maintain that these poems nevertheless presuppose the existence in Israel of a conception of the Messiah, since it is in accordance with the Messianic pattern that they describe and extol David and the other historical kings, who are depicted more or less as the realization of the Messianic hope, or as kings who have attained or will attain to the heights of the Messianic ideal.

In the texts themselves there is simply no foundation for this theory; and no measure of probability can be claimed for it on exegetical grounds. Gressmann argues as follows:[1] the descriptions of kings in the Psalter include not only contemporary historical references, but also many superhuman, mythical traits which must be derived not from the earthly ruler, but from a mythical, heavenly figure. In reply to this it may first be observed that even if the figure had traits which had to be explained as borrowings from a mythical figure, from a deity of some sort, it would not necessarily follow that this figure was an eschatological Messiah, or that the king in question was thought of as a Messiah because of his borrowed divine plumes. In the second place, the strongly mythical, superhuman colouring is no proof of the existence of any other figure from which it might have been derived for the royal portraits in the psalms. The same extravagant and celestial language is applied by Babylonian and Egyptian poets to their kings; and their descriptions are not drawn from any Messiah, for these peoples had neither eschatology nor a Messiah (see below, p. 127). A comparison with the more or less divine kings of other peoples ought to make it immediately clear that the mythical traits have not been borrowed from any quarter. As we shall see below, they belong to the oriental conception of the king, simply because he was a 'divine king', a superhuman being,

---

[1] See Gressmann, *Der Messias*, pp. 7ff.; cf. *Ursprung*, pp. 251ff. In his review of *Der Messias* in *Deutsche Literaturzeitung* 13, ix, 1930, cols. 1729ff., Hölscher gives a short, pointed, and factual criticism of Gressmann's exegetical and chronological treatment of the individual passages, such as Gen. xlix and Num. xxiv, in which Gressmann thinks that the Messianic idea is presupposed.

---

were fulfilled or realized in Christ, though this was not in the mind of the writer. As elsewhere (see below, p. 172 n. 1), Wolff here treats the problem as one of Christian doctrine rather than of Old Testament criticism.

a superman endowed with abnormal gifts and power, precisely what oriental peoples meant by a 'god': a being with super-human power or 'mana'.[1] The mythical traits and colouring in the portrait of the king are derived from the divine realm, because that is where the king belongs: he has faculties, characteristics, and endowments which ancient man could express only by mythi-cal ideas and in mythical terms. They belong to the king, not because he is a Messiah, but simply because he is an oriental king.[2] We shall discuss this oriental conception of the king in greater detail in the following chapter.

It is therefore bad scientific method to do as Gressmann, Sellin, and others have done, and to base our inquiry into the origin of the conception of the Messiah on an assumed oriental Messianic theology of which we know nothing, but which is supposed to have influenced the Psalmists and other royal bards. On the other hand, there are good grounds for the connexion (to which Gunkel and Gressmann drew attention) between the royal psalms and the oriental conceptions of kingship, and for the prominence given to this idea in recent study. There is, in fact, a close connexion be-tween the idea of the Messiah and the ancient Israelite conceptions of the king and kingship, which in turn are closely linked with the general oriental idea of the king.

2. *The Authentic Messianic Prophecies*

The true sources for the Old Testament conceptions of the Messiah are *the prophetic books*; and it is by the traditio-historical and literary criticism of these books[3] that we may discover whether there was any conception of a Messiah in the pre-exilic age.

At this stage we shall not discuss the origin and antiquity of the hope of restoration, of the belief in a Messiah, and of eschatology. It will suffice to establish the date of the actual Messianic prophe-cies in the prophetic books. It is of course impossible to undertake here any detailed exegetical and critical discussion of individual passages; we must be content to indicate the probable result of such an inquiry.

The passages which have to be considered are the following:

---

[1] This is the primary sense of the general Semitic term *'ēl, ilu*, etc., and of the Egyptian *neter*. See Beth in *Z.A.W.* xxxvi, 1916, pp. 129ff., xxxviii, 1919–20, pp. 87ff.

[2] This was first maintained by the present writer in *Ps.St.* II, pp. 297ff., and proved in detail by Engnell in *Divine Kingship*.

[3] On the prophetic books and their relation to the original sayings of the prophets, see Mowinckel in *N.T.T.* xliii, 1942, pp. 65ff.; *Prophecy and Tradition*, pp. 36ff.

Isa. iv, 2; vii, 10–17; viii, 8b, 10b; ix, 1–6; x, 21; xi, 1–9; xi, 10; xvi, 5; xxxii, 1–8; lv, 3f.; Jer. xvii, 25; xxiii, 5f. = xxxiii, 17f.; xxx, 9, 21; Ezek. xvii, 22–4; xxxiv, 23f.; xxxvii, 22–5; Hos. iii, 4f.; Amos ix, 11; Mic. iv, 8; v, 1–3; Zech. ix, 9f.[1]

The decision which of these passages belongs to the pre-exilic age is important, not only for a survey of the probable historical development of the Messianic faith, but also for the solution of a major problem which has been discussed during the past generation or more, namely the age and origin of the Messianic faith. Is it of pre-exilic or post-exilic origin? Yet ultimately the question has only a relative interest. For, as we shall see below, even if the Messianic faith belongs, in the main, to the age of Judaism, its actual content goes back to conceptions which are much older. As was indicated above in relation to the royal psalms, we have in the Old Testament a series of sayings and conceptions which may be regarded as preliminary stages in the development of the Messianic faith and as the ideological basis of that faith. The question will then be whether those sayings which appear to be pre-exilic are to be regarded as genuine products of the Messianic faith, or as belonging to the preparatory stage of its development.

As we shall see, several of the passages mentioned above have been handed down in collections of prophetic sayings attributed by tradition to prophets who lived before the collapse of the state and the monarchy in 587. The question then arises, is this tradition correct in every instance? This critical question cannot be evaded. It is a fact that the prophetic books consist of collections of prophetic sayings, which were handed down over a long period by word of mouth within the circles of these prophets' disciples, until at last they were written down and finally edited. During this process of transmission there were added sayings which originated within the circle of disciples, and come from later anonymous prophets.[2] It is therefore an assured and inescapable result of criticism that each of the extant prophetic books includes sayings which are later than the prophet with whose name the collection is associated. We need only refer to the book of Isaiah, the latter part of which (xl–lxvi) is undoubtedly the work of a prophet who lived 200 years later than Isaiah (the so-called Deutero-Isaiah), and of the circle of his disciples.[3]

[1] Bentzen, in *A.f.O.* vi, 1930, pp. 28off., tries to find the Messianic expectation in Mal. iii, 1, by a modification of the text. This is too precarious.
[2] See above, p. 15 n. 3, and also the survey in *G.T.M.M.M.* III, pp. 33ff.
[3] See *G.T.M.M.M.* III, pp. 185ff.

Of the passages mentioned above only two or three can be attributed on good grounds to the pre-exilic period.

There is no ground for doubting that Isa. vii, 10–14 goes back to Isaiah's own time, and contains reliable tradition.[1] Isa. ix, 1–6 also belongs to the period of the monarchy, as will be shown at greater length below (pp. 102ff.). We shall therefore return to both these passages, and see that they really express the old ideal of kingship, which is the ideological background of the Messianic faith. They are not Messianic in the strict sense.

Many critics regard Isa. xi, 1–9 as Isaianic. If it is, then we are dealing again with the preparatory ideological background of the Messianic faith. But the fact cannot be ignored that both here and in Job xiv, 8 the word *geza‘* means the stump of a tree which has been felled, from which a new shoot is to issue, and that Jesse's family tree is here regarded as hewn down, with only a stump remaining. This must mean that the royal family is no longer a tree, but only a stump; i.e., it is no longer a ruling house, but it will be restored. Thus the passage presupposes the fall of the monarchy.[2]

Concerning the date of Isa. xxxii, 1–8, nothing can be said with certainty. But the passage is not primarily a prophecy, still less a Messianic prophecy, but a wisdom poem which describes in general terms the blessing enjoyed in the reign of an upright king, of any upright king. It is based on the current ideal of true kingship; and it was only in the later Isaianic tradition that the poem came to be interpreted as a specific promise of the upright king of the future for whom they were then hoping.[3]

All the other Messianic passages are post-exilic. This is certainly true of the passage in Deutero-Isaiah (lv, 3f.), of Zech. ix, 9f., and of the passages in Ezekiel. These last come in all probability not from the exilic prophet Ezekiel, but from the circle of disciples who were responsible for the transmission of the

---

[1] As against Gressmann, *Der Messias*, pp. 136ff.; Kraeling in *J.B.L.* l, 1931, pp. 295ff. It does not, of course, follow that because Isaiah here expresses his belief in the miraculous power of Yahweh, the passage is legendary.

[2] Pedersen, *Israel* III–IV, p. 678 and Hammershaimb in *St.Th.* III, 2, 1949/1951, p. 141, point out that *geza‘* may also be used of the living stem of a plant, so that the word does not necessarily imply the fall of the dynasty. It is true that in Isa. xl, 24, the word is used of the stock or slip which might take root in the earth. But this does not alter the fact that in Isa. xi, 1 and Job xiv, 8, the word denotes the hewn stump from which new shoots sprout. Moreover, even the slip is a stem which has been cut before it takes root and sprouts. There ought to be no doubt about this, in view of the primary sense of the root *gz‘*: to cut, cut off, clip.

[3] See Mowinckel in *Z.A.W.* xlv, 1927, p. 49; *G.T.M.M.M.* III, pp. 167f.

17

book, and who made Ezekiel's sayings the basis of a prophetic appeal to the community, related to conditions in Judea after the consolidation of the community there.[1]

Isa. iv, 2 is part of a passage which is actually a secondary paraphrase of some words of Isaiah applied to a later age. It presupposes the existence of the Diaspora. The alien rule and dispersion of the post-exilic age are also presupposed by Isa. x, 21; xi, 10; and xvi, 5. There, too, we have later paraphrases of Isaianic themes.[2]

Isa. viii, 8b–10 is in all probability a later expansion of the original words of Isaiah in *vv.* 5–8a, which it interprets in the light of the Immanuel prophecy in vii. At all events the last word in *vv.* 8b, 10, *'immānû'ēl*, is not intended as the name of the future king or used as a vocative (so A.V. and R.V. in 8b). As the Massoretic vocalization and the context show, the word is used in its general sense, '(but) with us is God', 'for with us is God'.[3]

Whether the end of the book of Amos (ix, 11–15) comes from Amos himself or from later tradition in the circles of prophetic disciples[4] has often been debated. Most scholars adopt the latter opinion. Recently Hammershaimb has attempted to infuse new life into the traditional view, but is obliged in the end to admit that there are good grounds for the later dating.[5] The matter is in fact quite clear. No exegetical skill can explain away the prophet's assumption that 'the tabernacle of David is (already)

---

[1] All recent interpreters of Ezekiel are agreed that a number of the speeches in the book reflect conditions in Judea after the return. Cf., e.g., Hölscher, *Hesekiel. Der Dichter und das Buch*; Bertholet, *Hesekiel*; and in *F.u.F.* xiii, 1, Jan., 1936, pp. 4f.; Torrey, *Pseudo-Ezekiel and the Original Prophecy*; Herntrich, *Ezechielprobleme*; Messel, *Ezechielfragen*. The nucleus of truth in Hölscher's penetrating but one-sided and artificial literary criticism of the book is that the sayings and name of Ezekiel were used as a rallying point for the prophetic activity carried on by his followers after the return to Judea. Possibly we owe the greater part of the book to the circle of his disciples (in Hölscher's terminology, 'the redactor'). But I attribute more of the tradition to Ezekiel than Hölscher does; and I also hold that the disciples often used as a starting point prophecies derived from the exilic prophet Ezekiel. I also attribute to him some of the sections which Messel refers to his post-exilic 'Ezekiel', and some of the peculiar oracles in xxv–xxxii, which Messel attributes to an unknown X, whose date and character he declines to establish. A review of Ezekiel criticism is given by Rowley in *B.J.R.L.* xxxvi, 1, 1953, pp. 146–90.

[2] On these passages see *G.T.M.M.M.* III, ad locc.; in greater detail, Cheyne, *Introduction to the Book of Isaiah*, ad locc.; Bentzen, *Jesaja* I, ad locc.

[3] See Mowinckel in *N.T.T.* xlii, 1941, pp. 131ff.; *G.T.M.M.M.* III, pp. 101ff. Much the same interpretation of the word is given by Bentzen (*Jesaja* I, pp. 69f.) in viii, 10; but in 8b he takes it as a proper noun.

[4] This is the real question, not whether ix, 11ff. is a later literary insertion into a written book which was already in existence. See Mowinckel, *Jesajadisiplene*, pp. 10ff.; *G.T.M.M.M.* III, pp. 619–21, 651.

[5] Hammershaimb, *Amos fortolket*, pp. 134ff., 139.

fallen', and therefore that the Davidic monarchy no longer exists. The passage is concerned with the restoration of the family and tabernacle of David.

If Hos. iii, 4f. comes from Hosea himself, the reference in it is not to the future Messiah but to the reigning 'David', i.e., the king of Judah at the time at which the conversion of the northern Israelites (to which the prophet alludes) will take place. But it is most probable that in the form in which Hos. iii has come down to us it must be classed with those sayings of the prophet which have been modified in the light of the conditions and needs of later Judaism.[1] The assumption then is that Judah is also dispersed and in exile; but the prophet expects that one day the monarchy and the dynasty will be restored, and then Israel, too, will submit to the new David.[2]

Mic. iv, 8 also presupposes the fall of the monarchy. The situation which is here prophesied to Zion is 'the former dominion, the monarchy over Jerusalem'. Consequently this dominion was no longer in existence in the time of the prophet.[3]

Mic. v, 1–3 must be interpreted in the same way. The context shows that the coming king's brothers are the 'remnant' which survives the great catastrophe which befell Judah in 598 and 587. They *have been* carried off; and therefore this prophecy foretells that they 'will return'.[4]

It is only in a very restricted sense that Jer. xvii, 25 can be called a Messianic oracle. It prophesies that if the people will observe the Sabbath, there will always be in the future 'kings and princes sitting on the throne of David'. Moreover, the oracle is considerably later than Jeremiah.[5]

Jer. xxiii, 5f. = xxxiii, 15f. (cf. Isa. xi, 1–9, 10) uses the word 'shoot' (*ṣemaḥ*) of the future king. This symbolic title also occurs in Zechariah, when in veiled prophetic style he uses Zerubbabel's name ('shoot from Babylon') in this way (iii, 8; vi, 12). There can be little doubt that Zechariah's references are the earlier.[6] He had a real point of historical association for the symbolic name; and with Zerubbabel he linked those expectations of the restoration and realization of the ideal monarchy which are so character-

---

[1] See *G.T.M.M.* III, p. 569.
[2] In *N.K.Z.* xli, 1930, pp. 812ff. Caspari expresses well-founded doubts concerning Gressmann's Messianic interpretation of Amos and Hosea.
[3] See Lindblom, *Micha literarisch untersucht*, pp. 81ff.; *G.T.M.M.M.*, pp. 681f.
[4] See Lindblom, op. cit., pp. 95ff.; *G.T.M.M.M.* III, pp. 685ff.
[5] See *G.T.M.M.M.* III, pp. 357f.; Volz, *Der Prophet Jeremia*, pp. 188ff.
[6] Cf. below, pp. 119ff., 160ff., and Additional Notes IV and VII.

istic of Jewish Messianic theology. Later this figure of Zechariah's became a technical Messianic term, at once veiled and allusive, after the fashion of the later eschatology and apocalyptic. The above-mentioned passages in Jeremiah, and probably also Isa. xi, 10, are thus dependent on Zechariah and later than his time.[1] As we shall see below (p. 161), it is possible that Isa. xi, 1–9 also dates back to Zechariah's time.

The other passages in Jeremiah (xxx, 9, 21) are also certainly post-exilic. They imply a situation in which for the time being Israel is under foreign rulers; but a time will come when 'David' will be raised up, i.e., the house of David will be restored as a royal house, which it therefore no longer was in the prophet's time.[2] We shall return to all these passages in the appropriate contexts below.

A preliminary survey of the sources thus shows that all the genuinely Messianic passages in the Old Testament date from the time after the fall of the monarchy and the destruction of the Israelite states. Of those passages which are commonly held to be Messianic, only Isa. vii and ix, 1ff. can with certainty be referred to the pre-exilic age,[3] but they are not Messianic in the strict sense. This may seem to the reader to be a *petitio principii*; but it is not. Anticipating the results of the inquiry in the following chapters, the argument may be stated as follows. 1. The conceptions of the king in the old royal ideology and in the doctrine of the Messiah are in all their main features identical. 2. The overwhelming majority of the Messianic passages belong to the post-exilic age, when the monarchy no longer existed. It is therefore at least possible, and in fact very probable, that the few remaining pre-exilic sayings about the ideal king are concerned with the actual historical kingship, and not with the Messiah. In a later chapter it will be shown that this view provides a full and satisfactory explanation of these passages.

---

[1] See *G.T.M.M.M.* III, pp. 371f.; on the post-exilic origin of these two passages see Volz, op. cit., pp. 230, 310ff.

[2] See *G.T.M.M.M.* III, pp. 291ff., 391f.; Volz, op. cit., pp. 306ff., 310ff.

[3] It is impossible to present here in detail the arguments which lead me to maintain the late dating of all the passages referred to; that would lead too far. I have, however, discussed the matter briefly in *G.T.M.M.M.* III, pp. 69ff., and in the notes ad locc. Berry in *J.B.L.* xlv, 1926, pp. 232ff., regards Isa. ix, 1ff. and xi, 1ff. as later than all the other Messianic passages, but his arguments lack cogency.

CHAPTER III

The Ideal of Kingship in Ancient Israel

IT has been observed above that there must undoubtedly be a logical and historical connexion between the concept of the Messiah and the ancient Israelite idea of the king as 'Yahweh's Anointed'. 'The Messiah' is simply 'the Anointed'. This raises the question of the meaning of the expression 'Yahweh's Anointed', which in turn involves an inquiry into what the ancient Israelite meant by a true king, into his ideal of kingship.

The present writer has already maintained in his book on the origin of eschatology (*Ps.St.* II) that the conception of the Messiah was derived from the ideal of kingship, or 'king-ideology', to use the term now in vogue. A few preliminary observations must now be made to clear the ground. We must distinguish between two problems: that of the origin of the actual *expectation* of a future saviour king or Messiah, and that of the source from which is derived the *content* of the Messianic figure with all its varied traits. In the present chapter it is the latter problem that we shall discuss, in order thereby to prepare the way for an answer to the former. This much can be said at once: the content of the Messianic figure was derived from the kingly ideal of ancient Israel as we see it with particular clarity in the place and function of the king in the public ritual of the national festivals.

The Israelite monarchy came into existence long after the nation had invaded Canaan; and Old Testament tradition bears witness to the fact that it was a copy of Canaanite kingship. When the people ask Samuel to anoint a king to rule over them, they say, 'A king will we have over us, that we also may be like all the nations' (1 Sam. viii, 5, 19f.). This is precisely what historical considerations would lead us to expect. In the time of Moses, Israel was a 'primitive' people as compared with her neighbours. Her social customs, her political institutions, and her material and spiritual culture were still at the level of simple, semi-nomadic life. In all these respects both the Canaanites and the neighbouring great powers, who represented the advanced civilization of the ancient east, had progressed much further. The settlement in Canaan involved an entirely new way of life; and its inevitable consequences were a new social structure, and new political institutions and agencies, which in turn called for new forms and fashions. It was from the Canaanites that the Hebrews learned what a king was like, first in the clash of war, when they often had to withdraw before their chariots of iron and their superiority in arms and organization, and later on in peaceful intercourse, and in 'covenant', when chieftain, peasant, and herdsman had opportunity in visiting the towns to admire the wealth, the splendour, and the power displayed in royal courts. In legal and commercial transactions they often had to resort to the tribunals of these kings, and they had to use or, of necessity, to submit to regulations for trade and agriculture which they had not had to develop when they were nomads. By observation and experience they learned that the monarchial system lay behind every attempt to establish a great empire, and that only a monarchy had the power to hold together scattered tribes and settlements, since only a king could have an army big enough for the purpose. It was precisely in the struggle against the Philistines, who threatened to put an end to Israel's independence, that there arose the pressure towards a closer association between the scattered settlements, tribes, and clans, so that the idea of the monarchy was practically forced upon men's minds.

Together with the monarchy it was natural (and, indeed, inevitable) that Israel should take over from the Canaanites a great many ideas and conceptions of kingship, the royal ideology, the 'manner (*mišpāṭ*) of the kingdom', its etiquette and customs, the whole pattern of life which was bound up with it. The Old Testament does not conceal the fact that in many ways it was a new and alien 'manner': indeed, Samuel announces explicitly the character of the new despotism.[1]

It has, however, become more and more apparent that Gunkel and Gressmann (see below) were right in pointing out that the ideal of kingship which Israel took over from the Canaanites was actually a special development of the common oriental concept of kingship. By way of background, therefore, we must first offer an account of the royal ideology of the ancient east.

[1] See the later of the two sources in the Samuel tradition, 1 Sam. viii, 11–17; x, 25ff.

IDEAL OF KINGSHIP IN ANCIENT ISRAEL

1. *The Royal Ideology of the Ancient East*

The Canaanite monarchy was not an indigenous creation, independent of foreign influences. The entire culture of the country was in large measure composite, mainly Syrian, but, like Syrian culture itself, subject to strong influence from Mesopotamia (Hurrian-Mitannian), from Babylonia and Assyria, from Asia Minor (Hittite), and from the neighbouring country of Egypt.[1] Closer examination reveals so intimate an interaction among all these cultures, that it is correct to speak of a common oriental culture, just as in the Middle Ages we speak of a common European Christian culture, and in our own day of a western culture which in its main features is uniform. Among those elements in the culture of the ancient east which in all essentials are homogeneous, we must include kingship with its special character and status.

On these grounds, and partly also on the basis of older works on religion and ethnology which deal with kingship and the cult,[2] a number of English and American scholars have taken up the question of the oriental concept of kingship. Reference must be made to the two collective works edited by Hooke: *Myth and Ritual* and *The Labyrinth,* and to Hooke's own work, *The Origins of Early Semitic Ritual.*[3] This last is a stimulating book, and contains a wealth of material, but shows a tendency to artificial schematization. The author maintains that the cult of all ancient near eastern religions was dominated by a coherent complex of ritual and myth, which served as a 'pattern' for all these religions, and which had its home in Babylonia. Babylonian cultic practice in historical times, and also Canaanite, Israelite, and other cultic systems are variations of this original 'pattern'. At its centre stands the king, himself divine, the offspring or the incarnation of the god, who in the cult *is* at the same time the god himself, so that in dramatic form he lives or endures the entire 'myth' of the god, his deeds and his experiences. The god is thought of particularly as the god of fertility and creation. The most important cult festival is that of the New Year, when the world is created anew. In it the king goes through the humiliation and death of

---

[1] This is clearly shown in Albright's books: *From the Stone Age to Christianity,* and *Archaeology and the Religion of Israel.* See also Millar Burrows, *What Mean These Stones?,* and Schofield, *The Religious Background of the Bible.*

[2] Above all, Frazer's works on these subjects: *Lectures on the Early History of the Kingship* and *The Magical Art and the Evolution of Kings.*

[3] Among other works on similar lines we may mention Hocart, *Kingship,* and *Kings and Councillors;* James, *Christian Myth and Ritual,* and *The Old Testament in the Light of Anthropology,* pp. 47ff.

the god (originally in actual fact, later in the person of a substitute king, who was really put to death, and finally only symbolically), his resurrection, combat, and victory, and his 'sacred marriage' with the fertility goddess, and thereby creates the world and makes its prosperity and blessing secure for the New Year. As we have seen, it is thought that this pattern left its stamp on the cultic practice of the entire Near East, including that of Israel, but partly in such a way that the pattern was 'disintegrated'. Individual practices, ideas, and phrases were taken over, more or less correctly interpreted or re-interpreted, so that, for instance, conceptions originally associated with the king came to be used of the ordinary worshipper, as a result of the tendency towards 'democratization' which is prevalent in all religion.[1]

The views of the 'ritual pattern' school as expounded in the works mentioned above have the character of a provisional thesis to be demonstrated by further research rather than an assured position based on detailed investigation. Against the background of these general theories, and along the same lines as the myth and ritual school, I. Engnell has undertaken, in his *Studies in Divine Kingship in the Ancient Near East*, a thorough investigation of the royal ideology of the ancient east. His treatment of the problem in relation to the Western Semites is based on a thorough acquaintance with the texts and an extensive knowledge of the history of religion. His book is valuable and important both because of the fullness with which the sources are presented and because it attempts a consistent interpretation of the royal ideology in terms of a clear principle. It also has the merit of not mixing religions and peoples, for it treats each area separately. In a series of treatises by Widengren, Engnell's ideas have been developed and amplified on a number of important points.[2]

It is obvious that there is a core of truth in this idea of a ritual pattern. The ancient Near East did in fact possess a common culture; and within this *Kulturkreis* there was a constant interchange of ideas and of cultural factors. Phenomenological study reveals

---

[1] Jastrow had already drawn attention to this process of democratization in Babylonian cultic rites and psalms in his *Die Religion Babyloniens und Assyriens* II, pp. 106ff., 117; and the same tendency in several different types of Israelite psalms was pointed out in *Ps.St.* VI, p. 74, and by Birkeland in *Die Feinde des Individuums in der israelitischen Psalmenliteratur*. Cf. also Engnell, *Divine Kingship*, Index, s.v. 'Democratization'; Frankfort, *Kingship*, pp. 197ff.

[2] *Psalm 110 och det sakrala kungadömet i Israel*; in *R.o.B.* ii, 1943, pp. 49ff.; in *Horae Soederblomianae* I, iii; in *S.E.Å.* x, 1945, pp. 66ff.; and also *Religionens värld*, pp. 249ff., 254ff. These theories of a ritual pattern and royal ideology are maintained almost to the point of caricature by Haldar, e.g., in *Studies in the Book of Nahum*.

an extensive common stock of ideas and forms in religion and the cult. Hugo Winckler and his so-called Pan-Babylonian school had already maintained that all the religions of the Near East were identical, and were ultimately Babylonian in origin. In them mythological and cultic expression was given to the scientific astronomy and astrology of ancient Babylonia, and to the conceptions of the world, life, religion, and history which were based on that science.[1] The Yahweh of the Old Testament was a god of the same type as Marduk, Tammuz, or the like; and the religious texts of Israel were to be interpreted in accordance with their supposed Babylonian patterns. The theories and the programme of the school found perhaps their clearest expression in Winckler's *Himmels- und Weltenbild der Babylonier als Grundlage der Weltanschauung und Mythologie aller Völker*, and in A. Jeremias's *Handbuch der altorientalischen Geisteskultur* and his *Das Alte Testament im Lichte des alten Orients*.

This grandiose hypothesis has long since been refuted by an extensive series of exact studies of the sources. The Pan-Babylonists made the mistake of forcing texts from different countries into a ready-made scheme, without due allowance for the varied spiritual structures of the different religions, without making the necessary study of them, or overlooking such as had been made. Nevertheless the underlying idea of a common oriental *Kulturkreis* was sound. H. Gunkel, H. Gressmann, and *die religionsgeschichtliche Schule* of biblical scholars saw and often proved that a good many of the religious ideas and literary forms in the Old Testament were actually of non-Israelite and frequently of Babylonian origin, and could be adequately understood only when interpreted against this background. The great discovery involved in Gunkel's interpretation of the Psalms was just this, that the different types of psalm presupposed definite cultic situations, which in part were attested by the legal parts of the Old Testament and in part could be reconstructed from allusions in the psalms themselves. This reconstruction could often be supported and supplemented from similar cultic acts in Babylonian religion, which had obviously been the 'cultic pattern' for those in Israel. On the basis of this discovery the present writer sought in his *Psalmenstudien* to present a more detailed picture of the cultic background of the psalms in the Old Testament, and, in particular, rediscovered the main

[1] See A. Jeremias, *Handbuch*, pp. 171ff.; *Das A.T. im Lichte des alten Orients*, 'Motiv-register', s.v. 'König'. Zimmern, *Zum Streit um die 'Christusmythe'*, is more sober; cf. also *Die Vergöttlichung des Königs Lipit-Ištars*, p. 2, with references to texts, note 2.

features of the ancient Israelite New Year festival, in which one of the chief ideas was the enthronement of Yahweh as king of the world, the symbolic representation of His victory over His enemies, both the forces of chaos and the historical enemies of Israel. The result of this victory was the renewal of creation, election, and the covenant, ideas and rites from the old fertility festivals which lay behind the historical festival. One of the most important elements in the symbolic ritual was the great procession, in which Yahweh, represented by His ark, 'went up' to His palace, the temple. This festival ritual shows so many striking similarities to the other New Year festivals of the ancient east that the present writer felt justified in concluding that *in this respect* the Israelite festival had been developed under the influence of Canaanite 'patterns', which, in their turn, depended on influences which were more or less common to the entire Near East. It seemed also to be a sound procedure cautiously to supplement the biblical evidence from Babylonian and other oriental sources, where these were really in harmony with the spiritual structure of Israelite religion. In *Ps.St.* II the opinion was also expressed that the real, living myth always has a connexion with the cult and the ritual, the myth being the expression and the epic elaboration of the existential realities which were experienced in the cult.

In the same connexion Gunkel, Gressmann, and the present writer dealt also with the Israelite ideal of kingship: Gunkel in 'Die Königspsalmen' in *Preussische Jahrbücher* clviii, 1914, in his commentary on the Psalms, and in his and Begrich's *Einleitung*; Gressmann in his *Ursprung*, and in *Der Messias*; the present writer in his *Kongesalmerne i Det gamle Testamente*, and in *Ps.St.* II, III. In these works I have sought to show that the 'mythological' conception of the king, which is found in Israel as well as elsewhere, is not to be regarded as the result of stylistic influence only (Gressmann's *Hofstil*), but was the expression of a real religious and sociological faith, and was closely connected with cultic life and experience. The ideal of kingship has to be seen as an element in those religious ideas which found their expression in the cult. Pedersen, too, in his *Israel* I–II, III–IV, has recognized the validity of most of the views and conclusions mentioned above.[1]

There is, then, in the writer's opinion, real ground for the theories of the ritual pattern school. What they have added to earlier investigations appears to be, in the first instance, the

[1] *Israel* III–IV, pp. 384–425, 428–36; cf. pp. 737–45.

combination of them with the views of Frazer and his school on primitive life and anthropology. They also reveal a tendency to generalize, and to overemphasize the unity of the culture of the ancient east. It is not to be denied that Engnell, Widengren, and other representatives of this school show a marked tendency to go beyond the evidence, and, it may be said, to push their theories rather dogmatically to extremes. They reduce the various religions and texts to uniformity, and construct a ritual pattern which is found everywhere, though it existed nowhere; and they do not take sufficient account of the frequently varying and distinctive structures of the different religions. The same thing said or done in different contexts takes on different meanings. This is true, above all, in religion. Yet in dealing with each individual religion, the advocates of the ritual pattern theory seem to *presuppose* a common oriental pattern into which the texts must fit. For instance, because Egyptian religion consistently treats the king as a divine being, and Sumero-Accadian religion does so rather less consistently, the same tendency must needs be found in other eastern peoples as well. But to interpret the scanty and fragmentary sources in the light of a partly conjectural Babylonian pattern, and to supplement the material in accordance with this pattern, is naturally a doubtful undertaking, which can hardly be carried out without dogmatic regimentation of the evidence.[1]

Closer examination, such as has been undertaken by Henri Frankfort in *Kingship and the Gods*, shows that there are profound differences between the Egyptian and Mesopotamian conceptions of kingship, and that if we are to avoid the danger of Procrustean generalizations, we must pay far more attention to the general structure of each of the various religions and cultures, and to the social conditions which lie behind them, than the ritual pattern school has done.[2] Individual expressions and statements about the king in Egypt and in Mesopotamia may resemble each other fairly closely; but the precise content of any given conception can be discerned only when it is considered in the context of the particular system of thought to which it belongs. If proper allowance is made for this, the picture of the Mesopotamian royal ideology appears rather different from that painted for example by Engnell.

[1] For a criticism of the extreme ritual pattern theory, see Albright, *From the Stone Age to Christianity*, p. 36, and now Frankfort's excellent Frazer Lecture, *The Problem of Similarity in Ancient Near Eastern Religions*.

[2] Cf. Frankfort, *Kingship*, pp. 1ff., and the critical notes, pp. 355 n. 13, 382 n. 5, 405 n. 1, 408 nn. 66, 67, 69.

In the static Egyptian view of life,[1] kingship is an essential factor in the eternal cosmic world order, and the basis of all ordered existence.[2] Only savages have no king. The order of the world and creation are expressions of an eternal law, *ma'at*, 'right order', which is active in both kings and gods. Life is in itself imperishable: death is but a transition.[3] Everywhere the object of the cult is to maintain and renew life when the powers of death threaten to prevail;[4] but in Egypt it appears rather as an affirmation that after a momentary disturbance the world order has again been stabilized through the activity of the divine power and law.

This happens because society always has at its centre the intense power of the godhead. Pharaoh, the king, is himself a real god, in whom all divinity is incarnated. This is manifest even in art, where Pharaoh is always represented in superhuman proportions as the only person who acts, makes war, storms fortresses, slays the enemy, offers sacrifice, and so on. He is the equal of the gods, and himself an object of worship.[5] Officially he is called 'the good god'. His title, 'Lord of the two lands', implies that he rules over the entire dualistic universe.[6] In himself he embodies and holds in harmonious equilibrium the two powers, Life and Death, the gods Horus and Seth, who are in conflict, and yet, by the very tension between them, create and renew life. He *is* Horus and Seth, 'the Two Lords';[7] he is 'Lord of Years',[8] 'Lord of all'. He is officially styled Horus,[9] and as such is the reborn god of death and life, Osiris.[10] As king, he may be said to span two generations, for he is at one and the same time father and son. By death he becomes Osiris, and exercises his beneficial activity as creator of fertility in field, herd, and nation; and as the living one he is at the same time Horus, the son who avenges Osiris and brings him to life again.[11] The king is identified with all the gods.[12] As the expression of the eternal order of creation from its very beginning, he is the son of the sun god Re, and so on.

This is all expressed in the titles which are applied to the king;[13]

---

[1] In addition to Frankfort's extensive researches into Egyptian kingship, we may refer to Erman-Ranke, *Aegypten*[2], pp. 6off.; Steindorff-Seele, *When Egypt Ruled the East*, pp. 82ff.; Engnell, *Divine Kingship*, pp. 4ff.

[2] Frankfort, *Kingship*, pp. 3ff.

[3] Cf. Brede Kristensen, *Livet fra döden*, pp. 7ff.

[4] Cf. Mowinckel, *Religion og kultus*, pp. 55ff. (= *Religion und Kultus*, pp. 6off.).

[5] Frankfort, *Kingship*, pp. 6ff.   [6] Op cit., pp. 15ff.   [7] Op. cit., p. 21.

[8] Op. cit., p. 32.   [9] Op. cit., pp. 38ff.   [10] Op. cit., pp. 181ff.   [11] Op. cit., pp. 38ff.

[12] Engnell, *Divine Kingship*, pp. 6f., formulates the thought with undue theoretical precision when he speaks of Pharaoh as identical with the 'high god' and with the 'god of fertility'.   [13] Frankfort, *Kingship*, pp. 36ff.

and it is also taken literally in a metaphysical sense. Re takes the form of Pharaoh, goes in to the queen, and of her begets the new king.[1] The king is divine from birth.[2] He is the sun god, who has 'shone forth' on the earth.[3] All goddesses may be regarded as his mothers. As Osiris-Horus, he is the son of Isis, who ought probably to be thought of as the personification of the royal throne, charged with divine power.[4]

Thus Pharaoh is the absolute master of the whole country, or 'the two lands'. In theory all power and property belong to him.[5] It is he alone who acts in war and peace.[6] As Osiris he is worshipped after death, for from him all blessing proceeds.[7] He causes the Nile to rise and overflow its banks, making the fields fruitful; and it is he who makes the corn grow.[8] He upholds justice (*ma'at*); '*ma'at* is in him'. According to a hymn to Pharaoh Merneptah, he maintains the whole natural order.[9] He it is, too, who gives life to men. He is the 'Ka' or life-force of all his subjects.[10] His own Ka is personified and worshipped as a god.[11] The god Re can be represented as Pharaoh's Ka.[12] Many mythical forms may be used to express the king's abundant resources of divine power. He has been suckled with the milk of goddesses, and with it has imbibed the life-force.[13]

The Egyptians also reckoned with dangerous periods of transition in life, when order and harmony with the divine powers had to be strengthened, and vigour renewed by means of the effective power of cult festivals.[14] The New Year was a transition period of this kind, at which every year the king's accession was celebrated.[15] Another important festival of renewal was the *sed*-festival, which has been called a 'jubilee', but which was celebrated at irregular intervals of years,[16] when the divine world order, the king's power, and his dominion over the earth had to be strengthened.[17]

Pharaoh is one with his transfigured, divine, life-giving ancestors, who live and work through him. This is expressed above all in the festival of Min, the god of the life-force, and particularly of procreative power. He, too, is Pharaoh.[18] Taken together, Pharaoh's ancestors form a collective source of power, to which

---

[1] Op. cit., pp. 42ff.   [2] Cf. Engnell, *Divine Kingship*, pp. 4f.
[3] Frankfort, *Kingship*, p. 57.   [4] Op. cit., p. 43.   [5] Op. cit., pp. 51f.
[6] Op. cit., p. 55.   [7] Op. cit., pp. 55, 59.   [8] Op. cit., p. 57.
[9] Op. cit., p. 58; cf. Erman, *The Literature of the Ancient Egyptians*, pp. 278f.
[10] Frankfort, op. cit., pp. 60, 68f.   [11] Op. cit., pp. 69ff.
[12] Op. cit., pp. 77f.   [13] Op. cit., p. 74.   [14] Cf. van Gennep, *Les rites de passage*.
[15] See Dürr in *Theologie und Glaube* xx, 1928, pp. 305ff.
[16] Frankfort, op. cit., p. 79.   [17] Op. cit., pp. 86ff.   [18] Op. cit., pp. 89, 188f.

each king is added at death.[1] The living king is 'the elder son', and as such is identical with the god Upwaut;[2] and it is through him that the ancestors bestow life and power.[3]

Therefore the king's death and his entrance into the world beyond (where he shares in the eternal, living circuit of Re and the heavenly ones), together with the accession of the new king, form a 'transition' of vital significance.[4] It is consummated in the accession festival, which has been called 'the Mystery Play of the Succession'.[5] In it there is re-enacted with complete realism, and with the same result, all that took place at creation, when the world order was established, and at the historical institution of the monarchy. The god, who at one and the same time has joined his ancestors and been reborn in his son, stands there again in the fullness of divine power, holding the world order in his hand and securing life and blessing. What takes place and is symbolically realized in the cult is this: Seth has killed Osiris; but as Horus, the new king avenges his father, triumphs over Seth, and unites in his own person the two essential powers of existence in settled harmony. World order and justice again repose securely in the divine king. This cult festival and its 'Mystery Play' are a creative drama.[6] Through the realistic symbolism of the ritual, what it represents actually comes to pass. It is essential that something should really happen[7] in order that harmony between the cosmos and society may be restored and secured; and it does happen, in that 'Horus' once again triumphs and takes his place on the throne.[8] To prepare the way for this change, the old king often takes as his co-regent the new king (usually the eldest son), who has been designated by the god. 'Osiris takes Horus in his arms'; and the heir apparent *is* already Horus, and is filled with new divine power.[9] Then, at his death, 'Osiris' transmits to 'Horus' his entire divine power and sovereignty. In this way the danger involved in even the shortest interregnum is avoided. The accession takes place immediately after the old king's death; and the coronation, which is also the outward symbolic transference of the fullness of divine power, has to take place at some appropriate new beginning in the natural order, a 'New Year' of some kind.

---

[1] Op. cit., pp. 90f., 95.   [2] Op. cit., pp. 92f.   [3] Op. cit., pp. 97f.
[4] Op. cit., pp. 101ff.   [5] Op. cit., pp. 123ff.
[6] Cf. *Ps.St.* II, pp. 19ff.; *Religion og kultus*, pp. 68ff. (= *Religion und Kultus*, pp. 73ff.); art. 'Drama, religionsgeschichtlich' in *R.G.G.*[2] II, cols. 2000ff.
[7] Cf. van der Leeuw, *Religion in Essence and Manifestation*, pp. 339ff., 447ff.
[8] Frankfort, *Kingship*, pp. 124f.   [9] Cf. Engnell, *Divine Kingship*, p. 5.

The dead king's crossing to the world beyond and his full identification with Osiris through the ritual of embalming and burial, and the new king's accession to the throne, are equally important elements in this new transition.[1] The entire world order has thereby been secured; the world has been created anew. As the order of nature is derived from the creator god, so the order and welfare of the land are derived from the king.[2] The new king is the Atum, the creator god.[3] All these accession festivities conclude with the coronation with the two crowns. Thereby the king receives all the fullness of Re's power and dominion: he *is* Re. This means that the creation of the world has again been accomplished. A new era of prosperity follows the menacing state of chaos which resulted from the king's death and the breach between nature and society.[4] All these interpretations of men's experience of reality find expression in the hymns sung in honour of Pharaoh as of any other god.[5] It follows, then, that the king, whether alive or dead, is an object of worship;[6] and similarly it is he who (in theory) carries out the entire cult, and is the priest of all the gods.[7] It is he who invokes and stimulates all the other gods to grant blessing to himself and his people.

Behind this conception of kingship lies a thought which is found among many primitive peoples, and particularly among the Hamitic tribes of Africa, with whom the Egyptians had close ethnological and cultural connexions. The thought is that of a mana-filled chief of the type called 'rainmaker-king', who after death remains a source of power, and who, *inter alia*, is incarnated in his successor, though he himself also exists elsewhere, and acts in other ways.[8] This is shown, for instance, by the fact that it is in his character as the dead king that Osiris is the power of nature

---

[1] Frankfort, *Kingship*, pp. 110ff.
[2] Cf. op. cit., p. 105.   [3] Cf. op. cit., p. 108.   [4] Cf. op. cit., p. 150.
[5] Op. cit., pp. 58, 60; for the hymn to the royal crown, which is also divine, and may be personified and regarded as identical with the various gods, see op. cit., pp. 43, 108; cf. also Erman-Ranke, *Aegypten*[2], pp. 72, 76, 466, 469, 471, 473, 479; Erman, *The Literature of the Ancient Egyptians*, pp. 10ff., 134ff., 254ff., 258ff., 274ff., 278ff.; Steindorff-Seele, *When Egypt Ruled the East*, p. 83.
[6] Cf. Erman, *Die ägyptische Religion*[2], pp. 92, 219, 229.   [7] Op. cit., p. 67.
[8] Cf. Frankfort, *Kingship*, pp. 18, 33f.; see also Index, s.vv. 'Africa', 'Africans', 'Hamites', 'Rainmaker-king'. Cf. below, p. 33 n. 3. For 'primitive' ideas about the rule of mana-filled chiefs and kings, and on the chief as a 'sacral' bearer of divine, creative energies, and possibly as the incarnation of a deified ancestor, see, among others, Frazer, *Adonis, Attis, Osiris* (*The Golden Bough* IV, that vast collection of material, which will always retain its worth, even if theories and interpretations change). See further Hocart, *Kingship*; van der Leeuw, *Religion in Essence and Manifestation*, pp. 214ff.; Widengren, *Religionens värld*[2], pp. 254ff. (generalizing a little too much); Briem, *På trons tröskel*, p. 56, referring to Junod, *The Life of a South African Tribe*.

and of life, and has become 'saviour' and giver of life to both great
and small, to man and beast and country.[1] It is probable that
Osiris really is a deified ancestral chief of this type, who lives on
in his descendants, and who represents and possesses in himself
the entire power of life and fertility in nature and society. In
Egypt these thoughts are carried further and developed theo-
logically, so that they are of central importance in the entire
conception of the world and society.

As early as the time of the ancient Sumerians, the idea of kingship in Mesopotamia[2] differed considerably from that of Egypt in
many ways. We are dealing here not simply with two variants of
a common oriental ideology of kingship, but with a basic difference
of principle, in spite of many similarities in detail to Egyptian
phenomena.

'The land of the two rivers' had no well-defined frontiers, and
lay open to the nomadic tribes of the desert and the mountain
tribes of the north and east. It was dependent on rain and the
weather; and the Euphrates and Tigris were not, like the Nile,
regularly recurring sources of blessing, but often dangerous and
destructive 'powers of chaos'. There was, therefore, both in life
itself and in men's view of it, much more of danger, suspense, and
fear than in Egypt. At any time, the powers of evil, through the
agency of drought, devastating floods, or enemies, might threaten
to lay 'the world' waste again. The cult was not, as in Egypt, an
affirmation that the powers of life had been strengthened and
existence stabilized after a momentary disturbance during the
'transition'. It was a factor of vital importance in a life and death
struggle. Every year the powers of chaos *did* get the upper hand,
nature and life *were* dead, and at the mercy of the powers of death;
and it was then that every resource must be employed in the cult,
so that the gods of life might again be victorious over the power
of chaos, and really create the world anew.[3]

In Mesopotamia, too, it is life that is a stake in the cult. The
object of the cult is to create and safeguard life and its continuance.

---

[1] Frankfort, *Kingship*, pp. 207ff., 212.
[2] For Mesopotamian kingship see Meissner, *Babylonien und Assyrien* I, pp. 45ff.;
Zimmern, *Die Vergöttlichung des Königs Lipit-Ištars*; Christliebe Jeremias, *Die Vergöttlichung der babylonisch-assyrischen Könige*; Contenau, *La civilisation d'Assur et de Babylone*,
p. 210; Labat, *Le caractère religieux de la royauté assyro-babylonienne*; Engnell, *Divine
Kingship*, pp. 14ff.; Widengren in *R.o.B.* ii, pp. 49ff.; Frankfort, *Kingship*, pp. 215ff.;
de Fraine, *L'aspect religieux.*
[3] Cf. Frankfort, op. cit., pp. 4f.

But the individual has no prospect of lasting life, as in Egypt: 'when the gods created man, they gave him death for his portion, but life they withheld in their own hands', says the Gilgamesh Epic. The aim of the cult is to safeguard the continued life of the world, of nature, and of the race in 'the land'. But even the gods need to be strengthened and renewed by the 'service' and 'food' of which the sacrifices consist. The gods created men to perform this service, and set a king over them. He is, indeed, 'the great man' (Sumerian, LUGAL), but nevertheless a man like other men. His task is to serve the gods, and carry out their will on earth.[1] Mesopotamian art, in contrast with Egyptian, always depicts the king as leader of his men, and yet as one of them: his army and his servants are active comrades in arms, and co-operate with him. His relation to the gods is that of a worshipper, not an equal: he represents his people before them.[2]

This theological conception is in harmony with the sociological and historical origin of the monarchy in Mesopotamia. Here too, of course, there is a background of the common primitive ideas of the mana-filled chief and leader of the cult, in whom the 'power' of the community is concentrated, and who is the channel of divine life and power to the community.[3]

Kingship developed in the earliest Sumerian cities from a primitive patriarchal democracy, under the leadership of the elders.[4] The real 'lord' is the god of the city. He is regarded as the actual owner of the common land which belongs to the tribe and the city. The king (the great man) seems originally to have been one of the elders who was designated as leader in a situation of particular danger or importance. His authority lasted only until this particular task was accomplished.[5] Behind him stood the temple congregation, the community of citizens. Even in the divine polity the kingship is conferred on Marduk, according to the Epic of Creation, as the result of a decision in the assembly of the gods.[6] But behind the congregation stands the god of the city. It is at his instance, and in defence of his land, and temple, and congregation that the king is to play his part.[7] Accordingly, we find that

---

[1] Cf. Gadd, *Ideas of Divine Rule in the Ancient East*, pp. 3, 34; Frankfort, op. cit., pp. 239, 332.
[2] Frankfort, op. cit., pp. 8f., 224f.
[3] Cf. van der Leeuw, *Religion in Essence and Manifestation*, pp. 115ff., 191–241; Frazer, *Lectures on the Early History of Kingship*, and *The Golden Bough*, pp. 264ff.; Hocart, *Kingship*; and others. Cf. above, p. 31 n. 8.
[4] Frankfort, op. cit., pp. 215ff.   [5] See Jacobsen in *J.N.E.S.* v, 1943, pp. 159ff.
[6] Frankfort, op. cit., p. 236.   [7] Frankfort, op. cit., pp. 221f.

D

even after the emergence of permanent personal rule, the rulers do not usually call themselves 'kings', but the 'vice-gerents' (Sumerian, ENSI; Accadian, *iššakku*) and priests (*šangû*) of the god of the city.[1] The real king is the god of the city.[2] When the city state expands and subdues other cities, each with its ENSI, and when the position of the king acquires a more political and military character, based as it is on force, a distinction may arise in practice between the king and the vice-gerent priest; but it is still the king who is the link between the god and the community. He has a sacral character, inasmuch as he is an intermediary between the god and the people.[3]

In Mesopotamia the king always retained this close and distinctive relation to the deity; and the conception of this relationship was moulded by theological ideas about kingship. Kingship in Mesopotamia was a sacral institution; and the king shared the holiness of the institution to such an extent that we are justified in speaking of his divinity.[4] This accounts, too, for the fact that some of the kings of the larger city states put the sign for 'god' (the divine ideogram) before their names.[5] Much less frequently the king is depicted in art with the attributes of a god, with horns, for instance, or as a figure of supernatural stature. As a rule he is presented as a man among men.[6] In so far as the Babylonian king is endowed with divine powers and qualities, he may be regarded as a 'divine' being; but he is not a 'god' in the same sense as Pharaoh. The express attribution of divinity by the use of the divine ideogram and other symbols is relatively so infrequent that we may well suspect Egyptian influence, which, however, has not altered the genuine Babylonian conception.

As already mentioned, the king is the vice-gerent and proxy of the gods, either of the city gods, or, in the larger states, of the supreme god. In accordance with the will of the god he administers and governs the whole land, which is really the god's property,

---

[1] Cf. Labat, *Royauté*, pp. 1ff.; Frankfort, op. cit., p. 223.
[2] Frankfort, op. cit., p. 221.   [3] Labat, op. cit., p. 8.   [4] Labat, op. cit., pp. 361ff.
[5] Labat, op. cit., p. 8; Frankfort, *Kingship*, pp. 224ff. The first is Naram-sin of the Accadian dynasty; later, the kings of the third dynasty in Ur, and several kings of Isin, Rim-sin of Larsa in his later years, Samsu-iluna of the Hammurabi dynasty, and a few Kassite kings. Assyrian and neo-Babylonian kings never use it. These tendencies towards deification have nothing to do with 'Semitic' custom, as Labat seems to think. They disappear as the Semites prevail in Babylonia. Nor are they (as Frankfort has pointed out, op. cit., pp. 225f.) a consequence of basic Sumerian conceptions and the beginnings of monarchy. There must, therefore, be a special reason for them, to which we shall return below.
[6] Frankfort, op. cit., pp. 3ff., 224f.; cf. above, p. 33.

or the world and mankind, whom the gods created for their own service (see above, p. 33). The gods had kingship in mind from the time of creation, even if it is not, as in Egypt, a fundamental element in the cosmic order itself.[1] From the very beginning the potent insignia of royalty lay 'before the throne of the god Anu'.[2] Among the mythical kings of primeval times we also find gods like Tammuz, Etana, and Gilgamesh.[3] The king is king 'of the land' (that is, of the whole world of men), of 'the four quarters of the world' (*šar kibrāt irbitti*), of the universe (*šar kiššati*): these latter two titles both belong originally to the gods.[4] In theological terms this means that kingship came down from heaven as a supernatural power embodied in the royal insignia, the crown (tiara) and sceptre.[5]

The dominant thought is that the king has been designated and chosen by the gods,[6] called by name, equipped with power, 'thought of' beforehand 'in the heart of the god'; he is the man 'after the god's own heart', and so on.[7] This idea can be expressed in different mythological forms. Gudea of Lagash calls himself 'the shepherd envisaged by (the god) Ningirsu, steadfastly regarded by (the goddess) Nanshe, endowed with strength by (the god) Nindar, the man described (?) by (the goddess) Baba, child borne by (the goddess) Gatumdug, endowed with dignity and the sublime sceptre by (the god) Ig-alima, well provided with the breath of life by (the god) Dunshagar, he whom his (special) god Ningishzida has made to appear in the assembly with (proudly) raised head'.[8] The king has been suckled by goddesses, taught by gods.[9]

In accordance with a common religious tendency, this divine election of the king is often regarded as predestination.[10] Nabonidus says that the gods Sin and Nergal have destined him for dominion from the time when he was in his mother's womb; and Ashurbanipal says that his name was uttered for kingship from time immemorial. This predestination may even be dated back to creation itself. In the introduction to the code of Hammurabi it is stated that when the great gods Anu and Enlil created the

[1] Frankfort, op. cit., pp. 231f.
[2] Gadd, *Ideas of Divine Rule in the Ancient East*, p. 34.
[3] See Meissner, *Babylonien und Assyrien* II, pp. 439ff.
[4] Frankfort, op. cit., p. 228.
[5] Op. cit., pp. 237ff. [6] Op. cit., p. 229. [7] Op. cit., p. 238.
[8] Gudea Statue B II, 8ff.; see Frankfort, op. cit., p. 238.
[9] Frankfort, op. cit., pp. 300f.; Labat, *Royauté*, pp. 58, 63ff.
[10] Frankfort, op. cit., pp. 238f.

world, 'they also uttered my name', that is, as a future king, just as at that time they also decided the destiny of the world, and 'pronounced the name of Babylon', that is, decreed that Babylon was to be the capital of the world. We are not concerned here with the pre-existence of the king, or with the question whether, as has been said, 'the enthronement of a king is always a repetition of a primeval act',[1] but rather with a singular and unusually strong expression of the religious belief in predestination, and the high estimate of the matter which is implied in that belief.[2] This is clear from the very fact that the expression alternates with the idea of election from birth.[3]

Nor is the idea that the king is 'born' of such and such a goddess, or is the 'son' of such and such a god, or is 'the man who is the son of his god', and the like[4] anything more than a 'mythopoeic' expression of the idea of election and of the close relationship between the king and the god which election establishes. This is obvious, for instance, from the many different ideas in the passage quoted from Gudea.[5] It is obvious, too, in the statement made by the Assyrian king Ashurnasirpal of himself, that he 'was born among unknown mountains', and that the goddess Ishtar brought him thence to be 'a shepherd of men'.[6] He was in fact the legitimate son of king Shamshi-adad, and born in the royal palace. The myth of the birth of the sun god is used here to express divine election and predestination. Nor is anything more implied when, for instance, in invoking the god, the king sometimes says, 'I have no mother; thou art my mother. I have no father; thou art my father'.[7] This does not mean that he has been super-naturally begotten and born of the deity in a literal, metaphysical sense. It gives vivid expression to the fact that he has none but

---

[1] See Additional Note II.

[2] It seems, on the whole, to be characteristic of the religious mode of expression and its relationship to the 'mythopoeic' way of thinking that it prefers to use categories of time in order to express judgements of value. What is old is valuable and 'right'. Age and primeval origin are proof of high value.

[3] Therefore, to use later theological terminology, we are here concerned with the 'ideal pre-existence' of the king in the divine decree. Surely this thought does not have its origin in the annual installation of the king which was associated with the yearly recreation of the world and the repeated experience of the primeval situation. We can deduce too much from cultic experience. The same religious estimate of vocation, expressed in terms of predestination, is present in the statement that Yahweh appointed Jeremiah a prophet 'before I formed you in the belly' (Jer. i, 5).

[4] See Engnell, *Divine Kingship*, Index, s.v. 'Son of the God'; Labat, *Royauté*, pp. 51ff.

[5] Cf. Frankfort, *Kingship*, pp. 238ff.

[6] Op. cit., p. 239; Mowinckel, *Kongesalmerne*, pp. 30f.

[7] Gudea Cyl. A II, 6f.; Engnell, *Divine Kingship*, p. 16, reads too much into the language.

the god on whom to rely.[1] The king's sonship is not understood metaphysically, as in Egypt. He is not the 'son' of any particular god, but may be regarded as the son of all gods and goddesses. The god is his 'creator', and has 'brought him into being'; but the god or goddess has not 'begotten' or 'conceived' him; but 'fashioned him with the hands in his mother's womb'.[2] There is a distinction between this mode of bringing into existence and the physical relationship of father or mother.[3]

Sonship signifies an intimate relationship of trust and obedience. As a 'son', the king is the object of care, love, and protection from the god or goddess (or from all the gods); and he owes them filial obedience in their service. He is chosen to be a son; but, in accordance with Babylonian ideas, this means that his relation to them is regarded as that of adoption.[4] Indeed, the formula of adoption is, 'You are my son, whom I have begotten'.[5]

The thought of the divine choice of the king appears in a purely mythical form in statements about several ancient Babylonian kings (in part mythical kings of primeval antiquity), or about legendary founders of dynasties, to the effect that they grew up in the garden of the gods as their favourites. This is doubtless a reflection of the cultic function of the king in tending the tree of life, or its cultic counterpart, and making it grow, that is as ensuring life and security on earth and for men.[6]

The election of the king implies that he has a definite vocation and a definite task, namely to represent the gods before men and vice versa.[7] This is what is meant by the statement that he has been 'sent' by the gods.[8] Obviously this does not imply that the king has come from heaven, or from the world of the gods.[9]

[1] Engnell's expression, 'divinization from nativity' (e.g., *Divine Kingship*, p. 17), like 'identity with the god', is therefore misleading. Labat also warns against making too much of the mythical forms (*Royauté*, pp. 55ff.).

[2] Frankfort, op. cit., p. 300.   [3] Labat, op. cit., p. 58; but see below, p. 43.

[4] Frankfort, op. cit., pp. 299ff.; Labat, op. cit., pp. 55f. Nor do the sources referred to by Christliebe Jeremias (*Die Vergöttlichung der babylonisch-assyrischen Könige*, pp. 5ff.) prove more than that the king was adopted and brought up by the gods.

[5] See the references in Gunkel, *Die Psalmen*, p. 7 (on Ps. ii, 7).

[6] Widengren, *Religionens värld*[2], p. 138; *R.o.B.* ii, 1943, pp. 58ff. It is possible that ideas drawn from the myth about the *Urmensch* are present here; see below, p. 55 n. 3. It may be that the mythical sometimes veils political reality, i.e. the king in question was originally a priest and the god's 'governor' (ENSI, *iššakku*) at the main temple of the city state, or a feudatory prince who had attained royal status.

[7] Cf. Frankfort, op. cit., pp. 252, 258ff.   [8] See Widengren in *R.o.B.* ii, 1943, pp. 69ff.

[9] For the idea of 'being sent' among the Semites, see E. von Dobschütz in *J.B.L.* xli, 1922, pp. 212ff. Of course the expression is not used in so specific a way as to justify us in deducing from it ideas about the sending of the prophets, or of the Messiah as one sent, as Widengren seems to think. The word is obviously a natural term to apply to any one with a divine mission.

Normally the vocation comes through an oracle; and the gods restrict their choice for the most part to the family of the ruling king, but are not inevitably committed to it. In actual fact the outcome of the struggle for power between the claimants to the throne would often decide whom the gods had chosen and sent.[1] He is actually equipped with divine power when he is designated crown prince, and when he is crowned.[2] The regalia, crown and sceptre, are 'divine'. They are charged with power and transmit power; and they can be regarded, in mythopoeic fashion, as gods. The Sumerians spoke of the goddesses Ninmenna and Ninpa, 'the Lady of the Crown', and 'the Lady of the Sceptre'.[3] At the coronation the king acquires a new nature, which is expressed in a new name.[4] He assumes command, for instance, by authority of King Ashur,[5] as a man divinely endowed, but still a man.[6]

The king is the intermediary between gods and men. By means of oracles (asked for or sent), he must discover the will of the gods and accomplish it on earth. He must represent men before the gods, and govern his realm in accordance with the law of the gods.[7] In principle, therefore, he is also priest (šangû),[8] even if there are professional priests,[9] who in practice carry out the daily routine which forms part of his duties. The king is their head;[10] and on all important occasions he takes the leading part in the cult, in which he has important functions, both at the annual festivals and at those of penitence and expiation. He also receives oracles directly, for instance, through dreams in the temple.[11] He conducts sacrifices and performs rites. In relation to the gods, he is 'servant', subordinate to them and dependent on them.[12] The god is his 'king' and 'lord'. But the title of servant also implies that he has a task to perform by the god's authority. The gods and the king are united by powerful bonds. The gods visit him in his palace; and he writes letters to them and submits his concerns to them.[13]

But he also represents the people before the gods, and is responsible for relations between them.[14] He must expiate and atone

---

[1] Frankfort, op. cit., pp. 243ff.
[2] Op. cit., p. 245. [3] Op. cit., pp. 245ff. [4] Op. cit., p. 246.
[5] Op. cit., loc. cit. Engnell's interpretation of the cry of homage during the coronation procession, 'Ashur is king' (*Divine Kingship*, p. 17), reverses the sense.
[6] Frankfort, op. cit., p. 248. [7] Op. cit., pp. 252, 258ff.
[8] Op. cit., loc. cit.; Labat, *Royauté*, pp. 131ff., cf. pp. 300ff.
[9] Labat, op. cit., pp. 134f.
[10] Labat, op. cit., pp. 202ff.; Frankfort, op. cit., p. 252.
[11] Labat, op. cit., pp. 147f., 255ff.; Frankfort, op. cit., pp. 251ff.
[12] Frankfort, op. cit., pp. 255ff. [13] Op. cit., p. 266. [14] Op. cit., pp. 258ff.

for the people's sins, and must personally submit to the rites of atonement.[1] He may even have to suffer death for the sins and impurity of the people. That is why the Assyrians had a 'substitute king' (*šar pûḫi*) when disaster threatened the land. He had, for instance, to take upon himself the dangers of evil omens, in order to avert the judgements which were threatening the king, or had already befallen him.[2] This may be a survival from the old primitive conception of the king as the mana-filled man who bears in his own person the power that creates good fortune for the entire community, and who must die when experience shows that power has left him. The same mode of thought is also found among the old Northmen.[3]

We see then that in Mesopotamia even the king's religious attitude to the gods differs from what we find in Egypt.[4] The conception of the king is most clearly seen in his position in the cult,[5] especially at the great New Year festivals, the ritual of which is known to us from the Babylonian festival of Marduk at the spring equinox.[6] As we have seen, the basis of the life of society is the establishment and maintenance of harmony between the powers of life; and society must be sustained by the positive forces of existence, the gods with their vital power.[7] But this harmony was not regarded as something stable, as inherent in the cosmic order itself. It was dependent upon the often inscrutable will of the gods. The gods 'decided the fate' of lands and peoples as they pleased. Admittedly their will was 'right' and 'justice'; but what right was was often beyond human comprehension.[8] The cult was a system instituted by the gods themselves to enable men to learn their will, to serve them, and to ensure their help.

But even in the gods' own world harmony has to be restored. In the beginning, they defeated the powers of chaos and death; but every year these powers escape again, and threaten life with

[1] Op. cit., pp. 26off.

[2] Labat, op. cit., pp. 103ff., 353ff.; Frankfort, op. cit., pp. 262ff.

[3] Cf. van der Leeuw, *Religion in Essence and Manifestation*, pp. 115ff.; cf. p. 217. Hooke's presentation of this idea (*The Origins of Early Semitic Ritual*, pp. 10ff.) is marked by undue theoretical generalization, and gives it a wider application than it had in Mesopotamia.

[4] Frankfort, op. cit., pp. 267f. This more sober interpretation of the sacral king in Babylonia and Assyria is also maintained by Ravn in *Illustreret Religionshistorie*[2], pp. 148ff.

[5] See the summary in Hooke, *The Origins of Early Semitic Ritual*, pp. 6ff.

[6] See Zimmern, *Zum babylonischen Neujahrsfest* I–II; Pallis, *The Babylonian Akîtu Festival*; Frankfort, *Kingship*, pp. 313ff. For more detailed references to literature, see Engnell, *Divine Kingship*, pp. 201f.

[7] Frankfort, op. cit., pp. 103, 277.   [8] Op. cit., pp. 278f.

drought, and flood, and all such things as make life hazardous. The changes in the life of nature show that sometimes the god himself falls into the power of the forces of chaos. This concerns not only the gods of fertility and vegetation properly so called. Even the great gods like Marduk may for a season be 'imprisoned' in 'the mountain', in the power of the forces of death.[1] 'The suffering god' is an essential aspect of Mesopotamian gods, not only of Tammuz, the god of fertility, but also of all the other gods of the power of life, who are in reality identical in character with him, and are sometimes simply Tammuz under other names, or at least could easily be identified with him.[2] At the height of summer nature itself shows that the god has departed, is 'dead', 'imprisoned', 'overpowered', has 'descended', and the like. His counterpart is the mother goddess and goddess of fertility, his 'mother', or 'sister', or 'beloved', who mourns for him, searches for him, and finally finds him and sets him free again.[3] The dying or suffering and rising god represents that side of the whole power of nature which creates and generates life in plants, animals, and men.[4]

In Babylonia, as elsewhere in the East, the chief annual festival was regarded as an actual re-creation of the world, a deliverance from the domination of the powers of chaos, which had again brought about the withering of nature and the death of the god of fertility, which had held Marduk 'prisoner', and now threatened all life and order with destruction. The god's advent, victory, and resurrection or deliverance, which are brought about through effectual rites, signify therefore that the world is created anew. The myth of creation is the *muthos* of the festival. In later times, the poetic epic of creation is its 'lection', or 'legend';[5] and the cultic 'drama' is a visible and more or less symbolic presentation of what is taking place; and as it does 'take place' in the drama, it becomes reality.[6]

---

[1] See Additional Note III.

[2] Frankfort, *Kingship*, p. 288. As a rule, a god is not originally limited to any particular natural process, but is from the beginning and always simply 'a god', i.e., one who represents all the life, and power, and holiness which society needs for its existence, the powers of nature, the institutions and ideals of society, and the sacred harmony which they express and maintain. Cf. op. cit., p. 279.

[3] Frankfort, op. cit., p. 283.

[4] Op. cit., pp. 285f.

[5] For the myth of creation as a cultic legend in Egypt, see Kees in *N.G.W.G.*, 1930, pp. 345ff.; in Babylonia, Meissner, *Babylonien und Assyrien* II, pp. 63, 96, 99, 104; Frankfort, *Kingship*, p. 319; in Israel, *Ps.St.* II, pp. 45ff.; Humbert in *R.H.Ph.R.* xv, 1935, pp. 1–27.

[6] See *Ps.St.* II, pp. 19ff., and art. 'Drama, religionsgeschichtlich' in *R.G.G.*²

In this drama the king plays an important part. For the gods and for society he is 'instrumental in procuring for the community the boon of a harmonious integration with nature',[1] with the order and powers of existence. Particularly important is his role on the day of atonement, the fifth of the twelve days in the festival sequence.[2] Here the king must first relinquish his office into the hands of the god, and then receive it back from him and be reinstated as king. On behalf of the people he must first do penance, be divested of his regalia, submit to humiliating treatment at the hands of the high priest, make a confession in which he protests that he has not sinned, that he has not neglected the worship of the god, that he 'has not injured Babylon', and so on. He then receives the promise of Marduk's favour, and is again arrayed in crown and sceptre and reinstated as king. The rite is a penitential ceremony, and at the same time symbolizes the lowest depths of the state of chaos and degradation. The whole established order of existence has been disintegrated, even kingship itself which was divinely instituted to help to maintain the harmony of existence. But at the same time the rite signifies the 'absolution', the beginning of the restoration of society and its 'world' through the restitution of its representative and link with the gods. The New Year festival is also a repetition of the king's coronation, as is evident from the fact that the first year of his reign was officially reckoned from the New Year festival following his predecessor's death. The rest of the preceding year was 'the beginning of his reign' his *rêš šarrūti*.[3]

By means of the rites of penance and lamentation, king and people share in the experience of Marduk's imprisonment and humiliation, which are the occasion of these rites.[4] The king heads the procession 'in search of the imprisoned god'.[5] In Assyria the king thus 'represents' the god Ninurta, who here takes the place which Marduk's son, Nabu, has in the liberation of the god. But this does not mean that he 'is' Ninurta in a literal sense.[6] He is his visible representative and champion in the cultic drama, just as he is normally the representative of the gods before men.

---

[1] Frankfort, op. cit., p. 318.
[2] Labat, *Royauté*, pp. 240ff., 323ff.; Frankfort, op. cit., pp. 319ff., 409 n. 14.
[3] See Dürr in *Theologie und Glaube* xx, 1928, pp. 313ff.
[4] Frankfort, op. cit., pp. 321f.
[5] Op. cit., p. 324.
[6] Cf. the commentary, *K.A.R.*, 307; see Labat, op. cit., p. 245. Here we read, 'The king, who is carried out of Ekur with the gold crown on his head, and sitting on the throne so that they can carry him, and who walks (*sic*) to the castle, (that is) Ninurta

Thus Marduk's 'liberation' and 'resurrection' from the underworld are celebrated, and in the great assembly of the gods the
fate is fixed once again, when dominion has been restored to
Marduk. The king here plays the part of 'master of ceremonies'
in the assembly of the gods.[1] This is the personal function of a
royal priest, not of a divine being.

The king also appears as leader in the campaign of the gods
against the forces of chaos. In Assyria, he sometimes represents
the chief god, Ashur himself, or his son Ninurta, in the war
chariot.[2] This, too, is doubtless to be understood as representation, and not as an actual identification of the king with the god.
In fact, both the god and the king are thought of as being present.[3]
The king is, so to speak, the commander of the god's army in this
combat of *ragnarok* (the judgement of the gods in the old Norse
mythology).[4]

The climax of the procession is a symbolic presentation of the
victory over Tiamat-Chaos.[5] The king must take part in it all
as the god's indispensable instrument, through whom human
society enjoys the benefit of the victory.[6] He is the link between
gods and men, and the representative of both. What happens to
the king symbolizes what has happened to the god. When the
king is borne in triumph on his throne from the temple to the
palace, the meaning is that 'Ninurta has avenged his father'.[7]

Another part of this festival was the 'sacred marriage', the
effectual symbol of the renewal of life.[8] Here the king appears

---

[1] Frankfort, op. cit., p. 325. [2] Op. cit., p. 327.

[3] King Sennacherib had this ritual scene portrayed on the copper doors of the house
(temple) of the New Year Festival in Ashur; and in an inscription he describes the
picture; see Frankfort, op. cit., p. 327. It seems to me to be most natural to interpret
the text as indicating that both the god and the king were represented, standing in
Ashur's chariot. This is confirmed by the beginning of the list of gods who took part
in the procession: 'Image of Ashur, going to war against Tiamat; image of Sennacherib,
king of Assyria.' This seems to imply two images, one of the god, and the other of the
king.

[4] I cannot find that Labat's examination of the commentary on the festival ritual,
K 3476 (*Royauté*, pp. 241ff.), provides any evidence that the king is Marduk incarnate.
He carries out the symbolical rites, and plays his part as representative of the god;
but nothing more. Even Labat (op. cit., pp. 244f.) has to admit the possibility of this
interpretation.

[5] Frankfort, op. cit., pp. 327f. [6] Op. cit., p. 328. [7] See above, p. 41 n. 6.

[8] Labat, op. cit., pp. 115ff., 247ff.; Frankfort, op. cit., p. 295.

---

who has avenged his father.' But this cannot mean that the king literally *is* Ninurta,
but that this part of the festival ritual *signifies* or *symbolizes* that Ninurta is victorious.
The commentary gives a theological and symbolical interpretation of all kinds of
detail in the ritual. We read, for instance, that the 'horses which have been yoked'
are 'the sceptres of Zu' (i.e., the storm bird, here representing the power of chaos).
Obviously the horses do not *embody* the sceptres.

sometimes (but not always, nor even as a rule) as the consort
of the goddess, chosen by her to be her bridegroom; and through
his intimate association with her he obtains, on behalf of the
community, a share in the divine fertilizing power, which he
transmits to the entire community.

The king assumes this role, not because, through the entire
cultic drama, he is supposed already to have become one with the
risen god, but because, on certain occasions, the goddess 'selects'
him, presumably by means of an oracle.[1] He then, no doubt,
represents Tammuz[2] or Marduk, but as a proxy. In a still higher
degree he represents human society[3] which, through him and his
divinization in the cult, shares in the renewed vital force which
belongs to Tammuz.[4] At this moment he 'is' also the 'son', the
'lover', and the 'husband' of the goddess. In the cultic hymns he
is therefore called 'Tammuz', as is stated, for instance, of King
Idin-Dagan of Isin.[5] He experiences what Tammuz has experienced, and is therefore filled with the same vital force, the same
faculty of creating and transmitting life, to which the resurrection
of Tammuz and his union with the goddess bear witness. But it is
as the representative of mankind that he has this experience. The
initiative in this nuptial act is taken by the goddess herself, the
king being even then her 'servant'.[6]

We may take it that this rite, too, goes back to the 'primitive'
conception of the mana-filled great chief whose mana is renewed
by immediate sexual intercourse with the goddess. If this be so, it
shows still more clearly that we cannot speak here of a real
'identity' of the king with Tammuz.

So intimate an association with the goddess naturally gives the
king concerned a lasting stamp of divinity; and there are grounds
for believing that it was precisely those kings who were selected
as bridegrooms of the goddess who continued to regard themselves
as divine and put the divine ideogram before their names.[7]

Here then we have the starting point for a further development
of the idea. There appears to be one single instance of the idea
that the king was the physical offspring of the god and the goddess.[8]

[1] Frankfort, op. cit., p. 297.
[2] Cf. the hymn to King Shu-Sin of Ur, translated and discussed by Falkenstein in
Die Welt des Orients ii, 1947, pp. 43ff.
[3] Frankfort, op. cit., p. 297.   [4] Op. cit., pp. 296, 299; Labat, op. cit., p. 280.
[5] Frankfort, op. cit., pp. 295f.; Labat, op. cit., pp. 249f. For Sumerian hymns of
homage to the king see also Kramer in *B.A.S.O.R.* 88, Dec. 1942, pp. 10ff.
[6] Frankfort, op. cit., p. 297.   [7] Op. cit., pp. 297ff.; see above, p. 34.
[8] Frankfort, op. cit., p. 301 (Eannatum of Lagash).

In particular, when one of the kings subdued other city states, it would, for political reasons, be natural for him to emphasize this divine character in relation to his vassals.[1] It might then come about that the vassal would erect a temple for his divine overlord, as did a vicegerent in Ur for 'his god' King Shu-Sin of Ur. So did Ituria, governor of Eshnunna, for King Shu-Sin: after the liberation Ituria rebuilt it, making it part of his own palace.[2] Dungi of Ur is once called 'the god of his country.[3] The great King Hammurabi himself is once called 'the god of kings'.[4] We hear, too, of the worship of the royal statues.[5] In accordance with normal primitive thought, a person's likeness is regarded as the bearer of his being and soul power, the perfect representative of the person himself. When the king's statue was erected in the temple of the god, it was in order that it might constantly represent the king himself 'before the god', remind the god of the king, and intercede on his behalf. Thus King Gudea instructs his statue in the inscription, 'Statue, say to my king' (i.e., the god). The king's 'life' is in the statue; but 'life' must be nourished with sacrificial food and drink. Such a statue was not really regarded as a god.[6] But a statue which was endowed with power and life in this way might sometimes be invoked with gifts to intercede with the gods.[7] To the ordinary man, the powerful 'divine' king might easily seem to be in the same position as the gods, since it was through him that all their blessing was conveyed to the people. The ordinary man enjoyed protection and life in the 'shadow' of the 'godlike' king, as the king himself lived under the protection of the 'shadow of the god'.[8] Consequently in proper names the king may often take the place which usually belongs to the god: 'The-king-is-my-life', 'Rim-sin-is-my-god', 'The-king-is-my-god', and

[1] Op. cit., pp. 301f.
[2] Op. cit., p. 302. Christliebe Jeremias, *Die Vergöttlichung der babylonisch-assyrischen Könige*, p. 17.
[3] Jeremias, op. cit., p. 16.   [4] Frankfort, op. cit., p. 302.
[5] Frankfort, op. cit., pp. 302ff.; Jeremias, op. cit., pp. 13, 15, 17, 18.
[6] An offering to a god was described as '(offering) to the god X', whereas gifts to the royal statue were described as 'to the statue of King Y', without any divine ideogram; see Frankfort, op. cit., p. 303.
[7] This is in accord with the well-known fact that cultic objects which are charged with power, such as the door or the door-handle of the temple, may be personified and invoked as intercessors; see Frankfort, op. cit., pp. 305f. For the statue or the memorial as a living being of divine character with a 'soul', see also Euler in *Z.A.W.* lv, 1937, p. 291.
[8] Frankfort, op. cit., p. 304. Against the interpretation of this statement advanced by Engnell (and by Christliebe Jeremias in *Die Vergöttlichung der babylonisch-assyrischen Könige*), see Frankfort, op. cit., p. 406 n. 35. Cf. also Oppenheim's treatise on 'the Shadow of the King' in *B.A.S.O.R.* 107, Oct. 1947, pp. 7ff.

the like.[1] Or a man may take an oath 'by the god and by the king',[2] thereby filling himself with the sacred power[3] which resides in the gods and in their representative the king. It is also understandable that such deified royal statues might become objects of worship after the death of the king, and that we hear of temples where the cult of great kings was practised after their death.[4] This comes from the same primitive idea of the dead ancestor or chief as a being filled with power and blessing, which also lies behind the worship of the dead Pharaoh (see above, p. 31), but of which only occasional traces occur in Babylonia.

As we have already said, the intention of the gods in creating kingship and the king is that he shall see to it that men render to the gods the 'service' which they were created to render. But the king should also care for the material and moral welfare of men. Hammurabi, 'who fears the gods', has been called to the throne 'to make justice prevail in the land, to destroy the evil and the wicked, that the strong should not harm the weak, to rise like the sun god upon mankind (lit., the black-headed), to give light in the land, and increase the well-being of men'.[5]

Through his good relationship with the gods, a relationship which is strengthened and made effective by means of the cult, the king is able to convey to men the blessings of nature, good crops, abundance, peace, and so on. He is the channel through whom the blessing flows down.[6] He is 'like a god'.[7] In poetic language he may be called 'the sun.[8] He is 'like the tree of life',[9] and so on. He does not himself create blessing, but he prays to the gods to give it;[10] and he imparts it by being the 'man after the gods' own heart', who in the cult establishes the mystical union between gods and men.

The Mesopotamian royal texts are full of effusive descriptions of the material, social, and moral prosperity which abounds in the land when the rightful king has come to the throne, or when he has performed his cultic duties in the right and proper way, and complied with the will of the gods: then they reward him with years of prosperity and with every conceivable blessing.

---

[1] Frankfort, op. cit., pp. 306f.

[2] Op. cit., p. 306; Labat, *Royauté*, p. 226. This custom seems to have lasted only for short periods.

[3] For this interpretation of the oath see Pedersen, *Der Eid bei den Semiten*, pp. 128ff.; *Israel* III–IV, p. 450.   [4] See Jeremias, op. cit., pp. 13, 16, 17, 18.

[5] Introduction to the Code of Hammurabi.

[6] Cf. Frankfort, op. cit., pp. 307ff.   [7] See the quotation, op. cit., p. 309.

[8] Op. cit., p. 308.   [9] See Additional Note IV.   [10] Frankfort, op. cit., p. 311.

When Thou, O faithful shepherd Gudea,
shalt have begun work for me on Eninnu, my royal residence,
I will call up in heaven a moist wind.
It shall bring thee plenty from on high
and in thy days the country shall spread its hands over wealth.
Wealth shall accompany the laying of the foundations of my
house.
All the broad fields will bear crops for thee;
dikes and canals will swell for thee.
Where the water has not been wont to rise,
On the high ground it will gush forth for thee.
Oil will be poured abundantly in Sumer in thy time,
Good weight of wool will be given in thy days.

says the god Ningirsu to King Gudea.[1] And when Ashurbanipal,
'the husbandman' of his land, had come to the throne, 'Adad
(the rain god) sent his rains, Ea opened his fountains; the grain
grew five cubits tall in the stalk, the ear was five-sixths of a cubit
long; heavy crops and a rich yield made the fields constantly
abound, the orchards yielded a plentiful harvest; the cattle brought
forth their young successfully,—in my reign there was fullness to
overflowing, in my years there was abundant plenty'.[2] There are
many such expressions of the 'blessing' (to use the Hebrew term)
which men thought themselves justified in expecting that the gods
would 'fix as the fate' of the righteous king and his people when
they met to 'fix the fate' in the 'assembly of the gods' in the
chamber of fate.[3] When *we* apply to this the term 'paradisal'
fertility, the metaphorical expression is *ours* and does not reflect
the ancients' own ideas. There is no 'paradise myth' behind these
hyperbolical expressions of oriental imagination. The Babylonians
had no conception of a primeval paradise, now lost, which the
new king restored when he inaugurated a new epoch.[4] It is just

[1] Gudea Cyl. A XI, 5ff.; cf. Frankfort, op. cit., pp. 257f.; cf. Thureau-Dangin in
V.A.B. I, pp. 100f.
[2] Rassam Cyl. I, 45; see Streck, *Ashurbanipal* II, pp. 6f.; cf. Frankfort, op. cit., p. 310.
[3] Like several others, Labat here uses the term 'the Messianic King'; but see
Additional Note I.
[4] A. Jeremias, *Handbuch*, p. 207; Gressmann, *Der Messias*, p. 220, *et al.*, has maintained
that the Sumerian and Babylonian texts refer to the king as the one who is to 'restore'
paradise to mankind. This is not correct; see Dürr, *Ursprung und Ausbau*, p. 103 n. 24,
with references to the literature. Vriezen arrives at the same conclusion in his *Onderzoek
naar de paradijsvoorstelling bij de oude semietische volken*, 'paradise as a garden with the
first man and the tree of life is typically prophetic'. This conception appears first
among the Persians, who (unlike the Egyptians and Babylonians) had a definite
eschatology.

conceivable that a few features in the description of the happy state under the righteous king may contain echoes of Babylonian ideas of the wondrous garden of the gods at 'the mouth of the rivers', which is mentioned in the Gilgamesh epic and elsewhere.[1] But such stylistic influence from one motif upon another is a very different thing from conscious identification of whole systems of ideas.[2]

If we would sum up in one word what the people expected of the king who had been chosen and endowed with power, we may use the Mesopotamians' own expression and call him 'the shepherd'. Hammurabi, for example, so describes himself. The king is to be 'the shepherd of the black-headed ones'. But we may also sum it up in the Hebrew expression 'the saviour of his people'. The king will 'work salvation', *yēša'*, in the true sense of the word, 'width', 'spaciousness'.[3] It means not only deliverance from earthly, cosmic, and demonic enemies, and from distress and misfortune, but good conditions, well-being, outward and inward prosperity, fertility in field, flock, and nation, quietness and order in the state, 'peace', and the like. When, in the course of the year, prosperity and vital energy have been exhausted, then the king, by performing and leading the appropriate, re-creating, cultic acts, seeks to ensure that the gods will again be victorious over the powers of chaos, create the world anew, and bless the land. By his vicarious and representative rites in the festival, he will atone for the impurity which has accumulated (see above, p. 41). Accordingly, every new king, and not least the founder of a dynasty, maintains that through himself the gods have brought prosperity, salvation, and abundance to land and people. We often find the king presenting himself as 'the saving shepherd' (*rē'û mušallimu*), or 'the shepherd who brings justice', 'the righteous or just shepherd', as Hammurabi calls himself;[4] just as it is often said of the gods that they 'save', i.e., provide all the good things which are needed for life and well-being. The adjective 'saving' is not a special term regularly applied to a king-god, like 'Soter' in the Hellenistic period. It is the natural linguistic expression to convey the function and work of the righteous king.

[1] The Gilgamesh Epic IX, 163ff.

[2] It is possible that the Sumerians, the Babylonians, and others had the idea that the blessed garden of the gods had its counterpart in the temple garden of which the king was the gardener; see Widengren, *R.o.B.* ii, 1943, pp. 58f. But that does not mean that the king is an incarnation of the king of paradise, much less that such an idea lies behind the royal ideology; see below, p. 81.

[3] See Pedersen, *Israel* I–II, pp. 330ff.

[4] Code of Hammurabi, Epilogue; cf. also Staerk, *Soter* II, p. 240.

We may sum up as follows. The king is not a god, as in Egypt; but he has been endowed with a divine vocation and with a super-human power and quality, which in some respects puts him on the same plane as the gods. He possesses a 'divinity' shared by no other mortals.[1] He is 'like a god'; he is 'the image of the gods.'[2] He has been filled with divine power, and has authority on earth from the gods, as long as he acts in accordance with their will, with 'justice'. Hymns may, indeed, be sung in his honour on his festival day;[3] But men do not pray to the king; on the contrary, they pray the gods to bless him.[4]

It follows from all that has been said, that in Mesopotamia the king was not a real god in the same way as in Egypt.[5] Nor is it the case, as some have maintained, that in the cultic drama the king is identical with the god, and that in the cult the god is incarnate in the king, so that it is the king who dies, and rises again, and is victorious over the powers of chaos, who creates the world anew, marries the goddess, provides fertility and life, and is worshipped as a god.[6] We cannot assert that the king generally plays the part of the god in the cultic drama.

But it is certain that in Babylonia, too, the king has a super-natural divine quality, which distinguishes him from other men. He is divine, a god to his land and people, the image of the deity, surrounded by the divine glory,[7] the breath of the people's life, as the Amarna Letters often put it, using an expression which reflects Egyptian ideas.[8] His throne is a 'divine

---

[1] Frankfort, *Kingship*, pp. 311f.

[2] See the sources referred to by Staerk, *Soter* II, pp. 502f.

[3] For Sumerian royal hymns, see Kramer, *Sumerian Mythology*, p. 13; Zimmern, *Die Vergöttlichung des Königs Lipit-Ištars*, pp. 3f.; Güterbock in *A.f.O.* xiii, 1936, pp. 26ff. n. 11; Langdon in *J.R.A.S.* 1931, pp. 367ff., cf. ibid., pp. 421ff. The style of these royal hymns is echoed in the royal inscriptions in the first person (the 'epiphany' style); see Mowinckel, *Statholderen Nehemia*, pp. 151ff.; *Eucharisterion* I, pp. 313f.

[4] See Stummer in *A.f.O.* iv, 1927, pp. 19ff.

[5] The above account of Mesopotamian kingship agrees in essentials with that given by de Fraine in *L'aspect religieux*. In Mesopotamia, the king *qua* king shared in the divine authority ('une participation fonctionelle de l'anûtu'); he was not considered a divine being *per se*. Real deification ('l'apothéose d'une divinisation') took place only with some kings of the first Accadian dynasty, the third dynasty of Ur, and some Kassite kings (cf. above, p. 34 n. 5). I have been unable to refer fully to de Fraine's valuable book.

[6] This seems to sum up fairly the views of Engnell, Widengren, Haldar, and others. Engnell often speaks of the king as being identical with the god. Labat, whose thought is usually clearer, also speaks of the king in the festival as being 'the national god incarnate' (*Royauté*, p. 240). But on the cult of the king, Engnell expresses himself more cautiously: 'the direct cult of the divine king cannot have been of great signifi-cance' (op. cit., p. 46). Engnell's criticism of Labat's still more cautious statement (*Royauté*, p. 372; cf. p. 368) does not seem justified.

[7] Cf. Christliebe Jeremias, *Die Vergöttlichung der babylonisch-assyrischen Könige*, pp. 9f.

[8] Detailed references are given by Alt in *P.J.B.* xxxii, 1936, p. 20 n. 2.

throne'.[1] In him all power and justice dwell; and he is the earthly administrator of the divine government.

From the time of his election in the womb and his accession, he is filled with supernatural, divine powers and qualities, so that he can always be the appropriate link between gods and men, and represent both in their mutual relationship. He becomes the palladium of the community, the bearer of its divine powers, the channel through which divine energy, vitality, blessing, and good fortune flow from gods to men. It is he who in his own person receives all this on men's behalf, and lets it stream out into the community. In certain respects a union of divine and human[2] takes place in his representative person.[3] Through him the powers of life come in visible and tangible form to human society. His person is imbued not only with justice and righteousness, but with the creative, life-giving, life-preserving, fertilizing powers, which are thus available for the land and the people. To that extent we may say hyperbolically that he creates life, fertility, and the like.[4]

It is through his participation in the cultic drama and the usual

---

[1] Accad. *kussī ilūti*; see Christliebe Jeremias, op. cit., p. 10.

[2] Frankfort, op. cit., p. 286; cf. also Labat's carefully considered summing up, *Royauté*, pp. 361ff.; notwithstanding his divine character, the king is a man subordinate to the gods; he 'is the link uniting gods and men, and to a certain degree shares in the divine character'.

[3] In view of the general tendency of primitive thought to regard the representative and the symbol as identical with what they represent (cf. Lévy-Bruhl, *Les fonctions mentales dans les sociétés inférieures*, pp. 68ff.), we might suppose that the Babylonians held that in the cult the god momentarily revealed himself in the king. But this identity would be only temporary, and could not be made the basis of an understanding of the entire royal ideology. We are not justified in simply identifying the Mesopotamian royal ideology with primitive ideas of a chief and medicine man, who is endued with mana and divine properties; cf. Nyberg's statement: 'Sacral kingship is not a primitive Semitic idea; it is a historical innovation, which was never native to the desert, but is an invention of agricultural and civilized countries' (*Sakkunnigutlåtandet angående ledig förkl. professorsämbetet i exegetik* (*Expert's Report on the Vacant Chair of Exegesis*), p. 13). Moreover, the thought of the ancient Babylonians had left the primitive, pre-logical stage behind, and had a far more 'rational' character, as may be seen from their attempts at science. Their approach to things was 'empirico-logical', to use Albright's expression (*From the Stone Age to Christianity*[2], pp. 82ff.; cf. pp. 123, 134f., 147, 228, 257ff., 365; *Archaeology and the Religion of Israel*, pp. 26ff.).

[4] In fact, Engnell's definition of the king's divinity (whenever he so much as attempts to give any clear definition; see *Divine Kingship*, p. 31) does not go much beyond this. Of course, Engnell is right in saying that the king is 'in no way just "another feeble creature," ' (Witzel's expression). But the question is not the legitimacy of this phrase, but rather the sense in which we must understand the 'identity' of the king with the god. If Engnell adheres to his definition, then the king and the god are simply not identical; but then Engnell's statements in many other parts of the book about the full identity of the god and the king become obscure or directly misleading. It may be that many differences of opinion to which Engnell alludes (Hocart, Langdon, Witzel, and others) are the result of the difficulty of expressing 'pre-logical' realities in terms of modern, rational ideas.

E

cultic acts that this 'divinization' takes place and is constantly renewed. In the cult, the king *is* not the god, but *represents* him, in some instances more palpably than in others, but never in such a way that the clear distinction between the god and the king is obscured. Here, as in other ways, he is the connecting link, representing both the god and the people. This is evident even from his role in the drama of the New Year festival, in which his 'divinity' is in general most prominent, and in which, in many ways, he appears as one who shares in the power and nature of the gods. But he appears even more clearly and consistently as the representative of the world of men. As the connecting link between both worlds, however, he manifestly shares the experience of the fate of the gods, their impotence, their struggle, their victory and triumph, the experience of the death and resurgence of life in the reality of the cult, which determines and creates the reality of daily experience.[1] In the sacred marriage he has the same experience as Tammuz, and, to that extent, is for the time being a 'Tammuz'; but it is not as a god but as a man that he has the experience. It is as the representative of the people that the experience comes to him; and through it he imparts to the whole community for which he stands a share in the renewal of the vital forces, the resurgence of life, the blessing and salvation of the new creation. That is why he acts as priest in so many important cultic situations (see above, pp. 33, 38). His supernormal equipment enables him at one and the same time to transmit the divine energies, and to receive them on behalf of the people, as, for example, when he performs the effectual rites of fertility.[2]

Through one-sided exaggeration of the 'divinity' of the king in eastern religions, and of his position as representative of the god in the cultic drama, several scholars have recently contended that it was inherent in the king's character as identical with the god, and in the royal ideology, that he should be the suffering, dying, and rising god; and they have spoken of 'the aspect of suffering' as a constant element in the royal ideology.[3] This is, in fact, a misunderstanding. The presupposition of the theory (the king's absolute 'identity' with the god) is incorrect; and the individual

---

[1] Cf. my review of Engnell's *Divine Kingship* in *N.T.T.* xlv, 1944, pp. 70ff.; Bentzen, *Det sakrale kongedømme*, pp. 34f.; *King and Messiah*, p. 26.

[2] Labat, *Royauté*, pp. 288ff.; Gadd, *Ideas of Divine Rule in the Ancient East*, pp. 49, 91f.

[3] Engnell, *Divine Kingship*, see Index, s.v. ' "Passion", penitence, and "death" of the king'; and in *S.E.Å.* x, 1945, pp. 31ff. (= *B.J.R.L.* xxxi, 1948, pp. 3ff.); Widengren in *S.E.Å.* x, 1945, pp. 66ff.

arguments advanced in support of the theory of the suffering and dying king are untenable.[1]

In other parts of the ancient east, too, we find the influence of the ideas about kings and kingship which were held in the ancient civilizations. We find it, for instance, among the Hittites of Asia Minor.[2] Here, too, the starting point is the ancient tribal system, with the chosen chief as the leading man in the assembly of warrior nobles. When the name of Labarnash, the founder of the dynasty, is used as a royal title, this is doubtless an echo of ancestor worship, and of the conception of the ancestor as filled with power and made divine. The king is the 'hero',[3] equipped by the deity with superhuman faculties. He is hedged about by tabus of many kinds, doubtless inherited from an older 'mana-chieftaincy'.

As the kingdom increased in political power, and began to take part in international relations, it was also influenced by ideas from the ancient civilizations: from the east through the extensive intermingling of the Hittites with the Hurrians of northern Mesopotamia, through ancient Assyrian influence in Asia Minor, and through strong Assyrian trading colonies there, and so on; from Egypt, *inter alia*, through direct political connexions in war and peace. The use of the winged sun's disk (Horus-Re as the sunhawk) as a royal symbol is the result of Egyptian influence. The king himself is the 'sun-majesty'. 'My sun' is his way of referring to himself in the official formula. Like the Mesopotamian kings, he may also be called 'the son of Teshub', the god of storm, rain, and war. The king's mother is called 'the mother of the god', i.e., of the divine king.[4] After death the king enters the world of the gods and 'becomes a god'; the expression simply means that the king dies. This is probably a combination of ancient ancestor worship with the Egyptian royal ideology. Traces of Egyptian

---

[1] See Additional Note V.

[2] See Götze, *Kleinasien*, pp. 8off; Engnell, *Divine Kingship*, pp. 52ff.

[3] See Götze, op. cit., p. 82: 'In der Bezeichnung "Held" kommt die Steigerung der menschlichen Eigenschaften zum Ausdruck, die den König an die Sphäre des Göttlichen heranführt'; cf. Engnell, *Divine Kingship*, p. 76. In the Ugaritic text SS, the new-born god is called *mt* = Heb. plur. *meṭîm*, Accad. *mutu* = 'man', 'hero'. Of course this has nothing to do with the conception of the *Urmensch*, as Engnell thinks (op. cit., p. 169, n. 3); cf. Mowinckel in *St.Th.* II, i, 1948/9, p. 80.

[4] See Engnell, op. cit., p. 58. It ought not to be concluded from this (as is done by Engnell) that the king was regarded as the issue of a (cultic) divine marriage. Nor does anything suggest that the king was regarded as divine from birth (op. cit., p. 57). On the whole, Engnell draws too sweeping conclusions from slender evidence, seeking, as far as possible, to find his common eastern pattern of royal ideology even among the Hittites; see, e.g., op. cit., pp. 55, 56, 57, 59, 61, 64.

influence seem to be frequent; but they are not integrated in a coherent theological system like the Egyptian royal ideology itself. As in Babylonia, offerings were made to the king's statue, thought of as charged with power. The king was the 'image' of the god.

It appears that we are here dealing with individual borrowed elements, rather than with any consistent ideology of a divine king. But it is clear that the Hittite king, too, was regarded as a superhuman, 'godlike' being, endowed with divine faculties and qualities.

Similar ideas to those of Mesopotamia are found in Canaan, Israel's immediate environment, whose culture the Israelite settlers had assimilated. Admittedly, we have little direct knowledge of the royal ideology, and of the part played by the king as the god's representative in the cult and in the mind of the community.[1] The Ugaritic texts provide the most rewarding sources. The first of these which call for consideration are the Karit Epic and the Dan'il-Aqhat legend. Some scholars have taken the Karit Epic as a purely ritual text for cultic use, relating to the sacred marriage, in which Karit is both god and king in one person.[2] This can hardly be correct. As the poem now stands it is not a ritual text, but a poetic epic about Karit, a legendary king and the founder of a dynasty,[3] who appears as a demigod, but is at the same time, in relation to the gods, a human being.[4] It is possible, and even probable, that behind the mythical, legendary King Karit there stands a divine figure of the same type as Aleyan-Baal, the dying and rising god of life: Albright has drawn attention to the fact that Nu'man, one of the epithets applied to Karit, is identical with one used of the fertility god Adonis.[5] If so, 'the god Karit' has undergone the same development as the Babylonian Gilgamesh, who 'was two-thirds divine and one-third human' and who went forth in order to escape death and yet had to die. Originally King

---

[1] See Additional Note VI.

[2] See Engnell, op. cit., pp. 143ff., with the summary of earlier interpretations; see also his study 'The Text II K from Ras Shamra' in *Horae Soederblomianae* I, i, pp. 1ff.

[3] With this interpretation, cf. the rather similar one by Pedersen, in *Berytus* VI, 1941, pp. 63ff.; cf. also his 'Kana'anaeisk Religion' in *Illustreret Religionshistorie²*, pp. 207ff.

[4] See my remarks in *N.T.T.* xlii, 1941, pp. 129ff.; xliii, 1942, pp. 24ff.; xlv, 1944, p. 73. Cf. de Langhe, *Het Ugaritisch Keret-gedicht*; H. L. Ginsberg, *The Legend of King Keret*.

[5] See Albright in *B.A.S.O.R.* 65, Feb. 1937, p. 28 n. 20; cf. W. von Baudissin, *Adonis und Esmun*, pp. 86ff.

Gilgamesh was the god of vegetation, 'the god Tree'.[1] In the same way the god Thor in Asgard has become in the folksong 'Thor, Knight of Hafsgård'. The Karit epic 'is unmistakably a legend about men'.[2] But Karit is no ordinary historical king. The theme of the epic is the securing of posterity to perpetuate the dynasty. Pedersen is surely right in taking Karit as a hero, claimed as ancestor by a dynasty which was still reigning at the time when the epic was composed. The poem treats of Karit, the ancestor of the royal house, who lives on in later kings, and of his military expedition to win the bride, 'the young woman', who 'will bear a son to Karit' and perpetuate the life of the dynasty. The birth of a son means that life and prosperity are assured for his land and people in the coming generation. 'The Keret text presents the life of the king as the bearer of society, by describing the wedding festival of the ancestor king, the birth of the family, the fertilization of the fields through the cult.' The same thought underlies the Dan'il-Aqhat legend.[3] 'Behind the accounts of Daniel and Keret in these two royal texts lies the interplay between the souls of the god and the king.'[4]

Whether Karit was originally a divine figure or a legendary king, the historical and legendary elements in the epic are in part presented in the form and the language of myth. The motif of the epic is derived from the 'sacred marriage', which was one of the chief features in the Canaanite cultic drama. The entire religion was dominated by the idea of the dying and rising fertility god, by the thought of 'life out of death'.[5] The myth and the cultic drama describe how Baal dies in the conflict with Mot, the power of death, and how his beloved, 'the virgin Anath', searches for him, how she defeats Mot, how Baal rises again or is born again in the son he begets by Anath, and, further, how he defeats the hostile powers of chaos, is enthroned on the divine mountain in the north as king of gods and men, how he is united with Anath, the mother goddess and goddess of fertility, how he re-creates the universe, symbolized by the restoration of his temple.[6]

[1] Mowinckel in *Act.Or* xv, 1937 pp. 140ff.
[2] Ginsberg, *The Legend of King Keret*, p. 7, foot. Both de Langhe and Ginsberg underestimate the mythical element in this epic. The correct view, that Karit and Dan'il are heroes, is also maintained by Eissfeldt in *Beiträge zur Arabistik, Semitistik und Islamwissenschaft*, pp. 267ff.
[3] See Ginsberg in *B.A.S.O.R.* 97, Feb. 1945, pp. 3ff.; 98, April 1945, pp. 15ff.
[4] The last two quotations are from Pedersen in *Illustreret Religionshistorie*², p. 210.
[5] Cf. Brede Kristensen's book with this title, demonstrating the existence of this idea in Egyptian and Greek religion.
[6] We are indebted to Hvidberg (*Graad og Latter i det Gamle Testamente*) and Engnell

Themes from this cultic myth have been used as formative elements in the plot of the epic of Karit,[1] just as the motif of the death of the god has been used in the description of the death of the son Aqhat in the Dan'il Epic.[2] Karit is the specially chosen and trusted 'servant'[3] and 'son'[4] of the supreme god El. He is one of 'the gods'.[5] As in Babylonia, the royal child has been suckled by goddesses.[6] His bride, 'the noble Virgin',[7] has several features which belong to the fertility goddess; and the birth of the son guarantees life and prosperity to the royal dynasty and the people, like the birth of the son of the god in the myth. The life and health of the king mean blessing and righteous rule ('judgement') in the land. This last element also occurs in the Dan'il legend.[8] The supreme god, 'the Bull El', is his father.[9] The goddess promises immortality to the king's son, and as many years and months 'as Baal when he is alive'.[10] There are vestiges of the cult of the king's dead ancestors.[11] In the literal sense these hero kings are not themselves immortal, although they are sons of El,[12] and although for them, as for all eastern kings, men wish everlasting life (i.e., exceedingly long life). We hear that both Karit and Dan'il must die. 'The king occupies a dual, or rather, an intermediate, position between gods and men'.[13]

Whether the king of Ugarit played a part in the cultic drama as the god's 'representative', we do not know for certain, though

[1] This is the kernel of truth in Engnell's cultic interpretation of the epic.

[2] There seems to me to be no ground for Engnell's statement (op. cit., p. 141) that Dan'il 'is here [i.e., in I D, col. I, 38f.] simply identified with Ba'lu'. The text speaks of Dan'il 'conjuring the clouds' (cf. Hos. ii, 23f.) in order to make Baal keep back the rain for seven years.

[3] See Mowinckel in *N.T.T.* xliii, 1942, pp. 24ff., with references to the texts.

[4] Krt A, 41, 59, 76f., 169; Krt C cols. I–II, 10f., 20–4, 105f., 110f. (according to Ginsberg's enumeration of the lines).

[5] Krt C I–II, 22.

[6] Krt B II, 25ff.

[7] *mtt hry*; Ginsberg translates 'Lady Hurriya'.

[8] Dan'il V, 4ff.; Engnell, op. cit., p. 137.

[9] Dan'il I, 24; Engnell, op. cit., p. 136.

[10] Dan'il VI, 26ff.; Engnell, op. cit., p. 138.

[11] Dan'il I 24ff.; Engnell, op. cit., p. 136.

[12] It is brought out clearly enough in the description of Karit's illness in Krt C I, 1ff. Cf. Ps. lxxxii, 6f. It is an inversion of the truth when Engnell states (op. cit., p. 138): 'the king—although he is "immortal"—has to "die" like everyone else, or, more exactly, *for* everyone else'. Being in himself mortal, the king has an unusually long life in virtue of his kingship, because he is full of divine power.

[13] Pedersen in *Illustreret Religionshistorie*², p. 207.

(*Divine Kingship*) for making clear these fundamental features in the Aleyan-Baal myth, and its cultic meaning. Cf. my critique of Hvidberg's *Graad og Latter* in *N.T.T.* xl, 1939, and Kapelrud in *N.T.T.* xli, 1940, pp. 38ff.; see also Kapelrud, *Baal in the Ras Shamra Texts*.

there may be some grounds for thinking so.[1] If so, we have the same identification in experience of the king (as representative of the cultic assembly) with the deity, which was also characteristic of the position of the Babylonian kings in the cult (see above, p. 50).

It has sometimes been maintained that this oriental royal ideology must go back to a specific myth about a celestial, divine, 'saviour king' of the future, of whom individual kings were regarded as realizations or incarnations. But no such general, oriental, saviour myth (eschatological in greater or less degree) ever existed.[2]

Equally untenable is the theory that the royal ideology was originally associated with or derived from an *Urmensch*. Nor is the myth of the *Urmensch* a concept common to the ancient east. The fact that descriptions of the *Urmensch* sometimes contain kingly traits is in no way connected with the royal ideology as such, or with its origin.[3]

In spite of the great differences between, for instance, Egyptian and Babylonian views of the king, there are certain common basic features. As we have seen, both go back to the primitive conception of the 'mana-chief' as a being endowed in a special way with power, and possessed of divine faculties and energies. In Egypt, the king has become an incarnate god; in Babylonia, he appears with greater or less distinctness as a deified man, a superman, standing between the gods and ordinary mortals. It is chiefly in this Babylonian form that the royal ideology occurs among other eastern peoples, though certain traces of Egyptian ideas and etiquette occasionally appear, particularly among the Hittites. Thus when some modern scholars attribute 'identity' with the

---

[1] The features adduced by Hooke (*Early Semitic Ritual*, pp. 35, 42) as evidence that in the cult the king appeared in the role of the god, are only vague possibilities lacking positive proof. Nor does Engnell's rendering of the texts in *Divine Kingship* provide certain evidence of this; all the evidence is obtained with the help of the ritual pattern scheme; cf. op. cit., pp. 112, 127, 136 foot, 139 foot, 141, 150, 151, 152 foot, 155f., 161, 167. Engnell's own summary of the evidence (op. cit., pp. 168ff.) is obviously only sufficient to show that Karit has the same 'divine' features as for instance all the other earthly kings of Babylonia, and that the epic is modified by conventional motifs from the divine myth; but from this no certain conclusions can be drawn as to whether at Ugarit the king was identical with the god and played the part of the god in the cult. Cf. also Pedersen's indefinite statement in *Illustreret Religionshistorie*[2], p. 207: 'It is probable that at any rate in the early period the king played the part of the leading god in the festival.'

[2] See Mowinckel in *St. Th.* II, i, 1948/9, pp. 76ff.

[3] For further details see *St. Th.* II, i, 1948/9, pp. 71ff. Against Engnell's assertion that *ben 'ādām* is a term denoting the *Urmensch* and a royal title, see Sjöberg in *S. T. K.*, xxvi, 1950, pp. 35ff.

deity to eastern kings, and regard the 'pattern' of royal ideology as both uniform and common to the whole Near East, we must qualify their views in several ways.[1] Nevertheless the fact remains that sacral kingship played an important part in all these ancient civilizations. Even among the Babylonians, whose thought was more 'rationalistic' than that of any other eastern people, there was ascribed to the king a superhuman, we may even say a supernatural, divine quality. The king was a kind of god on earth. He had divine faculties and qualities. He was the representative of the gods before men, as he was the representative of men before the gods. He was the channel through which the power and blessing of the deity and of nature flowed to society; and he had an important and active part to play in the cult, whereby every year the gods created the world anew, and kept the universe and society in harmony with each other. Naturally, these thoughts often appear in mythical forms, in accordance with contemporary modes of thought and expression.

2. The Israelite Ideal of Kingship: Yahweh's Anointed

It is against the background of these eastern conceptions of kingship that the Israelite conception has to be considered.[2] When Israel came from the desert into Canaan, assimilated Canaanite culture, and finally, as the Old Testament sources themselves state, adopted kingship after the Canaanite model, it goes without saying that she also adopted and imitated Canaanite ideas of kingship, its forms and etiquette, and the like, just as the Roman emperor became the prototype of the national kings of the Teutons, the kings of the Franks, the Saxons, and others, and just as Charlemagne in his turn was to determine the character of the old Norse monarchy. The *Hofstil* in Israel would naturally be a more or less faithful imitation of that of Canaan, which in turn was only a special form of that found throughout the Near East,

[1] We are probably justified in saying that Widengren (*Religionens värld*[2], pp. 254ff.) ascribes too great general phenomenological importance to the developed ideology associated with sacral kingship. He rightly says that some fundamental ideas seem to be common to a particular level of culture. But the inquiry into sacral chieftainship ought to have been related more closely to the mana-filled chief and medicine man, and to the cult of ancestors, than Widengren has done.

[2] This was first maintained by Gunkel in *Preussische Jahrbücher* clviii, 1914, pp. 42f., and by Gressmann in *Ursprung*, pp. 250ff. See also Mowinckel, *Kongesalmerne*, pp. 20ff.; *Ps.St.* II, pp. 298ff.; Gunkel-Begrich, *Einleitung*, pp. 155ff.; Pedersen, *Israel* III–IV, pp. 33ff. The strong emphasis on this point of view by Hooke and his collaborators (*Myth and Ritual*, Index, s.vv. 'King', 'Kingship'; *The Labyrinth*, Index, s.vv. 'King, Divine') represents a one-sided exaggeration of the views of earlier scholars.

as it developed in the great states on the Euphrates and Tigris, and on the Nile.[1] This style and etiquette were an expression of the conception of sacral kingship.

But Israel did not take over either Canaanite religion,[2] or the sacral kingship which was connected with it, unaltered. In Yahwism the royal ideology underwent profound changes. Even in the purified, Yahwistic form of the tradition in the Old Testament, there are many indications that the forms and ideas associated with the monarchy, which were originally adopted in the court ceremonial of David and Solomon, were strongly influenced by common oriental conceptions. But we must also be prepared to find that many ideas were adopted in a sense different from that which they originally carried in Canaan or Babylonia. Many a cultic rite may have been dissociated from its original context[3] when it was appropriated for Yahwism, so that it now appears either as a survival or with a new meaning. This meaning is determined not by what it may have signified in another context, but by its context in the structural unity of which it now forms a part. As for expressions and phrases in the royal etiquette, many of these may have been just rhetorical or poetical forms, adopted simply because they belonged to the traditional literary style.

For we must not forget that the Israelite monarchy also inherited traditions from the old chieftainship of the semi-nomadic period and the time of the settlement.[4] In the traditions about Saul, the account of his simple household, court, and bodyguard are reminiscent of the establishment of an ancient chieftain rather than of an oriental king's court.[5] The chieftainship was in a measure hereditary. But the position of a tribal chief or sheikh depended primarily on his personal qualities, his ability to lead, advise, and help, and to settle disputes within the tribe or between tribes and clans.[6] All the traditions about the Judges show that they attained their position because, in a given historical situation, they were able to rally the tribe, or several tribes, around themselves, to beat off the enemy, and thus 'save' their people. In

[1] Cf. Gressmann, *Der Messias*, pp. 44ff.
[2] The view presupposed by Haldar (e.g., in *The Notion of the Desert in Sumero-Accadian and West-Semitic Religions*) is just as monstrous as was that of H. Winckler in his remarks on Israelite religion in his *Geschichte Israels*, or in *K.A.T.*[3], pp. 204ff., passim.
[3] See above p. 24. Cf. further Frankfort, *The Problem of Similarity in Ancient Near Eastern Religions*.
[4] Cf. Pedersen, *Israel* III–IV, pp. 41ff.
[5] See Buhl, *Det israelitiske Folks Historie*[7], pp. 185f.; cf. McCown, *The Ladder of Progress in Palestine*, p. 209.
[6] Cf. Pedersen, *Israel* III–IV, pp. 213ff.

time of peace they retained the authority thus gained; and the example of Gideon shows that it could also be transmitted to sons, provided they were able to uphold their father's 'honour'. But apart from the influence which the chieftain's honour won for him (and in honour there were of course included wealth, a good and numerous family, and personal moral qualities such as resourcefulness, courage, sagacity, knowledge of the traditions of justice, generosity, skill as a negotiator, and the like), his position was that of a *primus inter pares*.

The comprehensive expression for all these qualities and activities was that he 'judged'. He was 'judge', i.e., ruler, and leader, and magistrate, by virtue of his ability to do *mišpāṭ*, and his inherent 'righteousness' (*ṣeḏāḳâh*). This chieftainship has been called 'charismatic',[1] as dependent on Yahweh's 'grace-gift'; and the legends[2] often emphasize that the Judges were called to the task of liberation by a revelation from Yahweh Himself. We also hear that they performed their heroic deeds because Yahweh's spirit came upon them and endowed them with unusual power and insight.[3] When the spirit seized them in the hour of crisis, the effect was ecstasy, a high tension of all the powers and faculties of the soul. Then they 'went in this their might', with Yahweh as their protector and helper (Judges vi, 14; cf. 1 Sam. x, 1–7). There is no mention of a permanent endowment with the spirit, but of an abnormal communication of power from time to time.

In his activity the chief was dependent on the fact that he represented ancient use and wont and conceptions of justice, and on the approbation of the leading men of the tribe, 'the elders'. He had no independent power to enforce his commands. His authority was founded on the trust he enjoyed, the spiritual influence he exercised, and the approbation of public opinion and the common sense of justice.[4] If he had the tribe or a personal following behind him, he might also enforce his will on other tribes (see Judges xii, 1ff.).

[1] See Alt, *Die Staatenbildung der Israeliten in Palästina*, pp. 9f.; Michelet, *Fra Mose til profeterne*, pp. 122ff.

[2] The term 'legend' is here used to translate the Norwegian *sagn*; and 'legendary' elsewhere usually represents *sagnaktig*. The use of such terms does not, of course, imply that the narratives so designated are wholly unhistorical. Cf. Bentzen, *Introduction to the Old Testament*[2] I, p. 233 n. 4 (Translator).

[3] See Linder, *Studier till Gamla testamentets föreställningar om Anden*, pp. 1ff. Linder is scarcely right in holding that in Israel this conception is older than that of the spirit in the prophets. See below, pp. 78f.

[4] Cf. Jos. xxiv, 15; Judges vi, 25–32; viii, 1–3; xi, 4–11.

Besides his activity as a judge, the chief was also in charge of the public cult of his tribe.[1] The ancient unity of chief and seer-priest is reflected in the traditions about Moses; the chief Ehud appears as the bearer of an oracle from Yahweh (Judges iii, 19); Gideon receives oracles (Judges vi, 11ff.); and Samuel is presented both as seer-priest and as judge (1 Sam. ixf. and viif.). The memory of this twofold office appears occasionally in the tradition when it gives to the individual judge a man of oracles, or prophet, to advise and support him (Judges iv, 4ff.; 1 Sam. ixff.).

This all shows, of course, that the chief is closely associated with the god of the tribe; more so in practice than his fellow-tribesmen. This is reflected, for instance, in such phrases as 'the god of so-and-so (the chief or ancestor)'.[2] Alongside of it we also find the thought and the expression, 'the god of my house (i.e., of my family)'.[3] And a great many personal names from nearly all 'primitive' Semitic national groups show that the god of the tribe was looked upon as the father, or brother, or kinsman of the one who bore the name.[4] But this does not mean that the god was supposed to have physically begotten this particular individual. Here terms like 'father' have a sociological reference, not an individual and physical one. The god is the father, and brother, and kinsman of the whole tribe. The expression points to the tribe's origin, inasmuch as the god is often looked upon as its ancestor; but he is not the father of the chief in a sense different from that in which he is the father of the whole tribe and of all its individual members.

The Israelite monarchy is the result of the fusion of the traditions of the old chieftainship with the laws, customs, and ideas of Canaanite kingship. Thence arose the early attempts at tribal kingship under Gideon and Abimelech; and Ishbaal's kingdom east of Jordan was of the same character.[5] In contrast with these, Saul represents a conscious attempt to create a comprehensive national kingship embracing all the tribes; and he probably had

---

[1] Judges vi, 24, 25ff.; viii, 24–7; ix, 27; xvii, 1–5.
[2] Cf. Alt, *Der Gott der Väter.*
[3] See Euler in *Z.A.W.* lv, 1938, pp. 300ff.
[4] See Robertson Smith, *Religion of the Semites*[3], pp. 45ff., 509ff.; von Baudissin, *Adonis und Esmun*, pp. 43ff.; shorter survey, e.g., in Schofield, *The Religious Background of the Bible*, pp. 64ff.; M. Noth, *Die israelitischen Personennamen im Rahmen der gemeinsemitischen Namengebung.*
[5] 2 Sam. ii, 8ff.; iv, 1ff.; cf. Eissfeldt in *La Nouvelle Clio*, 1951, pp. 110ff.

behind him the old Israelite amphictyony of ten tribes.[1] This appears to be the kernel of the tradition about the solemn choice of a king at Gilgal and Mizpah (1 Sam. x, 17ff.; xi, 12ff.). On the other hand, the kingship of David and Solomon represents a national and religious syncretism. The powerful position of David's dynasty was based on hereditary control of the Canaanite city state of Jerusalem, which lay outside tribal territory;[2] and Solomon's administrative division of the realm had as its object and result the complete fusion of the Israelites with the native population.[3] The temple was a 'royal temple', and gave expression, according to the Canaanite pattern, to the close connexion between the national god and the king.

But in Israel the tension between the traditions of chieftainship and those of kingship, and, in general, the hostility of the 'desert ideals' to the monarchy were always present.[4] This is evident in the opposition between the old standard of justice and the despotic *mišpāṭ* of the new monarchy. In the affair of Naboth they clash in the persons of Elijah and Ahab (1 Kings xxi). The opposition is still more plainly seen in the theory that Yahweh alone should be king in Israel, and in the clear awareness that kingship was a Canaanite innovation, thoughts which find expression in one of the collections of traditions about Saul and Samuel (1 Sam. viii; x; xii; xv). When the cultic functions were transferred to the king, and the chiefs entered his service, it was left to the circles of old seers and prophets to conserve the traditions of nomadic times, or rather, what they believed these traditions to be. In the traditions about Moses he is not, as has been maintained,[5] a partial reflection of the figure of the king: on the contrary, he represents the ideals and traditions which were opposed to the monarchy. It was this prophetic opposition which constantly renewed the claim that the king's task was to submit to and maintain 'the justice of Yahweh', and not to claim to be more than he was, or to exalt

---

[1] On this amphictyony see Noth, *Das System der zwölf Stämme Israels*. But Noth is wrong in maintaining that it was a federation of twelve tribes; according to Judges v it consisted of only ten; see Mowinckel, *Zur Frage nach dokumentarischen Quellen in Josua 13–19*, pp. 21f.

[2] Cf. Alt, *Die Staatenbildung der Israeliten in Palästina*.

[3] Cf. Alt, in the *Kittelfestschrift*, pp. 1ff.

[4] Cf. Budde, 'Das nomadische Ideal im alten Israel' in *Preussische Jahrbücher* lxxxv, 1896; Nyström, *Jahwismus und Beduinentum*, pp. 79ff. This point is also rightly emphasized by de Fraine in *L'aspect religieux*.

[5] E.g., Pedersen, *Israel* III–IV, pp. 662f.; Engnell, *Gamla testamentet* I, pp. 98, 134, with references to the literature.

himself over his 'brethren'.[1] It is emphasized that it was 'a warrior chosen from among the people' that Yahweh exalted when he made David king (Ps. lxxxix, 20). King Ahaz is a man like other men, asserts the prophetic tradition; and in the moment of danger 'his heart and the heart of his people shook as the trees of the forest shake before the wind' (Isa. vii, 2, 13). That the bodies of the kings have been interred beside Yahweh's temple is for Ezekiel the gross 'defilement' which has called down Yahweh's punishment upon the city (Ezek. xliii, 7ff.).

It is, therefore, only to be expected that, if not at the outset, at least in the course of time, the common oriental royal ideology would undergo in Israel quite fundamental changes under the influence of Yahwism and the wilderness tradition, and that many of the forms which were borrowed would acquire a modified or new content. In consequence, those common features which do exist must not be interpreted solely in terms of the meaning they had in Babylonia or Egypt, but in the light of the entire structure and the fundamental ideas of Yahwism. Rites originally associated with the worship of the king may have been adopted in the Israelite cult without any thought of their original meaning.[2]

In the ancient Aramaic inscriptions from north Syria we have an interesting analogy which corroborates the way in which the old nomadic view of the relation between the king and the god prevailed over the oriental royal ideology. These inscriptions bear witness to the invasion of the semi-nomadic Aramean tribes into the small states of northern Syria, and their usurpation of political power in the tenth and ninth centuries B.C. They shed much light on the relation of the king and the royal family to the gods. Euler sums up the results of his thorough investigation in the following words: 'The king is not held to be of divine origin, and consequently is not the son of any god whatsoever. No text hints at anything of the kind.'[3] Nor does the king become divine after

---

[1] 1 Sam. viii, 10ff.; x, 25; cf. xii, 1ff.; Deut. xvii, 14–21, 'his brethren'; Jer. xxii, 13, 'his neighbour' (compatriot).

[2] In the search for such rites, scholars sometimes read into the evidence what they are looking for. So, e.g., when Hooke (*J.M.E.O.S.* xvi, 1931, pp. 23ff.) finds Yahwistic reaction against Canaanite rites of the deification of the king in Exod. xx, 26; xxiii, 19b; Lev. ii, 11. It is correct to speak here of reaction against the ritual of the Canaanite cult; but to find any reference to the king is arbitrary.

[3] See Euler in *Z.A.W.* lvi, 1938, p. 296. Engnell's polemic against Euler (*Divine Kingship*, p. 205) takes for granted what needs to be proved (viz., that the conception in these inscriptions is the same as that in the general oriental pattern), and does not take account of the essential point, that we are dealing here with a new, recently immigrated people with its own conceptions.

death; he is the agent of the divine will, entirely subordinate to the god, but not a more or less 'identical incarnation' of him.

In spite of all this, however, it is clear that, even in the official Israelite conception of the king, the idea which is central and fundamental is that he is a superhuman, *divine* being.[1] The king is also an *'elōhîm*, a powerful, superhuman being. He is a god; and is, at least once, directly addressed as such (Ps. xlv, 7). Like the deity, he is also called 'lord' (*'āḏôn*);[2] and he is called 'Yahweh's son'.[3] Sometimes the prophetic poet may describe the king's filial relationship to Yahweh in purely mythological figures. 'On the holy mountain I have begotten you from the womb of the morning,' says Yahweh to the king, according to one reading in the oracle in Ps. cx. The language used is probably derived from the myth of the birth of the new sun god on an 'unknown mountain', as is recorded of the Assyrian king Ashurnasirpal.[4] The birth of the new king brings back to the earth the fertility of the garden of the gods, and the peace which originally reigned among animals.[5] It is but natural that the birth of the king should be described in pictures taken from the birth of the god. The new god belongs to the garden of the gods on the divine mountain (Mount Zion) in the far north ('on the sides of the north'),[6] a conception which is

[1] Cf. Mowinckel, *Kongesalmerne*, pp. 25ff.; *Ps.St.* II, pp. 298ff.; Pedersen, *Israel*, III–IV, pp. 485, 498f.; Lods in *R.H.Ph.R.* x, 1930, pp. 209–21. Johnson (in *The Labyrinth*, pp. 71ff.), Engnell, Widengren, and others lay great stress on this fundamental idea; and in principle they are right. But their excessive emphasis on the correspondence of the Israelite ideal of kingship with 'the general oriental pattern' (particularly concerning the identity of the king with the god) is exaggerated and unhistorical. On the other hand, North's attempt to minimize the religious aspect of the Israelite conception of the king (*Z.A.W.* l, 1932, pp. 8ff.; cf. his paper in *A.J.S.L.L.* xlviii, 1931, pp. 1ff.) gives the impression of attempting to explain away the evidence, and does not seem to take sufficient account of the connexion with ancient oriental cult and religious vocabulary. The same is true, to some extent, of the sober paper by Lauha in *S.E.Å.* xii, 1947, pp. 183ff.; and of that by Puukko in *Teologisk Tidskrift* (Åbo), 1947.
[2] Ps. cx, 1; Jer. xxii, 18; xxxiv, 5; Gen. xl, 1; Isa. xxii, 18, etc.
[3] Ps. ii, 7; cf. cx, 3, in the text of the Hexapla (see *B.H.*[3]).
[4] See Mowinckel, *Kongesalmerne*, pp. 20, 135ff.; cf. Jastrow, *Die Religion Babyloniens und Assyriens* II, pp. 112ff., and above, p. 36.
[5] Isa. vii, 14–17 (see below, p. 110); xi, 6–9 (see below, p. 182).
[6] Ps. xlviii, 3. On the garden and the mountain of the gods, see Gunkel, *Genesis*[4], pp. 33ff. The idea of the mountain of the gods in the north, 'the northern mountain' (*ṣāpôn*) was taken over by Israel from the Canaanites. In Ugarit the idea and the name were connected with the mountain Ṣapân or Ba'al Ṣapân (Accad., *Ba'lu ṣapûna*) = Mons Casius (see Eissfeldt, *Baal Zaphon, Zeus Kasios und der Durchzug der Israeliten durchs Meer*; Lauha, *Zaphon. Der Norden und die Nordvölker*, pp. 10ff.; Morgenstern in *H.U.C.A.* xvi, 1941, pp. 47ff), where, after his resurrection, Baal takes his seat on the throne, and becomes king over gods and men (cf. Hvidberg, *Graad og Latter i det Gamle Testamente*, pp. 27, 30ff.).

now also known from Canaanite sources. The 'rise' of the royal family is likened to the rise of the sun in the east.[1] It seems also to have been customary to swear by the name of the king.[2]

It is in the light of the fundamental thought of the king's divinity that all the other features in the conception of the king have to be understood. Even if these features did not owe their historical origin to it, they were naturally associated with it in the mind of the Israelite.[3]

The Israelites' attitude to their king is most characteristically expressed in the term used of his relation to Yahweh, *Yahweh's Anointed*. Anointing was an act which first and foremost ratified the king's status as the chosen of Yahweh, and as duly installed.[4] It was a holy ceremony, a cultic act, which conveyed extraordinary 'holy' or 'divine' faculties and qualities.[5] It was an essential element in the cultic installation of the king.

The anointing of the king[6] was performed at the holy place, in Jerusalem normally in the temple. That one of the king's sons (usually the eldest) whom Yahweh had designated by an oracle[7] was conducted in solemn procession to the holy place, where the ceremony took place 'before Yahweh'. The king's son was mounted, and surrounded by the bodyguard, on foot and in war-chariots.[8] We may assume that the holy spring of Gihon (now the Virgin's Fount) down in the Kidron valley was originally the site of the anointing and installation of the kings of Jerusalem.[9] It seems that even in later times the ceremonial at the installation of the kings of Jerusalem included a rite of purification at the spring and of drinking its holy water which was imbued with

---

[1] Bentzen (*S.E.Å.* xii, 1947, p. 43) is right in finding this pun in Mic. v, 1: the *môṣā'ōṭ* of the royal family *mik-ḳeḍem*.
[2] Ps. lxiii, 12; see Gunkel, *Die Psalmen*, ad loc.
[3] For literature, see above, p. 56 n. 2, and further, Dürr, *Ursprung und Ausbau*, p. 74; Bentzen, *Det sakrale kongedømme*; Widengren in *R.o.B.* ii, 1943, pp. 49ff. In *Divine Kingship* Engnell only hints at the Israelite conception of the king. The same may be said of Frankfort's sketch (*Kingship*, pp. 337ff.), which, in contrast to the main parts of his book, is not based upon any critical study of the sources, but simply expresses a traditional, popular view. Although Frankfort is right in emphasizing the differences between the royal ideology in Israel and elsewhere, he completely overlooks the many far-reaching similarities.
[4] Ps. ii, 6. Cf. de Boer, *Het koningschap in Oud-Israel.*
[5] Cf. Gadd, *Ideas of Divine Rule in the Ancient East*, pp. 49f.
[6] The sources are the accounts in 2 Sam. xv, 10ff.; 1 Kings i, 32–53; 2 Kings xi, 9f. Cf. *Ps.St.* II, pp. 6ff.; von Rad in *T.L.Z.* lxxii, 1947, cols. 211ff.; Widengren, *Psalm 110 och det sakrala kungadömet i Israel.*
[7] 1 Sam. x, 1ff.; x, 20ff.; 2 Kings ix, 6ff.; Pss. ii, 7; cx, 1 ff.
[8] 1 Kings i, 33; Zech. ix, 9; 1 Kings i, 5, 38; 2 Kings xi, 8.
[9] 1 Kings i, 33; cf. Bentzen, *Studier over det zadokidiske Praesteskabs Historie*, p. 9.

power and able to bestow increase of strength.[1] This was probably in preparation for the main act in the temple. In the temple court the 'runners' (the guard) lined the route between the altar and the temple (2 Kings xi, 11). The priest led forth the king's son and made him ascend the dais[2] in view of all the people. At this point, presumably, the prophet uttered the oracle concerning Yahweh's choice and legitimation of the king,[3] and the priest placed the diadem ('the crown') on his head and handed 'the testimony' to him,[4] which contained his divine appointment and the ground of his royal prerogative. The priest then anointed him and so made him king.[5] As the king now stood there 'in holy array',[6] the whole people paid him the solemn act of homage, the trumpets rang out, the people clapped their hands, uttering the $t^e r\hat{u}'a\underline{t}$ $mele\underline{k}$, 'the shout of a king':[7] 'Solomon is king!' 'God save the king!' (lit. 'May the king live!')[8] Sacrifice was offered; and the sacrificial feast was celebrated with rejoicing, possibly both before and after the anointing.[9] Then followed the other main part of the festival, the solemn procession from the holy place to the royal palace, and the accession to the kingly office. With dancing gait,[10] to the accompaniment of fanfares, 'so that the earth rent', the ascent was made to the palace. There the king took his seat on the throne, which symbolized the mountain of the world,[11] and thus assumed his place 'at Yahweh's right hand' (Ps. cx, 1). He received the congratulations of his bodyguard and his people (1 Kings i, 47). We may also conclude from Ps. ii that at this point he issued a proclamation in which he communicated Yahweh's decision, referred to his legitimate, divine installation, and admonished his vassal kings and chiefs to pay homage to him and to submit to his own and Yahweh's overlordship: 'for I have been established as His king upon Zion, His holy mountain'.[12]

[1] This may be inferred from Ps. cx, 7; see Widengren, *Psalm* 110 *och det sakrala kungadömet i Israel*, pp. 22ff.

[2] 2 Kings xi, 14; 2 Chron. xxxiv, 31. Similarly in Assyria; see Frankfort, *Kingship*, p. 247.

[3] This may be inferred from Ps. cx.

[4] 2 Kings xi, 12; see von Rad in *T.L.Z.* lxxii, 1947.   [5] 2 Kings xi, 12 (G).

[6] Ps. cx, 3; see Widengren, *Psalm* 110 *och det sakrala kungadömet i Israel*, pp. 9, 12ff.

[7] Cf. Num. xxiii, 21; *Ps.St.* II, p. 43; Humbert, *La ' Terou'a': analyse d'un rite Biblique*, pp. 34f.

[8] 1 Sam. x, 24; 2 Sam. xv, 10; 1 Kings i, 39; 2 Kings ix, 13; xi, 12.

[9] 1 Sam. ix, 22ff., xi, 15; 2 Sam. xv, 12; 1 Kings i, 9, 19.

[10] 1 Kings i, 40 (G); 2 Sam. vi, 14f.

[11] See Widengren, *Psalm* 110 *och det sakrala kungadömet i Israel*, pp. 5ff.

[12] Ps. ii, 6. In the Ugaritic texts, Baal announces his enthronement in exactly the same words; see II AB, col. VII, 43 (cf. Hvidberg, *Graad og Latter i det Gamle Testamente*, p. 34).

The day was celebrated by the people as a festival.[1] With it there was also associated the king's extirpation of his enemies (2 Kings ii, 1ff.), and, in some instances, the granting of an amnesty:[2] the day of his enthronement was to be a day of joy.

Anointing was the really sacramental act in this festival ritual. Through it Yahweh's choice was confirmed and consummated, the king was 'made king',[3] and divine power and equipment were conferred upon him.[4] He who has been anointed by Yahweh has thereby been established as chief and ruler over His people (1 Sam. x, 1), and has received power to 'deliver it from its enemies round about' (1 Sam. ix, 16). To him 'belongs all that is best in Israel' (1 Sam. ix, 20). His sceptre of kingship is a 'righteous (i.e., legitimate) sceptre'.[5] Being anointed, he is tabu and sacrosanct. It is sacrilege and a capital offence to lay hands on him.[6] Even to cut off the skirt of his cloak is sacrilege (1 Sam. xxiv, 6). Compared with the king the ordinary man is just 'a dead dog, a flea' (1 Sam. xxiv, 15).

Behind this, of course, lie the common primitive ideas of the mana-filled chief and medicine man surrounded by tabus. But in Israel the tabus and sacred character of the king have a different basis. In ancient Israel, when a man was equipped with supernatural powers, it was thought that it was Yahweh's spirit that had 'come into him', had 'clothed itself with him', had been 'poured out into him', and the like. It is the charismatic, divine equipment with power, the ability to perform superhuman deeds, the quality of 'holiness' as a miraculous power and as a faculty akin to that of a divine being, which is expressed by this conception (probably Egyptian in origin)[7] of the life-giving, wonder-working, power-filled 'wind' or 'breath' of the deity, or, more hypostatically conceived, His 'spirit'. Just as the sacred martial ecstasy of the ancient heroes, and the sacred frenzy of the prophets were explained as the effects of Yahweh's spirit (as can be seen in the narratives about the heroes in the Book of Judges and about Saul in 1 Sam. xi), so anointing was related to endowment with

---

[1] 1 Kings i, 45; 2 Kings xi, 20; 1 Sam. xi, 15.
[2] 1 Sam. xi, 13; 1 Kings i, 50ff.; cf. 2 Kings xxv, 27ff.
[3] Cf. 2 Kings xi, 12: the chief priest 'made him king', *wayyamlîkô* (for M.T.'s *wayyamlîku*).
[4] 1 Sam. x, 1–6; Isa. xi, 2ff.
[5] Ps. xlv, 7. In the Baal myth, even the sceptre of the usurper Mot is described by the regular, traditional expression 'a righteous sceptre' (I AB, col. VI, 29).
[6] 1 Sam. xxvi, 9; 2 Sam. i, 14ff.; iv, 9ff.
[7] See Hehn, in *Z.A.W.* xliii, 1925, pp. 210ff., and below, p. 78.

F

the spirit. The later tradition says explicitly that when David was anointed, 'the spirit of Yahweh leaped upon him'. When the earlier tradition relates that the first experience which Saul had after being anointed was that Yahweh's spirit came upon him, so that he 'raved' in ecstatic frenzy together with the nĕḇî'îm (1 Sam. x), the writer certainly does not regard it as a mere coincidence, but as the appropriate and natural consequence of the anointing. In Isa. lxi, 1, too, the prophet presupposes as generally acknowledged the connexion between anointing and endowment with the divine spirit.

In virtue of his endowment with the divine spirit, the king is filled with superhuman power. He receives 'a new heart'; he is changed into a new man (1 Sam. x, 6, 9). He receives a soul filled with supernatural power instead of an ordinary human soul. He receives a new disposition expressed, according to oriental custom, in the giving to him of a new name[1] which indicates his new, intimate relationship with the god who has chosen him, and whom he represents.

Through his anointing and endowment with the divine spirit, the king also receives superhuman wisdom. 'As an envoy (angel) of Yahweh' he discerns all things, and accomplishes what he wills (2 Sam. xiv, 17ff.). He knows the future.[2] 'Eternal' (i.e., extremely long) life is attributed to him.[3] Wonderful experiences are his; and he can do what others cannot do.[4] He rules 'by the strength of Yahweh',[5] and performs mighty, superhuman deeds on earth.[6] The anointing expresses Yahweh's 'choice' of him 'to be king over His people'.[7] He is the 'man after Yahweh's own heart'.[8] In the legend about the birth of Saul ('the requested'), the founder of the monarchy, we hear an echo not only of the thought of election from the womb, but also of the idea that the conception of the heir apparent was the result of a wonderful divine intervention and of predestination. The 'requested' saviour

---

[1] On change of name among the Hebrews at the king's enthronement, see Honeyman in J.B.L. lxvii, 1948, pp. 13ff.; in Egypt, Frankfort, Kingship, p. 103; among the Sumerians, op. cit., p. 246; cf. above, pp. 35, 38.

[2] Ps. ii, 7; 2 Sam. xxiii, 1ff.

[3] 1 Kings i, 31; Pss. xxi, 5; lxxii, 5; cf. Jenni, Das Wort 'ōlām im Alten Testament, pp. 57ff.

[4] 1 Sam. x, 1ff.; cf. xi, 6f.

[5] Cf. Mic. v, 3 (of the future king).

[6] Ps. xc, 5f.; 1 Sam. xi, 6ff.

[7] Pss. xlv, 8; lxxxix, 21; 2 Sam. vii, 8. On the election of the king, see Rowley, The Biblical Doctrine of Election, pp. 95ff.; cf. Alt in V.T. i, 1951, pp. 2ff.

[8] 1 Sam. xiii, 14; xv, 28; xvi, 1ff.; Ps. lxxxix, 20ff.

king was born as a gift from Yahweh to the childless mother.[1] At the anointing, as we have seen, there is proclaimed the oracle or 'decree', telling of his election by Yahweh (see above, p. 64).

The king stands in a closer relation to Yahweh than anyone else. He is His 'son' (Ps. ii, 7). In mythological language it is said that Yahweh has 'begotten' him, or that he was born of the dawn goddess on the holy mountain (Ps. cx, 3; see also pp. 62, 75). The people say to the king, 'Yahweh *your* God'.[2] He is the servant of Yahweh in a different sense from anyone else.[3] As the son of Yahweh, the God of all the earth, he has a rightful claim to dominion over the whole world.[4] In David's supremacy over the other small states in and around Palestine, nationalistic religious circles in Israel and Judah saw a foretaste of the universal dominion over the peoples, which as goal and as promise was implicit in the election of the king as Yahweh's Anointed and deputy on earth. Hence the prophetic author of Ps. ii can describe the situation at the accession of a new king in Jerusalem as if in fact all the kings and peoples of the world were plotting to throw off the yoke of Yahweh and His Anointed, but were awed into submission by Yahweh's words promising the throne to the chosen king, and threatening His opponents with destruction, unless they submit in time and 'kiss his feet with fear and serve him with trembling'.[5]

The endowment which Yahweh has bestowed on the king may be expressed in two words, the 'righteousness' and 'blessing' of the king. 'Righteousness', 'being right', means living by Yahweh's

---

[1] 1 Sam. i. It was observed long ago that the legend of the birth of Samuel was originally associated with Saul, the first king. This is evident from the explanation of the child's name in i, 20–8: 'I have asked him (*še'iltiw*) from Yahweh', 'he is one who is asked (*šā'ûl*) of Yahweh', which is really an explanation not of the name *Šemû'ēl*, but of *Šā'ûl*. See Hylander, *Der literarische Samuel-Saul-Komplex* (1 Sam. 1–15) *traditionsgeschichtlich untersucht*, pp. 12f.

[2] 2 Sam. xiv, 17; see Birkeland, *Die Feinde des Individuums in der israelitischen Psalmenliteratur*, pp. 124f.

[3] Used of David: Pss. xviii, 1; xxxvi, 1; lxxxix, 4, 21; of Solomon: 1 Kings iii, 7ff.; of Zerubbabel: Hag. ii, 23; Zech. iii, 8; of some other king or of the king or leader of the people in general: Pss. lxix, 18, 37; xxvii, 9, and elsewhere; see Birkeland, *Die Feinde des Individuums in der israelitischen Psalmenliteratur*, pp. 124f. Of the king of Babylon: Jer. xxv, 9; xxvii, 6; xliii, 10; cf. the corresponding expressions used of Cyrus, 'the friend of Yahweh', Isa. xliv, 28 (pointing *rē'î* for *rō'î*); 'the beloved of Yahweh', xlviii, 14. See *G.T.M.M.M.* III, note on Hag. ii, 23a.

[4] Pss. ii, 8; lxxii, 8–10; lxxxix, 20ff.

[5] Ps. ii, 11f. As Bertholet has observed, the meaningless words *wᵉnaššᵉḳû bar* must precede *wᵉgîlû*, and the whole read *wᵉnaššᵉḳû bᵉraglāw*. Morgenstern's objection (*J.Q.R.* (N.S.) xxxii, 1942, pp. 371ff.) that *nāšaḳ* is nowhere else construed with *b*, and that therefore Bertholet's ingenious proposal is groundless, is scarcely valid. Morgenstern's own emendation is much farther from the consonants of the received text. On the kissing of the feet as a token of subjection and homage, see Gunkel, *Die Psalmen*, p. 8.

justice and according to Israelite custom. In the widest sense it includes the will and the ability to maintain the customs, rights, and prosperity of the community under the covenant, the ability to 'judge', i.e., to rule rightly, to do the right thing, and in general to maintain due order in affairs. Yahweh Himself gives to the king His own judgements and righteousness, i.e., His own ability to rule justly (Ps. lxxii, 2). The royal sceptre is the 'sceptre of righteousness' (Ps. xlv, 7).

The righteousness of the king includes first of all the ability to 'save his people from their enemies round about' (1 Sam. ix, 16; x, 1). The chosen king is the invincible warrior, filling the places with dead bodies. With his mighty sceptre he rules from Zion in the midst of his enemies: Yahweh makes them his footstool (Ps. cx, 2, 5f.). All his enemies will be clothed with shame (Ps. cxxxii, 18). His hand finds out all his enemies. His right hand finds out those that hate him. When he but shows his face, he makes them as a fiery oven. Their offspring he destroys from the earth, and their seed from among the children of men. When they plot evil against him and frame a malicious scheme, they achieve nothing; for he makes them turn their backs when he takes aim at them from his bowstring (Ps. xxi, 9ff.). At home and abroad he secures to his people justice, prosperity, and salvation.

The true king judges Yahweh's people with justice, relieves the oppressed, the helpless, and the unprotected, gives justice to the widow and the fatherless, protects them from the oppression of the wicked, and avenges them when their rights have been violated and their blood shed (Ps. lxxii, 2–4, 12–14). Therefore the righteous (i.e., good people) will flourish in his days, and the land will enjoy great prosperity (Ps. lxxii, 7).

The righteous king also conveys good fortune; he is an 'îš maṣlîaḥ (Gen. xxxix, 2). This element is also included in the term ṣaddîḳ. He possesses blessing and the powers which bestow good luck, and is therefore able to impart blessing to his surroundings. He is radiant like a star, and like a comet in the firmament of nations determines their destiny (Num. xxiv, 17). He will be as the light of the morning when the sun rises (2 Sam. xxiii, 3f.; Mic. v, 1). He will come down like rain upon the mown grass, like showers that water the earth. In his time there will be abundance of corn on every hill in the land; its fruit will shake like Lebanon; and men will blossom forth from the cities like the grass of the earth (Ps. lxxii, 6, 16). Under his shadow the people will live safely; he is the breath of their nostrils (Lam. iv, 20). Without him the people would be as water spilt on the ground, which cannot be gathered up again (2 Sam. xiv, 14). But under such a king, the land and the people, his 'household', reap all that the Israelite wished for himself, all that he meant by *peace* or *wholeness* (*šālôm*) and blessing: fertility of man, beast and crop, health, a large family, rain and sunshine and a succession of good seasons, good living conditions, good relations between old and young, master and servant, victory over the enemy, spoils of war, honour and reputation, dominion over the neighbouring peoples, loyalty and contentment amongst the brethren under the covenant, on every hand the fear of God, decent living, good demeanour, and sound morals, the maintenance of justice for everyone and the protection of the weak, the extermination of all who play false, of all sorcerers and villains—in a word, all that is meant by the word *yēšaʻ*, salvation, (literally, 'wideness', 'spaciousness', i.e., favourable conditions, both in external political relationships, and in internal social, moral, and religious conditions). Thus the king is the saviour to whom the people look for salvation, both in the negative sense of deliverance from enemies, danger, and need, and in the widest positive sense of good fortune and well-being. It is his duty to provide this *yēšaʻ*.[1] This is the picture which the royal psalms give of the king and his 'righteousness'.

Considered from one point of view, then, the king is more than human. He is a divine being, possessing this superhuman quality because Yahweh has 'called' and 'chosen' him to be the shepherd of His people, and has made him His son, has anointed him and endowed him with His spirit. He performs the will of Yahweh, and transmits His blessing to land and people. He represents Yahweh before the people.

But as a human being, a man from among the people (i.e., a representative man from the chosen people of Yahweh) he also represents the people before Yahweh; and gradually the main stress comes to be put on this aspect of his vocation.

According to the common primitive mode of thought, which Israel naturally shared in the early period, the chief, the ancestor, and after them the king, were each, so to speak, the visible embodiment of the supreme ego, society. The entire soul of the society is embodied in the king in a special way; and, in particular, the

[1] Cf. Pedersen, *Israel* III–IV, pp. 46, 81.

ancestor lives on through him. Land and people are his household and family, just as the family is the household of the ancestor or the household-father (*'aḫî-bêṭ-'āḇ*). *Bît-Ḫumri*, 'the household of "Omri" ', is the oldest name given to Israel by the Assyrians, who first encountered it during the Omrid dynasty. Just as the family lives in the ancestor or the head of the family in whom its 'soul' is concentrated, so the soul, honour, and power of the people are concentrated in the king. He is the breath of his people's life; and they live under his shadow (Lam. iv, 20). To have to live without such a source of power entails profound unhappiness, and is like being deprived of the cult and the other symbols of the divine presence (Hos. iii, 4). The concerns of the king, therefore, are the people's concerns. His honour is their honour, his defeats their shame. King and people have common interests, and are, in a sense, identical, since the entire people is embodied in the king. It is for the king to make a normal existence real for them—their 'wholeness' (*šālôm*), their peace and happiness, their desire for self-assertion (*ṣeḏeḳ, ṣeḏāḳâh*), their immanent blessing. Blessing, happiness, and righteousness are centred in the king. He should be in accord with the 'soul' of the people, with the character which is typical of them as a whole and to which they lay claim. He should in his own person realize the nature and essence of their being, what is characteristic of them, their destiny and vocation, to use modern terms. Since Israel, through her faith in election and covenant, became conscious of her special vocation, of being chosen by Yahweh for a glorious future, it would naturally be the king's task to make real to the people her peculiar character and destiny in the world. In other words, the king became (or should have become) the visible bearer and expression of the religious and moral ideals of Israel.

If the king fulfilled this requirement, it would again react on the people by virtue of that mutual participation in each other's soul which, in ancient thought, existed between the leader and the community.[1] The people would become what their kings were. If the king was righteous, pious, and godly, the people would be the same. If the king turned from the commandments of Yahweh and worshipped Him wrongly, or worshipped other gods, then the people would also be ungodly and guilty. This is the fundamental idea of the Deuteronomistic Book of Kings.[2]

[1] Cf. Lévy-Bruhl, *Les fonctions mentales dans les sociétés inférieures*. We might here borrow a term from traditional dogmatics and speak of a *communicatio idiomatum*.

[2] Cf. 1 Kings xi, 12f., 32; 2 Kings xx, 6; xxii, 18f.

This applied whatever might be the actual inner attitude of the individual to Yahweh and His law. The king, therefore, had great responsibility. He held in his hands the destiny of his people, according to the kind of man he was. The piety of the king was reckoned by God as the merit of the people. His sins infected the whole people and led to their destruction.[1] The true king knew that he was pledged to Yahweh's law, and that he ought to represent the ideal of piety and righteousness which lived in the mind of Israel (Ps. ci). When the psalmists praise him in the royal psalms, they do so because in him this ideal is embodied. They do not in fact speak of any particular king, with the defects which, unfortunately, many of them had, but of the ideal of the king as he ought to be, 'a man after Yahweh's heart'.

Both as representative of the people, and in virtue of Yahweh's choice of him, of his sonship, his divine equipment, and his sacred character, the king of Israel-Judah (like kings everywhere else in the ancient east) was clearly the mediator between his God and his people. Such a king might boldly draw near to Yahweh as a representative mediator without forfeiting his life, which would have been the fate of anyone else who sought to 'see Yahweh' (cf. Jer. xxx, 21). In other words, the king is a priest-king, the true chief priest of his people.[2] Several traditions make it plain that the king (or his sons) acted as priests and were theoretically the legitimate priests and responsible for carrying out the cultus.[3]

It is only to be expected that the king should appear as leader of the cultus just at the great national religious festivals. On ordinary days he would leave his cultic functions to a professional priest, a 'Levite'. For practical reasons this would be necessary at the great state temples, because of the gradual development and extension of the cultus there. But, as has been suggested above, we also see that, as the cultus and the central sanctuary increased in importance, so the professional clergy became more conscious of their vocation and increased their claims to power. Before long they consciously tried to force the legitimate holder of the office, the king, to content himself with the position of protector of the cultus and guarantor of the expenses involved in it, while the professional priests claimed for themselves all the economic advantages, a share in the sacrificial gifts, in the first-fruits, the tithes, and so on, and the spiritual authority over the people which was

[1] Cf. 2 Kings xvii, 7ff.; xxi, 10ff.; xxii, 16f.
[2] Cf. Morgenstern in *A.J.S.L.L.* lv, 1938, pp. 1ff., 183ff.
[3] 1 Sam. xiii, 9f.; 2 Sam. vi, 17f.; vii, 18; 1 Kings viii, 54f.

the consequence of the power and right to perform sacrifices, to proclaim the law and justice of Yahweh, and to bless or curse in the name of Yahweh.[1] We ought probably to bear in mind these very real spiritual and material consequences when the oracle of installation in Ps. cx promises to the king that he is to be 'a priest for ever after the order of (or, more correctly, 'on behalf of', or 'for the sake of') Melchizedek'. The king made a point of securing his divine right to the priesthood, based on his being the legitimate successor and heir of the ancient king of Jerusalem, Melchizedek, who was also the priest of El Elyon, possessed the power of blessing, and was entitled to tithes. The central part played by the king in the official cultus is seen quite clearly in the tradition about the removal of the ark of Yahweh to Jerusalem, and also in the tradition about the consecration of the temple by Solomon, who personally offered both sacrifices and prayers, and pronounced the blessing over the people, all of which were priestly functions. King Ahaz himself arranged the details of the temple and cultus; and King Hezekiah, on his own authority, did away with a cultic object which, according to temple tradition, dated back to Moses himself.[2]

Being a priest endowed with divine power, the king became the channel through which blessing flowed from the deity to the people. He was the point of union between God and the congregation. Gradually the main stress came to be placed on this human side of the king's office. This was partly due to the fact that his subordination to Yahweh was more strongly emphasized than was usual in the oriental royal ideology. The king was in a

---

[1] Deut. xxxiii, 10; x, 8; Num. vi, 22ff.

[2] 2 Sam. vi; 1 Kings viii; 2 Kings xvi, 10ff.; xviii, 4. We have interesting evidence about the functions of the king at the feast of Succoth (the harvest and New Year festival), if Widengren is right in his opinion (in *Horae Soederblomianae* I, iii, pp. 12ff.) that the Samaritan Succoth ritual (see Cowley, *The Samaritan Liturgy* I–II, pp. 782ff.), with its close parallels to Deut. xxvi, 1ff., really represents an ancient and pure tradition from the old festival at Bethel. In this Samaritan ritual it is 'the king of Israel' who places the basket with the tithes on the sacred spot before Yahweh and says a prayer which corresponds in all its main features with Deut. xxvi, 5ff. We cannot, however, exclude the possibility that this is an example of midrashic archaizing by Samaritan traditionalists (cf. the many 'archaeological' midrashim in the Talmud), and is based on Deut. xxvi itself. The strange circumstance that the king has to give the basket to 'the priest' arouses suspicion. If this really were an example of old Israelite ritual, we might expect the king himself to be the priest who had to place the basket beside the altar. On the other hand, it is beyond all doubt that the liturgy in Deut. xxvi reflects very ancient customs; and it seems quite possible that in earlier times the king said this prayer, and that it was originally framed to fit the king's part in the liturgy of the festival. We then have, as Widengren maintains, a clear instance in Deut. xxvi of the democratization of royal rituals, i.e., the use by the ordinary worshipper of ancient royal rites and phraseology.

special way Yahweh's servant or slave; and, as we have seen, analogies of this are to be found in royal texts from Mesopotamia. The term expresses the position of trust held by the king as the deputy of Yahweh, and also his complete dependence on and subordination to Yahweh. That is why the prophetic promises to the king, both at the regularly repeated festivals and on the special cultic occasions such as the days of humiliation and prayer before war,[1] constantly emphasize the fact that the good fortune and blessing of the king are dependent on his obedience to the will and law of Yahweh.[2] The conditions of good fortune are godliness and righteousness, in the sense of a right relationship with Yahweh.

> When a just man rules over men,
>   ruling in the fear of God,
> then shall the sun rise in the light of the morning,
>   his splendour in a morning without clouds.
> \<As the grass sprouts\> after rain,
>   as the tender grass springing from the earth,
> \<so am I toward Yahweh,\>
>   so is my house with God.

The poet puts this into the mouth of the royal ancestor David (2 Sam. xxiii, 3–5). The king may expect to enjoy the everlasting favour of Yahweh, as long as he keeps His commandments and does not neglect His statutes.

Although the blessing was generally regarded as an inherent power, it nevertheless came to be looked upon more and more as a gift from Yahweh. The blessing was of Yahweh's own making. It was the reward of obedience to the commandments of Yahweh, of piety and godliness. 'Yahweh has remembered (his) offerings and accepted (his) burnt sacrifice', 'rewarded (him) according to (his) righteousness, according to the cleanness of (his) hands', because 'all His judgements were before (him), and (he) did not put away His statutes from (him), but was blameless before Him and kept (himself) from (his) iniquity'.[3]

But if the king departs from Yahweh, the power and good fortune of a king will fail him. Instead of the good spirit of a king with which Yahweh has endowed him, an evil spirit from Yahweh

---

[1] See Mowinckel, *Kongesalmerne*, pp. 63ff.; *Ps.St.* III, pp. 78ff.; *Offersang og sangoffer*, pp. 316ff.; Lods in *Mémoires de l'Institut Français du Caire* lxvi, 1934, pp. 91ff.
[2] Pss. xx, 7–9; xxi; xxviii,6–8; lxiii, 6–9; lxxxix, 20–38; cxxxii, 11–18.
[3] Hos. ii, 10; Pss. lxxxix, 20f.; cxxxii, 12; xx, 4; xviii, 22–5.

will trouble him, and a destructive strife arise between king and people (Judges ix, 22ff.; 1 Sam. xvi, 14).

Just because king and people are truly one, the king embodying the supreme ego of the people, the destiny of king and people will be the same in good and evil. If the king is righteous and blessed, the whole people will be blessed, and righteous, and happy. If the king is ungodly and does what is evil in the sight of Yahweh, then the whole people will be infected with ungodliness and misfortune, and must suffer all the adversity which is the result of the king's sin. The whole record of the monarchy has been written from this point of view.

Extravagant descriptions of the good fortune of kings, with the same emphasis on its conditions, are also to be found in other oriental religions and in their royal ideology. We must recognize that practically every trait in the above picture of the king has obvious parallels in the other oriental peoples. No doubt a certain divinity was ascribed to the king in Israel too, the feature having been derived from surrounding cultures and religions through Canaanite channels.

Brief reference may be made to a few details. Anointing itself,[1] the sacramental act which more than anything else linked the king with Yahweh, seems originally to have been adopted from the Canaanites,[2] and was probably also practised among the Egyptians and the Babylonians.[3] The lion throne of Solomon on a podium with seven steps was originally meant to be the throne of the God of heaven on the top of the mountain of the world with seven terraces, symbolized by the tower of the temple with seven stories. The king sits on the Deity's own throne (Ps. cx), or, in more prosaic terms, on a throne of the same divine type as Yahweh's throne.[4] David's title *dawidum* (for the word was originally applied as a title)[5] was also a foreign borrowing, like the

---

[1] See Gressmann, *Der Messias*, pp. 2ff.; Hempel, art. 'Salbung' in *R.G.G.*².

[2] See Knudtzon, *Die El-Amarna-Tafeln*, No. 51, p. 319.

[3] See Bertholet, *A History of Hebrew Civilization*, p. 113; Meissner, *Babylonien und Assyrien* I, p. 63; Frankfort, *Kingship*, p. 247.

[4] See Gunkel-Begrich, *Einleitung*, p. 151. Yahweh's throne is a *cherub-throne* (see Pedersen, *Israel* III–IV, pp. 247ff., 439ff., 651ff.), as are the thrones of other oriental gods. The Israelite royal throne is also a cherub-throne (op. cit., pp. 77ff., 676f.), and David's throne still is in the synagogue painting of Dura-Europos (see Rachel Wischnitzer, *The Messianic Theme in the Paintings of the Dura Synagogue*, Fig. 34).

[5] In the Mari texts from the first half of the second millenium B.C. the word *dawidum* is an appellative with the meaning 'chief', 'prince'; see Dossin in *Syria* xix, 1938, pp. 109ff.; cf. Engnell, *Divine Kingship*, pp. 176ff.; Bentzen, *Det sakrale kongedømme*, pp. 54f.

word *Kaiser* from *Caesar*. The term may possibly be connected with *Daud* or *Dod* (cf. the personal name Dodijah, i.e., Yahweh is Dod),[1] the name of a god who was identified with Yahweh, and perhaps originally indicated the chief or king as an incarnation of his deified ancestor.[2] The Davidic dynasty acted as the true heirs of the ancient king of Jerusalem, Melchizedek, at once priest and king.[3] When the Epistle to the Hebrews speaks of his having neither father nor mother, this is scarcely an invention of the author based on the fact that the Old Testament does not mention his family, but rather an ancient tradition which survived in Judaism and was really intended to express his close relation to the deity (cf. above, p. 35, on King Gudea of Lagash). According to one interpretation, Psalm cx says that the king was born of Shahar, the goddess of the glow of morning, and appears as the fertilizing and life-giving 'Dew': 'Dew', *Tal*, seems to have been the Canaanite name for the god of fertility.[4] From many such details it can be shown that the ceremonial of the Israelite kings and of their courts, and the public institutions of Israel were influenced by Canaan, Egypt, and other countries.[5]

But, as we have said before, it is one thing to determine the ideas and terminology which Israel borrowed from alien sources, but quite another to determine what she did with them. The very fact that there is a change of emphasis in the presentation of the royal virtues is significant. In the oriental conception of the king, particularly in Assyria and Mesopotamia, martial traits are dominant. Even in Israel we find the picture of the king wounding the heads of many countries and filling the places with dead bodies (Ps. cx, 6), and breaking the peoples with a rod of iron (Ps. ii, 9). But the ethical demands made on the king are far more prominent.

This strong emphasis on the religious and moral factors in the king's good fortune is the result of a profound change in the royal ideology caused by the peculiar character of Yahwism. The

---

[1] 2 Chron. xx, 37; abbreviated *Dôdô*, Judges x, 1; 2 Sam. xxiii, 24; 1 Chron. xi, 12, 26.

[2] *Dôd* is a term for a near kinsman, as are *'āb* = 'father', *'āḥ* = 'brother', *'am* = 'kinsman', etc. Originally it meant 'beloved', 'darling' (in the inscription of Mesha, Albright translates 'chieftain'; see *A.N.E.T.*, p. 320). On such deified ancestors, see Frankfort, *Kingship*, pp. 33ff.

[3] Ps. cx, 3. On the interpretation, see Mowinckel, *Kongesalmerne*, pp. 171 ff. (cf. Index); *Ps.St.* III, pp. 88ff.; Widengren, *Psalm 110 och det sakrala kungadömet i Israel*.

[4] See Widengren, op. cit., pp. 9ff.; Engnell, *Divine Kingship*, p. 82.

[5] See Gunkel-Begrich, *Einleitung*, pp. 150–4; von Rad in *T.L.Z.* lxxii, 1947, cols. 211ff.

effect is seen primarily in the conception of the divinity of the king.

If we compare the common oriental conception of kingship with that found in Israel, we find that it is characteristic of the latter that all naturalistic elements in the relation of God and the king have been discarded, and that the concept of identity or physical incarnation (which might well be found in the Canaanite environment, so strongly influenced by Egypt) is absent. In the cult the king was primarily the representative of the people before Yahweh, and only secondarily the representative of Yahweh. Yet the Israelites did not discard the idea that the king really *was* the representative of Yahweh in the cult as well as in the political and social life of the nation, or the ancient idea of the king as a super-man with supernatural equipment or divine powers, standing in a peculiarly close relationship of sonship to Yahweh. They often continued to express this in terminology and ideas which originated in the oriental royal ideology and which reflected more mytho-logical conceptions.

Only occasionally do we find in such mythological pictures any indication of an interpretation in physical and natural terms of Yahweh's relation to His son. The Israelite view of the king is akin to the Babylonian rather than the Egyptian view. The king is manifestly a man, 'one chosen from the people' (Ps. lxxxix, 20), subordinate to Yahweh, and dependent on Him for everything. The growing tendency in Yahwism to give all honour to Yahweh and to subordinate to Him all that is human[1] has reduced the mythological element in the court etiquette. From the very first (or, at least, from a quite early date) it prevented the divine character of the king from resulting in any idolatrous worship of man in rivalry with the worship of Yahweh. In the Old Testament we find no trace in the cult of any worship offered to the king, even though laudatory songs may have been sung in his honour.[2]

This will all become clearer if we consider what the Israelites meant by 'a god'. They could use the word 'god' (*'elōhîm*) of many kinds of subordinate supernatural beings, such as the dead soul, the ghost that might be raised: 'I saw a god coming up out of the earth,' says the woman with a familiar spirit to Saul, when the ghost of Samuel appears.[3] The word may also be used of a

---

[1] Cf. Pedersen, *Israel* III–IV, pp. 615ff.   [2] Ps. xlv; cf. Ps. xxi. See below, p. 87.
[3] 1 Sam. xxviii, 13. In the Ugaritic texts, II D, I 27, 45, a ghost (*'ib* = Heb. *'ôb*, E.VV., 'familiar spirit') is called a 'god'; see Albright, *Archaeology and the Religion of Israel*, pp. 106, 123 n. 31.

demon which causes disease.[1] It is used to indicate the lower, heavenly beings (literally, 'the sons of God') surrounding the throne of Yahweh, who are sent out by Him as His messengers,[2] corresponding to the angels of later times (Judges xiii, 22). Even of man as such the poet may say that Yahweh has 'made him but little lower than a god' (A.V., 'than the angels', Ps. viii, 6). But this saying in itself shows that there is an essential difference between such a 'god' and Yahweh. What is characteristic of a 'god' is superhuman, supernatural power and insight (Gen. iii, 5, 22). A god is holy,[3] and partakes of all the attributes and qualities of holiness. Man's likeness to 'god' in Ps. viii consists primarily in his dominion and authority over all other creatures, in the all but divine glory and honour expressed in dominion over creation. The prophet is an *'iš 'elōhîm*, 'a man of god (of divinity)', i.e., 'a divine man',[4] because he is endowed with divine insight and power.

What then distinguishes all these 'gods' from Yahweh? First of all, the fact that Yahweh is the only one who really *is*, 'He who is what He is' (Exod. iii, 14), who is 'He', as Deutero-Isaiah repeatedly says,[5] the only one who is really stirring, creating, acting, and working behind all that is happening, in nature as well as in history.[6] There is also the point which is so clearly seen in Ps. lxxxii, where Yahweh 'judges among the gods': 'You are

---

[1] This is obviously the case in Job. xix, 22.

[2] *bᵉnê 'ēlîm* or *bᵉnê 'elōhîm*, Pss. xxix, 1, lxxxii, 6; Gen. vi, 2, 4; Job i, 6, xxxviii, 7; Deut. xxxii, 8 (reading *'ēl* with G, V, for *yiśrā'ēl*). The expression is also found in Phoenician (Karatepe inscriptions; see Eissfeldt, *El im ugaritischen Pantheon*, p. 7) and Ugaritic texts (op. cit., pp. 63ff., cf. pp. 2of.). It means quite simply those who belong to the divine category, 'the divine beings'; cf. *bᵉnê haṣ-ṣôrᵉpîm*, 'the members of the goldsmiths' guild', 'the goldsmiths'; *bᵉnê han-nᵉbî'îm*, 'the members of the prophetic community'. It does not mean, as Morgenstern thinks (*H.U.C.A.* xiv, 1939, pp. 29ff., 40ff.), gods of a younger generation; cf. the Ugaritic *dr bn 'lm*, 'the family of the divine beings'.

[3] Pss. xvi, 3; lxxxix, 6–8; Deut. xxxiii, 3; Zech. xiv, 5; Job v, 1; xv, 15; Dan. iv, 5f., 10, 14f, 20; v, 11; viii, 13; Ecclus. xlii, 17.

[4] 1 Sam. ii, 27; 1 Kings xiii, 1; Judges xiii, 8; 1 Sam. ix, 6ff.; 1 Kings xii, 22; 2 Kings iv, 7; Jer. xxxv, 4. The genitive is attributive.

[5] Isa. xli, 4; xliii, 1of.; xlviii, 12; cf. xliii, 12f.; xliv, 6. Clearly it was precisely this meaning which Deutero-Isaiah found in the name 'Yahweh' when he represented Yahweh as saying, 'I am He'; it is 'Yahweh-He' who is 'the first and the last'; by all His mighty deeds and fulfilled prophecies Israel can realize 'that I am Yahweh', the One 'who performs this'. It is very probable that Deutero-Isaiah is here really in agreement with the original meaning of the name: *yahweh < yahuwa = ya hu(wa)*, 'O He'; see my remark in Otto, *Aufsätze das Numinose betreffend*, pp. 11ff.; similarly Morgenstern in *J.B.L.* lxii, 1943, pp. 269ff.; Montgomery in *J.B.L.* lxiii, 1944, pp. 161ff.

[6] 'To be' (*hāyâh*) does not in Hebrew denote mere existence in the abstract sense, but the expression of oneself in creative activity. 'I am' means 'I assert myself through deeds', 'I work', 'I make or create things'. Cf. Ratschow, *Werden und Wirken, eine*

gods; and all of you are sons of the Most High. But you shall die like men, and fall like one of the princes.' When man in paradise had gained divine insight and wisdom, Yahweh prevented his attaining perfect likeness to God by refusing him immortality. Any other 'god' *may* die, even if normally he is immortal. Even the 'divine' earthly king is mortal; but Yahweh is 'the living God', 'the holy God who does not die'.[1]

Therefore, in spite of all the mythological metaphors about the birth of a king, we never find in Israel any expression of a 'metaphysical' conception of the king's divinity and his relation to Yahweh. It is clear that the king is regarded as Yahweh's son by *adoption*. When, in Ps. ii, 7, Yahweh says to the king on the day of his anointing and installation, 'You are My son; *I* have begotten you today', He is using the ordinary formula of adoption, indicating that the sonship rests on Yahweh's adoption of the king. The act of adoption is identical with the anointing and installation. The king is chosen as the adopted son of Yahweh (Pss. xlv, 8; lxxxix, 21). Yahweh Himself has taken care of him like a mother and father, has educated him, teaching him, among other things, the art of war (Ps. xviii, 35).

It is not only the idea of adoption that bears witness to this, but also the fact that the king's divine equipment is traced back to the spirit of Yahweh (see above, p. 65). The idea itself is old, as can be seen in the stories about the Judges, the ancient heroes whose abnormal equipment and powers are explained in this way.[2] We find the same conception among the Canaanites, the Babylonians, and the Egyptians.[3] Even in the pre-Israelite period, the ecstatic manifestations of the power with which prophets were endowed were explained by the idea of the life-giving and creative 'breath' or 'spirit' of the deity. When Israel believed that the spirit of Yahweh was in the king, this was not merely a direct continuance of the idea of the endowment of heroes and judges with the spirit. It was certainly already connected with the thought of Yahweh's spirit as the source of the ecstatic inspiration of the *neḇî'îm* or prophets. But as an explanation of prophetic inspiration it has

---

[1] Hab. i, 12, original text; see B.H.[3]. M.T. is a 'correction of the scribes' (*tiḳḳûn sôperîm*), and, as usual, a false one, dictated by dogmatic prejudice.
[2] Cf. Linder, *Studier till Gamla testamentets föreställningar om Anden*, pp. 1ff.
[3] See Hehn in *Z.A.W.* xliii, 1925, pp. 210ff., and above, p. 65 n. 7.

Untersuchung des wortes hajah als Beitrag zur Wirklichkeitserfassung des Alten Testaments. There is certainly a more than incidental connexion between *hāyâh* and *ḥāyâh* (to live). For the ancient Hebrews, life meant will and activity.

here clearly replaced an older, Canaanite conception, of which it must be regarded as a conscious Israelite transformation. There are many indications that the Canaanites believed that the god in question himself entered into the *nābî* 'and worked through him.[1] But such a view was incompatible with the Israelite faith in the sublime transcendence of Yahweh. It was therefore replaced by the thought of His representative, the spirit, which He 'sends' and 'pours into' the *nābî*.[2] When the idea of the spirit is transferred to the king, this means that the king is not one with Yahweh, or an incarnation of Him, but endowed by the spirit of Yahweh with supernatural powers.

An additional, though indirect, argument against the theory that the Israelite king was regarded as identical with Yahweh, or was equated with Him in the cult, is the prophetic polemic against kingship in its empirical manifestation (Jer. xxi, 11–xxiii, 6; Ezek. xxii, 25 G; xxxiv). In the book of Ezekiel, in which the historical kings of Judah are rebuked for their sins more vehemently than in any other prophetic writing, the climax of the attack is the accusation of blasphemy, because they put the royal palace side by side with the temple; they have even put the royal tombs there, so that they have defiled Yahweh's holy name by their idolatry and by their carcases (Ezek. xliii, 7–9).[3] What would Ezekiel have said if the kings had made themselves the equals of Yahweh, and had played the part of God, and had had divine worship offered to them in the cult? The records inspired by the prophets, and also the Deuteronomic narratives, do not charge the kings with self-deification, but with tyrannizing over their subjects.[4] Even Ezek. viii, which gives a detailed description of all the abominations in the temple, says nothing about the deifica-

---

[1] So, e.g., clearly in Wen-Amon's account of the prophet at Byblos; see Ranke in *A.O.T.B.*, p. 226; Wilson in *A.N.E.T.*, p. 26. Traces of the idea of ecstatic possession by the god himself are also found in the phraseology and the forms of the Old Testament; see Hölscher, *Die Propheten*, pp. 140ff., 147ff.

[2] See Mowinckel in *G.T.M.M.M.* III, p. 13.

[3] Neiman (*J.B.L.* lxvii, 1948, pp. 55ff.) has tried to demonstrate that in the Old Testament, as in Canaanite, *peger* often means not 'carcase', 'corpse', but a cultic 'stele', and finds this meaning in Ezek. xliii, 7, 9. It fits the context perfectly in Lev. xxvi, 30, but seems less certain in the Ezekiel passages. Even if Neiman were right, the passage would not refer to 'idolatrous stelae', as he renders it, but more probably to votive stelae with the king's image as representations of intercessory prayer; see above, p. 000. Even then we should have an instance, not of the deification of the king, but of an image in Yahweh's temple representing a human being, in the eyes of the prophet an unseemly thing.

[4] Cf. 1 Sam. viii; xii. Cf. Noth, *Ueberlieferungsgeschichtliche Studien* I, p. 57. The favourable attitude which Deuteronomy, in spite of everything, here adopts to the monarchy would have been impossible if kings had been guilty of direct self-deification.

tion of the king, and does not allege that the king had usurped the prerogatives of Yahweh.

Though the king is described as the channel of fertility and of the felicity of paradise, yet we find in Yahwism no trace of any mythological or cultic identification of the king with the fertility god. Thus there is in the Old Testament sources no evidence whatsoever that the king was identified with the tree of life, which in its turn is supposed to be identical with the deity.[1] That the king was the representative of Yahweh in the cult did not imply in Israel what 'representing' may formerly have signified in primitive thought: that the representative *was* the person whom he represented. The great prophets would never have thought of maintaining that they *were* Yahweh, although they did emphatically maintain that they had been authorized and sent by Him as His envoys. Similarly, the religion of Israel could never tolerate the thought that the king was identical with Yahweh or acted as if he were. He represents Him in the sense that he receives divine power and equipment from Him, and conveys His blessing. Yahweh has indeed made man 'little lower than a god', as Ps. viii puts it; and, in still higher measure than ordinary men, the king is a god on earth. But the distance between Yahweh and an ordinary god is as great as that between ordinary men and the 'divine beings' (*b*ᵉnê *ᵉlōhîm*).

We have already referred to the king's priestly office. This is, of course, expressed in the part he plays in the cult, in which he is the leader. Through the cultic acts, and especially through the enthronement ceremonies, the king is endowed with divine power and made the instrument of blessing and salvation. It is therefore important that the power with which the king is endowed should be constantly maintained and renewed.

There are several indications that in Israel, as in Babylonia,[2] the enthronement of the king was repeated as an annual festival, probably in connexion with the chief festival of the year, the autumn and New Year festival, which was also the festival of the enthronement of Yahweh.[3] This festival was celebrated as a re-enactment of creation, and as the establishment of fertility of

---

[1] See Additional Note VII.
[2] See Pedersen, *Israel* III–IV, pp. 746ff.; Dürr in *Theologie und Glaube* xx, 1928, pp. 305ff.; Frankfort, *Kingship*, pp. 318ff. Cf. above, pp. 41f.
[3] Volz, *Die biblischen Altertümer*, p. 452; Pedersen, op. cit., p. 432; Böhl, *Nieuwjaarsfest en koningdag in Babylonien en in Israel*; Dürr, op. cit., pp. 319ff. In Judah, too, at least

every kind, of well-being and of blessing for land, flocks, and people; to this we shall return. Then earth, and nature, and all growing things were created anew as at the first. It was therefore quite natural that the installation of the king and the New Year festival should be regarded as the preservation and re-creation of the primeval splendour. To the Israelite, all the glory of the earth was summed up in the thought of 'Yahweh's garden', 'the garden of God', told of in the ancient creation myths.[1] At that time earth itself was 'paradise'. No wonder, then, that the enthronement or birth of a new king is taken as an omen that the conditions of paradise are about to return: both the child and his people 'will eat curds and honey' (Isa. vii, 15, 22. See below, pp. 110ff.), the food of the gods, and wild and tame animals will live peaceably together (Isa. xi, 6–9. See below, p. 182).

But this does not mean, as some have held, that the thought of the king as 'king of paradise' forms an essential part of the concept of kingship, or that the royal ideology has its roots there. The parallel with the garden of god is only one of the features associated with the concept of kingship both in Babylonia (see above, p. 47) and in Israel, because the king is divine and is described in terms of different myths about gods. There is a connexion between divinity and the garden of god; therefore the king and the blessings of his rule are described in terms of the latter.

Still less may we conclude from this that the king was regarded in Israel as an incarnation of the *Urmensch*, even if it is true that the *Urmensch* is sometimes associated with paradise. None of the passages in the Old Testament which have been adduced as evidence of this idea proves that the king is the *Urmensch*,[2] or that this conception was the source of the Israelite royal ideology.

Somewhat more important, however, than the connexion between the New Year festival and its oriental pattern is the character which the festival acquired in Israel. In Yahwism it was, in fact, completely transformed. Its basis in the natural order is, indeed, still clear, even in Israel: what is created is, in the first instance, life on earth, fertility, crops, the cosmos. But the Canaanite thought that the god himself is renewed has disappeared; and

[1] Gen. xiii, 10; Isa. li, 3; Ezek. xxviii, 13; xxxi, 8f.; xxxvi, 35; Joel ii, 3.
[2] See Mowinckel in *St.Th.*, II i, 1948/9, pp. 71ff.

towards the close of the monarchy, the interval between the death of the old king and the next New Year festival was reckoned as 'the beginning of the reign' (*rēšît mamlekût*, Jer. xxvi, 1) of the new king, the next New Year festival being the beginning of his first year. See Mowinckel in *Act.Or.* x, 1932, pp. 177ff.

G

what the king obtains in the cultic festival is not primarily new life and strength, but the renewal and confirmation of the covenant, which is based on Yahweh's election and faithfulness, and depends upon the king's religious and moral virtues and constancy. To the renewal of nature there has been added another element of increasing importance, the renewal of history. It is the divine acts of election and deliverance in the actual history of Israel which are relived in the festival. Election and the covenant are ratified. In the cultic drama the historic events are experienced anew; and victory over the political foes of contemporary history is promised, guaranteed, and experienced in anticipation.[1] It is Israel's future as a people that Yahweh comes to guarantee; and the king is His instrument.

This entailed an essential change in the cultic drama and in the role of the king. In Canaan the drama enacted the god's own fortunes, his birth, conflict, death, resurrection, victory, and cultic marriage with the goddess. It is possible that in all this the king played the part of the god (see p. 55, above). But it is more probable that, as in Babylonia, the cultic drama was in large measure presented by means of symbolic rites, as, for example, Adonis gardens.[2] In Egypt, too, the resurrection of Osiris was represented by the raising of the Osiris pillar.[3] In Israel we find no trace of the representation of the fortunes of Yahweh by the king. The Jerusalem cult had its own drama, which presented vividly and realistically Yahweh's epiphany, His conflict and victory, His enthronement, and His re-creation of the world, of Israel, and of life on the earth. To this drama of the New Year festival we shall return in another context. But here Yahweh was not presented bodily, in flesh and blood. His advent, His epiphany, and His presence were made perceptible to experience and faith by means of symbols, above all by the festal procession with the sacred box, the ark. In an earlier age, the ark may possibly have contained some pictorial representation of Yahweh Himself; but in later times, at least, symbols were substituted: the ark itself, an empty chair of state, some sacred object such as the lots for the holy oracle, or something of the kind.[4] The cultic dance which

[1] See *Ps.St.* II, pp. 54–74, 146ff.; Noth in *Christentum und Wissenschaft* iv, 1928, pp. 301ff.
[2] On the Adonis gardens see von Baudissin, *Adonis und Esmun*, pp. 88f., cf. Register I; further, Baumgartner in *Schweiz. Archiv für Völkerkunde* xliii, 1946, pp. 122ff. (based on the material collected by E. Lewin).
[3] See Erman, *Die ägyptische Religion*[2], pp. 22, 64; Frankfort, *Kingship*, pp. 169ff.
[4] See Mowinckel in *R.H.Ph.R.* ix, 1929, pp. 212ff.; *Act.Or.* viii, 1930, pp. 257ff.

David performed was, from the standpoint of ritual, an ancient means of creating power and victory, and in David's time may for Israelite thought have expressed and guaranteed the ecstatic divine power which flowed into David and the people through the presence of Yahweh. But David did not share in that power because he was thought of as having become one with Yahweh. The dance was performed 'before Yahweh', and in His honour.

Probably Yahweh's victory over the enemy was presented dramatically by means of a sham fight, as was done among neighbouring peoples.[1] Some passages in the festival psalms seem to point to this.[2] But in virtue of the marked historical emphasis which is characteristic of Yahwism from the beginning, it is not the conflict with chaos and the dragon which is enacted (as, for instance, in Assyria; see above, p. 42), but Yahweh's victory over His own historical enemies and those of Israel. This can be deduced from the text of a similar dramatic episode from the cult contained in Ps. cxxxii. The institution of the cult of Yahweh in Jerusalem, and the first entry of Yahweh and the ark into the city are here enacted. The king assumes the role not of Yahweh but of David. He appears at the head of the Israelite army, seeking the ark which has been lost in the conflict with the Philistines, and brings it up in triumph to Jerusalem to its place in the temple.[3] Presumably something similar took place in the sham fight. When the king led the hosts of Israel, the priests, and the temple staff, and with a greater or less measure of symbolism enacted the deeds of Yahweh, His emblematic and archetypal triumph over His enemies past and present (the actual and possible enemies of Israel), and when with realistic symbolism he shattered the bow and cut the spear in sunder, and burned up the shields with fire (Ps. xlvi, 9f.), he did so in the power of Yahweh, but not through any cultic or mystical identity with Him. That the phrase 'the acts of Yahweh' may be taken in this sense is shown by an expression such as 'the wars of Yahweh' as applied to Israel's victories over her enemies.[4]

But both in Ps. cxxxii and in other cultic contexts, Israel's king generally appears as the representative of the congregation before

[1] On the important role of such mock battles and sham fights and the king's part in them, see Engnell, *Divine Kingship*, Index, s.v. 'Sham fight'. A vivid description of an Egyptian cultic combat is given by Erman, *Die ägyptische Religion*[2], pp. 64f.

[2] Pss. xlvi, 9f.; xlviii, 9f.; see *Ps.St.* II, pp. 112ff.

[3] See Mowinckel, *Kongesalmerne*, pp. 75ff.; cf. Bentzen, in *J.B.L.* lxvii, 1948, pp. 37ff.

[4] Num. xxi, 14. On 'the Book of the Wars of Yahweh', see Mowinckel in *Z.A.W.* liii, 1935, pp. 138ff.

Yahweh, not as the representative of Yahweh before the congregation. He dances and sings and plays 'before Yahweh', and leads the festal procession (2 Sam. vi, 5, 14ff.; cf. Ps. xlii, 5). In the cultic drama he represents David: Yahweh is represented by His holy ark, by the 'footstool' before the throne on which He is invisibly seated.[1] The king intercedes with Yahweh for the people, standing before Him as a servant. It is not he but the cultic prophet who in the festival ritual speaks Yahweh's words to the congregation (*Ps.St.* III). In Ps. cxxxii we hear the temple prophet's intercession for the king and his oracle to him in Yahweh's name.[2]

It is the king who receives Yahweh's promises, His blessings, and His power; and he transmits them to the community which he represents.[3] But in misfortune, too, he is the representative of his people and has to bear their fate. On the days of humiliation and prayer and in the atonement liturgies, it is the king who, as a corporate personality, vicariously bears and lays before Yahweh all the misfortune, suffering, and distress which have befallen the people. They become his personal suffering and distress, making him ill and weak. He can describe the afflictions of Jerusalem as if they were his own private afflictions, and entreat Yahweh to help and save him from distress.[4]

In order to grasp clearly the essential difference between the royal ideology in Israel and that found elsewhere in the east, or, in other words, how the religion of Israel transformed the ideas which it acquired from its environment, we must consider an essential difference between the Israelite conception of God and that of other oriental religions. This raises the question mentioned

---

[1] Ps. cxxxii, 1–10. On the throne within the temple see Isa. vi, 1ff.; Ezek. i; and cf. Pedersen, *Israel* III–IV, pp. 246ff.; H. Schmidt in *Eucharisterion* I, pp. 120ff.

[2] It is, therefore, misleading when Canney (in *J.M.E.O.S.* xvii, 1932, pp. 41ff.), in dealing with this ritual drama, speaks about a 'magical' activity.

[3] Pss. cxxxii, 11ff.; lxxii; cf. xx, 8f.; xxi, 10; Isa. lv, 3.

[4] This may be inferred from Ps. cii. The 'I' of this psalm (the worshipper), if not a king (the psalm may be post-exilic), is at all events the cultic representative of the congregation, its leading man, and as such has the same position as the king in former times, and uses the vocabulary of the royal ideology. The worshipper represents Zion, the congregation. The affliction and sufferings of Zion are also his suffering and 'sickness'. The climax of the psalm is the prayer about the restoration of Jerusalem and Israel. Since it is emphasized that the time of favour has now come (*v.* 14), we may hold that the psalm belonged to the cultic prayers at the harvest and New Year festival, when men were on the threshold of the new era of grace and the year of favour (Isa xlix, 8; lxi, 2). Observe also the emphasis on Yahweh's 'sitting' on His throne, on His 'arising' to save Zion (*vv.* 13f.), and His 'appearing in glory' (*v.* 17; the idea of epiphany); and note the allusion to the creation in *v.* 26. A gloss or a textual variant

above (pp. 41f.), how the 'experiences' of the deity in the cult were conceived. We saw that it was a common feature in oriental religions and their cultic pattern that the god fought, suffered, died, and rose again to new life, and that all this was visibly expressed in the cultic drama.[1] In the Pan-Babylonian school half a century ago,[2] and also quite recently, scholars have sought to maintain that this took place in Israel too, and that Yahweh was a dying and rising God,[3] and consequently that the suffering, death, and resurrection of the king formed part of the royal ideology as we see it reflected in the cult.[4]

It is, however, quite out of the question that Yahweh was ever regarded in Israelite religion as a dying and rising God. The invaders from the desert always felt that there was an essential difference between the gods of the Canaanites and 'the God of the fathers', who revealed Himself to them on Mount Sinai, and whose justice or 'manner' was the traditions and morals of the wilderness period. The Old Testament explicitly states wherein this difference consists. The 'gods of the peoples' may, as Ps. lxxxii puts it, 'die like men, and fall like one of the princes', and will do so when Yahweh appears to judge the earth. For the Canaanites, the expression 'the living god' meant 'the god who has come to life again':[5] for Israel it meant 'the God who always lives, and creates life out of His own life'.[6] Yahweh is 'the holy God who

---

[1] Cf. the systematic (and therefore too theoretical) summary in Hooke, *Myth and Ritual*, p. 8.

[2] See above, pp. 24f. This view is frequently found in the works of Hugo Winckler, e.g., his *Geschichte Israels in Einzeldarstellungen*.

[3] See Additional Note VIII.

[4] This consequence of the supposed general oriental ritual pattern has been drawn both by Engnell (*B.J.R.L.* xxxi, 1948, pp. 3ff.) and by Widengren (*S.E.Å.* x, 1945, pp. 65ff.). Although Engnell (*Divine Kingship*, p. 210 n. 2) rightly rejects the idea that the Israelites thought of Yahweh as a dying and rising god, he nevertheless maintains that their royal ritual was derived from a pattern which had this conception of the god. But even this modified form of the hypothesis is untenable in the general way in which Engnell expresses it. Riesenfeld, too, maintains (*The Resurrection in Ezekiel XXXVII and the Dura-Europos Paintings*) by *a priori* reasoning that in Israel the king died (symbolically) and rose again in the New Year festival; and he quite arbitrarily reads this idea into some passages where the text gives no indication of it. See further my *Offersang og sangoffer*, pp. 569f.

[5] See von Baudissin, *Adonis und Esmun*, pp. 466ff.

[6] Op. cit., pp. 450ff.

---

in v. 14 explains the time of favour (v. 14a) as the 'time of the festival' (v. 14b). In 14b two textual variants have obviously been conflated: *kî 'ēṭ bā' lᵉhenᵉnāh* and *kî bā' môᶜēd lᵉhenᵉnāh*. The psalm seems to belong to the early post-exilic age: the greater part of Jerusalem is still lying in ruins, the servants of Yahweh are represented as in bonds and appointed to death (vv. 21f.) 'the nations' triumph over them and refer in oaths and curses to the example of their misfortune (v. 9): in brief, the Jews are languishing under the oppressive and infamous domination of foreigners. But it is also possible to date the psalm in the period 598–587 B.C.

does not die' (Hab. i, 12; see p. 78 n. 1). It is characteristic that whereas in the Babylonian cult we hear of the king and his men going out to seek for the god who is imprisoned in the realm of the dead,[1] in the processional Ps. cxxxii it is the ever-powerful ark of Yahweh, the symbol of His active presence, that 'David' and his men are thought to have been seeking and then to have found.

However much Israel may have adopted the cultic pattern and myths of Canaan, she definitely rejected or radically transformed all those conceptions and rites which presupposed or expressed the death and resurrection of the deity.[2] In keeping with this is the fact that primitive ideas about the divinity of the dead (a fundamental feature in all ancient Semitic religion[3]) were suppressed in Israel to such an extent that a great gulf was fixed between Yahweh and the dead. With the dead and the realm of the dead, Yahweh and Yahwism have nothing to do.[4] This thought is emphasized so much that it almost conflicts with the idea of the supreme power of Yahweh over the whole universe.

In Israel, as in Babylonia, the sources afford no evidence for the idea (found in Egypt) that the king is one with the dead god, and that he was represented in the cult as suffering, dying, and rising again, or that in enacting this role he ever represented Yahweh.[5] There is not even any proof of the disintegration of such a pattern in Israel: i.e., of the theory that Israel adopted but reinterpreted a cultic pattern which originally had this meaning. This view has admittedly been recently maintained by some scholars.[6] Some of the psalms of lamentation are cited as evidence, and are interpreted as referring to 'cultic suffering', as lamentations uttered by the king, because as the substitute for the deity

[1] See Frankfort, *Kingship*, p. 317; cf. p. 323.
[2] This is very clearly maintained by Pedersen, *Israel* III–IV, pp. 440ff.; cf. pp. 466ff., 484, 737ff. Cf. also Engnell, *Divine Kingship*, p. 210 n. 2; Baumgartner in *T.Z.* iii, 1947, pp. 98ff.; Birkeland in *S.E.Å.* xiii, 1948, pp. 43ff.
[3] See Robertson Smith, *Religion of the Semites*[3], pp. 544ff.; Wellhausen, *Reste arabischen Heidentums*[2], pp. 383ff.; Pedersen, *Israel* III–IV, pp. 477ff.; *Illustreret Religionshistorie*[2], pp. 154, 160, 203ff. The same idea lies behind the conception of the tribal deity as the original ancestor of the tribe; see Robertson Smith, op. cit., pp. 39ff. Among the Bedouin the ancestor of the tribe *is* its god, and his grave its cult-place; see Musil, *Arabia Petraea* III, Index.
[4] Pss. vi, 6; xxx, 10; lxxxviii, 11–13; cxv, 17. Cf. Pedersen, *Israel* III–IV, pp. 485f.
[5] This seems to be Widengren's opinion in *Religionens värld*[2], pp. 311f.; cf. 1st ed., pp. 223 n. 2, 225. In *R.o.B.* ii, 1943, pp. 70, 72, Widengren says that Ps. lxxxviii is not actually a cultic text giving direct expression to this thought, but that the content and the phraseology are determined by rituals of this type.
[6] See, e.g., Johnson in *The Labyrinth*, p. 81; Widengren in *S.E.Å.* x, 1945, p. 66; cf. also Engnell, *Divine Kingship*, p. 170 n. 4, p. 210 n. 2, and in *B.J.R.L.* xxxi, 1948, pp. 4ff.

he has been overpowered and put to death in the cult by the powers of chaos, to which life succumbs every year, but from which it is again delivered through the cultic drama. But this interpretation of the psalms is false. The worshipper, undoubtedly often the king himself, does not here lament over suffering and death which he undergoes symbolically in the cult, but over actual present distress brought upon him by earthly enemies, foreign nations and traitors within the state, or over ordinary illness and the danger of death. When the worshipper at times describes himself as already swallowed up by Sheol and in the realm of the dead, his language is, from *our* point of view, metaphorical; but the figure is realistic in that it is based on the common Israelite notion that a person who is sick or threatened by death has already given lodgement to death, and is at the mercy of the powers of death, unless at the last moment Yahweh snatches him away. This is so, even although the actual poetical expression of this idea probably goes back ultimately to the cultic representations of the descent of the vegetation deity to the underworld;[1] but this does not alter the fact that these psalms speak of actual sufferings and earthly dangers, not the feigned sufferings of the cultic myths.

Thus there is no evidence that in Israel the king was regarded as Yahweh, much less the dying Yahweh, or that there was any representation in the festival ritual of the cult of the suffering and death of the king.

On the whole we may regard it as symptomatic that the only poem in honour of the king which the Psalter contains is the marriage psalm (xlv), written in order to express 'good words', the wish for blessing on the bridal couple. In Israel it was considered seemly to praise *Yahweh* in Zion (Ps. lxv, 2); and he who gloried (i.e., uttered the praises of that in which he found his honour and pride) must glory in Yahweh (Jer. ix, 22f.), not in any man or in any other god.[2]

We may therefore safely maintain that in the legitimate religion of Israel, the real Yahwism, any kind of identification of the king with Yahweh was repudiated. Undoubtedly the Israelite cult

---

[1] On the 'death' of the worshipper in the psalms of lamentation see Gunkel-Begrich, *Einleitung*, pp. 187ff.; Bentzen in the *Eissfeldtfestschrift*, pp. 57ff.; and further, my *Offersang og sangoffer*, ch. VII, 6, where the theory of feigned suffering in the cult is refuted.

[2] Ratschow (*Z.A.W.* liii, 1935, pp. 171ff.) tries to interpret Ps. xlvii as belonging to the cult of the king, but can do so only by means of radical and unjustified alteration of the text.

had very many forms and expressions which originally implied a far more intimate relation between the king and the deity than Yahwism could admit. But the utmost caution should be observed in arguing from a community of outward form to identity of meaning and thought. We have a good instance of this in the imperial etiquette of Christian Byzantium. The most important of the outward forms of imperial state (attire, metaphor, the throne and its surroundings, the 'appearance' at the great festivals and audiences, the decoration of the surroundings) were derived from the divine kingship of the ancient east.[1] But that the Emperor was regarded either by himself or by the Church as Christ incarnate or as a truly deified man is, of course, out of the question. So it was in Israel: the king was 'a god on earth', and all the forms of the royal etiquette emphasized the fact; but in every way he was subordinate to Yahweh, and in relation to the only truly living One he was a mortal man.

At times this may not have held good in some syncretistic circles, and perhaps even in the official cult of the Northern Kingdom.[2] It is also conceivable that in the time of David and Solomon the cult at Jerusalem was considerably more Canaanite than we can prove today. But at any rate we can see that the representatives of Yahwism, who upheld the old 'Levitical' traditions, reacted against this tendency at a very early period. The first anti-Canaanite purification of the temple and the cult is mentioned as early as the time of King Asa (1 Kings xv, 12f.). It is quite probable that the extant texts have been expurgated of traces of earlier Canaanite tendencies. What is more important is that the rites themselves were expurgated: that must have been a natural consequence of the purification of the cult. As has already been observed, when similarities occur between individual expressions and metaphors in our texts and corresponding features in Babylonian rituals, we must beware of concluding that we are dealing with the same cultic pattern and the same religious ideas and cultic practices. Details in texts and rituals must be seen and interpreted in relation to the entire new structure of which they form a part—in this instance, Israelite religion with its peculiar character. As has been said above, it rejected every attempt to make Yahweh a dying god and the king His 'identical' representative.

---

[1] Cf. L'Orange, *Fra antikk til middelalder*, pp. 63–129; *Apotheosis in Ancient Portraiture*, pp. 90ff.; *Keiseren på himmeltronen*, pp. 132ff.

[2] Cf. Hvidberg, *Graad og Latter i det Gamle Testamente*, pp. 81ff.; *Den israelitiske Religions Historie*, pp. 70ff., 111.

We may in conclusion sum up in the following terms the essential qualities which Israel required of a true king. The king is the natural, official leader of the public cult of the nation, even if on ordinary occasions the priest officiates in his stead. He is the channel through which Yahweh's blessings flow to the people, being conveyed primarily through his cultic functions. The presupposition and condition of this is that he should be loyal to the laws and justice of Yahweh. Although in virtue of his equipment (anointing and Yahweh's spirit) he is 'divine' and more than an ordinary human being, and although as leader in the cult he is the representative of the Deity, yet in a still higher degree he is the representative of the people in the presence of the Deity: he prays, intercedes, offers up sacrifice, and receives power and blessing. The covenant is concentrated in him; and through him and his line the promises are mediated. Through him the congregation stands before God and meets God.

If the king is what he ought to be, he is also the guarantee of the people's future and good fortune, its 'righteousness' and 'peace'. He is the leader in war, and in the power of Yahweh subdues all enemies. He is the supreme judge, the guardian of justice and righteousness. He is the guarantee of fertility and prosperity. All the victory and blessing which Yahweh creates for His people by His advent at the festival are brought to realization by the king, if he is a righteous king after Yahweh's heart. Then the association works as it ought, and Yahweh bestows power and good fortune for the maintenance of peace, justice, and prosperity. Neither the king nor the cult creates these things; Yahweh Himself creates and bestows them through the sacramental cultic acts and through the king's right relation to Yahweh.

It is also characteristic of Israel that the religious and moral conditions of all this are very strongly emphasized in the royal psalms, the official ritual texts at the royal services. Almost every aspect of the demands, promises, and requirements associated with the king appears in Ps. lxxii, a psalm of intercession and blessing:

> Inspire the king with thine own judgements, O God,
>   with Thine own righteousness the king's son,
>   that he may rule Thy people with righteousness,
>   and see that Thy poor has his right.

May he do justice to the poor of the people,
   and succour those who are needy;
<may he smite the wicked with the rod of his mouth,>
   and break in pieces the oppressor.

May he <prolong> (his days) while the sun endures,
   as the moon, throughout all generations.
May he come down like rain upon the mown grass,
   like showers that water the earth.

In his days <justice> will flourish,
   and abundance of well-being without <bound>;
the mountains will bring forth well-being;
   the hills <will yield> right order.

He will have dominion from sea to sea,
   and from the River to the ends of the earth.
The beasts of the wilderness will bow before him;
   and his enemies will lick the dust. . . .

All kings will fall down before him;
   all nations will serve him;
for he will deliver the needy when he cries,
   the poor, and him that has no helper.

He will have pity on the needy and the poor;
   and will save the lives of the poor:
from oppression and violence he will rescue them;
   and precious will their blood be in his sight. . . .

May there be abundance of grain in the land;
   may it wave on the tops of the hills;
may its fruit <flourish> like Lebanon,
   and its sheaves be as the grass of the earth.[1]

Instead of 'may he', we might translate 'he will', as is done above in the latter part of the psalm. The thought oscillates between the word of blessing and the word of prophecy, the blessing being in itself a prophecy which creates the future.

---

[1] Ps. lxxii, 1–9, 11, 14, 16. In *v.* 4b a hemistich seems to have been lost; in the translation above it has been supplied from the parallel passage in Isa. xi, 4. *V.* 3 breaks the connexion between *v.* 2 and *v.* 4, and is logically connected with *v.* 7; it is transposed above: read *ya‘ᵃlû gᵉḇā‘ôṭ. V.* 5: see *B.H.*³, n.a. *V.* 7: see *B.H.*³, nn. a, c. *V.* 12: see *B.H.*³, n.a. *V.* 16: see *B.H.*³, n.d-d.

The king's promise in the presence of Yahweh on the day of his enthronement (his 'charter') corresponds to these claims and expectations:

> I will sing of loyalty and just rule;
>> unto Thee, Yahweh, will I make music.
> I will give heed to the way of integrity.
>> O when wilt Thou come unto me?
>
> I will walk with integrity of heart
>> within my house;
> and I will set no harmful thing
>> before my eyes.
>
> I hate <him who> makes (his ways) crooked;
>> he shall not cleave to me (i.e., be my associate).
> A perverse heart shall depart from me;
>> I will know no evil man.
>
> Him who secretly slanders his neighbour
>> I will destroy.
> The man of haughty eye and proud heart,
>> with him I will not <share my meal>.
>
> My eyes shall be upon the faithful in the land,
>> that they may dwell with me.
> He who walks in the way of integrity
>> shall (be allowed to) be my servant.
>
> But he shall not dwell within my house
>> who practises deceit;
> and he who lies shall not be established
>> before my eyes.
>
> Morning by morning will I destroy
>> all the wicked in the land,
> cut off all who commit godless crime ('āwen)
>> from the city of Yahweh.[1]

Even if every individual feature in this picture, taken separately, represents ancient Israelite ideals, and also has parallels in the demands made by other eastern nations on their kings, yet the way in which precisely these demands are combined and empha-

---

[1] Ps. ci. V. 3: see B.H.³, n.a. V. 5: see B.H.³, n. b-b (G,S); M.T., 'I will not endure' (the proud-hearted) depends on the mistaken idea that Yahweh is the speaker in the psalm.

sized, and the king regarded as protector and friend of the needy and the humble reveals the influence of the prophetic movement on the official religion. It is therefore also clear that the prophets did not hesitate to direct their criticism even against sacral kingship,[1] and to assess individual historical kings in terms of the demands of Yahwism and its ideal of kingship. The king did not receive his office in order to exalt himself, to act arrogantly, to emulate the grandeur of great despots, or to oppress his fellow-countrymen (his 'neighbours'), but in order to prove by his actions that he 'knew Yahweh'. This is clear, for instance, from the words addressed by Jeremiah to King Jehoiakim:

> Woe to him who builds his house by unrighteousness,
> his chambers by injustice,
> who forces other men to work for nothing,
> holding back their wages,
> who says, 'I will build me a spacious palace,
> with roomy chambers and with windows wide,
> panelling it with cedar
> and painting it with vermilion.'

> Is it for you as king to vie
> <with Solomon> in panelling with cedar?
> Did not your father eat and drink (i.e., enjoy himself like a
> normal man)
> and he ruled justly and lawfully?

> Did he not uphold the rights of the poor and needy?
> Then it was well with him.
> Is not that the true knowledge of Me?
> says the inspired word of Yahweh.

> But you have neither eyes nor heart
> for aught but selfish gain,
> and shedding innocent blood,
> and doing oppression and violence.[2]

---

[1] See, e.g., Pedersen, *Israel* III–IV, pp. 142ff.; Graham, *The Prophets and Israel's Culture*, pp. 69ff.

[2] Jer. xxii, 13–17. For the text, see *G.T.M.M.M.* III, p. 799. *V.* 15a must originally have mentioned with whom Jehoiakim vies; and the line is metrically short: add *'et šelōmōh*. The meaning of *v.* 16b is not quite clear. Either he lived a decent life like an ordinary man; or he enjoyed himself with all good things. In the old Aramaic Hadad inscription, l. 9, 'eat and drink' means to enjoy a quiet and happy life; see Euler, *Z.A.W.* lvi, 1938, p. 299.

These verses summarize briefly the negative and positive aspects of the authentic Israelite ideal of kingship, which culminates in 'the knowledge of Yahweh'.

It would be a mistake to overlook the fact that these ethical features (the emphasis on the king's duty to uphold justice and righteousness and to protect the poor and needy) are also present, and sometimes even prominent, in other eastern royal ideologies. In Egypt, as we have seen, the king was the incarnation of the divine cosmic law (*ma'at*) itself and of Ma'at the goddess of justice. It was he who provided for order in the world and maintained law and 'justice'. The good fortune, peace, and welfare of 'the two lands' were his concern. But this is much less prominent than the king's glorious divine power. The impression is given that the ethical side of the matter is subordinate. The king provides for justice, not because it is a religious and moral duty or charge, but because it belongs to his divine nature. As a god he possesses all power and creates all good fortune and blessing; and what he does is always in itself 'just', because he, the incarnate god, does it. 'All that I commanded was as it should be,' says Amenemhet.[1] The king *is* himself *ma'at*, he *is* the cosmic law,[2] and there appears to be no moral law over him. If he maintains *ma'at*, the consequence to which most importance is attached is that he creates abundant crops in the land.[3]

The ethical aspect is considerably more prominent in the Assyro-Babylonian royal inscriptions.[4] The gods called Hammurabi to be king, 'in order that I should make justice shine in the land, destroy those who do violence and commit crimes, prevent the strong from harming the weak, rise like the sun-god over the black-headed ones, diffuse light in the land, and promote the welfare of the people' (Code of Hammurabi I, 32ff.). The king's task is to be the 'shepherd' of his people, to care for it, and to uphold justice against injustice, violence, and disorder.[5] Nevertheless, a study of the Assyro-Babylonian royal inscriptions[6] reveals a striking lack of emphasis on this idea.

The Babylonian kings lay the main stress on their cultic acts: the building and restoring of temples, gifts for temple and cult,

---

[1] See Frankfort, *Kingship*, p. 57. [2] Cf. Frankfort, op. cit., pp. 51f., 277f.
[3] Frankfort, op. cit., p. 57.
[4] Frankfort, op. cit., pp. 277ff.; Labat, *Royauté*, pp. 221ff.
[5] See Gadd, *Ideas of Divine Rule in the Ancient East*, pp. 38, 42ff.
[6] Cf. Mowinckel, *Statholderen Nehemia*, pp. 124ff.; *Eucharisterion* I, pp. 278ff.

offerings and prayers, and so on. The Assyrian kings emphasize above all their warlike exploits and boast of having subjected foreign nations and countries to the dominion of the god Ashur. To this we may add that the very conception of the character of 'justice' and 'blessing' had a different basis in Babylonia and Assyria from what it had, for instance, in Israel.[1] We may put it in this way: the gods stand above justice; 'justice' or 'blessing' is what the gods purpose; but that is often arbitrary and incomprehensible. It too often seems as if 'what seems to man to be wise is contemptible in the eyes of the god, and what seems evil in the judgement of man is good in the eyes of his god'.

In Israel, too, Yahweh is the source of justice and blessing, and in the thought of the pious He is supreme over these qualities. But the real belief of the, eading minds is that Yahweh is not arbitrary. There is a norm in His relation to mankind. He may be 'known', even if He is 'the hidden god'. The standard is the goodness and righteousness of His covenant,[2] in spite of everything. The tension remains; but faith in the morality of God's justice is maintained: that is the 'solution' in the poem about Job.[3]

Thus the relation between religion and morality has a different basis in Israel from what it has in Babylonia and Egypt; and this, of course, affects the content of the religious ideal of kingship. Two points express what is distinctive of the Israelite ideal: the king is absolutely subordinate to Yahweh and in everything dependent upon Him and His covenant blessing; and the king's essential task is to be the instrument of Yahweh's justice and covenant blessing among men. He is a true king in so far as he 'knows Yahweh' and the law of His moral being.[4]

It is, therefore, entirely in accord with the Israelite conception that the king's humility is emphasized. Just as it is the king's duty to sustain the humble and the oppressed, so he must himself be humble and meek. His strength resides not in horses and chariots, but in the name of Yahweh his God. Not splendour, but justice to the lowly is the essence of kingship.[5]

And yet, when we consider the picture of the king which is

---

[1] See Frankfort, *Kingship*, pp. 278f.
[2] See Mowinckel, *Die Erkenntnis Gottes bei den alttestamentlichen Propheten*, pp. 31ff.
[3] See Mowinckel, *Diktet om Ijōb og hans tre venner*, pp. 19–42.
[4] Cf. Mowinckel, *Die Erkenntnis Gottes bei den alttestamentlichen Propheten*, p. 8.
[5] Cf. Zech. ix, 9f.; Mic. v, 3, 9f.; Pss. xx, 8; xviii, 28; and see Pedersen, *Israel* III–IV, pp. 91ff.

given in the royal psalms, and see how, for example, Ps. ii, the psalm of anointing, promises the king world dominion, and what abundant blessings Ps. lxxii expects from him, there can be no doubt that even in ancient Israel he was regarded as more than mere man. He was like 'an angel of Yahweh' (2 Sam. xiv, 20), like a god on earth. He was the pledge of a happy future. Yahweh has chosen this man as the instrument in the fulfilment of His plans for the world. Here we are dealing not merely with the language of the court (*Hofstil*),[1] but with a genuine faith.[2] The poets do not say these things simply to flatter the king: they mean them. They speak of the king as he ought to be, and of what would follow if he were like that. Then he would be the willing and fit instrument of Yahweh for the fulfilment of His gracious plan of salvation for His people, which is based on His gracious election and covenant. We may put it differently, and say that if the king in all his conduct is 'a king after Yahweh's own heart' (and this condition is often emphasized), then he is not only a frail man, but is in accord with the mind of Yahweh, with the divine archetype of kingship.[3] Then, so long as he abides by the covenant, all the miraculous power of Yahweh is at his disposal.

The Israelite conception of and belief in kingship are the expression of the desire for some visible human evidence and guarantee of Yahweh's covenant and of His active presence with His people. Yahweh deals with the nation through one of its own members. Israel's own interpretation of her ideal of kingship is given by the author of the Deuteronomic history in his view of history; if the king abides by Yahweh's law, the people will prosper; if the king breaks the law and fails Yahweh, the ruin of the people will follow. Thus Israel's conception of kingship really points forward to Him who was its true fulfilment.

But this brings us to yet another important aspect of the conception of kingship with which the next chapter will deal.

[1] As Gressmann puts it, *Ursprung*, pp. 250ff.
[2] See Mowinckel, *Kongesalmerne*, pp. 139ff.; von Rad in *Z.A.W.* lvii, 1939, p. 217.
[3] See von Rad, op. cit., p. 219.

CHAPTER IV

The Future Hope

1. Realized and Unrealized Elements in the Ideal of Kingship

IT is important to recognize that from the very beginning the ideal of kingship in ancient Israel had a certain relation to the future; or, more precisely, it was never fully realized; but there always remained something to be desired. It is of the nature of an ideal that it can never become present reality, but always belongs to the future. At the very moment when you believe that it is already present, it ceases to be ideal; and the ideal itself escapes into the future and so asserts its own nature. It may be associated with something which is later seen not to correspond to it. Thus it lives in the borderland between present and future.

Several of the royal oracles which have been handed down to us assert that they will be realized only if the king cleaves to Yahweh and walks according to His commandment and will.[1] But the curse may light upon the king himself and make him ill-fated; he may fall into sin and become a wrongdoer (cf. Saul). Admittedly the court poets could sing of more than one king, praising them in effusive language as righteous and godfearing kings after Yahweh's own heart. But experience often showed that the king's good fortune did not always avail to protect the people from enemies, misfortunes, civil dissension, and injustice. But there must then be something wrong with the king himself and his righteousness. Thus, quite naturally, the thought of the fulfilment of the ideal came to be associated with the next king, the heir, the newborn prince, the new king on the day when he was enthroned and anointed. The descriptions of the kingly ideal which have been handed down are for the most part either idealized descriptions of the great kings of the past (which in effect means David), or wishes and promises for the new king. At the enthronement of the king, the temple prophets promise him all the royal fortune and blessing, power and honour which are proper to a son of Yahweh

---

[1] Pss. xviii, 21–7; lxxxix, 31–5; cxxxii, 12.

(Pss. ii; cx).[1] Year by year as the festival came round (coinciding with the annual enthronement festival of Yahweh, the New Year festival) these promises were repeated (Ps. cxxxii, 11ff.). The same thing took place on days of humiliation and prayer, before war, and in need and danger (Ps. xx). The congregation uttered on behalf of the new king its good wishes for blessing, describing how both at home and abroad he would make the ideal come true (Ps. lxxii); and the king himself offered to Yahweh a kind of charter, in which he promised to be a true king, to walk in Yahweh's way, and to make His justice a reality in the land (Ps. ci).

But as a rule these hopes and promises would not be fulfilled. The author of the Book of Kings passes very unfavourable judgements on most of the kings of both Israel and Judah. And the real condition of both country and court is shown as clearly as one could wish by the fiery denunciations of the prophets of doom, even if they too have so great respect for the sacrosanct ideal of kingship that they seldom attack the king himself explicitly and by name.

We may therefore maintain that precisely because the ideal of kingship was so lofty, and because the king was regarded as a divine being, of whom, accordingly, divine virtues and divine help were expected, the ideal of kingship became something which haunted everyday reality as the object of dreams, wishes, and longings, something for whose realization the people would hope in every new king and prince, or at least something which would at some time be fulfilled. For one day the true king must surely come and put everything right, as according to saga and poetry it had once been under the first king of Jerusalem, David, the founder of the dynasty.

In this form (as a vague dream of the possible realization of an ideal at some time in the future) the conception of a coming 'Anointed of Yahweh' existed in Israel quite early in the monarchic period. Naturally it cannot be older than the monarchy itself. It comes from a time when the common oriental ideal of kingship had been naturalized in Israel, and when the tension between ideal and reality was making itself felt, so as to prompt the wish that in spite of the unpleasant facts the ideal of kingship would be realized.

But we must mention here another factor which helped to give

[1] This may also be deduced from Ps. lxxxix, 21ff. and 2 Sam. vii; see Mowinckel in *S.E.Å.* xii, 1947, pp. 220ff.

97

the kingly ideal its future reference, namely, its connexion with the cult.[1] The occasions in Israelite life at which the king was presented to sight and thought as the realization of the ideal were the great festivals, when, as mediator between Yahweh and the people, and as representative of the latter, arrayed in holy attire, he received Yahweh's renewed promise of divine equipment, of the renewal of the covenant, and of every conceivable kind of good fortune for himself and his people in coming days. In particular, on two important cultic occasions the king thus represented the future hopes and prospects of the dynasty and the people. These were the festival of anointing and the great annual festival, the harvest and New Year festival, the festival of Yahweh's epiphany.

At the anointing, on the coronation day, he received the promise of a filial relationship to Yahweh, of victory over all his opponents, of world dominion, of 'everlasting priesthood', of the seat of honour at Yahweh's right hand. Promises of this kind have been preserved in the oracles of anointing, such as Psalms ii and cx.[2]

At the great annual festival, the foundation of the dynasty and the covenant with David (which also represented the covenant with the people) were experienced anew. Then the king received again the promise of his dynasty's everlasting reign, of Yahweh's favour, of victory, peace, and blessing for people and king, for priesthood and laity, for field and flock. The future was created and secured. Evidence of this is provided, for instance, by the festival liturgy in Ps. cxxxii.[3] But at the annual festival it was also the future of the whole people which was created anew. Fate was reversed; all things became new; a 'year of favour' was at hand. The invisible pledge of all this was the chosen of Yahweh, the king, 'David', with whom Yahweh would never break His covenant.[4]

Thus the fact is that at certain culminating and turning points in Israel's life the prevailing ideal of kingship crystallized into a present expectation and a specific promise of a definite person, who had already come or would come soon, and who was supposed to be the full realization of the ideal. To this the terms 'Messianic hope' or 'Messianic faith' have been applied. But this

[1] See *Ps.St.* II, pp. 297ff.
[2] See *Ps.St.* III, pp. 78ff.
[3] See *Ps.St.* III, pp. 30ff. On the covenant with David as parallel to the covenant on Sinai, see below, pp. 165f.
[4] Isa. lv, 3. On the oracles at the annual festival, see *Ps.St.* III, pp. 30–64.

is misleading, because the word 'Messiah' then loses its most important element, the eschatological element (see above p. 3). It is more accurate to see in this crystallization of the kingly ideal a preliminary stage of the true Messianic faith. From the standpoint of historical fact they belong to the more general stage of development, that of the royal ideology, not to the more specific, that of belief in a Messiah, which was produced by particular historical conditions and experiences against the background of the more general conception of the kingly ideal with its future reference.

But in order to understand the origin of the Messianic faith, it is important to see how the ancient Israelite ideal of kingship, being imperfectly realized, might take precise form at certain supreme moments and in times of emergency. It goes without saying that these decisive turning points in Israel had a cultic character.

In the faith of ancient Israel as we know it (which, in this connexion, means the form given to this faith by the spiritual leaders in Jerusalem under the monarchy), the realization of the kingly ideal was associated with the house of David, to which belonged the covenant and the promises,[1] since it was the chosen and anointed 'family of oil'.[2] The re-establishment of the nation's prosperity and of its prospects at the great annual festivals was also the re-establishment of the prosperity and prospects of David's house, represented by the contemporary bearer of the royal dignity. For the existence of the covenant people, the existence of the royal house with its 'peace' and 'righteousness' was a vital necessity. To the mind of the Israelite, the continuance and 'everlasting' character of life was bound up with the family. The content of the cultic and prophetic promises to the king and the royal house is that the dynasty will endure 'for ever' and 'stand before Yahweh', that there will always be sons sitting on the throne of their ancestor.[3]

A man's aim (and not least the king's) was to secure the life of his family. This was true of the Canaanites. To find a suitable wife who 'will bear a son to Karit' is the main theme in the Ugaritic epic of Karit. Here we see that the motif is found even in the world of the gods, for, as we have said, Karit is at once the

---

[1] Isa. lv, 3. On the interpretation, see Mowinckel in *G.T.M.M.M.* III, and below, pp. 165f.
[2] Cf. Zech. iv, 14; and see interpretation in *G.T.M.M.M.* III.
[3] 2 Sam. vii, 12–16, 25–9; 1 Kings viii, 25; Pss. lxxxix, 29–38; cxxxii, 11f., 17f.

deified ancestor and the god in the form of a hero. Both in Ugarit
and in Egypt the myth of the deity plays upon this motif: the son
is one with the father, and also the continuation of his life. It is
therefore natural that in the east the birth of a prince who is heir
to the throne is one of the great occasions in the life of the dynasty
and the nation. There are many echoes of this in oriental royal
inscriptions and in the Old Testament traditions. It is this motif
which creates the tension in the story about David and Bath-
sheba, about David's despair over the death of the first son, and
about the safe birth of the next, Jedidiah, 'the beloved of Yahweh'.
The same motif occurs elsewhere. That the story of the birth and
childhood of Samuel dealt originally with the birth of the later
King Saul, is still apparent from the explanation of the name in
1 Sam. i, 20, 'he who has been asked of Yahweh'. There is no
doubt, as several scholars have recognized and maintained, that
this explanation of the name really arose in order to explain the
name Šā'ûl, Saul.[1] The promise of sons who will be worthy successors of their father is also a leading theme in the oracle for the
royal wedding in Ps. xlv:

> Your sons will take the place of your fathers;
> you will make them princes over all the earth (or, land).

We are explicitly told that the court and temple prophets hailed
the birth of the prince with promises of good fortune from Yahweh.
The birth of Jedidiah-Solomon was certainly not the only occasion
when this happened.[2]

From the brief account which the narrator gives of this, we may
conclude at least this much, that the content of these promises was
Yahweh's goodwill to the child and thus to the dynasty which he
was to continue. They confirmed and renewed such prophecies
as were usually heard in the cult, at the enthronement of the king,
and at the annual festival: prophecies of Yahweh's everlasting
favour, of the everlasting dominion of the dynasty, and of the good
fortune and blessing to be brought on the land and the people by
the rule of the newborn child; cultic promises such as we find in
Pss. cxxxii and lxxxix, of which Nathan's oracle in 2 Sam. vii is
a narrative echo.[3]

[1] See Hylander, *Der literarische Samuel-Saul-Komplex* (*1 Sam. 1–15*) *traditionsgeschichtlich untersucht*, pp. 12f.; Mowinckel in *G.T.M.M.M.* II, p. 151.
[2] 2 Sam. xii, 24f.; the interest of the narrators in princes is also apparent in passages
like 2 Sam. iii, 2–5.
[3] *Ps.St.* III, pp. 35f., 110. It is not the case, as earlier literary critics tended to hold,
that Pss. lxxxix, 20ff.; cxxxii, 11ff., and other passages show literary dependence on

THE FUTURE HOPE

It is natural to suppose that, in such promises to the newborn prince, the kingly ideal would appear in its most glorious form. All kinds of expectations may be associated with the child while he is still new-born: as yet he has revealed nothing which can cast a shadow on these hopes. In the reigning king, both good and evil may be seen: everyday reality is always inferior to the splendour of the ideal and to soaring hopes and longings. But the ideal lives on, because its ultimate ground is religious reality and faith. The hope can never die. Without such an ideal of kingship, without the faith that in some measure it is always realized because Yahweh stands behind it, and that one day it will be fully realized, without that hope, ancient Israel could not live. That faith and that hope were the concentrated expression of her view of life and her religion. If Yahweh's promises and His covenant of 'righteousness', 'wholeness', 'prosperity', and 'salvation', are to be realized at all, it must be through kings who fulfil Yahweh's righteousness on earth and are the bearers of His blessing for land and people.

The great kings of the past, who had fulfilled something of the people's hope and faith, were still surrounded by the lustre of the full ideal of kingship. And since it was the custom for the birth of a prince to be greeted by prophetic promises, it was a regular poetic device to describe these great kings through the medium of a prophecy of their birth and appearance by some seer of the past. Such literary descriptions in prophetic and poetic style are known to us both from Egypt[1] and from Israel. In Israel it was natural

[1] It is these Egyptian prophecies (*vaticinia ex eventu*) about kings of the past, that have given rise to the untenable theories about an Egyptian messianic hope and eschatology. See above, p. 14, and below, ch. V, 1, p. 127 n. 3, p. 128 n. 1. Both the historical facts of which they treat and also psychological factors give rise to the recurrent pattern found in them: the time of misfortune which the new king brings to an end, and the time of blessing which he inaugurates. Hence the existence of such literary oracles gives no ground for concluding that there existed what is called a mythical pattern derived from a '*soter-muthos*', still less a myth with an eschatological

Nathan's prophecy in 2 Sam. vii, but rather the reverse. The legend records in narrative form how Nathan conveyed to David a promise which in form and content corresponds to that which was addressed, in the ritual, to a new king at his anointing. See further Mowinckel in *S.E.Å.* xii, 1947, pp. 220ff. Of course this does not rule out the possibility that Nathan actually did convey such promises to David, e.g., when he was solemnly installed as king in Jerusalem, which must have taken place after David had captured the city and entered into the heritage of the ancient King Melchizedek. A psalm like cxxxii shows that similar promises were made to the king at the annual festival, which was also the annual celebration of his accession. But it does mean that Nathan's prophecy cannot be taken as an independent historical tradition of what Nathan actually said to David on this occasion; still less does it mean that by the methods of literary criticism we can hope to recover a shorter 'original' form of the prophecy. From the literary and traditio-historical point of view, 2 Sam. vii is a faithful cult-historical reflection of a common cultic situation.

that David should be celebrated in this way. Among these poetical descriptions in the manner of prophetic promises we must include the prophecy of the 'star' or the 'comet', which was to 'rise out of Israel', in the Balaam lays, and the 'ruler' from the tribe of Judah in the Blessing of Jacob.[1]

2. *Specific Applications of the Kingly Ideal*

Among the extant texts which have from ancient times been regarded as Messianic there are some which must be regarded not merely as descriptions of the future, but as contemporary applications of the current ideal of kingship and the current expectation attached to the royal house and its representative. These came into existence in quite specific historical and cultic situations. First and foremost there are those passages which are associated with the birth of a prince.

The Birth of the Child (Isa. ix, 1–6). In form this passage is a blend of a prophetic message and a hymn. The glorious nature of the message makes the prophet cast it in the form of a song of praise, a hymn of thanksgiving to Yahweh for the work of salvation which He has already wrought through the birth of the child. But, as in the psalms of thanksgiving, he is actually speaking to the people.

The prophet begins[2] by giving a picture of the national situation as night and darkness; but at the same time he announces the dawning of the light.

> The people who walked in darkness
> have seen a great light;
> those who dwelt in a land of deep gloom
> upon them the light has shone.

The metaphor is taken from the conception of Sheol, the realm of the dead. It is the 'land of shadow' or 'gloom', the deep night in which the people are now living. When salvation is described as a sunrise, as a light shining in the night at the moment when the deliverer is born, it is plain (as we see below) that this metaphor has been derived from the myth of the sun god, the god of life, and of his victorious invasion of the nether world, Sheol, to rouse

[1] Num. xxiv, 7b, 17; Gen. xlix, 10; see above, pp. 12f.
[2] On the text, see *G.T.M.M.M.* III, pp. 785, 832 ('Rettelser').

reference, as Staerk holds (*Soter* II, pp. 234ff.). The 'pattern' is created by the nature of the facts: the ideal must have a dark background, that it may shine all the more brightly.

the dead. We find a variant of the same conception in Ps. cx, where behind the description of the king there lies the picture of the new god of fertility, 'the dew', *Tal*, born of the goddess of the 'glow of morning'. The Canaanite Baal, too, is both sun god and fertility god. He was dead, and in the realm of the dead; but he came to life, rose again, and brought back light to the world. Thus the background of the prophet's metaphor is ultimately the pre-Israelite conception of the king as the representative of the sun god and fertility god. In the comparison which follows, between the jubilation over the birth of the child and the rejoicing at the harvest festival, there is an echo of the conception of the association of the divine king with fertility. The Israelite prophet has forgotten the origin and the original meaning of these ideas; they have become merely metaphorical, depicting misfortune and the sudden, brilliant dawn of deliverance. The prophet does not need to mention the kind of misfortune he has in mind, for his audience knows it as well as he does himself; but the allusions which follow make it plain. It is the oppression of foreign rule. Beside the metaphors of the yoke on the neck of draught cattle and the driver's stick, there is a quite plain reference to the noisy military boots and the bloodstained garments of the army of occupation.

All this misery, says the prophet, is now ended in an instant. When the light is seen breaking into the darkness of Sheol, rejoicing already rises to heaven. Here hymn is joined with promise, as the prophet praises Yahweh for the salvation which He has already wrought through the birth of the child.[1]

> Thou hast multiplied the rejoicing,
>   and increased the gladness,
>   in Thy presence they rejoice as at harvest,
>   as men rejoice when they divide booty.[2]

The harvest and New Year festival when the crop has been safely gathered in, and the dividing of booty after a successful military expedition were from ancient times for the Israelite life's two supreme experiences, the former from the peasant's point of view, the latter from that of the warrior and the Bedouin. So now, rejoicing arises from the people who hitherto have been dwelling

[1] von Rad thinks that the 'Thou' in *vv.* 3f. is strange; *T.L.Z.* lxxii, 1947, col. 216. But see above, p. 102, on the literary form of the oracle.
[2] For the text of the first line see *B.H.*³ in loc. n.a-a.

in darkness. Presently we hear the reason. The coming of the light means that foreign domination is broken.

> For the yoke that weighed him down,
>   the bar that lay on his shoulder,
> and his oppressor's rod Thou hast broken
>   as in the day of Midian.

This last expression probably refers to the old stories about Gideon slaying the Midianites and delivering Israel from their domination and their forays (Judges vii f.). The prophet already sees the enemy defeated and driven out of the country. All his unclean, accursed equipment, which he has had to leave behind or throw away in his flight, is collected and burnt up to deliver the land from uncleanness and the curse:

> For every tramping soldier's boot
>   <shall be destroyed with fire.>
> And every garment stained with blood,
>   shall be fuel for the flames.[1]

But what is the reason for this sudden change of fortune? What is the light which has dawned on the oppressed people? We are now told:

> For a child has been born to us,
>   a son has been given to us;
> the token of royalty shall be on his shoulder,
>   and his name shall be called 'Wonderful Ruler',
> 'Divine Hero', 'Father for ever',
>   and 'Prince of peace and well-being'.

A son is born! By the birth of the child, light has dawned upon them in the darkness. The certainty of deliverance and salvation has been created within them, so that they already rejoice in anticipation of the coming victory and prosperity. The association of the myth about the birth of the sun god with the idea of the birth of the royal child is not accidental. By the birth of the child, salvation and a glorious future are guaranteed.

To this fact direct expression is given by the names which the prophet already gives to the child, names which he will assuredly win for himself when he sits on the throne of his fathers. In the east, as is clear particularly from Egyptian sources, the ceremony

---

[1] On the text, see *G.T.M.M.M.* III, p. 785.

of enthronement included the bestowal by the deity of names which expressed the king's nature, his relationship to the deity, and his destiny; and clearly this custom also formed part of the coronation ritual in Judah.[1] That is what the prophet is referring to here. Even now, by anticipation, he bestows upon the new-born prince the royal names which Yahweh has destined for him and which he will one day bear. They are 'Wonderful Ruler' (literally, 'Counsellor'),[2] 'Divine Hero', 'Father for ever', 'Prince of Peace and Good Fortune' (both ideas are included in the Hebrew *šālôm*, 'peace',[3] which really means, wholeness, fullness, perfect conditions). The first and last of these names are immediately intelligible to us: to rule over the land and the nation in war and peace, to have the right counsel in every situation, and to carry it into effect, to secure 'peace' and 'happiness' by victory in war and by prudent and just government were always the tasks of kings in ancient Israel. But even the first name, 'Wonderful Ruler', seems to hint that here these qualities are present in a wonderful, superhuman degree. The other two names show quite plainly that divine equipment is meant. The second name, *'ēl gibbôr*, may be translated as 'Heroic God' or as 'a God of a Hero', i.e., 'Divine Hero'; by analogy with 'Wonderful Ruler', the latter interpretation is the more likely. But in either event, the heroic power which the child will possess is characterized as divine. In form the name offers a precise parallel to the epithet applied to Aleyan-Baal in the Ugaritic texts: *'ilu ġaziru*, 'the victorious or heroic god',[4] the god who is victorious over his enemies and raises life out of death again. The third name, 'Father of Eternity', may according to normal Hebrew usage be interpreted 'Father for ever', i.e., one who for all time acts as the father of his people or his worshippers. But here, too, we have analogies which point in a somewhat different direction. The Egyptian king-god also bears the title 'Prince of Eternity' and 'lord of infinity'[5] and in the Ugaritic texts the supreme god, El, is also called 'Father of Years' (*'abu šanimi*). 'Eternity' in Hebrew does not denote the infinite, empty, abstract, linear prolongation of time which we associate with the word, but is equated with 'time' in all its infinite com-

---

[1] See von Rad in *T.L.Ƶ.* lxxii, 1947, cols. 215f.
[2] On 'counsel' = 'govern', 'lead', 'rule', see Pedersen, *Israel* I–II, 128ff., cf. Index, s.vv. 'counsel', 'counsellor'.
[3] Pedersen, op. cit., pp. 263ff.
[4] See Engnell, *Divine Kingship*, p. 110 n. 3.
[5] So Gressmann, *Der Messias*, p. 245.

prehensiveness. The word can therefore also mean 'the course of the world' (aeon) or simply 'the world' itself as a totality of time and space. To the Hebrew, 'time' is not an empty formal notion, a concept or category in the Kantian sense, but is inseparable from its entire content. 'Time' is all that exists and happens in time. It is the sum of the content of the years. 'Father of Eternity' and 'Father of Years' are therefore identical conceptions. They indicate the one who produces, directs, and is lord of the ever-changing years, who lets the years with all their content of events follow each other in constant succession, who thus produces and directs 'eternity', the entire fullness of events and reality. It is evident that such a name really belongs to a god, and not just any god, but *the* god, 'the high god', 'the supreme god', 'the father of the gods' (see below, pp. 182f). That the Jews, too, knew and used this title is apparent from a number of passages.[1]

Thus the newborn child is a ruler, a king, with divine attributes and divine equipment. What kind of child is this, then; and what are his task and his vocation?

> To increase the dominion,
>   and \<make\> good fortune endless,
> upon the throne of David,
>   and in his kingdom,
> to establish it with justice and righteousness
>   from henceforth and for ever
> the zeal of Yahweh of Hosts
>   will perform this.

The child will sit on the lofty throne of David's kingdom as a scion of David. He is called to extend his dominion and to create endless 'peace' (*well-being*) for his dynasty, and for its realm and empire, and thereby also for the people over whom the dynasty rules, and to restore the kingdom of David, which for the present, at least, is abased and subdued, to its ancient splendour. He will perform this as ruler of the kingdom, by displaying precisely those virtues which are required in a ruler: to execute 'justice', 'righteousness', and 'judgement', to provide 'justice' for his people, and by 'judging' them to deliver them from their adversaries, so to rule that well-being ('ideal conditions') is restored and maintained. He will also, if need be, 'give judgement against', and so

[1] Tobit. xiii, 6, 13; xiv, 7; Ecclus. xxxvi, 22 (17); see Charles *A.P.O.T.* I, ad locc., and cf. Bousset, *Relig.*[2], p. 358 n. 2.

destroy, not only foreign enemies, but any malefactors who exist within the nation, and protect all his subjects against the violation of their rights as members of the covenant people.[1] The ideal which is now to be realized through this child is the old ethical ideal of a king or ruler in Israel: to establish and maintain conditions of righteousness and bliss at home and abroad.

The first part of the prophecy would lead us to expect an explicit statement that it is the newborn king who in his time will perform all this; and this is in fact stated. The logical subject of the infinitives in *v.* 6 ('to increase the dominion', and so on) is 'he', the child of the preceding verse. But finally it is explicitly emphasized that this task is to be performed through the zeal of Yahweh of Hosts: Yahweh Himself will intervene, and deliver, and establish justice through the newborn child. Here the transforming power of revealed religion is apparent. A newborn king, who is described as a divine being with divine titles and faculties, who has appropriated the characteristics, achievements and name (i.e., the *muthos*) of the sun god and supreme god, is nevertheless only an instrument in the hands of 'Yahweh, God Almighty', who is the Author of all: he is a scion of David, a mere man. The mythical conceptions and metaphors have been transferred to the royal child of David's line; but in the last resort the power and the glory belong to Yahweh. It is He who accomplishes all; and without Him even the divinely equipped prince is nothing.

It is entirely in keeping with the transformation by the Yahweh religion of the old king-god motif that the prophecy does not include any description of the actions and achievement of the new king when he has reached man's estate. The announcement of his birth sums up all that there is to say. The very birth of the child is the guarantee of the coming salvation. The underlying conception has this element in common with the myth to which it ultimately goes back. In the Canaanite myths about the birth of the divine child (as we can discern them, for instance, behind the Karit Epic), all the emphasis is laid on the birth of the child. In virtue of his birth, the new age, the new year, life and blessing have arrived. This is clearly in accord with the cultic character of these myths, when at the time of the cultic festival the 'new' god of the new year is born and his birth is proclaimed as 'good

---

[1] On the meaning of righteousness and justice as virtues and functions of a ruler, see Pedersen, *Israel* I–II, pp. 336ff.

tidings'[1] for the people, then the new *is* present, then the dead god, his father, *is* alive again, life *is* reborn, blessing *is* already secured and will soon burgeon in the sight of all when the 'windows' of heaven are opened[2] and the life-giving and fertilizing rain begins to pour down. This feature of the myth, that all the emphasis is laid on the birth itself and on the salvation which it promises and guarantees, was of value to the Israelite prophet who adopted these ancient thought-forms to express his promises about the birth of the royal child. It was in keeping with what was for him the supreme fact, that it was the saving zeal of Yahweh which had intervened through this event to deliver His people from the night and death of misfortune.

Is the prophet speaking of what belongs entirely to the future; or does he apply his prophecy to a child already born? It is impossible to reach any certain conclusion on the evidence of the Hebrew verbal forms. Hebrew 'tenses' do not, like ours, express distinctions in time. Both the 'perfect' and the 'imperfect' in Hebrew can indicate events in the past, present, or future, according to context. In this passage the perfect and corresponding forms occur. They are used to emphasize that the events are thought of as real and must be described as such. Therefore the perfect, and particularly the corresponding consecutive imperfect (which also occurs here), are the usual means of describing what has happened (historic tense), and tend to become a real 'tense' denoting the past.[3] The style of this prophecy points in the same direction. The wording of *v.* 5, 'a child has been born', which expresses the chief point in the prophecy, is precisely in the style of a message. In everyday life it was in such terms that the news of the birth of a child was given to the father (Jer. xx, 15; Job iii, 3); and we may assume that in similar fashion kings informed each other of happy family events, in order that they might receive congratulatory embassies from friendly princes.[4] If we read the text of Isa. ix, 1–6

[1] This is the expression which the Ugaritic texts themselves use: *bšrt = bᵉśōrāh*. See Mowinckel in *N.T.T.* xl, 1939, pp. 205ff.; Engnell, *Divine Kingship*, pp. 116 (the news that the temple = cosmos is built), 126 (the birth of the new god, 'the calf'), 132 (the birth of the saviour god), 133 (do.: 'Lo, the damsel beareth a son.').
[2] These windows feature also in the Ugaritic texts. The restoration of the universe is symbolized by the erection of the temple which Baal builds, according to the myth; and it is an important point that the windows in the roof must be rightly placed. See Hvidberg, *Graad og Latter*, pp. 31f., 39, 47; Engnell, op. cit., pp. 102, 106.
[3] Nyberg (*Hebreisk grammatik*, p. 280) observes that the regular sequence of perfect and consecutive imperfect in Isa. ix, 1–6 cannot possibly express a prophecy of the future, but must refer to events which have either already taken place or are contemporary with the utterance.
[4] Cf. such congratulatory embassies on the occasion of victory, the accession of a

as it stands, without thinking of the traditional Christian interpretation, the immediate impression which we receive is undoubtedly that it describes something which has already happened. It
is the birth of a prince in Jerusalem which has occasioned this
promise. It expresses clearly and in classic form the ideas which
were associated in Israel with the bearer of kingship, and the
wishes and expectations which were quickened when a new heir
to the throne was born, not least in hard times, when the land was
threatened by the violence and injustice of the enemy, and all
thoughts were turned towards the future. Just as every year the
day of the New Year festival was expected to be 'the day of
Yahweh', which would bring the turn of their fortune,[1] so the
birth of every new prince was a starting point for the realization
of men's faith in the king's divine equipment and his vocation to
bring 'salvation', 'to establish justice' in the land. Here clear
light is shed on that unrealized element in the ideal of kingship,
which in time produced the Messianic hope. We are dealing with
an ideal of kingship and a hope which in the last resort are supra-
mundane, and which, in accordance with the spirit of revealed
religion, came at last to express the recognition that no human
king can bring that ideal and hope to fulfilment, but that 'the
zeal of the Lord God Almighty' must perform it, as the prophet
here clearly sees. There was, therefore, every justification for the
later Jewish interpretation of this passage as referring to the future
Messiah, and for the Christians who from the beginning recognized
that it had found its real fulfilment in Christ.

Of course it is impossible to identify the prince whom the prophet had in mind.[2] The prophecy does not describe this 'scion of
David' as he really was, but expresses the hope of what he might
become. Tradition has ascribed this saying to Isaiah. That is just
possible; but several factors tell against it; not only its context
and its secondary association with Isa. vi, 1–viii, 19,[3] but also

[1] Amos v. 18ff. See further pp. 142, 145, below.

[2] An interpretation of Isa. ix, 1ff. in terms of historical events is given by Dietze
in *Manasse*, but without any proof that the prophecy refers to the birth of King
Manasseh. The historico-ideological interpretation of the passage (and also of xi, 1ff.)
advanced above is shared in its essentials by Margaret B. Crook in *J.B.L.* lxviii, 1949,
pp. 213ff. She holds that these passages were connected with the enthronement of
King Joash of Judah, *circa* 837 B.C.; but the conventional and general features in the
description do not support so precise a dating.

[3] See Mowinckel in *G.T.M.M.M.* III, pp. 65, 104; cf. 'Komposisjonen av Jesajaboken Kap 1–39', in *N.T.T.* xliv, 1943, p. 163.

new king on the death of his predecessor, recovery from sickness, and the like; 2 Sam.
viii, 9f.; x, 1f.; 2 Kings xx, 12f. Embassies announcing the birth of a child are mentioned in the Amarna Letters and elsewhere.

particularly the fact that the prophet does not here attach to the promise any conditions of penitence and conversion, as Isaiah elsewhere always does.[1] But at least it comes from a prophet within the circle of his disciples, and was connected at an early stage with the tradition of Isaiah's sayings. It expresses the thoughts, expectations, and convictions which arose in the prophetic movement in the period after Isaiah.[2] It expresses what God had given to one of these later prophets to say, which in fact points beyond what he as yet could perceive. That God Himself must perform the work, establish justice, bestow salvation, but that He will do it through a divinely equipped man, a man who is really more than man, 'a greater than Solomon', 'a greater than Jonah' —that is what this prophet recognized. But *who* the child should be, was still hidden from him. It has been revealed to the Church; and there is every justification for reading this promise to the congregation as the first lesson at Morning Prayer on Christmas Day.

The Immanuel Prophecy (Isa. vii). The Immanuel prophecy in Isa. vii sheds clearer light on this wonderful royal child.[3]

The situation is the threatened assault on Judah by Ephraim and Damascus. King Ahaz does not dare to trust in Yahweh's help, but wants to appeal to the King of Assyria, which, to Isaiah, is synonymous with arrogance, unbelief, and contempt for Yahweh, setting the power of man above the power of God. But Isaiah does not give up hope of turning Ahaz to the right way. Yahweh Himself, in His longsuffering, will give him a sign, so that he does not even have to choose one: does he dare to accept it and yield himself to God? Then comes the sign: 'Behold the young woman has conceived, and she will bear a son (or, the young woman who has conceived will bear a son), and she will call him Immanuel

---

[1] See Mowinckel in *G.T.M.M.M.* III, pp. 70f., 105. von Rad, *T.L.Z.* lxxii, 1947, col. 216, points out that the hymnic mode of address to Yahweh (see above, pp. 102f.) is not found elsewhere in Isaiah. In Deutero-Isaiah this blend of promise and hymn is very common.

[2] See Mowinckel, *Jesajadisiplene*, pp. 46ff.; cf. 108ff.

[3] References to sources and literature relating to what follows are given in my article on the Immanuel prophecy in *N.T.T.* xlii, 1941, pp. 129ff. R. Kittel's monograph, *Die hellenistischen Mysterienreligion und das Alte Testament* is of fundamental importance for the interpretation. Stamm (*R.T.Ph.* (N.S.), xxxii, 1944, pp. 97ff.) still maintains the view which I formerly held (*Profeten Jesaja*, pp. 26ff.), that the child was the prophet's own. On the basis of the psalm superscription *'al 'alāmôt*, Fahlgren (*S.E.Å.* iv, pp. 13ff.) interprets *hā-'almâh* as referring to some female temple-singer. Fahlgren makes too much of the parallels in the Ugaritic texts. See also Hammershaimb in *St. Th.* III, ii, 1949/51, pp. 124ff., and the bibliography there (p. 142). Hammershaimb's interpretation of the prophecy is rather similar to my own.

(With-us-is-God). Curds and honey he will eat till (he is old enough) to have discretion to refuse what is bad and choose what is good. For before he has discretion to refuse what is bad and choose what is good, the land whose two kings you dread will be desolate.'

There has been much discussion of the identity of the young woman and the child. Is she the king's wife, or Isaiah's, or some woman who happened to be present, or any woman who is going to give birth to a boy in the near future? Instead of beginning with this question we ought rather to consider *what kind* of woman and *what kind* of child are here referred to. We then see that here, as in Isa. ix, 1–6, all the emphasis is laid on the birth and the name of the child, not on what will happen later. We are not told that he will reign as king over Israel, or indeed that he will be of royal rank, or that he will deliver the people from distress. On the contrary, it is stated that before the child is old enough to distinguish between what is useful and what is harmful (i.e., in a few years), the enemy will be destroyed by Yahweh. Since the sign is intended to make Ahaz believe absolutely in Yahweh, surrender himself to Him in complete trust and obedience, and in virtue of this choice decide to adopt the right attitude in the contemporary situation, it is clear that the sign must come to pass soon, and not, for instance, after the event, simply to confirm the divine direction, as in Exod. iii, 12.[1] This also means that a direct Christological interpretation is out of the question. Isaiah cannot here be referring to the birth of Jesus more than seven hundred years later. He foretells that since King Ahaz has not had sufficient courage and fear of God to make him ask for a sign from Yahweh, Yahweh Himself will give him a sign without delay. 'The young woman', already with child, will bear a son and give him a name expressing absolute trust that Yahweh protects His people. 'Immanuel', 'with us is God', was a familiar ejaculation in the liturgies of the sanctuary. With this cry the woman would greet the birth of her child, expressing her certainty of the truth which it conveyed: in that age, the first exclamation after the birth of a child was regarded as an omen of its destiny and its character.[2] With this ejaculation the congregation would greet the advent and presence of the deity at the festival, particularly the harvest and enthronement festival, as may be inferred from the refrain of the Epiphany

[1] The passage is so interpreted, e.g., by Duhm, *Jesaja²*, and formerly by the present writer; see *Profeten Jesaja*, pp. 26ff.　[2] Cf. Gen. xxix, 31ff.; xxxv, 16; 1 Sam. iv, 19ff.

and New Year psalm (Ps. xlvi). As has been said, we are not told that the child will reign as king, or deliver the people from the enemy. In this context, the value of the sign lies in the birth of the child and the name conferred on him. His birth is the token that henceforth God is with us.

What kind of child can this be? Some indication is given by *v.* 15. We are told that he will eat 'curds' (boiled up butter to which aromatic herbs have been added)[1] and honey. Some have followed Usener in interpreting this as the food of the gods, and accordingly have taken it for granted that the child is divine. There is certainly some truth in this. The expression is conventionally used to describe the fertility of the promised land.[2] In Babylonian rituals, cream or butter and honey are used as cultic ingredients;[3] and in the Canaanite texts from Ugarit, similar expressions are used to describe the fertility of the land, when Baal comes back to life, and the rain pours down on the earth,[4] the expressions here being almost exactly the same as those in the Bible. 'These two parallels indicate that the term has from ancient times been used for a choice food, which could please "both gods and men".'[5] Greek myths, too, tell of the newborn divine child who was nourished on milk and honey.[6] In the later Jewish period, milk and honey are mentioned as the food of the blessed in paradise.[7] But the expression is, in fact, ambiguous. In the myths about the newborn divine child, it is because the child has been abandoned in the wilderness that he has to be kept alive by such food. In those times, as today, the Bedouin used to give milk with honey in it to a nursling when the mother died or had no milk.[8] Accordingly, what is said about the child's food suggests that there is something unusual about him; he is not an *ordinary* human child. But it also indicates that for some time the child is to be in need and danger. Before the downfall of the enemy there will be a time of distress in which the child will be as one motherless and forsaken, and yet miraculously sustained by the powerful divine food of the wilderness, which can keep even deserted children alive.

[1] See Dalman, *Arbeit und Sitte in Palästina* VI, pp. 307ff.; cf. Mowinckel, in *N.T.T.* xlii, 1941, p. 135 n. 1.   [2] Exod. iii, 8, 17; xxxiii, 3; Deut. vi, 3; xi, 9; xxvi, 15; etc.
[3] See Zimmern, in *K.A.T.*[3], p. 526.
[4] See the text in AB III, 6ff.; cf. Mowinckel in *N.T.T.* xlii, 1941, p. 147; Hammershaimb in *St.Th.* III, ii, 1949–51, pp. 136f.   [5] Hammershaimb, ibid.
[6] See Gressmann, *Der Messias*, p. 158, with references to the material in Usener.
[7] Sib. V, 281ff.; 2 En. viii, 5f.
[8] See Mowinckel in *N.T.T.* xlii, 1941, pp. 135f., with references to the literature and the sources; Jaussen, *Coutumes des Arabes au pays de Moab*, p. 17 n. 1.

Thus the statement about the food gives no clear indication whether the child is really a divine or a human child. But the allusive brevity of the prophecy, in which important matters such as tribulation and desertion are presupposed, shows clearly that Isaiah is here referring to conceptions and narratives which were familiar to his hearers. From the bare reference to the child's food they realize the situation in which he is to be placed after his birth, and we are aware of the wonderful deliverance which he will live to see. They know something of what *we* are not explicitly told: why the child has been forsaken; who feeds him with milk and honey, and so on.

The expression, 'the young woman', *hā-'almâh*, with the definite article, is more explicit. The article may, admittedly, be used generically: a woman, some woman, any woman, the particular woman now referred to. But the most natural interpretation is that the article refers to a definite figure known to the king: the young woman you know, or have heard of, or of whom we all know. But then the reference cannot be to *any* woman, nor, according to the original sense, can it well be to any earthly woman. That some ordinary woman who gives birth to a child in those days should have the dauntless faith to call her son Immanuel, in spite of the imminent danger, could hardly be regarded as more likely to convince the king than the dauntless faith and certainty of the prophet. If Ahaz was disposed to dismiss Isaiah's faith as mere fanaticism, he would be still more inclined to dismiss the faith of an ordinary woman, or of any other person.

The situation becomes clear if we assume that Isaiah is here referring to a well-known popular belief of the time, about a supernatural woman who would bear a son whose birth would be an omen of a great and happy transformation. That there is something wonderful about the woman and about the birth of the child was suggested by the translators of the Greek Old Testament when they went beyond the proper sense of *'almâh* and rendered it by 'virgin': *'almâh* means a woman of marriageable age, whether married or single, whether virgin or not.

As has been said, there are several myths from antiquity which tell of the wonderful birth and upbringing of the new god, of how the divine child was deserted or carried off and kept alive on 'milk and honey' by herdsmen or by other divine beings.[1]

---

[1] The material has been collected by Usener in 'Milch und Hönig' in *Rheinisches Museum* (N.F.) lvii, pp. 177ff.; see also E. Norden, *Die Geburt des Kindes*.

Of these myths, those which have in recent years been most familiar in their original form are those from the immediate neighbourhood of Israel, from Ugarit in Phoenicia; and doubtless they were not confined to that country, but in many varying forms gave expression to a fundamental feature of all Canaanite religion. In them we are told of the wedding procession and nuptials of the fertility god (the dying and rising god), and of the birth of a son, who is the god himself in a new form, and whose birth guarantees the renewal of life, the triumph of life and of the powers of good over death. In the epic of Karit (which is, in a way, a variant of the themes of this myth presented in the form of poetic legend) the god has become a royal hero, and the event has acquired a kind of historical framework. The young woman (*galmatu* = Heb. *'almâh*) is the stock expression for the goddess who gives birth to the child.[1] The word also occurs in Ugaritic as the *name* of a goddess, who is a variant of the typical Canaanite mother-goddess and goddess of fertility, who also bears the name of 'the virgin Anath'. She is called 'the virgin', although in the myth she is the beloved of the god and bears his son: indeed, she even appears as the goddess of love. The reason is, of course, that in the myth, and in the cult which the myth reflects, all these things take place anew every year. At every New Year festival the cultic congregation meets her again as 'the virgin Anath'. That it is this goddess, 'the young woman', who bears the child and is the mother of the new, resurrected god, is plainly stated in another text which corresponds word for word with Isaiah's message in vii, 14: 'Behold, the young woman will bear a son' (*hl glmt tld bn*).[2] Thus there is something in the old translation of 'the woman' as 'the virgin':[3] Greek-speaking Jews must have known that behind the expression lay the idea of a woman who was a mother and yet ever became virgin again.

We know that many of the ideas which were associated with this cycle of myths were well known in Israel, and have left many traces in Israelite fantasy, thought, and metaphor, and to some

---

[1] See Mowinckel in *N.T.T.* xlii, 1941, pp. 144ff., cf. also Coppens, *La Prophétie de la 'Almah.*

[2] NK i, 7; see Engnell, *Divine Kingship*, p. 133. Cf. Dan'il's words in II D II, 11ff.: *yld bn ly*, 'a son is born to me'; cf. Isa. ix, 1 (so Hammershaimb in *St.Th.* III, ii, 1949/51, p. 127).

[3] On this 'return to tradition' see also von Bulmerincq's survey of recent exegesis of Isa. vii in *Acta et Comm. Univ. Tartuensis*, 1935. Although in the Karit Epic the context shows that Karit's future wife was still a virgin, this does not of course prove that the word *galmatu* as such means 'virgin', as E. J. Young seems to think (*Westminster Theological Journal* xv, 1952/3, pp. 122–4).

extent in religious practice.[1] Anath was also worshipped in Israel; and among the Jews on the island of Elephantine in Upper Egypt, as late as about 400 B.C., she was regarded as Yahweh's consort, sharing His throne, and bearing the name Anathyahu. Mourning rites for the dying god, Hadad-Ramman or whatever name he may have borne, are mentioned in the Old Testament.[2] Accordingly we may safely assume that such tales were known in Israel also, telling of a mysterious, supernatural 'young woman', in some unknown place, possibly on the 'mountain of the gods' where paradise lay,[3] a woman who would one day in a wonderful way bear a child whose birth would be the herald of a new age of bliss when all enemies would be overcome and God Himself would dwell among His people. These would be conceptions similar to those underlying St. John's symbols in Rev. xii concerning the 'great sign in heaven', a woman 'clothed with the sun, and with a crown of twelve stars on her head', who gave birth to a boy who was 'caught up to God and to His throne', while the woman fled to the wilderness to a place prepared for her by God.[4]

It is conceptions of this kind that Isaiah adopts here. Yahweh is about to perform a most wonderful sign. 'The woman', of whom ancient tradition tells, is now to bear a son; and the birth of this child will guarantee that 'God is with us'. Relying on this, 'the woman' (or whoever may be responsible for naming the child) will give him this name, Immanuel. But the sign will only be given on condition that even now it is accepted in faith, that the king really dares to commit himself completely into the hands of God, trusting in Him alone, at least to this extent, that he will have no dealings with Assyria until the sign has taken place. The sign is conditional upon this faith. It presupposes faith and is intended to create faith, to create certainty and security about the future. The implication of this is that, if the king will not receive the offer with so much faith, then there will be no sign. This is entirely in agreement with the fundamental law of religion, that without faith no miracle takes place. Only faith, however weak, is able to see the miracle and the sign. Unbelief and doubt see only an ordinary, unimportant 'accidental circumstance'; or they see nothing at all.

[1] Cf. Hvidberg, *Graad og Latter i det Gamle Testamente*, and bibliographical references.
[2] Zech. xii, 11; references to literature in Gesenius-Buhl[16].
[3] See Gunkel, *Genesis*[4] on ii f.
[4] Cf. Mosbech, *Johannes's Aabenbaring*, pp. 229ff.

But the sign does not foretell a 'Messiah' in the strict sense of the word. None of the functions which characterize the Messiah are ascribed to the boy. He becomes a sign simply by being born. It is the wonderful circumstances and happenings ordained by God in connexion with his birth which make him a miracle from God. But did Isaiah really think of, and so believe in, the existence of such a 'young woman' and in the birth of such a wonder-child? There is no reason to think otherwise, even if to modern ears it seems fantastic. Isaiah believed in the existence of equally fantastic, supernatural creatures: the six-winged seraphim in the temple, the flying, fiery, poisonous serpents or basilisks of the desert, and probably also the cherubim, those fabulous creatures which combined features from lion, ox, eagle, and man.[1]

Nevertheless we may assume that Isaiah has here rationalized the old mythical ideas, or, rather, that he has used them as a means of expressing more natural things and circumstances.[2] The word *'ôt*, which Isaiah applies to the sign, does not necessarily imply that it is to be a miracle in the strict sense: it can be used of natural, everyday things which become signs that Yahweh is about to do something important.[3] We have already seen that among the Canaanites these ideas of the promise of deliverance through the birth of a child were transferred to the founder of the dynasty and to the earthly king, the 'son' of the deity and his supernaturally equipped, 'divine' representative, Karit. It is certainly an exaggeration to say that here and in the corresponding cultic rites the king is identical with the god, and is himself a cult god:[4] still less is this true of the Israelite view of the king.[5] Nevertheless, as we have seen, both in Canaan and in Israel the king was divine in nature. It would be natural to speak of him in metaphors and ideas drawn from the mythology of the gods. Important as were the resurrection and rebirth of the god for the Canaanites, and the personal manifestation of Yahweh, 'the living God', to recreate and to save, for the Israelites, of equal importance for both was the conviction that the blessing and power of the deity were visibly represented in the divinely equipped royal dynasty

[1] Isa. vi, 2; xxx, 6; Ezek. i.
[2] Here my interpretation of Isa. vii differs from the one which I advanced in *N.T.T.* xlii, 1941.
[3] 1 Sam. x, 2ff. See Keller, *Das Wort OTH als "Offenbarungszeichen Gottes"*, pp. 51ff.
[4] Even Hammershaimb (op. cit., pp. 126ff.) is guilty of this exaggeration of the content of the royal ideology; cf. above, pp. 37ff.
[5] See above, pp. 76ff., 80, 84ff.

and in its contemporary representative, the reigning king. And important as was the rebirth of the god in his son for Canaanite faith and cult, of equal importance for Canaanites and Israelites was the continued existence of the royal dynasty in glorious sons. Both in the Karit Epic and in the kindred Dan'il poem from Ugarit, everything turns on the birth of a son to the king and founder of the dynasty.[1] In Israel, too, the prophetic poet promises the king at the wedding feast that glorious sons will in time succeed their father (Ps. xlv, 17); and the birth of the king is described in mythological terms; for the prophetic psalmist can say that the king was begotten by Yahweh or born of the goddess of the glow of dawn (Pss. ii, 7; cx, 3). The prophet associates supernatural, divine conceptions with the new-born prince and expects his birth to lead to wonderful things (Isa. ix, 1ff.; see above, pp. 102ff.). In Israel it is above all the dynasty of David which is the bearer of the divine promises and election, in which the individual king shares solely because he belongs to the dynasty.[2]

In the situation to which the promise in Isa. vii refers, the continued existence of the Davidic dynasty is at stake.[3] The enemy's plan was to depose Ahaz, and make another, the son of Tabeel (possibly an Aramean), king in Jerusalem. But if this is so, then the only probable, indeed, the inevitable conclusion is that in the Immanuel prophecy Isaiah is not thinking of a purely mythical, supernatural woman and a supernatural child, but of an actual, earthly woman and a human child.[4] Since these conceptions were already associated with the dynasty long before his time, and since they certainly existed in this form in the national consciousness, it can hardly be doubted that the reference is to the wife of King Ahaz, to the queen, and not simply to any of the ladies of the harem. In the Karit Epic it is to the future queen, the ancestress of the royal dynasty, the 'noble virgin', who 'is to bear a son to Karit', that the term *galmatu* (the young woman) is applied. The myth emphasizes that the son is really the king himself (originally the god himself) born anew. There is no need to assume that the queen was present at the end of the conduit on the way to the Fuller's Field, where the meeting between the prophet and the

---

[1] Cf. Hammershaimb, *St. Th.* III, ii, 1949/51, pp. 126ff.

[2] Cf. 2 Sam. vii; Pss. lxxxix, 20ff.; cxxxii, 10ff. On 2 Sam. vii, cf. Mowinckel in *S.E.Å.* xii, 1947, pp. 220ff.

[3] This is rightly emphasized by Hammershaimb, op. cit., p. 132.

[4] Like 'the Anointed' and 'the Servant of the Lord', 'Immanuel' has been subjected to the curious 'collective' interpretation in terms of the people Israel; see Skemp in *E.T.* xliv, 1932/33, pp. 94f.

king took place. Nor is it necessary to assume that either Isaiah or anyone else knew that she was with child. Probably Ahaz had just succeeded to the throne and was at the time very young, possibly only sixteen.[1] It is conceivable that a son had not yet been born to him, and that he was expecting the queen to ensure the continuance of the line. During the dramatic episode between Isaiah and the king, when so much is at stake, Isaiah becomes intuitively certain that the queen is with child, that she will bear a son, and that Yahweh intends this as a token that the promise stands secure, that the wicked designs of the enemy will come to nothing, and that all the good fortune and salvation which, in accordance with the covenant, are associated with the birth of a prince will again be realized. *If* the king dares to commit himself and the country to Yahweh's omnipotence, she will bear a boy whose birth is the fulfilment of all the thoughts and wishes which were associated with the king and the royal child. Then the new-born child will be the ideal king whose very existence is a guarantee that 'with us is God'.

The prophet does not here predict a Messiah, but a prince who realizes the idea of the king as the connecting link between God and the people, as a channel of blessing, and a palladium for his people. To this extent there is a measure of truth in the old Jewish interpretation of the Immanuel prophecy as a promise of the birth of King Hezekiah. He is the prince for whose birth everyone is waiting, and who, according to custom, will be greeted with shouts of exultation as rapturous as those with which, in the Ugaritic poem, King Dan'il receives the news of the birth of his son;[2] he will be hailed with the cultic shout, 'With us is God', and receive the honourable name Immanuel. Through him, through the very fact of his birth, victory and the future will be assured. But, as in several of the old myths, a time of affliction will come first. Perhaps mother and child will have to flee into the wilderness, as in the apocalyptic symbol in Rev. xii; but in a wonderful way the child will be kept alive on 'curds and honey'. The affliction will not last long. 'Before the child has discretion to refuse the evil and choose the good, the land before whose two kings you are in dread (i.e., the land of the two hostile kings) will be deserted.' Then the good fortune of the Davidic kingdom will

---

[1] According to 2 Kings xvi, 2 (M.T.) he became king at the age of twenty; but see Mowinckel in *G.T.M.M.M.* II, pp. 410f.; cf. Mowinckel, *Act.Or.* x, 1932, pp. 227ff., 231f.

[2] II D II, 11ff.; I K I, 143ff.; see Hammershaimb, op. cit., pp. 127, 130.

return; 'then will Yahweh bring upon you, and upon your people, and upon your father's house (wonderful) days the like of which have not been since Ephraim broke away from Judah', i.e., since the glorious age of the Davidic kingdom.[1]

If only the king dares to believe! Ahaz did not dare. Instead he sent messengers to the king of Assyria with 'all the silver and gold that was found in the house of the Lord and in the treasuries of the palace, and sent it as a present to the king of Assyria', and bade the messengers say to him, 'I am your servant and your son. Come up and deliver me from the hand of the king of Aram and from the hand of the king of Israel who are attacking me' (2 Kings xvi, 7f.). Thus the condition attached to the sign was neglected; the son who was born did not become such an ideal king; and the experience that 'God was with them' did not come to Judah. Here again, the promise of such a child was truly fulfilled only in Jesus. By that time the Immanuel prophecy had for long been interpreted as a Messianic prophecy.

The Prophecies about Zerubbabel. The prophecies discussed above both presuppose that the house of David was still in power as the ruling dynasty in Jerusalem. They are not 'Messianic' in the strict sense. But prophetic sayings have been handed down which had their origin against the background of the new situation which arose when the Davidic kingdom had collapsed, and which may therefore be said to represent the transition to the true Messianic prophecies, namely the promises made by the prophets Haggai and Zechariah to the governor Zerubbabel, who was of David's line. Yet they cannot be taken as an expression of the Messianic hope, for they neither presuppose nor proclaim it; but they lay the foundation for it and create it. The facts do not justify the common interpretation[2] that Haggai and Zechariah virtually lay on Zerubbabel's shoulders the mantle prepared for the Messiah, and announce, 'Now Messiah has come'. The specific expectations of a coming, eschatological Messiah did not yet exist. What these prophets do is to proclaim, 'In this man the house of David will be restored in its ancient glory. Once again we shall have a king who will fulfil the ancient ideal of kingship.' In their predictions the ideal again takes concrete form in a definite person in a

[1] On this point, too, with regard to *v.* 17, my interpretation differs from that adopted in *N.T.T.* xlii, 1941, and *G.T.M.M.M.* III. The verse is correctly interpreted by Hammershaimb, op. cit., pp. 137f.

[2] E.g., Gressmann, *Der Messias*, pp. 256ff. (mistakenly regarding Zerubbabel as a David *redivivus*), or Sellin, *Das Zwölfprophetenbuch.*

definite historical situation. To that extent they confirm the interpretation offered above of Isa. ix, 1–6 and vii. The ideal of kingship at one and the same time belonged to the present and had a future reference, and might at any time be applied to a historic person. The difference is that in Haggai and Zechariah the Davidic kingdom has been destroyed; but they regard the new historical situation as its restoration by Yahweh, and as already in process of being realized. The new ideal king of the ancient line is already present.

The Persian king, Darius, had sent Zerubbabel, David's descendant, to Jerusalem as governor of Judea, probably to secure the loyalty of the Jews during the great revolt after the death of Cambyses. But in Jerusalem he encountered a wave of religious nationalism. It was Yahweh Himself who had shaken the earth in order to overthrow the kingdoms of the nations and to restore Israel. Poverty, bad harvests, and oppression would soon be at an end. If only they would now set to and rebuild the temple, and so manifest their zeal for God's cause and proclaim their independence of the Persians, Yahweh Himself would come and dwell in the midst of His people, and let the fullness of blessing pour down on the land.[1]

In the advent of the descendant of David these prophets see a guarantee that the time of bliss has now begun. He is 'the Servant of Yahweh' (Hag. ii, 23; Zech. iii, 8), carrying His counsels into effect, 'the signet of Yahweh', as it were giving validity to His decisions, the 'chosen one' (Hag. ii, 23). Referring to his name Zerubbabel (the shoot from Babel), Zechariah announces that he is *semaḥ*, the Branch, the Rod,[2] which has shot up again from the stump of David's fallen family tree, showing that life and the energies of life have been renewed, just as in the cult the sprouting branch indicated the resurrection of the vegetation god. Where he treads there will be abundant growth (*yiṣmaḥ*, vi, 12); there will again be fertility and abundance in the country (Zech. viii, 4f., 10–13). Zerubbabel will finish the temple (Zech. iv, 7ff.; vi, 12). Like the oil-pipe which conveys the oil to the lamp, he will mediate Yahweh's blessing and His wonderful power to the people (Zech. iv, 1–6a, 10b–14). Zechariah already has in readiness the crown with which Zerubbabel will be crowned;[3] and his

---

[1] Hag. ii, 6–8, 18f., 21f.; Zech. i, 15–17; ii, 3f., 13–17; vi, 8; viii, 3, 20–3.

[2] Zech. vi, 12f.; iii, 8. This play on words is doubtless Zechariah's own; see below, pp. 160–5.

[3] Zech. vi, 9ff. I find it impossible to regard Rignell's defence of M.T. (*Die Nachtgesichte des Sacharja*) as satisfactory.

visions seem to contain reflections of the ritual of the enthronement of the king,[1] as in the enthronement oracle, Ps. cx.[2] Zerubbabel will be king over the restored Jerusalem, and will gain
power and renown. From distant lands foreigners will come to
join in building the temple of Yahweh; the hostile world power
will be destroyed before him; for his sake Yahweh will again before
long, 'shake both heaven and earth and overthrow the throne of
kingdoms, and destroy the power of the kingdoms of the nations,
and overthrow the chariots and those that ride in them; and
horses and riders will fall, every one by the sword of his brother'—
Israel will again subdue other nations.[3] But these political ends
will be attained only through Yahweh's action, without the help
of man: 'not by might, nor by power, but by My spirit, says
Yahweh of hosts'. There appears to be nothing to support the
view that Zerubbabel attempted to stir up a revolt against the
Persians; possibly he was deterred by these very warnings of the
prophet.[4]

Here, too, we see the ancient, extravagant, religious ideology of
kingship applied to a historical person, whom the prophets saw
every day, and who played an insignificant enough part in the
actual politics of the Empire. It is the mantle, not of the Messiah[5]
but of the ancient Israelite kings (designed, in fact, for a king-god)
that they throw over the shoulders of Zerubbabel the governor,
because he belonged to the ancient, chosen 'family of oil', which
Yahweh anointed and established among His people as bearers of
kingship. The message of Haggai and of Zechariah has nothing
to do with eschatology. What they are waiting for is a complete
historical revolution in the Near East, attributed, of course, to the
guidance of Yahweh and to the intervention of His miraculous
power, but developing within the course of empirical history and
working through normal human means. 'By His spirit' Yahweh
will guide events so that the world powers destroy each other in
the chaos which has arisen all over the east as a result of the death
of Cambyses; and Israel alone will remain unscathed and will
reap the benefit. This may be described as a fantastic and un-
realistic expectation, but that does not make it eschatology. The
religious interpretation of historical events always seems to the

[1] See May in *J.B.L.* lvii, 1938, pp. 173ff.
[2] See Widengren *Psalm 110 och det sakrala kungadömet i Israel.*
[3] Zech. iv, 6 aβ –7; vi, 13, 15; Hag. ii, 21f.
[4] So Bentzen in *R.H.Ph.R.* x, 1930, pp. 493ff.
[5] The expression is used by Bentzen (ibid.) and others.

worldly-wise to have something of the fantastic about it; but a religious interpretation of the world is not necessarily the same as an eschatological one. What distinguishes the pictures in Zechariah's night visions from those in the Revelation (which in large measure have been derived from Zechariah) is precisely the fact that in Zechariah the horses, riders, etc., are beings which really exist, and are always at hand, working as Yahweh's instruments like the angels, but as a rule, like Yahweh Himself, working behind and through natural agencies, whereas in the Revelation they have become apocalyptic entities, which do not come into existence, or, at least, into action, until the last times, their object being to precipitate the final catastrophe.

3. The Source of the Messianic Conceptions

It is impossible to read the expressions applied in the Old Testament to the king, Yahweh's Anointed, and to become familiar with the picture sketched above, without being struck by their close similarity to our usual ideas of 'Messiah', and to the general Messianic conceptions of the Church. The best proof of this is the fact that all these sayings, and especially the royal psalms, have been interpreted in traditional Christian theology as prophecies of the Messiah, and are still popularly interpreted in that way. The connexion between the royal ideology and the conception of the Messiah is quite evident. The royal ideology is the older, and the conception of the Messiah the more recent. It is thus clear where the content of the Messianic idea originated.

Both the content and the form of the conception of the Messiah are derived from the Israelite (and, ultimately, the oriental) conception of kingship: of that there can be no doubt. The correspondence between them is not confined to the prophecies which have been discussed in the previous section, but extends to the entire conception or 'ideology' of kingship. We can see how easily this ideology might become the expression of the hope and expectation of the people and the prophets, and how easily it could acquire immediate relevance through contemporary events and situations which turned men's thoughts to the future—and to the immediate future. In all the instances mentioned above, the ideal conception of kingship has been given immediate relevance by the presence of affliction in greater or less degree, accompanied by a measure of hope. It is affliction, the need for help, and the hope of a change in the situation, which makes the royal ideology relevant because of its reference to the future, and presents to the imagination the picture of an ideal king either in the immediate future or as already present.

It ought now to be possible to sum up the conclusions of all that has been said in the foregoing chapters. First, we have seen that we must distinguish between genuine Messianic prophecies and those which speak of the idealized and empirical king in Israel or Judah. The majority of the passages which popular theology interprets as Messianic are in fact concerned with the king of actual historical experience. Secondly, we have seen that those ideas which were associated in Israel with the king share all their essential elements with the concept of the Messiah. This will be still more evident when we come to describe the Messiah concept itself. The only essential difference is that the ideal of kingship belongs to the present (though it clearly also looks towards the future), whereas the Messiah is a purely future, eschatological figure. Clearly there is a historical connexion between these two complexes of ideas. Either the content of the kingly ideal was derived from the concept of the Messiah, or, vice versa, the content of the Messianic concept was derived from the kingly ideal. The latter alternative is manifestly the right one. 'Messiah' is the ideal king entirely transferred to the future, no longer identified with the specific historical king, but with one who, one day, will come.

Most of the earlier critics were convinced that the Messianic concept was comparatively late; but, on the other hand, they did not understand the royal ideology and the royal psalms. Other scholars, and particularly the so-called religio-historical school, maintained that the royal ideology was 'Messianic', i.e., that the kings were regarded as Messiahs and described in the metaphors and forms of the Messianic ideology. They thought that in Israel both eschatology and the Messianic concept were ancient, older than Israel itself, common to the whole orient, and that the oriental ideal of kingship reflected the Messianic conceptions. But this view (which was shared by Gressmann, Gunkel, Sellin, Jeremias, Staerk, and others) cannot be right. In the first place, we have seen that there was no ancient oriental eschatology. Apart from Israel, the first people to have an eschatology were the Persians; and Persian influence on the religion and culture of the east does not begin until the sixth century. But if there existed no eschatology which was common to the ancient east, neither was there any eschatological king, or 'Messiah'.

Secondly, the oriental ideology of kingship is very ancient. It is already fully developed in the Sumerian period. It is also ancient in Israel. We find it in the oldest sayings about the king, in very old psalms, like Ps. cx; and it is natural to suppose that it was taken over when kingship itself was adopted after the Canaanite pattern.

In the third place, we have seen that (according to the most probable critical dating of the sources) the genuine Messianic sayings in the Old Testament belong to a relatively late period, most of them (perhaps all) to the time after the fall of the monarchy.

The only justifiable conclusion, then, is that the substance of the Messianic hope was taken from the royal ideology, and not vice versa.

This brings us to the next question: how did the Messianic *hope* as such originate; why did any Messianic expectation arise in Israel at all; what were the historical and intellectual conditions which produced it (or, to put it in more theological terms, were the occasion of its emergence as an essential part of revealed religion), and which caused the prophets to be led to such thoughts and expectations? In order to answer this question clearly we must examine the whole subject of the Jewish future hope. If the Messiah is an eschatological figure, the problem of the origin of the Messianic hope cannot be separated from the problem of the content and origin of eschatology itself.

CHAPTER V

The Early Jewish Future Hope

AS we have seen, the Messianic faith was from the first associ-ated with the Jewish hope of a future restoration. That this was really so will be still more evident when we come to describe the content of the Messianic faith. At every point it is bound up with the future hope and with eschatology. Therefore, as part of the background, we must sketch the Jewish hope of restoration.

The expression 'future hope', rather than 'eschatology', has been deliberately used in the title of this chapter; for a distinction must be made between the two. A future hope which is national, as the Jewish hope undoubtedly was, need not be eschatological; that is, it need not be regarded as something which belongs to 'the last things', which coincides with the end of the present world order, and introduces or fashions a new world of a different kind.

It is also clear that there is an essential difference between the view of the future in the older parts of the Old Testament on the one side, and on the other, that found in the later portions, such as Daniel, and in later Judaism. The future hope had a history. Any description of it must take account of the problem of its origin and its content down through the ages. Since, however, our present purpose is to indicate the background of the conception of the Messiah, we must limit ourselves to a short outline.[1]

First, we must understand clearly the terms which we use. Eschatology is a word which has occasioned much confusion; and we must begin by defining it. Eschatology is a doctrine or a complex of ideas about 'the last things', which is more or less organically coherent and developed. Every eschatology includes in some form or other a dualistic conception of the course of history, and implies that the present state of things and the present world order will suddenly come to an end and be superseded by another of an essentially different kind. As a rule this new order has the character of a fresh beginning, a *restitutio in integrum*, a

---

[1] See Additional Note IX.

return to the origins, without the corruption which subsequently overtook and deformed the original creation. Eschatology also includes the thought that this drama has a universal, cosmic character. The universe itself, heaven and earth, is thrown into the melting pot. It follows that this is not brought about by human or historical forces, or by any immanent, evolutionary process. The transformation is definitely catastrophic in character, and is brought about by supernatural, divine, or demonic powers. In Christian terms, the new situation is the work of God: it is God's will that is accomplished, and His plan for the world which reaches its fulfilment.[1] Later Judaism had an eschatology of this kind which is presupposed by the preaching of Jesus. When and how did it arise; and what was its essential content?

1. No Pre-prophetic or Prophetic Eschatology

For a long time there has been diversity of view about the origin of the Israelite and Jewish future hope and eschatology; and some of the views held have been fantastic.

Sellin,[2] for instance, thinks that the future hope and the idea of the Messiah go back to the revelation of God to Moses on Sinai. We *may*, of course, hold this, since everything which came into existence within the Jewish religion is in some way rooted in the character and origin of the Mosaic religion itself. But there is no specific historical value in such vague general statements about 'origins'. It is saying little more than, for example, that such and such a specific species of animal originated in the primitive cell: it is undeniable, but scientifically worthless.

The older school of literary criticism maintained that the future hope did not become a factor of importance until after the states of Israel and Judah lost their independence. This view is supported by the fact that, in the main, the earlier 'writing prophets' had no eschatological message, but uttered prophecies related to the contemporary historical situation, and were prophets not of bliss but of doom; and further, by the fact that the eschatological promises included in the books which contain their sayings very often bear clear marks of later origin.

---

[1] For this definition of eschatology, cf. Hölscher, *Die Ursprünge der jüdischen Eschatologie*, p. 3. The heart of the matter is missed if we define it as Widengren does in *Religionens värld*[2], pp. 333ff. ('a summing up of conceptions of the last things, in the sense of all that follows death'), and by relating this to thoughts of the individual's destiny after death. This is a secondary use of the word eschatology.

[2] See Sellin, *Der alttestamentliche Prophetismus*.

In opposition to this view, Gressmann,[1] and with him *die religionsgeschichtliche Schule*, held that even the prophets of doom seemed to assume in their hearers some knowledge of a 'popular eschatology', which they took as their starting point, modified in various ways, and applied to the contemporary situation. This popular eschatology was thought to have been a more or less rudimentary variation of a general oriental eschatology, ultimately Babylonian in origin, and to have included from the outset two elements: disaster (the destruction of the world) and salvation (restoration), 'the time of the curse' and 'the time of the blessing'.[2] These two parts of the future expectation were thought to have been taken over in Israel separately and without any inner organic connexion, and yet as elements with a traditional association with each other in a pattern which was held to have belonged to 'prophecy' throughout the entire ancient east. This was the explanation of the abrupt and disconnected juxtaposition of prophecies of disaster and prophecies of salvation which the literary critics found so awkward. Many important facts tell against this theory, not least the fact that it has not been shown that there is the slightest trace of this supposed common oriental eschatology, either in Babylonia and Assyria or in Egypt.[3]

The rare incidental prophecies which naturally are also to be found in these two cultures, and which some have wanted to take as evidence of the existence of an eschatology, do not prove anything of the kind. They can be explained much more naturally in another way, partly as political prophecies with a contemporary reference (and what ancient people does not have such prophecies?), partly as literary imitations of such prophecies, as *vaticinia ex eventu*, and as literature for entertainment.[4]

[1] Gressmann, *Ursprung*. [2] So Jeremias, *Handbuch*, pp. 205ff., and Staerk, *Soter* I–II.
[3] Against the theory of an Egyptian eschatology and an 'Egyptian Messiah' (Gressmann in *Geisteskultur*, xxxiii, 1924, pp. 97ff.), see von Gall's sober examination of the sources on which, for instance, Jeremias (*Handbuch*, pp. 219ff.) relies, and his decisive criticism of this hypothesis (*Basileia*, pp. 48f.). The evidence for a Babylonian eschatology is still feebler: it is presented, e.g., in Jeremias, *Handbuch*, pp. 205ff., 225f.; cf. Staerk, *Soter* II, pp. 167ff. No specific textual evidence is offered other than the supposedly Messianic descriptions of the time of prosperity on the occasion of a new king's accession. How these are to be interpreted has been shown above (pp. 45–7); cf. von Gall, op. cit., pp. 43ff., and Dürr, *Ursprung und Ausbau*, pp. 4ff., 16ff. There is no ground for believing that eschatological ideas are applied to the present in these passages. Nor is there any cosmic or eschatological character in the regular alternation of ages of good and bad fortune to which Widengren refers (*Religionens värld*[2], p. 358); it arises from an attempt to interpret historical events in the light of the cultic conceptions of death and the new creation; see p. 128 n. 1. Against the hypothesis of a Babylonian eschatology and 'Messianism', see also Zimmern in *Z.D.M.G.* lxxvi, 1922, p. 44, and Labat, *Royauté*, p. 299.
[4] Cf. Wiedemann, *Die Unterhaltungsliteratur der alten Aegypter*, p. 28.

THE EARLY JEWISH FUTURE HOPE

Equally decisive against Gressmann's theory is the fact that from
the beginning Israel's future hope had a dominant idea which
held misfortune and salvation together in organic unity. That
idea was the kingly rule of Yahweh (see below, pp. 143ff). The
supposed 'prophetic pattern' does not in fact originally belong to
prophecy, but is a typical eastern attitude to history,[1] which arose
from the annual cultic experience of an ever-recurring time of
chaos and new creation. This would naturally also find expression
in literature which presented a survey of the events of the past in
the form of prophecy. As we shall see, the same experience certainly lies behind the idea of the kingly rule of Yahweh. But it
was only in the course of the history of Israelite prophecy that this
'pattern' became one of its leading ideas, and that too in connexion with the rise of a religious hope for the future and of
eschatology. That is why it provided the principle on which
tradition arranged the individual sayings of the prophets in larger
collections of prophetic books.[2] The use of the pattern as a principle of arrangement in the prophetic books does not justify us in
drawing any conclusions about the character of prophecy, the
origin of eschatology, or the supposed existence of an ancient
oriental eschatology.

The theories of Gressmann and Sellin rest on the assumption
that there are passages in the prophetic books, and occasionally
elsewhere in the Old Testament, which either are genuinely
eschatological utterances, or were so interpreted. The traditional
Christian view of the origin of the future hope is based on the
same assumption: the concept of the Messiah and the Messianic
hope came into existence because at an early period God proclaimed through the bearers of His revelation a series of Messianic
promises in which believers put their trust. Therefore even primitive
Christian theology (e.g., the Epistle to the Hebrews) believed that
the patriarchs lived in the hope of the Messiah, and that this hope
formed an essential part of their religion (Heb. xi; cf. John viii, 56).

[1] See Güterbock in Z.A. (N.F.) viii, 1934, pp. 2ff.; Stamm in T.Z. ii, 1946, pp. 18f.;
cf. p. 14. The thought of this kind of pattern of world history is maintained by Zimmern in K.A.T.³, pp. 392f.; Meyer, Die Mosesagen und die Lewiten, pp. 651f., Die Israeliten
und ihre Nachbarstämme, pp. 451ff. From it exaggerated conclusions are drawn concerning the interpretation of Israelite prophecy by Gressmann (Der Messias, pp. 72f.,
417ff.) and others. Against such exaggeration, see von Gall, Basileia, pp. 43ff.,
Mowinckel, Prophecy and Tradition, pp. 79ff.; Sjöberg in S.E.A. xiv, 1949, pp. 30ff.
Frankfort, Kingship, p. 398 n. 43, doubts whether this general view of history existed
in Mesopotamia.
[2] On the pattern of the collections in the prophetic books, see Mowinckel, Prophecy
and Tradition, pp. 79ff.

It is, of course, an unassailable theological thesis that the concept of the Messiah came into existence because God revealed such
thoughts and dreams to His saints. But a general statement of
this kind does not take us far towards a real historical understanding. What the theologian also wants to know is: How old is
this conception? Did it come into existence all at once, or has it
a history? What human and historical agencies did God use?
By what historical paths did He lead His prophets on to such a
conviction?

Our approach to the critical study of the Old Testament books
may be more or less conservative or radical. But any scholarly
treatment of them must reckon with the fact that practically every
prophetic book contains sayings, not only by the man whose name
it bears, but also by a whole circle, and from various times.

The work of tradition criticism and of literary criticism in distinguishing between earlier and later elements in the material
handed down to us, and in attempting to arrange the tradition
according to the changing periods in revelation history, and to
discover the line of development in that history, is an absolute
necessity if the historical study of theology is to be carried on.
It is a fact that there is constant change in the understanding of
historical connexions and lines of development. Even within
revelation history there are changes in the understanding of that
history itself; and Judaism had a different conception of the
development of its own revelation history from that contained in
the oldest historical traditions, e.g., that of the Yahwist. There is,
therefore, no ground for assuming that precisely that interpretation of the development which is advanced by the author of the
Deuteronomic history from Deuteronomy to 2 Kings[1] is *the* only
right and definitive view. Even in the course of revelation history
there is a developing comprehension; and the older interpretation
is superseded by the new.[2] This is referred to by Jesus Himself,
when He speaks of truths which His disciples were not yet ready
to understand, and of the Spirit of Truth who would afterwards
lead them into all the truth. It is, therefore, clear that critical
discussion of the eschatological passages in the prophetic books
has drawn attention to a real problem, and that a critical, exegetical discussion of the individual eschatological sayings (real or

[1] On this view of the extent of the history, see Noth, *Überlieferungsgeschichtliche Studien*
I, pp. 54ff.
[2] Cf. Mowinckel, *Det Gamle Testament som Guds ord*, pp. 23ff.

K

supposed) is a necessary preparation for an understanding of the origin and growth of eschatology and the concept of the Messiah.

The question whether eschatology is or is not to be found in the prophets must not be confused with the problem whether the prophecies of bliss in the older prophetic books are authentic sayings of the prophets concerned (Amos, Hosea, Isaiah, etc.), or arose within the circle of disciples in the process of tradition.[1]

As will be shown later, this much is certain, that at least some of the prophets of doom expected a restoration of Israel some time after the disaster. Nor is it improbable that they uttered glowing prophecies about the king. But this has nothing to do with eschatology or the Messianic faith. The question still remains, whether all the promises which have been handed down come from the prophet in question. No simple solution is possible, either on the ground of an ancient eastern pattern of history with a constant alternation between periods of good and bad fortune (see above, pp. 127f.), or because this pattern seems also to have been used to present historical events in the form of prophecy, or may perhaps also have been used as a pattern for predictions of the good fortune which a new king's reign would bring.[2] The dating of the prophecies of bliss in the prophetic books must be decided in each individual instance.[3] Whatever view we hold about the age of any individual saying in the prophetic books, it is established as a result of the historical and critical study of Old Testament tradition and literature during the past generation that there is no eschatology in the strict sense in the early, pre-prophetic age. Israel's religion did not originally have an eschatology. It was pre-eminently a religion for life in this world, realistic, sturdy, and robust.

Nor did the earlier of those prophets whose sayings are extant proclaim an eschatology, any more than they imply knowledge of a popular eschatology, or a learned Babylonian eschatology.

[1] On this traditio-historical approach, as opposed to one of purely literary criticism, see Mowinckel, *Prophecy and Tradition*, ch. II, especially, pp. 66ff.

[2] In support of this, reference is commonly made to the text *K.A.R.* 421, translated in *A.O.T.*², pp. 283f. Labat (*Royauté*, p. 297 n. 101) holds that broadly speaking no Babylonian or Assyrian prophecies have been handed down. But of course they did exist, e.g., in connexion with a king's enthronement, and as cultic promises, partly for the regular cultic festivals, partly on occasional cultic days, such as days of penitence and prayer in distress and misfortune. Cf. Haldar *Associations*, pp. 1–73. But the Irra texts to which Haldar refers (op. cit., pp. 70ff., following Ebeling in *B.B.K.* II, i, 1925) are not real prophecies either, but mythical poems related to the normal cultic promises following the habitual pattern: after the misfortunes of the age of chaos, good fortune is now at hand.

[3] Cf. Sjöberg in *S.E.Å.* xiv, 1949, p. 39.

Gressmann's attempt at reintroducing eschatology into the study of the prophets is a failure. In this the position of the older generation of literary critics was undoubtedly sound, although their 'literary' approach was one-sided and in part mistaken.[1] The prophets of doom were always concerned with contemporary events. Their starting point was always the given, concrete, historical situation, and nearly always the political situation. They were national prophets, not private fortune-tellers and medicine-men concerned with the trivial affairs of private individuals. They foretold the future; but it was the immediate future, which arose out of existing, concrete reality. Yahweh had opened their eyes and ears, so that they saw and heard Him in the events of the history of that age. They saw events as the outworking of God's government of the world; and they had been sent to proclaim what God intended to do next, His purpose and plan in what had already begun to happen. Their message to the people was: 'Take now, to-day, the right attitude to Yahweh, and so to what is happening; for He has already risen to perform His work, and you, His own people, are the object of His work.'

In a message of this kind there is no room for eschatology, not even in the sense that they proclaimed that in and through historical and political events the last things were at hand, the end of days, the destruction of the world, the restoration of heaven and earth. In their time there was no conception or doctrine of any end of the world or last things.[2] If they had themselves announced any such doctrine as something new, hitherto unknown, they would have expressed the matter much more clearly than in fact they did. They speak of the destruction of Israel at the hand of Assyria or Babylon by the direction of Yahweh, not of the destruction of the world. They make it abundantly plain that this is not the last word about history or the course of the world. The world and history still run their course, and Assyria and Babylonia continue to exist, even after the destruction of Israel. Admittedly Israel was to all intents and purposes their 'world' and that of their hearers; and a catastrophe which shattered that world was for them a catastrophe of world-wide dimensions. It could therefore be described in the most impressive language, mustering all those cosmic powers and terrors which can only be mobilized by

---

[1] On this point, cf. Mowinckel, *Prophecy and Tradition*.

[2] The expression $b^e a h^a r \hat{i} t$ hay-$y \bar{a} m \hat{i} m$, 'at the end of the days', occurs only in late passages, or late editorial links; see the references in Gesenius-Buhl[16]. The expression is probably influenced by Persian usage; see von Gall, *Basileia*, pp. 91ff.

Yahweh, but which He actually does mobilize whenever He is accomplishing some end in history, even if the profane eye does not perceive it.[1] But in all this nothing implies the end of the present world order. Amos, for instance, reckons with the possibility that Yahweh may choose a new people when Israel has been destroyed (Amos ix, 7). Isaiah speaks of the 'remnant' which will live on in history,[2] and Jeremiah gives advice about the continued life of the people after the deportation in the everyday world of history.

In the prophetic books, the eschatological sayings in the strict sense all belong to the later strata, and come from the age of post-exilic Judaism. This is evident from the fact that they treat of the restoration of Israel after the catastrophe which had befallen the people in 587, and that they do not foretell that catastrophe, but presuppose that it already belongs to the past.

The fixed point for all who have maintained that an eschatology existed before the appearance of the great prophets is the saying of Amos in v, 18 about those who 'wait for (desire) the day of Yahweh'.[3] But in fact there is here no reference to an eschatological day of Yahweh at some indefinite point in the future. The expression still has its contemporary connexion with the cult and with cultic experience. 'The day of Yahweh' originally means the day of Yahweh's manifestation in the festal cult at the New Year festival; and this connexion with the festal cult is still quite clear from the context in which the saying is found in Amos.[4] Because on every day of Yahweh in the festival the people experienced His coming, which guaranteed victory over enemies, deliverance from distress, and the realization of peace, good fortune, and favourable conditions, therefore, whenever the people were in distress, they would long for the coming days of Yahweh which would bring the 'change of fortune'.[5] And in so far as the term might denote any appearance of Yahweh to save and bless, we may speak of

[1] Judges v, 4f., 20; 2 Kings vi, 16f.; Isa. xxii, 11.
[2] Isa. vii, 3; x, 21f.; xxviii, 16ff; xxx, 15f.; i, 10-17, 18-20, 21-6, 27-31. Cf. Mowinckel, *Profeten Jesaja*, pp. 66ff.
[3] In *Ps.St.* II I myself still shared this erroneous interpretation of Amos v, 18, and on that basis put forward a dating of 'eschatology' which was too early and untenable; see op. cit., pp. 318 (foot), 319; cf. p. 272.
[4] Amos v, 18-27; *vv.* 18b, 19 are probably an explanatory addition; see Mowinckel in *G.T.M.M.M.* III, pp. 638f. For our present purpose the point is immaterial. The connexion between the day of Yahweh and the cult is sufficiently clearly indicated by the sequel, *vv.* 20ff., the denunciation of the festivals. This denunciation is the chief point in the passage, and it is in this connexion that Amos speaks of the day of Yahweh.
[5] Hölscher (*Die Ursprünge der jüdischen Eschatologie*, pp. 12ff.) was the first to recognize that in Amos v, 18 the day of Yahweh has its original cultic connexion.

the beginning of the separation of the idea from the cultic festival. Whenever distress arose, the people would long and pray that there might now come a day of Yahweh,[1] when Yahweh would show Himself as He really was, and make an end of His own enemies and those of Israel. But in no circumstances can this be called a developed future hope or an eschatology with a definite content.[2]

2. *The Origin of the Jewish Hope of Restoration*

Before Judaism acquired a genuine eschatology it had a hope for the future which was fundamentally religious. Certain features in the content of this hope are also characteristic of eschatology; yet in essential points they differ from each other. Out of the future hope eschatology developed.

But the earlier Jewish future hope was a hope for something which had not yet come. From the first it had the character of a hope for the restoration of Israel from the grave misfortune which had befallen her, a hope of the national and political deliverance of the people from oppression and distress, and for a moral and religious purification and consummation, a future with every conceivable happiness, glory, and perfection. It is different from the hope, or rather the belief, implied already in the election and covenant faith, that the nation would always have a future—as different as is the natural, buoyant optimism of a growing culture from the 'futurism' of an already disintegrated culture, to use Arnold Toynbee's expression.[3] But it has an essential presupposition in common with the optimism of earlier times; for it is rooted in the election and covenant faith and in Yahweh's covenant promises as the soil from which it grows.[4] The covenant and election faith is in itself something distinct from the hope of the future and of restoration which the Old Testament contains. The latter, the genuine future hope, presupposes the destruction of the nation. It is always *a hope of restoration*.

[1] Cf. Isa. ii, 12. The indefinite expression '*a* day of Yahweh' (*yôm le YHWH*) shows that here the expression has not yet become an eschatological term. Isaiah goes still further in the same direction as Amos, reversing the customary meaning of the day: since Yahweh is a holy God who upholds justice, His day means a retributive settlement with Israel itself: Israel is 'Yahweh's enemy'.

[2] Pidoux (*Le Dieu qui vient*) has renewed the attempt to maintain a pre-prophetic eschatology, but without adding anything to the old argument of Gressmann and Sellin. He rejects the aid to understanding the idea of a 'God who comes' which results from the recognition that every year Yahweh 'came' in the festal cult.

[3] See Toynbee, *A Study of History*, Abridgement of Volumes I–VI, pp. 431ff., 515ff.

[4] In this sense we can agree with Sellin that the future hope and eschatology are ultimately based on Yahweh's revelation at Sinai, and on the promises therein implied, and the faith in the people's future thereby created (see above, p. 126).

But in investigating its origin we must distinguish between the hope of restoration itself and the specific conceptions of its content, of what restoration would mean in detail, of the nature of the future perfection. As we shall see, this specific content of the idea was older than the faith in restoration which it embodied. In other words, the restoration hope, which had as its background the destruction of the nation, acquired a specific content through the transference to a new 'setting in life' of a group of concepts which already existed in another context.

In the sequel we shall first consider the origin or, rather, the historical background, of the restoration hope itself; and then examine the content which it acquired, and which actually helped to create it. The positive religious factor is combined with the negative one of misfortune.

As has been said, the prophets of doom had no eschatological message. They announced the destruction of Israel and Judah as independent nations. The first of them, Amos, and probably also Hosea, did so unconditionally and remorselessly. In Isaiah a new note is heard: a remnant will be converted and be saved. The first presupposition of this belief was the election and covenant faith. Yahweh could not let His chosen people go. He had something great in store for them, an enduring and glorious future. In the earliest period there had been something naïvely anthropocentric about this faith in the covenant and providence. Yahweh was bound up with His people and could not, after all, let them go. In the prophets of doom this faith acquired a deeper insight; Yahweh could not abandon His own plan and His own goal. 'God remains faithful; He cannot deny Himself.' Yahweh is the world's Ruler and God; and He has a purpose, a plan, an end in view. If He is truly God, His will and His plan must prevail, with or without His people. Amos hinted vaguely at the possibility that Yahweh might choose another people. Isaiah knew that Yahweh had the will and the power to order events so that the election would hold good. He knew that there were some among the people, himself and the children Yahweh had given him (Isaiah viii, 18), who had said 'Yes' to the will and the call of God, and were willing to submit to His plan for Israel, even through affliction. Therefore they could wait for Yahweh and hope in Him, even if He hid His face from the house of Jacob (Isa. viii, 17). Time and again Isaiah tries to lead the people to conversion, so that the remnant may be big enough. Even in dire distress, after Hezekiah has capitulated and Sennacherib has had to treat the city with unexpected leniency,[1] he holds fast to the fact that Yahweh has, of His undeserved grace, 'left us a remnant' (Isa. i, 9). Yahweh has laid the corner stone of His house, the building of God's people on Zion; and if the people will believe in Him, yielding Him their trust, their will, and their obedience, and relying on Him in every situation, that trust will never be put to shame. Even if only a small remnant holds fast to such a faith, from that remnant Yahweh will create a new Israel on the old foundation, on which is written the very word faith (Isa. xxviii, 16).

After Isaiah the prophets of doom never gave up this faith in the future. We find it again in most of the disciples of Isaiah,[2] even in those who announced the unconditional destruction of the people, amongst whom was Jeremiah. Immediately before the Chaldeans captured Jerusalem, when he had become quite certain about the outcome of the war, he received a 'word', a communication, from Yahweh, telling him, 'houses, and fields, and vineyards shall again be bought in this land' (Jer. xxxii, 15). He associated this hope with those who were carried away to Babylonia. They were 'the remnant' from which the new people would spring in a wonderful way known only to God (Jer. xxiv; xxix). We see how, even while the Chaldean supremacy lasted, the prophets sought in contemporary history for signs that Yahweh had now arisen to make an end of their oppressors and restore His people, and how they proclaimed this faith in sublime language, not least when the advance of the Medes and Persians began to threaten Babylon.[3]

A message of this kind may be rooted in a genuine faith in God, or in the national instinct of self-preservation, or in optimism, or in wishful thinking. For Jeremiah, as for Isaiah, this faith was assuredly no lightly won optimism. With the most intense mental anguish, and through lifelong persecution he had to proclaim remorseless doom on the nation, including their being carried off to exile and the utter devastation of their native land. He had no illusions about his nation's reserves of strength or innate possibilities and did not allow for any inherent spiritual power of restora-

[1] 2 Kings xviii, 13–16. See Mowinckel, *Profeten Jesaja*, pp. 5ff.
[2] Mic. vii, 7; Zeph. iii, 9–11a; Nahum; Habakkuk; Isa. x, 5–19; x, 27b–34; xiv, 27–9; xvii, 12–14; xxix, 1–8; xxx, 27–33; xxxi, 5–9; Zeph. ii, 13–15; Mic. iv, 8–13; iv, 14–v, 5. See Mowinckel, *Jesajadisiplene*, pp. 35, 43ff., 56ff., 61ff., 46ff.; *G.T.M.M.M.* III, ad locc.
[3] Isa. xxi, 1–10; xiii f.; and possibly in some of the other passages which are mentioned above in n. 2.

tion. His faith for the future was wholly and solely founded on God, and His faithfulness and power, and His will to maintain His own righteousness and His own purpose.

But there were also those within the prophetic movement who took up this idea in a more facile way. It accorded so well with the wishes and the self-esteem which they shared with the whole nation. The representatives of nationalistic religion among the disciples of Isaiah (Nahum, Habakkuk, and others) were confident that the tribulations of the Assyrian and Chaldean period would end with the victory of Yahweh, which was identical with the triumph of Israel. During this period, faith in the future took root in many circles in several forms, ranging from the most superficial national optimism, the hope of an early return (Jer. xxix), to the prophetic hope against all hope (Jer. xxxii).

To begin with, the catastrophe of 587 had a paralysing effect; but not on those who had foreseen it. In the defeat itself Jeremiah and his few friends saw the triumph of Yahweh. Gradually hope revived, although the motives were not the same as before.[1] From that time onward, the hope of restoration became a constant element in the prophetic message. The true prophecy of doom had achieved its end, or, rather, God's object in it had been attained. The task was now one of positive, constructive work. It was a matter of using the experience to evoke a genuine national repentance and of maintaining courage and hope, so that the people might not lose itself in despair and be merged in heathenism. The prophecy of restoration takes up both of these tasks. The first is characteristic of Ezekiel, the Trito-Isaianic prophetic circle (Isa. lvi–lxvi), and Malachi, in whom there are often echoes of the old prophecy of doom and punishment. The second task is taken up by practically all restoration prophecy. Even while the Chaldean Empire was still supreme, the prophets were eagerly looking for signs in contemporary history which might indicate a change of fortune.[2] After the fall of Babylon in the autumn of 538, Deutero-Isaiah (Isa. xl–lv) sings his song of triumph about the impending restoration of Jerusalem and Israel to undreamed-of glory. Yahweh Himself will now come and work the great miracle which will make all the nations of the earth pay homage to Him and His elected people.

The restoration under Cyrus and Darius, and the establishment

---

[1] See Mic. vii, 8–20; Lam. i, 21; iii, 22ff.; iv, 21f.
[2] Isa. xxi, 1–10, 11f.; xiii, 1–22.

of a Judean province, with a descendant of David as governor in Jerusalem, was the first step towards the realization of the hope, even if the realization fell far short of the Deutero-Isaiah's dazzling promise. The restoration of David's kingdom in all its splendour is the assured content of the prophecies of Haggai and Zechariah; and this hope survived later in spite of all disappointments, although there might be controversy about it within the community, and although some had only contempt for the enthusiasts who would not give up hope (Isa. lxvi, 5).

The chief features in the hope are in the main constant. Yahweh had for all time chosen Israel for Himself[1] and guided her history[2] towards a definite goal, the glorifying of Israel in the world for the honour of Yahweh's own name, so that all nations might own Him as the only true God.[3] Here the monotheism of the prophetic movement gave to the future hope a goal, a *telos*. Although Yahweh chastises His people, He does not lose sight of the goal. Chastisement disciplines and purifies them so that they may become worthy to be His people and to increase His honour.[4] By the rebuilding of the temple under Zerubbabel, Yahweh has given His people a pledge, a guarantee that the full restoration, the fufilment of the ancient promises, will one day be realized. The kingdom of David will then be established in its ancient glory, with its ancient boundaries, and will again subdue the neighbouring peoples, and receive homage and tribute from distant nations. The exiles will return, and Israel be reunited with Judah. Homage will be paid to Yahweh as the only true God by all nations. From all parts of the earth pilgrims will stream to Jerusalem. Merchandise, gold, and produce from every land will be amassed there as tribute to Yahweh, His temple, and His servants. All blessing, and fertility, and well-being will prevail in the land. Disease and misfortune will be banished. Everyone will enjoy the fruit of his work in peace, sitting in safety under his vine and his fig-tree. All sinners and offenders will be rooted out of Yahweh's people.

> None will do evil or act corruptly
>   in all my holy mountain;
> For the land will be full of the knowledge of Yahweh
>   as the waters cover the ocean's bed. (Isa. xi, 9.)

[1] Isa. xli, 8f.; xliii, 1; xliv, 1f., 21; liv, 7–10.
[2] Isa. xliii, 14; xliv, 28; xlv, 4; xlvi, 9–13; xlviii, 12–15.
[3] Isa. xl, 21ff; xli, 28f.; xlii, 5–9; xliii, 7, 10–12, 21; xliv, 6, 8; xlv, 5–7, 14f., 21–5; xlvi, 9; xlviii, 12; xlix, 26; li, 5; lxi, 11.
[4] Isa. xl, 27ff.; xlii, 1, 24–7; xlviii, 1–11; xlix, 14ff.; li, 17ff; lii, 1–6; lvii, 16–19.

3. *The Religious Basis and Transformation of the Future Hope. Its Connexion with the Experiences and Ideas Associated with the Cult*

A future hope such as this has two poles, politics and religion. But we must not forget that to the ancients these were not two separate departments of life, but two aspects of the same thing. Even in politics man has to do with the will of God; and it is God who is at work in historical and political events. Even so, there is a difference of emphasis, or, if you like, of emotional attitude to the subject, and of the motives for taking an interest in it. It may be the outcome of experience of God and of devotion to Him; but it may also arise chiefly from an interest in the temporal, in one's own well-being and power, or those of one's nation.

The political aspect of the Jewish future hope is unmistakable.[1] But as has already been observed, it also had a religious aspect from the very beginning. Ultimately it is rooted in the experience of God which came to an Isaiah, a Jeremiah, or a Deutero-Isaiah. In the east many peoples had a national religion and a national god whose favour or wrath occasioned the good or bad fortune of the people. Many of them lost their freedom and their country; and naturally all of them wanted to regain their freedom. But none of them produced a future hope and an eschatology which survived for thousands of years and became part of the world's spiritual heritage. It was the religion of Israel, not its national and political aspirations, which created the future hope.

Accordingly the religious basis of the hope is prominent from the outset. It is proclaimed as a promise from Yahweh. It is through His faithfulness and power that it will be realized. Prophecy is the true bearer of the future hope; and together with the law this hope becomes the leading element in Judaism. By it the pious lived; and from it they drew strength when oppressed by time and circumstance.

Moreover, the very content of the future hope was increasingly characterized by purely religious motifs. Not that it ever lost its political side: it retained that as long as Judaism survived, and retains it even today. But together with it, and in part overshadowing it, there are elements which may be called purely religious and ethical.

This appears in full vigour as early as Deutero-Isaiah, who lifts the whole conception of restoration up into a supra-terrestrial

[1] On the political aspect of the idea of the remnant, see Müller, *Die Vorstellung vom Rest im Alten Testament.*

sphere, presenting it as a drama of cosmic dimensions. Behind the conflict of Cyrus with the Chaldeans and Babylon the prophet sees the victorious conflict of Yahweh with His adversaries. These enemies are not only human beings and earthly powers; for behind the latter stand the heathen deities and all creation's evil, cosmic forces, which are embodied in the adversaries of Cyrus and of Yahweh, the oppressors of Israel. The future of Israel is at stake in this great encounter between Yahweh and His enemies. The end of the conflict is the glorification of Israel as a means to Yahweh's own glory. It is, in fact, for Yahweh's glory and Israel's freedom that Cyrus unwittingly engages in the struggle. It is for this that Yahweh has called and anointed him, 'though he did not know My name'.

Here Deutero-Isaiah was able to start from a developed system of ideas which was already in existence. He derived both the framework and the details from a feature of Israelite religion which was already central as early as the period of the monarchy, namely those ideas and experiences which were associated with the most important festival in the temple cultus at Jerusalem, the autumn and New Year festival (the feast of Tabernacles), the festival of the manifestation (epiphany) of Yahweh, *hag YHWH*, also regarded as *the festival of Yahweh's enthronement*.[1]

The natural basis of the festival was the approaching rainy season in the autumn. The year was at an end; the crops had been gathered in; the year's blessing was, so to speak, used up. All vegetation was now withered; the soil was burnt dry and dead;

---

[1] On the festival and its content, see Mowinckel, *Ps.St.* II, pp. 44ff.; *Offersang og sangoffer*, pp. 118–91. On the relation of Deutero-Isaiah to these ideas, see *Ps.St.* II, pp. 238ff., 251ff., 256ff., 263f., 273ff., 283ff., 292ff.; *G.T.M.M.M.* III, pp. 188f. The cultic interpretation of the 'enthronement psalms' (the *YHWH mālak* psalms) on which the reconstruction of the 'enthronement festival' is based, and from which Gunkel emphatically dissociated himself (*Einleitung*, pp. 100ff.), seems to be gaining increasing acceptance. Lucid and, in a measure, more fully developed presentations of the ideas and background of the enthronement festival are given by H. Schmidt in his *Die Thronfahrt Jahves am Fest der Jahreswende im alten Israel*, and by E. G. Kraeling in *J.B.L.* xlvii, 1929, pp. 133ff. The theory of a festival of this kind has also been given substantial support by the insight into the Canaanite background of the Israelite cult provided by the discoveries at Ugarit; cf. Kapelrud in *N.T.T.* xli, 1940, pp. 38ff. Among recent works which discuss the problem, reference may be made to Dürr's paper in *Liturgisches Leben* vii, 1935, pp. 128ff. Pap's contention (*Das israelitische Neujahrsfest*) that no New Year festival existed in pre-exilic Israel is in manifest conflict with the evidence of the sources. That such a festival really did exist is the conclusion reached by Snaith in *The Jewish New Year Festival*. But Snaith seeks to maintain that the 'enthronement psalms' have no connexion with this festival, but are, on the contrary, all dependent upon Deutero-Isaiah and are to be interpreted eschatologically. But form-critical and stylistic investigation makes it sufficiently clear that the dependence is on Deutero-Isaiah's side.

brooks and springs were empty; cattle began to suffer want on the pastures. The original state of chaos, before 'the Lord Yahweh sent rain upon the earth', was about to return; the evil powers with their 'curse' (death) were prevailing over life. It was then that Yahweh came and revealed Himself, giving Himself to His own and making Himself known by His mighty acts. In and through the effectual rites of the cult, in which God's coming and conflict were displayed in dramatic symbolism, His appearance, His combat, and His victory really took place. He engaged in conflict with the powers of chaos, and defeated them as He did at the beginning, crushing or chaining them. He recreated the world; and behold, soon afterwards the autumn rains came, soaking the earth, watering its furrows, making it fertile and productive. The God of life had triumphed over the hostile powers of death and created the world anew.

Even in the ancient Canaanite period this triumph of the god of fertility and life was regarded as the conflict of a king with his enemies, and his restoration of his kingdom: the deity is king over the kingdom which he himself has created. Israel transferred the same thought to Yahweh. Yahweh comes to His people in the festival. It is then that again and again He 'becomes King'[1] as is proclaimed by the enthronement psalms which belonged to this very festival. He comes and triumphs over all His enemies, over the sea, the dragon, and death, as well as over historical enemies (the nations) which are thought of as attacking His city, but as destroyed by Him outside the walls of Jerusalem (the myth of the conflict with the nations).[2] After the victory He enters His palace, takes His seat on His throne, and assumes the royal power, which is His though Death has sought to usurp it. He sits in judgement on His enemies, destroys them, and exercises His absolute kingly sway for the blessing and well-being of all creatures. He has now reversed the fall. Life can begin anew at the point where it began at Creation, before the wickedness of evil powers and of men had corrupted all and forfeited the blessing.

It is in these terms, as *Yahweh's cosmic conflict, victory, and enthronement*, that Deutero-Isaiah describes what is about to happen. Behind the world empire promised to Cyrus as a reward for his victory over Babylon and his liberation of the Jews, the prophet sees the combat in which Yahweh now engages after having 'been silent for long', His victory, and His entry into Zion at the head

[1] See Additional Note X.   [2] Pss. xlvi; xlviii; cf. ii, 1f.; see *Ps.St.* II, pp. 57ff.

of the exiles (Isa. xlii, 10ff.). He sees the herald who announces the King's entry:

> How beautiful upon the mountains
> are the feet of him who bears good tidings,
> Who proclaims peace, who says to Zion,
> 'Your God has become King.' (Isa. lii, 7.) [1]

He regards the condition of Israel in exile as a result of the renewed dominion of the powers of chaos in the world (xlii, 13–15). It is as if the world were doomed to destruction (li, 6). But then, as in the festal hymns, we hear that Yahweh is coming with bliss and restoration for Israel, but ignominy and ruin for His own and Israel's enemies. The enemies, in historical terms, are Babylon and the Chaldeans, but they are also described as the primeval deep and the dragon. Deutero-Isaiah often says that Yahweh will now make springs in the wilderness for the returning exiles; but he also speaks in terms of the myth of the primeval deep about Yahweh combating rivers and pools and making the land dry (xlii, 15). In the repeated debates between Yahweh and the false gods, which Deutero-Isaiah depicts for his hearers, debates which end with the ignominious defeat of the false gods who are without reply, [2] there is echoed from the enthronement psalms the idea that Yahweh's coming means ignominious defeat and judgement on the false gods (cf. Ps. lxxxii).

It is not difficult to see that the ideas of the enthronement festival must have been ready to hand for Deutero-Isaiah as the specific content of his promises and his faith in restoration. From early times the festival and the experiences which it imparted were imbued with expectation about the future. [3] Through Yahweh's coming in the festival, the community, so to speak, shared by anticipation in the prosperity of the coming year. The experiences of the festival looked forward to the coming year. The rituals and liturgies of the festival were full of promises about the glory brought by Yahweh, and thus assured for the future. [4] This conviction was based on the covenant between Yahweh and Israel, which was the foundation of Israel's faith and of its very existence. Accordingly, every year the community experienced in the festival

---

[1] Text as *G.T.M.M.M.* III, p. 792.
[2] Cf. Köhler, *Deuterojesaja stilkritisch untersucht.*
[3] This aspect of the festival's meaning is not emphasized with sufficient clarity in *Ps.St.* II. I may be allowed to refer now to my *Offersang og sangoffer*, ch. V, 11.
[4] See Pss. lxxxi; lxxxii; cxxxii; ii; cx; and cf. *Ps.St.* III, pp. 30ff.

the assurance that Yahweh could not fail His people; the nation which had Yahweh as its God was sure always to have hope and a future. The future hope was there, latent in the covenant, and in the ever-renewed experiences of the festival. Thus we find that as early as the time of Amos, when misfortune befell the people, hope was linked with Yahweh's new 'day' in the festival;[1] and within Isaiah's circle of disciples the form and content of promises made in difficult times were often drawn from the ideas connected with the enthronement of Yahweh.[2] Thus in misfortune, when there was need of a spiritual foundation for life, it was from the experience and the certainty afforded by Yahweh's enthronement festival, against the background of the covenant faith, that hope for the immediate future could grow and derive its content. There the prophets found the content of the message of hope which they had to deliver. Conversely (and quite naturally and logically), when eschatology had emerged, it was the restoration of Israel and the fulfilment of the eschatological hope to which the community looked forward and of which it was reminded at the autumn festival.[3]

But faith and hope are always created in distress. There had first to be a disaster so great, so crushing, and so lasting that again and again it thrust into the distant future the fulfilment of the promises which were inherent in the festal experiences; for hope could no longer rest content with what was afforded by the days of the festival and the year, with what lay within the scope of contemporary reality. There had to be a disaster which would force into existence the hope of, and faith in, an absolute, final, and unsurpassable day of Yahweh, if not this year or next year, yet assuredly some time, when punishment and chastisement had attained their end, when Yahweh would again remember His

---

[1] Amos v, 18. See Mowinckel in *G.T.M.M.M.* III, pp. 638f.

[2] See Mowinckel, *Jesajadisiplene*, pp. 89ff.

[3] Pss. xiv, 7; liii, 7; xc, 16; cxxix, 5ff.; cxxx, 8. See further, Mowinckel, *Offersang og sangoffer*, ch. V, 10–11. It is, therefore, with justice that scholars often draw attention to this element of expectation in the experiences of the autumn festival; e.g., Bentzen in *S.E.Å.* xii, 1947, pp. 38f., Volz, *Das Neujahrsfest Jahwes*, p. 15. It is not, however, justifiable to describe this as 'eschatology'. Only subsequently, in Judaism and in the later psalms, did the festival acquire a genuinely eschatological note alongside the others. It is also significant that in *Jésus transfiguré* Riesenfeld, who without more ado repeats the assertions of earlier scholars, cannot adduce a single Old Testament passage to support the contention that cult and eschatology were connected: he does not note the psalms referred to above. All the passages he cites represent later Judaism, and accurately reflect its outlook; but they prove nothing about the character of the autumn festival in the earlier period. It is a mistake completely to disregard historical perspective and to condemn it as 'historicism', as if scientific biblical study could discard the historical approach.

promises and His covenant, would again graciously let His countenance shine upon His people, and proclaim the great, final year
of favour (Isa. lxi, 2; xlix, 8).

That is what has happened in Deutero-Isaiah. For him the
ideas associated with the enthronement festival have come to life
again as a message about the future for his own time, and as a
promise of restoration.[1] They became the natural vehicle of the
message of consolation and joy which he had to proclaim. Here
the future hope is from the very outset based on religion, even if
it also has political and national aspects; and subsequently the
experiences and ideas conveyed by the enthronement festival (its
ideology) remain the inexhaustible source of the prophetic message about the future, as is clearly shown, for instance, by Isaiah
xxxiii.[2] Point by point all the elements in the future hope and in
eschatology can be traced back to corresponding conceptions in
the enthronement festival.[3] This accounts for the fact, which Gunkel
and Gressmann had noticed,[4] but for which neither of them could
offer a satisfactory explanation, that ideas about creation and
primordial time pervade eschatology. The appearance and enthronement of Yahweh mean a re-enactment of the events of
primordial time: creation; victory over the deep, and dragons, and
the power of death; recreation of the cosmos, of blessing, of life—
and of Israel. Eschatology is a reinterpretation of the mythology
of primordial time, as is clearly expressed in the *Epistle of Barnabas*:
'Lo, I make the last things like the first.'[5]

4. *The Content of the Future Hope*

The fundamental idea in the future hope is always *the kingly
rule of Yahweh*, His victorious advent as king, and His reckoning
with His enemies. Yahweh's victory is followed by the manifestation of His kingship. He appears as king and takes possession of
His realm. The prophet speaks about the wonderful processional
way for the royal entry into the temple, which is now to be laid
through the desert when Yahweh returns from His conflict with
Babylon. He borrows metaphors from the royal entry on the day
of enthronement, when the victorious Yahweh becomes visible

[1] See *Ps.St.* II, pp. 238, 251ff., 256ff., 282ff., 288ff., 292ff.; similarly Gyllenberg in
S.E.Å. v, 1940, pp. 87f.

[2] See *Ps.St.* II, pp. 235ff.

[3] See *Ps.St.* II, pp. 228–314.

[4] This appears already in the title of Gunkel's book, *Schöpfung und Chaos in Urzeit und
Endzeit*, and in the quotation from *Barnabas* vi, 13 which is its motto.

[5] *Barnabas* vi, 13. Cf. *Ps.St.* II, p. 229f.

and manifest for the eye of faith (by the appearance to the outward eye of His cultic symbol, the ark, the processional shrine) moving forward amid shouts of homage, 'Yahweh has become King!' The prophet sees it in enlarged and glorified form: the whole world sees and pays homage to the king, its creator and God. Nature, too, trees, mountains, and water, which He has now re-created, hail His procession.

As in the enthronement hymns, Yahweh's battle and victory are regarded by Deutero-Isaiah as a *righteous judgement*, an *act of justice*; but for Israel, judgement and justice are synonymous with salvation.

This is also regarded as a *new creation*. As in the enthronement psalms, Yahweh has become king of the world, because He Himself has created this kingdom of His: as He was 'the first', who created in the primordial age, so now He is 'the last', who now creates anew. The new order is described more or less distinctly as a paradisal order. The restoration is a return to the original perfection, the last things become like the first. As a conscious principle for the understanding of the last things, this sentence is derived from the later theory of ages, and from dualism;[1] but in Deutero-Isaiah it already operates inevitably as an unconscious formative principle,[2] precisely because he takes as the framework of his thought ideas from the enthronement festival, the festival in which was celebrated Yahweh's recreation of the perfection which existed at creation. The *wonderful fruitfulness* which is to be (a leading thought in the autumn and New Year festival) applies also to the nation.

This is all regarded as the *making of a new covenant*, a re-enactment of the old covenant on Sinai, and of the covenant with David. In the end Yahweh will receive homage from the whole world and be recognized as the supreme, the secret, the saving God. The honouring of Yahweh as king is the final goal of history (Isa. xlviii, 9–11).

From that time onwards the thought of the kingly rule of Yahweh, *the Kingdom of God*, was the central religious idea in the Jewish future hope. As king, Yahweh will gather His people and lead them home; as king, He will then be enthroned in their midst; to pay homage to the king, Yahweh, the Lord of hosts, all nations will stream to Jerusalem on the day of His festival.[3] The

---

[1] See below, pp. 182, 263ff.; cf. p. 270ff.   [2] Cf. Isa. xli, 22; xlii, 9; xliii, 18.
[3] See Mic. ii, 13; Zeph. iii, 15; Zech. xiv, 16f.

kingly rule of Yahweh is the central idea round which are grouped all other ideas and conceptions, and by which they are explained. The details in Jewish eschatology often seem to lack organic coherence; but once this central idea is recognized, the whole picture becomes clear.

The whole picture of the future can therefore also be summed up in the expression, *the day of Yahweh*.[1] Its original meaning is really the day of His manifestation or epiphany, the day of His festival, and particularly that festal day which was also the day of His enthronement, His royal day, *the* festival of Yahweh, the day when as king He came and 'wrought salvation for His people'. As the people hoped for the realization of the ideal of kingship, particularly when reality fell furthest short of it, so, from a quite early period, whenever they were in distress and oppressed by misfortune, they hoped for and expected a glorious 'day of Yahweh' (cf. Amos v, 18ff.), when Yahweh must remember His covenant, and appear as the mighty king and deliverer, bringing a 'day' upon His own and His people's enemies (cf. Isa. ii, 12ff.), condemning them to destruction, and 'acquitting' and 'executing justice' for His own people.[2] In the future hope, and later in eschatology, 'the day of Yahweh' (or simply 'that day') becomes the term which sums up the great transformation, when He comes and restores His people, and assumes kingly rule over the world.[3] Arising out of the idea in the enthronement festival that all the hostile powers will gather together in order to destroy Jerusalem, but will be annihilated by Yahweh outside the city walls,[4] eschatology also says that in the last days the heathen will gather with hostile arrogance for a similar final onslaught, or that their hearts will be hardened by Yahweh, so that they conceive this presumptuous plan, in order that He may annihilate them all at one stroke in the valley of Hinnom, the unclean site of the sacrifices to Molech, or, as it is also called, the valley of Jehoshaphat, or the valley of the threshing instrument,[5] where apostate and ungodly Jews will also receive their punishment.[6] Thus does Yahweh 'judge' the nations.

The specific features in the description of the future are those

[1] See above, pp. 140, 143; cf. p. 132.
[2] Cf. *Ps.St.* II, pp. 65ff., 165.
[3] Cf. Ezek. xiii, 5; Joel i, 15; Zeph. i, 7ff.
[4] Pss. xlvi; xlvii; cf. lxxvi. See above, p. 140; cf. p. 147.
[5] Joel iv; Zech. xii; xiv.
[6] Isa. lxvi, 23f. On the details in Deutero-Isaiah's predictions of the future, see *Ps.St.* II (see above p. 143 n. 1); cf. *G.T.M.M.M.* III, pp. 186ff.

L

which emerge when these ideas drawn from cultic experience are applied to actual historical situations in which the Jews were placed. The national and political restoration for which they hoped, and in which they believed, is depicted in patterns drawn from the ideology of the enthronement festival. The main features are as follows: the political and national deliverance of Israel,[1] the restoration of the dynasty and kingdom of David,[2] the reunion of the two kingdoms,[3] the destruction of the heathen powers,[4] the return of the Diaspora,[5] the religious and moral restoration of the people, including judgement on sinners and traitors,[6] marvellous, even paradisal[7] fertility of land, people, and cattle,[8] peace among the nations,[9] the transformation of wild animals,[10] the restoration and glorification of Jerusalem as the religious and political centre of the world:[11] the 'city of paradise' set on the highest point of earth,[12] to which pilgrims come from all the nations of the earth to pay homage to the God of Israel,[13] the king in Zion,[14] where they

[1] Isa. ix, 3; x, 27; xiv, 25; lii, 2; Jer. xxx, 8; Ezek. xxxiv, 27.

[2] The kingdom: Isa. xi, 13f.; Jer. iii, 18; xxxi, 27; xxxiii, 7; Ezek. xxxvii, 15–22; Hos. ii, 2f.; iii, 5; Obad. 18; Zech. viii, 13; ix, 10–13; x, 5f.; xi, 4–17; xiii, 7–9; cf. Hos. ii, 1, 16–25; xiv, 2f., 9; Jer. xxxi, 5f.; Ezek. xx, 42; xxviii, 25; xxxvi, 28; xxxvii, 25; Isa. viii, 23; xlix, 8, 19; lvi, 7; lvii, 13; lx, 21; lxv, 9f; Obad. 19; Mic. vii, 14; Zech. x, 10; Ezek. xlvii, 13–xlviii, 29; Amos ix, 8. The dynasty: see all the so-called Messianic passages above, p. 16.

[3] Isa. xi, 13f.; Jer. iii, 18; xxxi, 27; xxxiii, 7; Ezek. xxxvii, 15–22; Hos. ii, 2f.; iii, 5; Obad. 18; Zech. viii, 13; ix, 10–13; x, 5f.; Hos. ii, 1, 16–25; xiv, 2f., 9; Jer. xxxi, 5f.

[4] Indicated by the assembling of groups of oracles on foreign powers: Isa. xiii–xxiii; Jer. xlvi–li; Ezek. xxv–xxxii; Zeph. ii; Zech. ix; cf. Amos i f. See below, p. 154.

[5] Isa. xliii, 5f.; xlviii, 20; xlix, 17f., 22; lii, 8, 11f.; lvi, 7; lvii, 13; lx, 4, 8f.; lxvi, 20; xi, 11f., 15f.; xiv, 1; xxvii, 12f.; xxxv, 10; Jer. iii, 18; xxiii, 3; xxx, 3; xxxi, 7–12; xxxii, 37; xxxiii, 7, 11; Ezek. xi, 17; xx, 34, 41; xxviii, 25; xxxiv, 11ff.; xxxvi, 24; xxxvii, 12; Hos. xi, 10f.; Mic. ii, 12f.; iv, 6f.; Zeph. iii, 19f.; Zech. viii, 7f.; ix, 11f.; x, 8–10.

[6] Isa. i, 18–31; ii, 20; iii, 11, 18–23; iv, 3f.; xvii, 8; xxvii, 9; xxix, 20; xxx, 22; xxxi, 6f.; xxxiii, 14–16; Zeph. i, 6; iii, 11f.; Ezek. xiv, 1–11; xx, 36–8; xxii; xxxiv, 17–22; xxxvi, 25; Jer. xxxiii, 8; Mic. v, 9–13; Zech. xiii, 2–6; Mal. ii, 10–13, 17–iii, 5; Isa. lvii, 1, 3ff; lviii, 1–7; lix, 2–8, 12–15; lxiv, 4; lxv, 2.

[7] Amos ix, 13; Joel iv, 18; Isa. vii, 21f. See Gressmann, *Der Messias*, pp. 155ff.; Mowinckel, *Ps.St.* II, pp. 284ff.

[8] Isa. xlix, 20; lx, 22; Jer. iii, 16; xxxi, 27; Ezek. xxxvi, 1ff., 33–8; Mic. iv, 7; Zech. viii, 4f.; Joel iv, 20; Isa. iv, 2; xxx, 23–5; xxxii, 15, 20; xxxv, 1f., 6f.; Amos ix, 13; Joel iv, 18; Zech. xiv, 10; Ezek. xlvii; also the reinterpretation of tradition in Isa. vii, 15–22a.

[9] Isa. ii, 4; Mic. v, 9ff.; Zech. ix, 10.

[10] Isa. xi, 6–9; Hos. ii, 20; Ezek. xxxiv, 25ff.

[11] Isa. xlix, 16–19; li, 3; liv, 1f.; lviii, 12; lx, 10; lxi, 4; lxii, 4, 6f.; Ezek. xxxvi, 33ff.— passages which are older than Nehemiah's building of the wall. In addition, Zech. xiv, 10f.; Ezek. xxxviii, 12 (cf. Ps. xlvi, 5); Zech. xiv, 9; Isa. liv, 5; lix, 19; Mic. iv, 1–3; cf. Pss. xlvi, 11; xlvii, 4, 6, 10; lxvii, 5.

[12] Isa. ii, 2ff.; Mic. iv, 1ff.; cf. Ps. xlvii, 2f.

[13] Isa. xlv, 14, 23; lvi, 7; lx, 3; lxvi, 18f., 23; ii, 2–4; Mic. iv, 1–4; Jer. iii, 17; Zeph. iii, 10; Zech. viii, 20–3; xiv, 16–19.

[14] Isa. xxiv, 23; lii, 7; Jer. iii, 17; x, 7, 10; Obad. 21; Zech. ix, 4–7; Zeph. iii, 15; Zech. xiv, 9, 16f.

will not hurt or destroy,[1] because they will all know Yahweh,[2] and all be consecrated to Him.[3] A new covenant is made,[4] and Israel is changed by the spirit of Yahweh.[5] At times, following Deutero-Isaiah, more emphasis is laid on the religious, super-terrestrial elements; and then it is explicitly stated that this decisive change of fortune[6] is the day of Yahweh,[7] 'that day'.[8]

This epiphany of Yahweh, which will eclipse all previous ones, is depicted in the traditional colours of cosmological mythology.[9] Sometimes the enemies are presented not so much as specific historical nations, but rather as the world power which is at once earthly and cosmic,[10] which is commonly identified with a more or less imaginary distant people about whom there are only rumours and fables (King Gog and Magog).[11]

When the world power has been destroyed outside Jerusalem,[12] eternal peace will prevail.[13] Suffering and disease will be at an end, and men will live to be more than a hundred years old;[14] peace and joy,[15] light,[16] and life[17] will prevail, when old things are passed away and heaven and earth have been created anew,[18] 'in those days',[19] 'at that time'.[20]

---

[1] Isa. xi, 9; lxii, 25.   [2] Isa. xi, 9; Jer. xxxi, 34.

[3] Isa. iv, 3; vi, 13; lxii, 12; lxi, 6; Zech. xiv, 21.

[4] Isa. lv, 3f.; Jer. xxxi, 31ff.; cf. *Ps..St.* II, pp. 288ff.

[5] Ezek. xi, 19f.; xxxvi, 26; xxxix, 29; Joel iii, 1ff.

[6] Deut. xxx, 3; Jer. xxix, 14; xxx, 3, 18; xxxi, 23; xxxii, 44; xxxiii, 7, 11, 26; Ezek. xvi, 53; xxix, 14; xxxix, 25; Hos. vi, 11; Joel iv, 1; Amos ix, 14; Zeph. ii, 7; iii, 20. Cf. Pss. xiv, 7=liii, 7; lxxxv, 2; cxxvi, 1, 4.

[7] Amos v, 18; Isa. ii, 12; Zeph. i, 8, 14ff.; ii, 2; Isa. xiii, 6ff.; Ezek xxx, 3; Joel i, 15; ii, 1; iii, 3f.; iv, 14; Obad. 15; Zech. xiv, 1.

[8] Isa. ii, 20; iii, 18; iv, 2; v, 30; vii, 18, 20f., 23; x, 20, 27; xi, 10f.; xii, 1, 4; xvii, 4, 7, 9; xxii, 20, 25; xxiii, 15; xxiv, 21; xxv, 9; xxvi, 1; xxvii, 1, 2, 12f.; xxviii, 5f.; Jer. iv, 9; xxx, 7f.; xlvi, 10; Amos ii, 16; viii, 9, 13; ix, 11; Obad. 8; Mic. ii, 4; v, 9; Zeph. i, 9f.; iii, 11, 16; Zech. ix, 16; xii, 3f., 6, 8f., 11; xiii, 1f., 4; xiv, 4, 6, 8, 13, 20. In many of these passages the expression is intended simply as a connecting formula for two contemporaneous events, a kind of temporal conjunction or adverb; but this is by no means always so, as Munch holds (*The Expression bajjôm ha-hû'*). In several passages it is clearly an eschatological formula; and the later prophetic tradition tended more and more to take it in the absolute and specific sense, as referring to *dies illa*: this is the New Testament use of the expression. See p. 268 n. 5.

[9] E.g., Isa. xiii; Joel iii, 3f.; iv, 15; Amos viii, 9; Mic. i, 2–4; Nahum i, 2–10; Hab. iii, 3ff.; Zech. xiv.

[10] E.g., Isa. xiv, 26; xxvi, 21; xxxiii, 12; xxxiv, 1ff.; lxiii, 1–6; Jer. xxv, 29–38; xlvi, 10–12; Obad. 15; Mic. v, 14; Isa. xxiv, 21f. (cf. Ps. lxxxii); xxvii, 1; Zeph. ii, 11.

[11] Ezek. xxxviii f.   [12] See above, p. 145; cf. p. 140.

[13] Isa. iv, 9; xi, 6–8; xxxii, 17f.; xxxiii, 6; lx, 17; lxv, 25; Jer. xxiii, 6; xxx, 10; Ezek. xxxiv, 25–7; xxxvi, 8ff., 29f., 33; Mic. iv, 3f.; iv, 5; Zeph. iii, 13; Zech. iii, 10; ix, 10; xiv, 11; cf. Ps. xlvi, 10.   [14] Isa. lxv, 20.

[15] Isa. xii, 3–6; xxxv, 5f.; lxv, 18f.; Jer. xxxi, 10–14; xxxiii, 9; Isa. xxv, 6f.

[16] Isa. ix, 1; xxx, 26; lx, 19f.; lxii, 1.   [17] Isa. lxv, 20, 22; xxv, 8.

[18] Isa. lxv, 17; lxvi, 22.

[19] Jer. iii, 16, 18; xxxi, 29; xxxiii, 15; Joel iv, 1. See above, n. 8.

[20] Jer. iii, 17; xxxi, 1; Joel, iv, 1.

It is not easy to decide how much is poetical description and how much actual reality in this picture of the future. Naturally, no line of distinction was consciously drawn. There is, for instance, no point in asking what Deutero-Isaiah would have said if he had used sober prose to express what he really expected to follow from Cyrus's victory over Babylon and the world empire which he was establishing. It is easy to point out the logical gap between the promise about world dominion made to Cyrus by Deutero-Isaiah in Yahweh's name, and Yahweh's world dominion through Israel, of which he also speaks. His thought and style are those of rhetoric and poetry, of myth and religion; and the same style is used by the circle of his disciples. But whenever a specific statement is made, the national and political considerations appear, though they may take a fantastic form. If we *were* to translate Deutero-Isaiah's message into sober prose, we might, for instance, express it in this way. Yahweh has called Cyrus and raised him up to fulfil His purpose in history. When Babylon has been conquered, the oppressed and the captives will go free, and God will then put it into the mind of Cyrus to allow the exiled Jews to return home and to rebuild Jerusalem and the temple of Yahweh. Then the ancient royal house will be restored, and Yahweh will endow the ruler with righteousness, piety, and every virtue; and then the happiness and greatness of ancient days will again prevail in our land, and foreign nations will once more pay homage to Him as their overlord.

This will all be realized within the present world order. Deutero-Isaiah takes it for granted that even in the blissful future Israel may have enemies who will attack her, but always without success (liv, 14–17).

Even in Deutero-Isaiah, universalism is limited by Jewish nationalism. Even in his religious message, it is emphasized that the God of all the world is *Israel's God*. The narrow outlook which this thought could assume in less profound (and less poetical) minds may be seen in the message of Haggai and Zechariah about restoration; in spite of the unfavourable situation in the Persian Empire (and this is explicitly emphasized), the completion of the temple will herald a world revolution, in which the Persian Empire will be overthrown, Zerubbabel will be made king, and Jerusalem become the religious and political centre of the world. But this will come about through a direct and miraculous divine intervention. This national and this-worldly element remains the heart of the future hope throughout the entire Old Testament period: God's kingly rule on earth through the world-hegemony of Israel and her Davidic ruler.

But the religious point of view came more and more to predominate and to permeate the political without displacing it entirely. The restoration of Israel and the realization of all the people's ideals were taken to be the essential factors in the kingly rule of Yahweh. It is to restore His people Israel and give it a place in the sun that Yahweh comes as king and establishes His kingdom. It is through the glorification of Israel that the glorification of Yahweh is achieved. The sight of the great miracle, which He works for His people in spite of all human probability, makes the other nations submit to Him, and come as pilgrims to His sanctuary to worship Him as the only true God, as alone worthy of the name of God. This has already become a leading idea in Deutero-Isaiah. The submission of the other nations to Yahweh means, in concrete terms, that when He comes and frees His people, the nations' power is crushed, and that the survivors submit to Israel and become Jews. Thus the kingly glory of Yahweh appears in visible and tangible form. It goes without saying that this also means that the other nations share in Israel's happiness and blessing (i.e., salvation). Deutero-Isaiah invites 'all the ends of the earth' to come to Yahweh and 'be saved' (xlv, 22). Yahweh's kingdom is His dominion over the world, exercised on this earth through Israel.

5. *From the Hope of Restoration to Eschatology*

But this hope of restoration is not yet eschatological. As a type of historical outlook, it is exactly what Toynbee has called 'futurism'. It is the daring escape into the future of the harrowed soul, paralysed by catastrophe, and crushed in spirit (Isa. lvii, 15), when the present has become intolerable, yet the soul will not let this world go.[1] In spite of his mythological and symbolical language and his cosmic perspective, Deutero-Isaiah is still limited by his presuppositions. In spite of his universal outlook, he is a Jew, affected by Jewish nationalism. The universal God is the God of Israel; and in spite of everything His kingdom is still a kingdom of this world.

But a change is beginning to take place. To borrow Toynbee's language, Deutero-Isaiah has at least indicated the way which

---

[1] Cf. Toynbee, *A Study of History*. Abridgement of Vols. I–VI, pp. 520ff.

leads from a purely this-worldly futurism on through 'self-transcendence' to 'transfiguration' or glorified transformation.[1]

The historical and religious presupposition of this is the exclusive fanaticism of Yahwism and the prophets, which made the tribal and national God, Yahweh, the only true God, or, in the language of revealed religion, which taught them that it was the one true God who had drawn near to them as Yahweh, the national God. Everything centres in Him and in His rule of the world. Everything happens for Israel's sake, not because Israel has any merit, but because it has pleased Yahweh to choose this people, and through it to reveal Himself and fulfil His purpose for the world, 'to glorify Himself'.

Yahweh is king in the restored Israel, in the kingdom which, from the religious point of view, is the fulfilment of Israel's future hope. Even today the thought of Yahweh as king is at the centre of the Jewish New Year festival, and is the main idea in the hope of Judaism. Jesus preached the kingly rule of God as near at hand. Thus the ideas of the day and the kingdom of Yahweh and of the restoration of Israel assume an increasingly other-worldly character, which is expressed by the mythological metaphors in the description of Yahweh's conflict and victory and of the paradisal conditions in the new Israel. It is on this earth and in Israel's land that it will be realized. But it will be achieved by a divine miracle (Zech. iv, 6). The conception of how the future hope will be realized increasingly loses the connexion with concrete historical reality which it still had in Deutero-Isaiah (the victory of Cyrus over Babylon) and in Haggai and Zechariah (the disturbances in the Persian Empire after the death of Cambyses). It is true that hope was rekindled whenever great events were taking place (the destruction of Edom by the Nabateans, Alexander's campaign, the fall of the Persian Empire); but the thought that help will come not from men but from Yahweh is increasingly prominent.

Granted that the mass of the people would usually think of the purely political and earthly side of the matter, would be concerned about deliverance from the Chaldeans, the Persians, the Seleucids, or the Romans, and would dream of vengeance on their oppressors (even in prophecies from the later Old Testament period there is this emphasis), nevertheless the chief tendency in the expression of these ideas is religious and other-worldly, bringing

[1] Op. cit., pp. 520, 526.

out the transcendent, miraculous aspect of restoration. The Trito-Isaianic circle speaks of a new heaven and a new earth; and even if this ought not to be taken entirely literally (for it is linked with ideas from the New Year festival indicating a renewal of the universe, which has become old, effete, and corrupt), yet it reveals the other-worldly, cosmic character of the future hope. This is in entire accord with its religious basis and the religious influence (derived from the disciples of the prophets and those who transmitted their teaching) with which it is permeated.

But again we must emphasize the deepest religious reason why this unquenchable future hope could be born and survive in Israel, in contrast with all the other nations who had likewise been crushed in the international politics of the east and in the clash of Empires. All these other nations also had cultic festivals at which they celebrated the coming of the deity, and experienced the certainty of the happiness and security which it guaranteed. How did it come about that from these experiences no eschatology developed, for instance, in Babylonian religion?[1]

The reason is to be found in Israelite religion, in its conception of God, and the distinctive historical character of that conception.[2] Through Moses and the historical events of the Exodus and the settlement, Israel had experienced Yahweh as a God of action, who of His own initiative came and revealed Himself, freely choosing Israel as His own people, and manifesting this choice through historical events.[3] The message of the prophets deepened and kept alive the faith that it was in the field of actual history that Yahweh would appear and act. He alone is active there. Yahweh is 'He'; He is unique. Together with the ideas of election and covenant, this means that Yahweh has a purpose in world history. All the ancient religions and civilizations, even those of Greece, conceived of the course of history as a circle, corresponding to the annual cycle of the life of nature. The Old Testament conceives of history as a straight line pointing to a goal. Thus the Israelites alone were able to devise a philosophy of history.

[1] Cf. Pidoux, *Le Dieu qui vient*, p. 50. This point is, however, invalid as an argument against the connexion between the enthronement festival and eschatology. In *Ps.St.* II, pp. 315ff., I had already indicated the distinctive factors in Israel's religion which account for this development in Israel.

[2] In the work just referred to this contention is soundly and beautifully advanced by Pidoux. But it is not sufficient to explain that an eschatology was developed. Account must also be taken both of Israel's distinctive historical experiences, and also of that complex of ideas (the concept of the enthronement) which provided the specific content of the hope of restoration.

[3] Cf. Galling, *Die Erwählungstraditionen Israels*, pp. 5–37, 63ff.

Yahweh is directing history towards a goal, the salvation of Israel. But in time this comes also to mean the salvation of the whole world (Isa. xlv, 22ff.). No human power can thwart Yahweh's will for the world. Even the prophets of doom did not give up this faith. Even if Yahweh did destroy His people, He would not be thwarted. In one way or another He would fulfil His covenant and His promises. Yahweh was too great, too real, too much master of the world, not to have the will and the ability to direct history in conformity with the purpose He had devised in the act of election.[1] The world is in His hand; and He knows what He wants to do with it. 'He did not create it to be a waste' (*tōhû*), a desperate and intolerable chaos; 'He formed it to be inhabited', to be a home for human beings (Isa. xlv, 18).

In this historical faith of the prophets, in *their* religious ideas, a creative factor was provided by the experiences in the cult, when Yahweh would come every year, revealing Himself and creating salvation. Yahweh had come once decisively, and again and again He had come. The promises of the festival had often not been realized in history; and yet Yahweh had come again and again. He came in every historical event; every mighty upheaval in world history was His 'day'. Yahweh lives, Yahweh can, and Yahweh will: that was the unshakable conviction of the prophets. They had known that experience in their own lives, which were utterly taken up into His service. Yahweh was 'righteous' and 'true'; and He could not make Himself unrighteous and false by breaking His word. 'The living God' must be a God of action, bringing to life again what He had smitten (Hos. vi, 1f.).

It was against the background of the destruction of the kingdom and the nation that this faith became fully conscious of itself as a stubborn faith, in spite of everything. Yahweh has forsaken His people and His city; but He will return. The hope of future restoration (and with it eschatology) arises when this faith is confronted with the brutal reality of history. The history of Israel is a tragic drama in which reality seems to gainsay faith, a constantly repeated disappointment. When faith rises up and overcomes the disappointment, the future hope and eschatology begin to be. The point is concisely and clearly put by Martin Buber: '*Die eschatologische Hoffnung . . . ist zwar immer Geschichtshoffnung; sie eschatologisiert sich erst durch die wachsende Geschichtsenttaüschung. In*

---

[1] Cf. Galling, op. cit., pp. 92ff.

*diesem Vorgang bemächtigt der Glaube sich der Zukunft als der unbeding-
ten Geschichtswende, sodann als der unbedingten Geschichtsüberwindung.'*[1]

Being *Geschichtsüberwindung*, the future hope takes possession of
history. In all the great events of history the prophets sought to
discern the coming of Yahweh (see above, pp. 131, 140); and
what would then happen is described in pictures drawn from the
experiences and hopes of the enthronement festival. The coming
of Yahweh in the cult is related to the present, and provides the
content of the expectation of the great coming of Yahweh which
will put an end to Israel's distress. The essential content and
theme of the future hope and of eschatology is the faith which
grew out of history and was corroborated by history, faith in a
living God who has a purpose and a goal in all that happens.

To this extent we are justified in saying that Israel's unique
conception of God as the God of history is the root of eschatology.[2]
Faith's own understanding of events enables us to go further and
say that because the true God came and revealed Himself to
Israel at the beginning of her history, and went on revealing
Himself to her and guiding her inner life and external history,
therefore in this nation, and here alone, there arose a hope for the
future, the heart of which is the conviction that this living God
has a positive goal for His creation, His election, and His covenant,
and that one day this goal will be reached.[3] In this divinely guided
history of the origin of the future hope and of eschatology, the
experiences and conceptions associated with Israel's cult also played
an important part. They provided material for the conceptions
of what Yahweh's final coming would involve.

We may say that the basis of an eschatology had actually been
laid when the future hope was thus permeated and fashioned and
motivated by religious faith, and in Deutero-Isaiah had received
its mythical and other-worldly character. But this was only the
stage of possibilities, not of fulfilment. Any sober historical consideration which avoids the confusion of different ideas will
recognize that Deutero-Isaiah himself does not yet present a true
eschatology. We miss the conception of a definite end to the

[1] Buber, *Königtum Gottes*, p. x.

[2] Dürr, *Ursprung und Ausbau*, p. 53; cf. Pidoux, *Le Dieu qui vient*, pp. 51ff. There is
thus a core of truth in Sellin's view that the experience of Yahweh's coming at Sinai
is the root of eschatology, *Der alttestamentliche Prophetismus*, p. 148. But of course
eschatology cannot be directly derived from it without reference to later history. A
definite future hope could arise only on the basis of the message of the prophets and
the later historical experiences; cf. above, p. 133 n. 4.

[3] This is also the fundamental idea in Pidoux's monograph, and gives it its value in
spite of its somewhat defective appreciation of the historical factors.

present order, and of a new world of an essentially different character from this one. The historical empires of Cyrus and of others have their place in Deutero-Isaiah's picture of the future.[1] What has been described in the preceding section is the vision of the future as it appears *to us* when we consider Deutero-Isaiah's message. It needed time to develop; and it could not do so fully until something new had been added to the old hope of restoration. It was not until the later period of Judaism that this took place; and it was in the teaching of Jesus that the new factor became dominant. Nevertheless what does begin to take place in Deutero-Isaiah is the severance of the future hope from historical reality, from the contingent, from any causal connexion with circumstances, so that it assumes an absolute character. It begins to be lifted up into the transcendent realm, to become something which is not a matter of 'rational' probability or possibility. It is certainly true that for a long time afterwards it was still related to the great historical and political events of the day. Whenever anything decisive took place, such as the fall of the Persian Empire, or an event which to the Jews, with their narrow political experience and outlook, might seem to indicate that something decisive was about to happen, such as the various disturbances in the Persian Empire, or the revolutions in the age of the Diadochi, then the future hope would be revived, and would express itself in prophetic poems, or new editions of old prophecies, foretelling the great change of fortune and the restoration of Israel, such as Isa. xxxiii; xv f.; xxxiv f. In particular, we may recall the grouping of earlier and later prophecies about the destruction of the most varied foreign powers into larger collections of 'oracles about the heathen', in order to give a picture of the fall of the world power or the heathen power in preparation for the restoration of Israel and the kingly rule of Yahweh.[2] But what was characteristic of the future hope in the later Old Testament period was the aspect which from the standpoint of human reason may seem unreal and fantastic, the fact that it was the wistful longing of an oppressed, suffering, longing people, yet a people deeply conscious of its religious destiny. Nevertheless we must emphasize that throughout the Old Testament period it continued in a large measure to have a this-worldly, national, and political character with the same features as in the earlier period of Judaism.

[1] Sidney Smith (*Isaiah Chapters XL–LV: Literary Criticism and History*, pp. 18f.) also rightly protests against the view that Deutero-Isaiah's message is eschatological.

[2] Isa. xiii–xxiii; xxiv–xxvii; Jer. xxv; xlvi–li; Ezek. xxv–xxxii; xxxviii f.

CHAPTER VI

The Place of the King in the Future
Hope: the Messiah

1. *The Origin of the Messianic Faith*

IT is against the background of the hope of national restoration (which is essentially this-worldly and political) that we must consider the Messianic expectation of early Judaism and the ideas associated with it. This is the problem alluded to above (p. 124).

Granted that the Messiah is a political and eschatological figure, and as such an object of hope for the future, there is obviously a connexion between this figure and the future hope as a whole. The Messiah is simply the king in this national and religious future kingdom, which will one day be established by the miraculous intervention of Yahweh. No objection of any weight has ever been raised against this formal definition. It means that the Messianic faith is by its very nature linked with Israel's hope of restoration.

Now we have seen that the characteristic Jewish future hope did not exist as a hope of restoration until there was a restoration to be accomplished. It originated and was developed after the fall of the state. Accordingly the Messianic hope in the strict sense arose at the same time as the hope of restoration, and as an integral part of it. This is entirely in keeping with the literary dating of the genuine Messianic oracles (see above, ch. II, 2). We have also seen that several of the eschatological descriptions culminate in the promise of the new scion of David who will be the head of the restored kingdom.

The historical connexion stands out clearly when we recall what was suggested above about the historical situations to which were related the unrealized elements in the ideal of kingship. Passages like Isa. ix, 1–6; xi, 1–9, or the words of Zechariah or Haggai about Zerubbabel, come as near as possible to being 'Messianic' expectation. The situations are times of affliction and distress;

yet hope was sustained by a faith in Yahweh which looked for the prince or governor whom Yahweh had appointed to realize the ideal, to be the king after Yahweh's heart, and the bearer of the promises to the dynasty and the nation.

We have also seen that practically all the passages in the Old Testament which express the hope of a Messiah who has yet to appear originated in that situation which for Israel was the worst of all the afflictions and punishments which had befallen the nation throughout its fateful history, namely the destruction of the state, the degradation of the royal house, the dispersion of the people and their subjection to foreign rulers: the exile and the Diaspora. That the Messiah belongs to the future means that he is part of the Israelite hope for the future. The Messianic faith is also the faith in the restoration of the state, the nation, and the monarchy; the two arose at the same time. This will become still clearer in the section on the scion of David. The restoration of the state means the restoration of the monarchy.

The hope attached to Zerubbabel came to nothing. The actual conditions after the return were but a feeble realization of Deutero-Isaiah's glorious promises. Thereafter the hope of restoration deliberately looks forward to a future not yet at hand, and gradually discards the connexion which the royal ideology previously had with empirical cultic experience. Not until much later, in a turbulent age, does it again become attached to a specific historical person.

It is, therefore, a fundamental principle for understanding the content of the Messianic conceptions, that whatever applies to the Israelite ideal of kingship also applies to the Messiah, but in a still greater measure. *The Messiah is the future, eschatological realization of the ideal of kingship.*

The restored Davidic kingdom was an ideal conception based on religion and permeated by religion; but in the thought of the earlier period it was nevertheless 'a kingdom of this world', established, it is true, by a miraculous divine intervention, yet through political means, through the historical and political circumstances of the age. It was to be realized entirely within the 'natural' course of world events, within 'natural' human history, which continued its course in accordance with the same 'laws' and 'forces' as before. It was idealized, embellished, enhanced (depicted as a Utopia, as secularized moderns would say), so that the guiding divine will and power behind the 'natural' events would stand out much more clearly than they did in the gloomy present. But still it was 'a kingdom of this world', as had been David's kingdom, and even the age of Moses and the patriarchs, in spite of all the interventions of Yahweh.

For Haggai and Zechariah, the coming kingdom of Zerubbabel is both at once. For Deutero-Isaiah, the restoration of Israel is the fulfilment of the everlasting promises of faithfulness made to David. From the religious point of view, Yahweh is king of the restored kingdom; but from the standpoint of everyday reality in national and political life, it is the ideal kings of David's line who will again govern Yahweh's people.

When we take all this into account, there can be no doubt that the expectation of a Messiah came into existence as a part of Israel's hope of restoration, and as a natural part of it. The Messiah is the ideal king of David's line, who reigns in the restored kingdom of his ancestor when the nation has been raised from her degradation and freed from foreign domination, when justice has been established and godliness and virtue again prevail in the land. The Messianic faith developed, along with the faith in restoration, out of the longing for a future realization of the ideal of kingship.

We must again refer to the forward-looking aspect of the ideal of kingship. That ideal was of such a kind that, when it was separated from its primitive mythological background and associated with a historical religion which laid supreme emphasis on the action of Yahweh in history (as was the case in Israel), everyday reality could not but give it something of the character of unrealized longing. But, even in Israel, hope and faith were always attached to the new bearer of the ideal, and to the new festival of Yahweh's epiphany, which was expected to improve conditions. Before the ideal of kingship could become the expectation of a future Messiah, it had to be separated from those possibilities which were associated with the next festival and the next king, yet never realized. The gulf between ideal and reality had first to become considerable and to be generally realized. Actual conditions had to become such that there no longer seemed to be any possibility of connecting the realization of the ideal with any reasonable probability. As always, faith comes into existence only when all human possibilities have been exhausted. The whole history of the monarchy had first to be enacted. There had to be a general awareness of the conflict between the culture of the monarchy on the one hand, together with the new social conditions of which it was at once a symptom and a contributory cause, and, on the other hand, the ancient desert ideals, the ancient ancestral culture, and the ancient 'justice of Yahweh' with its brotherhood and fellowship. (Then the longing for a specific future realization of the ideals could arise and take shape. Then the gulf between the power and honour which the king was supposed to possess and to obtain for his people, and the modest position which he really occupied in the international politics of the east became tragically plain. Things had to come to such a pass that there appeared to be no future for the representatives of David's line: those who really wielded power, and those who could be expected as their successors, were such that hope could no longer be connected with the normal succession. In other words, the Messianic faith as a faith in a future descendant of David (a purely future figure), who would restore the monarchy and blessing to the dynasty, implies the fall of the state and the monarchy, and foreign rule as the normal state of affairs.

The experience of the disruption after Solomon's death does not adequately account for the Messianic expectation and faith. For in spite of the disruption, the Davidic dynasty and its representatives were still regarded by the leading circles in Judah as the bearers of the covenant promises, as the true tokens of the covenant between Yahweh and His people. That this was also the general view is shown by the fact that after each of the few palace revolutions which took place in Jerusalem the people put the legitimate heir of David on the throne. It is these actual historical kings of the period after the disruption who are described in the royal psalms with all the superhuman features of the ideal of kingship. The existing Davidic dynasty was considered the fixed point in the nation's life, Yahweh's own guarantee for all time to come.[1] This conception of the Davidic dynasty leaves no room for any expectation of a specific, future, ideal king, for a Messiah in the strict sense, but only in the sense implicit in the forward-looking element in the kingly ideal itself. It was not until the fall of the Davidic monarchy that this forward-looking element (which was implicit in the ideal of kingship from the beginning) could develop into a Messianic expectation, a faith in the restoration of the fallen kingdom to its ancient splendour under a king who really fulfilled the ancient ideal of kingship in all its fullness.

[1] See Pedersen, *Israel* III–IV, pp. 86ff.

THE KING IN THE FUTURE HOPE: MESSIAH

But alongside the fact of God's guidance of the nation through its peculiar historical experiences, another element must be emphasized, namely the distinctive character of Yahwism, its faith in election and covenant. For there was implicit in it the germ of the faith that God had a great future in store for His people, and that those conditions and circumstances would be realized which summed up the ideal, and which corresponded to the moral standards and desires of righteous and pious men, and therefore to Israel's ancient Yahwistic morality and justice, in short, the faith that God's promises are genuine, and that God's purpose must be fulfilled. But as yet this faith is neither eschatology nor the Messianic faith, and must not be confused with the latter. But it is *faith*, faith in God's purpose, and will, and power to attain His end, the faith out of which eschatology itself arises, and which is the religious core of eschatology.

2. *The Scion of David*

It is in keeping with the character of the future restoration of the Davidic kingdom that its king is not a divine being from above but *a mortal man of David's line*. What has been said above concerning the origin of the Israelite future hope makes it quite evident that Staerk, for instance, is entirely wrong in maintaining that 'the Old Testament belief in a coming saviour cannot be separated from the eschatological aspect, the change and re-creation of the course of the world'.[1] In so far as old Testament eschatology has as its background the destruction of the nation and is formed around the hope of restoration as its nucleus, to that extent the Messiah is a political figure of this world, and has nothing to do with a change in the course of the world or an eschatological new creation. In so far as the future hope and eschatology borrowed material from the other-worldly hope of a new creation and a new world and were gradually conformed to that hope, to that extent does the kingly rule of Yahweh, not the Messiah, become the central idea and the dominating conception. As scholars have long maintained, this central conception really makes the figure of the Messiah superfluous, so long as the subject is viewed from the standpoint and experience of early Judaism. The thought of

---

[1] See Staerk, *Soter* I, p. 40. What is said above indicates that I dissent from the main thesis of this book, so far as it deals with the Old Testament, and also my reasons for doing so. Cf. my critical notes in *N.T.T.* xlv, 1944, p. 71 n. 1, p. 238 n. 47, p. 243 n. 164. The character of the present work forbids discussion of details or more extended examination of Staerk's hypothesis; but occasional reference is made to it.

the need for a revelation of God through an atoning mediator still lay beyond their experience of life and beyond the revelation of God which they had been led to apprehend. The meaning of the Messianic figure was from the beginning derived from the national and political aspect of the future hope. It was only later in revelation history (in consequence of new experiences of man and God which came to God's people in the course of that history, and as a result of the continued preparatory revelation which that history itself was and mediated) that the Messiah was drawn into the central position and became the other-worldly saviour and mediator of a new world order.

As many passages show,[1] the ideal future king, the 'Messiah', was always thought of in the Old Testament as a scion of David, 'a shoot from the stump of Jesse', descended from the ancient Bethlehemite line. Sometimes, too, it appears that the expectation was directly connected with a particular descendant of David who was alive at the time. It is possible that Isa. ix refers to an actual newborn prince of the ancient dynasty. It is at all events certain that Zechariah and Haggai associate all the expectations of an ideal future with a specific historical person, Zerubbabel, the grandson of King Jehoiachin (1 Chron. iii, 18f.). Haggai promises him that once again (i.e., in addition to the insurrections which broke out after the death of Cambyses) Yahweh will shake heaven, and earth, and all the nations, so that the riches of all the peoples will be gathered in the temple of Jerusalem as tribute; then He will overthrow kingdoms, and thrones, and those who have hitherto held power, and in their stead make His chosen servant, Zerubbabel ben Shealtiel, a signet on God's hand, one who will execute and put into effect on earth the decrees of Yahweh (Hag. ii, 6f., 21ff.). For Zechariah, 'Yahweh's servant, the Shoot' (referring to the name Zerubbabel, 'the shoot from Babylon'; see below, p. 164) is 'he that cometh', the Anointed, who will always stand by the Lord of the whole earth (Zech. iii, 8; iv, 14). The prophet even now has the crown ready with which the 'Shoot' is to be crowned; 'under him everything will shoot up', and 'he will bear the mark of honour, and will sit and rule upon his throne' (Zech. vi, 10–13). The wonder-working spirit of Yahweh will level his path and break down all opposition; and as a sign that all this is going to happen he will be able to complete

[1] Isa. xi, 1, 10; ix, 6; xvi, 5; lv, 3f.; Mic. v, 1; Jer. xvii, 25; xxiii, 5; xxxiii, 17; xxx, 9; Ezek. xxxiv, 23f.; xxxvii, 24f.; Amos ix, 11.

the building of the temple and put the top stone in place (Zech.
iv, 6f.; vi, 12f.). Then the heathen nations will submit to the scion
of David and to Israelite supremacy; 'they will be spoil to their
servants' (Zech. ii, 4, 13; vi, 8); 'many nations will be joined to
Yahweh in that day, and will become My people' (Zech. ii, 15).

It is possible that the promise in Isa. xi, 1ff. about 'the shoot
which will come out of the hewn stump of Jesse' also belongs to
the same period and refers to the 'Shoot', Zerubbabel, or one of
his descendants. But of course it may be also a purely future
expectation.

When Zechariah uses the term 'Shoot' as a title of the ideal
king, he is also thinking of legitimate descent from David's line.
In Phoenician, ṣemaḥ ṣedek, 'the rightful shoot', denotes the legitimate heir to the throne, who is also chosen by the deity;[1] and in
the Aramaic royal inscriptions from North Syria the ṣedeḳ of the
king indicates his right of succession to the throne.[2] That this
usage was also well known in Israel and in Judaism is shown by the
later prophecies in the book of Jeremiah (xxiii, 5f. = xxxiii,
14–16), which refer to Zechariah's ṣemaḥ prophecy and predict a
ṣemaḥ ṣaddiḳ, a legitimate Shoot for David; the adjective means
'rightful' as well as 'righteous', 'just'. The prophet emphasizes
both the moral qualities of the future king and also his legitimacy
as the rightful heir of David and inheritor of the promises made to
David.[3] On the other hand, nowhere in the Old Testament is
there any suggestion that the Messiah was thought of as David in

---

[1] See Lidzbarski, *Handbuch der nordsemitischen Epigraphik* I, p. 422, No. 2, 11; Gressmann, *Der Messias*, pp. 253f. The same thought underlies the reference to Karit (the
Ugaritic demi-god and royal ancestor) *šph lṭpn*, '*Lṭpn*'s (i.e., El's) shoot' (II K I–II,
10; see Eissfeldt, *El im ugaritischen Pantheon*, p. 35).

[2] See Euler in *Z.A.W.* lvi, 1938, pp. 277ff.

[3] Widengren (*R.o.B.* ii, 1943, p. 61) sees in these prophecies the influence of an ancient oriental myth identifying the king with the mythical tree of life, a 'shoot', 'twig',
'branch', of the divine tree of paradise. This theory about a mythical conception
appears to me to have no very secure foundation. It can hardly be safe philological
and historical method to combine all kinds of figures which describe a person as, or
liken him to, a 'twig', or a 'shoot', regardless whether the person is a god or a king,
or whether the twig is alive or cut off. Besides, the figure is in itself altogether too ready
to hand, and may well be supposed to have occurred independently in the most varied
contexts. If Widengren's method were to be followed to its logical conclusion, the
unfruitful branch of John xv, 6, which 'is cast out as a branch and withers' and finally
is thrown on the fire, might be taken as an offshoot of the ancient oriental Messianic
king; or the many '-grens' (branches) and '-kvists' (twigs) (the reference is to Swedish
surnames ending in '-gren' and '-kvist') who rest in Swedish churchyards might be
regarded as evidence of the influence of the royal ideology of the ancient east on
Swedish Lutheranism and its hypothetical cult of the dead. There is no justification
for the assumption that Zechariah made a conscious allusion to any ancient oriental
myth about the king when he devised his conceit about the 'Shoot from Babylon' as
the royal Shoot under whom 'all things will shoot up'. See also below, p. 164.

person, returning in a wonderful way.[1] It is not in accordance with Old Testament thought that a man who has died a natural death should return.[2] The Messiah is a scion of David, not David himself in person.

It needs to be emphasized that in the Old Testament, and particularly in its older parts, the Messiah is not a supernatural being who comes from above. He is indeed depicted in mythical colours; but we find not more, but rather less of the mythical style than is usual in the ancient oriental conception of the king. As we have seen, the literal sense which it may originally have conveyed was weakened in Israel; and the divinity of the king was not conceived as anything more (nor yet as anything less) than a divine adoption of an ordinary man and his endowment with power. The natural aspect in the mythical form was in Israel transferred to the personal and moral sphere. That the king, in spite of his divine quality, was an ordinary man of this world was not felt to be either a paradox or a problem. This is true no less of the Messiah, the future king, the more so since it was not the older, more mythical, Canaanite form of the conception of kingship which formed the background of the idea of the future king when it emerged, but rather the conception held in the later monarchy, or after the end of the monarchy, when the influence of the prophets, the sole lordship of Yahweh, and the growing sense of the distance between God and man had forced the mythical element in the ideal of kingship on to the moral plane.

It is therefore not true to say that the Messiah is thought of in the Old Testament as a 'divine child', as a 'pre-existent' being from remote antiquity.[3] But as we shall see below, it is true that in so far as the future hope becomes eschatology, and the king is lifted up above the sphere of empirical reality, to that extent are mythical features increasingly included in the conception of the king, so that the Messiah again approximates to the ancient oriental king-god. It is the longing for a superhuman helper and a growing understanding of the 'otherness' of the future kingdom and of the divinely miraculous character of its realization that lie behind this 'mythologizing' and emerge in the promises on which they have left their stamp. We shall discuss this in greater detail below.

[1] As is held by Schmidt, Der Mythus vom wiederkehrenden König im Alten Testament, and Gressmann, Der Messias, pp. 232ff. See further below, pp. 163f.
[2] Cf. Job vii, 7f., 21; x, 21f.; xiv, 7, 12, 14.
[3] As Staerk does; see the summary of his views in Soter I, pp. 4of.

3. The Name and Titles of the Future King

The name and titles which are applied to the future king are in accord with his descent from David. In the Old Testament his name is not Messiah, but *David*, or the scion of David.

Sometimes this king of the age of restoration is simply called David.[1] It has been maintained (e.g., by Gressmann, Moore, Staerk, and others) that the prophets are here thinking of a resurrected or reincarnated David, a David redivivus in person. That is improbable. The thought would be unparalleled in the whole range of Old Testament thought,[2] and so novel that it must have been emphasized and commented on if *that* had been what these prophets meant. This is evident from Isa. liii, where a unique resurrection miracle of this kind is in fact announced, but is also emphasized with all the writer's resources as something unheard of and unprecedented. But it was an ancient Israelite idea that the ancestor lived on in his descendants. It is David's 'blessing', his inmost being, his royal soul, his royal honour, his royal good fortune, that are inherited by his sons, just as the disciples of the prophets inherit a greater or less portion of the 'spirit' manifested in their master, as with Elisha and Elijah (cf. 2 Kings ii, 9–15). As the people may be called 'Jacob' or 'Abraham' (Mic. vii, 20) because the 'weight', the 'soul', the blessing, and the nature of Abraham and Jacob live on in them, so too, he who in any age represents David's line and his status may be called David. In Ps. cxxxii the reference is obviously to the reigning descendant of David; for the psalm prays for the favour of Yahweh on this anointed one 'for Thy servant David's sake', so that 'the anointed one' cannot here be identified with 'Thy servant David'. Yet later in the same psalm this anointed king is called 'David'. The two expressions are in synonymous parallelism to each other; and when the promise is given that Yahweh will clothe 'his' (i.e., 'David's') enemies with shame, but make 'his crown glitter', the very background of the psalm (intercession with promises) shows that in fact 'David' is here the contemporary king of David's line, the one who, according to the same psalm, plays the part of David in the religious drama of the enthronement festival. In the titles of the psalms, the expression

---

[1] Jer. xxx, 9; Ezek. xxxiv, 23f.; xxxvii, 24; Hos. iii, 5.
[2] Moore (*Judaism* II, p. 326) refers to Malachi's promise that Elijah would come before the last times. But there is a difference between Elijah and David. Elijah did not die, but still lives in heaven. David both died and was buried, and 'saw corruption', as Peter says in Acts ii, 29, 31; cf. above, p. 162, and n 1.

'for David' (it should be so translated) is used meaning 'for the use of the king'. This interpretation is further corroborated by the fact that the term *dawidum* = *dāwīḏ* has been found in Mesopotamian texts from Mari on the Euphrates as a title of princes, a title used as a proper name, and partly regarded as such, like Augustus, or conversely Caesar (see above, pp. 74f). 'David', as the name of the Messiah, means nothing other than 'David's scion'.

Sometimes, too, the cryptic yet suggestive title 'Shoot' (*ṣemaḥ*) is used.[1] The term is first used by the prophet Zechariah, and later in one or two obviously secondary Messianic passages. Some interpreters hold that this is in itself an ancient Messianic term;[2] but this is out of the question during the period when no ancient Messianic idea existed. Nor can this theory be supported by reference to any ancient eastern ideology of kingship.[3] For even if the vegetation god who rises again, and *possibly* also the king as his cultic representative, may be compared to a shoot or a tree which shoots up again, it is a very different thing to use the 'Shoot' as a *term* for the god or the king. In Zechariah, the real connexion between the expression and the prophet's promises about Zerubbabel ('the Shoot from Babylon') as king of Israel is so evident, and the use of cryptic allusions, instead of a public announcement about him by name, is so intimately associated with the political situation, that there can hardly be any doubt that this play on words was devised by Zechariah himself. This remains true even if it was an ancient usage in the east to call the king a 'legitimate shoot' of the old family tree (see above, pp. 161f.). Later the prophetic disciples interpreted this play on words as an expression for the future king of the restoration.

The expression indicates, as we have seen above (pp. 161f.), the legitimacy of the king. But it also includes something more. Zechariah himself says explicitly what he implied by it: 'under him everything will shoot up'. That this name might suggest associations with the thought of reawakening nature, as did the name of the Canaanite god of vegetation, is just possible. But the ethical element is also present. When we also find the variant *ṣemaḥ ṣeḏāḳâh*, 'the shoot of justice or righteousness', it implies above all what was always an important aspect of the Old Testa-

---

[1] Zech. iii, 8; vi, 12; Isa. iv, 2; cf. Jer. xxiii, 5; xxxiii, 15. See Buda in *Biblica* xx 1939, pp. 10ff.

[2] So, e.g., Horst in Robinson-Horst, *Die zwölf kleinen Propheten*, p. 223.

[3] As Widengren would do; *R.o.B.* ii, 1943, p. 61.

ment conception of 'righteousness', namely salvation, the felicity which is brought, restored, and maintained by the 'righteous' ruler, and also the ethical qualities which are the basis of his power to confer good fortune.

Only once is the future king given a name which expresses the character and source of his kingship: 'Yahweh is our righteousness', i.e., our righteous champion and saviour (Jer. xxiii, 6). We shall return to this below (pp. 177ff.).

4. *The Scion of David as a Sign of the Restoration of David's Line*

In the early Old Testament future hope, the king is in reality not a specific individual person, the unique one who will have no successor. What we find there is, in fact, not the coming of an individual Messiah, but a restoration of the Davidic kingdom under the sway of the house of David. This is clear from such passages as Jer. xvii, 25; xxxiii, 15ff.; Isa. lv, 3f.; Amos ix, 11; Mic. iv, 8. It is 'the fallen tabernacle of David' that is to be raised again. In Jer. xvii, 19ff. an undoubtedly post-exilic prophet speaks *in the plural* of 'kings and princes sitting on the throne of David'. In connexion with the 'righteous Shoot' (the one who 'will execute judgement and righteousness in the land'), which Yahweh will cause to grow when once the time of chastisement has expired and He fulfils His promises to Israel and Judah, we hear that 'David will never lack a man to sit upon the throne of the house of Israel'. Thus the dynasty will always exist, and always bring such 'righteous Shoots' to rule over the restored people of Yahweh. That this cannot be taken in any other sense becomes quite clear when in the sequel a similar promise is made to the priesthood, 'the Levites': 'Nor will the priests, the Levites, lack a man before me to offer burnt offerings, to burn cereal offerings, and to perform sacrifice continually' (Jer. xxxiii, 14–18).

When the exiles have returned and the state of bliss is being established, then, says Deutero-Isaiah, Yahweh will again make a covenant with His people:

I will make an everlasting covenant with you,
the sure promises of favour to David.[1]
Behold, I have made him a witness to the peoples,
a leader and commander over the peoples. (Isa. lv, 3f.)

[1] *ḥasᵉdê ḏāwīḏ han-neʾᵉmānīm*. On the covenant with David, see Pedersen, *Israel* III–IV, pp. 89ff., and Index, s.v. 'Covenant'; Rost in *T.L.Z.* lxxii, 1947, cols. 129ff.

The covenant with David is described here as $h^a s\bar{a}\underline{d}\hat{i}m\ ne^{,e}m\bar{a}n\hat{i}m$ true deeds of favour (E.VV. 'sure mercies'), sure promises of grace, indicating that he and his dynasty would rule over tribes and nations. Now Yahweh re-establishes this covenant with Israel. This of course does not imply the thought, which has sometimes been read into the passage, that the nation will now take the place of the dynasty and inherit the promises made to David, but rather that these promises have again become valid and effective. Now as always, David and his dynasty represent the people; and in David the nation has the visible expression of its unity, its embodiment, and its palladium. The promises made to David are the essential content of the covenant with the people. In and through the covenant with David the covenant with the people is also confirmed. It is not expressly stated in the Old Testament that the covenant with David is identical with the covenant on Sinai, including and continuing it; but the idea itself is present, and is clearly brought out in the statement that the promises of the Davidic covenant are the essential content of the covenant which Yahweh will now make 'with you', i.e., with the Jews. This is also true of Jer. xxx, 21f., where the result of the coming of the future king is described in the very words which are used elsewhere to express the content of the covenant on Sinai: 'and you shall be my people, and I will be your God'.[1] Thus when Isa. lv, 3f. promises the re-establishment of the Davidic covenant, the meaning must be that the Davidic dynasty (to which the promises applied just as much as to David personally)[2] as the true embodiment of Israel will again become the royal house and gain dominion over other nations as of old. It is 'the former dominion, the kingdom over Jerusalem', which will 'come to the daughter of Zion', when Zion once again has a king in her midst, when a ruler has arisen from the ancient dynasty of Bethlehem, says the book of Micah (iv, 8; v, 1–3). The work of Yahweh presaged by the birth of the royal child in Isa. ix, 1–6 is

> To increase the dominion
> and <make> good fortune endless,
> upon the throne of David,
> and in his kingdom.

The same prediction is made when it is emphasized that in the

---

[1] Exod. xix, 5f.; Lev. xxvi, 12; Jer. xxiv, 7; xxxi, 33; xxxii, 38; Zech. viii, 8; Ezek. xi, 20; xxxvi, 28; Hos. ii, 25, etc.

[2] See 2 Sam. vii; Pss. lxxxix, 20ff.; cxxxii, 11ff.

restored kingdom (by contrast with the unhappy present) the king 'will come forth from his (i.e., Jacob's) midst' (Jer. xxx, 21); Israel will no longer have to obey foreign kings.

It is one of the distinctive features of prophetic vision and the prophetic word that general truth is expressed in concrete form. The vision of the prophet is fixed on the one figure in whom the restored Davidic kingdom first takes visible, concrete shape before his mind's eye. What interests him and his audience is the beginning, the dawn of a new age; and therefore he describes this brilliant forerunner, with whom everything begins, without thought or mention of the obvious fact that for all time he will be succeeded by equally brilliant descendants of David. But on occasion it is stated that he is one of an endless succession. In Jer. xxiii, 1–3 the prophet (here, too, undoubtedly post-exilic) promises that Yahweh 'will gather the remnant of My flock from all the countries whither I have driven them'; and then continues, in direct contrast with the bad 'shepherds' whom the people have previously had, and who 'have scattered My flock, and have driven them away, and have not cared for them', 'I will set shepherds over them who will shepherd them', i.e., give them kings who will rule over them. In the Old Testament, as in the east generally, the figure of the shepherd undoubtedly represents the king. Accordingly the restored kingdom will have new kings who will be better than their predecessors. But then there rises before the prophet's mind the first of this new line of kings, under whose rule the age of bliss will be inaugurated:

> Behold, the days are coming, says Yahweh,
> when I shall raise up for David a righteous Shoot;
> and he will reign as king and wisely attain his aim;
> and he will execute justice and righteousness in the land.
> In his day Judah will be saved,
> and Israel will dwell in security.
> And this is the name by which he will be called,
> 'Yahweh our Vindication'.

Obviously Zechariah did not think that Zerubbabel would be immortal, even if he became the 'Messiah' of the restored kingdom. When a member of the Deutero-Isaianic circle describes the bliss of the future kingdom, saying,

> No longer will there be in it
> an infant who lives but a few days,

167

> nor an old man who has not completed
> the wonted span of life;
> for the youngest will die a hundred years old,
> else he will be deemed a sinner accursed (Isa. lxv, 20),

he clearly does not assume that men will be immortal in this kingdom of bliss; and it should be equally clear that he does not except the king.

That this is so is confirmed by the idea which sometimes appears in later Judaism in connexion with the thought of a Millennium, namely that the Messiah will die when the Millennium ends.[1] This idea has been regarded as very remarkable, as indeed it is from the standpoint of later Judaism, for which the Messiah had become 'the Son of Man', a pre-existent, heavenly, eternal being. But precisely because this idea is at variance with the general outlook of later Judaism, it must be ancient, a relic of an earlier conception. It is, in fact, quite natural and intelligible in the light of the early Jewish future hope, in which the Messiah is simply the first in the endless line of David's descendants, who will succeed one another on the throne of the glorious restored kingdom.

The early Jewish 'Messiah', then, is no specific individual. In fact, like the king in the royal psalms, he is a type. Beyond him we can discern the whole line of 'Messianic' successors who have the same ideal character as the first 'righteous Shoot' from the stump of Jesse.

Moreover, in the 'Messianic' passages referred to above, where the name 'David' is applied to the Messiah, this means, as we have seen, the scion of David, or, more precisely, all the 'Davids' who are to be in the happy kingdom of the future.

All the Old Testament promises make it clear that the Messiah is really a royal figure, a ruler. It is therefore a misuse of the word 'Messiah' and a misrepresentation of the Old Testament conception of the future to speak of a 'prophetic' or a 'priestly' Messiah alongside the kingly one.[2] The latter is a particularly misleading and unhistorical use of the term. In the theocratic programme for the future in Ezekiel, the 'prince' is a this-worldly figure, too unimportant and insignificant to be of any interest in a historical account of the Old Testament expectation of a Messiah. He is rather an example of the undistinguished substitute conceived of

---

[1] 2 Esdras vii, 28ff.; cf. xii, 34; 2 Bar. xxx, compared with xxix, 3. See Bousset, *Relig.*[2], p. 332.

[2] As do Gressmann (*Der Messias*) and Staerk (*Soter* I).

in those circles which were no longer interested in the Messiah as an element in the future hope (because he would conflict too much with their theocratic and priestly ideals and desire for power),[1] or perhaps, more accurately, as part of a religious and political programme, which would have existed in the same form whether or not there had been any Messianic hope at all. The prince in the book of Ezekiel has no connexion with the idea of the Messiah, and has no place in a survey of its history. There is therefore every justification for the statement[2] that Ezekiel xl–xlviii deals not with the last age, but with a historical interregnum, and with a prince as he actually was in the dreary interval between the return and the establishment of the glorious kingdom.

5. *The Kingly Rule of the Scion of David and the Kingly Rule of Yahweh*

The Messiah of the Jewish future hope and of Jewish eschatology is, as we have seen, a figure who belongs to the this-worldly, political side of the hope of restoration and deliverance, but who must, of course, be understood in the light of the general religious outlook, like everything else of significance in Israelite life. Religion and politics were not two distinct spheres, but politics was regarded as an outcome of man's place in the world as defined by religion. Man was God's creation and servant, a member of that order of creation which was wholly determined by God and directed by and to God.

As we have seen above (pp. 140–9), the fundamental thought in the Jewish hope of future restoration (even in its national and political form) is the idea of the kingly rule of Yahweh, 'the kingdom of God'.[3] All the other conceptions are grouped round this central one; and in the light of it their organic connexion can be understood. This has remained true in Judaism to this day. That it was also true in the time of Jesus is shown quite simply by the evangelists' summary of His message: 'the kingly rule of God is at hand.'

This being so, it might be concluded that there was a conflict between this central idea and the thought of the kingdom of the Messiah; and there was in fact a tension between them. In later Judaism this tension is reduced by the thought that the kingdom of the Messiah is an interregnum before the coming of the kingdom of God (see below, pp. 277, 321, 324, 326).

---

[1] Staerk seems to agree on the latter point; see *Soter I*, p. 41.
[2] See Procksch in *Z.A.W.* lviii, 1940–1, p. 99. [3] See *Ps.St.* II, pp. 220ff.

But in the earlier period this tension is not so apparent, precisely because, considered from the religious point of view, the future kingdom is essentially the kingly rule of Yahweh. Whenever the conception is dominated by this religious point of view, the practical, earthly form of the kingdom recedes into the background. For Deutero-Isaiah, the picture of Yahweh's glorious, royal 'appearance' and salvation overshadows all the concrete details of everyday experience. It is only incidentally that he mentions that it also involves the re-establishment in Israel of the kingly rule of the Davidic line: he takes it for granted. It is through the gloriously endowed king, who will inherit the covenant promises made to David, that the kingly rule of Yahweh will be exercised in the daily life of the future.[1]

In the description of Israel's future, the king is naturally the supreme figure, symbolizing and expressing the restoration of the kingdom in its ancient glory on the basis of the old covenant. Yet the restored kingdom is much more glorious and secure, because in the monarchy, in the constant presence through the ages of 'David' on the throne in Jerusalem, renewed and concrete visible expression is given to the election of and covenant with Israel, and to all the promises and possibilities which these implied. The future kingdom is founded on a renewal and fulfilment of precisely this concrete expression of the covenant, 'the sure promises of favour to David' (Isa. lv, 3f.).

The scion of David is so natural an element in the description of the future, that he is often not mentioned but tacitly assumed. This is so, for instance, in the passage in Deutero-Isaiah just referred to about the restoration of the Davidic covenant.

Yet it is remarkable that there are relatively few references to the 'Messiah' in the Old Testament descriptions of salvation and the state of bliss. In this, Deutero-Isaiah's attitude is really characteristic. He even gives the ancient Israelite royal title, 'Yahweh's anointed', to Cyrus: the new king in Jerusalem is only indirectly referred to. Still more remarkable is the fact that the future king is hardly ever described as re-establishing the kingdom. Only one of the 'Messianic' passages (Isa. ix, 1–6) appears to

[1] If this is the point of Engnell's statement that 'Yahweh and His anointed are one', and that this accounts for the two aspects of 'Messianism' (*Gamla testamentet* I, p. 146 n. 1), then this statement is not without truth. But it is misleading, since it is calculated to obscure the two aspects, which are at all events sufficiently distinct to be separate from each other chronologically in later Judaism. The statement leads Riesenfeld to fuse the two aspects (*Jésus transfiguré*, pp. 56f.).

imply that the king who is now born will be instrumental in throwing off the yoke of the oppressors and destroying tyranny. But it is significant that even here it is Yahweh ('Thou', *v.* 4) who achieves this. The thought is proleptic: Thou hast done it; that is, in principle, through the birth of the royal child. Yet the thought may well be that it is the child who will actually carry it out, so that light will dawn on those who dwell in a land of deep gloom. All the other passages either state directly or imply, without actually saying so, that Yahweh Himself is directly responsible for the establishment of the future kingdom of bliss, the gathering of the dispersed, and everything else that is associated with it.[1] In all of them the king is mentioned only as the ruler of a kingdom which has already been established. Even in Isa. ix, 1–6 the last word is that it is 'the zeal of Yahweh' that will 'perform this'.

This apparently remarkable fact is explained by the originally political character of the future king. Since, in the thought of the east, the existence of a realm implies a king (the wise man Agur expresses his amazement that the locusts can march forth in ordered array without having a king: Prov. xxx, 27), the future king is mentioned (or tacitly taken for granted) as one of the greatest and most conspicuous glories of the restored kingdom. But in general the future kingdom is conceived of in the Old Testament in religious rather than political terms. As we have seen, the religious point of view predominates increasingly. This involves an emphasis on the miraculous character of the kingdom. The kingdom will be established by a miraculous divine intervention: it will be God's own work, not the work of man. This is particularly clear in Deutero-Isaiah, and still more in those who came after him. So paradoxical is Yahweh's action that He even uses the heathen Cyrus as His 'anointed' instrument in restoring Israel. Because the kingdom is restored by a miracle wrought by Yahweh, there is hardly ever any question of the king's establishing the kingdom. He is the future kingdom's greatest visible good, the abiding pledge of Yahweh's faithfulness and active presence; but he does not establish the kingdom.

Accordingly there is for the thought of Israel and the Old Testament no conflict between the kingly rule of Yahweh and that of the Messiah, just as, ideally, there is no conflict between Yahweh's

[1] Isa. xvi, 5; lv, 3f.; Jer. xxiii, 1–6; Ezek. xvii, 22–24; xxxiv, 23f.; xxxvii, 22–5; Zech. ix, 9f.

kingly rule and that of His son, the anointed, earthly king.[1] If
the king is what he ought to be, he is the obedient, faithful,
'righteous', and power-filled instrument for carrying out Yahweh's
will on earth and exercising the daily functions of His kingly rule.
This is also true of the future king. Nowhere are his status and
power so emphasized that they threaten the exclusive dominion
of Yahweh or the monotheism of the Old Testament.

Naturally, thought may dwell on the one or the other of these
two aspects, Yahweh's kingly rule, or His kingship as exercised
through the future king; but they are never felt to be two distinct
things. When the Messiah stands in the foreground, it is because
reference is made to the national and political side of the future
kingdom, or because emphasis is laid on the value of having a
fully qualified intermediary between Yahweh and His people,
like the priest-king of earlier times (Jer. xxx, 21; see below, pp. 238ff).
But the greater the prominence given to the religious point of view,
the greater is the emphasis on the idea which became the focus
and centre of the future hope when Deutero-Isaiah adopted the
enthronement mythology: it is Yahweh who is king in the future
kingdom.[2] It is He who is its founder, and who rules and governs
('judges') in it. This is the general view in Old Testament
descriptions of future conditions (the end time) and their realization, even where Yahweh is not explicitly called king. It is
Yahweh who blinds, hardens, and destroys the hostile world-
power;[3] it is He who will gather His people from all lands and
realms;[4] it is He who will thenceforth dwell in the midst of His
people,[5] and Himself keep watch on those who rule and judge;[6]
and He will be to His people sun, and light, and wall, and defence.[7]

In so far as the religious side of the future hope is emphasized,
the ideal, earthly king of David's line recedes into the background
behind Yahweh Himself. From the standpoint of the general

[1] In Z.A.W. liv, 1936, pp. 168ff., Wolff presents the problem, not in Old Testament
terms, but with an emphasis and sharpness which arise from a Christian interpretation
of the Messiah; and he discusses it in terms of dogmatic theology rather than historical
criticism. The main point in his conclusion is, of course, sound: that it is Yahweh's
work which is accomplished through the Messiah. On the other hand there is no
historical justification for his idea that the Messiah is a form of the manifestation
(*Erscheinungsform*) of Yahweh (op. cit., p. 191).
[2] Isa. lii, 7 (cf. xl, 9–11); xliii, 15; xli, 21; xliv, 6; xxxiii, 17, 22; xxiv, 23; Zeph. iii, 15;
Isa. lxii, 3; Zech. xiv, 9, 16f.
[3] Isa. xlix, 25f.; li, 12ff; lii, 12; xli, 13; xlix, 16ff.; lxiii, 1ff.; lxvi, 15f.; xxxi, 5–9.
[4] Ezek. xxxiv, 12ff.; xxxvii, 21; Isa. xlix, 10ff., 22, 25.
[5] Ezek. xxxvii, 27; Isa. liv, 5; lx, 14; lxii, 11; Zeph. iii, 15.
[6] Ezek. xxx, 15ff.; Isa. xxxiii, 21f.
[7] Isa. xxx, 19f.; Zech. ii, 8f.

scheme of religious thought which provided the material for the specific development of the future hope, one might be tempted to say (as has in fact been said) that the Messiah is Yahweh's *alter ego* or *Doppelgänger*. If this is intended to suggest that the Messiah is an alien element in the picture, it is wrong. From the beginning the Messiah is associated with the hope of restoration. But it is true that in so far as the purely religious aspect becomes dominant, the Messiah recedes into the background and remains there as a relic of the this-worldly, political aspect of restoration. That is why we find the Messiah left out of many descriptions of the future kingdom without any sense of loss.[1] The figure of the Messiah in the earlier period is therefore the best illustration of the two sources of the Jewish future hope, on the one hand a natural, national, political hope based on religion, and on the other the purely religious experience of Yahweh's enthronement and kingly rule, and the projection of that experience into the future as the religious development of the content and ground of the hope.[2]

In the earlier Jewish future hope, then, the Messiah does not actually establish the future kingdom, but is the Davidic ruler in the restored Israel, in so far as it is thought of as political and this-worldly. Only rarely is he regarded as Yahweh's instrument in crushing the enemy and establishing the state of bliss (Isa. ix, 1ff.; see above, pp. 102ff.). This of course does not mean that it was commonly thought that the Messiah would *not* take an active part in establishing the kingdom, but only that the emphasis was not laid on this aspect of the royal figure. In the restoration Yahweh Himself dominated the scene and all attention was directed to Him. Of course David's descendant *may* be regarded as the instrument Yahweh will use, not only as governing and defending in Yahweh's strength, but as the royal deliverer who will lead Yahweh's campaign against His enemies. But, on the whole, the passive part played by the king in the establishment of the future kingdom is characteristic. Zechariah's word to Zerubbabel (iv, 6) provides an apt comment: '"Not by might and not by power (i.e., by human power), but by My (wonder-working) spirit", says Yahweh.' Generally speaking it is only after the restoration that the future king comes into action.

---

[1] This is discussed at greater length below, pp. 337ff.; cf. above, p. 170.
[2] This dual character is not presented with sufficient clarity in *Ps.St.* II, where only the origin of the *content* of eschatology (Yahweh's kingly rule over a newly created world) is examined. Insufficient attention is given there to the political aspect of the future hope and the question of the political background against which it arose.

6. *The Equipment, Call, and Work of the Future King*

The future king is thought of as endowed with superhuman *divine powers and qualities* in at least as great measure as the idealized historical king. Everything which has been said above about the ideal of kingship applies to him as well. It is only by chance that one or another feature in the picture is not mentioned in the relatively few 'Messianic' sayings in the Old Testament.

X But there is all the more justification for completing the portrait of the future king in accordance with the portrait of the king in the psalms, for example, in that these psalms and similar poems and prophetic utterances about the king came to be interpreted in Judaism as promises of the future king or Messiah. There is clear evidence of this from the circle of Isaiah's disciples, namely in Isa. xxxii, 1–8. This passage is not really a prophecy, but a wisdom poem describing the good fortune and blessing of a country where there is the right kind of king, who 'reigns in righteousness'; and the poem gives a concrete example of such righteous rule by indicating the appropriate lot which will befall 'the fool' and 'the noble man'. The king is here thought of in terms of the customary ideal of kingship, as he is described, in greater detail, in the so-called 'last words of David' (2 Sam. xxiii, 1ff.), a passage which is also characterized by the style and thought of wisdom poetry.[1] In the circle of Isaiah's disciples the poem Isa. xxxii, 1–8 was interpreted as a prophecy about the ideal future king, and in the course of transmission it was put together with earlier and later prophetic utterances by Isaiah and his successors. The opening line, *hēn leṣedeḳ yimloḳ-meleḳ*, 'when the king reigns in righteousness', has been interpreted as a prophecy: 'Behold, the king (or, a king) will reign in righteousness.' In the course of transmission a poem like this could (or had to) be taken in this way, because at that time the Jews no longer had a king, much less a righteous king; and therefore descriptions of the ideal king could only be interpreted either of one of the idealized kings of the past (which practically meant David), or of the scion of David, who would come in the future when Israel had again become a free, pious, and righteous nation.

Another instance of a 'Messianic' interpretation of earlier prophecies is perhaps to be found in a passage in the book of Ezekiel (xxi, 32), a threatening word against the ruler of Judah, whose turban will be torn off, his crown thrown down, and his

---

[1] See Mowinckel in *Z.A.W.* xlv, 1927, pp. 30ff.

kingdom reduced to ruins 'until he comes whose right it is, and to whom I shall give it'. This passage probably alludes to the expected righteous scion of David (see above, pp. 160f.) as contrasted with the post-exilic governors and 'princes',[1] who ruled by the favour of the kings of Persia but found no favour in the eyes of the prophets of restoration. But it is also probable that Ezekiel here had in mind older prophecies about David, such as the familiar Shiloh passage (Gen. xlix, 10), and the prophecy about the 'star out of Jacob' in the lays of Balaam (see above, pp. 12f.), and interpreted them as prophecies about the coming scion of David in the age of restoration.[2]

In every point the descriptions of the future king correspond with the ideal of the royal psalms. The future king is more than an ordinary man. He has a *divine nature*. He can be called 'divine hero', and his ability as 'counsellor' (i.e., governor and ruler) is 'wonderful' (Isa. ix, 5). Just as the historical king can be regarded as the incarnation of his entire dynasty, so that men wish him everlasting life (see above, pp. 64, 69f), so, too, the newborn future king can have the promise of the honourable name, 'Father for ever' (Isa. ix, 5), the one who will for all time govern his people and his country as a father.

The source of this divine equipment is not a supernatural conception or birth, but the fact that '*the spirit of Yahweh rests upon him*'.[3] With it come all the royal virtues,

a spirit of wisdom and discernment,
a spirit of counsel and strength,
a spirit of knowledge and reverence for Yahweh (Isa. xi, 2).

This charismatic endowment (to use an expression from New Testament theology) of the future king is the source of all his powers. The gift of the spirit manifests itself in superhuman powers which are physical, intellectual, and moral.[4] To sum up, it may be said that the future king 'rules in the strength of Yahweh,

---

[1] See above, p. 18 n. 1.

[2] Cf. Genesis Rabbah 28, on Gen. xlix, 10: 'Shiloh is King Messiah.' See Weber, *Jüd. Theol.*[2], p. 356.

[3] Cf. Koch in *Biblica* xxvii, 1946, pp. 241ff.

[4] This is rightly emphasized by Staerk, *Soter* I, pp. 3f. But neither this feature nor the other which Staerk emphasizes in the same connexion (the intimate relation of the future king to God) gives any ground for the conclusion that the king '*therefore*' (!) has the characteristics which the myth attributes to the *Urmensch*, and 'is therefore, as the one who brings in paradise, himself the *Urmensch* returned'. See above, pp. 55, 81.

in the majesty of the name of Yahweh his God' (Mic. v, 3). His mere word and the breath of his lips suffice to slay the violent and the wicked (Isa. xi, 4).

Having this endowment, he can display superhuman, heroic strength as a warrior in *the defence of land and people* (Isa. ix, 5), for early Judaism did not think of the blissful age of restoration as free from the need of defence against foreign hostility and envy (Mic. v, 3f.). The thought occasionally occurs that it is this 'Messiah' who will break the yoke of the oppressors and set Israel free; at all events the promise of the birth of the royal child associates deliverance with the appearance of the wonder child, though even here it is Yahweh who has broken the yoke and the rod of the oppressor. This has already been achieved by Yahweh ideally in the birth of the child; and therefore the prophet already hears in spirit the rejoicing at the celebrations for the royal child, anticipating the celebration of victory on the day when the prophecy implicit in his birth is fulfilled.

As divine hero and victor, the king secures *peace* for his people. Alluding to the heavy boot of the Assyrian armies, the prophet promises that all the military equipment of the oppressor, the trampling boots of the soldiers and their bloodstained garments, will become fuel for the fire (Isa. ix, 4; see above, p. 104). The king 'will be peace' (Mic. v, 4). He is the 'prince of peace'; and one of the later prophets sees him ride into the city as a king of peace, upon the foal of an ass. Thus he secures peace for the future:

> He will banish the chariot from Ephraim
> and the war horse from Jerusalem;
> and the battle bow will be banished;
> and he will enjoin peace upon the nations
>   (Zech. ix, 10, reading the first word as *wᵉhikrît.*).

It is clear from the context, which says that the king will abolish war and the instruments of war from Israel, destroying war-lords by his power, that the ass on which he rides is not simply an animal of peace in contrast to a war-horse. The ass or mule is the royal mount of ancient times (see Judges v, 10; x, 4, etc.). There reappears here an ancient feature of the royal ideology, which was reflected in the cult in the early Canaanite period. In the ritual texts from Ugarit, the 'saving' king-god Dan'il, who brings the blessing of fertility and also justice for widows and orphans, comes mounted on a saddled ass.[1] Thus there is conscious archaism in the prophet's reference to the saviour king. The future king becomes the king of peace because he has power to banish war and war-lords.

But the 'peace' (*šālôm*) of which the prophet speaks here, comprises more than the mere prevention of war and victory over enemies. The word also includes all good fortune and well-being, safety and security, good order and morality in the nation, fellowship ('wholeness') and brotherhood, in short whatever may be described as material well-being and sound social and moral conditions. Again and again this external and internal well-being is described, when 'the Shoot of Yahweh will be beautiful and glorious, and the fruit of the land will be the pride and glory of the survivors in Israel' (Isa. iv, 2).[2]

> And in his days Judah will be saved,
> and Israel will dwell in security;
> and this is the name by which he will be called,
> 'Yahweh our Vindication' (Jer. xxiii, 6).

'Salvation', or rather 'width, spaciousness' (*yēša'*), here includes not only deliverance, preservation, and victory in war, but also every kind of well-being, good fortune, and ideal conditions. The words 'right' and 'righteousness' (*sedek*, *sᵉdākâh*) have the same suggestion of well-being, and of favourable internal and external conditions; and in the passage just quoted 'vindication' implies the 'right and good fortune' which are so often associated with the reign of the future king.[3] In short he will be a 'light' to his people, who have so long dwelt in deep gloom (Isa. ix, 1). This material blessing, which was conceived of in ancient Israel as the result of the blessing which was inherent in the king's person, is described in the book of Ezekiel (xxxiv, 23ff.): 'I will set one shepherd over them, my servant David, who shall feed them . . .; and I, Yahweh, will be their God . . . I will make a covenant of peace with them, banishing wild beasts from the land, so that they may live securely in the wilderness and sleep in the woods. And I will settle them round my own hill, blessing them with showers of rain at the right season. The trees of the field shall bear fruit; the earth shall bring

---

[1] See Engnell, *Divine Kingship*, p. 141, and references.
[2] With the conception of the king as 'the Shoot of Yahweh', cf. King Karit as the 'Shoot' of the god El; see above, p. 161 n. 1.
[3] Cf. Isa. ix, 5 (*šālôm*); xvi, 5; xxxii, 2; Jer. xvii, 25ff.; xxiii, 4–6; xxxiii, 15; Ezek. xvii, 23; xxxiv, 25ff.; xxxvii, 25ff.; Mic. v, 3f.; Zech. ix, 9.

forth its crops; and they shall be secure in their land. . . . And they shall no longer be a prey to the nations, nor shall the wild beasts of the land devour them; but they shall dwell securely, and none shall make them afraid.'

It may also be noted that on occasion it is explicitly emphasized that this good fortune will be the lot of the united Israel, the two kingdoms which once were one under David's sceptre (Ezek. xxxvii, 22; Jer. xxiii, 6).

The kingly rule of the future king, like David's, will extend over other distant and alien nations. Sometimes, like the psalmist, the prophet has a vision of a universal empire:

> His dominion will be from sea to sea,
> and from the River to the ends of the earth.[1]

This is the ancient phraseology which is actually derived from the Babylonian royal style: from the ocean in the east to the ocean in the west, on earth's circumference, and from the River (i.e., Euphrates) at its centre to all its farthest borders, encircling the world. From all nations they will come to do homage to the king, and to the God who has given him his power.[2] He will be the splendour and glory of his people, and an ensign for the peoples to which the nations will resort (Isa. iv, 2; xi, 10).

This is brought about not least by the renown of his righteous rule which brings good fortune. It is on this aspect of the work of the Messiah that the main emphasis is laid. In a word, his task in the future kingdom is to 'judge' Yahweh's people. That means defending them from any attack or encroachment, driving the enemy back when he ventures forth, and ruling the land with justice and righteousness for the good fortune and success of the people. It is perhaps, after all, this ethical aspect which is the most prominent feature in the picture of the future king. When it is stated that he re-establishes and lays the foundation of the Davidic kingdom 'with justice and righteousness' (Isa. ix, 6), the context shows that the main emphasis still falls on the victorious power (ṣeḏeḵ, righteousness) by which he wins for his people 'justice' and 'salvation'. But the ethical and social side of 'righteousness' is quite evident in the promise about the Shoot which comes forth from the stump of Jesse:

---

[1] Zech. ix, 10; cf. Ps. lxxii, 8. See also Isa. lv, 4; Ezek. xvii, 23; Amos ix, 12; Mic. v, 3.
[2] Isa. xi, 10; Ezek. xxxvii, 28; Mic. v, 3; cf. Isa. xlv, 22ff.; xlviii, 9, 11; ii, 2f.

He will not judge by what his eyes see,
nor decide by what his ears hear,
but he will judge the needy with righteousness,
and decide with equity for the poor in the land.
He will smite the violent with the rod of his mouth;
and with the breath of his lips he will slay the wicked.
Righteousness will be the girdle of his loins,
and faithfulness the girdle of his waist
(Isa. xi, 3–5, reading *'ārīṣ* for *'ereṣ* in *v.* 4).

This appears again and again.[1] The righteousness of the future kings as 'good shepherds' is contrasted with the injustice and misrule of the historical kings (Jer. xxiii, 4). Tradition puts into Jeremiah's mouth a saying which manifestly alludes to the pitiful last king of Judah (Zedekiah, 'Yahweh is my vindication'), and prophesies the name which the future king will win by his righteous and auspicious rule, *Yahweh ṣidḵēnû*, 'Yahweh our Vindication' (Jer. xxiii, 4ff.).

Accordingly his rule will also result in a *moral revival* in the land. The same passage in Jeremiah says that in virtue of his divine endowment he will 'deal wisely and gain his end' (*hiśkîl*, Jer. xxiii, 5): every man in his appropriate station will do his duty and be a blessing to the whole community (Isa. xxxii, 3–8). But this is only one aspect of the *religious revival* which will come about when Yahweh again makes a 'covenant of peace', an 'everlasting covenant', with them, when He becomes their God, and 'David' their king and the people walk in Yahweh's laws and observe His statutes.[2] This religious aspect of conditions in the future kingdom is emphasized in the Ezekiel passage from which the above phraseology is taken (Ezek. xxxvii, 24ff.): '. . . I will set my sanctuary among them for evermore. My dwelling place shall be with them; and I will be their God, and they shall be my people. And the nations shall know that I, Yahweh, sanctify Israel.'

Then the godly and righteous king of Israel's own dynasty will be the true and legitimate priest, the mediator between the people and God; and the covenant made at Sinai will again become a reality.[3] In the promise to Jacob in Jer. xxx, 21f., the prophet (not Jeremiah, but a post-exilic prophet) says:

---

[1] See Isa. ix, 6; xvi, 5; xxxii, 1; Jer. xxiii, 4f.; xxxiii, 15; Ezek. xxxiv, 22f.; Zech. ix, 9.
[2] Ezek. xxxvii, 24; cf. also Jer. xxiii, 6; xxx, 9, 21f.; xxxiii, 16.
[3] Jer. xxx, 21f. See above, p. 165 and n. 1.

> Their prince shall be one of themselves;
>   their ruler shall come from among them.
> I will grant him access, and he shall approach me . . .
>   And you shall be my people (as of old),
>   and I will (again) be your God.

Here we find a close connexion between the priestly function of the king and the establishment of the new covenant. The words about Israel being Yahweh's people and Yahweh their God were commonly used in the earlier parts of the Old Testament to express what was implied in election and covenant. The point of the passage is that when a covenant has again been made between Yahweh and Israel in the age of restoration, it will function normally, because the people will again have a legitimate king of their own dynasty (in contrast with the foreign rulers of the present) a king whom Yahweh will permit to approach Him in order to perform the priestly service as mediator, as leader in the cult, as intercessor, as one who transmits blessings, and, in all probability, revelations. How important this thought was for Judaism can be seen from an addition, made in the text as transmitted, to the saying about the part played by the future king as priestly mediator, emphasizing that no ordinary man could dare to undertake it.[1] When Israel once again has such a mediator to offer expiation, then no more wrong or injustice will be committed, for 'the land will be full of the knowledge of Yahweh' (Isa. xi, 9; see above, p. 137).

We find here an important feature in the equipment of the future king, his *knowledge of God, da‘aṭ ’elōhîm*. This simply means that he lives constantly in personal fellowship with God, deriving all his power, his aims, and the very nature of his being from this fellowship.[2] In the prophecy just quoted, this 'knowledge of God', which is at once the sum and the source of all else, shows that the picture of the future king was supremely influenced by the spirit of the great prophets. The knowledge of God, immediate union with Him, and acquaintance with His nature and will, together with the willingness to conform to His will and to express it in act, is the source of every virtue and blessing: it is the true crown of the future king.

It is from prophecy that this feature in the picture of the Messiah is derived, and not, as has been maintained, from any

[1] Jer. xxx, 21; see Mowinckel in *G.T.M.M.M.* III, p. 392.
[2] See Mowinckel, *Die Erkenntnis Gottes*, pp. 6ff.

mythical conception of the *Urmensch*, or from ancient ideas about sacral kingship.[1] This is a fact, even if the prophetic emphasis on the knowledge of God as a fundamental royal virtue may have had links with earlier ideas about the king as the possessor of 'sacral knowledge of God', i.e., as custodian of the sacral and ritual oracle. The king is also required to know Yahweh; but in the oriental conception of the king more emphasis is laid on the deity's knowledge (i.e., choice) of the king. In Israel the knowledge of Yahweh was increasingly regarded as the special function of the priest and the prophet, particularly the prophet.[2] It was the prophets who advanced the knowledge of God as *the* essential demand on the king, the nation, and each individual in the nation;[3] and from the prophets it was taken over as a fundamental feature in the picture of the future king.

7. *Mythical Elements in the Conception of the King*

What has just been said does not, of course, mean that there are no mythical elements in early Judaism's conception of the future king; nor does it imply any depreciatory estimate of the mythical, as if Old Testament ideas had to be protected from mythical elements. The thought and language of the Old Testament (and of religion generally) are unthinkable apart from the thought and language of myth. Throughout the ancient east the conception of the king and the royal ideology were mythical. Mythical elements in the conception of the future king are to be expected as the natural way of expressing his divine equipment and power. What is superhuman can usually only be spoken of in the metaphorical picture-language of myth.

Accordingly, it goes without saying that all the mythical features, which in earlier times belonged to the conception of the king, were transferred to the Messiah (the future king), and in a measure became even more prominent, coming to life again, as it were, as the future king receded farther from prosaic everyday reality. The superhuman, miraculous, divine aspect then became more prominent than in the sacral, earthly ruler.

This is shown, for instance, by the fact that the prophet deliberately uses material from the ancient myths in depicting the future king. But as a rule this applies not to new features but to ancient conceptions which were formerly associated with the conception

---

[1] Against Staerk, *Soter* I, p. 3.   [2] See Mowinckel, *Die Erkenntnis Gottes*, pp. 9ff.
[3] Op. cit., pp. 8, 35ff.

of the king. We merely refer here to a few prophetic sayings which show the influence of the myth about paradise and the primordial age, and the myth about the miraculous birth of the divine child.

The thought of *paradisal conditions* and *peace among animals* occurs in the passage in Isaiah which immediately precedes the passage quoted above:

> The wolf will dwell with the lamb;
> and the leopard will lie down with the kid;
> the calf and the young lion will graze together;
> and a little child will lead them.
> The cow and the bear will be friends;
> their young will lie down together.
> The sucking child will play happily
> over the hole of the asp,
> and on the viper's den
> the weaned child will put his hand (Isa. xi, 6–8).[1]

The idea underlying this description appears to be that the ideal king corresponds to the king of paradise in the old myths, even though no such myth of the king of paradise occurs elsewhere in the Old Testament. When the true king comes, paradise is restored. Admittedly it is not stated in so many words that the king is thought of as the *Urmensch*; but it is not unlikely that we have evidence here that the royal ideology was sometimes influenced by the conception of the king of paradise or *Urmensch*.[2] Naturally the fact of such influence does not in any way indicate the origin of the ideal of kingship.

In such promises about the ideal king, we also find the thought of the king's *divine character*, and ancient expressions for this idea. Among the names which are applied to the royal child in Isa. ix is *'aḇî 'aḏ*, usually rendered 'Everlasting Father'.[3] This naturally recalls the ancient Canaanite title of the supreme god El, 'Father of Years' (*'ab šnm*),[4] and the Egyptian title of the creator god Ptah, 'Lord of Years', 'Lord of Eternity'.[5] The same idea undoubtedly lies behind all these expressions. The fact that 'per-

---

[1] Reading *yir'û* for *ûmᵉrî* in *v.* 6, *tiṭrā'ênâh* for *tir'ênâh* in *v.* 7, and omitting *wᵉ'aryeh kabbāḵār yōʾḵal teḇen* as a gloss in *v.* 7.

[2] See above, pp. 55, 81; cf. below, pp. 186, 383.

[3] Literally, 'father of perpetuity', commonly taken as an attributive genitive.

[4] A I 8; B IV 24; see H. Bauer in *Z.A.W.* li, 1933, p. 82 (cf. liii, 1935, pp. 54ff.). The translation 'Father of Years' is not undisputed; see Eissfeldt, *El im ugaritischen Pantheon*, p. 30 n. 4.

[5] See Frankfort, *Kingship*, p. 32.

petuity' is here synonymous with 'years' shows that what is meant is not our abstract, timeless conception of 'eternity', but that '*ad*, like the usual word '*ōlām*, here means 'time' with all its content, everything that happens in it from the very beginning on into the unfathomable future.[1] The creator God is lord and author of all that happens during this endless time. The prophet confers the same title of honour on the royal child. As king he will prove to be the beneficent lord and author of the age of bliss and its glorious progress. It is a title which really belongs to the god who regains and exercises dominion over the world. When applied to the king, it is obviously used in a modified sense. The meaning of the expression can perhaps best be rendered 'continual providence'; and naturally it is only on behalf of Yahweh and by His power that the king can be such a 'providence' (cf. above, pp. 106f.).

There are also other passages in which the thought of the fertility of paradise and peace among the animals has influenced descriptions of the future king's rule.[2]

In the conception of the Messiah, other mythical elements appear. When the saying in Isa. ix, 1–6 is interpreted of the future king, the conception of *the birth of the new sun god and life god*, and of his victorious invasion of Hades in order to raise the dead to life, is made to reflect the contemporary situation as an expression of the future king's saving work.

The Messianic interpretation of the *Immanuel prophecy* also brought a new influx of mythical features from the ancient royal ideology. The disciples of Isaiah who collected and arranged the tradition[3] of Isaiah's sayings from the period of the Syro-Ephraimite war[4] had already taken the Immanuel prophecy to apply to the wonderful king of the future. By placing the promise about the royal child of David's line immediately after Isaiah's sayings in this period,[5] they intended to bring out a connexion between the two prophecies: in the birth of the royal child they saw the fulfilment of the Immanuel prophecy. Thus 'Immanuel' is no longer merely a sign; and the emphasis is no longer on his birth, where

[1] On the Hebrew conception of eternity and time see Pedersen, *Israel* I–II, pp. 487ff.; cf. above, pp. 105f.

[2] Ezek. xxxiv, 25f.; cf. Amos ix, 13, and below, pp. 270, 276; cf. 383.

[3] On the collection and transmission of the prophetic sayings by the prophets' disciples, see Mowinckel in *N.T.T.* xliii, 1942; cf. *Z.A.W.* xlix, 1931, pp. 244f.; Birkeland, *Zum hebräischen Traditionswesen*.

[4] On Isaiah's 'testimony' in vi, 1–ix, 6, see Budde, *Jesajas Erleben: Eine gemeinverständliche Auslegung der Denkschrift des Propheten (Kap. 6, 1–9.6)*: Mowinckel in *G.T.M.M.M.* III, pp. 64ff.

[5] Isaiah's own conclusion to the collection is viii, 16–19, 20b–23a.

Isaiah had laid it. He becomes the future king, who one day will come and reign in the restored kingdom, and may also be Yahweh's instrument in delivering Israel from her enemies and establishing the kingdom, as in the prophecy about the birth of the child in Isa. ix, 1–6. 'The young woman', too, returns to the supernatural world of myth to which she originally belonged. The note of mystery in the prophecy may have contributed to this interpretation. It is therefore extremely likely that the later disciples of Isaiah, who were responsible for the tradition, also thought of the child's birth as more or less similar to the various mythical accounts of wonderful divine princes, with which they were to some extent familiar. The Old Testament itself knows of wonderful births brought about by the miraculous power of Yahweh. There are, for instance, several narratives about barren or aged women having children through Yahweh's miraculous power, contrary to all expectation or natural probability: Sarah, Hannah, Manoah's wife, and Elisabeth.[1] Manoah's wife's son, Samson, is explicitly said to have been a holy person 'consecrated to God', a *nāzîr* from his mother's womb, from his very conception (Judges xiii, 5); and when we are told that 'Yahweh's spirit began to stir him up' in his early youth (Judges xiii, 25), it may be that the narrators thought that he was a holy man because of an endowment with the spirit received when he was still in the womb. In Jewish thought it was Yahweh's *rûaḥ*, His spirit or breath, which was the instrument in His creative work, by which the changing generations on earth were brought forth and given life (cf. Ps. civ, 30). The note of mystery in the Immanuel prophecy, and the fact that it is the mother and not the father that is mentioned, could, and almost certainly would, suggest the idea that this scion of David came into existence as a result of a specially wonderful exercise of Yahweh's own power, at least as wonderful as the birth of Isaac, Samuel, or Samson.

The prophecy about the ruler from Bethlehem in Mic. v, 1–3 (in which there is also an allusion to the king's 'rising' like the sun) also seems to suggest that the future king would come into existence in a wonderful way. When it is emphasized that

> his rising is from of old,
> from ancient days <his going forth>,[2]

---

[1] Gen. xviii; 1 Sam. i; Judges xiii, 2ff.; Luke i.

[2] Supplying, *metri causa*, some expression parallel to *môṣā'ōṭāw*; see *G.T.M.M.M.* III, pp. 686, 821.

the meaning is probably that in him the ancestor is, as it were, recreated in a wonderful way. He brings to fulfilment what the dynasty was in its origin (in ancient eastern thought anything was seen at its truest and best in its origin). The nation's misfortune, it is said, will last only until this scion of David is born:

> Therefore He will give them up till the time
> when she who is in travail brings forth.

But then Yahweh brings the exile and dispersion to an end, allows the king's dispersed brethren to return, and establishes the glorious kingdom in which the one who is born will rule by the power of Yahweh. Again it is the mother, 'she who is in travail', that is mentioned, and not the father; and again it is the child's birth, and not any work of deliverance performed by him, that is in itself the decisive turning point in the fortunes of the people. There can hardly be any doubt that the prophet is here referring to ideas similar to those which lie behind both the Immanuel prophecy and, in a measure, Isa. ix, 1–6. But here they have clearly been transferred to the 'Messiah' in order to bring out the miraculous element in his person and the fact that a new era is inaugurated by his very birth. It is not impossible, as has been maintained, that in Mic. v, 1–3 the prophet bases his message directly on a 'Messianic' interpretation of Isa. vii.

The fact that the Greek-speaking Jews of Alexandria rendered *hā-ʿalmâh*, 'the young woman' in the Immanuel prophecy, by ἡ παρθένος, 'the virgin', shows that they, too, were aware of the mythical ideas from which Isaiah had derived his sign, and that they went further in emphasizing the miraculous character of the birth of Immanuel, regarded as the future king. When Isaiah spoke of 'the woman' who would bear a son, he did not himself consciously think of her as a virgin; but later on, when this idea was read into his words, it was in accord with the original ideas about 'the young woman's' son.[1] The interpretation in the Septuagint is ultimately derived from 'the virgin Anath'. This means that the ideas here presented to us were probably known outside the Hellenistic milieu. So far as we can see, the Palestinian Jews were also familiar with them, even if rabbinical orthodoxy later pushed them into the background.

[1] This was maintained by Kittel in *Die hellenistischen Mysterienreligion und das Alte Testament*, pp. 13ff. While Kittel naturally thinks of a Hellenistic milieu for these ideas, their pre-Israelite, Canaanite origin has now been proved by the Ras Shamra discoveries.

It is impossible to tell how widespread was this form of the idea of the wonderful nature and origin of the future king. But it agrees substantially with the ancient Israelite conception of the king as Yahweh's son. The 'Messiah' is no less wonderful or divine than the king, the anointed son of Yahweh.

But on the other hand it is a mistake to exaggerate the mythical elements in the figure of the Messiah in the Old Testament, as the religio-historical school often did. Attention has been drawn above to some results of this tendency;[1] and there are probably good grounds for emphasizing that within the Old Testament there is nothing to indicate that the concept of the Messiah originated in ideas about the mythical *Urmensch* and his return as an eschatological saviour.[2] Neither the charismatic wisdom of the future king in Isa. xi, 1–9, nor his 'rising from of old' in Mic. v, 1ff. provides any support for such a theory. In the tradition of the ancient east others besides the *Urmensch* are regarded as wise (moreover, 'wisdom' is only one of the charismatic spiritual gifts of the king in Isa. xi, 1ff.); and the passage in Micah does not speak of the origin of the king as an individual, but of the origin of the dynasty in remote antiquity, in the time of Jesse, and not before creation, as it ought to have been if the reference had been to the *Urmensch*.

The relationship of the myth of the *Urmensch* to the Messiah of later Judaism is another question, to which we must return below (ch. X, 19).

---

[1] See above, pp. 80, 81f., 84ff., 159, 162.

[2] This is one of the main contentions in Staerk's *Soter*, and one of the presuppositions of his further theories. See also p. 181, above. Bentzen also goes beyond what is probable in the light of the sources when he assumes that originally the idea of the *Urmensch* was associated with the Messiah and the royal ideology. See *Det sakrale kongedømme*, pp. 116f.; *S.E.Å.* xii, 1947, pp. 43ff.

CHAPTER VII

The Servant of the Lord

FROM the very beginning of the Christian era the prophecies in Deutero-Isaiah about the special Servant of Yahweh (*'ebed YHWH*) have been applied to Jesus Christ;[1] and we must therefore define our attitude to them. From the historical point of view the question is not, Do these prophecies refer to Jesus of Nazareth? but rather, Are they intended to be Messianic in the sense which the word has in the Old Testament and in Judaism? Their relationship to Jesus is another question, which cannot be considered until the first has been answered.

It may be said at once that these prophecies were not intended to be Messianic, but that Jesus gave them decisive importance for the concept of the Messiah. How this came about the present chapter will show.[2]

1. *The Servant Songs*

These poems consist of four passages, which contemporary opinion almost unanimously distinguishes from the rest of Deutero-Isaiah, as follows: Isa. xlii, 1–4; xlix, 1–6; l, 4–11; lii, 13–liii, 12.[3]

[1] Direct quotations in the New Testament: Matt. viii, 17; Luke xxii, 37; John xii, 38; Acts viii, 32f.; Rom. xv, 21; 1 Pet. ii, 22. Allusions and applications: Mark ix, 12; Acts ii, 33; Rom. v, 19; Phil. ii, 7, 9; 1 Pet. ii, 24f. For further detail, see H. S. Nyberg in *S.E.A.* vii, 1942, pp. 12f.; and for interpretation in the early Church, see Wolff, *Jesaja 53 im Urchristentum. Die Geschichte der Prophetie 'Siehe es siegt mein Knecht' bis zu Justin.*

[2] Surveys of the various interpretations of the Servant through the ages are given, e.g., by Cornill in *T.R.* iii, 1900, pp. 409ff.; Lindhagen in *S.T.K.* viii, 1932, pp. 350ff.; Mowinckel in *Act.Or.* xvi, 1938, pp. 1ff.; Eissfeldt in *T.L.Z.* lxviii, 1943, cols. 273ff.; Volz, *Jesaja* II, p. 188 (where Dietze is not mentioned among the advocates of the Uzziah theory); and now, above all, by C. R. North in *The Suffering Servant* and in his supplementary survey in *S.J.T.* iii, 1950, pp. 363ff. Reference may also be made to Coppens, *Nieuw licht over de Ebed-Yahweh-Liedern*, and Rowley in *O.T.S.* viii, 1950, pp. 110ff. = *The Servant of the Lord*, pp. 59ff.

[3] Other delimitations of the passages, and the interpretation of additional passages as Servant Songs (see, e.g., Gressmann, *Der Messias*, pp. 287ff.; Fischer, *Isaias 40–55 und die Perikopen vom Gottesknecht*, p. 287; Rudolph in *Z.A.W.* xliii, 1925; p. 91; cf. also *Z.A.W.* xlvi, 1928, pp. 156ff.) are the result of faulty exegesis and inadequate attention to formal and stylistic factors; see Mowinckel in *Z.A.W.* xlix, 1931, pp. 93ff. and in *D.T.T.* ix, 1946, pp. 150ff., 160ff. Against Bentzen's interpretation of li, 9–16 as a

It was Duhm in his commentary on Isaiah (cf. *Die Theologie der Propheten*, pp. 287ff.) who first recognized that these passages (and possibly some others) form a separate group within the collection of Deutero-Isaiah's sayings which came into being in the circle of his disciples;[1] and this is now almost universally accepted by Old Testament scholars.[2] However the Servant may be interpreted, there is general agreement that the Songs speak of a special Servant of Yahweh, or of the Servant Israel, regarded from a definitely individual point of view and in the light of his call, which in several ways distinguishes this picture of him from the usual conception of the servant Israel in Deutero-Isaiah.

To discuss this at greater length would take us too far. I take it for granted that these four poems form a special group, that they treat of the same figure, the Servant, uniformly conceived, and that they must be interpreted in their own light and in relation to each other, without any preconceived theory of their relation to the other sayings in the Deutero-Isaianic collection. Our present concern is the content of the passages, not the literary problems of authorship and date. Whether they come from Deutero-Isaiah himself or the circle of his disciples (to which the so-called Trito-Isaianic sayings in Isa. lvi–lxvi bear witness) is a matter of subordinate interest. The point is that they cannot simply be interpreted in terms of what 'the servant of Yahweh' means elsewhere in Deutero-Isaiah, but must be considered independently.

It is therefore a matter of no moment whether the Servant Songs come from Deutero-Isaiah (i.e., the unknown prophet be-

---

[1] See Mowinckel in *Z.A.W.* xlix, 1931, pp. 87ff., 242ff.

[2] Recent exceptions are Caspari, Kissane, and Sidney Smith. Caspari (*Lieder und Gottesprüche der Rückwanderer (Jesaja 40–55)*) discards any sort of unity in the conception, and holds that the Servant in Deutero-Isaiah denotes Israel in the most varied relations to Yahweh; there exists no separate group of passages about the Servant of the Lord in a special sense (cf. Mowinckel in *Act.Or.* xvi, 1938, pp. 31f.). Kissane (*The Book of Isaiah* I–II) links each individual Servant passage with its present immediate context, and so arrives at varying interpretations of the Servant in the different Songs: Israel in xlii and xlix; the prophet himself in l, 4ff.; the Messiah in liii—the last of which at least can claim no support from the context. S. Smith (*Isaiah Chapters XL–LV: Literary Criticism and History*) holds that 'the Servant' probably refers to an individual, but that it need not be the same person in every passage: in xlix, 1–6 and l, 4ff. the prophet speaks of himself; probably liii also refers to the prophet himself, but if so must come

---

Servant Song, see Mowinckel in *Z.A.W.* xlix, 1931, pp. 108f., 255; *D.T.T.* ix, 1946, pp. 164f.; *G.T.M.M.M.* III, pp. 241f. Stevenson (in *Exp.*, 8th Series, vi, 1913, pp. 209ff.) would interpret li, 4–6 as a Servant Song; but the speaker there is unquestionably Yahweh ('*My* righteousness', '*My* salvation'). Stevenson is right in finding close connexions with the Servant Songs in thought and expression; but what the passage shows is that the Servant Songs are 'dependent' on Deutero-Isaiah and attribute to the Servant tasks which Deutero-Isaiah attributed to Yahweh Himself. See further North's summing up in *The Suffering Servant*, pp. 127ff.

hind the sayings in Isa. xl–lv) or from another prophet, e.g., a member of the circle of Deutero-Isaiah's disciples. For the intuitive vision which dawns on the prophet's inward eye conveys a conception of this special Servant which is different from Israel regarded as 'Yahweh's servant' or 'the servant', and from Cyrus when the title is applied to him too.

First we summarize the content of the Servant Songs.

First Song

Behold, My Servant whom I uphold,
  My chosen in whom I delight!
I have put My spirit upon him;
  right religion will he bring forth to the nations.
He does not cry, or lift up his voice,
  or make his voice heard in the street;
a bruised reed he does not break,
  and the dimly burning wick he does not quench.
He brings forth right religion as truth requires,[1]
  not burning dimly, or being bruised,
until he has established right religion in the earth;
  and for his instruction the far coasts wait (xlii, 1–4).[2]

---

[1] Literally, 'in accordance with truth'; see Sidney Smith, op. cit., p. 164. Begrich's interpretation (*Studien zu Deuterojesaja*, p. 163), 'he announces the (judicial) sentence as truth', is impossible, since *mišpāṭ* does not here mean 'sentence' but 'right religion'; cf. p. 219 n. 4 below.

[2] Many include xlii, 5–7 in the first Servant Song; but both stylistic and exegetical arguments tell against this; see North, *The Suffering Servant*, pp. 131ff. The passage was originally addressed to Cyrus; see Haller in *Eucharisterion* I, pp. 262f.; Mowinckel in *G.T.M.M.M.* III, ad loc. But it has an indirect relevance, since the figure of the Servant is consciously drawn as a fulfilment of those expectations which Cyrus did not satisfy; see Hempel in *Z.S.T.* vii, 1929, pp. 631ff.; cf. also Mowinckel in *Z.A.W.* xlix, 1931, p. 94 n. 4. Barnes also recognized that xlii, 5–7 was about Cyrus (*J.T.S.* xxxii, 1931, pp. 32ff.; cf. *J.B.L.* xlvii, 1929, pp. 133ff.); but he held that xlii, 1–4 could also be interpreted of Cyrus in the light of the 'context'; similarly Sidney Smith, op. cit., pp. 54ff. But there is no 'context', in this sense, linking the individual sayings (see Mowinckel in *Z.A.W.* xlix, 1931, pp. 87ff.); and the contrast between the call of the Servant in *vv.* 1–4 and what is said of Cyrus elsewhere is clear enough. The 'definitely liturgic-formal context' of which Engnell (*B.J.R.L.* xxxi, 1, 1948, p. 14) finds that xlii, 1ff. forms a part, and which, on his view, appears to consist of xl–xlvi, is merely postulated, not proved. Engnell's argument is as superficial as the attempts of earlier exegetes to find connexions within and between the chapters in the prophetic books,

---

from another hand; xlii, 1–4, like xliii, 5–9, relates to Cyrus. Caspari's view is the result of reading far too much into varying shades of meaning, and of a logical, modern approach which fails to appreciate the complex character of Hebrew concepts. Kissane's method represents a neglect of the understanding which has been gained in recent years of the detached character of the individual prophetic words, and of the composition of the prophetic books, and is a return to out-of-date literary theories; cf. Mowinckel in *N.T.T.* xliii, 1942, p. 65, and *D.T.T.* ix, 1946, pp. 142ff. Smith's view is best described as a variation of the so-called autobiographical interpretation first advanced by the present writer (cf. below, p. 248 and n. 3).

In this first poem Yahweh is the speaker. In form it is an oracle in which a prophet receives his call, a direct word from Yahweh in which the prophet is told of his call and of the character of his special task. The style and structure of such an oracle are an imitation of the royal initiation oracle by which a king is called, as in Pss. ii and cx, and in the sequel to the present passage (xlii, 5–9), the oracle in which Cyrus is called.[1] Yahweh presents the person concerned to the people, and speaks of his endowment with the spirit, and his task to bring forth 'right religion to the nations'. Here *mišpāṭ* is not something which is 'announced' (so North). The verb *yôṣî'* indicates the *establishing* of something; and *mišpāṭ* here means 'right religion' (as is shown by the parallelism with *tôrâh*, 'instruction', i.e., in the right way, the laws of God), the knowledge of what God requires, and so also the good fortune and ideal conditions which will result when God's will is obeyed. In this passage 'truth' (*'emeṯ*) is practically synonymous with 'right religion'. It is Yahweh's truth, which can be trusted, and which is shown to be true when it is fulfilled.[2] The task is universal. The right religion is to be established in the earth among the nations; and the whole world ('the far coasts') is already actually waiting for his preaching about God's way. The mention of his task and equipment leads also to a fuller account of the way in which he works, and so of his character. In contrast with the ecstatic popular prophets, he does not appear in the streets and the market place, crying and shouting; nor does he announce

---

[1] See Mowinckel in *Edda* xxvi, 1926, p. 257; *Ps.St.* III, pp. 78ff.; Bentzen, *Jahves Tjener*, pp. 11, 21f.; *Jesaja fortolket* II, p. 32; *King and Messiah*, pp. 49f. Naturally this stylistic connexion between the royal initiation oracle and the oracle of the prophet's call does not prove that the poet thought of the Servant as a king, as Engnell holds (*B.J.R.L.* xxxi, 1, 1948, pp. 14f.). The oracle in which Jeremiah is called also falls into the same stylistic tradition; but that does not mean that he claims royal status. On the Servant and the royal ideology, see below, pp. 219ff.

[2] Cf. Pedersen, *Israel* I–II, pp. 337ff. The word *mišpāṭ* is rightly explained by Hertzberg in *Z.A.W.* xl, 1922, pp. 256ff.; xli, 1923, pp. 16ff.; see xli, p. 41 n. 1. North (*The Suffering Servant*, pp. 140f.) would probably have been less sceptical if he had studied Pedersen more closely.

---

and does not come to grips with the real problems; nor does it go beyond pointing out the association of certain catchwords and connexions in phraseology. There is equal justification for demonstrating 'connexions' between individual psalms in the Psalter. Bentzen (*St.Th.* I, 1947, p. 184) has not fully understood Gyllenberg (see p. 143 n. 1), when he there interprets his statements, 'that the Deutero-Isaiah book is an imitation of a liturgy for the New Year Festival'. Gyllenberg is speaking, not of the 'book', but of the ideas contained in it. Engnell, too (*B.J.R.L.* xxxi, 1, 1948, pp. 5f.), regards the Servant of Yahweh texts as '*a prophetic re-modelling* of a liturgical composition belonging to the Annual Festival', dealing with the cultic suffering, death, and resurrection of Tammuz.

doom and destruction, but glad tidings which make the bruised
reed rise again, and bring the dimly burning wick into flame.

Second Song

Hearken, ye far coasts, to me;
 and give heed, ye peoples, from afar!
Yahweh has called me from the womb;
 from my birth He has made mention of my name.

He made my mouth like a sharp sword;
 in the shadow of His hand He hid me.
He made me a polished arrow;
 in His quiver He concealed me.

And He said to me, 'You are My Servant,[1]
 by whom I will get myself glory.'
And I was honoured in the eyes of Yahweh;
 and my God Himself became my strength.[2]

But I said, 'In vain have I laboured;
 for nought and vanity have I spent my strength.
Yet surely my cause is with Yahweh;
 my recompense is with my God.'

And now, thus says Yahweh,
 who formed me from the womb to be His Servant,
to bring back Jacob unto Him,
 and that Israel to Him should be gathered:

'Too light is it that you should be My Servant,
 to raise up the tribes of Jacob;[3]
I will make you a light to the nations,
 that My salvation may reach to the end of the earth'
        (xlix, 1–6.).[4]

---

[1] See Additional Note XI.

[2] *V.* 5b is here transferred to follow *v.* 3. In its traditional position 5b is in any case
parenthetical, and breaks the connexion between the introduction of Yahweh as the
speaker in 5a, with the accompanying explanation of why He created the Servant,
and 6, which contains Yahweh's words extending the scope of the call. The statement
that the Servant was honoured by Yahweh and endowed with His power is in substance
connected with the reference to the call and to Yahweh's intention to get Himself
glory by the Servant. If 5b is transferred to follow 3, the whole passage falls into
regular and logical strophes of two full lines each.

[3] *V.* 6a is too long for a normal full line, and as the text stands has three members;
whereas the other full lines have two members. We can either regard the words 'that
you should be My Servant' as an explanatory addition, or take 6aβ, 'and to bring
back the preserved in Israel', as a variant of the preceding member. 6aβ is omitted
above.

[4] On the delimitation of the poem, see p. 187 n. 3; cf. Mowinckel in *Z.A.W.* xlix,
1931, p. 104 n. 2 (cf. also p. 246), refuting Gressmann, Fischer, and Rudolph, who

Here the Servant is the speaker; and he is addressing the whole world. He tells of his election from birth and of his prophetic equipment. He says that there was a time before he appeared as a prophet, a time when he was only held in readiness by the Lord, like a sword in the scabbard, or an arrow in the quiver, until (probably through a special prophetic experience) he received the explicit call to appear to Israel as 'the Servant'. Thus there came to him the clear consciousness of the purpose of his whole life. The call he received (as we are told below) was 'to bring back Jacob unto Him (Yahweh), and that Israel to Him should be gathered' and 'to raise up the tribes of Jacob'. If we consider this in the light of what is said in the first poem about his equipment and his manner of working, it is clear that there is no allusion here to any political or military activity. The words do not refer to any new Exodus; and the Servant is not thought of as a new Moses.[1] It is by his prophetic word that he will act; and the bringing back of Jacob to Yahweh means primarily that the Jews will be converted to Yahweh. But the words about gathering in the dispersed suggest that this will lead in due course to the restoration of the nation Israel, when it will be gathered together again in the homeland. The text does not suggest that the Servant himself is thought of as leading those who return. In speaking of his call the Servant mentions the support and strength which the Lord has given him in his work. But he also tells that at last the work seemed to him to be in vain, so that he was near to despair, and had to set all his hopes of success, of his 'cause', on the Lord alone. This has brought him to what is the main point in this passage, the answer which the Lord has given to his complaint and prayer. The Lord will entrust him with a still greater and more glorious mission. It is too limited an aim merely to convert Israel and bring her back to the Lord, thereby gathering together the dispersed people and raising up the tribes of Jacob. The Lord will make him a bearer of light, a preacher of true religion, and so a mediator of salvation for all peoples, that the whole world may share in the salvation.

[1] As Sellin once held; see *Mose und seine Bedeutung für die israelitisch-jüdische Religionsgeschichte*, pp. 77f. The idea reappears in Bentzen (*Jesaja fortolket* II, pp. 81f.) in connexion with a different interpretation of the Servant.

---

include in the passage *vv.* 7–9 or 7–9a. Staerk (*Z.A.W.* xliv, 1926, pp. 245ff.) is also opposed to this delimitation, but for other reasons. Bentzen (*Jesaja fortolket* II, pp. 82–84) interprets xlix, 7–13 also as a Servant poem which is formally independent, but is nevertheless connected with xlix, 1–6; against this, see Mowinckel in *D.T.T.* ix, 1946, pp. 154, 160f.

Thus this Song looks back and reflects upon the Servant's first call to be a prophet (which is more directly described in the first poem) and upon his work, and goes on to record the actual words of the new call. The fact that the prophet himself proclaims it in words like 'thus said Yahweh to me' may be compared with the account of the royal initiation oracle in Ps. ii and the accounts given by the prophets of the oracles by which they were called. The announcement of a new oracle about the call and its aim, as an answer to the prophet's complaint about difficulties in fulfilling the call, has its nearest model in Jeremiah's complaints about persecution and difficulties, and in the answers which Yahweh gives him.

Just as these passages in Jeremiah have their formal models in the psalms of lamentation with the answering oracles sung at the sacrifice of purification for sick, persecuted, or other afflicted persons, so this Servant Song is modelled on the psalms of thanksgiving sung when the thank-offering was made by one saved from distress and danger. The person who had been delivered would tell of his afflictions, his lamentations, and his prayers to Yahweh for help. The fact that the help is here referred to as a promise by Yahweh, and not described in a narrative about His direct intervention, accords with the style of the psalms of lamentation rather than with that of the psalms of thanksgiving.

Third Song

My Lord Yahweh has given me the tongue of a disciple,
    that I should give strength to the weary;
My Lord Yahweh has opened my ear,
    that I should know how to speak the (right) words;
He wakens my ear morning by morning,
    to listen as disciples do.[1]

And I was not rebellious,
    nor turned away backward.

---

[1] The poem clearly has six strophes each consisting of three full lines. As the text stands the first strophe is in disorder. 'My Lord Yahweh has opened my ear' (perfect), referring to the original and decisive act, stands now as *v.* 5aα in contrast with the imperfect (present) in 'He wakens my ear morning by morning', etc. But this is an unnatural and clumsy sequel to *v.* 4, and is not logically connected with what follows in *v.* 5. The three infinitives *lāḏaʻaṯ, lāʻûṯ,* and *lišmōaʻ* are clearly meant to be independent, co-ordinated expressions of purpose each related to one of the three narrative principal clauses in *vv.* 4, 5aα, whereas in M.T. *lāḏaʻaṯ* stands as subordinate to *lāʻûṯ* and defining it more exactly, and *dāḇār* has to be translated irregularly as if it were *bᵉḏāḇār,* 'with a word'. Above, *dāḇār* has been transposed to follow *lāḏaʻaṯ* as object, *v.* 5aα is transposed to follow *dāḇār.* The superfluous *yāʻîr* is omitted (following Volz).

I gave my back to the smiters,
   and my cheeks to those that plucked out (the beard);
my face I did not hide
   from insult and spitting.

For my Lord Yahweh Himself will help me;
   therefore I shall not be put to shame;
therefore have I set my face like a flint,
   and I know that I shall not be ashamed.
Near is my Vindicator;
   who can gain a verdict against me?[1]

Who will take proceedings against me?
   Let us stand up together (in court)!
Who would be my adversary?
   Let him come near unto me!
Lo, they shall all wear out as a garment;
   the moth shall consume them.
Whoever among you fears Yahweh,
   let him listen (reading *yišma'*) to His servant!
He that walks in darkness,
   and has no ray of light,
let him trust in the name of Yahweh,
   and lean upon his God.

Behold, all you who kindle fire,
   who make burning shafts,
begone into the flame of your own fire
   and among the shafts you have lit!
This shall be your fate at my hand:
   You shall lie down in torment (l, 4–11).

This poem falls into two parts. In *vv.* 4–9 the Servant himself speaks about his mission, to strengthen by his word 'the weary', those who stand in need of salvation (that is all Israel), and especially feel their need of it and long for it. He also describes his equipment as a preacher and teacher instructed or inspired by Yahweh.[2] As elsewhere in later Judaism, the conceptions of the learned ('the wise') and of the inspired, who are endowed with

---

[1] *V.* 9aβ makes a natural sequel to *v.* 8aα in antithetic parallelism. See also the language of Rom. viii, 33f.; *Barnabas* vi, 1; and in Irenaeus, *Adv. Haer.* IV, 55, 4. *V.* 9aα is simply a repetition of *v.* 7aα and does not fit into the regular strophic structure.
[2] Cf. Isa. viii, 16. To use the obscure passage 2 Sam. i, 18 to explain *limmūdîm*, as Engnell does (*B.J.R.L.* xxxi, 1, 1948, p. 20 n. 2), and to discard the traditional and the most obvious interpretation, is unsound method; see Bentzen, *King and Messiah*,

the spirit, are blended. But he speaks especially of the insults and indignities to which he has been subjected in his work, and of his bearing under persecution. Finally he expresses his confident assurance that Yahweh will 'justify' him, i.e., maintain his cause by the outcome of events, directing them so that his prophecies come to pass, and find a well-prepared flock of believing adherents, whereas his adversaries are put to shame and brought to nought. As often happens, this 'judgement', brought about by God's guidance and by the issue of events, is described in terms of a case at law.

The literary form of this section is in the main that of the individual lament: the description of affliction, the affirmation that the worshipper is in the right, and the certainty that his prayer will be heard. But there is this difference, that the psalm of lamentation is addressed to God, whereas this poem is addressed to men, to the Servant's hearers. The literary form of the psalms is combined with prophetic themes, the prophet's account of himself and allusion to his call, as in the second poem. The entire passage is a vehicle of prophetic preaching, with the intention of addressing an appeal to men: make the right response to the Servant and his message.

The second part, *vv.* 10f., must on no account be regarded as a new poem. In form and content it is linked with what precedes. Several scholars have held that it is a later addition to the poem. This is not unlikely. It strikes a much harder note than the rest of the Servant poems, and the style is less assured; Yahweh is sometimes referred to in the third person, and sometimes appears abruptly speaking in the first person. It is possible that this ending comes from the circle of traditionists who inserted the Servant poems into the Deutero-Isaianic collection.[1] If so, another disciple of the prophet is speaking in this second section, partly in the name of Yahweh, corroborating the faith and assurance of the Servant. To this extent the structure of the whole poem in *vv.* 4–11 corresponds to the psalms of lamentation in which prayer and

[1] See below, pp. 253f. (cf. p. 251 and p. 245 n. 5). Fischer (*Alttestamentliche Abhandlungen* VI, pp. 82f.) and Rudolph (*Z.A.W.* xliii, 1925) also hold that *v.* 10 is secondary. Staerk (*Z.A.W.* xliv, 1926, pp. 243f.) also regards *vv.* 10f. as a 'redactional' reinterpretation of the preceding Servant poem to make it apply to Israel (cf. p. 245 n. 5). North (*The Suffering Servant*, p. 135) also regards *vv.* 10f. as secondary.

p. 53. The Servant is 'instructed' by Yahweh like the others who are 'instructed', i.e., the prophets. It is quite clear that the 'instruction' is thought of as inspiration, an 'opening of the ear'; cf. Isa. xxii, 14. The expression has nothing to do with the royal ideology (against Engnell, see Bentzen, loc. cit.).

assurance are confirmed by a direct oracular response, a literary form which Jeremiah, more than any other prophet, imitated.[1] But here the answer is not directed to the Servant himself, but to his hearers; and it states explicitly the admonition to which the first part only alluded indirectly. The godly who still live in 'darkness', in affliction and distress, are exhorted to take to heart the Servant's preaching, to believe in his message, and hope in Yahweh as he himself has done. The persecutors and scoffers are threatened with a destruction which will certainly be their lot— if they are not converted.

It is the prophetic aspect of the Servant's mission which is particularly prominent here, but from the standpoint of a more comprehensive prophetic ideal than that of earlier times. Here we meet the prophet as a preacher, and as something of a pastor, devoting himself particularly to 'the weary'. It is the disciplined listening to God early, 'morning by morning', and the whole-hearted surrender, obedience, willingness, and absolute trust in God's help even in distress which give the faith and power which will not yield or succumb to adversity, and which can also help with rightly guided words those who are weary and stumbling.

Finally the most distinctive poem:

The Fourth Song

Behold, My Servant will attain his aim,[2]
　　will be exalted, and lifted up, and be very high;
as many stood aghast at him,[3]
　　so will the nations be amazed at him.[4]

Before him even the great will be silent;
　　kings will shut their mouths at him;

---

[1] Cf. Jer. xv, 10–21; xx, 7–13.

[2] *yaśkîl*, literally 'deal wisely (so as to attain his aim)', fulfil his task wisely. Naturally such an expression can often be used of the king; but that does not mean that in itself it is a term proper to the royal ideology, as Engnell holds (*B.J.R.L.* xxxi, 1, 1948, pp. 24–6). The fundamental meaning 'to display insight' (in the 'primitive' sense) (internal causative) is indisputable, and it is this fundamental meaning which explains the term *maśkîl* in the Psalms, not vice versa, as Engnell claims.

[3] The 'so' (*kēn*) which corresponds to 'as' (*ka'a̓šer*) in *v.* 14aα is not the *kēn* in *v.* 14aβ, but that in *v.* 15. In its present position *v.* 14aβb is parenthetical, and *kēn* must then be given the sense 'to that extent'. But since *kēn* in the latter sense following *ka'a̓šer* would be misleading, and a parenthesis of this sort would obscure the meaning, and, further, since *v.* 14aβb makes the strophic structure at the beginning of the poem uncertain, and a full line (two members) is required to give regular strophic structure (see below, p. 198 n. 8) in liii, 1f., everything supports Duhm's view that lii, 14aβb has been displaced in transmission, and originally followed liii, 2, which also speaks of the Servant's 'appearance' (*mar'ēhû*).

[4] On *yazzeh*, see Engnell, *B.J.R.L.* xxxi, 1, 1948, pp. 29f.

for what had not been told them they will have seen,
and what they had not heard they will discern.

Who could have believed what we heard?
Who could have seen here the arm of Yahweh?
For he grew up as a sapling in dry ground,[1]
and as a root out of arid soil.

He had no form or stateliness that we should look at him,
nor yet appearance that we should desire him,
so inhumanly marred was his appearance,
he no longer resembled man.

He was despised and forsaken of men,
a man of pains and acquainted with sickness,
as one from whom men hide their faces,
he was despised, and we did not esteem him.

Yet *ours* were the sicknesses that *he* carried,
ours the pains that *he* bore;
while *we* accounted him stricken,
smitten of God, and afflicted.

But *he* was pierced for our rebellions,
he was crushed for our iniquities;
the chastisement that won our welfare was upon him,
and by his stripes there is healing for us.

All we like sheep have gone astray,
each to his own way we have turned;
But Yahweh caused to light on him,
brought upon him[2] the iniquity of us all.

He was harshly treated, yet bore it humbly,
and opened not his mouth,
as a lamb that is led to the slaughter,
as a ewe that before her shearers is dumb,

[1] Reading *bᵉḥārāḇāh*. No matter how *lᵉpānāw* in liii, 2 is changed or interpreted (cf., e.g., Nyberg in *S.E.Å.* vii, 1942, p. 49), the sense remains: a sapling which grows up in the most unfavourable conditions, and therefore is stunted and wretched in appearance. Cf. North, *The Suffering Servant*, p. 123.
[2] In spite of Nyberg's rejection of the requirement of regularity in Hebrew verse (op. cit., pp. 38ff.), the law of parallelism (thought rhyme) within the full line is a fact, and it requires a new verb in v. 6b in place of the sign of the accusative; therefore read *he'ᵉṭāhû. V.* 7b is a dittograph. The defence of the line on metrical grounds advanced by Köhler and others does violence to the law of parallelism.

From protection and right(s) he was taken away,[1]
and who reflected (any longer) on his fate?[2]
For he was cut off from the land of the living;
for our rebellions he was stricken to death.[3]

His grave was made with the wicked,
with evil-doers his sepulchre, [4]
although he had done no violence,
nor was any deceit in his mouth.

Yet it pleased Yahweh to bruise him;
He has relented,[5] (and will acquit him):[6]
If he (lit., 'his soul') pays the guilt-offering (as a pledge),
he will see his seed, he will prolong his days.[7]

When the purpose of Yahweh is fulfilled through him,
(He will deliver) his soul from distress;
he will see (light and live long),
and be satisfied with what he desires.[8]

---

[1] Engnell's interpretation of *mēʿōṣer ûmimmišpāṭ* in *v.* 8 as a hendiadys = 'a judge-ment of violence' is by no means obvious; and the rendering of *min* as 'by reason of' is improbable, as is North's rendering, 'after'. *ʿōṣer* in the sense 'protection' (Yahuda) can be supported by the meaning of the verb in 1 Sam. ix, 17, where it undoubtedly means 'to rule over' *sensu bono* = to be protector and lord of.

[2] On the interpretation of *dôr*, see Nyberg, op. cit., p. 53. The word occurs in the Ugaritic texts with the undoubted sense of 'family'; see Eissfeldt, *El im ugaritischen Pantheon*, pp. 15f, 63ff.

[3] In spite of Nyberg's defence of the grammatical construction in *v.* 8b (op. cit., pp. 55f.), the meaning which he finds here ('from those for whom my people's sin is leprosy'!) does not make sense in this context, and is ruled out by the fact that through-out the whole section *vv.* 1–10a a plural subject ('we') speaks, and not Yahweh or the poet alone. The sense makes textual emendation necessary: read *mippᵉšāʿênû* for *mippešaʿ* ʿ*ammî*, *lammāwet* for *lāmô* (cf. G), and point *nuggaʿ*; see *B.H.*³.

[4] On *v.* 9aβ see Mowinckel in *G.T.M.M.M.* III, p. 793, and p. 201 n. 3. *bᵉmōṯāw* can hardly be pointed *bāmāṯô* (Ibn Ezra), since *bāmâh* does not mean 'burial mound' anywhere else in the Old Testament; it is an abbreviation of *bêṯ-mōṯāw* (or *bêṯ-mōṯô*); the original text had no vocalic consonants, but the plural may be of amplification.

[5] On the interpretation of *heḥᵉlî* see Nyberg, op. cit., p. 58.

[6] The full line in *v.* 10aα is too short as it stands. The regular parallelism within each full line in this poem justifies the view that *v.* 10aα also consisted of a full strophe. The words in brackets in the translation simply indicate the interpretation of *heḥᵉlî*; see the preceding note.

[7] Here I follow M.T. (contrast the translation in *G.T.M.M.M.* III; and see the list of corrections there, p. 833). On the interpretation of *v.* 10 aβ, *ʾim tāśîm*, etc., see Nyberg, op. cit., pp. 58f.; the literal rendering is 'if his soul will set a guilt-offering (as a pledge)'; cf. p. 203 n. 1.

[8] Since, *pace* Nyberg (op. cit., pp. 38ff.), I regard the double full line as a prevalent rule in Hebrew metre, and since Isa. liii provides a series of clear examples of this simple, basic, strophic form (see *vv.* 1–2a, *v.* 3, *v.* 4, *v.* 5, *v.* 6, *v.* 7, *v.* 8, *vv.* 11b–12a; 12b), the structure of the poem indicates that *vv.* 10–11aα consist (or originally consisted) of 4 full lines (2 strophes). The new full line must begin with *yaṣdîḳ*, since that half line continues up to and including *lᵉrabbîm* and cannot contain any more words; so that *bᵉḍaʿtô* goes with what precedes. M.T. is clearly right in that *ʾim tāśîm ʾāśām napšô*

My Servant will stand forth as righteous before the many,
  because he bore their iniquities;
therefore will I divide him a portion among the great,
  and he will divide the spoil with the mighty—

because he poured out his life unto death,
  and was numbered among the rebellious;
yet he bore the sin of the many,
  and interposed for the rebellious (lii, 13–liii, 12).

The passage begins with a speech by Yahweh (lii, 13–15),
which in the familiar style of oracles predicts great and incredible
events, which before long will befall the Servant, and will cause
wonder of a very different kind from that occasioned by his previous fate, not mingled terror and disgust but the deepest respect.
A more detailed account is given in liii, 1ff., where certain persons
('we') bear witness to their past experience of the Servant and to
what they now expect to happen. The speakers cannot be the
nations which are mentioned in lii, 14f., as we should have to
suppose if the Servant were identified with Israel: that the Servant
should have suffered for the sake of the nations conflicts with the
view of Israel held by Deutero-Isaiah and by the prophets as a
whole (Isa. xl, 2; xliii, 24). The speakers have themselves seen the
Servant grow up in their midst; therefore they are Jews.[1] They
have already 'heard' what the foreign nations and kings had not

---

[1] North (*The Suffering Servant*, pp. 150f.), while holding the individual interpretation
of the Servant, nevertheless identifies the speakers with the nations of lii, 13ff. His
arguments are general observations lacking cogency, and appear in a very different

---

and *yir'eh zera' ya'ªrîk yāmîm* go together as protasis and apodosis. Thus these two half
lines (members) form a full line (period); but in that case some word must have been
omitted after the bald *heḥᵉlî* (see above, n. 5). Thus the following strophe (double
line) extends from *wᵉḥēpeṣ* in *v.* 10b up to and including *bᵉda'tô* in *v.* 11 (see above).
V. 10b is a prefixed circumstantial clause. 'The righteous one', *ṣaddîk*, is, of course,
the Servant himself. The subject in *v.* 11aβ is *'abdî*: 'My Servant will show himself to
be righteous (*yaṣdîk*, internal causative) (and so stand) as righteous before the many';
with this is connected the circumstantial clause in *v.* 11b, 'although he bore' or 'because he bore'. Since according to the strophic structure in double lines *v.* 11b from
yaṣdîk onwards goes with *v.* 12a (see above), *vv.* 10b and 11a as far as *bᵉda'tô* (see above)
must have formed two full lines of which *v.* 10b is the first half line. It is clear that some
word is missing here: *yir'eh* has no object; to take *yiśba'* as an object clause to *yir'eh*
(Nyberg, op. cit., p. 59) has no parallel in Biblical Hebrew. To take *bᵉda'tô* as *birᵉ'ūtô*
is not an emendation, since *dālet* and *rēš* were identical in the early square script, and
vowel letters were not in use. Thus the second half line is *yiśba' birᵉ'ūtô*. In the
two middle half lines there is no object for *yir'eh*, nor is there a predicate before *mēʻᵃmal*.
At all events it is clear that *vv.* 10b–11a deal with the same thought as *v.* 10a. The
similarity between *v.* 10a and *vv.* 10b–11a is so great that we may complete the lines in
v. 11a in accordance with *v.* 10a and add, for example, *yaṣṣil* and *'ôr wᵉya'ªrîk yāmîm*,
or the like, even if Nyberg is right in holding that we can hardly appeal here to G as
attesting another supposedly original text.

yet heard (lii, 15). The speakers are the poet-prophet himself and the circle of Jews who share his view of the Servant; and the speech is addressed in the first instance to the other Jews.

What they have to relate is a 'report', 'something heard' (*šemū'āh*). The word may denote knowledge imparted by a God-given audition, or a prophetic inspiration; but here it means rather a report, a tradition which they have heard within their own circle,[1] and which, through the prophetic author of this Song, they are now spreading abroad. It is a message about the Servant, a kerygma. But what is first related is not the unheard-of thing alluded to in the opening lines, but the Servant's miserable life on earth. This speech takes the form of a belated funeral dirge; belated because the Servant is described as having been dead and buried for a considerable time.[2] In the first part of the poem (up to and including liii, 9) the poet adopts the standpoint of one narrating past events. For him the whole earthly story of the Servant here belongs to the past, as is shown both by the retrospective character of the funeral dirge and also by the tenses (perfect and consecutive imperfect).[3] But this poem appears to be exactly the reverse of the usual funeral dirge: the dead man's beauty, courage, and manly virtues, which made men love him and miss him, are not celebrated here as in other poems which thus became bitter laments over loss. This Song tells how unimpressive, hideous, and despised the Servant was; not a tree in blossom, but a parched shoot; not a lion or an eagle (the figures used for instance in the lament over Saul and Jonathan), but a gentle lamb. He was neither high-born nor manly, and had no fascinating influence upon man; on the contrary, he was unimpressive and gentle. Moreover, he was stricken by a foul disease which

[1] Isa. liii, 1. On the interpretation of the word, see Nyberg, op. cit., pp. 48f.

[2] See Jahnow, *Das hebräische Leichenlied im Rahmen der Völkerdichtung*, pp. 256ff. Begrich (*Studien zur Deuterajesaja*, pp. 50ff.) takes the psalms of thanksgiving to be the model.

[3] Bentzen is therefore wrong in stating (*Jesaja* II, pp. 100, 105) that the whole poem is prophetic in character, and in supporting this contention by an appeal to the 'connexion' with what precedes. This 'connexion' is purely imaginary. The death of the Servant in *v.* 8 also belongs to the past, i.e., from the standpoint which the poet imaginatively adopts; but this does not, of course, preclude the possibility that the whole passage is an ideal description of what has yet to be fulfilled in the future.

light when account is taken of the formal characteristics of the poem: 'a belated funeral dirge' expressing a confession of faith and a kerygma (see below, pp. 203, 206ff.). To express the content and aim of the message proclaimed by the prophet and his circle, there is no real point in dwelling upon the question *how* 'nations and kings' express their overwhelming astonishment at the destiny of the Servant.

brought disgrace, possibly leprosy,[1] 'smitten of God and afflicted', as they believed. The text does not make it clear whether he died of the disgraceful disease, or by violence, perhaps as a victim of the 'lynch-law' of his adversaries, or by normal condemnation and execution, after being accused of some crime. If the last, it is natural to suppose that the accusation was connected with his preaching, which would then have given offence to prevailing opinions. At all events, after sore afflictions he died the death of a noted sinner,[2] and was interred in the burial place of foul criminals.[3] He was forgotten by men, without family or renown. All this he bore without a murmur, without replying to the scorn and derision which were commonly inflicted (for apotropaic reasons) on one 'smitten by God'. Unlike Job, he did not even try to maintain his 'righteousness'.

But now the poet announces *a great new truth* which has been discerned by himself and others ('we'), an insight which they share, and which they are now spreading abroad together with the message about the Servant and his teaching, as a 'tradition' which they have themselves received (see above, p. 200 n. 1 and p. 252); his suffering and death are not really the merciless end of

---

[1] The identification of the disease with leprosy and the corresponding interpretation of *nāgûaʿ* in *v*. 4 (cf. *negaʿ* or *nuggaʿ* in *v*. 8) as indicating leprosy were first advanced by Duhm; and among those who have followed him is Nyberg (op. cit., pp. 52ff.). This interpretation is not certain, and is challenged by Engnell, Bentzen, and North. Engnell's objections (*B.J.R.L.* xxxi, 1, 1948, pp. 31f.) are based on the preconceived theory that the fate of the Servant is described in terms of the pattern of the Tammuz ritual, rather than on exegetical considerations. The question is of no great moment. The main point is that the Servant's death was such that normal Jewish belief saw in it a judgement of God.

[2] With the aid of modern logical considerations and of modification of the text, Marmorstein (*Z.A.W.* xliv, 1926, pp. 260ff.) will have it that the text did not originally relate the death of the Servant, but only physical sufferings. This is arbitrary. In *v*. 8 it is explicitly stated that he was 'taken away', 'cut off from the land of the living', 'stricken to death'.

[3] Nyberg (op. cit., pp. 56ff.) defends M.T. ('with *a rich man* was he in death'; Nyberg renders, 'they gave him a grave among the ungodly, and *together with* the wealthy class when he died') by pointing out that in the thought of the prophets 'ungodly' and 'rich' are synonymous terms. It is of course true that the prophets often inveigh against the rich (i.e., the powerful members of the community); but it does not follow that the words 'ungodly' (*rāšāʿ*) and 'rich' have become semantically equivalent. There is no example of this, either in the Old Testament or the New. Moreover, Nyberg's interpretation and translation presuppose that in early Judaism the rich *qua* 'ungodly' had their own burial place, and that one who died like the Servant in what appeared to be a state of ungodliness and impurity was interred in the burial place of the rich. This is clearly out of the question. Since the rich exercised power and authority in the community, they would obviously have prevented an unclean leper or other *rešāʿîm* from being interred in their burial place. In the light of the new MS. *DSIa*, it is obvious that *ʿsyr* = *ʿsyr* = *ʿōsê raʿ* (*B.H.³*). *ʿAyin* and the other gutturals are here more frequently omitted at the end of a syllable, because they were no longer pronounced. See Hempel in *Z.D.M.G.* ci, 1951, p. 140.

an earthly life which held everything that is of any value (that would be the judgement of the ancient Israelite, and of the funeral dirge); but death is his great work, the achievement because of which the others ('the many', the whole community, the people)[1] are now in his debt and have gained an entirely different conception of the Servant. The suffering is a positive element in the work to which he was called and is 'the purpose of Yahweh' (liii, 10f.). The new truth is this: the Servant did not suffer for his own sins; 'he had done no violence, nor was any deceit in his mouth'. For Jewish thought this does not mean that he was sinless —no human being is;[2] but that he had committed no such gross sin as could justly be punished by so great sufferings. He had been 'upright' like Job or Abraham, and, like Jeremiah confronting God, might have maintained his 'righteousness' in relation to his enemies and persecutors. Even the emphasis on the silence of the Servant seems to suggest his 'righteousness' and innocence. Usually, of course, a person who was stricken by misfortune would defend himself by apotropaic curses directed against the person responsible for his misfortune. There are many instances of this in the psalms of lamentation.[3] The misfortune was supposed to be caused by wicked enemies and demons; and the curses were held to be a legitimate means of breaking the power of the author of the misfortune, so that the misfortune might release its hold upon the victim and fall instead upon its own author.[4] Even where the disease was looked upon as a punishment from Yahweh, passionate lamentations were the rule (cf. Job). But in the Psalms the worshipper sometimes asserts that he has not opened his mouth against his enemies, mentioning this as a 'factor of righteousness' in his favour.[5] Originally this was a precautionary measure. The author of the suffering might be Yahweh Himself; and if so, the worshipper would be in danger of cursing God. But the psalmists also plead their quiet waiting upon God in affliction,[6] taking the suffering as His admonition. In Israel silence and stillness (as contrasted with the 'noise' of sinners and of the

---

[1] 'The many' (not 'many'; the article is omitted in poetical style) is the community as contrasted with the single individual, and so = 'all'.

[2] Cf. Job iv, 17ff.; xv, 14f.; xxv, 4–6.

[3] See Gunkel-Begrich, *Einleitung in die Psalmen*, pp. 226ff., especially p. 228; Mowinckel, *Offersang og sangoffer*, pp. 250ff.

[4] Pss. vii, 15–17; ix, 16; lvii, 7; cf. Prov. xxvi, 27; Ecclus. xxvii, 25f.

[5] Pss. xxxviii, 14f.; xxxix, 2, 4, 10; see Mowinckel, *Offersang og sangoffer*, pp. 207, 231ff., 259.

[6] Pss. lxii, 6; cxxxi; cxxiii; cf. Mowinckel, *Der Knecht Jahwäs*, pp. 57f.; *Offersang og sangoffer*, pp. 216f. Bentzen in [*D.*]*T.T.* v, 1932, pp. 199ff.

powers of chaos) became to some extent the typical religious attitude, a mark of piety and uprightness, the attitude which was characteristic of the ideal of humility.

If, then, the Servant was 'righteous' and innocent, it was not for his own sins that he suffered, but for those of others, of his fellow-countrymen, 'the many'. The punishment, the sickness, the suffering, and the scorn, which they really ought to have borne, were borne by him (liii, 4, 8, 12). Yahweh allowed all to fall upon him that they might escape. He gave his life *vicariously* as a guilt-offering (*'āšām*) for the others (liii, 10), perhaps without himself being aware of it, but, at all events, by Yahweh's decree. The poet's words may also imply that he thereby gave his life (his 'soul', i.e., himself) as a pledge to Yahweh that the others might escape,[1] to win for them 'peace', the restoration of the normal relationship with Yahweh, pardon, good fortune, well-being, a full life (liii, 5). If so, this agrees in general conception with the passage about the priestly service of the future king; to be a mediator between God and man means 'to give one's life as a pledge' (Jer. xxx, 21f.; see above, pp. 179f, and below, pp. 238ff.).

In proclaiming this new truth the poet finds the funeral dirge the most natural form to use in order to look back and pass a final verdict on the Servant and his work. The lament in the funeral dirge becomes an accusation, the self-accusation of the poet and his hearers. Thus the Song becomes *a vindication of the Servant's honour*; for everyone must now understand that the ignominy, the wretchedness, the humility, the apparent lack of self-assertion ('righteousness') were really his titles of honour. This new insight is the presupposition and the explanation of the certainty with which the impending restoration is proclaimed later in the poem. In this way the funeral dirge becomes at the same time a confession of sins. The speakers now realize and confess that it is for *their* sins that the Servant has suffered. Thus the Song includes here elements from the psalms of penitence and lamentation, and also an assertion of innocence as in the lamentations of the innocent, but with this essential difference, that it is the innocence not of the speakers but *of the Servant* that is attested; it is not for his own misdeeds that he has suffered. The emphasis is not on the confession of the sin of the worshippers, but on the testimony to the innocent suffering of the Servant on behalf of, and for the benefit

---

[1] See Nyberg's interpretation of liii, 10 aβ. Nyberg takes *śîm*, 'to set', as a verb used absolutely, meaning 'to give a pledge', and compares Job xvii, 3; op. cit., pp. 58f.

of, others. In this way the Song becomes a profession of faith in the Servant and his sufferings, and in their significance for the speakers.

Accordingly, just as the penitential psalms usually ended in the assurance of being heard (*Gewissheit der Erhörung*),[1] often followed by a reassuring oracle from Yahweh, so here the poem ends with the speaker's assurance that the Servant will receive the 'reward' which, according to Jewish belief, must come to the pious and the innocent, and still more to the person who, through his innocence and righteousness, has made the others innocent and righteous by bearing their penalty. This assurance leads immediately to a direct *promise from Yahweh*, who now gives an explicit undertaking concerning the restoration of the Servant which was alluded to in the opening words. With this part of the poem there begins what for the poet still lay in the future; it is prophecy. This is corroborated by the literary form (the assurance of the penitential psalms is applied to the future), and by the tenses; from *v.* 10 onward the imperfect (the normal tense for expressing the future) is used.

First there is announced the divine purpose in the suffering and death of the Servant. It was by the gracious purpose of Yahweh that the Servant was bruised for the sins of the others. This was necessary that they might recognize their sins, do penance, and be converted to Him; and thus it has become possible for Yahweh to show mercy to the others. That is why it is announced that Yahweh will now justify the Servant, i.e., show the whole world that he was a man who 'acted wisely and attained his aim' (*hiśkîl*, translated above 'attain his aim') through faith in God. Just because he was willing to 'pay the guilt offering', Yahweh will order events so that he will 'stand forth as the righteous man he really is' (*yaṣdîḳ, v.* 11b). He will not be deprived of the reward of the righteous.

For a great miracle will take place, whereby the others will realize that the Servant was in the right, and that he suffered for their sakes. Kings and nations will be amazed when they hear of and see the miracle. Yahweh will raise the dead man from the grave;[2] his greatness and his honour will be restored; he will see

---

[1] See Gunkel-Begrich, *Einleitung in die Psalmen*, pp. 132, 243ff., 351ff.; Mowinckel, *Offersang og sangoffer*, pp. 219ff., 231f., 257ff.

[2] P. Volz (*Buddefestschrift*, pp. 180ff.) denies that Isa. liii speaks of the resurrection of the Servant, holding that the reference is to a reward in the hereafter; but in his commentary, *Jesaja* II, p. 179, he modifies his view to the extent of saying that it is

his seed (presumably this refers to his spiritual children),[1] prolong his days, see his work crowned with success, and reap all the glory that an eastern poet could possibly describe.[2]

What is described is a special miracle wrought by God for the sake of the Servant, in order that his work may prosper. A general resurrection is not presupposed. That is what makes the resuscitation of the Servant so wonderful, and enables it to produce results so convincing and so decisive. It was in accordance with the general tendency of the Old Testament thought that piety and undeserved sufferings like those of the Servant could not go unrewarded if God was righteous. What is new here is that the poet makes this assertion concerning one who is already dead, and who, therefore, according to common belief, was irrevocably branded by God as a sinner. Here the belief in a resurrection emerges in the Old Testament for the first time,[3] but only as an unheard of exception on behalf of this one man.

The resurrection of the Servant is the crown of the divine purpose. It is also the decisive miracle through which the Servant's work attains its end, to be a blessing and a remedy for the others. His resurrection will convince the whole world of his innocence, and so make his fellow-countrymen admit that his suffering and death must have been caused by the sins of others, by *their* sins. His resurrection will call forth the recognition of sin, the penitence, and the conversion which are expressed in the belated funeral dirge. The great miracle will make men share the view of the Servant which the poet and his circle now have. As formerly he was despised, so now he will be highly esteemed; and a corresponding earthly glory and good fortune will be his reward. In spite of the spiritualizing of the reward which is expressed in the second poem (where the reward consists of a yet greater and more difficult mission, and of its result, the salvation of the whole world), Jewish thought could not discard the ancient belief in a connexion between piety and earthly good fortune. It is this reward of piety

---

[1] Cf. Isa. viii, 16, 18; and Mowinckel, *Profeten Jesaja*, pp. 19f.

[2] Isa. lii, 13; liii, 10, 12. On the formula 'long life, progeny, success, and honour' as the traditional expression of the Israelite desire for 'life', see Marmorstein in *Z.A.W.* xliv, 1926, pp. 262ff.

[3] Job explicitly rejects the thought that resurrection is possible (xiv, 10–12, 14). Neither in Ps. lxxiii nor in Ps. xvi is there any mention of resurrection after death. The earliest passage is Isa. xxvi, 19 (cf. xxv, 8) presumably of Hellenistic date; also Dan. xii, 2, 13. Cf. Birkeland in *St. Th.* III, i, 1949/50, p. 72.

---

doubtful if the text speaks of a resurrection. Rudolph rightly argues against this view (*Z.A.W.* xliii, 1925, pp. 93ff.).

(cf. *v.* 12) that the Servant will receive in return for his faithfulness and his sufferings.

Thus the end of the poem is linked with its opening. Through something they have 'heard', the poet and his circle are convinced that this miracle will take place. It is this assurance that the poet expresses in the introductory strophe in the form of an oracle from Yahweh Himself. The whole section (liii, 1–9) speaks of events which (from the standpoint adopted by the poet in this poem) have already happened, as is shown both by the use of the dirge and by the tenses (consecutive imperfect and perfect). The Servant has lived and suffered, and is dead and buried. From the standpoint of the poet and the speakers, what is still a proclamation concerning the future (the prophecy itself) does not begin until liii, 10 (as the tenses show: consecutive perfect and imperfect), having been hinted at in the opening lines with their prediction of the impending miraculous exaltation. For the poet, the resurrection and the reward still belong to the future; and his supreme concern is with the proclamation of this prophecy about the future.

The aim of this proclamation is manifest. The poet wants to bring his hearers to the same view and the same faith that he and his circle share. They must embrace the Servant's 'instruction' and message, believing that he is in the right and that he is really the chosen Servant of Yahweh, whose claims and instruction are the real condition of Israel's salvation.

Taken as a whole the Song is in form an 'inverted' funeral dirge, with elements from the penitential psalms, set within a framework of promise. In content it is a 'kerygma', a 'message', a grateful confession of faith in the Servant, and a proclamation about him and his work by those who have been healed by his sufferings and death; and it is set forth as a testimony to the other Jews, but in reality, as the other poems show (xlii, 4; xlix, 6), to the whole world.

2. *The Work of the Servant*

Let us now try to see as a whole the picture of the Servant which these poems present. What is he? And what is his work?

He has received from Yahweh a quite *special* task. That is why he is His Servant, not in the more passive sense which the word has in Deutero-Isaiah when it is applied to Israel: the worshipper of Yahweh, secure under His favour and protection, able to trust in Yahweh, and because of her historical experiences a witness to

the election, the favour, and the faithfulness of Yahweh, and to
His will and power to save Israel and to bring to fulfilment His
plan for the world; but in an active sense: he who has been chosen
and equipped for a special work in Yahweh's service.[1] He is
Yahweh's 'deputy', an effective instrument for the realization of
Yahweh's purpose, and thus for glorifying Him in the world
(xlix, 3).

Yahweh has chosen him for this service from his mother's womb
(xlii, 1; xlix, 1), endowed him with His spirit (xlii, 1), trained his
tongue (l, 4; xlix, 2), and made him fit for his mission like a sharp
sword and a polished arrow (xlix, 2). For this service Yahweh
upholds him (xlii, 1) and gives him strength (xlix, 4, 5b).

His service is a ministry of the word (xlix, 2; l, 4, 10; cf. xlii, 2).
He has a message from Yahweh to proclaim; and he receives daily
revelations bearing on that message (l, 4, 5a).

In the first instance his ministry is addressed to the people and
community of Israel (xlix, 5; cf. l, 4); later it is extended to include
all the nations of the world (xlix, 6; xlii, 4). By his preaching
(l, 4; xlii, 4; xlix, 2) the Servant will 'bring forth right religion'
(i.e., the true religion and the state of bliss which accompanies it)
on the earth (xlii, 3f.). In this way he will lead back to Yahweh
the preserved in Israel, i.e., lead them to true penitence and godliness, and thereby make possible the complete restoration and ingathering of those who have been scattered abroad (xlix, 5f.).
More than this, his preaching will reach out to all the peoples of
the earth, who are longing for the true religion (xlii, 4), and be
the means of their salvation. He will be 'a light to the nations'
(xlix, 6). This clearly denotes some kind of active missionary
calling.

The content of the Servant's message is in harmony with this.
It is not harsh words of doom (xlii, 2f.), but promises of consolation for the encouragement of the weary (l, 4). It is a message of
salvation like that of Deutero-Isaiah, but is, in fact, more definitely
universalistic in its scope. It includes all nations; but no longer
are there suggestions that the nations will become Israel's vassals.
Deliverance from error and from the consequences of sin, remission
of the punishment for sin, and the establishment throughout the
world of the propitious rule of true religion and of a right relationship to God: that, in short, is the content of the message.

Thus the mission of the Servant has a bearing on Israel's hope

[1] See Mowinckel in *G.T.M.M.M.* III on Isa. xli, 8a.

of restoration. Its aim is the realization of what was for Deutero-Isaiah the essence of the hope of restoration from both the national and the religious standpoint: that all Jews should accept the message in faith and rally to the God of their fathers; that the nation should be restored, the exiles return home, the dispersed be gathered together; that the heathen should accept the religion of Yahweh in enthusiastic wonder over the great work of salvation; that Yahweh should be honoured throughout the world, and His name be hallowed, as the only true God in heaven and on earth.

It is the task of the Servant by his message to co-operate in the accomplishment of this wonderful work. It is with his message that it begins. By it he will 'bring back Jacob unto Him (Yahweh), and gather Israel to Him' (xlix, 5). The fruit of his message (or 'teaching') will be the turning away of the people from despondency, doubt, and unbelief, and perhaps even from actual apostasy and other sins. But his message will also have meaning for the heathen. When we read that 'for his instruction the far coasts wait', and, again, that Yahweh will also make him 'a light to the nations, that My salvation may reach to the end of the earth', it is clear that it is by his message that he will be a light to the heathen and convey salvation to them.

But the Songs tell of more than the message of the Servant. The poet knows, too, that the Servant meets the greatest difficulties and sufferings in carrying out his mission. He has good reason for becoming weary (xlii, 4). He has to endure opposition, derision, blows, and ill-treatment, and has many enemies (l, 5ff.). Sometimes he even thinks that all his endeavours are in vain (xlix, 4). We hear that he is a man of humble station, without earthly grandeur or reputation, outwardly unimpressive and insignificant (liii, 2f.), even repulsive in appearance (lii, 14b). For he has been stricken by disease, misery, and sore pains (liii, 3f., 7), so that, in accordance with normal Israelite and Jewish standards, his associates and countrymen regard him as one whose sin has been brought to light, whom God has smitten and branded (liii, 4). According to the accepted view, he is 'unclean', excluded from the community. In fact, 'sin' has been laid on him. (Jewish thought could not as yet distinguish between uncleanness and sin; something of the ancient material and objective view of sin still survived.) At last the Servant dies from his painful disease, and is buried in an ignominious fashion in the burial place of unclean malefactors (liii, 7–9; cf. p. 201 n. 3).

But to all this he quietly submits, and does not weary in adversity (xlii, 4). He receives power to stand his ground again after his times of despondency (xlix, 4). The poet makes him tell us that it was at such a time that he received from Yahweh the assurance of a still greater call than that of leading Israel back to the right way, the call to be a light to the nations and a means of making Yahweh's salvation universal (xlix, 5f.). He has willingly accepted blows and derision, knowing all the time that in the end, in one way or another, Yahweh would help him, vindicate him, and put his adversaries to shame (l, 5ff.). It is explicitly emphasized, and finally admitted by those who misjudged him, that all this has befallen him in spite of the fact that he was no 'sinner' in the pregnant Israelite sense of the word (liii, 10), but really a righteous man and 'honoured' in Yahweh's eyes (xlix, 5). He bears his sufferings, because they come as a necessary consequence of the mission which must and shall be accomplished (l, 5ff.).

In the fourth Song the poet announces that to him and his circle there has been conveyed the recognition of the true character, the value, and the work of the Servant. When others see the restoration and glorification of the Servant, they, too, will all understand. This involves the recognition that the Servant was really guiltless, and therefore did not suffer for his own sins but for those of others. Accordingly, his sufferings and death were vicarious, made atonement for others, and brought them back (or will bring them back) to 'peace' and communion with Yahweh.

How does the poet think that this will come about? Wherein, precisely, does the atoning effect of the Servant's vicarious work consist?

It is clear that the poet expresses his thoughts in sacrificial and legal phrases and conceptions. The Servant has 'poured out his soul' (i.e., his life), and has pledged his life as a guilt-offering ('āšām).[1] He has become their surety. This presupposes the ancient belief that an offence can be atoned for by vicarious payment of compensation ('āšām), or guilt-offering, or rite of purification (sin-offering), such as Job used to perform for sins which his children might have committed (Job i, 5). In this way the one who

---

[1] Isa. liii, 10; see above, p. 198, and n. 8.

makes atonement becomes the 'redeemer' ($g\bar{o}$'$\bar{e}l$) of his kinsman.
According to the ancient mode of thought the family, the tribe,
or the people is a unity; and thus the decisive factor in atonement
for an offence is not that the culprit should himself pay the penalty
but that the community to which he belongs should do so.
Accordingly, one with whom he is in fellowship can intervene as
his redeemer. The more eminent the deliverer is, the more valuable
is his action on behalf of the other. The utter guiltlessness of the
Servant gives a special value to what he does. His guiltlessness is
his 'merit', his 'righteousness'. Indeed, he has increased it by his
patient silence in suffering (see above, p. 203). But he has done
even more. He has *voluntarily* accepted suffering, not only in the
certainty of ultimate triumph, as in the third Song, but because (so
the poet holds) he has known or surmised something of the purpose
of the suffering. He has come forward as 'deliverer' for the sake
of the others. Since such vicarious action is possible, it has been
decreed by the wonderful counsel of Yahweh that the Servant
should bear the diseases and afflictions, the punishment for guilt,
which the others ought to have borne for their sins. The poet and
his circle have now realized that if the community ('we') had
really been punished as it deserved, the individual members would
have had to endure many more and worse diseases and afflictions
than they have in fact done. But the Servant has borne them on
their behalf, and thereby has won for them 'peace', or, to put it
figuratively, 'healing'.

So in the poet's thought it is not the wrath of God which has
imposed the suffering on the Servant. But, according to the
thought of ancient Judaism, every sin bears within itself the seed
of misfortune, a 'fruit', or 'guilt', which in time overtakes the
culprit and (or) his family. The sins of Israel are so many and so
great, that, if nothing were done to atone for them and to 'purify'
the people, she would succumb under the burden of her guilt.
Therefore it 'pleased' God in His clemency to establish a purpose
or plan, by which a redeemer should bear the burden of guilt
which would have been too heavy for the people.

What is here described is an act of free grace on God's part.
It is His plan that is realized; and it is for this that He has created
and equipped the Servant. In order to make this thought clear,
the poet naturally uses metaphors from current contemporary
ideas about atonement and the forgiveness of sins, i.e., sacrificial
language. But these expressions are not to be taken literally.

They are, at all events, in some degree symbolic and metaphorical. As has been said (p. 205), the poet has in mind the psychological effect of the Servant's work, which will produce a change of mind in his fellow-countrymen, as it has already done in the poet and his circle. The resurrection and glorification of the Servant will convince them that he was guiltless, and so make them realize that he has suffered as a deliverer on behalf of the others.[1] The poet realized that the sin of men was too great, and the holiness of God too serious, for salvation to be man's own work. His point of view here is that of Jeremiah and of the book of Ezekiel (see below, pp. 238ff.). Therefore he announces that God Himself will create an instrument, the Servant, who by his preaching, suffering, and death will bring about the conversion which would otherwise never have happened.

As we have seen, this takes place because they see him glorified; and, as a result, they see the guilt of their own sin, and realize how great it must be to have brought such sufferings upon the righteous one. For suffering and sin are inseparable; and since the righteous one has had to suffer, it must have been for our sins. This is what they acknowledge in the belated funeral dirge. The conviction of sin brings them to penitence and conversion, and leads them back to Yahweh. Thus, what we have here is no longer the primitive idea of the connexion between the community and the individual, according to which one may take the place of another, so long as atonement is made. The thought is rather that of the psychological and moral effect of the Servant's work, bringing about the conversion of the people, and so atoning for their guilt.

Accordingly, there is no mention here of what is often present in primitive, sacrificial religions, the thought of a change wrought in God Himself, so that His attitude is modified as a result of the death of the Servant, as medieval theologians held. The thoughts and expressions derived from the language of sacrifice and from its substitutionary theory are sublimated and lifted to a higher plane.[2] The atoning worth of the Servant's action depends on whether his fellow-countrymen appropriate it, so as to see their own guilt and thereby be moved to conversion and penitence. From the first it is God Himself who purposes this and brings it

---

[1] On the suffering of the pious as a vicarious atonement in Jewish theology, see Moore, *Judaism* I, pp. 546ff.; Sjöberg, *Gott und die Sünder*, pp. 174f.; Marmorstein in *Z.A.W.* xliv, 1926, p. 264.

[2] Cf. Taylor, *Jesus and His Sacrifice. A Study of the Passion Sayings in the Gospels*, p. 42.

all to pass.[1] It is because the Servant's sufferings open the eyes of the others and bring them to repentance, that the righteous Servant justifies the many (assuming that the traditional translation of liii, 11 is correct).[2]

This subjective, psychological interpretation of the atoning effect of the Servant's sufferings and death is supported, for example, by the occurrence of similar ideas in Judaism. The apocryphal Wisdom of Solomon speaks of the demeanour of the righteous and the ungodly at the judgement after the resurrection. The self-confident, clever men now see that the poor, despised, righteous man,[3] whom they oppressed during his earthly life, and whose sufferings they derided, is now acquitted, whereas they themselves are condemned. 'Troubled with terrible fear', and 'amazed at the marvel of his salvation, they shall say within themselves repenting' . . .

> This was he whom aforetime we had in derision,
> And made a by-word of reproach:
> We fools accounted his life madness,
> And his end without honour:
> How was he numbered among sons of God!
> And how is his lot among saints!
> Verily we went astray from the way of truth,
> And the light of righteousness shined not for us . . .
> We took our fill of the paths of lawlessness and destruction,
> And we journeyed through trackless deserts,
> But the way of the Lord we knew not.[4]

Here, too, it is the sight of the exaltation of the despised and suffering righteous ones, when 'they receive a glorious kingdom and a diadem of beauty from the Lord's hand', which makes the ungodly and proud clever men realize that the despised men are right and they themselves wrong. Admittedly the thought of vicarious atonement is not present here; for that there is no place at the last judgement. But the 'wise man' is here thinking, in the same way as the poet-prophet of Isa. liii, of the effect which the

---

[1] Cf. Lofthouse: 'The one real actor in the drama is Jahveh himself' (*J.T.S.* xlviii 1947, p. 174).

[2] The meaning is the same, even on the interpretation adopted above.

[3] Wisd. of Sol. v, 1ff. refers to the suffering righteous in general, not to the 'son of God' regarded as the Servant of the Lord (as Huntress holds in *J.B.L.* liv, 1935, pp 117ff.). To that extent, this righteous one is a Lazarus figure rather than a Servant of the Lord.

[4] Wisd. of Sol. v, 2ff. Translation by Holmes in *A.P.O.T.* I.

exaltation of the blameless and despised sufferer will have in making the ungodly recognize the truth, though here it is too late.

It is also right to emphasize that here, as elsewhere, 'subjective' and 'objective' are not contradictory but correlative ideas. They express two aspects of the same thing. 'Objectively', the Servant's atoning work is wrought by God Himself. It is He who both plans and prepares it, and knows what it will lead to. For those at whom it is directed (Israel), the aim is realized when the impression made by God's miracle, wrought through the Servant, produces the desired end, that change of mind which is the condition of forgiveness and restoration. God's work through the Servant makes them seek reconciliation with God.

3. *Prophet, not Messiah*

This Servant, who has a task to perform with the rest of Israel, whose mission it is to speak to those who fear God (i.e., the Jews), and whom the other Jews have seen grow up, live, and die before their eyes, who died of leprosy and was buried among malefactors, is clearly no collective entity. He is not the nation, or the congregation, or a particular class or group within the nation. There is no need to enter here into this aspect of the discussion about the Servant.[1] Nor is he the 'ideal' as distinguished from the empirical Israel.[2] Such a distinction is Platonic, not Hebraic. The Servant is regarded and described as a specific individual. This is clear, not only from all the purely individual and personal traits in the

---

[1] See Additional Note XII.

[2] This is rightly maintained by Peake (*The Servant of Yahweh and Other Lectures*, p. 67). The conception of the Servant as a personification of the 'ideal' or the 'spiritual' Israel has often been adopted, even in earlier times; so, e.g., Cölln, Thenius, Anger, Knobel, Vatke, Ewald, Kosters, Cheyne ('the genius of Israel'), and others. For more recent attempts to unite the individual and the collective interpretations, see p. 215 n. 2. These expressions, 'the ideal Israel', 'the spiritual Israel', etc., are generally used with the utmost vagueness. If they are used in a Platonic sense, of the transcendental 'idea' of Israel, by contrast with its empirical reality, then the thought is entirely alien to ancient Israel. If what is meant is an 'idealized' presentation of Israel (in the popular sense of the term), then it is quite inconceivable that the 'idealized' Israel should accomplish a task the object of which is 'the real Israel'. If 'the spiritual Israel' means the believing kernel of the nation, by contrast with the great mass of the unbelieving or the unresponsive, who are Israelites only 'after the flesh', the difficulty is that this kind of distinction does not appear elsewhere in the Old Testament; for Deutero-Isaiah, all Israelites are real Israelites, even if they are bad Israelites (see the references in p. 214 nn. 3, 4). The distinction between 'Israel after the spirit' and 'Israel after the flesh' presupposes in effect a spiritual dualism which did not appear in Judaism until the Hellenistic period. All these attempts at modernizing distinctions arise because it is felt that other passages in Deutero-Isaiah make it necessary to begin with the identification of the Servant with Israel in some sense (see Additional Note XII).

picture,[1] but also indirectly, since every collective interpretation leads to absurdities.

In the first place, it is obvious that the Servant cannot be a poetical 'personification' or a means of presenting the nation Israel in terms of the ancient conception of the community.[2]

No Old Testament prophet, not even Deutero-Isaiah,[3] could say that Israel suffered innocently, or that she bore her sufferings silently and patiently, or, least of all, that her sufferings were incomprehensible. All the prophets saw clearly that Israel deserved to suffer as the logical result of her sins; and this is explicitly emphasized by Deutero-Isaiah.[4] It is also evident that the Servant has a vocation of which Israel is the object. He is to achieve something for and with Israel; and Israel will be converted to Yahweh as a result of the Servant's work.[5] He is one on whom those who fear God will set their hope (l, 10). Nor will it do to say that the Servant is a personification of the prophetic order, as several scholars have maintained.[6] The poet, who himself comes forward as a prophet, could not possibly say that the prophetic order, or 'prophecy', is dead, and will at some time arise and be honoured again. The Servant is certainly a prophet, as we shall see presently; but he is an individual prophet and not a collective abstraction.

In recent times a clearer understanding of the ancient con-

---

[1] These traits are still individual even if they apply in a general way to the pious, and are to that extent 'typical', as Volz maintains (*Jesaja* II, p. 183). But Volz exaggerates this 'typical' element. The metaphors and phrases may, admittedly, be used of other pious sufferers; but it is quite obvious that the story which the poet-prophet tells of the Servant is about unique events which happened once for all.

[2] Cf. Gressmann, *Der Messias*, pp. 316f.

[3] See Isa. xl, 2; xliv, 18, 22; xliii, 8, 22–5; xlv, 9f.; xlviii, 1, 4, 8–10; liv, 8; lv, 7.

[4] Isa. xl, 2; xlii, 18, 24f.; xliii, 8, 22–8; xlv, 9f.; xlviii, 1–11; li, 17–20; liv, 9; lv, 7; cf. xlii, 19–23 (Trito-Isaianic).

[5] See Isa. xlix, 5f., and above, pp. 192, 206ff. These verses have played an important part in the discussion between the supporters of the individual and the collective theories. Budde, in particular, has tried to show that they are compatible with the collective interpretation (see his commentary on Deutero-Isaiah in *H.S.A.T.*[4] I, p. 678; *Die sogennanten Ebed-Jahwe-Lieder und die Bedeutung des Knechtes Jahwes in Jes.* 40–55: *Ein Minoritätsvotum*; and most recently his review of Eissfeldt's *Der Gottesknecht bei Deuterojesaja (Jes.* 40–55) *im Lichte der israelitischen Anschauung von Gemeinschaft und Individuum*, in *T.L.Z.* lviii, 1933, cols. 324f. Rejecting what is undoubtedly, for reasons of grammar and sense, the most probable interpretation, Budde would take Yahweh as the logical subject of the infinitives *lᵉšôbēb* in *v.* 5, *lᵉhāḳîm* and *lᵉhāšîb* in *v.* 6. But if that is the sense, we cannot understand why, in place of 'Israel' and 'Jacob', we do not find simply 'you'. There is no ground for denying that the language used distinguishes between the Servant (you) and 'Israel' or 'Jacob', or that it is much more natural to take the *lᵉ* before the infinitives as expressing purpose and not of attendant circumstance ('in that I bring back', etc.), as Budde holds.

[6] E.g., Gesenius, de Wette, Wiener, Umbreit, Schenkel, Farley.

ception of 'corporate personality'[1] has led scholars, such as Pedersen, Eissfeldt, and Wheeler Robinson, to try to combine the individual and collective interpretations.[2] The Servant *is* the prophet, who will bring about the conversion of the other Israelites, and 'he *is* Israel created to be the Servant', says Wheeler Robinson.[3] Nyberg holds that 'the Servant is Israel in the sense of the ancestor as well as the people; in him the experiences of a whole people are concentrated'.[4] Bentzen maintains that he 'is Deutero-Isaiah and Israel, the new Moses ('Messias' in radically changed form) and the congregation, for whom he is ready to die, in one single person, the Patriarch of the new race'.[5] They appeal to the well-known fact that, both in the Israelite patriarchal traditions and in similar traditions among other eastern peoples in both ancient and modern times, the ancestor and founder of the nation represents the entire community, so that the experiences of the family, the tribe, and the nation throughout the ages can be presented as those of the 'supreme ego' (represented as an individual), and can be transferred to the ancestor as a story about him personally.[6] But then we must not forget that the story-teller conceives of it all as a story about the individual ancestor; and at the moment when he so conceives it, Jacob, for example, is not at the same time ancestor and people, but an individual person, who

[1] The classical work is Pedersen's *Israel* I–II; cf. also Wheeler Robinson in *Werden und Wesen des Alten Testaments*, pp. 49ff.; Johnson, *The One and the Many in the Israelite Conception of God*, where, however, the identification of individual and community is exaggerated (see Snaith's criticism in *J.T.S.* xliv, 1943, p. 82).

[2] Pedersen, *Israel* III–IV, pp. 603ff. Pedersen's view was anticipated by Eissfeldt in *Der Gottesknecht bei Deuterojesaja*. Against Eissfeldt, see Mowinckel's review of the book in *A.f.O.* xi, 1936/7, pp. 81f. See further, Wheeler Robinson in *Werden und Wesen des Alten Testaments*, pp. 49ff.; Bentzen, *King and Messiah*, pp. 48ff. The 'both-and' position is also maintained by Nyberg in *S.E.Å.* vii, 1942, pp. 5–82, where he greatly over-emphasizes the kingly and ancestral features in the Servant. Pedersen's approach is followed by Wheeler Robinson (see Additional Note XII) and Engnell in *B.J.R.L.* xxxi, 1, 1948. Ström in *Vetekornet* directly identifies the individual and the community, in what is a pure caricature of Pedersen's fundamental view; see C.-M. Edsman's well-founded criticism of Ström in his review of *Vetekornet* in *Kyrkohistorisk Årsskrift*, 1944, pp. 356ff., and in the article 'Evangeliskt och katoliskt om Corpus Christi, kyrkan och den enskilda' in *S.T.K.* xxi, 1945, pp. 272ff., where he points out the many misleading generalizations and inconsistencies in Ström's definitions and interpretations. Attempts to revive the collective interpretation of the Servant, but more along the older lines, are made by Farley in *E.T.* xxxviii, 1926/7, pp. 521ff. (idealized prophecy), Peake in *The Servant of Yahweh and Other Lectures*, Waterman in *J.B.L.* lvi, 1937, pp. 27ff., Snaith in *Studies in Old Testament Prophecy Presented to T. H. Robinson*, pp. 187–200 (the Servant is 'the righteous remnant', which in Deutero-Isaiah is represented by Jehoiachin and his fellow-exiles of 597 B.C.).
Young's criticism of Eissfeldt in *Westminster Theological Journal* xi, 1948, pp. 135ff., misses the point, because he is unfamiliar with the ancient mode of thought, and therefore his arguments are too modern and rationalistic, i.e., supposedly orthodox.

[3] *Werden und Wesen des Alten Testaments*, pp. 59ff.   [4] *S.E.Å.* vii, 1942, p. 75.
[5] *King and Messiah*, p. 67.   [6] See Additional Note XII, and p. 213 n. 2.

experienced what the nation also experienced later, and carried out various exploits such as his descendants also accomplished. To *us*, looking at the characters in the light of the study of the history of tradition, they *are* both. But for the narrators of the patriarchal sagas, Abraham *is* the man Abraham, and Jacob *is* the individual Jacob, in whom the hearers recognize themselves as they are in their best moments, but who are nevertheless not 'identical' with the nation, in any other way than we modern Norwegians or Englishmen are, when we 'identify ourselves with' (i.e., become aware of our connexion with) our own nation in its past history, and with the exploits then accomplished. It is also possible to exaggerate the mythical and irrational character of ancient thought. For instance, even if Bentzen were right in his view that the Servant is thought of as a new Moses, the Servant would not therefore, in the poet's thought, actually *be* Moses himself, or the Israel of the Mosaic period, still less a resuscitated Moses,[1] or *Moses redivivus*; he *is* the Servant, who in the future will have as momentous a task to perform with 'Israel' as Moses had in the past. If we start from the ancient conception of the unity of the nation and the individual, of 'Israel' as a type embodied in the ancestor, the nation, and its individual members,[2] the view that the Servant is 'Israel', and has a mission to a quite different unbelieving 'Israel', is utterly improbable, indeed impossible. The 'type' is present in the

---

[1] Cf. *King and Messiah*, p. 66.

[2] What Pedersen means by 'type' must be understood in the light of primitive thought, and not of Platonism. It is, of course, true that the conception which really primitive peoples have of the people or community has a certain similarity to the Platonic teaching about ideas (cf. V. Grønbech, 'Primitiv Religion' in *Illustreret Religionshistorie*[2], p. 23), a similarity which is perhaps particularly evident in the Persian conception of the 'bull's soul', the primal, heavenly bull. In primitive thought the reality which is given consists of wholes which are also entities. As in fairy stories, it is not '*a* bear', but '*the* bear', the 'eternal' bear. Each entity has its own definite character and type. 'The man' is different from 'the lion'; 'Israel' is a different type from 'Moab'. The type 'Israel' is an eternal reality. It is manifested in the ancestor, in the nation in its varying historical situations, and in individual Israelites, particularly in representative men such as chiefs and kings. We may try to express this in modern terms by saying that the ancestor lives on in the nation and in all its individual members, and that the king, for example, embodies the entire nation. Israel is a corporate personality (to use Wheeler Robinson's expression); and in certain situations this corporate personality may be manifested in a representative person, such as the ancestor or the king. This is what Pedersen means when he calls Israel an 'ideal quantity' (*Israel* I–II, p. 475). But this is rather different from Plato's distinction between the 'idea' and the (inferior) empirical reality. Through sin, Israel may forfeit her 'type'; but then it ceases to exist. It is normally in concrete reality, in historical exploits, etc., that the essence of 'life' of the type is manifested. It is the duty of the individual to realize the type in his life, in unity with the whole community; and between individual and community there is no contrast. Those who hold the collective interpretation of the Servant fail to appreciate this correspondence between type and reality.

ancestor, the nation, and the individual members; but it has no existence outside any of them, as a sort of metaphysical being. It cannot be imagined as a 'person', in contrast with the empirical Israel, to which it has a mission to fulfil. The view of the Servant held by Pedersen and the other neo-collectivists is therefore untenable.

Nor is there anything in the texts themselves to compel us to accept so unnatural an interpretation. That the Servant in xlix, 1–6, should be, as Wheeler Robinson holds, at one moment the prophet, labouring to convert his fellow-countrymen, and then, the instant he receives the new mission to be 'a light to the nations', suddenly be changed into Israel, or come to think that he *is* in fact Israel since he is the 'representative' through whom she will realize her mission—that is not only a rather difficult idea to conceive; it is also quite unnecessary, since the text itself does not call for a mental leap of this kind in order to be understood.

As depicted by the prophet in the four poems, the Servant *is* neither the ancestor nor Israel (no matter how many features he may have borrowed from the conception of the ancestor), but a person who has, both now and in the future, a task to perform towards Israel.

But there is *some* truth behind the idea that the Servant is Israel, in that he has the standing and importance of one who represents the entire nation, such as a king, or, in the cult, a priest or a prophet. There is an intimate connexion between the Servant and his people Israel. In this sense we may say that the Servant is a 'corporate personality', since, as we have seen, he represents the the whole nation. His work is of decisive importance for the fate of the nation; and to that extent it may be said that the nation acts through him. He suffers what the nation ought to have suffered; what befalls him befalls the nation through him. His sufferings and death are the sacrifice, the *'āšām* offered for the sins of the nation; and his resurrection will result in new life for Israel by leading to its conversion. But that does not prevent his being considered an individual with a task to perform towards the nation Israel. When the word 'servant' is used of Israel in other passages in Deutero-Isaiah, it does not have this individualistic character. It leads only to confusion if we fuse the two 'servants' in Deutero-Isaiah, and feel bound to cover both by a single explanation. The Servant is an individual; but one who represents the whole nation, whose fate is decisive for its fate, and through whom its conversion and the renewal of its life will be realized.

What kind of person, then, is the Servant? He is regarded and described as a *prophet*. This is obvious from what has been said above about his mission and work. He has the endowment which is supremely characteristic of the prophets, endowment with Yahweh's spirit (xlii, 1). He delivers 'direction', *tôrâh*,[1] and has the tongue of a disciple (l, 4), i.e., a disciple of some prophet (viii, 16), or of someone taught by the spirit. Tongue and speech are his instruments, made fit by Yahweh for His service (xlix, 2). Yahweh has called him from his mother's womb, another prophetic feature (Isa. xlix, 2; cf. Jer. i, 5). Daily He opens his ear, so that he may receive revelations (l, 4). The title 'Yahweh's servant' is also used elsewhere of the prophets.[2]

If we consider the content of his prophetic mission, we may

---

[1] Isa. xlii, 4; cf. i, 10; xlii, 3; viii, 16; see Mowinckel in *G.T.M.M.M.* III, n.a on Isa. i, 10.

[2] Isa. xliv, 26; xx, 3; 2 Kings ix, 7; Jer. vii, 25; xxv, 4; xxvi, 5; xxix, 19; xxxv, 15; Amos iii, 7, etc.; see von Baudissin in the *Buddefestschrift*, pp. 3f.; of Moses, Deut. xxxiv, 5; Joshua i, 1; Num. xii, 7; Mal. iv, 22, etc.; see von Baudissin, op. cit., p. 3; of Joshua, Joshua xxiv, 29; of the patriarchs, Exod. xxxii, 13; Deut. ix, 27. In all these instances the underlying notion is that of a prophet. On 'servant' as a designation of the king, see above, p. 67 n. 3. On the prophetic features in the Servant, see also Bentzen, *King and Messiah*, pp. 48ff. It is remarkable that Nyberg in *S.E.Å.* vii, 1942, pp. 63ff. does not raise the question of the category to which the poet held the Servant to belong, but is content to inquire into the 'groups of motifs', from which the conceptions may have been borrowed. This confusion of exegesis with the history of motifs must necessarily be misleading. The primary question must always be, 'What does the writer himself mean?' not, 'What is the source of the individual elements in his conception?' How wrong Nyberg's approach to the question is can be seen (*inter alia*) by what results from it, when he goes on to say that the title of 'servant' was taken over from a Canaanite title which was specially applied to the founder of the dynasty and of the cult (op. cit., p. 79). That is not in itself impossible; but it is of no importance for the interpretation of the Servant; for it is out of the question that Deutero-Isaiah, or a member of his circle, should have thought of the Servant as the founder of a new cult. The cult of Yahweh needed no new 'founder'. Besides, so many intermediate stages and changes of meaning intervene between the original Canaanite title of 'servant', and the Servant in Deutero-Isaiah, that the latter cannot be interpreted in terms of the content of the former. What is sound in Nyberg's view is that the use of the expression in the Ugaritic texts shows that the title always indicates a close connexion with the deity, and a special task derived from him. Engnell, too, who regards the Servant as a royal figure (*B.J.R.L.* xxxi, 1948), has to admit that several traits in the Servant suggest a prophetic figure; but he holds that they arise ultimately from the fact that the king (as he says) is a 'primeval prophet'. Engnell thinks that, in order to maintain that the Servant is conceived as a prophet, it must first be shown that these royal and prophetic traits have passed through a process of 'disintegration', and can also be used of persons who are not kings (op. cit., p. 15 n. 1). To this a reply is offered by Bentzen in *King and Messiah*, p. 108 n. 77. Since I hold that the Servant poems must be interpreted in their own light, without reference to the contexts in which, as it happens, they now stand, I must reject the argument (dissenting here from Bentzen, op. cit., p. 49) from *mᵉbaśśēr* (xli, 27). This word, which here refers to Deutero-Isaiah himself, is undoubtedly a designation for a prophet, like *mubassiru* in Accadian (see Haldar, *Associations*, p. 33).

justifiably speak of a new ideal of prophecy: not the diviner, but the missionary preacher of true religion. The transition to this prophetic ideal is seen in the circle of Deutero-Isaiah's disciples,[1] the so-called 'Trito-Isaiah', in which, in all probability, we must look for the author of these Songs (see below, pp. 253f.).

He is also more than an ordinary prophet, since what matters is not only his preaching and his message, but his person, and what is achieved through his life. His suffering and death are also essential to his work; they were necessary in order that Yahweh's purpose of salvation might be fulfilled. But even this extension of his work is in the prophetic line, as we shall see below.

Several scholars[2] have tried to discover in the Servant features from the figure of the king, or even maintained that he was thought of as a king, or as a royal representative of his people.[3] There are, in fact, no unmistakable royal features to be found.[4] The nearest approach to such is the promise that he will 'be exalted, and lifted up, and be very high', that 'the nations will be amazed at him', and 'before him even the great will be silent; kings will shut their mouths at him' . . . 'therefore I shall divide him a portion among

---

[1] Isa. lxi, 1ff.; cf. Mowinckel in *G.T.M.M.M.* III, p. 17.

[2] Above all Sellin, and, in a different way, Gressmann, Dürr, Rudolph, and, most recently, Nyberg, Engnell, Coppens, and de Leeuw. In recent discussion the parallel drawn by Dürr, between the Servant and the king as atoning in the cult by suffering, has been of particular importance. See below, pp. 221ff.

[3] In particular Engnell, following Dürr, has tried to interpret a number of individual features in the Servant passages in terms of the cultic side of the royal ideology (see *B.J.R.L.* xxxi, 1948, pp. 1ff.). In *King and Messiah*, pp. 48ff. Bentzen refutes Engnell's one-sided views and assumptions; cf. also above, p. 190 n.1, p. 218 n. 2. As a rule, the features in question can be interpreted much more naturally as referring to a prophetic figure. Engnell regards the idea of suffering as itself a sign of the royal ideology; on this point, see above in the text. Another error in method, which Engnell commits in his discussion of the subject, is that he does not distinguish between the Servant poems and the other Deutero-Isaianic sayings, and will not recognize that two different conceptions of the servant are involved; see Additional Note xii; xli, 27; xliii, 4; xliv, 1ff.; and xlix, 7ff. are irrelevant to the subject, quite apart from the question whether Engnell is right in finding there allusions to the royal ideology. He is, in fact, mistaken; cf. Bentzen, op. cit., pp. 58ff. North, *The Suffering Servant*, pp. 139ff., emphasizes rather more strongly than Bentzen the supposed political features in the description of the Servant's work; but he makes too much depend upon the interpretation of the expression 'bring forth *mišpāṭ*' xlii, 1, 3, which, he holds, 'seems to exceed the functions of any king or prophet known to us' (op. cit., p. 141). He also believes that the expression, 'raise up the tribes of Jacob', must point to 'a political restoration', since a tribe is a political entity (op. cit., p. 146). The latter conclusion is not necessary. For instance, it is possible to work for the restoration of a people through 'moral rearmament', which is not really a form of political activity. North does not appear to arrive at any definite conclusion.

[4] Begrich, *Studien zu Deuterojesaja*, pp. 163f. interprets *mišpāṭ yōṣî* as 'announces the sentence as just', and as referring to Yahweh's sentence on the heathen; and he holds that the metaphors of breaking the rod and extinguishing the lamp in Isa. xlii, 3, are legal symbols for condemnation, a view which Bentzen also accepts (*Jesaja* II, p. 33). But not one of the passages to which Begrich refers (Isa. xiv, 5; Ecclus. xxxv, 18; Prov.

the great, and he will divide the spoil with the mighty', or, as perhaps it should be rendered, 'Therefore I assign him the great for his portion, and give him the strong as spoil' (lii, 13–15; liii, 11f.).

But this is future, and speaks of what the Servant will be, not of what he is or has at some time been. Nor does it exceed the honours which might be accorded to any ordinary Israelite or oriental, if he was 'a man whom the king delighted to honour'. Then 'the royal apparel is brought, which the king has worn, and a horse which the king has ridden, and on whose head a royal ornament is set. The apparel and the horse are given to one of the king's most noble princes, that he may array in this apparel the man whom the king delights to honour, and bring him on horseback through the open square of the city, and proclaim before him, "So is it done to the man whom the king delights to honour!" '. Afterwards the king may even give this man the royal seal, and so appoint him Grand Vizier over 'his whole house', so that 'all the princes of the provinces, and the satraps, and the governors, and the royal officials' do his will, because fear of him has fallen upon them'; for such a man has become 'great in the king's house, and his fame spreads throughout all the provinces, for he becomes more and more powerful' (Esther vi, 7–10; viii, 2; ix, 3f.). In this account from Esther of how the Persian king Ahasuerus (Xerxes) exalted the Jew, Mordecai, we have a more or less contemporary and authentic description of how the Jews

---

xiii, 9; xx, 20; xxiv, 20; Job xviii, 5f.; xxi, 17f.) displays or even alludes to any connexion with forensic conceptions or legal terminology. When the 'staff' or sceptre of kings and tyrants is said to be broken, the metaphor obviously points to military operations. The extinguishing of a man's lamp in his tent merely means that the tent is deserted, and the man and his 'house' extirpated; but the metaphor affords no clue to the way in which this has happened. The metaphor depicts the condition of the lost man's tent, and not some symbolic act which brought about this condition or ratified it. Similarly, Snaith (in *Studies in Old Testament Prophecy Presented to T. H. Robinson*) thinks that the prophet speaks here about the execution of justice in the sense of strict justice (le'emet), and that 'wait' means that the Gentiles are waiting with dread for this execution of justice. It is clear that in xlii, 3, the metaphors do not point to any action by the Servant as a judge, but to his preaching as a prophet, preaching which is for edification, not condemnation. The 'judgement' and 'instruction', which he 'brings forth' and 'establishes', denote (as Bentzen, at least, realizes) the true religion; cf. Volz's reference to the Arabic *dín*, which also means both 'judgement' and 'religion'. Of any act of condemnation or sentence (Begrich) there is no mention. Lindblom (*The Servant Songs in Deutero-Isaiah*, pp. 15–17) also finds 'juridical terms' in xlii, 3, and holds that xlii, 1ff., describes kingly activity, an idea which is influenced by his view of xlii, 5–9 as the prophet's own interpretation of xlii, 1–4; see Additional Note XII. On the interpretation of xlix, 1–6 as presenting the Servant as leader of the returning exiles, see above, p. 192. de Leeuw (*De Koninklijke Verklaring van de Ebed-Jahweh-Zangen*) does not seem to have advanced any argument for the royal interpretation of the Servant other than those examined above and in the following pages.

of that period imagined that a man was honoured, before whom even the great and the kings (the Jews regarded the great satraps of the empire as kings, and more than kings) must be silent because of his wonderful exaltation, and who (in the military metaphor) would have the great as his portion, and give the strong as spoil, i.e., would receive power and authority over high-born and power-ful men. The author of the Songs about the Servant of the Lord was a Jew, and thought in the conceptions and metaphors of the day. When he wants to describe the unexpected and wonderful exaltation of a man from the deepest contempt to the highest honour and recognition, it is these conceptions and metaphors from the royal court which are ready to hand. The fact that he uses them does not mean that he thinks of the man in question as a reigning king.

By way of analogy, we may refer to the way in which the writer of Wisdom describes the exaltation of the righteous after the last judgement:

> Therefore they shall receive a glorious kingdom,
> And a diadem of beauty from the Lord's hand
> (Wisd. of Sol. v, 16).

The righteous will one day receive royal rank and adornment as the reward of their righteous piety; but the writer does not, of course, imply that they are actually kings. It would be quite mis-leading here to say that the righteous as such are thought of and described in terms of the oriental royal ideology.[1]

Attempts have also been made to find in the Servant's fate another (and contrasted) feature from oriental kingship, a feature which is supposed to explain the whole of the poet-prophet's thought about the Servant: it is precisely as a sufferer that the Servant is a king, the very suffering being a fundamental element in the royal ideology. It was part of the Babylonian New Year ritual that, on the sixth day of the festival, the king was led by the chief priest into the temple, in front of the chapel of the god Marduk. There he was stripped of his royal insignia, which the priest laid down before the god. On behalf of the god, the priest slapped the king on the cheek and treated him with dishonour; and the king had to kneel, and make a confession of sin, and offer a prayer of penitence. He then received absolution; and his king-ship was restored to him, in return for a promise to care well for

[1] Dürr, *Ursprung und Ausbau*; cf. his *Psalm 110 im Lichte der neueren altorientalischen Forschungen.*

Babylon and the temple of Marduk. On that condition, Marduk would overthrow all his enemies before him. He was then arrayed again in his regalia.[1] It has been maintained (the Catholic scholar, Dürr, was the first to do so) that the thought of the Servant's vicarious atonement through humiliation and degradation was influenced by these rituals from the Babylonian New Year festival,[2] and that this very feature provides the explanation of the figure of the Servant: he is the king, who, on behalf of his people, atones, suffers, and dies, but is restored to life. Such phraseology has been used, particularly by Engnell and Widengren, in maintaining the idea of the Servant as king. Complex, ancient associations are supposed to be involved; and we must therefore examine this hypothesis more closely.

Whereas Dürr contends merely that the Servant of the Lord is depicted in the guise of the penitent king, who suffers and makes atonement, Engnell regards the ritual itself as a cultic expression of the death and resurrection of the king, and accordingly holds that in this ritual he is identical with the god, as he supposes him to be elsewhere in the cult. He believes that the cult had this form and this significance, not only in Babylonia, but also in Canaanite Ugarit, and in Israel.[3] The Servant is thus the king-god in his atoning passion, death, and resurrection,[4] which Engnell regards as typical elements in the kingly character, and as part of the religious, royal ideology as it is expressed in the cult. Widengren seems to share this view.[5]

In my opinion, the evidence that in the cult the king was held to be identical with the god in his suffering, death, and resurrection, is very slight.[6] Even for Babylonia it merely suggests that, as in the mystery religions, those who took part in the cult shared in the experience of the god as they witnessed the enacting of his

[1] Zimmern, *Zum babylonischen Neujahrsfest* II; Pallis, *The Babylonian Akitu Festival*.

[2] See Dürr, *Ursprung und Ausbau*, pp. 125ff.; most recently Nyberg in *S.E.Å.* vii, 1942, pp. 66ff.; Widengren, in *R.o.B.* ii, 1943, p. 71; Engnell, *Divine Kingship*, pp. 152 n. 1, 170 n. 4, 176 n. 4.

[3] *Divine Kingship*, Index, s.vv. ' "Passion", penitence, and "death" of the king'.

[4] Op. cit., Index, s.v. 'Ebed Yahweh'; see especially pp. 152 n.1, 170 n. 4, 176 n. 4; cf., however, *B.J.R.L.* xxxi, 1, 1948, p. 6.

[5] *R.o.B.* ii, 1943, p. 71; cf. *S.E.Å.* x, 1946, pp. 66ff.; see alo *Religionens värld*², pp. 311f. The advocates of this supposed 'ideology of the cultic death of the king' find much of their material in cultic texts concerning the dying Tammuz, which are to be found in Witzel, *Tammuz-Liturgien und Verwandtes*. Rowley, too, finds in the Servant features from the suffering king (*The Servant of the Lord and Other Essays on the Old Testament*, pp. 61–88).

[6] See my review of the books by Engnell and Widengren, in *N.T.T.* xlv, 1944, pp. 70ff.; see also above, pp. 41, 48ff., 84ff.

fortunes.[1] The texts do not support the substantial identity which Engnell assumes, and which would mean that in the cult there was no consciousness of any distinction between the god and the king. The king may, indeed, have played the part of the *victorious god*. As the god's earthly vicegerent, he was also his champion, and represented him in his conflict and victory; but the king's death was not enacted. It is quite out of the question that in Israel such a conception should have existed and found expression in the rituals of the cult (see above, pp. 84ff.). Both in Babylonia and elsewhere, the rituals show quite clearly that the king's part in the cult was primarily that of a man, interceding and sacrificing as an intermediary on behalf of the people.

In the penitential ritual of the Babylonian New Year festival, it is quite clear that the king appears as the representative of men before the god, humiliating himself before him, and being restored by him. The texts do not suggest that his atoning penitence and self-humiliation on behalf of the people are regarded as a spiritualized 'death'. It *could*, of course, have been so regarded in the thought and language of religion, as the New Testament sometimes regards conversion as a 'death'; but there is no necessary identity between the two ideas. There is, therefore, no ground for regarding the ritual of atonement at the New Year festival as an expression of the resurrection of the king and the god of vegetation,[2] or for maintaining that the suffering was an essential feature of the royal ideology.

Nor is there any ground for regarding the Babylonian ritual, with the king's atoning penitence and humiliation at the New Year festival, and the mythical conceptions which may possibly lie behind it, as the pattern of the description of the Servant of the Lord. There is nothing to suggest that the Babylonian rite of atonement was used in the temple at Jerusalem during the monarchy, although, of course, on many occasions the king acted

---

[1] Cf. also Bentzen, *King and Messiah*, pp. 26ff.

[2] Nor may we draw this conclusion, as Dürr (*Ursprung und Ausbau*, p. 140) and Engnell (*Divine Kingship*, Index, s.v. '*šar pûhi*') appear to think, from the fact that in certain circumstances it was customary, in order to avert dangers which threatened the king, to choose a substitute king (*šar pûhi*), who was arrayed in royal insignia, and was perhaps sometimes killed as a sacrifice. See Labat, *Royauté*, pp. 103ff.; Frankfort, *Kingship*, pp. 262ff.; and cf. above, pp. 38ff. The redemption of the life of the king and the people by the sacrifice of a substitute has nothing to do with the death and resurrection of the vegetation god, and does not prove that the king's atonement and penitence were regarded as a cultic death. Gadd (*Ideas of Divine Rule*, pp. 48ff.) also regards the repeated investiture as a ceremony by which power was renewed, not as a resurrection.

as the cultic representative of the people on days of penitence and at festivals of atonement.[1] An instance of this has been mentioned above,[2] namely Ps. cii, which obviously reflects a penitential rite in which the people is embodied in its leader to such a degree that the oppression of Jerusalem may be presented as his own personal suffering and illness. Certain features also suggest that this psalm belonged to the penitential rites of the New Year festival. But in the texts there is nothing to suggest that the king was dethroned and reinstated, much less that he was supposed to die and rise again. As the representative and embodiment of Jerusalem, he bears her sufferings, and performs the atoning rites and prayers, which will induce Yahweh to intervene and save. There is here no mention of any vicarious suffering, still less of vicarious suffering, which, as in Isa. liii, is misunderstood and unappreciated.

The most that can safely be said about such cultic 'patterns' is that the work of the Servant must be considered against the background of the general ideas of fellowship and mutual responsibility between the community and its representative, ideas which are expressed both in penitential ritual, such as lies behind Ps. cii, and in the conception that the penitence and atonement of one may avail for the others whom he represents. It is perhaps incorrect to call this 'vicarious suffering', at least in terms of a strictly legal theology. The representative of the community can do penance on its behalf precisely because he is its representative and embodiment. But gradually such ideas are rationalized. The vicarious element can survive, even after the ancient view of 'corporate personality' has passed away. In the same way, animal sacrifice can be interpreted as 'vicarious', which does not accord with its original significance.

The conception of a vicarious office, as we find it in the religion and cult of Israel, is, therefore, one of those general ideas which underlie the Servant's vicarious atonement. Just because it formed part of the general theory of the cult, it could easily be adopted as an explanation of the guiltless suffering of the Servant. But this provides no explanation of the origin of the idea of the Servant's death and resurrection; and still less are we justified in concluding that the king was the model for the portrait of the Servant. Even before the time of Deutero-Isaiah, there had for long been in

---

[1] Dürr, *Ursprung und Ausbau*, pp. 139f.
[2] See above, p. 84 n. 4. The annual Day of Atonement (*yôm kippūrîm*), on the tenth of Tishri, originally formed part of the New Year festival; see *Ps.St.* II, pp. 83ff.

Israel others besides the king who could make vicarious atonement. The part played by the High-priest in the ritual of atonement in Lev. xvi (P) certainly goes back, in its main features, to a considerably earlier period.

In this context we may also point out that there is an essential difference between the Babylonian king's ritual penitence and humiliation and the suffering of the Servant. Before the king was abased, he was king; and he became king again afterwards. It was a drama in three acts: exaltation, abasement, and again exaltation. In the Servant's life there are only two acts: a time of ever-increasing abasement, followed by elevation to a height above anything previously attained. Even if the Babylonian ideal of kingship was one of the specific cultic data which provided the general cultic background for the origin of the idea of the atoning worth of the Servant's suffering, there is still nothing to show that it was precisely *this* specific datum which, in the first instance, determined the poet's conceptions; and there is nothing in his description to show that he thought of the Servant as a penitent and atoning king.

Even the title, 'Servant', has been taken as evidence that the Servant is thought of in terms of the royal ideology.[1] It is, of course, true that, both in the east generally and in Israel, the king is the 'servant' of the deity in a special sense.[2] Not only is he a worshipper; but he has a specially intimate relationship to Him, and an honourable task to perform for Him.[3] This is also the content of the conception of the Servant of the Lord. As we shall see later, there is probably some connexion between the Servant's status and title, and the same title in Canaanite religion and mythology. But there is nothing to suggest that the title of Servant was meant to indicate royal status. As a title of honour, and as an expression of an active mission, the 'Servant of Yahweh' is applied in the Old Testament, as we have seen, first and foremost to the prophets.[4]

[1] Engnell, *Divine Kingship*, p. 152 n. 1.
[2] See above, p. 67 n. 3. On the expression in Babylonia, see p. 38.
[3] See Mowinckel in *N.T.T.* xliii, 1942, p. 25. On the servant conception in the Old Testament and in the Semitic east, see Lindhagen's exhaustive treatment in *The Servant Motif in the Old Testament: a Preliminary Study to the 'Ebed Yahweh Problem' in Deutero-Isaiah.* Lindhagen produces abundant evidence to show that, in the east, 'servant' denotes a vassal king, and thus designates the king as the vassal of the god. Obviously; but it does not follow that every *'ebed* is a vassal king, and that every *'ebed* of a deity is a king.
[4] See above, p. 218 and n. 2. Widengren in *R.o.B.* ii, 1943, pp. 70ff., also maintains that the Servant is thought of first and foremost as a king who suffers, dies, and rises again. He argues from the fact that the Servant is compared with the tree

Some scholars have also maintained that the figure of the Servant as a withered shoot has been derived from the royal ideology. Strictly speaking, this figure denotes the dying god of vegetation; but it is argued that the god is represented in the cult by the king. *Therefore*, this figure shows that the Servant is a royal personage. But even if the conception of the tree of life, which dies and blossoms again, and that of the king-god who dies and comes to life again, are the ultimate background of the form in which the thought of the Servant's death and resurrection is expressed, this still does not prove that the Servant was thought of as a king. For in both Babylonian and Israelite religion these figures underwent a process of 'democratization'; i.e., in the rites and prayers of the cult, they were used at first to describe the king's relationship to the god, to support faith in his deliverance from affliction, and to justify prayers for that deliverance; but later the rites and the language came to be applied to ordinary men and their relationship to the god.[1]

The same is true of the influence of the form of the psalms on the thought of the Servant's death and resurrection, and on its development (to this point we return below). It is true that, both in Babylonia and Israel, the vivid language of the psalms about the deliverance of the worshipper from the realm of the dead was

[1] This is admitted by both Widengren and Engnell. It follows that the point ceases to be relevant to the historical and exegetical interpretation of the Servant's identity, and affects only the ultimate origin of this or that feature in the portrait.

(or 'shoot') which withers (and comes to life again; though this latter point is not mentioned in the text); and finding here (perhaps rightly) an echo of the ideology and cultic symbolism of the vegetation god, he goes on to maintain (like Engnell) that, in the cult, the tree represents the king. But the sources quoted by Widengren and Engnell do not provide any support for this; see my review in *N.T.T.* xlv, 1944, pp. 77f. Widengren makes further reference to a number of supposed royal traits in the Servant. But his treatment is too superficial. In Isa. lxi, 1ff., the speaker is not the king, but the king's herald, i.e., the prophet. The royal functions cannot without more ado be transferred to the herald or prophet. Accordingly, Isa. xi, 1–9 does not prove anything about the Servant. When Widengren refers to 'Isa. xlii, 1–7 . . ., xlv, 1–7 and xlix, 1–13', he is confusing two quite different matters. The first Servant Song consists of xlii, 1–4 not xlii, 1–7. In *vv.* 5–7 there is a complete change of subject, as is shown by the new introductory formula, and by a consideration of the stylistic structure of the prophetic oracles. What we have here is an oracle to Cyrus; see Haller in *Eucharisterion* I, pp. 262ff.; Mowinckel in *Z.A.W.* xlix, 1931, pp. 94ff.; *G.T.M.M.M.* III, p. 211. xlv, 1–7 is also an oracle about Cyrus, and proves nothing about the conception of the Servant, although it is true that the author of the Servant Songs transfers to the Servant-prophet tasks which Deutero-Isaiah has attributed to the king (Cyrus); see below, pp. 224f. Nor can xlix, 1–13 be used as evidence. The Servant Song consists only (*pace* Engnell, *B.J.R.L.* xxxi, 1, 1948, p. 18) of *vv.* 1–7. Once more, a new subject is introduced at *v.* 8, which was originally addressed to Israel. It is unfortunate that Widengren and Engnell do not give more heed to questions of style, and to the study of the history of literary genres, which help us to define the limits of the individual prophetic sayings with greater certainty.

originally applied to the king. But in both religions the psalms and the rites associated with them came to be used of ordinary mortals. The 'royal style' in the psalms, and the echo of it in the description of the Servant's destiny, do not therefore in any way prove that he was thought of as a king.

There is yet another way in which the sufferings of the Servant have been taken to prove that he is depicted and conceived as a king. In Babylonia these sufferings are characteristic of the god Tammuz. But, it is argued, in the cult the king is identical with Tammuz; therefore the Servant is the suffering king in the cult.[1] The syllogism lacks cogency, because, as we have seen (see above, pp. 84ff.), there is no valid evidence either that the king in Israel was Tammuz, or that his part in the cult involved suffering. It is true that there are certain features in the description of the Servant which go back ultimately to the conception of Tammuz (to this we return below); but this has no bearing on the question whether the Servant is depicted as a king.

There is, however, some truth in the contention that certain royal traits have been transferred to the Servant. The point is not only that he will one day be exalted to be the equal of kings, but that, of his mission as Servant, it is said that he will be a light to the nations, and bring forth right religion in the earth (xlii, 4; xlix, 6). It is well known that, both in Israel[2] and elsewhere in the east, the king is regularly described as the sun rising on mankind, giving light and warmth, and creating life.[3] In particular, the Babylonian sun god Shamash is also connected with justice and law.[4] There is nothing surprising in the transference of these ideas to the Servant, since the author of the Servant Songs explicitly transfers to the Servant those expectations and metaphors which Deutero-Isaiah had applied to King Cyrus (see below, pp. 244f.). The decisive fact is not the origin of these expressions in the 'royal style'. In the Servant Songs they have acquired a new meaning, which is determined by the prophetic call. It is by his proclamation of the true religion that the Servant becomes the light of the nations, and the means of establishing right conditions

---

[1] Engnell, *B.J.R.L.* xxxi, 1, 1948, pp. 4ff.

[2] 2 Sam. xxiii, 3b, 4; Ps. lxxii, 5, 17; cf. Ps. ci, 8; Mic. v, 1b.

[3] In Egypt, the king is the son and incarnation of the sun god. Among the Hittites his official title was 'the Sun'. Hammurabi was installed as king 'to rise like Shamash (the sun god) over the black-headed people (mankind), and to light up the land' (Code of Hammurabi I, 40); etc.

[4] See Meissner, *Babylonien und Assyrien* II, p. 20; Schroeder in *Z.A.W.* xxxiv, 1914, p. 69f.

in Israel and to the ends of the earth. The Servant is a prophet, who will bring to Israel the salvation which was in ancient times expected of the king, and more than that; but he will accomplish it by methods quite different from those used by the king, or the future king, for the deliverance of his people.

In the main, then, the Servant is depicted as a prophet, and not as a king.[1] If it can be shown that, in the east, prophetic powers and titles were often associated with the king, that is here of no importance. In Israel a clear distinction had come to be made between king and prophet. The author of the Servant Songs represents the outlook of the prophetic circles in an age when there were no kings. For *him* the functions and powers which he attributes to the Servant are clearly prophetic.

Admittedly, the Servant has this formal connexion with the future king or 'Messiah', that he is associated with the realization of the future hope. But in this he plays a part which far exceeds what is usually ascribed to the future king, in that he is not merely a leading figure in the restored nation, but himself directly instrumental in the restoration of Israel, and co-operates in the fulfilment of the future hope. Again, the means employed by the Servant in the fulfilment of his task differ from those usually attributed to the 'Messiah'. The Servant works by the prophetic message, the divine word. It is said, of course, of the Messiah in Isa. ix, 1–6, that he uses his mouth as his instrument, but there the point is that he kills his adversaries with 'the breath of his mouth'; he is the warrior who fells them, not the missionary prophet who convinces them.

Since there is also not the slightest indication that the Servant was thought of as a scion of David,[2] it follows that he is not thought of as a 'Messiah' in the Old Testament sense. Rudolph, for instance, is quite wide of the mark in holding that the Servant's task in relation to Israel is that of a general, a statesman, and a ruler, as well as a prophet and a teacher. There is not the slightest suggestion that the Servant will use military and political means in 'bringing back' Israel.

Similarly, Bentzen is wrong, when (partly following Nyberg) he thinks of the Servant as a new Moses, who will lead back the

[1] This is emphasized by Lagrange in *Le judaïsme avant Jésus-Christ*, pp. 379f.

[2] I disregard Gressmann's fantastic notion that the background of the Servant conception is King Josiah and an annual festival of lamentation for him (*Der Messias*, pp. 324f.). All that is needed to refute this view was said by Hölscher in his review of Gressmann's book in *Deutsche Literaturzeitung* 13, IX, 1930, cols. 1729ff. Cf. Bentzen, *King and Messiah*, pp. 63f.

exiles to Jerusalem in person, and re-establish Yahweh worship
there.[1] The Servant's task is not political, but purely spiritual.
He is the prophet who will bring about the conversion of Israel;
and then Yahweh will provide for the home-coming and restoration of Israel.[2] In the Servant we find no trace of the political
element, which was always present in the 'Messiah' of the Old
Testament, even when the religious element was predominant.
As we have said, we may at most speak of metaphors drawn from
the political sphere, from oriental court life, or from predatory
tribal expeditions. The Servant is neither 'an exilic Messiah', as

[1] *King and Messiah*, pp. 65ff. To a certain extent Bentzen here takes up again
Sellin's idea of the Servant as a new Moses; but he discards Sellin's fantasies about
the martyr death of the historical Moses. He appeals to the well-known fact that,
on occasion, Deutero-Isaiah thinks of the home-coming of the exiles as a new Exodus
through the wilderness (cf. *Ps.St.* II, pp. 198, 335); and he maintains that in xlix,
5f. and 8–12 the Servant is described as the new Moses or Joshua, who leads the
people back and brings about a new apportioning of the land after the return. This
latter point is wrong: xlix, 8–13 deals, not with the Servant, but with Israel; and the
passage is quite independent of xlix, 1–6 (see above, p. 191 n. 4). The logical subject of
the infinitives in *vv.* 8b and 9a is Yahweh Himself. The clause, 'I have formed you
and made you a covenant of the people' (*v.* 8c), would not be sufficient to show that
the poem deals with the Servant, even if it were original, which it can hardly be.
The basic passage, xlii, 6, deals with Cyrus. The thought in xlix, 8ff. is that in the time
of His favour Yahweh has heard Israel's prayer and has begun to help them to restore
the land, to repopulate the desolate cities, and to bring the prisoners out of the prison.
In xlix 5, there is no mention of bringing the dispersed people back to Canaan, but
rather of bringing them back to Yahweh, i.e., converting them. *V.* 6 must be understood in this light. The return of those who have been delivered is here a consequence
of conversion, and, *in that sense*, it is the Servant's work. But there is no suggestion in
the text that the Servant is literally thought of as leading the people through the desert.
It is quite another matter that certain traits from the figure of Moses may have been
present to the mind of the poet, when he painted his picture of the Servant. To this
we shall return later. When Bentzen uses the expression 'Moses redivivus', he presumably does not mean literally a resurrected or reincarnated Moses, but simply what
he calls elsewhere 'a new Moses'. How the ancients themselves would have thought
of the matter is shown by the words of the angel to Zacharias in Luke i, 17, concerning
the Baptist: 'He will go before Him in the spirit and power of Elijah', i.e., he will be
equipped with the same spirit and power as Elijah had. The same interpretation must
be put on the words of Jesus in Matt. xi, 14, 'he is the Elijah who is to come'. (In the
English edition of his book, Bentzen makes it clear that the above is the sense in which
he uses the term 'Moses redivivus'; see *King and Messiah*, p. 66 [Translator].)

[2] Cf. Rudolph in *Z.A.W.* xliii, 1925, p. 98. In support of his view, Rudolph contents
himself with referring to Isa. xlii, 1–4, 6, 7a; xlix, 6b; and liii, 10, 12a, and further
(op. cit., p. 102) to xlix, 8, 9a. The interpretation of liii, 10–12 is discussed above
(pp. 220f.). xlii, 1–4 says nothing about political activity; see above, and pp. 190f.;
also Mowinckel in *Z.A.W.* xlix, 1931, p. 94 n. 4. xlii, 6f. is not part of the first Servant
Song, but deals with Cyrus; see above, p. 189 n. 2. Of xlix, 6b, the same may be said as
of xlii, 1–4: it mentions the prophetic and religious activity of the Servant; see above,
pp. 192f. Staerk rightly makes the same point in *Z.A.W.* xliv, 1926, pp. 245f. Like
xlix, 7, xlix, 8, 9a has no connexion with xlix, 1–6, or with the Servant poems as a
whole, but belongs to an independent poem, xlix, 7–13; see Mowinckel in *Z.A.W.*
xlix, 1931, p. 104 n. 1. Accordingly, my own former statements about 'Messianic
features' in the portrait of the Servant (*Der Knecht Jahwäs*, pp. 31f.) are misleading.
I made them because I did not then realize that xlii, 5–7 does not belong to xlii, 1–4
(op. cit., p. 2 n. 8; cf. pp. 7f.).

Rudolph calls him,[1] nor, in Gressmann's phrase, 'a prophetic Messiah', unless we take the term 'Messiah' in a sense entirely different from that which it has elsewhere in the Old Testament, and throughout the whole of the Old Testament period, and read into it a New Testament content. But such inaccurate use of terms is misleading, and therefore objectionable by scholarly standards.

In fact, the poet's conception of the Servant goes far beyond anything that the other prophets of Judah ever thought or imagined about their 'Messiah'. It is not of a 'Messiah' that the poet speaks; but he has a vision of a prophetic figure who would in time include within himself and supersede the Jewish Messiah.

But the picture of the Servant also includes features which go beyond the usual picture of the Old Testament prophet. The prophet is a man of words, a man with a message to proclaim. But the Servant reached the climax of his vocation, when he no longer proclaimed a message, no longer 'opened his mouth', but remained silent,

> as a lamb that is led to the slaughter,
> as a ewe that before her shearers is dumb (liii, 7).

The Servant's life is his real work.

But we may recognize in this a link with earlier ideas about a prophet's person. Since his words possessed an active power, the prophet did not only predict coming events; as God's agent, he brought them to pass. Originally, the prophet had this significance because of his 'power-charged actions'. When he performed symbolic acts (such as shooting 'an arrow of victory for Yahweh, an arrow of victory against Aram'), according to ancient Israelite thought, these acts brought to pass the events which they represented, and which the accompanying words described. The prophet could himself be a powerful 'symbolic' agency of this kind. For example, Yahweh made Isaiah walk 'naked and barefoot for three years', in order to bring down the same ignominy on the allies of sinful Israel, the Ethiopians and Egyptians (Isa. xx). Jeremiah had to walk about with an iron yoke upon his neck, in order to illustrate and bring to pass the fate which awaited Judah and the other peoples of Western Asia, slavery under the yoke of the king of Babylon (Jer. xxxvii f.). But the prophet's whole person

---

[1] Neither a 'Messiah' nor 'exilic'; see below, pp. 254ff.

and life may be a sign of this kind.[1] He is no longer his own master. Yahweh may even devastate his personal life in order to use him in this way as a powerful 'portent' to attain His purpose. So it is with Jeremiah. Yahweh forbids him to marry and have children, or to have any human or social intercourse with his neighbours, to go to a house of mourning, or a party, or a wedding. In short, he cuts himself off from his natural environment, from all the sources of his life, and sacrifices his entire natural life, in order to be a vehicle of the message of doom which he has to convey to his people. That he felt it to be a grievous disaster and curse is evident from his complaints about his mission, as he sits alone because Yahweh's hand is upon him, and he is filled with Yahweh's own indignation.[2] In the same way, Ezekiel has to swallow a scroll 'with lamentations, and mourning, and woe written on the front and on the back'. He has to let all the disaster which will befall Jerusalem afflict his own person, lying bound three hundred and ninety days for Israel, and forty days for Judah, and 'bear their punishment'. 'And behold I shall put cords upon you, and you will not turn from one side to the other, till you have completed the days of your siege.' During this time he will eat bread by short weight, and drink water by short measure, and disregard the rules of cleanness, because this will also be Jerusalem's lot during the siege. Yahweh will take away from him the desire of his eyes, his wife; and he may not mourn for her, or do honour to her memory in accordance with customary decorum. In this way, Ezekiel will be a portent to the Jews, indicating that the same fate will befall them all, the loss of wives, sons, daughters, and kinsfolk without their being able to lift a finger to help them.[3]

In this way, the prophets often had to share the burden of punishment for the people's sin. The suffering and the martyrdom to which the prophets (particularly Jeremiah, so far as we know) were exposed in fulfilling their mission, were endured by them because of the people's sin, certainly not willingly, and with a strong sense of the injustice of it, but still as a consequence of their efforts to bring the sinful people to conversion, penitence, and salvation. They had to make their whole lives and their very selves to be a powerful 'sign', which would bring about the

---

[1] Isa. xx, 3; viii, 18; Ezek. xii, 6, 11; xxiv, 24, 27; Zech. iii, 8; cf. Keller, *Das Wort OTH als "Offenbarungszeichen Gottes"*, pp. 49ff.
[2] Jer. xvi, 1–13; xv. 17; xx, 7b.
[3] Ezek. iii, 8–10; iv; xxiv, 16ff.; cf. also xii.

realization of Yahweh's punitive will for the people (see above, pp. 230f.). It meant suffering and martyrdom for the sake of the people, the suffering of the righteous on behalf of others. But there is no question here of atoning suffering.[1] Thus, what is said of the Servant of the Lord goes far beyond the normal suffering of the prophets. He becomes the necessary means of bringing about others' confession of sin, conversion, and salvation, by voluntarily (yet perhaps without himself knowing why) allowing his own life to be destroyed, and suffering an undeserved and ignominious death, deprived of descendants and renown, being 'taken away from protection and right'.

Yet this idea is based on the experience of the prophets and their deepening insight. It has been mentioned above (p. 228f.) that some scholars have seen in the Servant a new Moses. To later ages, Moses was the prophet *par excellence*, the pattern for all prophets.[2] An important element in the tradition about Moses is his constant intercession for the sinful people. He is even ready to die, in order to appease the wrath of Yahweh against the people; and the punishment for their sins falls on him as well.[3] It is quite possible that the memory of these ideas helped to form the portrait of the Servant in the mind of the poet-prophet.

It has sometimes also been maintained that Jeremiah was the pattern for the description of the Servant of the Lord.[4] As a major explanation it is incorrect. But the two are alike in bearing unmerited suffering for the sake of the people, although they were 'righteous' and in their suffering were guiltless. What distinguishes the attitude taken to the sufferings of the Servant from that of Jeremiah and the other earlier prophets to what they had to endure, is that the author of the Songs has found the *explanation* of the suffering. It has a positive purpose in God's plan for the salvation of the people and of all peoples, whereas Jeremiah could but moan in his pain. Only after the wildest attempts at rebellion did he attain humble submission to the incomprehensible God, and even then did not discern any purpose in his suffering.

.   .   .

---

[1] Cf. L. B. Paton in *J.B.L.* xlv, 1926, pp. 111ff.

[2] Deut. xxxiv, 10; cf. xviii, 15; Hos. xii, 14; Isa. lxiii, 11f.

[3] Exod. xxxii, 31ff.; Deut. ix, 17ff., 25ff.; i, 37; iii, 26; iv, 21. See Bentzen, *King and Messiah*, p. 66.

[4] Duhm in *Das Buch Jesaia*[1]; Volz, *Jesaja* II, p. 188; most recently by Nyberg in *S.E.Å.* vii, 1942, p. 80. The idea is advanced in a somewhat artificial way by Farley in *E.T.* xxxviii, 1927/8, pp. 521ff.

All that has been said above justifies the view that the figure of the Servant in some sort sums up the entire prophetic movement and its experiences down through the ages. This is the core of truth in the wrongly expressed idea that the Servant is 'the personification of the prophetic order or of the prophetic movement'. The ideas revealed in the description of the Servant constitute a climax in Old Testament prophecy. The whole line of revelation history in prophecy and in Israel's spiritual history leads up to the thought of the innocent, suffering Servant of God, who, by his message, his suffering, and his death, reconciles men to God, 'intervenes', 'pays the forfeit of his life'. What later ages expected of the true prophet was that he should stand in the breach for the people, and avert Yahweh's wrath.[1] According to the later view, this was what Moses tried to do, offering his own life to achieve it (see above; Exod. xxxii, 1–14, 30–2). Time and again, several of the prophets felt themselves impelled to the service of atoning intercession, even after judgement of death had been passed on the ungodly people.[2] Thus, elements from the tradition about the prophets and men of God in the past may well have been incorporated in the poet's description of the Servant.

It is by no means impossible, but rather probable, that some influence was also exercised by the thought of other persons 'intervening' with God on behalf of the community by means of intercession and rites of atonement (features from the functions of priest or king as cultic mediator). We shall return to this point below (ch. VII, 4). But there is no evidence in the texts that such influence came from the Babylonian ideas and rites mentioned above.

The general background of the conception of the Servant has been referred to above. It is the ancient Israelite conception of the common life of society. All the members of the nation form a unity, a totality, an organism. Therefore, one member can atone for another, as long as they all willingly and consciously identify themselves with him, his person, and his work. Accordingly, it was natural for the poet-prophet both to describe the Servant in prophetic terms, and also to express his interpretation of the Servant's work, the redemptive purpose of his death, in metaphors and phrases drawn from the vocabulary of sacrifice, where we moderns might have preferred to use psychological categories and terms.

[1] Ezek. xiii, 5; xxii, 30; Ps. cvi, 23.
[2] Amos vii, 2, 5; Jer. iii, 22–5; vii, 16; xi, 14; xiv, 13f.; cf. Isa. lxiii, 7ff.

THE SERVANT OF THE LORD

4. The Historical Background of the Thought of the Servant's Resurrection and the Atoning Significance of His Suffering

What has been said above about the Servant as 'the ideal prophet' still leaves unexplained how the unheard-of notion of his resurrection from the dead could arise in the thought and faith of the poet. But this idea, too, has its precedents in earlier Old Testament thought.

We must first consider ideas and expressions from the psalms of lamentation and thanksgiving. In accordance with the ancient Israelite thought of illness and misfortune as akin to death,[1] those who are suffering, or those who have been healed, speak of their illness (or of other menacing, deadly dangers) as a descent into Sheol, a sojourn in the grave, a real death.[2] From this state of death they pray to God to deliver them; or they thank Him because He has done so. From our modern point of view, it might be said that these are only figures of speech; and certainly there was in ancient Israel no expectation of a general resurrection. But it is equally certain that men were firmly convinced that God could work such a miracle if He wanted to do so.[3] In the reality of ordinary, everyday life, it did not happen. But it could happen; and then the effect, and the consequences for the relationship of men to such a God, would be even greater than what the psalmists often described as the consequences of the healing and deliverance for which they prayed. In this connexion, it is also worth noting that the psalms often describe in vivid language how God's miraculous deliverance of the sick or the afflicted will make kings and nations be amazed and praise the God who performs such

[1] Pedersen, Israel I–II, pp. 153f., 443ff.; cf. also Index, s.v. 'death'.
[2] Cf. Gunkel-Begrich, Einleitung in die Psalmen, pp. 185ff., and references to sources.
[3] See 1 Kings xvii, 17ff.; 2 Kings iv, 18ff.; cf. xiii, 20ff. On the Old Testament belief in resurrection, see Nikolainen's discerning, but somewhat rationalizing book, Der Auferstehungsglauben in der Bibel und ihrer Umwelt I, pp. 96ff., and Birkeland's valuable review in S.E.Å. xiii, 1948, pp. 43ff. (see also St.Th. III, i, 1949/50, pp. 60ff.). Birkeland is entirely right in his contention that the preparation for such a faith is present both in the Canaanite conceptions of the death and resurrection of the god (see below, pp. 235f.) and in the faith in Yahweh as 'the living God' or 'the God of life', who constantly renews 'life', and raises it from death when He comes in the festal cult. But what is involved is 'life' in general, the life of the cosmos, of nature, and of the people, not the life of the individual. Riesenfeld (The Resurrection in Ezekiel XXXVII and in the Dura-Europos Paintings, pp. 3ff.) tries to establish a connexion between these two thoughts, by supposing that the king, as the embodiment of the people, symbolically died and rose again in the ritual of the New Year festival. Against this arbitrary theory, see above, pp. 50, 84ff., and Additional Note V. Riesenfeld antedates the sources, and also obscures the issue by confusing individual resurrection and the renewal of 'life' in the festal cult. On resurrection in the Psalms, see Ch. Barth, Die Errettung vom Tode in den individuellen Klage-und Dankliedern des Alten Testamentes, and my Offersang og sangoffer, pp. 240ff.

234

mighty acts. Ps. xxii is an adequate illustration of this; cf. Ps. cii, 16ff., where the worshipper is a representative of the people (Zion), and describes in even stronger terms than Ps. xxii, the impression which his deliverance will make among nations and kings.

We are therefore justified in saying that, from one point of view, the Servant is described after the pattern of the innocent sufferers in the psalms of lamentation. He is the ideal innocent sufferer.[1] But the psalms still regard this suffering from a negative point of view. It is unreasonable and incomprehensible, something to be avoided. Accordingly, this formal pattern provides no explanation of the positive value of the Servant's suffering.

Yet there is a certain connexion. The innocent sufferer in the psalms is very often the king, who represents the people.[2] In the crisis brought about, for example, by the attack of the enemy, he is described as the person who is chiefly threatened or afflicted by the disasters; in fact, he suffers on behalf of all. And in the ritual of days of penitence and expiation, it is the king who, on behalf of the whole people, humbles himself and does penance before Yahweh. He brings before God the need of all. It is his wonderful deliverance that makes all the godly rejoice, and makes kings and nations praise Yahweh.

It is very probable that the conception, in the psalms, of deliverance as a resurrection from death, owes something to the influence of general eastern ideas about the dying and rising god, his descent into Hades, and his return to life to restore life. It is probable, too, that there is here a conception which helped to mould the thought of the death and resurrection of the Servant of the Lord.[3] We have seen (above, p. 82) that the worship of such dying and rising fertility gods was also a fundamental feature in Canaanite religion. From Ras Shamra-Ugarit we have different versions of the myth about such gods. The religious idea is not merely the belief in the resurrection of the god himself, but also the meaning which it has for men. Through the resurrection of

---

[1] See Mowinckel, *Der Knecht Jahwäs*, pp. 53f.; cf. Stamm, *Das Leiden des Unschuldigen in Babylon und in Israel*, pp. 40ff.

[2] See provisionally Birkeland, *Die Feinde des Individuums in der israelitischen Psalmenliteratur*, pp. 114ff., 128ff.; in greater detail, Mowinckel, *Offersang og sangoffer*, ch. VII.

[3] This was first maintained by Gressmann (*Ursprung*, pp. 328ff.), and later by many others, most recently by Nyberg, Engnell, and Widengren. See Engnell's *Divine Kingship*, where he sets out the sources, and his paper in *B.J.R.L.* xxxi, 1, 1948. The idea is referred to with caution by Böhl, *De "Knecht des Heeren" in Jesaja*; cf. Gressmann in *Z.A.W.* xlii, 1924, pp. 156f.

the god, or his coming to life again in his son, life itself is raised from the dead, blessing is created anew, salvation is won for men. They share in this salvation by taking part in the cultic representation of the death and resurrection of the god, in the rites of mourning and the festal joy, in 'weeping and laughter';[1] and they experience the same fate, and are filled with divine power in the rejoicing, the ecstasy, and the display of power in the festal drama at the high places. In all parts of the east there were heard laments and hymns of rejoicing in honour of deities of this kind, who were everywhere alike in their character, whether called Tammuz or Marduk as in Babylonia, Osiris as in Egypt, Adonis as in Phoenicia, or Aleyan-Baal as at Ugarit. In a special way, through the king as the representative of the community, and through his central role in the cult, the people experienced and shared in the god's resurrection power, were filled with life, and rescued from the threat of death. Through him they all experienced the fate of the god; and the god became the 'archetype' of the people.[2] As in Israel (see above, pp. 234f.), so in Babylonia this idea was used to describe the 'state of death' experienced by the sick and afflicted, from which they were raised up by the god when cured or delivered from affliction.[3]

The description in Isa. liii of the humiliation, death, and resurrection of the Servant is also influenced to some extent by the style of such psalms. From one point of view, that chapter is written in the style of a 'belated dirge' in honour of the Servant—belated, since the Servant is described as dead and buried long before, and because the Song is a recognition of the glory and the achievement of the dead man, which the speakers confess that they ought to have made long ago. It has been maintained[4] that the noteworthy, and (in the Old Testament) very unusual idea of one person dying and rising again for the salvation of his covenant brothers arose under the influence of such mythical conceptions, which thus acquired a new and deeper meaning. There is every reason to believe that this is true. It is supported by the similarity

---

[1] Cf. Hvidberg, *Graad og Latter i det Gamle Testamente*, and references to the literature. Baumgartner surveys the Ras Shamra discoveries and the most important literature in *T.R.* (N.F.) xii, 1940, pp. 163ff.; xiii, 1941, pp. 85ff., 157f.; *T.Z.* iii, 1947, pp. 81ff., and my review of Hvidberg's book in *N.T.T.* xl, 1939, pp. 16ff.

[2] Cf. above, pp. 39, 43, and especially pp. 49f.

[3] Cf. Böhl, op. cit.; Gressmann, in *Z.A.W.* xlii, 1924, pp. 156f.

[4] E.g., by Gressmann, both in *Ursprung* and in *Der Messias*; similarly Dürr, *Ursprung und Ausbau*; most recently Nyberg in *S.E.Å.* vii, 1942, p. 64, and Engnell in *B.J.R.L.* xxxi, 1, 1948.

in both style and thought, a similarity which extends even to details. As the Babylonian Tammuz is compared to a tamarisk which had no water to drink in the garden, and whose crown sent out no branches over the steppes, so it is said of the Servant that

> He grew up as a sapling in dry ground,
> and as a root out of arid soil (liii, 2).

The other expressions which describe the lowliness and wretchedness of the Servant in his sufferings can be paralleled in the Sumerian and Accadian psalms to the dead Tammuz.[1] But of course these similarities do not prove that the Servant was thought of as a dying king-god. They are conventional poetical terms which are applied to the Servant as appropriate in descriptions of suffering. But the very existence of such conceptions, applied to the dying and rising god, *may* have helped to give rise to the thought of the Servant's resurrection, or rather may have provided expression for the thought when it had arisen in the prophet's mind as an inspired postulate of faith. What actually happened was that the ancient myths, with their concepts and phraseology, were ancillary influences, when the thought of the Servant's suffering, death, and resurrection emerged. But this latter thought is on another and a higher plane than the Babylonian and Canaanite myths, on the personal, moral plane, not the amoral plane of nature.

Not only the main idea of death, resurrection, and the meaning of salvation, but also the Servant's title is paralleled in the Canaanite myths. In the epic poem about the legendary or mythical King Karit, who was probably originally a form of the dying and rising god Aleyan-Baal, or Tammuz Adonis, and bears his name Na'man or Nu'man, the Lovely One,[2] this divine king constantly bears the title, *'bd 'il*, 'The servant of El (the supreme god)'. Here, 'servant' does not mean merely the worshipper of the god, but also his favourite and representative, who is under his special protection. We may also note that the Babylonian king, who represents the people in penitential atonement, is also called the 'servant' of the god.[3] Probably the fact that in the old myths and legends the conception of a saving death and resurrection was connected with one called 'the servant of the god', helped the

[1] See the collection of such phrases made by Engnell in *B.J.R.L.* xxxi, 1, 1948, pp. 26–9.
[2] See Albright in *B.A.S.O.R.* 63, Oct. 1936, p. 28 n. 22. Ginsberg adopts a different view (*The Legend of King Keret*, pp. 35f.).
[3] See Dürr, *Ursprung und Ausbau*, pp. 137, 149 n. 59a.

prophet of Isa. liii and his circle to grasp the idea that a similar destiny awaited the special 'Servant of Yahweh', whom they knew, or for whom they were hoping.[1] This assumes that the Servant was already known as Yahweh's servant; and being a prophet, he would be so known, as we have seen above (p. 214 and p. 218 n. 2).

In the light of these ideas in the prophets and the psalms, to which we have referred, the question might well arise concerning the meaning of those sufferings which befell the pious. The psalms do raise this question, but usually offer no answer. Yahweh's ways are past finding out. In the wisdom poetry the question is taken up. Job's three friends advance the usual answer: the sufferings of the righteous are disciplinary trials, chastisements, and warnings.[2] But here the whole question is the meaning of the suffering for the person concerned. Job denies that the usual answer can have universal validity. It was only in later Judaism that it became customary to speak of the suffering of the righteous as atoning for others.[3]

The question naturally arises whether, in the earlier Messianic conceptions of the coming deliverance, there were any tendencies which might have led to so novel a reorientation in the future hope as the thought of the Servant of the Lord and the value of his suffering for others, even if this reorientation is away from the Messianic hope. The answer is that there is such a point of connexion; and here elements from the conception of kingship enter into the portrait of the Servant.

Among the sayings about the future king, there is the passage in Jer. xxx, 21f. (see above, p. 172), in which his priestly office as intercessor between Yahweh and the re-established Jacob is emphasized in a way rather different from that of Ps. cx. In the psalm, the priesthood of the king is considered rather from the king's own point of view, as the source and ratification of his position of exalted power. But the passage in Jeremiah reflects a very different underlying religious attitude. The ancient sense of the need of a sacral mediator between the people and the deity was not the expression of a feeling of essential unworthiness in the community, so that it needed a mediator of an essentially different character from itself. When, at Mount Sinai, Moses is asked to

---

[1] See Mowinckel in *N.T.T.* xliv, 1943, pp. 24ff.
[2] See Mowinckel, *Diktet om Ijōb og hans tre venner*, pp. 19ff.
[3] See Sjöberg, *Gott und die Sünder*, pp. 174f.

speak with Yahweh on behalf of the people, the reason is that the tokens of the theophany which they have already experienced have overwhelmed them and filled them with holy awe. Moses is able to go, because he has already spoken with Yahweh, and therefore knows by experience that he does not run the same risk as the people, of being killed by the dangerous divine revelation (Exod. xx, 18–20). In ancient times, the chief or the king, being the leader of the cult, was also the natural individual embodiment of the collective supreme ego of the people, just as the fellowship of the covenant is objectively represented in the person of the natural leader of the people. When, by a cultic act, Yahweh has made a covenant with Moses and the elders of Israel, He has thereby also made a covenant with Israel (Exod. xxiv, 1, 9–11). The covenant with David is identical with the covenant with Israel. But, of the two, the covenant with Israel is fundamental, whereas the covenant with David is a later specific instance of it, which, as Deutero-Isaiah promises, will be re-established by Yahweh's act in once again treating Israel as His chosen one, bound to Him by covenant. It was not *necessary* that the king should act as cultic leader. In place of him, any really representative person might act as the embodiment of the community, and as the connecting link with the deity: the priest, the tribal sheikh, the chief of the family, the head of the house. The cult and its duties were felt to belong to more normal conditions. But in the passage from Jeremiah, the meaning is that, because of the sins of the people, the covenant has been suspended, and with it the direct relationship with Yahweh broken, until the king returns. In the present evil age, before the new covenant is established, the people cannot have immediate access to Yahweh and His blessings. The passage clearly reflects the ever-deepening consciousness of sin in post-exilic times. The passage is therefore rightly interpreted in the gloss which has been added: 'for who would (dare to) engage his heart to approach me, says Yahweh' (Jer. xxx, 21b). As long as the community is under the judgement and wrath of Yahweh, none of its members dare risk his life by appearing before Him. Therefore Yahweh must Himself appoint and authorize a man for this task, a king of David's line; and through his constant intercession in the cult, the new covenant will be upheld for ever.

The explicit formulation of the covenant, which will be renewed when 'Messiah' comes, puts this passage in line with others from about the same time, partly in the short collection of promises in Jer. xxxf., partly in the book of Ezekiel, which speak of the new covenant which Yahweh will make with the people at the restoration,[1] save that these sayings have advanced a stage further in the recognition of what was lacking and what was needed before restoration could take place. Here we meet a tendency among the disciples of the prophets, who recognize that it is not enough that the people should be freed, and a king of David's line be restored: if salvation is to come, the people must become a new people from within. Yahweh must take from the breast of each one of them the stubborn, selfish, unbelieving, and disobedient heart of stone, and give them a heart of living flesh instead. To discard the metaphor, they need a new spirit, and only God can give it. It is not enough that God's commandments are written on tables of stone, and are laboriously inculcated, discussed, and interpreted. Under the new covenant, God will put His law in their inward parts, and write it on their hearts, so that they need no longer teach each other, saying 'know the Lord', for they will all know Him. God's commandments must invade men's lives through the emotions and the heart, so that obeying them becomes natural and a matter of course. When this happens, 'I will be their God, and they shall be my people'. Of special importance is the explanation Yahweh gives, why and how this can take place: 'for I will forgive their iniquity, and will remember their sin no more' (Jer. xxxi, 34). The factor in the people's life which hinders the renewal of the covenant and the realization of Israel's hope is their unforgiven sin. Here, again, we meet the growing consciousness of sin and the longing for atonement which marked the postexilic age, which also finds expression in the development in the Priestly Code of the sacrificial system into an ordinance of atonement.

The passage about the priestly office of the future king must be understood in the light of these sayings, as is shown by the emphasis which they all lay (partly in identical terms) on the thought of the renewal and content of the covenant (see Jer. xxx, 22 and xxxi, 33). In the period from which these passages come, the priest's most important function is to 'approach' Yahweh in order to make atonement for sin. Sin makes it a fatal act to approach Yahweh, even in the cult, which from ancient times was held to be the safe and obvious way of approach without

[1] Jer. xxxi, 31–4; Ezek. xxxvi, 25ff.; xi, 19; xviii, 31.

forfeiting one's life, provided the prescribed rules were observed (cf. Exod. xxviii, 35). Now, it was the priest's task to attend to all the necessary offices of atonement. The laws lay such emphasis on the importance and value of their atoning offerings and ceremonies, and these cultic acts form so important a part of the daily and festival services, that one might well imagine that the community must have a sense of security and forgiveness, as being freed from sin. Yet time and again we meet the signs of conviction of sin, as an almost dominant feeling in the life of the post-exilic community. Men did not feel quite safe, in spite of all the daily endeavours of the priests after atonement. This attitude is the background to the longing which underlies a promise like that in Jer. xxx, 21f. In certain prophetic circles, particularly those which preserved the idea of the future king as the central blessing in the restored commonwealth, the thought would sometimes arise (as an extension of the ancient ideas associated with kingship) that this king would be a better king, and a more acceptable mediator between the community and God, one who could approach Yahweh, bringing atonement for sins, so that the new covenant could function normally.

It is in this setting that we must view the origin of the Songs about the Servant of the Lord. Behind them we discern the longing, the hope, and the certainty felt in some prophetic circles concerning one who will effect a new and better atonement for the sin of the community, a person who is not a 'Messiah', but who advances from another sphere within the future hope, and displaces the ideal king. For, as we have seen, a feature which is central in the conception of the Servant is the thought of the conversion of Israel, and of the need to do something to achieve it, the thought of the need of reconciliation between Israel and God, and the thought of a mediator who could effect this atonement, and thereby, also, the conversion of Israel and its religious and moral renewal.

5. *The Historical and Religious Background of the Conception of the Servant*

Throughout the above description of the person, mission, and work of the Servant, and of the conceptions associated with them, the question of the authorship of the poems has not been raised. All that has been said remains valid, whether the Songs come from Deutero-Isaiah or from another prophetic author, possibly one of his disciples. The interpretation of the content and message of the poems is in itself independent of the question of authorship. This point ought to be taken for granted, once it is realized that the individual prophetic sayings are independent units, which, as a rule, both can and must be understood each in its own light,[1] and were not originally presented as parts of a connected 'book' or extended 'speech'.[2]

In the following discussion of the historical basis and the specific historical background of the poems, the argument will be based on a conception of their age and authorship, which will be dealt with in a later section. Strictly speaking, this support is unnecessary. Our view of the authorship is, in fact, the result of a purely exegetical examination of the thought of the poems, in relation to the sayings and thought of Deutero-Isaiah. But to keep these two questions entirely separate would lead in part to repetition, and in part to a confusing presentation of the argument. Accordingly, in the discussion which follows, reference will sometimes be made to points which arise from the inquiry to be made below, namely, that the Servant poems are rather later than Deutero-Isaiah, and are best understood as a later development, and, in part, modification of his thought and message.

There was as yet no organic connexion between all the prevailing Jewish ideas about suffering, atonement, and restoration described above. A 'catalyst' was needed. Here it is obvious that an important part was played by general historical and religious conditions and experiences within the Jewish community.

We shall understand more clearly the longing for a saviour and mediator, if we try to see the Servant against the background of Deutero-Isaiah's glorious promises, irrespective of whether they come from a later period in his own life, or from one of his disciples (see above, p. 241).

[1] See Mowinckel, *Prophecy and Tradition* pp. 36ff.

[2] Accordingly, Sidney Smith (*Isaiah Chapters XL–LV*, p. 54 n.) is wrong in maintaining that a correct interpretation of the poems must of necessity be based on the assumption that they belonged to the Deutero-Isaianic collection from the outset. This does not agree with his admission, 'that each complete utterance is logically independent and must be judged by itself, without preconception, is one of the great advances due to recent work' (op. cit., p. 22), a statement which is also not in accord with his rejection of *Gattungsforschung* (op. cit., p. 11). It is, therefore, by a misunderstanding (caused in part by the mode of expression in my article in *Z.A.W.* xlix, 1931) that Sidney Smith holds that I reached the conclusion that the Servant poems are not by Deutero-Isaiah, on the basis of my theory of the arrangement of Deutero-Isaiah's sayings according to catch-words. I had reached that conclusion long before, as a result of a comparative, historical examination of the ideas which they contain.

With exuberant enthusiasm, Deutero-Isaiah had announced that Yahweh would soon fulfil, through Cyrus, Israel's hope for the future, in a manner far exceeding all her expectations and all practical probability. Deliverance is already at hand. Yahweh is on His way; He has already given the world into the hands of Cyrus; Cyrus will soon send the exiles home, restore Yahweh's temple, and build His city. Then Yahweh Himself will come as king, and enter into His house. From the ends of the earth, gifts will flow thither, and homage be rendered. Israel has already done 'double' penance for her sins (xl, 2). She has already been converted, and is a people 'who understand what is right, and have My law in their hearts', and on whom Yahweh, after a moment of wrath, has had compassion with everlasting love (li, 7; liv, 7f.). The glory will now exceed all imagined bounds.

The temple was really rebuilt. A company of Jews returned. A scion of David was for a time governor in the province of Judea. And that was all! None of the wonderful things happened which had been prophesied by Deutero-Isaiah, Haggai, and Zechariah. Conditions were cramping and oppressive; the times were drab and cheerless. Before long, the pious felt that they were in a minority. Their brethren 'hated them for My name's sake', and derided them for the hope of restoration by which they lived. In the community, all the old heathen practices and ungodliness were rampant.[1] Neither the fall of Babylon nor the victory of Cyrus, neither the return nor self-government, neither the restoration nor the scion of David had achieved anything. What then?

It is to this situation that the Songs about the Servant of the Lord apply. Some one is needed who can 'bring Israel back to Yahweh', one who, in the power of Yahweh's spirit, and with the right words, can give strength to the weary, one who does not 'break a bruised reed' or 'quench the dimly burning wick', one, who can 'bring forth right religion', the true, upright piety, faith and righteousness, both in and beyond her borders. Some one is needed to 'step into the breach' for the sinful people, one through whom the miracle may take place to make them confess their sin and be recalled from the paths in which they have strayed, one who can intervene on behalf of sinners. Before the restoration can take place, there must be conversion, and atonement for their hostility to God. But how? Who is to accomplish it?

The Songs about the Servant of the Lord presuppose that the

[1] Isa. lxvi 5; lvi, 9ff; lvii, 1ff.; lviii, 1ff.; lix, 1ff; lxiii, 10ff., 17; lxv, 1ff., 11f.; lxvi, 3.

prophetic circle, or Deutero-Isaiah himself,[1] was perplexed both
about the 'Messianic work' of Cyrus, of which Deutero-Isaiah
had spoken, and about the political 'Messiah' generally. What
was needed was another mediator of salvation than the people
had hoped and waited for. 'The arm of Yahweh' must appear,
and 'arm itself with power' in a different way and by different
means than those of which Deutero-Isaiah had thought, if his
words had hitherto been rightly interpreted.[2] Before 'righteousness' or 'judgement', in the sense of 'salvation' or 'restoration',
can come, 'judgement', in the sense of right religion and godliness, must be restored and propagated.[3]

It is at this point that we may speak of the importance of these
Songs for the Messianic expectation. They are not Messianic, in
either the earlier or the later Jewish sense of the term. But they
look for and predict a figure who actually replaces the Messiah,
or rather, who will be what the Messiah in the earlier period was
never thought of as being, namely, a true mediator of salvation,
one who brings salvation to the people, who mediates that religious
and moral conversion and transformation, without which there
can be no salvation, and in which salvation supremely consists.

Deutero-Isaiah had intended that Cyrus should lead back the
exiles, and gather together the dispersed. In these Songs, it is the
Servant who is to do this.[4] For Deutero-Isaiah, it is Cyrus whom
Yahweh has 'called by name', and who will 'fulfil Yahweh's
will'. In the Songs, it is the Servant who has been called by
Yahweh and entrusted with this mission.[5] Deutero-Isaiah had
thought that Cyrus would 'bring forth right order' by his sword,[6]
or that Yahweh would do so by His miraculous power,[7] and even
then he was probably thinking, as elsewhere, of Cyrus as Yahweh's
instrument in history. In the Songs, it is the Servant who will
'bring forth right religion (judgement, right order) 'by his quiet
and patient preaching (xlii, 1ff.). Deutero-Isaiah says that Yahweh
Himself proclaims judgement (*mišpāt*) and instruction (*tôrāh*) to
the far coasts; and it is for His 'arm', and the 'judgement' which
it brings, that the coasts are waiting. It is Yahweh's 'judgement',
His establishing of right order by His miraculous word (*mišpāt*

[1] This is Hempel's view in *Z.S.T.* vii, 1929, pp. 631ff.
[2] Isa. li, 9; lii, 10 (lix, 16; lxiii, 5), taken along with liii, 1.
[3] Isa. xli, 2 (with note in *G.T.M.M.M.* III) and xlii, 2, 4.
[4] See Isa. xlii, 7; xlv, 13; together with xlix, 5ff.
[5] See Isa. xlv, 3f.; xliv, 28, contrasted with xlix, 1; liii, 10.
[6] Isa. xli, 2f.; xlii, 6; liv, 13.
[7] Isa. xlvi, 13; li, 14f.; cf. xlii, 1ff.

parallel to *tôrâh*), which is 'the light of the nations'. The poet
of the Songs knows that it is the Servant who will establish right
order, and for his 'instruction' (*tôrâh*) that the far coasts are waiting.[1] In Deutero-Isaiah, it is before Israel that kings and nations
will arise and prostrate themselves, marvelling at Yahweh's mighty
work. In the Songs, it is before the Servant, when he is wonderfully exalted, that this will happen.[2] In short, what Deutero-Isaiah
regarded and expected as a work of 'Yahweh's Anointed, Cyrus',
or as a direct result of the revelation of Yahweh's mighty power,
to be seen in the fall of the Chaldean empire and the victories of
Cyrus, all this the author of the Servant Songs expected to come
from the Servant's prophetic preaching, his patient, vicarious,
atoning suffering, and death, and the resurrection which Yahweh
would grant to His 'righteous' Servant, in vindicating him before
the eyes of all the world. Sometimes word for word, the poems
echo thoughts and expressions from Deutero-Isaiah's preaching
about Cyrus, and apply them to the Servant. 'My righteous,
saving act (*sedeḳ*) is near,' says Yahweh in Deutero-Isaiah; 'near
is my Vindicator' (*maṣdîḳî*), says the Servant about Yahweh.[3]
Israel's enemies will be eaten up by the moth and the worm, says
Deutero-Isaiah; the Servant uses the same metaphor about the
destruction of his enemies.[4] The compilers and editors of the
prophetic words preserved by the circle of disciples have gone
further in this direction, and interpreted Deutero-Isaiah's words
about Cyrus and Israel as sayings about Yahweh's servant, i.e.,
about the special Servant of the Lord who is the subject of the
Songs.[5] The Servant has been set up as a contrast to Cyrus, and,

---

[1] Isa. li, 4ff., contrasted with xlii, 4.   [2] See Isa. xlix, 7, contrasted with liii, 13.
[3] Isa. li, 5 and l, 8.   [4] Isa. li, 8 and l, 9.
[5] The juxtaposition of the Servant Song, xlii, 1–4, and the Cyrus oracle, xlii, 5–7, is
evidence of this. In xlviii, 16b we probably have an original Cyrus text, which has
been altered and reinterpreted as a word about the prophetic equipment and mission
of the Servant. The interpolation of li, 15f. also introduces the Servant as the agent
in the new 'creation' of the world and of Israel. It is clear that these verses are an
editorial link, because *v.* 15 is a verbatim quotation from Jer. xxxi, 35, which is later
than Deutero-Isaiah (see Mowinckel in *G.T.M.M.M.* III, pp. 291ff., 389, 397ff.),
and because *v.* 16a = Jer. i, 9b (cf. also Isa. vi, 7). Moreover *v.* 16 has echoes of Deutero-
Isaiah's words in li, 13, which must therefore have been interpreted of the Servant by
the compilers or editors. Similarly, the gloss in xlix, 8b is intended to make xlix, 7–11
a Servant oracle. In xlii, 19f., on the other hand, the people Israel is the 'servant',
to whom there are applied individual features from the special Servant; and we thus
have a 'collective' re-interpretation of the Servant, like the gloss 'Israel' in xlix, 3,
and xlii, 1 (G). See further, *G.T.M.M.M.* III ad loc. Another re-interpretation of
the Servant is presented by G and the theological tradition behind it: the Servant is
identified (in the light of l, 4ff., and lx, 1ff.) with the prophet himself, i.e., for the
translators, Isaiah, who in this way becomes an important eschatological figure; see
Euler, *Die Verkundigung der leidende Gottesknecht aus Jes.* 53 *in der griechischen Bibel.*

in general, as a contrast to the way in which the mode of restoration is presented in Deutero-Isaiah.[1]

This contrast with earlier expectations is worked out in detail; and it may well be that there is influence both from ancient ideas about the fading and withering of the vegetation god, and from the impression made by the historical person who perhaps lies behind the Servant (see next section). The Servant is the opposite of all that is humanly great and exalted, of all that is lordly, and mighty, and masterful. He is not impressive or attractive; he has no outward glory or majesty, but is unclean, despised, and forsaken of men. The dirge does not describe him, as is usual, as a flowering tree, but as a root in arid soil; not as a lion or an eagle (cf. 2 Sam. i, 23), but as a ewe, dumb before her shearers (see above, p. 200). But when he has been 'vindicated' (justified), he will be the spiritual deliverer of Israel, and a light for the nations, who will be won for the true religion by the miracle wrought on him by Yahweh.

6. *Is the Servant a Historical Person?*

Clearly it will never be possible fully to explain the origin of an idea like that of the Servant of the Lord in terms of historical preparation or contributory conceptions and modes of thought. It will always be a mystery how there arises in the mind of a prophet a creative idea which profoundly influences the future. What can be said about 'historical preparation' is only a partial help towards understanding the thoughts, experiences, and needs, which had to be present in the environment, and in the minds of men, before such an idea could be received and become influential in revelation history.

Imperfect as our historical explanations may be, however, it is natural to inquire whether the emergence of such an idea would not require more specific and definite causes than the rather general historical development and the merely formal similarities in other ideas, to which reference has been made. In other words, did the prophet relate his prophecies to any specific person, who by his life and death may have been the 'catalyst', which caused the figure of the Servant to be presented to the mind of the prophet, who thereby realized what the Servant would mean for his nation and for mankind? The question may also be put in this way: is

[1] Hempel deals with this point in *Z.S.T.* vii, 1929, pp. 631ff.; but he holds that it is Deutero-Isaiah himself who, in the Servant Songs, corrects his earlier view.

the Servant a historical person who in the prophet's time had
already lived his life, or does he belong wholly to the future?
We have already seen *what* the Servant is, we now inquire *whom*
the prophet conceived him to be.

As in Isa. vii, we must again maintain that the prophet neither
saw nor sought to describe the historical Jesus of Nazareth. The
Servant is not crucified, but dies of a disgraceful disease. After
his resurrection, the prophet expects him to receive earthly glory
and reputation, to enjoy long life as a human being, to have offspring, to be honoured by kings and princes, and so on. Thus, the
prophecy about the Servant is not directly Christological. We
may say that this, like the other Old Testament prophecies, is
only indirectly Christological. In Jesus Christ they are fulfilled
in a way beyond anything the prophet ever imagined. It is a *new*
fulfilment that comes to pass. God creates something new, a new
reality, which fulfils the prophecy in a higher sense than that of
which the prophets and their contemporaries were aware. God,
who inspired their thought and its expression, saw farther than
they did; but this can be realized only when the higher fulfilment
has come. In its light we can then see that God's thoughts were
higher than those of the prophets.

Nor is the Servant a Messiah in the Old Testament sense of the
word, as we have already seen. He is neither a king nor a scion
of David; and he has nothing of that political element which is
essential to the Messiah throughout the Old Testament period.

Scholars have tried in the most diverse ways to find a concrete
historical person whom the prophet may have had in mind in
describing the Servant, or who at least was the original of the figure
or of some of its essential traits: Moses, the leprous King Uzziah,
Isaiah, Jeremiah, the captive King Jehoiachin, Cyrus, Zerubbabel,
an unknown teacher of the law in the earlier age of Judaism, some
unknown prophetic figure during the Exile, the prophet Deutero-
Isaiah himself.[1] It is quite possible that certain earlier prophets,
such as Moses, and especially Jeremiah, served to some degree as
models for the portrait of the Servant (see above, p. 231). As we
have seen above, there is also some ground for the view that the
entire prophetic movement left in men's minds the picture of the
ideal prophet which was the final outcome of its historical achievement and experience, and that this helped to fashion the figure of

---

[1] See the surveys referred to above, p. 187 n. 2. Coppens revives Sellin's idea that
King Jehoiachin was the prototype of the Servant, but limits this to the first three
Songs. For the Fourth Song, the model is King Zedekiah.

the Servant. Recently, Nyberg and Bentzen have emphasized the element of contemporary history which lies behind the figure. In a measure, he reflects the experiences of the prophetic circle in the age of the poet-prophet himself, when the monarchy had gone and the priesthood was diminished, so that prophetic circles to a considerable extent exercised the spiritual leadership of the people.[1] But it is quite improbable that the prophets thought of a definite person in the *more remote past*, considering the note of contemporaneity, and the direct relevance to the present and the immediate future, which were characteristic of true prophecy, and also the fact that the prophet here makes his contemporaries say that they have themselves seen the Servant growing up and living his life in their midst.[2] The identification with the prophet himself[3] is very natural, because in two of the poems (xlix, 1ff. and l, 4ff.) the Servant speaks in the first person. But it is refuted by the fact that in ch. liii the death of the Servant (assuming that he is a historical person) is described as having already taken place. On a historical interpretation of this kind, what belongs to the future is the real miracle, the resurrection and exaltation of the Servant. The use of the first person in the two poems can also be explained in another way, as we shall see below (pp. 251f.).

The strongest indications that a historical person was the original of the Servant are the following: 1. the concrete character of the description, and the vivid impression of something actually experienced and witnessed; 2. the literary types used: the oracle in which the prophet is called, and the prophet's message about further oracles of this kind; his lament because of opposition, together with his assertion of innocence and assurance that he is heard and Yahweh's promise of help; his fellow-countrymen's belated dirge, with their penitential confession and believing testimony to the saving significance of the Servant; 3. the grammar of

---

[1] Cf. Nyberg in *S.E.Å.* vii, 1942, pp. 79ff.; Bentzen, *King and Messiah*, pp. 68ff.

[2] The view that a prophetic personality from *contemporary* history lies behind the picture of the Servant has been maintained in recent times, e.g., by Kittel, *Gestalten und Gedanken in Israel*, p. 414; Rudolph in *Z.A.W.* xliii, 1925, and xlvi, 1928; and Nyberg (see last note).

[3] This identification was first made, with supporting arguments, by the present writer in *Der Knecht Jahwäs*, and has been accepted by Gunkel (*Ein Vorläufer Jesu*), Balla (in *Eucharisterion* I, pp. 245ff.), Haller (ibid., pp. 261ff.), Sellin (in *N.K.Z.* xli, 1930, pp. 195ff., in a somewhat modified form: the first three Songs being by Deutero-Isaiah himself, the fourth about him by Trito-Isaiah), Begrich (*Studien zu Deuterojesaja*), Wolff, *Jesaja 53 im Urchristentum*), Bentzen (in *Jesaja* II; cf. *King and Messiah*, pp. 64ff. and others. Sidney Smith also interprets the Second and Third Songs as sayings of Deutero-Isaiah about himself, and the Fourth Song as written about him by one of his disciples after his death (so Elliger and Sellin), but takes the First Song as about Cyrus (see above, p. 188 n. 2, p. 189 n. 2).

ch. liii, in which the earthly life of the Servant is described in those verbal forms which are used of events which have actually happened (the perfect and the consecutive imperfect), whereas from v. 10 onwards the description of his resurrection and exaltation passes over to the imperfect and consecutive perfect, which are used particularly of future events. It seems that, for the prophet, the earthly life and work of the Servant, his death and ill fame, belong to the past and the present, whereas to the future belong his resurrection and exaltation, and the effects of this miracle—the confession of his adversaries (l, 9ff.; lii, 15), the conversion and restoration of Israel (xlix, 6; liii, 10ff.), and the fulfilment of the greater task given him by Yahweh: 'that My salvation may reach to the end of the earth' (xlii, 3f.; xlix, 6). All this points to a real historical person, who lived, worked, suffered, and died, who is dead and buried, but who, according to the prophet's message in these poems, will one day rise again and be highly exalted.

We must admit, however, that it is conceivable that the Servant is a purely future figure, seen by the inspired imagination of the prophet. The Hebrew verbal forms do not necessarily indicate any definite time, but may all be used of past, present, or future, according to the point of view adopted by the speaker. It frequently happens that a prophet, in describing future events, imagines them so vividly, and presents them with such lively poetic force, that they appear already to have taken place (perfect tense). This happens especially when the prophet adopts the role of a poet, and puts his prophecy, for example, in the form of a thanksgiving by the congregation for deliverance, as if the deliverance had already been experienced, or puts into the mouth of the people the prayer of penitence which he longs to hear them utter. So it may be that the author of the Servant Songs takes the spiritual experiences of the prophetic movement down through the ages, together with the ancient ideas of supernatural saviours who suffer, die, and rise again, and in his inspired imagination crystallizes them all in the thought of, and the longing for, one who in his own person will gather up all the sufferings of the godly, all their faith, and confidence, and obedience, all they had endured for the sake of the community, all their yearning for atonement and forgiveness, and all their hope—will gather up all this in one great, personal, vicarious act of self-commitment, which God will reward by wonderfully restoring him, and by which the eyes of the whole people will be opened, Israel led to conversion and restoration, and true religion spread to all the nations of the earth.

But there is no denying that the emergence in the Old Testament of so unusual a conception can best be understood if we assume that it was linked with a definite person known to the prophet, one who had in some measure fulfilled the idea of the Servant which was present to the prophet's mind. Here, too, 'the myth became flesh' (to quote Nyberg's characterization of Israel's spiritual history)[1] before it was again spiritualized in the inspired imagination of the prophet.

This much, then, might be said of this historical servant of Yahweh. He was a prophet from the same circle as the author of the Songs, which in all probability was the Isaianic and Deutero-Isaianic circle, which was responsible for the tradition about Isaiah, and the collection and formation of the book of Isaiah. Probably this prophet lived some time after Deutero-Isaiah (see below); where, we cannot say; presumably in Palestine. He held it to be his mission as a prophet to win his countrymen to true conversion to Yahweh, and a trusting and obedient observance of Yahweh's commands, which would lead to the spread of this true religion to other nations. It may be that in his environment active missionary work was being carried on. Like every prophet, he found the work heavy and seemingly hopeless; and sometimes he despaired of everything. But God sustained him, deepened his sense of vocation, and gave him a yet greater goal and wider vision. God did this, too, in the sufferings, the disease, and the ignominy which were his lot. He was enabled to maintain his faith, and at least discerned that there was a positive divine purpose in his sufferings. They, too, being vicarious and redemptive, would serve to bring Israel back. After his death, his disciples (at first, perhaps, only one of them) recognized the divine purpose. He who had been misunderstood and rejected was in a special sense Yahweh's Servant, the mediator of salvation and restoration to Yahweh's people; indeed, to all mankind. It was for the guilt of others that he had suffered; and, as in the myths of ancient times, God would perform a great miracle, raising him from the dead; and by his very exaltation he would draw others to himself.

The poet has, of course, idealized the portrait. Every prophetic interpretation and transformation of historical reality is an idealization. To contemplate an event in the light of inspiration, and to interpret it prophetically, is to lift it to a higher plane than that

[1] *S.E.Å.* vii, 1942, pp. 81f.

of empirical reality. Therefore we shall never be able to distinguish with certainty between what the historical Servant himself thought and perceived of the meaning of his life, and what
deeper purpose the poet-prophet, or the believing circle before
him, found in the actual events of history. The entire spiritual
experience of the circle, the prophetic movement, and of Israel
throughout revelation history, left its impress on the portrait, even
if a historical person was its original. The portrait of the Servant
is the supreme spiritual legacy of the prophetic movement, its
ideal goal.

It is this circle's tradition and message about the Servant and
his soteriological significance that the author of the four Songs
proclaims, or, at times, makes the Servant himself proclaim by
putting the words into his mouth. It is significant that it is precisely the supremely personal experiences in this prophetic record
that he makes the Servant himself describe: anxiety, doubt, help
to stand fast amid suffering, derision, and persecution, confidence
in the help of God and the triumph of his cause, the revelation of
the wider mission (xlix, 1–6; l, 4–11); whereas he makes the circle,
and all those in Israel who have come to a recognition of the truth,
express the interpretation of the Servant's work and his self-commitment, its atoning and saving power (liii), the profession of
faith in the Servant, the proclamation of his work as the way to
salvation for others, which they must accept in faith, in order that
in his chastisement they may find their true welfare, and healing
by his stripes.

May we, perhaps, suppose that in the two poems in the first
person we have the Servant's own sayings, describing the personal
revelation of his call from Yahweh, whereas in the other two
poems it is the poet (and through him the circle, 'we') who
speaks? Or should find in all four the tradition, interpretation,
and faith of the circle? The existence of such an Isaianic circle
(appearing here as a Deutero-Isaianic circle) is a fact demonstrated by direct and indirect evidence.[1] Such a circle must be
postulated as the religious and sociological background of the
poems. In the ancient east, a circle of this kind is not simply a

[1] Isa. viii, 16ff. The indirect evidence is Isa. lvi–lxvi, the so-called Trito-Isaianic
passages, which on the one hand present great similarities in thought and poetical
form to Deutero-Isaiah, but on the other hand differ from it considerably in historical
background, and in poetic and prophetic power. They give the strong impression that
they come from a generation later than Deutero-Isaiah, and are therefore best explained as prophecies from a circle of Deutero-Isaiah's disciples at a somewhat later
period.

fortuitous and indefinable group of people with the same outlook, but a quite definite body, with a more or less fixed organization, a 'family' or 'house', as it would be called in ancient Israel, a 'sect', in the oriental sense of the word, without the suggestion of schism and heresy which is associated with the Christian use of the term. Such a circle recognizes a definite authority (in this instance the Isaianic tradition, the sayings, both of the master himself and of later disciples, contained in the book of Isaiah), and forms a religious fellowship, being, in other words, a cultic association. Similarly, the ecstatic exercises of the old prophetic guilds were not only a technique belonging to the prophetic office, but were regarded as a form of religious service, a worshipping of Yahweh and an experience of His presence.

In this circle (perhaps a smaller circle within the Isaianic circle) the Servant became a central figure. It may be that he had already become such during his lifetime, before disease and impurity made even his own followers regard him as one 'stricken, smitten of God, and afflicted'. Only after his death did he become of supreme significance, when it was revealed to the circle what the sufferings of the Servant really meant, and what kind of future lay before the one who had been despised and rejected. Perhaps this recognition divided the older Isaianic circle, producing from it a smaller 'Servant circle'.

This recognition came to be the central idea in the 'theology', the expectation, the very religion of the circle; but, in accordance with the outlook of ancient Judaism, its cultic life as a religious community would also be affected. When the circle met, the life, death, and saving significance of the Servant would be preached: this is implied in the word 'tradition' ($\check{s}^e m\bar{u}\,{}^c\bar{a}h$), which comes at the beginning of the Fourth Song. His mission and work were made real for their thought and meditation, not only by the penitential psalm about his death, with the assurance of his resurrection, but also by the prophetic oracles of vocation, which expressed his divine task and the promise attached to it, his exemplary faithfulness in suffering and humiliation, and his stead-fast belief and confidence in God. Here it would be natural to put into the mouth of the Servant words about the promises associated with his call, and about his steadfastness and unshaken faith in God, and, as it were, to allow him to appear himself in the pro-phetic circle and proclaim the conviction which God had given him and was now giving them, that his cause would triumph, and would lead to Israel's conversion, ingathering, and restoration, and to the spread of true religion among all people. This cultic interpretation enables us to understand the use of the first person in the Second and Third Songs.

There are other examples in the history of religion of a central figure of this type being introduced as speaking in the first person in a cultic circle, even if he is no longer visibly present on earth.[1] In this way, his spiritual presence is vividly brought home to the minds of the members of the circle.

7. *The Poet-Prophet and His Circle*

In what has been said above, we have given some indication of the author of the Servant Songs. A prophet who saw so clearly something entirely surpassing and even contradicting important features in Deutero-Isaiah's message can hardly be Deutero-Isaiah himself.[2]

The literary forms used in the Servant Songs are also different from those commonly used by Deutero-Isaiah. We do not find in them the hymns which are so frequent in the latter; but, on the other hand, no such combination of literary forms as occurs in Isa. liii is to be found in Deutero-Isaiah.

The poet must be one of the prophets from Deutero-Isaiah's circle, one of the first or second generation of his disciples. For the poet does not merely present a contrast to Deutero-Isaiah; on the contrary, he not only follows Deutero-Isaiah, but goes beyond him in his central ideas: the restoration of Israel, Yahweh's wonderful purpose of salvation, universalism in both his doctrine of God and his conception of salvation. He also has the same poetic and pictorial gift as Deutero-Isaiah. We notice that he adopts figures and phrases from Deutero-Isaiah, and that not only in

[1] One example is the song of the pearl in the *Acts of Thomas* (see Hennecke, *Neutestamentliche Apokryphen*, pp. 521ff.; James, *Apocryphal New Testament*, pp. 411–15) in which Christ appears speaking in the first person, in what is manifestly a cultic song. In the Gnostic *Odes of Solomon* this conception is also present; see *Odes* ix; x; xviii; xxii; xxviii; xxxi; xxxiii; xli; xlii, in which Christ (the Anointed One) is introduced as speaking sometimes throughout the poem, sometimes in part of it. Note also the literary relationship between *Ode* xxxi and Isa. l, 4ff.

[2] Lofthouse (in *J.T.S.* xlviii, 1947, pp. 169ff.) gives good grounds for the view that the author of the Servant Songs cannot be Deutero-Isaiah. But he can hardly be right in dating the Songs in the darkest period of the Exile (i.e., *before* Deutero-Isaiah), because the dependence of the Songs on Deutero-Isaiah is as clear as the features which distinguish them. Rudolph (in *Z.A.W.* xliii, 1925, pp. 111ff.) recognizes that the Songs must be later than Deutero-Isaiah's (other) utterances; but since he holds that the poet is Deutero-Isaiah himself, he takes the view that the poet modified and supplemented his earlier sayings by adding the Songs to them. So also Hempel in *Z.S.T.* vii, 4, 1929, pp. 631ff. But the view maintained above seems more natural.

order to impart to them a fresh nuance: cf. the simile of the garment eaten up by moths, describing the disintegration of the enemy; the thought that he 'will not be put to shame', will not let himself be overwhelmed by a feeling of shame; the interrogative pronoun 'who', in the sense 'if anyone'; the use of 'fire' as a metaphor for punishment; 'the far coasts', in the sense 'the whole earth'; 'chosen' (favourite), as a parallel term for 'servant'; 'the arm of Yahweh', as an expression of His omnipotence; etc.[1]

It appears, then, that in this circle of disciples, the Songs were associated with the tradition about the words of Deutero-Isaiah, and that the attempt was made to combine the two by the insertion of small editorial links.[2]

Thus the Servant Songs come from a prophet in that circle of Deutero-Isaiah's disciples, to which the Trito-Isaianic prophecies in lvi–lxvi belong. This is corroborated by a distinct and striking linguistic similarity between these prophecies and, in particular, ch. liii.[3] It is also corroborated by the marked spiritual affinity between the Servant Songs and the prophet's description of himself, and testimony to his call, in the familiar passage Isa. lxi, 1ff.

The spirit of my Lord Yahweh is upon me;
because Yahweh has anointed me,

[1] Isa. l, 9 and li, 8 (cf. li, 6); l, 7 and liv, 4; l, 8 and xliv, 10; l, 11 and xlvii, 14; xlii, 4 and xl, 15; xlii, 1 and xliii, 20 (of Israel); liii, 1 and xl, 10; li, 5; lii, 10. The phrase about Yahweh's word being put in the Servant's mouth, li, 16, alludes also to the emphasis on His word in the Songs (l, 4; xlix, 2).

[2] See above, pp. 244f. and p. 245 n. 5. The method by which the Songs have been interpolated into the collection by means of catchwords (Sellin in Z.A.W. lv, 1934, pp. 180f.), but not by the system of catchwords used in the Deutero-Isaianic collection (see Mowinckel in Z.A.W. xlix, pp. 245ff.), might suggest that the insertion took place after the latter had been committed to writing. But it is not strictly necessary to draw this conclusion. Rudolph (in Z.A.W. xliii, 1925, pp. 112ff.) also notes the inconsistency between the content of the Servant Songs and their present contexts, and also the editorial additions which the interpolation has made necessary, both in the Songs and in the Deutero-Isaianic passages. Cf. also Staerk (in Z.A.W. xliv, 1926, p. 243), whose arguments, however, are based on an untenable view of the composition of the book (against which cf. Gressmann in Z.A.W. xxxiv, 1914, pp. 254ff.). The view that Deutero-Isaiah's sayings were arranged on the catchword principle is opposed by Elliger in Deuterojesaja in seinem Verhältnis zu Tritojesaja, pp. 219–72. It is obvious that there are many instances in which the validity of individual catchwords may be disputed; but this is less important than the fact that Elliger himself is obliged to admit that the catchword principle affected the collection and arrangement of the material. Similarly, Sidney Smith's illustration of catchwords in xl, 9–11 (Isaiah Chapters XL–LV, p. 111) fails to dispose of the theory as a whole.

[3] See Elliger, op. cit.; Sellin in N.K.Z. xli, 1930, pp. 145ff. The fact that most of the examples occur in the Fourth Song is a natural consequence of the fact that it is the longest. North (The Suffering Servant, p. 173) rightly holds that Elliger's linguistic statistics do not prove that ch. liii is the work of the same 'man' as lvi–lxvi, or of another than the author of the first three Songs. But if Trito-Isaiah is regarded not as an individual but as a circle, to which the author of the Servant Songs also belonged, the linguistic evidence supports the connexion.

has sent me with good news for the afflicted,
to bind up the broken-hearted,
to proclaim liberty to the captives,
and release to those who are bound,
to proclaim a year of grace from Yahweh,
a day of vengeance from our God.

If the explanation of the use of the first person in two of the Servant Songs is that they were composed by the Servant himself, it may well be that this prophetic saying also comes from the Servant, and sheds light on his sense of call.[1] At least, the passage reveals something of the thoughts about the prophetic call, which were current in the circle to which the author of the Songs belonged.

In deliberately referring to the words of Deutero-Isaiah, yet reinterpreting and going beyond them, the prophet intended the Songs to convey the new revelation which amplified what the master had said by means of the portrait of the mediator of salvation, the Servant, who would accomplish what was not achieved by Cyrus, or by the restoration of the temple, or by the governor of David's line—that conversion to Yahweh, without which the glad tidings of the full salvation and restoration of Israel could not be realized.

8. *Relationship of the Songs to the Messianic Idea*

Thus the message about the Servant far surpasses everything in the Old Testament message about the Messiah (the future king), his person, and his work. The Servant's task is to do the very thing which was not expected of the future king, and which experience had shown that none of the historical persons such as Zerubbabel, with whom the future hope was associated, could perform: to bring Israel back to Yahweh. The Servant will do this, not as a victorious king, but by his suffering and death. From the Jewish point of view, a suffering Messiah is a contradiction in terms, and therefore 'a stumblingblock to the Jews'. That is why Judaism never interpreted the Servant of the Lord as the Messiah without drastic modification of the text and the portrait, a point to which we must return later.

[1] The similarity to the Servant Songs has often been felt; and the present writer admitted (in *Der Knecht Jahwäs*, pp. 16ff.) the possibility of attributing Isa. lxi, 1ff. to Deutero-Isaiah and associating it with the Servant Songs. Cannon (in *Z.A.W.* xlvii, 1929, pp. 284ff.) seeks to show that Isa. lxi, 1–3 really is a Servant passage. Against this, however, is the thought of 'a day of vengeance from our God', which is not entirely in accord with the Servant's message.

It is going too far to say that the Servant makes the Messiah superfluous in the conception of the future. In the Old Testament period, no one expected the Messiah to be instrumental in establishing the kingdom of God. What the Messiah cannot do, the Servant of the Lord will do. Therefore the thought of the Servant is in itself compatible with the idea of a future king as the supreme figure in the restored kingdom. The poet-prophet would hardly think of the two conceptions as overlapping. Probably he never consciously thought of the relationship between them. At least, there is no evidence to suggest that he did. But we may certainly hold that a man, who looked forward to a mediator of salvation like the Servant, would have little interest in a Messiah in the Jewish sense of the word. He had seen something at once more exalted and more profound than the Old Testament Messiah. Accordingly, the thought of the suffering Servant of the Lord had, broadly speaking, no influence on Messianic conceptions in the Old Testament and Judaism. That influence is first seen in Jesus.

The influence of the Servant on the conception of the future leads to a very important result. The Servant displaces the king, and himself becomes king. The poet-prophet does not say so explicitly; but something of the kind must have begun to dawn more or less clearly upon his mind. He knows that kings and princes will be silent, shutting their mouths in amazement, when they see the glory and honour which are bestowed upon the one who was despised and rejected. He announces that the Servant will have 'the great for his portion, and the strong as spoil' (or perhaps we should translate [Yahweh] will 'divide him a portion among the great, and he will divide the spoil with the mighty') (liii, 12). The Servant will receive princely rank and dignity, and be not only the equal, but the overlord of kings, one before whom they spring to their feet and shut their mouths in reverence.

What no Messiah, as conceived by the Jewish national religion, could perform, the Servant performs. He is victorious, not only over his opponents, but over the souls of men. He wins the hearts of his own people and of his enemies, as he has already won the hearts of the poet-prophet and the prophetic circle. They tacitly discard the Messiah, and quietly replace him by the Servant, as the overlord of kings and the plenipotentiary of God.

As we have seen, it is nevertheless possible that the conception of the Servant was in many indirect ways influenced by the ancient oriental ideal of the sacral king and by the thought of the king's suffering and exaltation. Far more important is the fact that the Servant is the legitimate child of the prophetic movement, and its supreme realization.

It is, therefore, with justice that the Church has from the very beginning seen in Jesus Christ the true fulfilment of these prophecies. In this she has followed Jesus Himself. Just because Jesus was something much more than the Jewish Messiah, and something essentially different, He found in the prophecies about the Servant of the Lord a prediction of His own mission and work. It was not until then that the figure of the Servant influenced the thought of the Messiah, by giving expression to an essentially new conception of the Messiah.

S

PART II

The Messiah in Later Judaism

CHAPTER VIII

The Eschatology of Later Judaism

AS in the earlier period, we must give, as a background to the figure of the Messiah, a sketch of the eschatological conceptions to which he belongs.

1. *The Future Hope and Eschatology*

In earlier Judaism we may speak of a *future hope and a hope of restoration*, essentially this-worldly, national, and political in character, but with important religious elements and a tendency to give a mythical other-worldly colouring both to details, and to the divine miracle which will bring it to pass. But we may justifiably speak of an *eschatology* in later Judaism. We have already seen that the change took place in principle when Deutero-Isaiah set the future hope in a new light by the religious character which he gave to it. He based the hope of national restoration entirely on religion, and regarded it as the outward and objective side of religious reality, namely Yahweh's epiphany, His coming as king to triumph over His enemies and establish His kingly rule or kingdom.

From the religious point of view, the primary and essential thing would be 'the day of Yahweh', His enthronement and kingly rule. The restoration of the nation and of the kingdom of David would be the visible outcome, the objective fulfilment, of the day of Yahweh. In fact, of course, the religious aspect might be degraded into a mere form, an 'ideology' for the national and political element; and no doubt it was merely that for many Jews down through the ages. But, to the religious mind, Deutero-Isaiah's conception means (though he himself may not have been conscious of the fact) that the object of the future hope becomes something absolute and definitive, which, being absolute, becomes 'the wholly Other', different from everything hitherto experienced on earth. Nothing can ever go beyond the kingly rule of God with its realization of God's purpose and will, of the meaning

of election and history, and thus of every material and spiritua
wish and ideal. The imagination and the intellect do not seek to
see anything beyond this. It is definitive and final. It comes
ultimately to be consciously thought of as 'the *eschaton*', what will
come to pass 'in the latter days',[1] when all things return to their
original state. To that age there is consciously applied in eschatology that fundamental principle which was inherent in the connexion with the New Year festival, and which is expressed with
essential simplicity in the *Epistle of Barnabas* (vi, 13); 'Behold, I
make the last things like the first.'

This absolute, final, unsurpassed, wholly other character in the
realization of the future hope can be expressed only in mythical
terms, metaphors, and colours. To see and express the wholly
other, intellect and imagination must lay hold of the thought and
form of myth. In this way the future state, in spite of its earthly
setting, is lifted up into an other, transcendent, mythical sphere.
We may say that this means that the powers, laws, and conditions
of myth (i.e., of the religious and poetical conception of reality)
are brought to fulfilment in the world of reality, that the world of
the gods, the divine world, is brought down to earth. The myth
is religion's authentic mode of speech, to express the truth about
the invisible realities by visible media. True religion can never be
entmythologisiert.

If, in spite of the scope of Deutero-Isaiah's conceptions, it seems
inaccurate to describe his message about the future as eschatological, the reason is that he himself was unaware of its ultimate
and supra-historical character, and expected it (as he himself
says) to be realized as a result of the victory of Cyrus over Babylon
Nor does Deutero-Isaiah announce the fulfilment of an already
existing eschatology as a result of the appearance of Cyrus,
as has been maintained, particularly by Gressmann. Prophets
have, indeed, often identified the fulfilment of an already existing
eschatology with the contemporary historical situation, saying,
'The last age has come, and all that we know about it will now be
fulfilled'. But then they presuppose the existence of an eschatological doctrine, which they reproduce. That is not true of Deutero-
Isaiah. He neither presupposes an eschatology nor consciously
creates one, saying, 'Now I announce to you what will happen at

---

[1] Gen. xlix, 1; Num. xxiv, 14; Deut. iv, 30; xxxi, 29; Isa. ii, 2; Jer. xxiii, 20; xxx, 24;
xlviii, 47; xlix, 39; Ezek. xxxviii, 16; Hos. iii, 5; Mic. iv, 1; Dan. x, 14; cf. Ezek.
xxxviii, 8.

the end'. He announces the national, religious, and moral restoration of Judah and Israel by the power of God in terms and conceptions which ultimately divorce that restoration from earthly reality and lift it up among the miracles of the divine world. Thus it *finally* becomes purely eschatological; but it is not yet so in Deutero-Isaiah. In him all the presuppositions are present. He can speak about the old or 'former' things and the 'new' things, the creative, saving acts of the past and those which are now to take place. These 'new' things are, admittedly, a repetition of the 'former' things, but in a much more glorious way, and on a worldwide scale, so that they appear to him as hitherto unheard of, as *das nie da Gewesene*.[1]

2. *Dualism*

The Jewish future hope became eschatological in the strict sense when it was linked to a dualistic view of the world. Dualism was unfamiliar to the ancient Israelite, though of course he was aware of the existence of evil powers, and knew that life was a constant struggle to maintain blessing against the curse.[2] Characteristic of the dualism of later Judaism is the thought of the two ages or aeons, 'this age' and 'the age to come' (*hā-ʿôlām haz-zeh* and *hā-ʿôlām hab-bāʾ*, ὁ αἰὼν οὗτος and ὁ αἰὼν μέλλων), which were separated by a sharp transition, and which had each its own definite time and character.[3] This aeon was under the dominion of evil powers hostile to God. Earlier Judaism held the evil world power to be embodied in the successive great heathen powers which ruled over the Jews. In later Judaism they were not distinguished, but regarded as the effect of a cosmic, transcendent principle of evil, Satan, the Devil, Beliar, Mastema, or whatever he might be called.[4] In this aeon the 'kingdom of Satan' prevailed. Paul can even call Satan 'the god of this aeon'.[5] In this aeon there prevailed misfortunes and evils of every kind; and it would reach its climax in the throes of the Messianic age,[6] a final intensification of the dominion of all evil powers hostile to God, and of all sin and wickedness. The coming aeon is the very reverse of this, the wholly

---

[1] Cf. Bentzen in *St. Th.* I, 1947, pp. 183ff.
[2] Pedersen, *Israel* I–II, pp. 441f., 453ff., 470ff.
[3] Bousset, *Relig.*[2], pp. 277ff.; Volz, *Eschatologie*[2], pp. 64ff.; Moore, *Judaism* II, p. 378, and Index I, s.v. 'World to Come'.
[4] Bousset, *Relig.*[2], pp. 381ff.; Volz, *Eschatologie*[2], pp. 86ff., and Index, s.v. 'Satan'; Moore, *Judaism*, Index I, s.v. 'Satan'.
[5] 2 Cor. iv, 4; John xii, 31; cf. xiv, 30; xvi, 11.
[6] Weber, *Jüd. Theol.*[2], pp. 350f.; Bousset, *Relig.*[2], pp. 286f.; Volz, *Eschatologie*[2], pp. 147ff., and Index, s.v. 'Wehe'; Moore, *Judaism* II, pp. 361f.

Other. In it, God would overthrow Satan's dominion,[1] fetter or destroy all his angels or demons, extirpate all sinners, end all sin, misfortune, and suffering, and establish His kingdom, assuming His kingly rule. Israel, or the pious, would receive as their reward all happiness and bliss[2] on a re-created earth or in a realm beyond, in paradise, or in heaven.[3] The Devil, his angels, and the ungodly would be thrown into Gehenna, and suffer eternal punishment.[4]

Thus we have here a dualism which is temporal, spatial, and ethical. In the present, there was a conflict between God and Satan. God had, as it were, withdrawn and left this world to Satan and his power for a pre-determined period.[5] The heathen world-powers were representatives of the transcendent power which was hostile to God.[6] Originally God had appointed the angelic powers to govern the nations as His deputies; but they had lapsed into pride and sin, governing unjustly,[7] and becoming servants of evil.[8] But when the period had elapsed, 'in the fullness of time', God Himself would assume the kingdom, and then the present evil age would be at an end.

This dualistic view of life and of the world was worked out in the course of the earlier Hellenistic period, no doubt under the influence of Persian religion,[9] which was consistently dualistic from the beginning. But the influence was that of Persian ideas, not in their pure and unalloyed form, but in the form which they acquired under the impact of the culture, philosophy, and world-view of Babylonia, that is to say, from 'Chaldean'[10] syncretistic religion, cosmology, and speculation. Here dualism has been combined with a doctrine of ages concerning the destruction of the world and its renewal after so many millennia, after which things return to their original state, and the 'last things become like the first'.[11] As a conscious principle, this sentence is the result of influence from dualism and the doctrine of ages.

[1] Bousset, *Relig.*[2], p. 288; Volz, *Eschatologie*[2], pp. 88, 309ff., 318.
[2] Volz, op. cit., pp. 359–406.
[3] Bousset, *Relig.*[2], pp. 324ff.; Volz, *Eschatologie*[2], pp. 408ff.
[4] Bousset, *Relig*[2], pp. 321, 328f.; Volz, *Eschatologie*[2], pp. 320ff.
[5] Bousset, *Relig.*[2], pp. 279, 288ff.; Volz, *Eschatologie*[2], pp. 135ff.
[6] Bousset, *Relig.*[2], pp. 250ff.; Volz, *Eschatologie*[2], pp. 83ff.   [7] Cf. Ps. lxxxii.
[8] Cf. Bousset, *Relig.*[2], pp. 574f.; Volz, *Eschatologie*[2], p. 170 and Index, s.v. 'Engel', die gefallenen'.
[9] Bousset, *Relig.*[2], pp. 571ff.; Böklen, *Die Verwandtschaft der jüdisch-christlichen mit der parsischen Eschatologie.*
[10] On the meaning of this term, see Jansen, *Die Henochgestalt*, pp. 13ff.; cf. Schnabel, *Berossos*; Bousset, *Relig.*[2], pp. 548, 588; Reitzenstein-Schaeder, *Studien*, p. 127.
[11] Cf. *Barnabas* vi, 13; see above, pp. 142f.

THE ESCHATOLOGY OF LATER JUDAISM

If more closely examined, however, this dualistic world-view in later Judaism is seen to be the result of tendencies in the earlier Jewish future hope, which was already dominated by the thought of a time when Yahweh's kingly rule would put an end to all the injustice, sin, and oppression which were prevalent since those who had power in the world had abused the retributive and punitive authority which Yahweh had given them, and were keeping His people enslaved and dispersed. The mythologically conceived picture of the change of fortune (*šûb šebût*) presented by Deutero-Isaiah and the latest prophets was interpreted by later Judaism (or, rather, by certain circles therein) in the light of dualism. Thus the whole picture of the future was lifted up into the transcendent, other-worldly realm, as a description of a world order and an age entirely different from the present one.[1]

In its religious structure, the eschatology of later Judaism actually reveals a more extreme form of dualism than that of Persia, a dualism which extends further into the nature of man and of creation, as a result of the clearer and more penetrating insight into the nature of sin which is characteristic of revealed religion. Persian eschatology presents us with a conflict between good and evil, in which man can freely take sides, and contribute to the result, God's victory over the evil power which, for some inexplicable reason, has existed from the beginning. In the eschatology of the Bible and of later Judaism, we find an entire re-creation of mankind and nature which, as the result of a fall and of the sin which has become their nature, have come under the power of evil, and would be destroyed if God did not intervene with His miracle of restoration, carrying through His original design in creation from the time when He saw that all things were 'very good'.[2] It must be noted, however, that the dualism which develops from the Old Testament approach is one-sided in relation to the full biblical view of the world as God's creation and as the place where His will will be done and His kingdom be manifested. In later Judaism there was a tendency to treat creation, the natural world as such, as evil. This tendency comes from the syncretistic, ascetic, gnostic milieu from which dualism itself was

---

[1] Messel (*Die Einheitlichkeit der jüdischen Eschatologie*) has sought to deny this two-sided character in later Jewish theology, and regards all the other-worldly, mythical elements as 'exaggerations', which really describe a state of bliss which belongs only to this world. But there is no evidence to support this. Messel's approach to apocalyptic is too intellectualistic. He has not entered into the life and atmosphere of this spiritual movement; cf. Gunkel's review in *N.T.T.* xvii, 1916, pp. 196ff.

[2] Cf. Staerk, *Soter* II, p. 148 n. 1.

derived; and its influence is particularly evident in the Jewish sects, such as Essenes, Mandeans, and other 'baptizers'.

3. The Influence of Theology

The addition of Persian dualism to the Old Testament hope of future restoration transformed the latter into an eschatology, a faith and doctrine about 'the last things', with the minimum of emphasis on 'doctrine'. But the development of eschatology was affected by one important factor which must be mentioned, namely theological, exegetical, and speculative learning based on the old prophetic sayings and books. It was within the circles of prophetic disciples, amongst whom the prophetic traditions were preserved, that the future hope was cherished. The latest phase of prophecy was, in large measure, an inspired revision, amplification, and interpretation of the earlier prophecy. It was spiritual learning, or 'wisdom'.[1]

Out of this wisdom (combined with elements of all kinds of ancient oriental learning on cosmography, astrology, angelology, and medical magic) there finally arose apocalyptic,[2] which may be described as inspired learning or revealed theology, with eschatology as its centre. This prophetic tradition with its eschatological outlook would read the ancient prophets in the light of the future hope, interpreting, for example, the predictions about Assyria in the book of Isaiah as referring to the last age before the restoration. Under the influence of the conception in the enthronement mythology of the climax of affliction before the coming of Yahweh,[3] there arose the dogma about a final attack on Jerusalem by all the heathen nations, whom Yahweh would destroy outside the city walls. This mythological dogma is already represented in the Old Testament in the prophecies about Gog and Magog, and in Deutero-Zechariah.[4] Under the influence of Persian dualistic conceptions, this developed into the idea of the last great universal tribulation, when all Satan's powers, all the spiritual forces of evil under heaven, would assemble to destroy God's people.

Another characteristic result of this theological interpretation of the prophetic words is the expression 'in that day',[5] so often used

---

[1] See Mowinckel in N.T.T. xliii, 1942, pp. 97f.; G.T.M.M.M. III, pp. 27ff., 31.
[2] Cf. Hölscher, Geschichte der israelitischen und jüdischen Religion, pp. 186–93; G.T.M.M.M. III, pp. 29ff.
[3] See above, pp. 140f.
[4] I.e., Zech. ix–xiv; see G.T.M.M.M. III, pp. 755ff.
[5] See below, pp. 268ff. and p. 268 n. 5.

in editorial links or interpolated into earlier sayings to make them refer to the last, great, eschatological day.

Precisely because later Judaism treated the entire Old Testament revelation as a unity[1] with a consistent teaching, and used the prophecies as predictions of eschatological happenings, it is legitimate to use earlier passages as evidence in an account of the eschatology of later Judaism.

4. The Last Things: A. The Earlier Tendency

The influence of dualism meant a considerable strengthening of the transcendental, other-worldly element in eschatology. In a far greater measure than before, salvation became a miraculous divine intervention outside history, distinct from the 'real' human powers, something utterly different in character from all that is experienced here. It is the fulfilment of all ideals and longings, yet far more than even the most exalted idealization of all earthly values. It is 'what eye has not seen, nor ear heard, nor the heart of man conceived'.

But it was never forgotten that the starting point for the future hope was faith in the restoration of Israel as a free people among the other nations, on this earth, in the land of Canaan. Thus there persisted in eschatology an unresolved tension, a gulf between those elements which were political, national, and this-worldly, and those transcendental and universal elements which belonged to the world beyond. Here we have two profoundly different conceptions of the future, one of which is older and more truly Jewish than the other. It is, therefore, a practical necessity in any historical account to describe them separately, as Bousset has rightly maintained in his *Die Religion des Judentums im neutestamentlichen Zeitalter*. These ideas were never systematically arranged; and any attempt so to present them would only result in an artificial picture.[2]

---

[1] Cf. Moore, *Judaism* I, pp. 235ff.; II, p. 327.

[2] In Schürer's classical work (*Geschichte des jüdischen Volkes im Zeitalter Jesu Christi*[4] I–III, which will always retain its value as a critical collection of the source material) this point is not yet clearly recognized. The first to do so, and to draw the consequences for a scholarly presentation, was Bousset (*Relig.*[1] 1903). Most recent scholars have followed Bousset more or less faithfully; cf. Volz, *Eschatologie*[2]; Hollman's popular sketch, *Welche Religion hatten die Juden als Jesus auftrat?*; Gressmann in the third edition of Bousset's book. Bonsirven's unified presentation of the two tendencies is, therefore, a retrograde step in historical scholarship (*Le judaïsme palestinien au temps de Jésus-Christ* I–II). The opposition which is less systematically offered by Küppers and Riesenfeld (cf. Additional Note XIII) does not provide cogent evidence, and is inadquate to disprove the point. Lagrange, on the other hand (*Le messianisme chez les juifs*, and still more clearly in *Le judaïsme avant Jésus-Christ*), reaches the same conclusion as

THE ESCHATOLOGY OF LATER JUDAISM

To quote G. F. Moore, 'For orderliness we may distinguish between the national form of the expectation, a coming golden age for the Jewish people, and what for want of a better word may be called the eschatological form, the final catastrophe of the world as it is and the coming in its place of a new world, which in so far as it lies beyond human experience of nature we may call supernatural. But it must be understood that in all the earlier part of our period the two are not sharply distinguished, but run into each other and blend like the overlapping edges of two clouds.'[1]

In all the confusing lack of system, with ideas of different kinds overlapping, and amid all the fantastic descriptions, there is, nevertheless, one common factor which is the essential point in the entire eschatology and in all eschatology, namely the belief that world history in the widest sense is the expression of a divine purpose, that God has a purpose, and that He will intervene in order to achieve that purpose. All else, all the varying, fantastic details, may be regarded as things which 'helped men to give reality to their faith through an imaginative presentation',[2] though these pictures were not deliberately and consciously invented for this purpose, but received as a tradition, and interpreted in the light of contemporary events.

The influence of the other-worldly dualism is least effective in the early period, during which the general assumption is that salvation, the restoration of Israel, will take place as a historical event belonging to this world, though miraculous in character.[3] Although 'Yahweh's day',[4] 'that day',[5] is described in terms

---

[1] Moore, *Judaism* II, p. 323.   [2] Moore, ibid.
[3] With what follows, cf. the concise and lucid survey in Hölscher, *Geschichte der israelitischen und jüdischen Religion*, p. 154.
[4] Isa. xiii, 6ff.; Ezek. xxx, 3; Joel i, 15; ii, 1; iii, 3f.; iv, 14; Obad. 15; Zech. xiv, 1.
[5] Isa. ii, 20; iii, 18; iv, 2; v, 30; vii, 18, 20f., 23; x, 20, 27; xi, 10f.; xii, 1, 4; xvii, 4, 7, 9; xxii, 20, 25; xxiii, 15; xxiv, 21; xxv, 9; xxvi, 1; xxvii, 1, 2, 12f.; xxviii, 5; Jer. iv, 9; xxx, 7f.; xlvi, 10; Amos viii, 9, 13; ix, 11; Obad. 8; Mic. ii, 4; v, 9; Zeph. i, 9f.; iii, 11, 16; Zech. ix, 16; xii, 3, 6, 8f., 11; xiii, 1f., 4; xiv, 4, 6, 8, 13, 20. In many of

---

Bousset, but makes too mechanical a distinction between the groups of source material, and is too prone to regard the two types of eschatology as belonging to two successive periods. This is in line with his defective appreciation of the religio-historical problem which underlies apocalyptic; and (in spite of his excellent account of its character as distinct from prophecy in *Le judaïsme avant Jésus-Christ*, pp. 72ff.) he tends too much to regard apocalyptic as a purely Jewish development of prophecy under the sway of the Law, and as typical of Judaism during the last century B.C. Similarly, he is too prone to regard Pharisaism as a 'renaissance' of the earlier 'Messianism', arising from (*inter alia*) a reaction against apocalyptic; and he does not show sufficiently clearly that Pharisaism is the logical continuation of a type of religion and a 'Messianism' which had existed throughout the history of Judaism, both before apocalyptic and alongside it.

drawn from the nature mythology of the divine epiphany,[1] the political and this-worldly element is very prominent. It is true that the enemies are often regarded as a unity, the heathen world power,[2] but, in accordance with the political situation, it is also a specific historical and political entity, including all the individual heathen nations of which the great power actually consisted. When Yahweh destroys them,[3] He will also judge the idolaters and the ungodly within the Jewish community.[4] Here the thought is in some measure coloured by the dualistic doctrine of catastrophe, which was combined with the earlier ideas of a final reckoning with the world power outside Jerusalem (the myth about the conflict with the nations).[5] The reckoning with the heathen becomes a sweeping world catastrophe, in which only Zion remains unshaken. All who worship Yahweh,[6] 'the remnant of Israel',[7] the righteous,[8] will find refuge and deliverance there. Then Zion and the temple will become Yahweh's throne; and He will rule there as a king,[9] on the mountain of the Lord,[10] where only the holy, elect ones may live.[11] The dispersed ones will

[1] Descriptions of a theophany: Gen. xv, 17; Judges vi, 21; xiii, 20; Exod. iii, 2ff.; xiii, 21ff.; xix, 18ff.; xxiv, 10; xxxiii, 18–23; 1 Kings xix, 11ff. In battle: Judges v, 4, 20f.; Exod. xiv, 24; Joshua x, 10f.; Judges iv, 14f.; vii, 22; 1 Sam. vii, 10; xiv, 15, 20, 23; 2 Sam. v, 20, 24. In the prophets: Isa. xiii; Joel iii, 3f.; iv, 15; Amos viii, 9; Mic. i, 2–4; Nahum i, 2–10; Hab. iii, 3ff.; Zech. xiv.

[2] Isa. xiv, 26; xxvi, 21; xxxiii, 12; xxxiv f., lxiii, 1ff.; Jer. xxv, 29ff.; xlvi, 10–12; Obad. 15; Mic. v, 14; Isa. xxvii, 1; xxiv, 21f.; Dan. ii; vii; viii; ix ff.; Ps. Sol. xvii, 24; Jub. xxiii, 23f.; xxiv, 28; 2 Esdras iv, 23; 2 Bar. lxxxii, 3ff.; Wisd. of Sol. xvi, 19.

[3] Isa. lxiii, 1–3; 1 En. xcii ff.; xc, 18; T. Dan v; T. Asher viii. See Bousset, *Relig.*[2], pp. 25ff.

[4] Isa. xxviii–xxxi; iii, 11; iv, 4; xxix, 20; xxxiii, 14; Amos ix, 10; Zeph. i, 6; iii, 11; Ezek. xiv, 1–11; xx, 36–8; xiv, 17–22; Isa. ii, 20; xvii, 8; xxvii, 9; xxx, 22; xxxi, 6f.; lvii, 3ff., 13; lxv, 1–4, 11ff.; lxvi, 3, 17; Ezek. xxxvi, 25; v, 9–13; Zech. xiii, 2–6; Isa. iii, 18ff.; xxix, 20; xxxiii, 10–14; Zeph. iii, 11f.; Ezek. xxii.

[5] See above, pp. 140, 145.

[6] Isa. xiv, 32; Joel iii, 5; iv, 16; Obad. 17; Ps. Sol. xvii; Ass. Mos. x. For rabbinic evidence, see Volz, *Eschatologie*[2], pp. 342ff. Further, 2 Bar. 2; xxi, 1; xxix, 2; xxxvi–xl; 1 Esdras xii ff.

[7] Isa. iv, 3; x, 20–2; xi, 11, 16; xxviii, 5; xxxvii, 31f.; Jer. xxiii, 3; xxxi, 7; Joel iii, 5; Mic. ii, 12; v, 6f.; vii, 18; Zeph. ii, 7, 9; iii, 12f.; Zech. viii, 6, 11f.; 2 Esdras vi, 25; vii, 28; ix, 8; xii, 34; xiii, 24, 26, 48f.; 2 Bar. xxix, 4; xl, 2; Sib. IV, 384.

[8] Bab. Yebamot 47a; 2 Bar. xiv, 13, 19; xv, 7; xlviii, 50; li, 3, 8; lxvi, 7; 2 Esdras vii, 17; viii, 52; 2 En. lxv, 8.

[9] Isa. xxiv, 23; lii, 7; Jer. iii, 17; x, 7–10; Obad. 21; Mic. iv, 7; Zeph. iii, 15; Zech. xiv, 9, 16f.; 2 Bar. xxi, 23, 25; Tobit xiii, 7; Ps. Sol. xi, 8; xvii, 30; 2 Esdras vii, 42, 87; viii, 30; 1 En. xxv, 3, 7; xxvii, 3; xlvii, 3; l, 4. Cf. Volz, *Eschatologie*[2], pp. 167f.

[10] Mic. iv, 1f.; Zech. xiv, 10; Ezek. xxxviii, 12; cf. Ps. xlviii, 3.

[11] Isa. iv, 3; xxix, 23f.; Joel iv, 17; Zech. xiv, 2of.; cf. n. (8). See further, 1 En. i, 1; v, 7f.; xxv, 5; Wisd. of Sol. iii, 9; 2 Bar. xxx, 2; lxxv, 5.

these passages, the formula is a secondary result of the editorial and theological re-interpretation of the prophetic words in eschatological terms. See above, pp. 267f. and p. 147 n. 8.

return;[1] Israel and Judah will be reunited; and the kingdom of David will be restored and will have dominion over the neighbouring peoples.[2]

The myths about primeval time also make their contribution, as is natural, considering the connexion between eschatology and the enthronement mythology.[3]   In Palestine, on Zion, paradise is recreated with the river of life.[4]   There is the centre of the world, from which God will exercise His dominion over the world.[5] All nations will make pilgrimage thither, to worship the only true God.[6] Eternal peace will prevail there,[7] under the sway of the prince of peace.[8] Nature will be blessed with teeming fertility.[9] All sorrow and pain will be ended. Gladness,[10] light,[11] and life[12] will prevail, when heaven and earth are restored to their original state.[13]

5. *The Last Things: B. The Dualistic, Apocalyptic Tendency*

In the Hellenistic and later Jewish period, the newer elements gradually asserted themselves. This is connected with the development towards individualism and universalism which took place in the religion of this period. Ever since the age of the prophets, there had been a tension between the nationalistic conception of religion and salvation, and the universalistic conception of God. But now Judaism was as much a religious community as a nation.

[1] Bousset, *Relig.*[3], pp. 270f. Shemoneh Esreh 10; Targ. Jon., Jer. xxxiii, 13; Targ. Ps.-Jon, Exod. xl, 10; Num. xxiv, 7; Deut. xxx, 4.

[2] Bab. Pesahim 118b; Abodah Zarah 3b.

[3] See above, p. 162.

[4] Ezek. xlvii, 1ff.; Joel iv, 18; Zech. xiv, 8; cf. Ps. xlvi, 5; further, Rev. xxi, 2, 10; iii, 12; Gal. iv, 26; Heb. xii, 22; Rev. xxii, 1f.

[5] Zech. xiv, 9; Isa. lix, 19; Mic. iv, 3; cf. Pss. xlvi, 11; xlvii; lxvii, 5. See also p. 269 n. 9.

[6] Isa. xlv, 14, 23; lvi, 7; lx, 3; lxvi, 18f., 23; Jer. iii, 17; Mic. iv, 2; Zeph. iii, 10; Zech. viii, 20–3; xiv, 16–19; Isa. xxvi, 6; cf. Ps. xlvii, 2.

[7] Zech. ix, 10; xiv, 11; 1 En. xc, 34; Luke ii, 14; Targ. Jon., Isa. xi, 6.

[8] 1 En. xc, 37; Targ. Jon., Isa. xi, 6.

[9] Isa. iv, 2; xxx, 23–5; xxxii, 15, 20; xxxv, 1f., 6f.; Amos ix, 13; Joel iv, 18; Ezek. xlvii; Rev. xxii, 2; 1 En. x, xxvii, 1; 2 Bar. xxix; T. Judah xxv; Sib. III, 581; V, 281; Sifre Lev. xxvi, 4f. (110a); Sifre Deut. xi, 14 (90a); xxxii, 12 (135a); Elijah Apocalypse vi, 11f.; Bab. Shabbat 30b; Ketubot 11b; Sib. III, 620ff., 659f., 744ff.

[10] Isa. xii, 4–6; xxxv, 5f.; lxv, 18; Jer. xxxi, 10–14; xxxiii, 9; Isa. xxv, 8.

[11] Isa. ix, 1; xxx, 26; lxii, 1; lx, 19f.; xxvi, 19; Zech. xiv, 7; Dan. ii, 22; 2 Bar. liv, 13; 1 En. xiv; lviii, 5f.; lxxi; xci, 16; 2 En. xx; xxxi, 2; T. Levi, xviii; Sib. II, 35f.; Bab. Hagigah 12a; Tobit xiii, 11. For 'light' as a metaphor for salvation, see Volz, *Eschatologie*[2], p. 365; of moral enlightenment, op. cit., p. 366.

[12] Isa. lxv, 20, 22; xxvi, 19; xxv, 8; Dan. xii, 2; 2 En. xlii, 6; T. Asher vi; 1 En. xxxvii, 4; xlii, 2, 5, 10; lviii, 3; 4 Mac. xv, 3; T. Asher v; Ps. Sol. iii, 12; 2 Bar. lvii, 2; lxxxv, 10; 2 Esdras vii, 48; Bab. Berakot 61b; Bab. Yom Tob. 15b.

[13] Isa. lxv, 17; lxvi, 22; *Barnabas* vi, 13; see also Volz, *Eschatologie*[2], pp. 359ff., and Index, s.v. 'Urzeit und Endzeit'.

As a result of the dispersion and missionary activity, it had congregations in every land; and when the emphasis came to be laid on the observance of the Law, so that a distinction was made even among those who were Jews by birth, the universalistic elements in the doctrine of God became more prominent and coloured the conceptions of restoration and salvation. Devotion to the Law, the existence of the Diaspora, and new social conditions were accompanied by a stronger tendency to individualism. It was personal decision and the conduct of life which determined whether a man was a true Jew, or a renegade and no better than a Gentile. An individualistic piety could no longer be content with the kind of salvation which was involved in the restoration of the people at some time in the future. It required salvation for the individual soul, corresponding to the decision of the individual.[1]

These new needs were met by those influences from Persian eschatology, which are represented in the apocalyptic literature. A new eschatology came into existence, dualistic, cosmic, universalistic, transcendental, and individualistic.

But the old view and the new appear nowhere in the literature as two distinct systems; and they certainly never actually existed as such in the minds of individuals. They are always intermingled in a quite unsystematic combination, so that the main emphasis is put sometimes on the one aspect, sometimes on the other.[2] Sometimes we also find conceptions which are intended to modify the contradictions and produce some kind of unity.[3] The fundamental idea is that of the two aeons or world-orders.[4] The present one is evil, transient, destined to end[5] at a time which the 'wise' can compute.[6] The coming aeon is eternal,[7] transcendental in character, bringing life, light, blessedness, joy, and peace.[8] Thus a solution is found for the problem of suffering, which had raised such difficulties for the earlier Jewish conception of a just apportioning of reward and punishment in this life. The present aeon

---

[1] See Bousset, *Relig.*[2], pp. 333ff.   [2] Cf. Moore, *Judaism* II, p. 323; and above, p.267.
[3] See below on the Millennium, p. 277.
[4] Bousset, *Relig.*[2], pp. 277f.; Volz, *Eschatologie*[2], pp. 64ff.; Bonsirven, *Le Judaïsme palestinien au temps de Jesus-Christ* I, pp. 310ff. See also 2 Esdras vii, 50; iv, 2, 27; vi, 9; ,iiv12, 47, 112f.; viii, 1f., 52; 2 Bar. lxxxiii, 8; Eph. i, 21.
[5] 2 En. lxvi, 6; Rom. xii, 2; 1 Cor. i, 20; ii, 6, 8; iii, 18; 2 Cor. iv, 4; 2 Esdras iv, , 5, 11 26f., 36f.; v, 50ff.; vi, 20; vii, 12f., 31; xi, 44; 2 Bar. xliv, 9, 12; liv, 21; Ass. iMos. , 18; xii, 4.
[6] Dan. ii; vii, 1ff.; ix, 22ff.; 1 En. x, 12; lxxxix; xc, 17; xci, 15; xciii, 3; 2 Esdras iv, 5; xiv, 11; 2 Bar. xxvii; liii ff. See Bousset, *Relig.*[2], pp. 283ff.; *Volz, Eschatologie*[2], pp. 141ff.
[7] 2 En. lviii, 5; lxi, 2; lxv, 7–10; lxvi, 6f.; li, 8; 2 Cor. iv, 18; 2 Bar. xliv, 11.
[8] See the references to the late Jewish sources in p. 270 nn. 10, 11 and 12; also Volz, *Eschatologie*[2], p. 359ff.

itself lies in evil; the eternal aeon will redress the balance.[1] The enemies and oppressors of the Jews (the political world power) are often looked upon as the manifestation of a mythical, cosmic power, at enmity with God. Whatever Gog and Magog may have meant in Ezekiel, this distant people now comes to denote the hostile, cosmic, world power as such.[2]

Towards the end of the present aeon, sin, wickedness, and misfortune will reach a climax. The powers of nature will fail. There will be bad seasons and poor crops. Ominous happenings of every kind ('signs in the sun and in the moon') will take place.[3] There will be rebellion and war, all men at strife with each other.[4] These are the throes of the Messianic age,[5] foreboding the last desperate resistance to God[6] by Satan,[7] his army,[8] and the evil world powers,[9] when God comes to put an end to him and the evil world order.[10] The old idea, derived from cultic experience, of the return of the powers of chaos, and their rage over the new creation, when Yahweh manifests Himself at the New Year, has been brought to the point at which it becomes absolute, extending to the very ground of all existence. In the last times, this evil aeon will show its true satanic nature in a life-and-death struggle against God and the godly.

There was also a widespread belief that in the last days the satanic power would appear in human form as an 'Antichrist'.[11]

[1] See Volz, *Eschatologie*[2], pp. 127ff., and references.

[2] See Volz, *Eschatologie*[2], p. 150.

[3] 2 Esdras v, 4–6, 8, 50–5; vi, 16, 21f., 24; 2 Bar. xxvii; xxxii, 1; 1 En. viii, 2; xcix, 5; c, 11; Jub. xxiii, 18, 25; Sib. II, 154f., 164f.; III, 538f., 633, 796–806; Josephus, *B.J.* VI, 285ff.; Apoc. Abr. xxix f.; Rev. vi, 12ff.; xi 6; 2 Mac. v, 2f. Cf. Bousset, *Relig.*[2], p. 287; Volz, *Eschatologie*[2], pp. 155f.

[4] 1 En. xcix, 4, 8; cx, 2; 2 Esdras v, 1–5, 9; vi, 24; ix, 3; 2 Bar. xxv, 3; xlviii, 32f., 35; lxx, 2f., 5f.; Jub. xxiii, 19; Sib. III, 633ff.; Dan. xii, 1; Mark xiii, 8. See Volz, *Eschatologie*[2], pp. 153ff.

[5] Matt. xxiv, 8. See Weber, *Jüd. Theol.*[2], pp. 350f.; Bousset, *Relig.*[2], pp. 286f.; Volz, *Eschatologie*[2], p. 147; Strack-Billerbeck I, p. 950; IV, pp. 974ff.; Moore, *Judaism* II, p. 361. The rabbis use the singular form: 'the travail of the Messiah'; see Moore, ibid., n. 2.

[6] Dan. xii, 1; 1 En. xc, 16–18; 2 Esdras xiii; T. Jos. xix; Sib. III, 663ff.; Rev. xii, 7–9; xiii, 17; xix, 19. See the connected account in Volz, *Eschatologie*[2], pp. 147–63.

[7] See Bousset, *Relig.*[2], pp. 289ff.; Volz, *Eschatologie*[2], p. 86.

[8] The fallen angels and their descendants: 1 En. x, 9, 12f.; xiv, 6; xv, 8; xvi, 1–4; xxi, 10; xli, 9; liv, 5f.; lxiv; lxviii; lxxxviii; xc, 21–4; identical with the astral powers: 1 En. xxi, 1–6; Isa. xxiv, 21–3. Cf. Bousset, *Relig.*[2], pp. 288f.; Volz, *Eschatologie*[2], Index, s.v. 'Engel, die gefallenen'.

[9] Dan. vii, 25; viii, 13f.; ix, 26; xi, 41ff.; Ps. Sol. xvii, 15ff.; Ass. Mos. viii f.; 1 En. lvi, 5; xc, 17; Ezek. xxxviii f.; 1 En. lvi; xc, 16; 2 Esdras xiii; T. Jos. xix; Sib. III, 663ff. On King Gog and Magog, see Volz, *Eschatologie*[2], p. 150.

[10] 1 En. lvi, 7; xc, 18f., 94ff.; Sib. III, 670ff.; Elijah Apocalypse vii, 1ff.; T. Asher vii; T. Dan v; Ass. Mos. x; Bab. Sanhedrin 95b. See Volz, *Eschatologie*[2], pp. 151f., 94.

[11] 2 Thess. ii, 3; Justin, *Dialogue with Trypho*, cx, 32; Sib. III, 63ff. See Bousset, *Der Antichrist*; *Relig.*[2], pp. 291ff., 589f.

Originally he was conceived as a man, as God's last, mighty opponent on earth, a godless, tyrannical ruler, or a false prophet leading men astray by his miracles. But gradually he came to be thought of as a supernatural being, a manifestation of Satan himself.[1] Antichrist might also be identified with some historical person, as was also the Messiah (see below). The early Christians regarded Nero and Domitian as the Antichrist; and it seems likely that the great antagonist of the Damascus sect, the 'man of untruth', the 'man of scorn', though himself a historical person, is described in terms of the Antichrist.

More and more the end was thought of as a 'judgement', not in the ancient Jewish sense of an act of power, victory over God's enemies, and their destruction,[2] but in the forensic sense of a judicial process,[3] in which God Himself, 'the Ancient of Days', will sit in judgement on men, angels, and demons, and finally will pass sentence on Satan himself.[4] Judgement will be passed according to men's deeds which are recorded in the heavenly records.

Both the living and the dead have to appear for judgement. The dead will rise in order to be judged. This thought, which just begins to appear in the latest parts of the Old Testament,[5] is characteristic of later Judaism;[6] but the fact that the Sadducees rejected it shows how new it really was, and how alien to earlier Judaism. The original Jewish idea of resurrection, as we meet it in Daniel, was that 'many', namely the most righteous and the worst sinners, should arise to everlasting life and to everlasting contempt, respectively. Here we see the religious root of the conception, to which the foreign, Persian influence served as a catalyst.

---

[1] See Bousset, *Der Antichrist*; *Relig.*[2], pp. 291ff.; Preisker, art. 'Antichrist' in *R.G.G.*[2] I, pp. 375f.; Volz, *Eschatologie*[2], p. 282.

[2] See p. 272 n. 10; cf. Volz, *Eschatologie*[2], p. 94.

[3] 1 En. x, 6–12; xxii, 4, 11; xxv, 4; liv, 6; lx, 6; lxxxiv, 4; xci, 7, 15; xcviii, 10; xcix, 15; c, 4; Jub. v, 10; lxxxiii, 11; xxxvi, 10; T. Levi iii; iv; Ass. Mos. i, 18; 2 En. vii, 1; xl, 12; xliv, 5; xlviii, 9; l, 4; lviii, 6; lxv, 6; lxvi, 7; 2 Esdras vii, 70, 73, 87; 2 Bar. v, 2; xx, 4; lvii, 2; lix, 8; lxxxiii, 7; lxxxv, 12ff.; Life of Adam x; xii; xxvi; xxxvii; xciii; Sib. III, 55; Wisd. of Sol. iii, 13, 17; iv, 6; vi, 5f. Bousset, *Relig.*[2], pp. 294ff.; Volz, *Eschatologie*[2], pp. 272–309.

[4] Dan. vii, 9–12; 1 En. i, 3–9; xc, 20–9; xci, 15f.; Jub. v, 13; 2 Esdras vii, 33f.; 2 Bar. xxx; xlix–li; T. Levi iv; Ps. Sol. xv; Ass. Mos. x; xii, 13; Sib. III, 73, 689–92; IV, 40ff., 183f.; 2 En. xxxix, 8; xlvi, 3; lxv; Rev. xx, 11–15.

[5] Isa. xxv, 8; xxvi, 19–21; Dan. xii, 2, 13.

[6] 1 En. xcii, 3; c, 5; li, 1–3; xxxviii, 1, 6; xlv, 1–3; lxi, 5; 2 Esdras v, 42; vii, 32f., 78–101; 2 Bar. l, 2; li, 1ff.; lii, 3; lxxxv, 12ff.; Sib. IV, 180f.; T. Sim. vi; T. Levi xviii; T. Jud. xxv; T. Zeb. x; T. Dan v; T. Benj. x; 2 Mac. vi, 26; vii, 9, 14, 36; xii, 43f.; xiv, 46. See Bousset, *Relig.*[2], pp. 308ff.; Volz, *Eschatologie*[2], pp. 229ff.; Moore, *Judaism* II, pp. 292ff., and Index, s.v. 'Resurrection'. Riesenfeld's attempt to derive belief in resurrection from the supposed cultic conceptions of the 'resurrection' of the god and the king is unsuccessful; see Birkeland in *St. Th.* III, i, 1949/50, pp. 60ff.

The prevailing thought in earlier Judaism is the resurrection of the righteous to take part in the bliss of the end time. But in the time of Jesus, belief in a general resurrection was prevalent, and was taken as the distinguishing mark between believers and unbelievers. It is God who raises the dead. The idea of resurrection brings out clearly the universalistic and ethical tendencies in the eschatology of later Judaism.

After resurrection and judgement, the pious enter upon eternal life.[1] In describing it, use is made, for the most part, of terms and metaphors drawn from an idealized earthly life. But the expressions used reveal the fumbling attempt to put into words something 'wholly other', something essentially different from the life of this aeon.[2] It is simply 'Life';[3] and sometimes this fact is explicitly emphasized. 'Light' and 'Life' become parallels and synonyms.[4] We meet with the ethico-religious idea of living together with God for ever in His kingdom, where all sin and injustice have been destroyed.[5] The evil are sentenced to eternal and irrevocable perdition.[6] The place of punishment, Gehenna (Gehinnom), originally the name of a valley outside Jerusalem,[7] becomes a cosmic place of torture.[8]

After resurrection and judgement, the new world appears. This means not only the new 'age' (aeon), but a real creation of a new heaven and a new earth.[9] That later Judaism understood this quite literally, can be seen from the references to a destruction of the world by fire, preceding the new creation or 'rebirth' (of

---

[1] Dan. xii, 2; Ps. Sol. iii, 12; ix, 5; xiii, 11; xiv, 10; xv, 13; 1 En. xxxvii, 4; xl, 9; lviii, 3; 2 En. lxv, 10; 2 Mac. vii, 9, 14, 36; cf. 2 En. l, 2; lxvi, 6; 2 Esdras xiv, 36; 2 Bar. xiv, 13; li, 3; Wisd. of Sol. v, 15, etc. See Dalman, *Words of Jesus*, pp. 156ff.; Bousset, *Relig.*[2], pp. 316ff.; Volz, *Eschatologie*[2], pp. 362ff., 407.

[2] Cf. Gunkel's review of Messel's *Die Einheitlichkeit der jüdischen Eschatologie* in *N.T.T.* xvii, 1916, pp. 196ff.

[3] 1 En. xcviii, 10, 14; Ps. Sol. ix, 5; xiv, 3, 10; xv, 13; 2 Esdras vii, 21, 67, 129, 137f.; viii, 6; xiv, 2; 2 Bar. xli, 11; xlix, 2; li, 11; lxxvi, 5; lxxxv, 15; 2 En. xlii 6; 4 Mac. xvii, 18; Sifre Deut. vi, 5 (73b). See Volz, *Eschatologie*[2], pp. 341f., 362.

[4] 1 En. v, 7; xxxviii, 4; lviii, 3; Ps. Sol. iii, 12; 2 Bar. viii, 50; 2 En. xlii, 10; cf. Dan. xii, 3; Wisd. of Sol. iii, 7; 1 En. cviii, 11–14; 2 En. lxvi, 7; 2 Esdras vii, 97, 125; 2 Bar. li, 1ff. See Volz, *Eschatologie*[2], pp. 365f.; Aalen, *Die Begriffe 'Licht' und 'Finsternis' im Alten Testament, im Spätjudentum und im Rabbinismus*, pp. 181, 254, 276, 311, 313.

[5] See below, p. 276.

[6] Dan. xii, 2; 1 En. xci, 15; ciii, 8; x, 6, 12f.; xc, 24f.; 2 En. ix f.; 2 Bar. iv, 12; li, 5; lxxviii, 6; lxxxiii, 8, 10–21; lxxxv, 13; 2 Esdras vii, 36, 75, 84; viii, 59. See Bousset, *Relig.*[2], p. 325.

[7] 2 Kings xxiii, 10; Jer. vii, 31f.; xix, 2, 6; xxxii, 35 (Molech sacrifice); cf. Joel iv, 1, 12, 14 (see Mowinckel in *G.T.M.M.M.* III, ad loc.), and Isa. lxvi, 25f.

[8] 1 En. xxvii, 2f.; liii f; lvi, 3. See below, p. 277.

[9] Isa. lxv, 17; lxvi, 22; 1 En. xci, 16f.; lxxii, 1; Jub. i, 29; l, 5; 2 En. lxv, 7; 2 Esdras vii, 75; 2 Bar. xxxi, 5; xxxii, 6; xliv, 12; lvii, 2. See Bousset, *Relig.*[2], pp. 321ff.; Volz, *Eschatologie*[2], pp. 338f.

the world).[1] Side by side with this idea (probably Persian in origin) of a world conflagration,[2] we also meet the idea of a new deluge,[3] from which only the righteous will be saved. It is not apparent how these ideas are to be logically combined with the thought of judgement and a place of punishment. But it was generally believed that the eternal life of the righteous would be lived out on the new earth, under the new heaven.

On the other hand, the boundaries between earth and heaven seem to disappear. From the way in which the new life of the new aeon is conceived, we see how two tendencies meet and contend, even in the new eschatology with its transcendental character. The new life is not, as it would have been in Greek or Gnostic thought, a purely spiritual one in contrast to the physical life in the body. It is rather a perfecting of physical, bodily existence on this earth, a restoration of the perfection which existed at creation, a transfiguration of bodily life, not the abolition of it. Jewish dualism, like that of the Greeks, is moral, spiritual, and intellectual, and not, like that of the Gnostics a dualism of matter on the one hand, and, on the other, a spirit which is pure and abstract, i.e., empty, and therefore meaningless. Thus the new aeon means existence in a re-created world, in which everything evil and imperfect has been destroyed, and which has become, spiritually and morally, what it was immediately after creation, when God saw that everything was 'very good', before sin invaded and spoiled God's creation.[4] This conception brings out the ancient Israelite realism, with its healthy opposition to the purely spiritual. The transcendental and superterrestrial never becomes the merely spiritual, abstract, invisible, intangible, and empty. The 'wholly other' in biblical religion never becomes that which can be expressed only by negations. Where, as in 2 Enoch, we find a tendency towards the incorporeal, Greek and Gnostic influences are present.

It is this conception of a perfection of creation through a

[1] Matt. xix, 28. This conception belongs originally to cosmic eschatology, before being applied to individual eschatology and to ethico-religious conversion. See Preuschen-Bauer, *W.B.N.T.*[4], s.v., with references to the literature.

[2] Sib. IV, 172; V, 155ff., 206ff., 247f., 344f., 447f., 512ff.; Ass. Mos. x, 6; Rev. xxi, 1. See Bousset, *Relig.*[2], p. 321; Volz, *Eschatologie*[2], p. 335.

[3] Cf. Bousset, *Relig.*[2], pp. 321f.; Volz, *Eschatologie*[2], p. 336, and Index, s.v. 'Sintflut'. The thought of Enoch as deliverer from the new deluge seems to underlie the description in 1 Enoch of Enoch as having foreseen the first deluge; see Jansen, *Die Henochgestalt*.

[4] Both Otto (*The Kingdom of God and the Son of Man*, pp. 197ff.) and Staerk (*Soter* II, pp. 458, 461f.) have rightly drawn attention to and emphasized this feature in the eschatology of later Judaism.

restoration of the original state of things that finds expression in the thought of paradise as the abode of the pious.[1] The ancient Israelite notions of a primeval, divine garden, high up on the divine mountain, were revived under the influence of new conceptions of Babylonian and Persian origin. Paradise is situated at heaven's uttermost bound, in the north. But sometimes it is thought of as situated in heaven itself, a conception which obliterates the boundary between the new heaven and the new earth. The idea of paradise also influenced the national Jewish eschatology. At the end of the ages the conditions of paradise return: Zion, or the entire Holy Land, is transformed into a paradise. The new Jerusalem is a heavenly city, which comes down to earth radiant with fabulous splendour.

Alongside and blended with these ideas of a transfiguration of the created, physical world (a 'corporeal eschatology'), we also find conceptions of a purely heavenly paradise, and a state of bliss for the souls of the dead, which begins immediately after death, 'in the abodes of the righteous, the holy, the elect' in heaven, as described in the Apocalypse of Enoch. These abodes already exist. This purely 'heavenly eschatology' (Otto) or 'animatistic eschatology' (Staerk) occurs occasionally in the Apocalypse of Enoch and in other writings; but it is not dominant.[2] It is undoubtedly the result of Persian influence.[3]

We have seen that in the realistic, earthly, ethico-religious idea of salvation there is a process of spiritualization. It is in keeping with this that blessedness, the true state of salvation, comes to be understood as fellowship with God, when God 'dwells among His people', the congregation of the saved. These ideas are expressed in sensuous terms, when it is said that the blessed will be 'as angels in heaven', will be clothed with the nature of light, will be like the stars, and so on.[4]

There were different views about the fate and location of the damned.[5] Sometimes we hear of eternal destruction,[6] sometimes

[1] 1 En. lxi, 12; lxx, 3f.; 2 Esdras vi, 26; vii, 28, 36ff.; xiii, 52, xiv, 9, 49; 2 En. viii f., etc. See Volz, *Eschatologie*[2], pp. 413ff.; Bousset, *Relig.*[2], pp. 324ff.

[2] Cf. Staerk, *Soter* II, pp. 462ff.

[3] Op. cit., p. 464. Following Otto, Staerk observes that both tendencies (the 'corporeal' and 'animatistic' eschatology) are also found in Persian teaching, side by side and blended with each other. This shows that these conceptions come from two different sources.

[4] See further, Volz, *Eschatologie*[2], pp. 394–401, with references to the sources; Bousset, *Relig.*[2], p. 321.   [5] Bousset, *Relig.*[2], pp. 309–21.

[6] 1 En. xciv, 1, 6f., 10; xcv, 6; xcvi, 6, 8; xcvii, 1; xcviii, 10, 14; xcix 1, 11; Ps. Sol. iii, 11; xiii, 11; xiv, 9; xv, 10ff.; 2 Esdras viii, 38; vii, 48, 61; 2 Bar. xxx, 5; 2 Mac. vii, 14, 16.

of eternal torture in Hades, the realm of the dead, in the outer darkness where there is weeping and gnashing of teeth because of the eternal cold.[1] We also hear of Gehenna,[2] the eternal fire,[3] which is fairly clearly distinguished from Hades, and located in the valley of Hinnom outside Jerusalem, where children had been sacrificed.[4] But Gehenna can also be conceived in cosmic terms, as belonging purely to the world beyond, and as always having been in existence. Here Persian ideas have been fused with Jewish teaching about the Valley of Hinnom or of Jehoshaphat, where the heathen powers will be destroyed,[5] and apostates punished with endless torture.

Finally, it must be noted that we often find an attempt to reconcile the nationalistic, this-worldly eschatology with the universalistic, individualistic, other-worldly eschatology, by means of the idea of the Millennium.[6] After a preliminary judgement, a Jewish Messianic kingdom will be set up on earth; and it will last for a thousand years under the rule of the Messianic king. Other periods, such as four hundred years, also occur. Then follows the general judgement, the destruction of the world, in which even the Messiah will die;[7] and everything returns to the primeval 'silence', i.e., to chaos. Then comes the new creation, the new heaven and the new earth, the resurrection, and the new state of bliss. This is the conception found in the Ezra Apocalypse.

Such attempts to reconcile the conflicting elements in eschatology are also characteristic of rabbinic orthodoxy in the early Christian period.[8] This orthodoxy, too, is based on dualism, though in a much milder form than that of apocalyptic; and its eschatology, though quite unsystematic, and varying considerably in details, is built around the thought of this aeon and the coming aeon.[9] The prevalent view, then, distinguishes between 'the days of the Messiah' and 'the coming aeon', putting the former between the two aeons.[10] Most of the traditional, this-worldly,

---

[1] 1 En. xlvi, 5; lxiii, 6; cviii, 14; ciii, 8; xcii, 5; Jub. vii, 29; Ps. Sol. xiv, 9; xv, 10; Matt. viii, 12; xiii, 42; xxiv, 51.
[2] Isa. lxvi, 24; 1 En. xxvii; xc, 26f.; 2 Esdras vii, 36. See Bousset, *Relig.*[2], p. 329; Volz, *Eschatologie*[2], pp. 328f., 332, 413.
[3] 1 En. x, 6, 12f.; xc, 24–6, c, 9; cviii, 4–6; 2 Esdras vii, 36f.; 2 Bar. xliv, 15; xlviii, 43; lix, 2; lviii, 13, etc.; Matt. v, 22; Mark ix, 43, 45, 47f.; Matt. xviii, 28; xxv, 41; Jude 7; Rev. xix, 20; xx, 10, 14f.; xxi, 8, etc.
[4] See above, p. 274 and the references in n. 8.   [5] See above, p. 147.
[6] Bousset, *Relig.*[2], pp. 330ff.; Volz, *Eschatologie*[2], pp. 71ff., 227, 273.
[7] See above, pp. 167ff., and below, pp. 285f.
[8] For what follows, see Moore, *Judaism* II, pp. 323–95.
[9] Moore, *Judaism* II, p. 378; see also Index I, s.v. 'World to Come'.
[10] Moore, *Judaism* II, p. 378; cf. p. 323.

national and political eschatology is included in 'the Messianic age'.[1] In speaking of this, the rabbis are rather reserved. The great catastrophe which ended in A.D. 70 with the destruction of Jerusalem and of the temple, and which resulted in the dispersion of all Jews, damped their enthusiasm, and taught them that the period of waiting might well be greatly prolonged. The attempts of the apocalyptists to calculate the time fell into disrepute.[2] Penitence, conversion, and strict obedience to the Law were now the supreme requirements.[3] The Messiah would come at the time appointed by God; and God would then bring to an end the dominion of the heathen. Descriptions of the glory of the age of restoration are infrequent, and for the most part restrained. They appear mostly in the exegesis of individual passages of Scripture, arbitrary, forced, unhistorical, hair-splitting, like all rabbinic exegesis, but sometimes containing legendary descriptions and amplifications of the text (midrash), and characterized by a blend of arid rationalism with mythical conceptions which were often far from poetical.

After the travail of the Messianic age, and before the nation is restored, God will extirpate all sinners from Israel.[4] This may be regarded as a judgement, in which both the Messiah and His forerunner Elijah[5] sometimes have a part to play.[6] In the restored Israel, glory, joy, and temporal blessings of every kind will abound.[7] The rabbis also write imaginatively of the great feast which God will make for His pious ones from the flesh of the two primeval monsters, Leviathan and Behemoth.[8] The dispersed Jews will return from every land;[9] but on the fate of the ten tribes there are varying views.[10] The day of freedom will have come. Israel will have independence under a wise and good king of the ancient royal line, and will enjoy all the divine blessings. The heathen nations will be subdued or converted to Judaism, and will never again be a menace to the people of God.[11]

But together with this, the religious aspect also appears. All peoples will then worship the true God.[12] The kingdom of heaven (i.e., of God), *malkûṯ šāmayim*, will have come; and His name will

---

[1] Moore, *Judaism* II, pp. 345f.
[2] Moore, *Judaism* II, pp. 352f. The interest which later rabbis had in these calculations shows that they were not finally discredited. See Silver, *A History of Messianic Speculations in Israel from the First to the Seventeenth Centuries.*
[3] Moore, *Judaism* II, pp. 350ff.   [4] Op. cit., p. 362.
[5] See below pp. 298f., and op. cit., pp. 357ff.   [6] Op. cit., p. 363.
[7] Op. cit., pp. 365f.   [8] Op. cit., pp. 363ff.   [9] Op. cit., pp. 366ff.
[10] Op. cit., pp. 368f.   [11] Op. cit., p. 371.   [12] Op. cit., ibid.

be hallowed all over the earth. Moore describes it in modern terms as 'the universality of the true religion, not alone professed by all men, but realized in their lives in all their relations to God and to their fellow-men'.[1]

Thus, in the fullness of time, the new aeon will come.[2] In the way in which it is conceived, the individualism of later Judaism emerges clearly. It is the individual that is involved. He will be acquitted or condemned according to what he has done as an individual.[3] The dead will be raised for judgement.[4] The heathen[5] and sinners will be condemned; but some held that in the end all Israelites would be saved.[6] Other scholars distinguished between an intermediate stage and the last judgement. Immediately after death, the pious go into the 'treasury', being 'bound up into the bundle of life'[7] in heaven,[8] or into the garden of Eden.[9] The wicked go into Gehenna, an evil and unhappy place.[10] At last comes the resurrection, when body and soul are re-united;[11] and then the final distinction is made between the righteous and the unrighteous. The damned will be eternally tortured in the fire of Gehenna, or destroyed after a shorter period of punishment there. The pious will enter into the heavenly glory, which is sometimes also called the garden of Eden (paradise). There is little description of the world beyond. Of the lot of the blessed it is said, 'The World to Come is not like this world. In the World to Come there is no eating and drinking, no begetting of children, no bargaining, no jealousy and hatred, and no strife; but the righteous sit with their crowns on their heads enjoying the effulgence of the Presence (Shekinah).'[12]

---

[1] Moore, *Judaism* II, p. 372.   [2] Op. cit., p. 378.
[3] Op. cit., p. 377; cf. Sjöberg, *Gott und die Sünder*, pp. 105ff.
[4] Moore, *Judaism* II, pp. 378ff.
[5] Not all the rabbis thought that the heathen would rise from the dead. Op. cit., pp. 385ff.
[6] Op. cit., pp. 387f.
[7] Borrowing an expression from 1 Sam. xxv, 29 (see Mowinckel in *G.T.M.M.M.* II, ad loc.); see Moore, *Judaism* II, p. 390; and further, Frazer, *Folklore in the Old Testament* II, pp. 503ff.
[8] Moore, *Judaism* II, p. 390.
[9] Op. cit., pp. 390f.   [10] Op. cit., p. 391.   [11] Op. cit., ibid.
[12] Bab. Berakot 17a; see Moore, *Judaism* II, p. 392. Cf. Mark xii, 25; Matt. xxii, 30; Luke xx, 34–6.

CHAPTER IX

The National Messiah

1. *Two Conceptions of the Messiah—The National Messiah*

AS in the Old Testament period, so in that of later Judaism, the figure of the Messiah is not an indispensable part of the future hope or of eschatology. In a whole series of religious writings which speak of the future hope, the Messiah does not appear; e.g., Daniel, 1 and 2 Maccabees, Tobit, the Wisdom of Solomon, Judith, Sirach, Jubilees, the Assumption of Moses, 1 Baruch, 2 Enoch or the Slavonic Enoch, and also considerable portions of 1 Enoch or the Ethiopic Enoch (i–xxxvi; xci–xciii the Apocalypse of Weeks; and the hortatory sections in xc–civ). This is also true of the writings of Philo.[1] In other writings the Messiah appears only occasionally, as a traditional element in the belief about the future, but without playing an important part.

This may seem remarkable, since eager Messianic expectation forms the background for the appearance of Jesus and the Gospel narrative generally. Yet it is not difficult to understand. In proportion as the main emphasis came to be laid on the religious aspect of the future hope, on the kingly rule of Yahweh, there would be little or no room for the Messianic king, in whom, after all, at least in the traditional belief, earthly and human features predominated. The earthly scion of David was not fitted to satisfy the deepest *religious* longings and needs. It was for the presence of God Himself in the midst of His people that men longed. This would be still more true when the national and political future was overshadowed by an eschatology which was transcendental, universalistic, and individualistic. It was not easy to disregard the fact that the Messiah was in origin a political figure belonging to this world, who could not easily be accommodated to the transcendental, other-worldly thoughts and longings of the new eschatology. Had it not been that in certain circles in the later period the conception of the Messiah was powerfully and decisively

[1] Cf. W. Manson, *The Epistle to the Hebrews*, p. 95.

influenced by other religious and eschatological ideas, it might well have passed out of eschatology altogether.

We shall return below to these entirely new aspects of the figure of the Messiah, aspects which are particularly closely associated with the term 'Son of Man'. It appears that, as in the general future hope of later Judaism there were two tendencies, originally quite distinct, but now fused with each other, so the conception of the Messiah in later Judaism manifests the same double character.[1] The one side is national, political, this-worldly, with particularistic tendencies, though universalistic when at its best. The other is super-terrestrial, other-worldly, rich in religious content and mythological concepts, universalistic, numinous, at home in the sphere of the 'Holy' and the 'wholly Other'. These two types of Messiah seldom appear in a pure form. In the circles and at the period from which our sources come, men were unaware that they were, in origin, separate types. von Gall's attempts to prove that this was not so,[2] as if the fusion of the two were due only to occasional, secondary additions, or attempts at theological harmonization, seem artificial and unconvincing. The thought of later Judaism is concerned with one and the same royal figure, who belongs to the end time, and appears under different names, and in whom this-worldly and other-worldly traits are blended. But it is quite obvious (and can be definitely proved) that two figures which were originally quite distinct have been fused. The fusion is never complete. In the various writings and the circles from which they are derived, one aspect or the other was dominant and overshadowed the other; and as a rule we are presented with one of the two Messianic figures, influenced by the other in greater or less degree.

It is therefore justifiable to consider these figures separately as two Messianic types, each belonging to its own circles in later Judaism, but to some extent allied with each other. To attempt to systematize the features in the two different conceptions and produce from them a uniform conception of the Messiah would give a wholly distorted impression of the facts. In the first place, it would not in fact be uniform or coherent, but full of conflicting elements at every important point; and secondly, it would provide us with a conception of the Messiah which never existed in that form in the thought of later Judaism, being simply a chimera produced by modern theological learning.

[1] See Additional Note XIII.   [2] von Gall, *Basileia*, chs. 9 and 10.

The other-worldly, universalistic eschatology described in the preceding chapter is found particularly in the apocalyptic literature. We may say with certainty of this literature that it was neither a popular literature nor a reflection of the religion of the masses of the people.[1] This entire literature is derived from the learned wisdom schools, which were occupied with the wisdom of the time, chiefly Chaldean in origin,[2] with non-Jewish religious traditions, and with mystical and spiritual experiences.[3] From this we may conclude that the ideas which they express, including that of the transcendental Messiah, were current in certain literary circles, among the learned (the 'wise', or the scribes), and in those circles in the upper classes and the religious sects which were influenced by them. Among the masses of the people, the older, this-worldly, national future hope prevailed. It appealed directly to popular sentiment and aspirations, particularly in evil times, when feeling ran high because of the pressure of alien rule, social and economic difficulties, and the reaction against the breach of ancient custom by the 'Hellenists' and foreigners, and their outrage of religious feeling. It was also among the masses of the people that the older, this-worldly national conception of the Messiah lived on.

But of course it also survived elsewhere; otherwise we should have known no more about it than might be concluded from the Messianic revolts (see below) and from the Gospels. In literary circles it survived and affected thought and aspiration. The Psalms of Solomon, the Testaments of the Twelve Patriarchs, the Targums, the ancient synagogue prayers, and, in a measure, the way in which the Greek translation of the Bible renders certain Old Testament passages, all bear witness to national Messianic ideas among the upper classes of the people. The same is true of the rabbinic literature, in which apocalyptic elements have been suppressed by normative Judaism with its more nationalistic and this-worldly spirit.

In particular, the Targums (the somewhat free Aramaic renderings of the Old Testament for use in the synagogues) provide evidence of the important place given to the Messianic idea in leading religious circles. Of course they apply to the Messiah both the royal psalms and the passages in which the future king is mentioned. They also treat in the same way passages which are not

---

[1] Cf. Bousset, *Relig.*[2], p. 256. [2] See above, p. 264 n. 10.
[3] See Hölscher, *Geschichte der israelitischen und jüdischen Religion*, pp. 186ff.

intended to be either eschatological or Messianic, such as the Balaam poems[1] and the Shiloh prophecy in Gen. xlix. Some other examples of Messianic interpretation may be noted. In Isa. x, 27, MT speaks of fatness breaking the yoke from the people's neck. This was interpreted of the Messiah breaking the power of the heathen. In Isa. xiv, 29, 'Messiah of the sons of Jesse' was read into the threatening words against the Philistines. In Mic. iv, 8, 'the former dominion' was promised not to Jerusalem (as in MT) but to the future Messiah, who was still hidden because of Israel's sins. The interpretation of the seed of the woman, in Gen. iii, 15, as the Messiah is derived from the Targums and Jewish theology. The bridegroom in the Song of Songs was interpreted in the Targums as the Messiah. Still more important is the fact that the Servant of the Lord in Deutero-Isaiah was identified with the Messiah; but, as we shall see below, this identification was then combined with a complete reinterpretation of the Servant.

The Targumic interpretation is here characteristic of all Jewish theology and religious exegesis. As G. F. Moore has pointed out, the rabbis assume that the entire divine revelation in Scripture forms an organic unity.[2] Wherever it was in any way possible, the rabbis read into the texts references to the Messiah, the son of David. Learned exegesis of this kind has contributed much to the picture of the Messiah in Ps. Sol. xvii f. But no attempt was ever made to co-ordinate and harmonize the ideas and conceptions at which they thus arrived by their exegesis, which would, indeed, have been an impossible task. There is, therefore, no reason why the historian of religion or of theology should try to construct a detailed and systematic rabbinic doctrine of the Messiah.

This interest in the Messiah was shared by practically all Judaism at that period. As we have seen, the Greek translation of the Old Testament shows signs of an interest which finds the Messiah even in passages where the original text has a quite

[1] See the references to the sources in Aalen, *Die Begriffe 'Licht' und 'Finsternis' im Alten Testament, im Spätjudentum und im Rabbinismus*, p. 232 n. 2. The Messianic interpretation of the royal psalms is not the only one. Thus the Targum interprets Ps. cx of David himself. 'The Lord has said in His word that He will make me Lord of all Israel. But then He said to me, "Wait for Saul, who belongs to the tribe of Benjamin, until he shall die"'. Or, according to another tradition, 'The Lord has said in His word that He will give me the kingdom'. So also R. Judah ben Shallum; see Strack-Billerbeck IV, pp. 452ff. There is no question here of an alteration of the text, as Danell seems to think (*St.Th.* IV, i, 1950/1, p. 94 n. 1), but of a free, paraphrastic rendering. There is no reason to think, like Danell, that this rendering is post- and anti-Christian.
[2] See Moore, *Judaism* II, p. 327; cf. also Staerk, *Soter* I, pp. 49f.

different meaning, or which interprets the language in a more other-worldly sense.[1]

2. *The Messiah a Historical Person*

The best proof of the diffusion of the Messianic expectation and of the political, this-worldly character of the conception is the fact that precisely in the later period of Judaism, when the transcendental features were present, time after time some historical person was regarded as the Messiah and aroused great Messianic excitement among the people.

The first evidence of this is the proclamation by Haggai and Zechariah of Zerubbabel as king of the restoration. That even in later times this kind of idea was quite acceptable is shown by the Talmudic interpretation of Isa. ix, 5 (the child who is born to us) as an allusion to King Hezekiah, who, according to the purpose of the Lord, should really have been the Messiah, with Sennacherib as King Gog, but was found to be unworthy.[2] The fact that the Hasmonean rule was widely held to be the fulfilment of the prophecies about the restoration of Israel, and that Simon was regarded as the Messiah and the first of a new Messianic line, is shown by the description of Simon's rule in 1 Mac. xiv, 4ff., which reads like a paraphrase of the Messianic prophecies in the Old Testament. The dignity of Messiah was on one occasion even attributed by one of the Pharisees to Phreoras, brother of Herod.[3] We may also recall the series of 'false Messiahs'[4] whom Josephus and the Roman authorities characterized as brigands, rioters, and saboteurs: Hezekiah, the 'robber-chief', as Josephus calls him, from whom Herod, when governor of Galilee, delivered the country,[5] but who was recognized as Messiah by Hillel;[6] further his son, Judas the Galilean from Gamala, and his brother, Menahem ben Hezekiah; the prophet Theudas in the time of the procurator Cuspius Fadus; the Egyptian Jew who led his followers to

---

[1] See Bousset, *Relig.*[2], pp. 303f.; cf. also Euler, *Die Verkündigung vom leidenden Gottesknecht aus Jes. 53 in der griechischen Bibel.*

[2] Bab. Sanhedrin, 94a.   [3] Josephus, *Antt.* XVII, 47f.

[4] Cf. E. Meyer, *Ursprung und Anfänge des Christentums* II, pp. 402ff.; Gillet, *Communion in the Messiah*, pp. 102, 225ff.; R. Meyer, *Der Prophet aus Galiläa*, pp. 70ff.; cf. below, p. 285 n. 3.

[5] Josephus, *Antt.* XIV, 160.

[6] Bab. Sanhedrin, 98b, 99a. Moore (*Judaism* II, p. 347 n. 2) thinks that this Hillel is another person than the famous Rabbi Hillel who was contemporary with Jesus. The Talmudists think that the Hezekiah to whom Hillel here refers is Hezekiah, king of Judah; but Gressmann is probably right in supposing that it is really Hezekiah the Galilean who is meant (See *Der Messias*, pp. 449ff.).

the mount of Olives, so that they might see the walls of Jerusalem fall down, but was put to the sword with his followers by the procurator Felix; another unnamed Jew, who appeared in the time of Festus and led his followers out into the wilderness, where they were cut down by the Roman soldiers;[1] and finally Simon bar Cochba, 'Son of a Star', who came forward claiming to be the fulfilment of the prophecy of Balaam about the 'star out of Jacob', and who was hailed as Messiah by no less a man than Rabbi Akiba.[2] Such Messiahs also appeared among the Samaritans.[3]

This all shows that the Messiah was generally regarded as an earthly man like other men. This is also the universal view of the rabbis, in spite of the impressive epithets which they apply to him.[4]

It has often been maintained that even the learned rabbis taught the Messiah's pre-existence; but this is incorrect.[5] In the rabbinic literature of the earlier Christian period we do occasionally find the thought of the 'ideal' pre-existence of the Messiah, i.e., his existence in the mind of God as part of His unchanging and eternal plan for the world; but there is no question of a literal and actual pre-existence (see further below, p. 334). The actual pre-existence of the Messiah was taught only in those circles in Judaism in which the Messiah was identified with the Son of Man. We shall return to this in the next chapter.

The fact that the Messiah was from the first regarded as an earthly being is shown clearly by the fact that in later Judaism he was often held to be mortal, as in the earlier form of the Jewish future hope (see above, pp. 165ff., 277). This conception appears in the attempts made to harmonize the older, this-worldly, national, future hope and the later, other-worldly, universalistic forms by means of the idea of the earthly Millennium (see above, p. 277). The Messiah was associated with this earthly kingdom of the end time. This was quite logical, for he had belonged from the beginning to the restored kingdom on this earth. Accordingly it is also stated that when this interim kingdom comes to an end, even the Messiah will die (2 Esdras vii, 28f.). Both the 'Messiah

---

[1] Josephus, *Antt.* XVII, 271; *B.J.* II, 118, 433ff.; *Antt.* XX, 97f.; Acts v, 36; xxi, 38; Josephus, *Antt.* XX, 169ff.; *B.J.* II, 266ff.; *Antt.* XX, 188.
[2] See Buhl, *Det israelitiske Folks Historie*,[6] pp. 437f.
[3] Josephus, *Antt.* XVIII, 85f.; Origen, *Contra Celsum* I, 57. See E. Meyer, *Ursprung und Anfänge des Christentums* II, pp. 409ff. On Jewish Messiahs in the Diaspora and in the Middle Ages, see Simchowitsch in *J.L.* IV, cols. 132f.
[4] See Moore, *Judaism* II, p. 349.
[5] Strack-Billerbeck II, pp. 334ff., where the rabbinic passages are quoted.

from Joseph' and the Samaritan Taheb are said to be mortal (see below, pp. 290f.).

Even at this period, of course, the Messiah is described as having all those superhuman features, which from ancient times formed part of the ancient oriental idea of kingship. An impression of this ideal is given by Ps. Sol. xvii, to which we shall often refer below. But these miraculous features are always thought of as extensions or idealizations of natural human ideals realized within human nature, although they result from the divine equipment which the Messiah will receive for his task. As the scion of David (see below), and as one who could be identified with an actual historical person, the Messiah is an altogether natural human being. When Justin, in his dialogue with the Jew Trypho, makes the latter say, 'among us everyone holds that Messiah will come as a man from men', he is expressing the prevalent Jewish view.

3. The Messiah's Descent. The Scion of David. Other Conceptions

Thus the Messiah was to be a human being. Nor was there any doubt, as a rule, that he would be of David's line. He was 'the son of David'. This is shown both by Jewish literature[1] and the popular conceptions which we find in the Gospels.[2] Mic. v, 1 gave rise to the belief that he would be born in Bethlehem.[3] In the rabbinical literature we occasionally find the idea (based on a literal interpretation of passages like Hos. iii, 5; Jer. xxx, 9) that David would return in person as the Messiah. This view can hardly have been popular, and it was rejected by other scribes.[4] In addition to David, some other of his pious descendants (long since dead) are mentioned as returning as the Messiah, namely Jehoshaphat and Hezekiah.[5] But here, too, we have to do with the private opinions of individual scribes.

For a short period it seemed that the thought of the son of David would become less prominent. This was when the Maccabean rule was at its height and had not yet lost that ideal quality and religious lustre which Judas and Simon had shed on it. As we have seen, there were many in that age who thought that the

[1] Ps. Sol. xvii, 4f., 21, 23; T. Judah xxii–xxiv; Shemoneh Esreh xiv, the *Haḇtnēnû* prayer; for rabbinical evidence see Bousset, *Relig.*[2], p. 260; 2 Esdras xii, 32; Targum of Jonathan on Isa. xi, 1; Jer. xxiii, 5; xxxiii, 15; Hos. iii, 5. Cf. von Gall, *Basileia*, p. 397.
[2] Mark x, 45; xi, 10 (with parallels); xii, 35 (with parallels); Matt. xii, 23; xv, 22; xxi, 15f.; Rom. i, 3; 2 Tim. ii, 8; Rev. v, 5; xxii, 16. Cf. *Didache*, ix, 2.
[3] Targum on Mic. v, 1; Matt. ii, 5; John vii, 41f. See Strack-Billerbeck II, pp. 335ff.
[4] Jer. Berakot 5a; Lamentations Rabbah on i, 16. See Moore, *Judaism* II, p. 326.
[5] Strack-Billerbeck II, p. 337 n.a.

glorious Messianic age was being realized. But the Hasmoneans were a priestly house, of the tribe of Levi, not Judah. The book of Jubilees knows nothing of a future monarchy of the house of Judah, but only of the house of Levi; and in the Testaments of the Twelve Patriarchs the new idea of a Levitical Messiah is found side by side with the traditional Messiah from Judah.[1] As Jacob, before he died, laid his right hand on Joseph's younger son, and thus gave him the birthright and the greater blessing (Gen. xlviii, 13ff.), so the book of Jubilees tells us that the dying Isaac blessed Levi and Judah, but gave the birthright to Levi: 'May the God of all, the very Lord of all the ages, bless thee and thy children throughout all the ages. And may the Lord give to thee and to thy seed greatness and glory. . . . And they shall be judges and princes, and chiefs of all the seed of the sons of Jacob;

> They shall speak the word of the Lord in righteousness,
> And they shall judge all His judgements in righteousness.'
>
> (Jub. xxxi, 13, 14a, 15a)

In the Testament of Levi it is put still more clearly:[2]

> Then shall the Lord raise up a new priest . . .
> And he shall execute a righteous judgement upon the
>   earth for a multitude of days.
> And his star shall arise in heaven as of a king,
> Lighting up the light of knowledge as the sun the day,
> And he shall be magnified in the world.
> He shall shine forth as the sun on the earth,
> And shall remove all darkness from under heaven,
> And there shall be peace in all the earth . . .

[1] Jub. xxxi, 13ff.; T. Reub. vi, 10–12; T. Levi xviii; see R. Meyer, *Der Prophet aus Galiläa*, pp. 62ff.; Eppel, *Le piétisme juif dans les testaments des douze patriarches*, pp. 98ff.; Leivestad, *Christ the Conqueror*, pp. 9ff. Bickermann (*J.B.L.* lx, 1941) denies that any such doctrine is to be found in the Testaments, and refers to T. Judah xxii, 2f. and T. Sim. vii (the latter generally regarded as not genuine). Black (*E.T.* lx, 1948/9, pp. 321f.) regards the whole chapter, T. Levi xviii, as a Christian interpolation. Charles (*A.P.O.T.* II; cf. art. 'Testaments of the XII Patriarchs' in *H.B.D.* IV, pp. 721ff.) finds allusions to the Maccabean priestly kingdom also in T. Levi viii, 11ff. As the text of the Testaments stands, the two Messiahs are to be found side by side. Charles has tried to show that the Messiah from Judah is due to secondary Jewish interpolations (apart from the still later Christian interpolations); and most scholars have agreed with him. But, as Beasley-Murray says (*J.T.S.* xlviii, 1947, pp. 1ff.), 'the juxtaposition of the Messiah from Judah and the Messiah from Levi is too deeply rooted in the fabric of the book for either to be discarded'. Cf. T. W. Manson, ibid., pp. 59ff.

[2] Text in Charles, *The Greek Versions of the Testaments of the Twelve Patriarchs*. On the text-critical problems, see Bousset in *Z.N.T.W.* i, 1900, pp. 141ff. Commentary in Charles, *A.P.O.T.* II; cf. Charles in *H.D.B.* IV, pp. 721ff.

And the knowledge of the Lord shall be poured forth
upon the earth, as the water of the seas . . .
For he shall give his majesty to his sons in truth for
evermore;[1]
And there shall none succeed them for all generations for
ever.[2]
And in his priesthood the Gentiles shall be multiplied in
knowledge upon the earth,
And enlightened through the grace of the Lord.

(T. Levi xviii, 2–5, 8–9a)

The 'new priest', whom the Lord will raise up, and who will
receive royal power and bequeath his majesty to his sons, is
evidently meant to be the founder of the Hasmonean priestly
monarchy of the house of Levi; and the status, and power, and
glory which are ascribed to him and his house are the same as are
elsewhere ascribed to the Messiah of the house of David.

It is characteristic of the nature of these ideas about a Messiah
of the house of Levi that they are concerned not with a single,
specific, ultimate individual, but with the founder of a dynasty and
his sons after him. It is the dynasty, not the first individual, which
will never be succeeded by any other ruler, i.e., by any other dynasty. It is in this sense that the Testament of Dan speaks of
the 'salvation' (i.e., the saviour) from the tribe of Levi,[3] who
'shall give you peace', and 'shall make war against Beliar, and
execute an everlasting vengeance on our enemies' (v, 9f.).

This thought also underlies the description in the Testament of
how in heavenly visions the ancestor Levi is installed as priest-king
over Yahweh's people. Levi is brought before the Most High and
installed as His son, His servant, and His priest. He is arrayed in
the holy garb of a priest-king and the insignia of royalty, the
sceptre, crown, and purple girdle, and equipped with righteous-

[1] The Greek text has 'the majesty of the Lord'; but this would mean 'the royal
majesty (dignity) that he has received from the Lord'. The original text probably
had 'his majesty (dignity)'. Hence the departure in this line from the rendering in
A.P.O.T. II.

[2] Note again departure from the rendering in *A.P.O.T.* II ('them' for 'him'). The
mention of the 'sons' (plural) to whom the priest-king gives his majesty, i.e., kingship
(see above n. 1), shows that von Gall (*Basileia*, p. 392) is right in taking αὐτῷ as a misunderstanding of a Hebrew *lāmô* as singular (=*lô*) instead of plural (*lāhem*).

[3] If Charles and others are right in taking this to refer to the Messianic king, the
words 'of Judah and' must be an interpolation. But T. W. Manson (see above, p.
287 n .1) takes *vv.* 4–10 as a Christian interpolation referring to the Holy Communion,
and explains *vv.* 11–14 in terms of the establishment of the Zadokite priesthood under
Solomon.

ness and wisdom, so that he may kindle the light of knowledge in Jacob, and be as the sun to the seed of Israel.[1] It is clear that the ancient enthronement ritual reappears here, and that certain features indicate a connexion with the royal ideology.[2]

But the Messianic kingdom of the Hasmoneans was a short-lived dream. Even before Pompey made an end of it, many had come to look upon the dynasty as a usurping one, secularized and hellenized as it had become. In the Psalms of Solomon it was regarded after its fall as a dynasty of ungodly tyrants, justly over-taken by the Lord's punishment.[3] Post-Hasmonean Judaism dis-carded the idea of a Levitical Messiah. Some scholars have held that the expression 'Messiah of (or from) Aaron and Israel' in the Damascus Fragments indicates that 'the congregation of the new covenant' in Damascus[4] knew of two Messiahs, one of the seed of Aaron, the other of the seed of David.[5] But this is incorrect. The expression means simply that the Messiah will come from the midst of the community itself ('those of Aaron and of Israel'), i.e., the community which consists of segregated priests and laymen.[6]

Besides the Messiah of the house of Levi, we sometimes hear of

---

[1] T. Levi iv, 2f.; v, 1–3, viii.

[2] See Widengren in *Horae Soederblomianae* I, pp. 1ff., where he shows that similar conceptions of enthronement have been transferred to Enoch at his enthronement and installation as heavenly scribe and Metatron (2 En. xxi, 3; xxii, 4–6, 8–10; xxiv, 1–3; xxxvi, 2; see op. cit., pp. 7ff.). Traces of this enthronement ritual are also to be found in 1 Enoch (li, 3; lx, 2; ch. lxxi does not belong in this connexion); see Widengren, op. cit., pp. 8ff.

[3] See Messel in *N.T.T.* viii, 1907, pp. 325ff.; Mowinckel, *Den senjødiske salmediktning*, pp. 21f., 24, 27ff.; Lindblom, *Senjudiskt fromhetslif enligt Salomos psaltare*. The Jewish discussions about the Hasmonean priest-kings are sometimes echoed in the rabbinic and apocryphal sayings about the Messiah, but by no means as often as Aptowitzer thinks (*Parteipolitik der Hasmonäerzeit*).

[4] See Hvidberg's excellent study, *Menigheden af den nye Pagt*, with references to editions and literature. The origin of the sect was dated by some scholars in the Maccabean or pre-Maccabean age, by others as late as the Middle Ages; see Hvidberg, op. cit., pp. 282ff.; Rowley, *The Relevance of Apocalyptic*, pp. 71ff. The latter opinion was held by Hölscher (*Z.N.W.* xxviii, 1929, pp. 21ff.) among others; the former, in itself the more likely to be correct, was advocated by E. Meyer (*Ursprung und Anfänge des Christentums* II, pp. 47ff.) and others, and has now been corroborated by the latest finds of documents in Palestine, the Dead Sea Scrolls; some of which clearly come from the same circles as the Damascus fragments. On this question, see Ginsberg in *B.A.S.O.R.* 112, Dec. 1948, pp. 19ff.; Brownlee, ibid., 112, Dec. 1948, pp. 8ff.; 114, April, 1949, pp. 9ff.; 116, Dec. 1949, pp. 14ff.; 121, Feb. 1951, pp. 8ff.; Burrows in *O.T.S.* VIII, pp. 156ff. On the date of the Scrolls (between *ca.* 175 and *ca.* 30 B.C.) see Trever in *B.A.S.O.R.* 113, Feb. 1949, pp. 6ff.; Birnbaum, ibid., pp. 33ff.; 115, Oct. 1949, pp. 20ff.; *J.B.L.* lxx, 1951, pp. 227ff.; Albright in *B.A.S.O.R.* 115, Oct. 1949, pp. 10ff.; cf. Burrows, ibid., 122, April, 1951, pp. 4ff. On the present state of the whole com-plex of problems, see Baumgartner in *T.R.* (N.F.) xvii, 1948/49, pp. 329ff.; xix, 1951, pp. 97–154; H. H. Rowley, *The Zadokite Fragments and the Dead Sea Scrolls* (with extensive bibliography).

[5] So especially Ginzberg, *Eine unbekannte jüdische Sekte* I, pp. 299ff.

[6] See Hvidberg, op. cit., pp. 273ff.

U

a Messiah ben Joseph, or ben Ephraim, who, according to the Jerusalem Targum of Exod. xl, 12, will defeat Gog in the last times. He is also mentioned elsewhere.[1] For instance, we hear that he will fall in the conflict with Gog. In reference to Deut. xxxiii, 17 (where Joseph is described as being like a vigorous firstborn bullock and his horns like those of a wild ox) this Messiah is also called 'the Horned' or 'Two-Horned One'.

How the thought of the Messiah ben Joseph arose is not clear. It might well be thought that it arose among the Samaritans as a counterpart of the Jewish Messiah of the house of David,[2] but that it was occasionally accepted in Jewish circles, partly because it could claim support from the interpretation of certain passages of scripture, partly because the Jews could regard the Messiah ben Joseph as one of the forerunners of the Messiah, like 'Taxo' of the house of Levi, whose task it then was to lead home the dispersed members of the ten tribes. Billerbeck holds that the conception originated among the scribes, simply as a result of an interpretation of passages like Deut. xxxiii, 17.[3] Torrey thinks that it arose from the Messianic interpretation of Isa. liii: a dying Messiah could not be the true Messiah ben David, but must be an antecedent Messiah, coming from Joseph, as the tribe which ranked next after Judah.[4] But, as we shall see, the rabbis did not interpret Isa. liii of the death of the Messiah; and accordingly, the idea of a dying Messiah from Ephraim can hardly have originated there. It would be more natural to suppose, like Moore, that the concept arose from what is said in Obad. 18 about the house of Joseph, which will become a flame and consume Edom.[5]

Perhaps the idea of the Messiah ben Joseph has a more concrete origin. As we have seen, it is sometimes said that he will fall in the battle against Gog. Besides Gog, we hear also of Armilus = Romulus = Rome.[6] It is also stated (referring to Zech. xii, 10)

---

[1] Targum of Song of Sol. iv, 5; vii, 4; and in Talmudic sources; see Weber, *Jüd. Theol.*[2], pp. 362ff.; Klausner, *Die messianischen Vorstellungen des jüdischen Volkes im Zeitalter der Tannaiten*, pp. 86ff.; Bousset, *Relig.*[2], pp. 264f. The *locus classicus* for this idea is Deut. xxxiii, 17; see Dalman, *Der leidende und sterbende Messias der Synagoge im ersten nachchristlichen Jahrhundert*, p. 19.

[2] So von Gall, *Basileia*, p. 388; also Bertholdt (as early as 1811) in *Christologia Judaeorum Jesu apostolorumque aetate*.

[3] Strack-Billerbeck II, pp. 290ff.   [4] See Torrey, in *J.B.L.* lxvi, 1947, p. 256.

[5] Moore, *Judaism* II, p. 371. Dix's attempt to find the idea of the Messiah ben Ephraim in Gen. xlix, 10b, 24b (*J.T.S.* xxvii, 1926, pp. 130ff.; cf. xxviii, 1927, pp. 223ff.) fails, *inter alia*, because it is based upon unjustifiable modifications of the text. Accordingly, H. Smith's attempt to find the idea in Matt. ii, 28 must also be rejected (*J.T.S.* xxviii, 1927, p. 60).

[6] See Hvidberg, *Menigheden av den nye Pagt*, p. 277.

that this Messiah will suffer death. This idea can hardly have arisen simply by exegesis of the Scripture passages referred to. There was no particular reason for interpreting the one 'whom they have pierced' in Zech. xii, 10 as a national, warlike Messiah, if the idea of his death was not already taken for granted on other grounds. Gressmann[1] held that it was the 'dynasty' of Galilean Messiahs mentioned above (p. 284), and especially Menahem ben Hezekiah, that gave rise to the thought of the dying Messiah ben Joseph, ben Ephraim, or ben Manasseh, as he is variously called; for they all fell in the conflict with the ungodly Rome, and Rome was at that time regarded as the fulfilment of the prophecy about Gog and Magog, or as Edom. Death in the struggle for liberty against the enemy would then be associated from the outset with this Messianic figure. The explanation is very attractive; the more so since it is explicitly stated that the Messiah ben Joseph will appear in Upper Galilee. At all events, the Messiah ben Joseph is not a prominent feature in the Jewish Messianic hope. Judging from the rabbinic sources, the idea of such a Messiah would seem to belong to a late period, perhaps in the Christian era.[2]

The Messiah ben Joseph would meet the need felt in some quarters for a Messiah even more warlike than the son of David was held to be (see below). Sometimes the rabbis called the Messiah ben Joseph the 'War-Messiah' ($m^e\check{s}i^ah$ $mil\dot{h}\bar{a}m\hat{a}h$), by contrast with the descendants of David.[3] But the true Messiah is and remains the Son of David.

4. The Names and Titles of the Messiah.

It was not until the later period of Judaism that the king of the end time came to be called 'Messiah' (ham-$m\bar{a}\check{s}i^ah$; Aramaic $m^e\check{s}i\dot{h}\hat{a}$'), 'the Anointed'. We frequently find the fuller form, 'the Lord's Anointed' ($m^e\check{s}i\dot{h}\hat{a}$' $d^a\underline{d}\bar{o}n\bar{a}y$), or, with a backward reference, 'His Anointed'.[4] The common occurrence (e.g., in the Targums) of the expression $malk\hat{a}$' $m^e\check{s}i\dot{h}\hat{a}$' shows that the term is about to

---

[1] In the essay 'Der unerkannte Messias' in *Der Messias*, pp. 449ff.

[2] See Gressmann, *Der Messias*, p. 457; cf. Weber, *Jüd. Theol.*[2], p. 363. Torrey's attempt to find the Messiah ben Ephraim in 2 Esdras vii, 28–31; 2 Bar. xxix; xxx; xl; 1 En. xc, 38; Dan. ix, 24–27; Zech. xii, 9–11, and in a supposed original text of Zech. iv, and so to trace this idea back to the early post-exilic period (see above, p. 290 n. 4) is not convincing.

[3] Pesikta 51a; Pesikta Rabbati xv, 75a; Canticles Rabbah on ii, 13.

[4] Ps. Sol. xvii, 32, 36; xviii, 5f., 7f.; 1 En. xlviii, 10; 1, 4; 2 Esdras vii, 48ff.; xii, 32; 2 Bar. xxix, 3; xxx, 1; xxxix, 7; xl, 1; lxx, 9; lxxii, 2. See Bousset, *Relig.*[2], p. 261; von Gall, *Basileia*, pp. 381, 384f.

become a personal name, 'King Messiah',[1] like 'King David' and similar expressions. But even as late as St. Paul's time, the conception oscillates between title and proper name: ὁ χριστός and χριστός. Other terms in the Targums are 'Messiah bar David' (son of David), 'the Messiah (or Anointed One) of Israel', 'the Anointed One of righteousness', i.e., the righteous Anointed One, *mešîḥā' dᵉsidḳā'*.[2] This title also includes the idea that he will establish 'righteousness', i.e., salvation and right order in religion and morals, and that he himself is therefore righteous (see below).

It is natural and understandable that the Messiah is also called 'the Son of David'.[3] This name often occurs in the Gospels. 'The Son of David' designates him as both the fulfilment of the ancient promises and the expression of the national hope of restoration.[4] The expression 'Messiah ben David'[5] is used, for example, to distinguish him from the Messiah ben Joseph (see above). But as in earlier times, the Messiah is also sometimes called 'David': it is a new David who arises.[6] On the expression in the Damascus Document, 'Messiah from Aaron and Israel', see above.

Occasionally the Messiah is also called 'the King' or 'the Great King'.[7] A name which was sometimes used was 'the Deliverer' (the Redeemer; Hebrew *gō'ēl*),[8] based on a Messianic interpretation of Old Testament passages, especially in Deutero-Isaiah, where Yahweh is called 'the Redeemer of Israel'. Probably the name 'Comforter' (*mᵉnaḥēm*)[9] has the same origin. The book of Enoch is also following Scripture when it calls the Messiah 'the Chosen One of God'.[10] In the Old Testament, both David

---

[1] Dalman's objection to this explanation of the phrase (*Words of Jesus*, pp. 293f.) is not decisive; cf. *ha-'ēl bêt'ēl* = 'the god Bethel'; see Gressmann in *Z.A.W.* xliii, 1925, p. 281.

[2] See Dalman, op. cit., pp. 237ff.

[3] See von Gall, *Basileia*, pp. 387, 397, with references to the Targums on 1 Kings v, 13; Isa. xi, 1; xiv, 29; Jer. xxiii, 5; xxx, 9; xxxiii, 15; Hos. iii, 5; Song of Sol. iv, 5. Cf. Luke i, 32; John vii, 42; Rom. i, 3; 2 Tim. ii, 8.

[4] Mark x, 47; xi, 10; Matt. xii, 23; xv, 22; xxi, 15f.

[5] E.g., Targum on Song of Sol. iv, 5; vii, 4.

[6] Strack-Billerbeck II, p. 337 n. β.

[7] Sib. III, 611; Ps. Sol. xvii, 47.

[8] See Bousset, *Relig.*², p. 262; von Gall, *Basileia*, p. 386; Weber, *Jüd. Theol.*², pp. 359f., with references to the sources.

[9] See Bousset, *Relig.*², p. 261; von Gall, *Basileia*, p. 386. Gressmann, *Der Messias*, p. 460, thinks that this Messianic title goes back to the name of Menahem ben Hezekiah; and following A. Geiger, he sees in this title the origin of the conception of the Paraclete, explained as 'the Comforter'. This latter opinion, at least, is wrong: παράκλητος does not mean 'comforter' but 'spokesman', 'advocate', in the wider sense of 'helper', corresponding to Hebrew *mēlîṣ*; see the present writer in *Z.N.W.* xxxii, 1933, pp. 37ff.   [10] 1 En. xxxvii–lxxi.

and the Servant of the Lord in Deutero-Isaiah bear this title, which the Targums interpret as referring to the Messiah (see below). But the title really belongs to the Son of Man, to whom it is also applied in the book of Enoch.

The description of the Messiah as the Servant of God or of the Lord is also the result of interpretation of Old Testament passages. The Targums understood the expression thus in several passages in Deutero-Isaiah,[1] both those which refer to the special Servant of the Lord and those which speak of Israel.[2] The title does not imply that leading ideas connected with the Servant of the Lord were transferred to the Messiah, as we shall see below in considering the Messiah of the Targums. It means neither more nor less than when it is applied in the Old Testament to David or to any anointed king (see p. 67 n. 3). It indicates one who has been chosen by Yahweh for an honourable task in His service, and to fulfil His will and counsel among men; and it follows naturally that it is specially used of the anointed king. As we have seen, the term can be applied in the same sense to heathen kings, such as Nebuchadrezzar and Cyrus, whom Yahweh uses as His instruments in furthering His purpose. The Targums and the rabbinic exegesis of later Judaism in general took no account of context or of historical background, but interpreted each individual passage in isolation and in the light of particular phrases. It is therefore not surprising that passages which contained what were clearly royal titles, such as 'the Chosen One', 'Yahweh's Servant', 'the called of Yahweh', and the like, were taken to refer to the Messiah. But we may not infer from this that the entire conception of, for example, the Servant of the Lord was transferred to the figure of the Messiah.

If the Samaritan Taheb is really a Messianic figure and not one of the forerunners of the Messiah (see below, ch. IX, 6), this name, 'the Restorer', is also easy to understand as a name for the national Messiah: he who 'restores the kingdom to Israel'.[3]

It is, however, most improbable that the Jews ever called the Messiah the 'son of God', although a Messianic interpretation of Ps. ii, might have suggested such a title.[4] In the rabbinic litera-

---

[1] Isa. xlii, 1; xliii, 10; lii, 13; liii, 10. See also 2 Bar. lxx, 9, 'My servant Messiah'.
[2] On other occasional names for the Messiah, sometimes enigmatic or half-humorous, such as Shiloh (Gen. xlix, 10), Yinnon (Ps. lxxii, 17), Haninah (Jer. xvi, 13), see Moore, *Judaism* II, pp. 348f.; Strack-Billerbeck I , pp. 64ff.
[3] Acts i, 6; cf. iii, 21; Mark ix, 12.
[4] Dalman, *Words of Jesus*, pp. 268ff. For further literature see Bieneck, *Sohn Gottes als Christusbezeichnung bei den Synoptikern*.

ture the term 'son of God' is used of the Messiah only in citations of Ps. ii and other similar passages which are interpreted Messianically. It is never used as a personal name for the Messiah.[1]

A Messianic title of this kind might be suggested by some passages in the Latin translation of the Apocalypse of Ezra, which speak of *filius meus (Christus)*,[2] 'My son (Messiah)'. But since this expression stands quite alone, it is most probable that the Christian translator used it to render the Greek word παῖς, which may mean both child and servant, the latter sense being the more frequent in later use. It would then correspond here to the Hebrew *'aḇdî*, 'My Servant', in the original.[3]

Besides these passages in 2 Esdras, there is only one other to be considered, 1 En. cv, where the Lord (=God) is represented as saying 'I and My Son'. But the whole of cv, 1f. is manifestly an addition to the real conclusion of the apocalypse in civ, 11–13; and it can hardly be doubted that this addition is of Christian origin, since it clearly presupposes the missionary command of Jesus in Matt. xxviii, 19f., and therefore tells us nothing about Jewish thought or linguistic usage.[4]

But even if these passages in 2 Esdras and 1 Enoch had originally expressed the idea of the Messiah as the Son of God, we must note that we should not then have to do with a normal Jewish title for the Messiah, but with an idea which was originally associated with the Son of Man (see below, pp. 368ff.), and which has left only occasional traces in Jewish Messianic theology. That being so, the Jews would understand the term in accordance with Old Testament ideas of the king as the *adopted son* of Yahweh, as in Ps. ii, i.e., as indicating not a metaphysical sonship from all eternity, but rather a divine election for a specially close and intimate relationship to God, and a call from Him to be fulfilled in His power.

[1] Strack-Billerbeck II, pp. 19ff. Huntress, too (in *J.B.L.* liv, 1935, pp. 117ff.), admits that the expression 'son of God' was not a common Messianic title in later Judaism. He is hardly correct in explaining this as the result of a reaction against Hasmonean pretensions.

[2] 2 Esdras vii, 28; xiii, 32, 37, 52; xiv, 9.

[3] See Drummond, *The Jewish Messiah*, pp. 285ff.; Violet, *Die Ezra-apokalypse*, pp. 74f. The word 'son' does not appear in the Arabic, Ethiopic, and Armenian versions. It may be assumed that it is a Christian interpolation in some manuscripts of the Greek version, and that the original text had only 'My Anointed'.

[4] Dalman, *Words of Jesus*, pp. 269f., takes *v.* 2 as a Christian interpolation. But the whole chapter is secondary. This is also proved by the newly discovered parts of the Greek text (of which the Ethiopic is a translation), where both cv and cviii are missing. See Bonner, *The Last Chapters of Enoch in Greek*.

5. When Will the Messiah Come?

To put the question another way: When will the signs be so sure and the end so near, that the Messiah's coming can be expected?

'The wise', who were familiar with the 'secret' (apocryphal) traditions and with the 'sealed books of revelation' could say much on that subject. They were the men who understood the chronological scheme of the two aeons, the secrets of the 'years' and 'weeks of years', the signs which foretold the end of this 'age', and had the key by which the signs could be interpreted. They could therefore calculate the times and discover the point which had now been reached. All of this was an essential part of the apocalyptic 'wisdom' and tradition, which belonged to the new, super-terrestrial, universalistic eschatology; and considerable portions of the apocalyptic literature are concerned with it. But for this very reason, these matters were unfamiliar to, and too profound for, the mass of the people, to whom the older, national, this-worldly Messianic hope was more congenial. Among them the chronological scheme of the book of Daniel does not seem to have been widely accepted. They would probably have agreed with the view expressed in the Targum on Eccles. vii, 24, that of the day and the hour no man knows, but only God Himself. He will raise up the son of David at the time known to Himself (or, according to another reading, which He has determined), on the day of grace, when His Anointed comes.[1]

But the wise man (the apocalyptist or scribe) can discern when the day is approaching, because it is preceded by a series of obvious omens.[2] It is this culmination of sin and wickedness which brings this world to an end, the last tribulation, so familiar to both the apocalyptists and the rabbis, and called by the latter 'the travail of the Messiah (or Messianic age)' (see above, p. 272): tumult and war, pestilence and famine, bad seasons and dearth, apostasy from God and His Law, the disruption of all moral order, and disorder even in the laws of nature.[3] Blessed is he who does not live to see them![4]

Many attempts were made, both by the apocalyptists after Daniel and by the rabbinic scribes, to calculate when the Messianic age would dawn. Daniel had interpreted the seventy years in

---

[1] Ps. Sol. xvii, 21; xviii, 5. See Messel's remarks in *N.T.T.* viii, 1907, p. 319.
[2] Strack-Billerbeck IV, pp. 977ff.
[3] 1 En. xcix, 4ff.; Jub. xxiii, 22ff.; 2 Esdras iv, 51–v, 13; vi, 18ff.; viii, 63–ix, 6; 2 Bar. xxv–xxix; xlviii, 30–37; lxx, 1ff.; Bab. Sanhedrin 96b, 37; 97a, 5.16.36.39. 41; 98a, 4.12.21.36; 98b, 2; and many other passages; see Strack-Billerbeck IV, pp. 981ff.
[4] 2 Bar. xxviii, 3; 2 Esdras xiii, 16ff.; Strack-Billerbeck IV, p. 986.

Jeremiah as seventy 'weeks of years'; and it is quite pathetic to see the courageous faith with which one addition to the text after another is made in the attempt to postpone from month to month the time calculated by Daniel.[1] We have the Apocalypse of Enoch with its division of the present aeon into ten periods, the Apocalypse of Ezra with its twelve world-periods, the cloud-vision of the Apocalypse of Baruch with its twelve periods, new interpretations of Daniel's seventy weeks of years, and so on.[2] The learned systems of calculation were numerous,[3] as were the miscalculations and disappointments.[4] Accordingly, men came to doubt whether such calculations were justified. The rabbis give warnings against them as impious and forbidden:[5] the wise men of the past deliberately concealed the date; the end will come when wickedness has reached its climax, or when all Israelites have become pious and righteous, or at the time when God so decides, when 'the time is fulfilled', in 'the fulness of time',[6] i.e., when the time has elapsed, which God has appointed for this aeon.

'The day' may be at hand; but it may also be distant. When times were hard and evil, pious men often thought that the day was too far off. Then they anxiously awaited its approach; and from their hearts and lips there arose again the old question from the psalms of lamentation: 'How long, O Lord?' and 'Wherefore, O Lord?'

Then was born the prayer that the Messiah might come. Israel could but humble herself before God and ask for His grace, 'hope in God, our deliverer', and ask Him to 'cleanse Israel against the day of mercy and blessing':

> Behold, O Lord, and raise up unto them their king,
> the son of David,
> at the time in which Thou seest, O God, that he
> may reign over Israel Thy Servant . . .
> May the Lord hasten His mercy upon Israel!
> May He deliver us from the uncleanness of unholy
> enemies![7]

[1] See Baumgartner in *Die christliche Welt* Nos. 31/32–37/39, 1925, col. 26.
[2] Dan. ix; 1 En. xciii, 1–10; xci, 12–17; 2 Esdras xiv, 11f.; 2 Bar. liii–lxxii; Sib. IV, 47ff., etc. See Strack-Billerbeck IV, pp. 986ff.; Volz, *Eschatologie*[2], p. 145.
[3] Strack-Billerbeck IV, pp. 999ff.; Volz, *Eschatologie*[2], pp. 143ff.
[4] See Volz, *Eschatologie*[2], p. 145.
[5] See Strack-Billerbeck IV, pp. 1013ff.; Volz, *Eschatologie*[2], p. 145; Moore, *Judaism* II, pp. 352ff.
[6] Gal. iv, 4. See Strack-Billerbeck III, pp. 570, 580; Moore, *Judaism* II, pp. 350ff.
[7] Ps. Sol. xvii, 21, 51; cf. *v.* 3 and xviii, 5.

In the Jewish 'Eighteen Prayers', which in its main features goes back to the time of Jesus, we also find the prayer that God will restore Jerusalem and establish the throne of David: 'the Shoot of David do Thou cause to shoot forth speedily'.[1]

The presupposition of these prayers is the conviction that Israel needs to be purified. Already in Ps. Sol. xvii the poet lays the main responsibility for the disaster, which is the background of the psalm, on the house of 'sinners', who had 'laid waste the throne of David in tumultuous arrogance', yet completely identifies himself with his people in their responsibility before God, and confesses frankly that 'for our sins, sinners rose up against us'.[2] Conviction and confession of sin on behalf of the entire community are leading themes in these psalms. The author certainly means to say that it is because of her sins that Israel has still to wait for the day of grace when the true Anointed One can come. Therefore the hour may be hastened by penitence and the fulfilling of the Law, by study of the Scriptures and good works; but it may also be delayed by sin and impenitence.[3]

The same thought occurs elsewhere. The Targums on Mic. iv, 8 know that it is because of Israel's sins that the appearance of the Messiah is delayed. One of the strict scribes says that if Israel would rightly repent for but one day, or keep a single Sabbath as the Law requires, then the Messiah would come.[4]

But besides the idea of more or less perfect penitence as a condition, we sometimes find the very natural thought that the Messiah will come when wickedness has reached its climax. We may compare the mediating view of Rabbi Johanan: 'Messiah, the son of David, will come only when the age has become wholly worthy (virtuous), or when it has become wholly guilty.'[5] That salvation will come when distress is at its worst, when the Messianic travail has reached its climax, accords with the view of the earlier prophets of restoration and of the prophetic disciples who collected the prophetic books. It is reflected in the arrangement of the books, where the threats of doom are followed immediately by

---

[1] Cf. *Authorised Daily Prayer Book*, p. 49; German translation in Else Schubert-Christaller, *Der Gottesdienst der Synagoge*, pp. 14ff.

[2] Ps. Sol. xvii, 5, 8. On the poet's association of himself with the sins of the people, see my *Senjødisk salmediktning*, pp. 22, 28ff., 32f.

[3] Strack-Billerbeck I, pp. 599, 600.

[4] Pesikta 163b; Shabbat, 118b; Sanhedrin, 97b; etc. See Weber, *Jüd. Theol.*[2], pp. 348ff.

[5] Sanhedrin, 98a; Jer. Taanit, 64a, with reference to Exod. xvi, 25 combined with Isa. xxx, 15. See Moore, *Judaism* II, pp. 350f.

prophecies of salvation; and thus it appears to be supported by these books. Ultimately the thought goes back to the conception in the enthronement festival of God's intervention and new creation when distress is at its worst.[1]

But in the last resort the hour must be left to God. Israel must not try to hasten the Messiah's coming by her own strength or by outward force, say the rabbis.[2] This is an echo of bitter experience in the many abortive Messianic revolts.

6. *The Forerunners of the Messiah*

Since the coming of the Messiah depends on whether Israel repents and is converted, it is necessary that there should first come men who can bring about conversion and restore everything to right order. The recognition of this, and the longing for those who will thus prepare the way, are the religious background of the rise of the wide-spread belief in the forerunners of the Messiah.[3] But the content of the idea, and the influence behind its origin and its development, lay in the many parallel Messianic conceptions, which needed to be harmonized with each other, and also in the exegetical treatment of earlier Old Testament expressions of a corresponding expectation of men who could prepare for Yahweh's coming to His people.[4]

This expectation is expressed in Mal. iii, 23f., as the ending of the collection of prophetic books, as prophecy's last word to Israel, so to speak: 'Behold, I will send you Elijah the prophet before the coming of the great and terrible day of Yahweh. And he shall turn the hearts of the fathers to their children, and the hearts of the children to their fathers, lest I come and smite the land with a curse.' This addition to the book is itself a re-interpretation of Malachi's own prediction (iii, 1ff.), that Yahweh will send His angel ('the angel of the covenant', as a gloss puts it) in advance,

[1] See Pss. xlvi and xlviii; and cf. *Ps.St.* II, pp. 57ff., 126ff., 254ff.; *Offersang og sangoffer*, pp. 149ff.

[2] Strack-Billerbeck I, pp. 598f.

[3] Strack-Billerbeck I, p. 756; IV, pp. 781f., 784f., 786; cf. Volz, *Eschatologie*[2], pp. 193ff.

[4] von Gall's attempt to trace the idea of forerunners back to the Persian idea of a number of 'Saviours' (Saoshyants) (*Basileia*, p. 377) is both unnecessary and improbable. Bousset is right in finding the origin of the idea itself in Malachi (*Relig.*[2], p. 266); but he, too, introduces unnecessary complications into the prophecy of Malachi by obscure parallels from comparative religion. Malachi's longing for a new and greater prophet than himself, who will understand better than he does how to prepare the way for God, and put Israel in a fit state to receive her God when He comes, is readily understood in the light of the prophet's own sense of inadequacy and the unworthiness of the community. Nevertheless there is an element of truth in the views of Bousset and von Gall; see below, p. 302.

to prepare the way for Him (alluding to the familiar prophetic cry of Deutero-Isaiah). We are not told in detail what will be the angel's task. No doubt it is in the first instance, to foretell the Lord's coming, and to remind men of the covenant and the Law. Then the Lord Himself will appear in His temple and give judgement, refining and purifying. An age which had no prophets felt the need of men of God, filled with the spirit, who could preach penitence and conversion with greater power and effect than the epigoni of the prophets (the learned custodians of tradition and the 'wise') felt that they could. Therefore they interpreted Malachi's words as a promise of a prophet of the old kind, one of the old prophets themselves; and whom was it more natural to expect than Elijah, who had not died, but had been taken up into heaven alive?

In later Judaism, then, Elijah has become the forerunner of the Messiah. Probably this idea is expressed already in Eccles. xlviii, 10; and at all events, we find Elijah mentioned by the Jew Trypho in Justin's dialogue as one who should come and anoint the Messiah for his work. In one version of the rabbinic legend about the birth of the Messiah, to which we shall return below, it is Elijah who detects who the newborn child is (see below, pp. 304f.). But Sirach already knows that Elijah will return; and it is probable that the Apocalypse of Enoch contains the same teaching.[1] The thought of Elijah as the forerunner of the Messiah seeems to have been widespread in Judaism; and it is presupposed in the Gospels as a common Jewish belief.[2] Of his role as 'the restorer' the rabbis have much to say.[3] For instance, he will decide questions about clean and unclean, and separate foreign elements from the Jewish nation.[4]

As a rule, other forerunners are mentioned together with Elijah. Most frequently Moses appears beside him.[5] From Deut. xviii, 15, in which Israel is promised that she can always rely on God to send 'a prophet like Moses' to show her the right way, it was easy for Jewish exegesis to discover that Moses would come again. The

---

[1] 'The young ram' in 1 En. xc, 31 (cf. lxxxix, 52; xc, 9); see Pedersen in *Islamica*, ii, pp. 422ff.

[2] Ecclus. xlviii, 10f.; Mark ix, 11f.; Matt. xi, 13f.; xvii, 10ff.; John i, 21, 25; cf. Luke i, 17; Jerusalem Targum on Exod. xl, 10; Targum of Jonathan on Deut. xxxv, 4. See J. Jeremias in *T.W.B.N.T.* III, pp. 930ff.; Bousset, *Relig.*[2], pp, 266f.

[3] Strack-Billerbeck IV, pp. 781ff.; Klausner, *Die messianischen Vorstellungen des jüdischen Volkes im Zeitalter der Tannaiten*, pp. 38ff.; von Gall, *Basileia*, p. 379.

[4] See Moore, *Judaism* II, pp. 357ff.; and p. 278 above.

[5] Strack-Billerbeck IV, p. 787; cf. Volz, *Eschatologie*[2], pp. 194f.; J. Jeremias in *T.W.B.N.T.* IV, s.v. Μωυσῆς.

expectation of Moses and Elijah as forerunners of the Messiah sheds light on the story of the Transfiguration of Jesus on the mountain, and also on the reference in the Apocalypse to the two witnesses.[1] The rabbis, too, (e.g., Johanan ben Zakkai) speak of Moses and Elijah.[2] Sometimes Moses is mentioned as the only forerunner.[3]

It is natural that Enoch should be mentioned together with Elijah. Of both it was told that they were taken up into heaven alive; and therefore they can return from heaven.[4] The expectation of such a return before the coming of the Messiah is extended in the Ezra Apocalypse to all men who have been taken up (*recepti*), who from their birth have not tasted death.[5] The Coptic Apocalypse of Elijah speaks of sixty forerunners of the Messiah.[6]

It is also possible that the Samaritans' Taheb (see p. 290 above), 'he who brings back', or 'the Restorer', was not originally a Messianic figure, but really belonged to those forerunners who would restore the life of the community, like Elijah.

Among the forerunners we may also include the mysterious *Taxo(n)*, 'the Orderer', who appears in the Assumption of Moses,[7]

---

[1] Rev. xi, 3f.; Mosbech, *Johannes's Aabenbaring*, pp. 192ff. Further references to the literature in Munck, *Petrus und Paulus in der Johannesapokalypse*. Munck tries to prove that the two witnesses are Peter and Paul.

[2] See von Gall, *Basileia*, p. 378; Munck, op. cit., p. 10.

[3] See von Gall, op. cit., p. 380, with references to the Samaritan tradition and to Sib. V, 256ff.; Volz, *Eschatologie*[2], p. 191.

[4] 1 En. xc, 31; cf. Bousset, *Der Antichrist*, p. 134; *Relig.*[2], p. 267; Volz, *Eschatologie*[2], pp. 197f.

[5] 2 Esdras vi, 26; see Volz, *Eschatologie*[2], p. 193; Stade-Bertholet, *Die Biblische Theologie des Alten Testaments* II, p. 443.

[6] A Baraita quoted by Klausner (op. cit., p. 71; cf. Volz, *Eschatologie*[2], p. 218) speaks of nine righteous men in the past, who have been taken up into paradise alive.

[7] On Taxo in Ass. Mos. ix, 1ff., see Bousset, *Relig.*[2], p. 266; Clemen in *A.P.A.T.* II, p. 326; Burkitt in *H.D.B.* III, pp. 448ff.; von Gall, *Basileia*, p. 381; Rowley, *The Relevance of Apocalyptic*[2], pp. 134ff., with further references. Lattey (*Catholic Biblical Quarterly*, January 1942, pp. 17f.) sees in Taxo a cipher for 'Shiloh' (Gen. xl, 10), taken as a name for a suffering Messiah. But the way in which Taxo is referred to in the Assumption of Moses seems to indicate that he was a historical person, and that the author had knowledge of his work and his death. From these he expected a miraculous result in the last days. Burkitt, Charles, and others see in Taxo a reflection of some historical person, such as Eleazar in 4 Mac. i, 8. Against this specific identification, see Rowley, op. cit., loc. cit. Torrey (*J.B.L.*, lxii, 1943, pp. 1ff.) finds in the word a cipher, 415, in a supposed Aramaic original, corresponding to a *ḥšmny*, 'the Hasmonean'= Mattathias the Maccabee. Against this, see Rowley in *J.B.L.* lxiv, 1945, pp. 141ff.; and cf. Torrey's reply, ibid., pp. 547ff. The interpretation of 'Taxo' in the Latin text as corresponding to a τάξων ('the Orderer') in the Greek 'original', from which the Latin text was undoubtedly translated (see Charles in *A.P.O.T.* II, pp. 409f.), is suggested by Clemen and Bousset. It might seem doubtful so long as no Hebrew word could be indicated, of which this τάξων could be the translation; but see the following note, and Mowinckel in *Supplements to V.T.* I, pp. 88–96. That the original of the Assumption of Moses was in Hebrew, seems to be beyond doubt; see Charles in *A.P.O.T.* II.

although no Messiah is mentioned in this apocalypse. Taxo(n) is a righteous man, who, in the last times, together with his seven sons, through prayer and self-sacrifice, will move the Lord to put an end to the tribulation and bestow salvation. The name cannot be explained from any Semitic language, and must therefore be a Greek translation of a Hebrew original. In all probability it represents the Hebrew *meḥōḳēḳ* of Gen. xlix, 10.[1] In the Damascus Document (viii, 8), this word is used with the meaning 'Lawgiver', or 'Orderer', one who maintains and expounds the Law through his *meḥuḳḳeḳôt*, and thus establishes right order, and sees that the congregation obeys the *ḥuḳḳîm* and *ḥuḳḳôt*.[2] He is identical with 'the student of the Law' (*dôrēš hat-tôrâh*), 'the Teacher of righteousness' (i.e., the right, or righteous, Teacher: *yôrēh ṣeḍeḳ*), who had played a great part in the reorganization of the sect in Damascus. The sect appears to have expected that this 'Orderer' and 'Lawgiver' would return at the end of time, once again to play the part of a *taxon*. Forty years would pass between his death and the coming of the Messiah.[3]

According to the Fourth Gospel (i, 21; cf. vi, 14; vii, 40) the Jews of the time of Jesus also believed in 'the Prophet' (the true Prophet), who was to appear before the Messiah, but who was explicitly distinguished from Elijah.[4] This expectation could be

[1] In Greek renderings of Hebrew or Aramaic writings, τάξις and τάσσειν have a special relation to *ḥuḳḳâh* or *ḥōḳ* and *tôrâh* (Aramaic *dāt*), and are used in parallelism with νόμος (e.g., 1 En. lxxii, 1, 35; lxxix, 1; cf. ii, 1; v, 4). See Aalen, *Die Begriffe 'Licht' und 'Finsternis' im Alten Testament, im Spätjudentum und im Rabbinismus*, pp. 159f. In the Septuagint, τάξις = *tôrâh* in Prov. xxxi, 26 (24), τάσσειν renders *ṣiwwâh* in 2 Sam. vii, 11; 1 Chron. xvii, 10; Isa. xxxviii, 1. Cf. Ecclus. xvi, 26, where Aalen rightly suggests a *ḥuḳḳîm* or *ḥuḳḳôt* behind the μερίδας = the cosmic orders or laws.
[2] The *meḥōḳēḳ* is identical with the 'Student of the Law' (viii, 8; ix, 8; see Hvidberg, *Menigheden af den nye Pagt*, pp. 26of., 292ff.), who is also the 'righteous Teacher' (viii, 10; see Hvidberg, op. cit., pp. 270ff.) or 'Teacher of the congregation' (*ywrh hyḥyd*). This last expression has been interpreted as 'the Teacher of the Unique One' (i.e., God; so Gressmann), and more often as 'the unique Teacher'; but in the Dead Sea Scrolls, which come from the same sect, *yḥd* is a term applied to the congregation, 'the many' (*plenum*) (see Burrows in *O.T.S.* VIII, pp. 172ff.), and *yḥyd* in the Damascus Document must have the same meaning. The spelling with a second *y* is either due to a later misinterpretation, or indicates a pronunciation like *yāḥēd*.
If this explanation of Taxo(n) is right, we may perhaps conclude that the Assumption of Moses originated in the same circles as the Damascus sect. Note that Taxo(n) and his seven sons hide themselves in a *cave* in order to pray for the people, but also to be able to live in accordance with their strict interpretation of the Law. The cave at 'Ain Feshkha was certainly not only a depository for the manuscripts, but also a hiding place for the leaders of the sect in times of persecution. The cave of Taxo(n) may well have been the cave at 'Ain Feshkha.
[3] Damascus Document ix, 39; see Hvidberg, op. cit., pp. 261ff.; Rowley, *The Relevance of Apocalyptic*[2], pp. 76f.; *The Zadokite Documents and the Dead Sea Scrolls*, p. 40. See also the *Habakkuk Commentary* on Hab. i, 5 (translation by Brownlee in *B.A.S.O.R.* 112, Dec. 1948, pp. 8ff.).
[4] Strack-Billerbeck II, pp. 363, 479f.; cf. Volz, *Eschatologie*[2], pp. 193f.

based on Deut. xviii, 15, where, as we have seen, reference is made to a future prophet like Moses. It is possible that there are other references to this Prophet, for instance in the people's decision that Simon the Maccabee should be leader and High Priest until a trustworthy prophet should arise, who could settle the question of the Messianic status of the Maccabees.[1]

Sometimes this prophet seems to have been identified with the Messiah himself. This was probably the case when the Jews wanted to make Jesus king, because they saw in Him 'the prophet who should come into the world' (John vi, 14).

But the idea of a forerunner contains one feature which can hardly be explained solely on the basis of Old Testament presuppositions, namely the not uncommon conception, referred to above, of several forerunners, sometimes two, often three: Moses, Elijah, and the Prophet. The thought of one forerunner could easily have arisen from conceptions peculiar to Judaism; but the Old Testament presuppositions do not explain why three such forerunners are spoken of as following each other. This seems to be connected originally with an idea which occurs in Persian religion and in several doctrinal systems in Jewish Gnosticism, the notion of several 'saviours' (Messiahs); and this, in turn, is associated with the doctrine of world-periods, which is also of Iranian and Chaldean origin. In Persian eschatology, four world-periods are mentioned, each of which has its saviour (Saoshyant), the last of whom is the true saviour, the three others being forerunners. The Jewish thought of three forerunners was determined by these conceptions.[2]

7. The Day of the Messiah and His Appearing

'The day of grace' (Ps. Sol. xviii, 10 (9)), when the Messiah will come, is also called 'the day of the Messiah' (e.g., 2 Esdras, xiii, 52). This term reappears in the New Testament as 'the day of Jesus Christ'.[3] The expression is formed by analogy with the earlier 'day of Yahweh', which, in turn, is analogous to 'the day of the king'. It means the day when Yahweh, or the Messiah, will appear as king, assume the royal title, and be acclaimed as king. When the royal day of Yahweh is mentioned, the thought is that He becomes king and is acknowledged as such, because he

---

[1] 1 Mac. xiv, 41; see von Gall, *Basileia*, p. 381; Volz, *Eschatologie*[2], p. 191; cf. R. Meyer, *Der Prophet aus Galiläa*, pp. 18ff.

[2] See the present writer in *N.T.T.* xlv, 1944, pp. 231f.

[3] 1 Cor. v, 5; Phil. i, 6, 10; ii, 16; 2 Thess. ii, 2.

has again accomplished His work as king. By a great act of salvation He has established and created His kingdom. This was the fundamental thought in the old harvest and epiphany festival, from which it was transferred to the future hope and to eschatology. 'The day of the Messiah' is evidently meant to be taken in the same sense. It means the day on which he has accomplished his Messianic work, crushed the enemy, saved his people, 'restored the kingdom to Israel' (about which the disciples, with their Jewish outlook, could still ask even after the Resurrection; Acts i, 6), and thus shown himself to be the Messiah.

It is to this revelation as Messiah that the Targums refer when they repeatedly say of his appearing that he 'reveals himself' (*'iṯgallî*).[1] This expression is also used elsewhere, and it indicates that the Messiah's appearing has a special character.[2] This, too, is reminiscent of the ideas associated in the Old Testament with Yahweh's epiphany, in that He 'makes Himself known' (*nôḏa'*),[3] revealing His character through His glorious appearing and His mighty, kingly acts. The day when the Messiah appears and accomplishes his Messianic work of salvation is the day when he 'is revealed' as what he is destined to be, as the Messiah. These expressions imply that it is this Messianic work which makes him the Messiah. He cannot be known and acknowledged as such until these actions have revealed his identity. By performing Messianic works he 'reveals his glory' (his dignity as Messiah), as the Fourth Gospel puts it (John ii, 17). The brothers of Jesus say to Him, 'Reveal yourself to the world'; by which they mean, come forward, and perform openly the Messianic works and miracles (John vii, 3ff.; cf. xiv, 22). According to Jewish thought, it is only then that He will become Messiah in the full sense of the term.[4] Before that time we may say that He is but *Messias designatus*, a claimant to Messianic status.

Besides this idea of manifestation through Messianic acts, we also find in later rabbinic literature the conception of a still more dramatic and striking manifestation. In one passage we read, 'At the time when King Messiah reveals himself he will come and stand on the roof of the temple'; from there he will announce to Israel the message of redemption.[5] The Temptation

---

[1] On the use of this word, see von Gall, *Basileia*, p. 400.
[2] 2 Bar. xxix, 3; xxx, 1; 2 Esdras vii, 28; Sib. III, 652.
[3] Ps. xlviii, 4; lxxvi, 2; see *Ps.St.* II, p. 458.
[4] This is rightly emphasized by Messel in *N.T.T.* xxi, 1920, pp. 67ff.
[5] Strack-Billerbeck III, p. 9.

narrative shows that similar ideas were known even in earlier times.

At this point we need only add that it is not improbable that in the expression and the idea of 'the revelation of the Messiah' (his epiphany or *parousia*) there are more profound, metaphysical elements, influenced by ideas about a heavenly being, 'the Son of Man', who will appear at an appointed time, revealing himself as he really is (see further, pp. 388f, below).

The pregnant expression, 'the day of the Messiah' (referring to the appointed day and hour when he will appear and reveal who he is), must not be confused with the more general and comprehensive plural, 'the days of the Messiah'. In comparison with '*the* day' this expression is secondary and weaker. In rabbinic usage it actually includes his entire reign as king; but here, too, special emphasis is laid on the day when he appears, and the great revolution takes place, when the kingdom is founded, set up, and consolidated: to this extent the original sense is still evident. We shall return below to the expression, 'the days of the Messiah'.

8. *The Hidden Messiah*

If it is the Messiah's work that makes him the Messiah and reveals him as such, then it is obvious that as a human being he may live part of his life without coming forward and being acknowledged as the Messiah, and possibly without himself realizing that he is the Messiah, without any 'Messianic consciousness', to use the technical, theological expression. The people cannot know in advance who is the Messiah. The Messiah is, as we have said (p. 303), the one whom God calls, raises up, and equips, bestowing upon him grace to perform the Messianic work. But like one of the old prophets, or like the Servant of the Lord, he himself may well have received the call and known in experience that the Lord has made him like a sharp sword and a pointed arrow, though hitherto He has hid him in His sheath, until he comes forward and carries out the Messianic work, or until by another designatory miracle God reveals him to all the world as the Messiah, and makes men acknowledge him as such.

That these ideas (which are of importance for an understanding of the Messianic consciousness of Jesus) were really current in Jewish circles may be seen from the references to the unknown Messiah which sometimes occur. In his *Dialogue with Trypho*, Justin Martyr (*ca.* A.D. 150) makes the representative of Judaism say, 'Even if the Messiah should have been born and be living somewhere (this is meant to be a hypothetical concession to the Christian assertion that Jesus was the Messiah), yet he is un-known;[1] indeed, he does not even know himself; nor has he any power, until Elijah comes, anoints him, and reveals him to all' (viii). In cx Trypho says, 'Even if men say that he has come, he will not be known for what he is until he becomes famous and renowned'. Here we have the two possibilities mentioned above. The Messiah is an ordinary human being (of David's line, we must assume), until a day when Elijah returns and anoints him king, as the prophets did in ancient times, and so makes him known as the Messiah; but afterwards he gives abundant evidence of his Messianic dignity by making himself renowned, i.e., by performing the work of the Messiah, and compelling all the world to acknow-ledge him.[2]

The same conception appears in the Ezra Apocalypse (see 2 Esdras xiii). The feature, which is certainly traditional,[3] that the Messiah (here called the Son of Man) will come up from the sea, is thus interpreted to the apocalyptist: 'Just as one can neither seek out nor know what is in the deep of the sea, even so can no one up-on earth see my Son [*or those that are with him*] but in the time of his day' (xiii, 52). For this apocalyptist, the Messiah is undoubtedly the pre-existent being, the Son of Man, who will be revealed by a miracle. But the expressions he uses here in xiii, and the thought which he here associates with the revelation of the Son of Man, are taken from the conception of the unknown earthly Messiah. As Justin says, it may well be that men will *see* the Messiah before he is acknowledged; but they will not see him as he really is, until he is revealed. This is also the original sense of the words used in the Ezra Apocalypse, even if the author understood them to mean that it is only when the Messiah is revealed from the world beyond that he can be seen at all by those who dwell on earth. There is also an allusion (though perhaps not rightly understood) in the Fourth Gospel to the Messiah's incognito (vii, 27).[4]

This thought of the unknown or hidden Messiah also occurs in the rabbinic literature. The commentary on the Psalms, Midrash Tehillim, interprets Isa. xi, 10 of the Messiah: 'It is Messiah, the

---

[1] ἄγνωστος: The word probably also includes the nuance 'unknowable'.
[2] On this interpretation of the evidence from Justin, see Messel in *N.T.T.* xxi, 1920.
[3] As Gunkel rightly emphasizes, in opposition to Messel's rationalization (ibid., pp. 75ff.); cf. his review of Messel's, *Die Einheitlichkeit der jüdischen Eschatologie*, in *N.T.T.* xvii, 1916, pp. 196ff.   [4] See Messel, ibid.

x

Son of David, who keeps himself hidden until the appointed time has come.'[1] After his birth he lives unknown,[2] no man knows where; some say in Rome, the very stronghold of the ancient enemy; others speak of a place in the far north; and others, again, speak of paradise, or some other place in heaven.[3] From this hidden, unknown, lowly, often degraded existence in suffering and want (see below) the Messiah will come forth and reveal himself on his day.

But these somewhat theoretical and hypothetical ideas about the hidden Messiah also took another, more specific, more legendary and fantastic form. The Messiah *has* already really come, though he is still unknown as he moves about among men. This appears already in the Targum on Mic. iv, 8, where the reason for his still being hidden is Israel's sins. The Targum on Exod. xii, 42 knows that the Messiah will come from Rome, a conception also found among the rabbis.[4] We hear, too, that the Messiah is thought to be sitting as a leper among the plague-stricken, outside the walls of Rome,[5] or wandering through the world as a beggar, until the time when he will become known and come forth as the Messiah.[6] But the same idea, in the age after Christ, resulted in a legend about the birth of the Messiah which exists in different versions. According to this, the Messiah is born on the same day as the destruction of the temple; only one person (in some accounts, an anonymous Arab; in another, Elijah) realizes who he is; but soon afterwards the child is taken away until the day when he will come forth as Messiah; and no one knows where he is now.[7] This narrative was also applied to the political Messiah, Menahem ben Hezekiah.

The source of this idea, that the Messiah is already wandering about unknown, is probably the longing for his day. But the epic formulation of it makes use of traditional motifs. The longing has laid hold upon the familiar oriental theme of the unknown saint, who lives despised among men, who do not suspect what kind of

---

[1] Strack-Billerbeck III, p. 315.

[2] Op. cit. II, p. 339; IV, p. 766.

[3] Op. cit. II, p. 340; I, pp. 160f., 481, 960, 1018; IV, p. 488.

[4] Op. cit. II, p. 340; Dalman, *Der leidende und sterbende Messias*, p. 41; von Gall, *Basileia*, p. 400.

[5] Bab. Sanhedrin xi, 98a, etc. Schoeps has shown (in *Biblica* xxix, 1948) that Symmachus's rendering of Isa. liii, 5, alludes to the idea of a leprous Messiah.

[6] See Gressmann, *Der Messias*, p. 451 n. 3, pp. 452, 458.

[7] This nativity legend is analysed by Gressmann in his essay 'Der unerkannte Messias', in *Der Messias*, pp. 449ff., with translations of the texts and references to the sources.

person he really is.[1] In the nativity legends, motifs concerning the
unknown child of the king or the god have provided material for
the development of the idea. A similar motif also played a part in
the development of the tradition about the birth of Jesus.[2] But
probably some part is also played by a mythological motif of the
same kind as underlies Rev. xii. We may conclude this from the
fact that the legend does not explain why the child is taken away;
that must have been explained by the narrative from which it is
derived. Rev. xii tells of a woman in heaven, who gives birth to a
child, who is caught up to God's throne and thus delivered from
the dragon who wants to devour him. This tale about the divine
child, who brings redemption and the new world, is very widespread. In the form which underlies the symbolism of the Revelation, we probably have to do with the new sun god, who signifies
the end of the dominion of the dragon (the state of chaos, winter,
flood or drought, and death).[3] It is also probable that the
oriental myths about the resurrected or reborn god of fertility and
life are included in the material which has contributed to this
story, the kind of myth which underlies the symbolism of the
Immanuel sign in Isa. vii. The same mythical motif appears in
the statements that the Messiah has been born, but is hidden for
the time being in heaven or in paradise (see above, p. 306), which
does not really fit the earthly son of David. In the development
of the legend of the Messiah's birth, with which we are concerned,
this myth served only as a single contributory motif. From it is
derived the feature for which the Messianic legends provide no
reasonable explanation: that the child disappeared soon after his
birth, having been taken away. In the myths this is explained by
the fact that he had to be saved from the dragon.

But even those who handed down this nativity legend sometimes asked themselves why the child was taken away again, and
the people's hope, which seemed to be assured at the very moment
when they experienced their deepest humiliation by the destruction of the temple, was postponed to the unknown future. One of
the variants offers an answer, which, however, is not an organic
part of the motif itself, but is the result of theological reflection,

[1] See Bousset in *A.R.W.* xxi, 1922, pp. 1ff.; further literature in Gyllenberg, *Herrens tjänare*, pp. 25f.
[2] See Gressmann, *Das Weihnachtsevangelium;* and cf. the survey in Klostermann-Gressmann, *Das Lukasevangelium*, on Luke ii, 1–20.
[3] See the survey of the various parallels and attempted explanations in Mosbech, *Johannes's Aabenbaring*, p. 229.

namely that the child will remain hidden until the time appointed by God has elapsed, and the end is at hand.[1] This is probably how most Jews would have answered the question. Sufficient penance has not yet been done for the sins of Israel; and until there is genuine conversion and obedience to the Law, the Messiah cannot 'be revealed'. That is precisely the reason why first of all there must come men who can evoke penitence and conversion, and put all things in order, namely those forerunners of the Messiah to whom we have referred.

9. The Equipment of the Messiah for His Mission.

It is possible for the Messiah to be the Messiah, and to save his people, only because, through his close relationship to God, he has acquired special equipment for his mission. In Ps. Sol. xvii, 42 (37) we read:

> For God will make him mighty by means of (His) holy spirit,
> And wise by means of the spirit of understanding, with strength and righteousness.

The Messiah will receive the holy spirit of God with all the gifts bestowed thereby. This is the source of his equipment for his mission.

Of course the Messiah is righteous.[2] From remote antiquity that formed part of the oriental ideal of kingship. He is called 'the Messiah of righteousness' (i.e., the righteous Messiah, $me\check{s}i\hbar\acute{a}$' $de\underline{s}i\underline{d}\underline{k}\acute{a}$'. Sometimes his righteousness also implies his just government and judgement of his people:[3] every man will get his due; peace and order will be maintained; the wicked will be punished; the good will live in peace, and will 'secure their livelihood, and keep their possessions'. Here the term 'righteousness' corresponds to what we moderns understand by it, with special reference to its application to legal and administrative activity. But, as a rule, something different is meant when the Messiah's righteousness is mentioned. From the beginning the term is closely associated with salvation, with establishing and maintaining for the people good conditions at home and abroad. The Messiah will obtain

---

[1] See Gressmann, Der Messias, p. 452.

[2] Ps. Sol. xvii, 25 (23), 28f. (26f.), 31 (29), 35 (32), 42 (37), 48 (43); xviii, 8 (7); Targum on Jer. xxiii, 6; xxx, 15; Agadat Shir hash-shirim IV, 11; Seder Rab Amram i, 9a (cf. 10b, 12a); Pesikta Rabbati 161b, 162ab, 163ab, 164a. See Dalman, Der leidende und sterbende Messias, p. 241.

[3] Ps. Sol. xvii, 28f. (26f.), 35 (32), 48 (43).

his people's 'right' against heathen oppressors, and any traitors, bandits, and sinners, who may exist in their own midst. He will save them from slavery and misfortune, and maintain this salvation and liberty in the face of all menacing perils; for it is Israel's 'right' to be free, rich, and prosperous, and the first among the nations. The righteousness of the Messiah consists in his saving his people: righteousness and salvation are identical.[1]

Not only his righteousness, but his wisdom is constantly emphasized.[2] The rabbis hold that the Messiah knows what is in men, and what is going to happen.[3] Wisdom and counsel imply the ability both to see what is right and to bring it about.

But the true essence and source of wisdom is the fear of God. This, too, is a gift of God's grace, a religious and moral quality. Therefore, whenever it appears in its fullness, it is accompanied by freedom from sin, a characteristic of the Messiah which the Psalms of Solomon emphasize:

> And he himself (will be) pure from sin, so that he may
> rule a great people.
> He will rebuke rulers, and remove sinners by the might
> of his word.   (Ps. Sol. xvii, 41 (36))

In accordance with normal Jewish thought, what is chiefly meant here is that freedom from sinful acts, which is possible to those who, in the fear of God, and enlightened by His holy spirit, conform to God's Law: in other words, 'righteousness' in the Jewish sense.[4] It is his endowment with God's holy and purifying spirit that keeps the Messiah righteous and free from sin. That the spirit of God will descend on him in all its glory, and give him his equipment and his powers, is also emphasized in T. Levi xviii, 7:

> And the glory of the Most High shall be uttered over
> him,
> And the spirit of understanding and sanctification shall
> rest upon him.

Because he has God's holy spirit, he is also himself holy, and his own spirit is a sanctified spirit. This indicates, first of all, the divine, superhuman, miraculous character of his equipment; but

---

[1] T. Judah xxiv, with reference to Mal. iii, 20.
[2] Ps. Sol. xvii, 42 (37); 1 En. xlix, 2f.; li, 3; T. Levi xviii; see Volz, *Eschatologie*[2], p. 221.
[3] Strack-Billerbeck II, p. 439.
[4] Cf. Ps. Sol. i, 2f., 'full of righteousness'; and see Messel in *N.T.T.* x, 1909, p. 127.

it also refers to a moral quality.[1] This is evident from the close association here with 'the spirit of understanding'. In Jewish thought, understanding and wisdom denote moral and religious insight and power: the knowledge of God means religious and moral character and action.[2]

In the main, it is the religious and moral ideal that the Messiah fulfils. His piety is shown in what was the heart of Jewish religion from the time of Isaiah onwards: that in the fear of God, and trusting in Him, he never falls into the sin of pride, which is characteristic of heathen powers, who trust in human might and understanding. But

> He shall not put his trust in horse and rider and
> bow . . .
> Nor shall he gather confidence from (?) a multitude(?)
> for the day of battle . . .
> His hope (will be) in the Lord: who then can prevail
> against him?
> (He will be) mighty in his works, and strong in the fear
> of God,
> (He will be) shepherding the flock of the Lord faithfully
> and righteously.
>
> (Ps. Sol. xvii, 37 (33), 44f. (39) f.)

Because he himself possesses wisdom and the fear of God, he can also be both leader and example to his people when they live

> Under the rod of chastening of the Lord's Anointed in
> the fear of his God,
> In the spirit of wisdom and righteousness and
> strength;
> That he may direct (every) man in the works of
> righteousness by the fear of God,
> That he may establish them all before the Lord,
> A good generation (living) in the fear of God in the
> days of mercy.
>
> (Ps. Sol. xviii, 8–10 (7–9))

Because he himself is holy, he can make his people holy also, cleansing them from sin, impurity, and heathenism, so that they may live a life dedicated to God, and also giving them the moral and religious quality which is implicit in holiness.[3]

---

[1] Cf. Stade-Bertholet, *Die Biblische Theologie des Alten Testaments* II, pp. 76, 409f.; Fridrichsen, *Hagios-Qadoš*, pp. 58ff.   [2] Cf. Mowinckel, *Die Erkenntnis Gottes*, pp. 5ff.
[3] Ps. Sol. xvii 28 (26), 32 (30), 35f. (32), quoted below, pp. 315–317.

John iv, 25 also mentions that Jews and Samaritans believe that the Messiah will teach his people a right understanding of the Law, a right insight into the fear of God, and piety, as he himself takes upon himself the whole Law and fulfils it. In learned circles, among the rabbis, it was probably this aspect of the Messiah which was most emphasized.[1] The Apocalypse of Enoch also knows that the Messiah has, as a gift of the spirit, the charisma of teaching.[2] Here the prophetic inheritance of the Messianic conception is evident (see below, pp. 321f.). It is possible that the Damascus sect held it to be an important task for the Messiah to preach, and to maintain sound doctrine and obedience to the Law. At all events we find that the rabbis sometimes think of him as a scribe and a teacher of the Law.[3]

The Messiah's equipment may be described in terms of ancient Israelite thought and vocabulary in a single word: there has been bestowed on him a special *blessing*:[4]

And the blessing of the Lord (will be) with him: he will
be strong and stumble not.

(Ps. Sol. xvii, 43 (38))

Therefore he will 'bless the people of the Lord with wisdom and gladness' (Ps. Sol. xvii, 40 (35)).

10   *The Work of the Messiah and His Kingdom*

The Messiah is the blessed king of David's line, equipped with the spirit and with the divine powers and qualities; and as such he exists for the sake of Israel. When he reveals himself it is with the glad tidings of Israel's redemption and her coming glory, of peace and salvation.[5] He has been sent to the house of Israel; his mission is the salvation of Israel.

This means, in the first place, to restore Israel as a people to her former glory; more, to gain for her the leading position among all the nations of the world. His first task, therefore, is to free his people from her enemies,[6] crushing the heathen world power which holds her in bondage. Clearly the Messiah of later Judaism

---

[1] Strack-Billerbeck III, pp. 570f., 577; IV, pp. 1f.; cf. pp. 796, 878, 885, 907, 918.
[2] 1 En. xlix, 3. See also Hvidberg, *Menigheden af den nye Pagt*, p. 262. with references.
[3] See Hvidberg, op. cit., pp. 262f., with references.
[4] On this fundamental idea in Israel's conception of life, see Pedersen, *Israel* I–II, pp. 182ff.; Mowinckel, *Diktet om Ijōb og hans tre venner*, pp. 5ff.
[5] Strack-Billerbeck III, pp. 8ff.; I, p. 607.
[6] Sib. III, 653; 1 En. xlvi; li–liii; 2 Esdras xi, 46; xii, 34; xiii, 5, 37f., 49; 2 Bar. xxxv ff.; lxx, 9; T. Jos. xix; cf. Volz, *Eschatologie*[2], pp. 223f.; Strack-Billerbeck III, pp. 576, 873.

plays a much more active part in the deliverance than the king of
the earlier future hope. This is very clearly expressed in the Psalms
of Solomon,[1] which come from the time after Pompey had ended
the rule of the Hasmoneans in 63 B.C., thus removing from the
earth this house of sinners, who had laid waste the throne of David
in their arrogance, as the writer says of this once celebrated
dynasty. The passage in Ps. Sol. xvii quoted above (p. 296)
continues thus:

> Gird him with strength, that he may shatter unrighteous
> rulers,
> And that he may purge Jerusalem from nations that
> trample (her) down to destruction
> Wisely, righteously he shall thrust out sinners from (the)
> inheritance,
> He shall destroy the pride of the sinner as a potter's
> vessel.
> With a rod of iron he shall break in pieces all their sub-
> stance,
> He shall destroy the godless nations with the word
> of his mouth.
> At his rebuke nations shall flee before him,
> And he shall reprove sinners for the thoughts of their
> heart.
>
> (vv. 24–27 (22–25))

This victory over the heathen is thought of as an act of war. As
a rule, the Messiah is not regarded as judge of the world in a legal
and forensic sense. When the statement is made (alluding to Isa.
xi, 4) that he will destroy the heathen with the word of his mouth,
the thought is not of a judicial act, but that when the heathen hear
his threatening war-cry, they will be reduced to impotence and will
flee.[2] It often sounds as if the victories were won by the Messiah
single-handed. But this would be too rash a conclusion. The expressions reflect the traditional court-style[3] as we meet it in the
I-style of the old royal inscriptions.[4] The same conception of the
Messiah's work is found in Jubilees, the Targums, and the Jewish
Sibylline Oracles.[5]

---

[1] See Gray in *A.P.O.T.* II, pp. 627ff. [2] Cf. Bousset, *Relig.*[2], p. 263.
[3] So, rightly, Leivestad, *Christ the Conqueror*, pp. 8f.
[4] Cf. Mowinckel in *Eucharisterion* I, pp. 297ff.
[5] E.g., Jub. xxxi, 17 (the Messiah from Levi); Jerusalem Targum I, II on Gen. xlix,
10; Jerusalem Targum I on Deut. xxv, 19; Lam. ii, 22; Isa. lii, 12; liii, 1, 3, 7, 11f.;
Sib, V, 108f.; III, 288ff., 632ff.

The Messiah's first task, then, is the destruction of the world powers. Here the Messianic conception of later Judaism differs from the earlier one. This is obvious in the Ezra Apocalypse and the Baruch Apocalypse, where it is the Messiah himself who, in a miraculous way, destroys the world power, Rome.[1] By contrast with the earlier conception, the view of later Judaism is that the Messiah will come, not after God has established the kingdom, but after the events which prepare for the great day, after the signs have shown that the day is at hand, after the climax of wickedness and sin and the appearance of the forerunners.[2] There is reason to think that the warlike spirit of the Maccabean line has influenced this new conception. Only occasionally, as, for instance, in the original kernel of 1 Enoch, do we find the view that the Messiah will not appear until after the great judgement. But, as we have seen, this does not mean that the Messiah is thought of as a judge. The ancient Jewish conception is that God himself, 'the Ancient of Days', is the judge of the world. The Messiah of later Judaism is God's victorious instrument in the establishment of the kingdom.

But the reckoning with the world power is also regarded as an act of judgement in which the Messiah takes part. This is so, for instance, when Rabbi Akiba holds that one of the judgement seats in Dan. vii, is for 'David', i.e., the Messiah.[3] The Apocalypse of Ezra, too, sometimes has this conception alongside the idea of annihilation: 'For at the first he shall set them alive for judgement; and when he hath rebuked them (i.e., convicted them) he shall destroy them.'[4] There is here a blend of lingering influences from the older conception of the judgement (see above, p. 273; cf. pp. 176ff.), and of elements from the conception of the Son of Man (see below, pp. 393ff.).

The world power which is to be destroyed is often called Gog and Magog,[5] with reference to Ezekiel. In nationalistic circles it was, of course, Rome that was meant; and it was also called Babylon or Edom, and identified with the last of the four world empires mentioned in Dan. vii (2 Esdras xii, 11). As the leader of this power, which is hostile to God, a specific person appears, an 'Antichrist' (see above, pp. 272f.), often called Armilus, which is no doubt a distortion of Romulus, the name of the first king of Rome.

---

[1] 2 Esdras xi, 1ff.; xiii, 1ff.; 2 Bar. xxxvi, 1ff.; xxxix, 1–xl, 4.
[2] See Schürer, *Geschichte*[4] II, pp. 612f., with references to the sources.
[3] See below, p. 352 n. 3. [4] 2 Esdras xii, 33.
[5] Jerusalem Targum II on Num. xi, 26; Jerusalem Targum I on Exod. xx, 11.

But thought is centred primarily on Israel's own land and people.[1] There is no great concern about the fate of the heathen. Only very occasionally is it stated that the survivors of heathen nations will be converted;[2] if anything is said about their destiny, it is usually to emphasize their destruction. But those who survive will be compelled to acknowledge the true religion and submit to Israel. Sib. III, 654 tells us that he will slay some and 'consecrate faithful vows to others', that is, compel them to submit and assure them of security and life under his dominion.

> He shall have the heathen nations to serve him under
>   his yoke;
> And he shall glorify the Lord in a place to be seen
>   of (?) all the earth.   (Ps. Sol. xvii, 32 (30))

The heathen will become tributary vassals under the Jews' Messiah. They may no longer live in Israel's land, being themselves unclean, and by their very presence making the land unclean. Fear will make them acknowledge and pay homage to the God of Israel; but the national Messianic hope had no great missionary interest.

This strong emphasis on the Messiah as a warrior (cf. the expression 'War-Messiah' used of the Messiah ben Joseph, p. 291, above), and the development of a more active conception by contrast with the earlier period (see above, pp. 169ff.) are no doubt indirectly connected with the new, transcendental conception of the Messiah which finds expression in the Son of Man. The fact that this universalistic and transcendental conception of the Messiah came to prevail in many circles (as we shall see later) made conservative circles, for their part, lay still greater emphasis on the national and political aspect of the future king, thus making him more of a military figure. A similar influence was exercised by the growing intolerance of everything foreign, which was a result of the Maccabean revolt and the Roman rule, and which made foreign dominion over the Jews seem increasingly obnoxious. In such circles the future hope would concentrate more and more on deliverance from alien rule. The Messiah would be primarily a royal deliverer, the enemy of Rome, a Zealot.

Referring to Num. xxiv, 17, the Damascus Document says that the Messiah will crush all the children of Sheth (i.e., the heathen),

---

[1] See Bousset, *Relig.*[2], p. 268.
[2] References to the sources in Bousset, *Relig.*[2], p. 269 n.1.

and that the rest of the sinners in Israel, who have survived the final catastrophe, will be put to the sword when the Messiah of Israel and Aaron comes.[1] This latter expression seems to indicate that it is God Himself who annihilates the heathen and sinners, or perhaps that the Messiah does it by his miraculous power, without direct military action.[2]

In later rabbinic theology the military features again become less prominent. Leadership in war is left to the 'War-Messiah' of the house of Joseph; or God Himself will overthrow the heathen by His miraculous power, whereas the Messiah will assume power[3] in the restored kingdom, and thereafter maintain peace.

Victory over the heathen means not only the liberation of Israel, but also the universal dominion of the Messiah. 'He shall have the heathen nations to serve him under his yoke', says Ps. Sol. xvii, 32 (30). The rabbinic literature, too, emphasizes his universal dominion, alluding to a number of biblical passages.[4] Jerusalem will then be the centre of the world; and all nations will come and do obeisance before the God of Israel, who will have become king of all the world. The passage from the Psalms of Solomon just quoted continues,

And he shall purge Jerusalem, making it holy as of
    old:
So that nations shall come from the ends of the earth
    to see his glory,
    Bringing as gifts her sons who had fainted,
And to see the glory of the Lord, wherewith God hath
    glorified her.[5]

The rabbis frequently describe the stern rule which the Messiah will exercise over the heathen. He is lenient towards Israel, but stern towards the heathen.[6] He will hold all nations under his yoke,[7] and quell every revolt with the breath of his mouth.[8] But

[1] Damascus Document ix, 10ff.; cf. Hvidberg, *Menigheden af den nye Pagt*, pp. 263, 267, 269.
[2] As in 2 Esdras xiii, 28; cf. Hvidberg, op. cit., p. 269.
[3] This is rightly emphasized by Hvidberg in discussing Ginzberg's view of the Messianic teaching of the Damascus Sect; see op. cit., pp. 274, 276f., with references.
[4] Numbers Rabbah 13 (170b); Genesis Rabbah 1 (196a); Pirke de-R. Eliezer 11 (6c); see Strack-Billerbeck II, pp. 147f.; and further IV, pp. 88, 895 n.d., 896 nn. h, i, 899 n.m.
[5] Ps. Sol. xvii, 33f. (30f.). See further Strack-Billerbeck III, p. 148 n.f.; IV, pp. 881, 895 n.f., 897 n.k., 889 n.l. Messel (in *N.T.T.* x, 1909, pp. 105ff.) underestimates the universalistic tendency in Ps. Sol. xvii.
[6] Strack-Billerbeck I, p. 64; III, p. 144; IV, p. 882.
[7] Op. cit. III, pp. 144, 148; IV, p. 882.
[8] Op. cit. III, pp. 144, 148, 641; IV, p. 882.

it is also said that he will be the light of the nations.[1] The peoples seek after him; and he will teach them to observe the most important of God's commands.[2]

The prevailing view is that the heathen will yield to him voluntarily; for the Messiah is the prince of peace; and when the heathen have been overcome, he has put an end to war.[3] His kingdom is a kingdom of peace and prosperity for both Israel and the other peoples.[4] He will be the good shepherd to his people.[5] He will restrain them,[6] and preserve them from all evil:

> (He will be) mighty in his works, and strong in the fear of God,
> (He will be) shepherding the flock of the Lord faithfully and righteously,
> And will suffer none among them to stumble in their pasture. (Ps. Sol. xvii, 44f. (40))

But occasionally it may be presupposed that even after his enthronement the Messiah may be obliged to restrain the princes, and to meet the enemy on a 'day of conflict'. But none shall prevail against him, because he puts his trust in the Lord (Ps. Sol. xvii, 37 (33), 41 (36), 44 (39)).

Therefore we also read:

> Blessed be they that shall be in those days,
> In that they shall see the good fortune of Israel which
> God shall bring to pass in the gathering together of
> the tribes. (Ps. Sol. xvii, 50)
> In that they shall see the goodness of the Lord which He
> shall perform for the generation that is to come.
> (Ps. Sol. xviii, 7 (6))

When the world power has been crushed, the dispersed can return;[7] and this, too, is now a result of the Messiah's work. The heathen themselves have to bring them back;

---

[1] Op. cit. II, p. 726.   [2] Op. cit. II, p. 438.
[3] Sib. V, 429ff.; cf. III, 706ff.; Jub. xxxi, 20.
[4] 2 Bar. lxxiii, 1; T. Judah xxiv; and further, Strack-Billerbeck III, pp. 9 nn.c.-o. 148 n.h.; IV, p. 910 n.ee.
[5] Ps. Sol. xvii, 44–46 (40f.); Exodus Rabbah ii, (68b) and other rabbinic passages Strack-Billerbeck II, pp. 536f.
[6] See the passages about the Messiah's painful work for his people, cited in Strack-Billerbeck II, pp. 287 nn.g., h.i.k., 289 nn.f.g.; Bousset, *Relig.*[2], p. 271.
[7] Cf. above, p. 269; and Strack-Billerbeck I, p. 591; IV, pp. 882, 907 n.f.g.; Bousset *Relig.*[2], p. 271.

And he shall gather together a holy people, whom he shall
    lead in righteousness,
  And he shall judge the tribes of the people that has been
    sanctified by the Lord his God.
And he shall not suffer unrighteousness to lodge any more in
    their midst,
  Nor shall there dwell with them any man that knoweth
    wickedness,
  For he shall know them, that they are all sons of their God.
And he shall divide them according to their tribes upon the
    land,
  And neither sojourner nor alien shall sojourn with them
    any more.
He shall judge peoples and nations in the wisdom of his
    righteousness . . .
And he (shall be) a righteous king, taught of God, over them,
And there shall be no unrighteousness in his days in their
    midst,
  For all shall be holy and their king the anointed of the
    Lord.   (Ps. Sol. xvii, 28–31 (26–29), 35f. (32))

After the fall of Jerusalem in A.D. 70 we also find that the
rabbinic literature attributes to the Messiah the restoration of
Jerusalem and the temple in their former glory.[1] In the Eighteen
Benedictions, prayer is made that the Lord in His great mercy
will have compassion on His people Israel, on Jerusalem the abode
of His glory, on the temple and on the kingdom of the righteous
Messiah, the scion of David.

The Messiah will be a righteous ruler over the returned and
restored people. He will judge his people with righteousness. He
is *meših̄ā' de ṣidḳā'*, the Messiah of righteousness, or the righteous
Messiah (see above, pp. 308f.). When he is also called 'The
Messiah of Thy (i.e., the Lord's) righteousness',[2] it is the thought
of the Lord's saving righteousness that is present (see above, p.
309). But again and again it is also stated that as a king who rules
and judges, the Messiah himself will bring forth justice and righteousness, and by his righteousness (in the sense of an ethical
quality) will fulfil God's righteousness (in the sense of His salva-

---

[1] Strack-Billerbeck I, pp. 1003f.
[2] See Bousset, *Relig.*[2], p. 258 n., according to the Jerusalem recension of Shemoneh
Esreh *v.* 14.

tion).[1] Sinners will be rooted out, together with the heathen. The land and the people will no longer be infected and desecrated by the presence of foreigners and immigrants. The people will become a holy people, in the sense not only of being separated and dedicated to the Lord, but of having moral qualities (see above, p. 309):

> In the assemblies he will judge the peoples, the tribes of the sanctified.
> His words (shall be) like the words of the holy ones in the midst of sanctified peoples.
> (Ps. Sol. xvii, 48f. (43))

Injustice will no longer dwell among the people; they will all be the sons of their God.

> (He will be) shepherding the flock of the Lord faithfully and righteously,
> And will suffer none among them to stumble in their pasture.
> (Ps. Sol. xvii, 45 (40))

He will lead them all in righteousness:

> And there will be no pride among them that any among them should be oppressed.
> (Ps. Sol. xvii, 46 (41))

Because he is filled with the blessing of the Lord (see above, p. 311), he himself is a blessing to his people, and will bless the Lord's people with wisdom in gladness. All the virtues, peace, righteousness, faithfulness, will flourish among the people (p. 310), because God has set him over the house of Israel to guide them in the right way. All this he creates and upholds by his chastisement.

Like the king in ancient times, the Messiah is the intermediary between God and the people, in that he intercedes for them and gains the divine forgiveness.[2] The Messiah of the tribe of Levi combines the call and inspiration of king, priest, and prophet;[3] a typical Jewish development of the idea. In the Targum's interpretation of Isa. liii (see below, pp. 330ff.), it is said that he gains the divine forgiveness of sins both by interceding on behalf of his people, and by causing them to observe the Law and do right. But there is no suggestion in Jewish literature that he has

---

[1] Ps. Sol. xviii, 8 (7); 1 En. xlvi, 3; xlix, 2; lxii, 2; lxxi, 14ff.; see above, pp. 308ff.
[2] Targum on Isa. liii, 4.
[3] T. Levi xviii; Jub. xxxi; cf. Josephus, *Antt.* XII, 299; *B.J.* i, 681.

any authority to forgive sin.[1] According to Jewish thought, to forgive sins is God's prerogative, and His alone. This is evident from the offence which was caused when Jesus appeared with full authority to say 'Your sins are forgiven'.[2]

Nor is the thought of the resurrection of the dead connected with the national conception of the Messiah. It is God who raises the dead. This is quite natural, since in Judaism belief in the resurrection is later in origin than the Messianic hope. Where we find indications of a connexion between the Messiah and the resurrection, it is the result of influence from the idea of the Son of Man.[3]

Nor is the national Messiah thought of as judge of the world; for judgement, too, belongs to God Himself (see above, p. 313). It is, therefore, very significant that the thought of the Messiah as judge of the world does not occur in the rabbinic literature, but only in the Apocalypse of Enoch, where the reference is really to the Son of Man, and not to the national Messiah.[4]

In a certain sense it may be said that all the blessings of the Messianic age are bound up with the Messiah; and from that point of view a comprehensive and detailed picture could be given of all the glory and happiness which later Judaism and the learned rabbis thought would come with the days of the Messiah.[5] But our present concern is to bring out those features in the conception of the future which are explicitly connected with the Messiah, and regarded as brought about by him; and there are a few special features, in addition to those mentioned above, which the rabbis attribute to the Messiah. As the Messiah was present from the first in the thought of God, and in His eternal purpose for the world, he is also, as the central figure in the last things, thought of at times as the first-born of creation (as in St. Paul),[6] as the end and goal of creation and of created things,[7] and as

---

[1] Some scholars think that the Damascus Document xviii, 8 expresses the idea that the Messiah will forgive the sins of the congregation (see Hvidberg, *Menigheden af den nye Pagt*, p. 268). It is more probable that the text (which is fragmentary at this point) refers to God Himself. The verb used is *kipper*, which with a human subject does not mean 'forgive', but 'make atonement' (see Stamm, *Erlösen und Vergeben im Alten Testament*, pp. 59ff.). If the Messiah is the subject in xviii, 8, then the reference will be to his intercessory prayer.

[2] Mark ii, 5ff. and parallels; cf. Strack-Billerbeck I, pp. 495f.

[3] Only once, and in a late document, is the Messiah spoken of as raising the dead; see Strack-Billerbeck I, p. 524; and below, pp. 337, 400f.

[4] Strack-Billerbeck I, p. 978; IV, p. 1100.

[5] Op. cit. IV, pp. 875–968.

[6] Op. cit. I, p. 65; III, p. 626; cf. pp. 258, 677.

[7] Op. cit. III, p. 626; IV, p. 994.

greater than the angels.[1] Therefore he is also sometimes regarded as the restorer (cf. the Taheb of the Samaritans) of those good things which existed at the beginning, but were lost through the fall of Adam:[2] the splendour of man's countenance which was a reflection of the glory of God, eternal life; the original proportions of the human body, the paradisal fertility of earth and of the trees, and the original power of the light of the heavenly bodies. In other passages these things form part of what God will Himself renew in the last times.[3] The Messiah will also cause to fall from heaven the manna, the miraculous food of the desert wanderings.[4]

Thus the Messiah is the supernaturally equipped instrument in the establishment of the kingdom of the end time, the restoration of the kingdom of Israel (Acts i, 6), the kingdom of God on earth. In that kingdom he is the perfect ruler. In the days of the Messiah[5] there will be all imaginable happiness; and righteousness, peace, and piety will prevail among men, both in Israel, and among the other nations, who submit to Israel's God and ally themselves with His people.

But there was an increasing tendency in Judaism to distinguish between the kingly rule of Yahweh (the kingdom of God) and the kingdom of the Messiah. This is connected both with a conservative influence and also with the projection of the kingly rule of God into the next world, which was strongly fostered by the new, otherworldly eschatology with its cosmic dualism (see above, pp. 270ff.). The more conservative tendency in the future hope in later Judaism (particularly among the rabbis), which represents a traditionalist, conservative reaction against many features in apocalyptic, maintained firmly that in the last things the real agent was God Himself. The day is 'the day of the Lord'; and the kingdom is the kingly rule of God or of heaven.[6] God is judge of the world. The resurrection is the work of God. God is creator of the new heaven and the new earth. It is God who brings back paradise, and who Himself then dwells in the midst of His people.

On the other hand, men could not disregard the fact that the kingdom of the Davidic Messiah was an earthly kingdom, though a glorified and idealized one. And they were aware of a profound difference between that kingdom and God's eternal, transcendental, other-worldly kingdom in a wholly new and different state

---

[1] Op. cit. II, p. 673. [2] Op. cit. I, p. 19; IV, pp. 887ff.
[3] Op. cit. IV, p. 891. [4] Op. cit. I, p. 87; II, p. 481; IV, pp. 890, 954.
[5] See above, p. 304, and the references below, p. 326 with n.3.
[6] Strack-Billerbeck IV, pp. 897f. nn.k.l.

of existence. This gave rise to the theological compromise mentioned above (p. 277). The Messianic kingdom becomes an interim kingdom before the real kingdom of glory under the kingly rule of God; and its duration is limited. It will be the conclusion of the present aeon. Sometimes it was supposed that the catastrophic transition to the new aeon would end the Messianic kingdom: when the days of the Messiah had elapsed, the Messiah and all other living men would die; then would come the resurrection, the establishment of the new aeon, and the eternal kingdom of God (see below, pp. 325f.). In spite of all attempts at idealization and all the fresh influences from the new eschatology, the Messiah and his kingdom were and remained this-worldly in character.

11. *The Influence of Prophet and Scribe on the Idea of the Messiah*

Thus the Messiah is a king, and his mission is that of a king. But in the later Jewish idea of the Messiah there are present certain influences from men's conception of the prophets. This is evident, for instance, from the fact that 'the Prophet who is to come into the world' sometimes seems to have taken the place of the Messiah (p. 302).

The thought of the Messiah as an intermediary between God and the people (pp. 238f., 318) is another mark of prophetic influence. In itself this status of intermediary is also a royal feature: the king is the leader of the cult, and represents his people before God. But prophetic ideas also play their part here. In Judaism the prophet became more and more the true intercessor and intermediary, at least in popular thought and in legend.

In the extensive Messianic interpretation of Old Testament passages of every kind, it was taken for granted that the national and political Messiah had prophetic characteristics. These characteristics are admittedly also associated with the conception of the king in the east and in Israel; but nevertheless the prophetic contribution is noteworthy, This is so when the Messiah's wisdom is emphasized.[1] He has all wisdom, and understands all mysteries (p. 309). He is superior to the angels.[2] He understands men's hearts.[3] 'Come and see a man who has told me all that I ever did. Can this be the Messiah?' asks the Samaritan woman (John iv, 29). And this wisdom is something which the Messiah has learned from God, not from men.[4] This wisdom has a markedly

[1] Op. cit., II, pp. 438f.
[2] Op. cit. III, p. 673.   [3] Op. cit. II, pp. 412, 438.
[4] Op. cit. II, p. 152; III, p. 36. Cf. Staerk, *Soter* I, pp. 69f.

Y

didactic character, which means, in later Jewish thought, that it is prophetic. 'When the Messiah comes, he will teach us all things', says the Samaritan woman (John iv, 25). This includes both how God ought to be worshipped, and how the Law is to be interpreted and observed.

When the people came to the conclusion that Jesus was truly 'the Prophet that should come into the world', the natural consequence was that they should proclaim Him king (John vi, 14f.). Thus, the Messiah is 'the prophet' κατ᾽ ἐξοχήν. This passage seems to imply that 'the Prophet', simpliciter, was a title of the Messiah. This is in harmony with the fact that Old Testament passages which spoke, or seemed to speak of a special prophet in the future (like Malachi's prediction of the return of Elijah, or the reference in Deuteronomy to the coming of a prophet like Moses), were by some interpreted Messianically,[1] whereas other scholars took them to refer to a prophetic forerunner of the Messiah (see above, pp. 298ff.).

Nevertheless it ought to be noted that whereas, in the earlier period, and particularly in the circle of the Servant of the Lord, more was said about the knowledge of God, that intimate relationship with God which brought an immediate understanding of, and unity with, the will and Law of God, in later Judaism more is said about the Messiah as a teacher, and of the spirit of teaching. Here, as generally in later Judaism, the prophetic element is formalized by tradition and the influence of learning.

When the equipment and mission of the Messiah are sometimes expressed in terms of the triple function of king, High-priest, and prophet,[2] this is a somewhat formal description; and its implications are not worked out in any detail. The bearing of the idea is indicated by the fact that the reference is to the Messiah of the tribe of Levi. It undoubtedly originated in Hasmonean court circles, and probably never enjoyed general currency.

In general, it should be noted that the influence of the interpretation of Scripture on the conception of the Messiah was always limited to occasional details. Admittedly the Jewish scholars themselves regarded their Messianic teaching as based on the revelation in Scripture; but in fact the Messianic hope and its essential content are a religious tradition, which is older than the

---

[1] See Staerk, *Soter* I, pp. 62ff. Staerk exaggerates the point, and, by generalizing and overlooking distinctions, draws hasty and sweeping conclusions from the evidence.

[2] T. Levi xviii; cf. Josephus, *Antt.* XIII, 299; *B.J.* i, 681. See Murmelstein in *W.Z.K.M.* xxxv, 1928, pp. 273f.; cf. xxxvi, 1929, pp. 51ff.; see above, p. 318.

sacred canon of Scripture. What the scholars did was to find in Scripture individual passages, which supported or amplified the conception of the Messiah which they had inherited. Their interpretation of Scripture was always more or less atomistic: an exposition of, or a deduction from, individual verses or sentences, without any appreciable reference to the context. They would interpret this or that psalm messianically; but this seldom meant that they had attempted to grasp the content of the passage in its entirety. This also applies to their treatment of the Servant of the Lord in Deutero-Isaiah. They had no difficulty in applying one verse to the Messiah, and the next, perhaps, to the people of Israel.[1] This explains why Isa. liii has, in the main, left little mark on the conception of the Messiah, in spite of the fact that the Servant was not infrequently identified with the Messiah. What men found in the Scripture texts was, broadly speaking, the Messianic concept which they already held (see below, pp. 330ff.).

12. *Was the Messiah an Eternal Individual?*

Is the Messiah of later Judaism really a specific individual who will have no successors; or is he, like the king of the restoration in the earlier period (see above, pp. 165ff.), a representative of the restored dynasty, and the first of an unending succession of similar rulers?

At least the Messiah of the tribe of Levi in the Testaments of the Twelve Patriarchs and the Book of Jubilees is regarded as the representative of his line. Here the eternal character of the Messiah denotes the eternal rule of the line. This is clear, for instance, from the fact that (according to 1 Mac. xiv, 41) the people proclaimed Simon prince and High-priest 'for ever'; that is, made the office hereditary in his line for the future.[2]

In spite of everything, the national Messiah was a man: and, according to Jewish belief, a man cannot live for ever; the few individuals (like Elijah[3] and Enoch) who were caught up into heaven are exceptions. Even in Ps. Sol. xvii, which attributes to the Messiah so many superhuman qualities, he is thought of as inaugurating the newly restored, eternal dynasty of David.[4]

[1] North's survey of the many rabbinic interpretations of the Servant (*The Suffering Servant*, pp. 9ff.) gives a clear impression of their inconsistencies and their unsystematic character.   [2] See Schürer, *Geschichte*[4] II, p. 616 n. 18.
[3] Ecclus. xlviii, 9–11. Staerk (*Soter* I, p. 69) thinks that Sirach here means that the immortal Elijah is the Messiah, or, at least, that this idea underlies his words. But Staerk offers no proof of this; for no proof exists.
[4] This follows from the implication that his span of life is limited; cf. *v.* 42 (37), 'throughout his days he will not stumble', i.e., throughout his whole life. Cf. Messel in *N.T.T.* x, 1909, pp. 105ff.

But there were several factors which led to the conception of the Messiah as a specific individual. First, there was the strong appeal and interest which the thought of the great transformation, the dawn of the Messianic age, had for religious thought and reflection. It was so great and decisive an event, that at first men had no inclination to go further and inquire what would follow afterwards, and whether this age of bliss would ever end. This question is first raised because of the need, in the interests of a theological system, to relieve the tension, for instance, between the this-worldly and the other-worldly forms of the Messianic hope. It was only natural that in the specific, individual prediction or description of the Messianic kingdom, the kingly rule of the Messiah came as a glorious climax, beyond which neither thought nor imagination sought to reach. In the moment of apprehending the idea, the Messiah was presented to the mind as unique and ultimate.

But, in addition, there was the influence of the new, other-worldly eschatology, with its belief in the resurrection, and its conception of the Son of Man, who is a specific individual, transcendental and eternal. This could, and did, cause the Messianic idea to develop in two directions. The attempt to reconcile the two views of the future by the idea of an interim kingdom, an earthly state of glory, as the end of the present aeon, could, of course, lead to the thought that the Messiah, who represented the this-worldly future hope, would be king in this interim kingdom. There was ascribed to him a precisely limited period of activity: a thousand years or five hundred years, in accordance with the varying chronological systems in learned circles; and thereby he necessarily became a specific individual, but one subject to temporal limitations. As we shall see below (p. 325f.), this idea occurs in several passages.

But, apart from the idea of an interim kingdom, the idea of the two aeons helped to make the Messiah not only a specific individual, but an eternal being. In that he was associated with the coming aeon and the resurrection faith, he became an eternal being, one who would rule in an eternal Messianic kingdom. By contrast with the present aeon, the coming aeon is eternal and unchanging; and, as a result of the resurrection faith, it was held that men would enjoy eternal life in this new aeon; and it was taken for granted that this was true of the Messiah, irrespective of whether or not the resurrection faith was applied to him (see below, pp. 326f.). He was an exceptional man, like Enoch, Elijah and others, who had been caught up to heaven, and shared in the life of paradise or heaven. Sometimes, too, the rabbis imagined that after his birth the Messiah was hidden in paradise, or with Elijah in heaven,[1] or that he was one of the righteous persons of the past who would return (see above, p. 281; cf. p. 302). In either event he had already had experience of life. He had become the sole Messiah, who needed no successor. This was a still more natural consequence when the Messiah was equated with the eternal Son of Man, for, as we shall see, the latter was an eternal being.

Throughout the rabbinic literature, therefore, it is taken for granted that the Messiah is unique and that he is eternal. If this is but seldom explicitly stated (for the most part by contrast with the Messiah ben Joseph, who falls in the conflict with Rome, and in order to emphasize the difference between these two figures),[2] the reason is that what is taken for granted does not need to be expressed. We can readily understand, therefore, why the rabbis sometimes attribute to the Messiah an ideal pre-existence (see below, pp. 334f.).

13. *The Suffering and Death of the Messiah*

In apocalyptic and elsewhere, ideas sometimes occur which are more closely connected with the older conception of the Messiah as mortal. This conception had a lasting influence. We have seen (above, pp. 277, 285, 321) that it was a logical consequence of the original, national, this-worldly conception of the Messiah, that when the tension between the two eschatologies was relieved by the idea of an interim kingdom, this was regarded as the conclusion of the present, transitory aeon, and the Messiah was king of the interim kingdom. The idea, which sometimes occurs in precisely those circles where the new, other-worldly eschatology had taken root, of the death of the Messiah at the end of the interim kingdom, is entirely in accord with the original view of the Messiah.

The thought is most clearly expressed in the Ezra Apocalypse. There the Messianic age is described in these terms: 'My Servant[3] the Messiah shall be revealed, together with those who are with him, and shall rejoice the survivors four hundred years. And it shall be, after these years, that my servant the Messiah shall die,

---

[1] Strack-Billerbeck II, p. 340.
[2] Bab. Sukkah 52a; see Weber, *Jüd. Theol.*[2], p. 366.
[3] *Filius meus* = '*abdî*; see above, p. 294. *A.P.O.T.* II renders 'my Son'.

and all in whom there is human breath. Then shall the world be turned into the primeval silence seven days, like as at the first beginnings'; and then follow the new aeon and the new life (2 Esdras vii, 28ff.).

From the standpoint of earlier Judaism, this thought is anything but surprising. It is the logical method of reconciling the old idea of the Messiah with the doctrine of the two aeons and with belief in the resurrection. The assumption here is, of course, that at the end of the seven days' silence (a repetition of the original state of chaos), the Messiah will rise with the rest of the dead, and will live and reign as God's vicegerent for ever.

The old idea that the Messiah is mortal recurs in the conception of the Messiah ben Joseph, who falls in conflict with Gog or Armilus. It was of this Messiah that the rabbis interpreted the saying in Zech. xii, 10 about 'him who they have pierced'.[1]

It is also said of the Taheb (or 'Restorer') of the Samaritans that he will rule over Israel until the dawn of the new aeon, and then will die in peace.[2]

The old ideas recur in the rabbinic literature in association with the expression 'the days of the Messiah'.[3] This is a general expression for the Messianic age, the age in which the Messiah is king. Originally it was identical with the end-time, the age of bliss, or, in terms of the later Jewish eschatology, the coming aeon. Nevertheless, the rabbis did not lose the conviction that the days of the Messiah, though a glorified and idealized age, belonged essentially to this world. Accordingly, the idea recurs, and with increasing emphasis, that the days of the Messiah really belong to the present aeon, and are its glorious conclusion. This is, in fact, the idea of the interim kingdom, or Millennium, in another form. This thought is very common in rabbinic theology.[4] Where the Messianic kingdom has become an interim kingdom, the resurrection of the dead (which is associated in apocalyptic with the appearance and rule of the Messiah)[5] is explicitly postponed to the period after the days of the Messiah,[6] very much as in the Ezra Apocalypse.

---

[1] See above, p. 321, and the references in Bousset, Relig.², pp. 264f.
[2] See Merx, Der Messias oder Ta'eb der Samaritaner, p. 41.
[3] See above, pp. 304, 320; and Strack-Billerbeck I, p. 602; IV, pp. 815, 830ff., 857ff., and Index, s.v. 'Tage des Messias'.
[4] 2 Esdras vii, 28ff.; Rev. xx, 4f.; Sanhedrin 99a, where the different rabbinic opinions are quoted. See also Moore, Judaism II, pp. 375f., with references.
[5] Strack-Billerbeck II, pp. 827ff.; IV, pp. 971, 1166.
[6] Op. cit., III, p. 827; IV, pp. 971ff., 1166.

That the rule of the Messiah will one day come to an end, and be replaced by something still more glorious, is thus a familiar thought in Judaism, and the result of the conflict between the older, this-worldly eschatology and the later, other-worldly type. Clearly it was also influenced by the old, fundamental conviction that the eschatological kingdom is really *God's* kingly rule. In the light of later Jewish thought there is no difficulty in understanding Paul's words: 'Then comes the end, when He (Christ, the Messiah) delivers the kingdom to God the Father, after He has destroyed every rule, and authority, and power' (1 Cor. xv, 24).

But the thought of the Messiah as an eternal being in an eternal kingdom was still prevalent. Certainly it was the dominant conception in the time of Jesus. This was the result of the influence which the idea of the Son of Man exercised on that of the Messiah. The surprising thing is that the thought of the Messiah as a mortal man held its ground so well. This is a clear testimony to the original, political, this-worldly character of the Messiah.

In Christian thought the death of the Messiah is inseparably associated with his suffering; and both have the character of vicarious atonement. This was not so in Judaism. There the death of the Messiah was not held to have any organic connexion with his sufferings; nor was there any question of an atoning death. In spite of statements to the contrary,[1] Judaism knows nothing of a suffering, dying, and rising Messiah.[2]

[1] See J. Jeremias in *Deutsche Theologie* ii, 1929, pp. 106ff.; Staerk, *Soter* I, p. 77; II, pp. 406ff.; Johansson, *Parakletoi*, pp. 113ff., 301f.; Riesenfeld, *Jésus transfiguré*, pp. 81ff., and 314ff., where a survey is given of recent discussion of the problem. Nearly all of those who maintain that the Jews were familiar with the idea of a suffering and dying Messiah make the mistake of confusing these two conceptions, failing to realize that the mortality of the Messiah and his sufferings are two distinct factors. Nor do they distinguish between the different conceptions of the Messiah. If the problem is to be solved, the national Messiah, the Messiah from Ephraim, and the Son of Man must not be confused; and the question of the unknown Messiah must also be considered separately. The problem has been discussed from the standpoint of Christian doctrine, rather than from that of the historical background of Jewish thought.

Jeremias and Staerk try to prove the existence of a Jewish doctrine of a suffering and dying Messiah, on the ground of the rabbis' Messianic interpretation of the Servant of the Lord, and of Isa. liii. But the rabbinic sayings on the subject do not go beyond what Dalman and Billerbeck have stated, as mentioned above. What the rabbis (like the Targum) found in Isa. liii was the pain and toil of the Messiah in his conflict, as a background to his glorification; but the emphasis was on the glorification; and there was no thought of the Messiah's atoning death. See below, pp. 329ff. Johansson and Riesenfeld do not adduce new material beyond what Dalman and Billerbeck have discussed; nor do they succeed in advancing new arguments for their interpretation. Riesenfeld admits that he can find only 'slight traces' of the supposed doctrine. But he boldly turns a somersault, and writes as if these 'traces' indicate that this doctrine of a suffering Messiah had 'not yet entirely disappeared from Palestinian Judaism' (op. cit., p. 84). He ought first to have proved that it ever existed there. What in fact he presents is only an assumption, based on an untenable interpretation of the Servant

It is true that the idea of the suffering of the Messiah does occur in Judaism; but the meaning is not the same as in Christianity. In its rendering of Isa. liii, 12 the Targum speaks of the Messiah's heavy and exacting task, in pursuance of which he hazards his life. But the thought is not of such sufferings as we have in mind when we raise the question of the Messiah's sufferings, but rather of the danger and the exertions which are the lot of the Messiah in the war with the heathen. In order to shatter the dominion of the world powers and crush the enemies of Israel, he hazards his life; but, in the end, he gains a triumphant victory. This was a natural thought for Jewish scribes, who interpreted a number of disconnected biblical passages of the Messiah. Both Isa. liii and the other passages about the Servant of the Lord spoke of travail and affliction. The Jew Trypho, in Justin's dialogue, admits that it accords with Scripture that the Messiah must suffer.[1]

It is essential to distinguish here between the Church's view of the Messiah's sufferings and that of the Synagogue. The Church has always proclaimed a Christ who suffers, *and dies*, and rises again. The view taken by the Synagogue is clearly (but perhaps too sharply) formulated by Strack-Billerbeck: 'When reference is made (i.e., in Judaism) to a suffering and dying Messiah, it is not, as might be thought, one and the same person that is meant, but, on the contrary, two different persons. The synagogue of ancient times knows of a Messiah who suffers but does not die; and it knows of a Messiah who dies, but of whom it is not said that he must suffer, that is, the Messiah ben Joseph.'[2] This is true, but

---

[1] See Staerk, *Soter* I, p. 81. But Staerk is mistaken in saying that Trypho accepts the idea of the death of the Messiah. He only admits that he has to suffer greatly in accomplishing his task. It must also be noted that Trypho's replies are not fully reliable evidence for Jewish belief. For apologetic purposes, Justin is concerned to let the spokesman for Judaism come as near as possible to the Christian interpretation of Scripture, and to show how the Jew is finally convinced by the Christian interpretation as an example to other Jews.

[2] Strack-Billerbeck II, p. 273f.; cf. Bonsirven, *Le judaïsme palestinien au temps de Jésus-Christ* I, pp. 381ff. On the Messiah ben Joseph see above, pp. 290f.

---

of the Lord as the Messiah, and of his sufferings as an echo ('disintegrated pattern') of the 'Messianic' sufferings of the king in the cult. The theories of Engnell and Widengren are here uncritically accepted as scientific dogmas. When the whole of the theory about the 'disintegrated, Messianic, cultic pattern' collapses, what Riesenfeld here alleges about the rabbinic view of Isaac as a meritorious atoning act on Abraham's part, ceases to have any significance for the question now under discussion.

Against this theory of a suffering Jewish Messiah, see also Sjöberg in *S.E.Å.* v, 1940, pp. 163ff.; ibid. vii, 1942, pp. 141ff.; *Der Menschensohn*, pp. 116ff. Cf. also above, pp. 321ff.

[2] Dalman, *Der leidende und sterbende Messias*, p. 360; Weber, *Jüd. Theol.*[2], p. 360; Schürer, *Geschichte des jüdischen Volkes im Zeitalter Jesu Christi*[4] II, pp. 648ff., with references; and especially Strack-Billerbeck II, pp. 273ff., where the sources are given in full. Cf. also Héring in *R.H.Ph.R.* xviii, 1938, pp. 419ff.

with this qualification, that in the earlier period the Messiah ben David was also regarded as a mortal man. But the suffering and the death are not organically connected with each other; and the suffering of the Jewish Messiah is not associated with a vicarious and atoning death.

In the time of Jesus, at all events, the thought of a suffering and dying Messiah was quite alien to the normal Jewish view. For many it was not merely incomprehensible, but offensive.[1] Somewhat later we find it in the sayings of individual rabbis, but in a different sense, and never as a doctrine which is universally accepted.[2] The starting point is the customary Jewish estimate of the suffering of the pious. All suffering has a certain atoning effect;[3] and the suffering of the righteous, like his pious acts, benefits his people as merit and as atonement. There is also the rabbis' conviction that all righteous men must suffer in order to be worthy of blessedness in the next world. As the one who is righteous above all others, and who is called to the greatest future glory, the Messiah must be prepared for afflictions and sufferings.[4] The Messiah suffers *qua* righteous man, but not *qua* Messiah.[5]

On the whole, for the rabbis the Messiah is still the victorious hero who inaugurates the glorious era. When the thought of the Messiah's sufferings appears (arising in part from the general considerations mentioned, and in part from passages like Isa. liii and Zech. xii, 10; xiv, 1ff.), these sufferings are associated, sometimes with his struggles in the conflict with the heathen, and with the throes of the Messianic age, the last great affliction which will befall all the pious (see above, pp. 272f.), and sometimes with the period during which the Messiah is still hidden, unknown, misunderstood, exposed to the derision of the heathen, poor, leprous, etc. (see above, pp. 306f.; but, as we have seen, this last thought is late and not prominent). By all these sufferings the Messiah, in company with other pious men who suffer, atones for part of the guilt of his people Israel. The thought of atonement as the peculiar work of the Messiah, or of an atonement for the sins of the world, never occurs.

The fact that the document which has most to say about the sufferings of the Messiah is the medieval Pesikta Rabbati (tenth

---

[1] Matt. xvi, 21ff.; Mark viii, 31; ix, 31f.; Luke xxiv, 20f.; Acts xvii, 3; 1 Cor. i, 23; Gal. v, 11; etc.
[2] See the references in p. 327 n. 2.   [3] See Sjöberg, *Gott und die Sünder*, pp. 169ff.
[4] Cf. Otto, *The Kingdom of God and the Son of Man*, p. 244.
[5] See Weber, *Jüd. Theol.*[2], pp. 326ff., with references.

century)[1] indicates that Christian teaching and Christian theology have in some degree contributed to the spread of this idea among the rabbis of the Christian era. And when in Pesikta Rabbati we find a pre-existent Messiah, whom Satan attempts to overthrow during his pre-existence in heaven, and who declares himself to be ready to go down and take upon himself every suffering, in order to save all Israel,[2] it is natural to assume influence from the saviour myths which appear in the Gnostic systems, and which also lie behind the conception of the Son of Man, to which we shall return.

These later rabbis extracted from Scripture their ideas about the Messiah's sufferings, precisely in order to provide a biblical counterblast to the Christian faith in the Jesus (who had died) as the Messiah. The Scripture does present the Messiah as suffering to atone for Israel; but he does not die upon a cross. The same idea and intention appear in Trypho's arguments in Justin's dialogue (see above, p. 328). This is a secondary tendency, in reaction against Christianity, not a genuinely Jewish feature, and certainly not a pre-Christian one.

But we have seen above that the Targums identify the Servant of the Lord in Isaiah with the Messiah, and that they use this expression as a Messianic title. Is this not evidence of the conception of the person and work of the Messiah, and does it not show that Judaism, too, had the belief in a Messiah who suffers, dies, and rises again? The answer (cf. above, p. 328) may be most simply found in the Targum's rendering of Isa. liii, the chapter which is most characteristic:[3]

'Behold my Servant Messiah shall prosper; he shall be high, and increase, and be exceeding strong: as the house of Israel looked to him during many days, because their countenance was darkened among the peoples, and their complexion beyond the sons of men, so will he scatter many peoples: at him kings shall be silent, and put their hands upon their mouth, because that which was not told them have they seen, and that which they have not heard they have observed.

'Who hath believed this our glad tidings? and the strength of

---

[1] Strack-Billerbeck II, pp. 347f.

[2] Op. cit., loc. cit.

[3] The rendering here followed is that of Driver and Neubauer in *The Fifty-third Chapter of Isaiah according to the Jewish Interpreters* II, pp. 5f.; cf. W. Manson, *Jesus the Messiah*, pp. 168ff., where the translations of M.T. and of the Targum are set out in parallel columns. Cf. also Nyberg's translation of the Targum in *S.E.Å.* vii, 1942, pp. 34f.; and see Seidelin in *Z.N.W.* xxxv, 1936, pp. 194ff.; Staerk, ibid., p. 308.

the mighty arm of the Lord, upon whom as thus hath it been revealed? The righteous will grow up before him, yea, like blooming
shoots, and like a tree which sends forth its roots to streams of
water will they increase—a holy generation in the land that was
in need of him: his countenance no profane countenance, and the
terror at him not the terror at an ordinary man; his complexion
shall be a holy complexion, and all who see him will look wistfully
upon him. Then he will become despised, and will cut off the
glory of all the kingdoms; they will be prostrate and mourning,
like a man of pains and like one destined for sicknesses; and as
though the presence of the Shekhinah had been withdrawn from
us, they will be despised, and esteemed not. Then for our sins he
will pray, and our iniquities will for his sake be forgiven, although
we were accounted stricken, smitten from before the Lord, and
afflicted. But he will build up the Holy Place, which has been
polluted for our sins, and delivered to the enemy for our iniquities;
and by his instruction peace shall be increased upon us, and by
devotion to his words, our sins will be forgiven us. All we like
sheep had been scattered, we had each wandered off on his own
way; but it was the Lord's good pleasure to forgive the sins of all
of us for his sake. He prayed, and he was answered, and ere even
he had opened his mouth he was accepted: the mighty of the
peoples he will deliver up like a sheep to the slaughter and like a
lamb dumb before her shearers; there shall be none before him
opening his mouth or saying a word. Out of chastisements and
punishment he will bring our captives near; the wondrous things
done to us in his days who shall be able to tell? for he will cause the
dominion of the Gentiles to pass away from the land of Israel, and
transfer to them the sins which my people have committed. He
will deliver the wicked into Gehinnom, and those that are rich in
possessions into the death of utter destruction, in order that those
who commit sin may not be established, nor speak deceits with
their mouth. But it is the Lord's good pleasure, to try and to purify
the remnant of his people, so as to cleanse their souls from sin:
these shall look on the kingdom of their Messiah, their sons and
their daughters shall be multiplied, they shall prolong their days,
and those who perform the Law of the Lord shall prosper in his
good pleasure. From the subjection of the nations he will deliver
their souls, they shall look upon the punishment of those that hate
them, and be satisfied with the spoil of their kings: by his wisdom
he will hold the guiltless free from guilt, in order to bring many

into subjection to the Law; and for their sins he will intercede. Then will I divide for him the spoil of many peoples, and the possessions of strong cities shall he divide as prey, because he delivered up his soul to death, and made the rebellious subject to the Law: he shall intercede for many sins, and the rebellious for his sake shall be forgiven'.

Nyberg rightly comments (*S.E.Å.* vii, 1942, pp. 35f.): 'The suffering Servant of the Lord is completely eliminated, and replaced by the victorious and triumphant Messiah, who, in the future, will come and restore Israel. The Targum knows only the exaltation, not the humiliation. . . . In this version, the sufferings, the sickness, the disfigurement, the violent and ignominious death, fall upon the heathen, the adversaries of Israel, and are brought about by the victory of the Messiah! The sheep which have gone astray in liii, 6 are the dispersed Israelites; and the lamb which is led to the slaughter and the ewe which is silent before her shearers are illustrations of how Israel's enemies submit to the Messiah. The power of the nations will depart from the land of Israel; the sins which Israel has committed will light upon her enemies; and the ungodly will be consigned to Gehenna. The remnant of the people will be purified and cleansed from sin; and the Messiah will be the people's intermediary and intercessor before the Lord, so that He may forgive them their sins. Israel is restored; the Messianic age dawns; the Israelites increase in numbers and in length of life; and the Messiah gains universal obedience to the Law among the recalcitrant. The heathen and their strong cities are overthrown; and the Lord allots their spoil to the Messiah, as a reward for risking his life in the fierce wars!'

Here in the Targum we have a complete rewriting of the text, bringing it at every point into agreement with the national, political conception of the Messiah. The only feature in the conception of the Messiah which may be derived from Is. liii is his intercession, which induces the Lord to forgive His people's sins. But this feature, as we have seen (pp. 84, 180, 240f.), does not go beyond what was ascribed to the king in ancient times. In the royal psalms we repeatedly find the king represented as interceding for the people, a role in which the ancient sagas depict David, Solomon, and Hezekiah.

It is also characteristic, first, that the Messianic interpretation of the Servant of the Lord is only one among several rabbinic interpretations;[1] second, that it is never taken far enough to produce a unified conception (see above, pp. 322f.); and third, that this interpretation was very often applied to the Messiah from Ephraim and his sufferings and death in conflict with the heathen.[2] The central idea in Is. liii was never clearly grasped, and did not have any decisive influence on the conception of the Messiah.

14. *The Varying Forms of the Conception of the Messiah*

Finally, it may again be emphasized that the différence between this national conception of the Messiah in later Judaism and that held earlier arises not merely from new elements, but just as much from a change of emphasis. The heightened opposition to everything foreign, and particularly to Rome, which had so abruptly ended the Maccabean dream of freedom, and the steadily increasing dominance exercised by the scribes and the rabbis in matters religious and spiritual, caused other elements in the conception of the Messiah (such as the martial or the transcendental) to receive more prominence. But it must be remembered that all the other features in the older conception of the Messiah are also present, even if they are more in the background. They formed part of the revelation in Scripture; and, as we have seen (pp. 266f., 283), the scribes found the Messiah in a number of passages, which originally did not refer to him, but to the king, or to other figures.

The new element in the conception consists first and foremost of those figures which are derived from the Son of Man, and which have been attributed to the Messiah, without any thought of system or logical consistency, in spite of the fact that in a number of important points they not only differ from the traditional conception of the Messiah, but are often even in fundamental disharmony with it.

As has been said, it is an advantage to present the two conceptions separately, in order to gain a clear and comprehensive view of them. But lest the distinction should be exaggerated and they should appear to be two independent figures, it is appropriate to mention at this point the most important features which were commonly attributed to the Messiah, but had in fact been borrowed from the Son of Man.

First, then, it was the association with the Son of Man which was primarily responsible for the idea of the Messiah as an eternal being (see above, pp. 323ff.).

[1] See North, *The Suffering Servant*, pp. 9–22.　　　[2] See North, op. cit., pp. 15ff.

As the Messiah became a unique and eternal individual, and came to have decisive significance for salvation, and not merely for the exercise of government in the kingdom of the redeemed, it was natural that Jewish theological speculation should also think of him as pre-existent.[1] It is easy, in the light of Old Testament presuppositions, to account for this idea. That any expression or vehicle of God's will for the world, His saving counsel and purpose, was present in His mind, or His 'Word', from the beginning, is a natural way of saying that it is not fortuitous, but the due unfolding and expression of God's own being.[2] This attribution of pre-existence indicates religious importance of the highest order. Rabbinic theology speaks of the Law, of God's throne of glory, of Israel, and of other important objects of faith, as things which had been created by God, and were already present with Him, before the creation of the world.[3] The same is also true of the Messiah. It is said that his name was present with God in heaven beforehand, that it was created before the world, and that it is eternal.[4]

But the reference here is not to genuine pre-existence in the strict and literal sense. This is clear from the fact that Israel is included among these pre-existent entities. This does not mean that either the nation Israel or its ancestor existed long ago in heaven, but that the community Israel, the people of God, had been from all eternity in the mind of God, as a factor in His purpose, as an 'idea' in the platonic sense. It is an ideal pre-existence that is meant. This is also true of references to the pre-existence of the Messiah. It is his 'name', not the Messiah himself, that is said to have been present with God before creation. In Pesikta Rabbati 152b it is said that 'from the beginning of the creation of the world the King Messiah was born, for he came up in the thought (of God) before the world was created'. This means that from all eternity it was the will of God that the Messiah should come into existence, and should do his work in the world to fulfil God's eternal

---

[1] See Weber, *Jüd. Theol.*[2], p. 353; Schürer, *Geschichte*[4] II, pp. 616f.

[2] Cf. Exod. xxv, 9ff.; xxvi, 30; xxvii, 8; Num. viii, 4; the tent of revelation is made in accordance with a pre-existing pattern in heaven; see Schürer, *Geschichte*[4] II, p. 618 n. 22.

[3] See Strack-Billerbeck II, pp. 334ff., where the rabbinic sources are quoted; cf. Weber, *Jüd. Theol.*[2], p. 198.

[4] Genesis Rabbah, i, 4; ii, 4; Leviticus Rabbah, xiv, l; Targum of Jonathan on Zech. iv, 7; Midrash Mishle 67c. See Weber, op. cit., p. 355; Dalman, *Der leidende und sterbende Messias*, p. 247; Klausner, *Die messianischen Vorstellungen des jüdischen Volkes im Zeitalter der Tannaiten*, p. 66; Schürer, *Geschichte*[4] II, pp. 617f.; Bowman in *E.T.* lix, 1947/8, p. 288.

saving purpose. Orthodox Judaism's thought about the pre-existence of the Messiah remained at this stage.[1]

In the Christian period we also find in Judaism the thought that every human soul, including the Messiah, existed beforehand in heaven.[2] It is a real pre-existence that is meant; but it is not something which distinguishes the Messiah from all other men.

But in accordance with a tendency of thought and speech in that age (and, in a measure, in all religion), the abstract conception of an ideal pre-existence, comes to be understood concretely. Popular thought does not distinguish between idea and reality, between ideal and real pre-existence.[3] The thought appears in mythical form, and depicts in concrete terms the manner of the Messiah's pre-existence in heaven. In the late writing Abodat hak-kodesh, the seer beholds the Messiah and Elijah in heaven, and hears them speaking of the time when the Messiah's appearance will be at hand.[4] And we have referred above (p. 330) to the conception in Pesikta Rabbati. It is the influence of the Son of Man which lies behind this, as we shall see below.

It is undoubtedly the influence of the Son of Man which leads to the interpretation in a Messianic sense of 'one like a son of man' in Dan. vii, 13, and of the expression *ben 'āḍām* elsewhere in the Old Testament.[5] This also led, in the rabbinic literature, to the inclusion in the conception of the Messiah of certain other alien elements; but this was sporadic and had no organic connexion with the rabbinic view as a whole. First and foremost, there is the view occasionally expressed by the rabbis, that the Messiah will be revealed in the clouds of heaven.[6] The name Anani, which occurs in the fifth and last generation after Zerubbabel in the Davidic genealogy (1 Chron. iii, 24), is interpreted as 'Cloud man' (*'ānān* = cloud) and taken to refer to the Messiah.[7] But this does

---

[1] See Dalman, op. cit., pp. 245ff. It is hardly possible to read anything more into Resh Lakish's explanation of Gen. i, 2; '"the spirit of God moved upon the face of the waters" is the spirit of the King Messiah'. Schürer, op. cit., p. 618, is probably wrong in thinking that this more abstract, idealistic idea (as contrasted with an older, more realistic idea in apocalyptic) is the result of a reaction against Christianity. There was always a difference between apocalyptic and rabbinic thought.

[2] Strack-Billerbeck II, pp. 340ff.

[3] Moore's view is almost the same (*Judaism* II, p. 344). For Jewish thought, real, personal pre-existence is not a problem, but a quite natural idea.

[4] See Weber, *Jüd. Theol.*[2], pp. 355f.

[5] See Moore, *Judaism* II, pp. 334f.; Bowman in *E.T.* lix, 1947/8, pp. 284ff.; and cf., e.g., the Targum on Ps. lxxx, 15.

[6] Sanhedrin 98a; Jer. Taanit 63d; cf. Sib. V, 414. See Moore, loc. cit.

[7] Sanhedrin 96b; Tanhuma Toledot 20. See Moore, op. cit., II, p. 336.

not mean that the rabbis regarded the Messiah as a heavenly king; he was, and continued to be, a natural descendant of David.[1] The reference is to a wonderful manifestation to the people, by means of a miracle wrought by God, like the revelation of the Messiah on the roof of the temple (see above, p. 303). This is indicated by the words of the Targum, 'This means King Messiah, who will be revealed', and by Rabbi Joshua ben Levi's combination of Zech. ix, 9 ('Behold, your king comes to you; . . . humble ('*ānî*) and riding on an ass') with Dan. vii, 13 ('Behold, with the clouds of heaven there came one like a man') in the following way: 'If they (Israel) are worthy, (he will come) with the clouds of heaven; if they are not worthy, (he will come) poor (insignificant), and riding on an ass'. For a people who are worthy, the Lord will perform the miracle of causing the Messiah to be revealed in radiant majesty; but to an unworthy people, the Messiah will come in humble fashion;[2] and, we may add, by such a people he will not be recognized until he has begun to perform the Messianic works (p. 303), which will free them from affliction, and make them worthy by rigorous purification.

The idea of the Son of Man and the Messianic interpretation of Dan. vii are also the source of the statement that the Messiah shares in the judgement of the world. Judgement, of course, is in God's own hands, and belongs to the coming aeon, which, according to rabbinic thought, follows the Messianic age.[3] This notion appears in rabbinic speculation about the plural 'thrones' in Dan. vii: the one is for the descendant of David, the Messiah (see above, p. 313). But as a rule the rabbis reject the thought that the Messiah (or the Son of Man) shares in the judgement.[4] It comes out more clearly in apocalyptic, where the Son of Man is sometimes called the Messiah, and judges the nations (see pp. 312f.; and cf. below, pp. 393ff.). The Messiah's action in destroying the heathen is probably also the result of influence from the idea of the Son of Man (see above, p. 313).

As the national, Davidic Messiah is not thought of as coming from heaven, so it is not normal Jewish doctrine that he will return thither. This accords with the fact that where the national aspect of eschatology is prominent, the kingdom of the Messiah

[1] Moore, op. cit., II, pp. 347ff.
[2] Cf. Lagrange, *Le Messianisme chez les juifs*, pp. 227f.
[3] See Moore, *Judaism* II, p. 339; and above, p. 277.
[4] Bab. Sanhedrin 38b, 98a; Jer. Taanit 65b; Midrash Tehillim, Ps. xxi, 7. See Lagrange, op. cit., pp. 224ff.

is always a kingdom which will be established here on earth. It is *here* that the Messiah will reign.

Here too, however, ideas of another type leave their mark. We occasionally find it said that the Messiah will restore paradise, which was lost by Adam's fall.

> And he shall open the gates of paradise,
> And shall remove the threatening sword against Adam.
> And he shall give to the saints to eat from the tree of life,
> And the spirit of holiness shall be on them.[1]

Here it is the thought of the Son of Man in his role as king of paradise which has influenced the idea of the Messiah. It may also be detected in 2 Esdras xiii, 12, 39ff., where the Messiah brings home the ten tribes (see below, p. 381f.).

This idea about the Messiah and paradise has a certain connexion with the view, which occurs once in the rabbinic literature, that at the resurrection the Messiah will awake Adam first,[2] or with the statement made in a medieval Jewish document that it is the Messiah who will awake the dead.[3] This is certainly the result of influence from the idea of the Son of Man (see below, pp. 399ff.). Elsewhere the rabbis say that in the days of the Messiah God will abolish death,[4] or that the resurrection will take place then.[5]

15. *The Place of the Messiah in Later Judaism*

We have already noted (pp. 170ff.) that the Messiah is often relegated to the background in Old Testament descriptions of the future, and that he does not appear in a considerable number of late Jewish writings (p.280). This raises the question of the place occupied by the Messiah in Judaism's future hope, and, in general, in its religious thought and piety.

The Gospels would lead us to believe that the idea was a dominant one, familiar to all, and the substance of a general hope throughout Judaism. But we must not forget that the Gospels reflect a particular milieu within Jewish religion and life. Therefore we ought not to be too prone to draw from the Gospels conclusions about thought in literary circles, or among the Pharisees or Sadducees. To a certain extent, the milieu of the Gospels

---

[1] T. Levi xviii, 10f. See Murmelstein in *W.Z.K.M.*, xxxv, 1928, p. 254.
[2] Strack-Billerbeck III, p. 10.
[3] Strack-Billerbeck I, p. 524; see above, p. 319 and n. 3.
[4] Exodus Rabbah, xxx, 3; see Murmelstein, ibid.
[5] See Moore, *Judaism* II, p. 379.

coincides with that represented by the apocalyptic literature and by certain more limited circles. This is evident from the part played, both in apocalyptic and in the Gospels, by the idea of the Son of Man. But we cannot simply assume that these circles were typical of Judaism as a whole. In 'normative Judaism',[1] at all events, apocalyptic fell into some degree of disfavour after A.D. 70 (see above, pp. 295f.).

Again, the fact that in the whole of the Wisdom literature the thought of the Messiah scarcely ever appears (see above, p. 280) gives food for thought. What brought it about that in certain circles the Messianic faith came to count for so little?

We have noted above that, even in the Old Testament, the future hope appears under two aspects. There is the purely religious aspect, which is focused on the thought of the kingly rule of God; and there is the more political aspect, in which the Messiah is more prominent. These are, in fact, two aspects of the same thing, two emphases within the same future hope; and they are not opposed to each other. As, in the religion of Israel, the central article of faith was the sovereign lordship of Yahweh, whereas in experience that lordship was exercised by His king, aided by His priests and prophets, so the heart of the future hope is that Yahweh will again decisively become king, and exercise His unchallenged kingship in the world, whereas the thought of the Messiah expresses the manner in which that lordship will be exercised in actual experience.

This implies, however, that the thought of Yahweh's kingly rule is, for thought and feeling, the more explicitly religious form of the future hope, whereas the thought of the Messiah comes to mind when men ask just how that prosperous future will take shape, and when the political and national side of the hope becomes prominent. The one form is decidedly theocentric; the other more anthropocentric.

This is undoubtedly the reason why, when the rule of the Messiah is taken for granted, only touched upon, or not emphasized, the thought of Yahweh's kingly rule is presented so clearly and boldly by the prophets, those heralds of God, who had stood face to face with God, and knew that their whole lives had been determined by Him.[2] Before the message of the advent and

---

[1] The expression is Moore's, and well represents his view in *Judaism*. Davies (in *E.T.* lix, 1947/8, pp. 233ff.) has clearly shown that we ought not to exaggerate the difference between apocalyptic and rabbinism.

[2] Cf. Isa. xl, 3, 5, 9; lii, 7; lxi, 1f.

kingly rule of Yahweh, everything else, even all the practical concerns of the kingdom, recedes into the background.

Deutero-Isaiah sees the whole drama of the future as the decisive day of Yahweh's enthronement, which is cosmic in its significance. From this all else is derived. The heart of his message is, 'He is coming. Your God has become king'; and that message is echoed by the circle of his disciples (in Isa. lvi–lxvi). Yahweh's coming as king and His triumphal entry by the new *via sacra* is also the central theme in the message of Isa. xxxiv f., which comes from the disciples of Deutero-Isaiah.[1] For the prophet of Isa. xxxiii, also, the supreme expression of the bliss of the future kingdom is that the redeemed may 'see the king in His beauty'. There can be no doubt who the king is:

> For Yahweh is our judge, Yahweh is our ruler,
> Yahweh is our king, who will save us.[2]

It is Yahweh's kingly rule over the world from His temple on Zion that is proclaimed in Isa. ii, 2–4 = Mic. iv, 1–4. The message of the book of Zephaniah reaches its climax in the announcement, 'Yahweh has become king in the midst of you (Jerusalem)' (iii, 15). In Zech. xii–xiv, the conclusion of the great drama of the end time is that all peoples will make pilgrimage to Jerusalem, do homage to the king, the Lord of Hosts, and take part in the celebration of His royal festival (xiv, 16f.). None of these passages mentions the future king, the Messiah.

We are, therefore, justified in saying that when the purely religious aspect of the future hope is prominent, the Messiah is, to a certain extent, neglected.

But, it might be objected, in all these passages the Messiah is taken for granted, as in Isa. lv, 3ff. In His development of historical events, Yahweh needs a king on the earth. That is true. But between what is taken for granted and what is emphasized there is a distinction which is important for thought, and feeling, and judgement. What is taken for granted is often *only* taken for granted.

This is in accord with the impression we derive from the literature of later Judaism. It is significant that it is chiefly the sober and matter-of-fact wisdom poetry and the historical literature which do not give expression to the thought of the Messiah.

[1] See Mowinckel in *G.T.M.M.M.* III, pp. 173ff.
[2] Isa. xxxiii, 17, 22. See *Ps.St.* II, pp. 235ff.; *G.T.M.M.M.* III, pp. 170ff.

This undoubtedly means that the Messiah did not occupy an important place in normal, everyday, religious thought and feeling in these circles.

But what was said above (p. 284) about the many political Messiahs shows that in time of gloom and unrest the thought of the Messiah emerged again in the depths of the national consciousness, setting men's thoughts in a ferment, in virtue of its national and political character. This is understandable. The pressure of evil times gave life to the longing for one who would deliver and restore. An expectation which belonged to the presuppositions of the corpus of inherited, traditional, religious conceptions, was again given contemporary relevance, but in a form corresponding to what every nationally minded Jew might wish, irrespective almost of the measure of his religious enthusiasm. In the same way, during war and occupation, Christian conceptions and ideas have taken on a new meaning, and have to some extent become vital again, even in circles where their conscious influence had previously been small.

There can be no doubt that the thought of the Messiah is not prominent in rabbinic literature. If we attempt (as we must do, if we would gain an orderly survey of the subject) to reduce the religious conceptions of the rabbis to some sort of theological system, it becomes clear that its centre is not the Messiah, but the Law. The rabbis' basic religious principle is the majesty of God, and His actual lordship over the world, and man's submission to it in the form of obedience to God's Law. Besides this, they live in hope of an age when this will be finally realized, when Israel will be restored, and the covenant promises will be fulfilled. The Messianic idea is an expression of this hope. But the dominant theme here is the theocentric thought of the complete and visible realization in actual experience of God's lordship over the world. It is this that will come to pass in the coming aeon.

It is here that we meet the idea that the Messianic kingdom is a more earthly, interim kingdom,[1] which forms a transition between the two aeons, more glorious than the present aeon, but far short of the glory of the coming aeon. This, in fact, became the prevalent, normative view in rabbinic Judaism.[2] The influence of the new, dualistic, transcendental eschatology is certainly at work here.[3] But it is not the sole factor. What in fact has hap-

---

[1] See above, pp. 277, 285, 321, 326.   [2] See Moore, *Judaism* II, pp. 375f.
[3] See Moore, loc. cit.

pened is that the two aspects of the older future hope, the kingship of Yahweh and the kingship of the Messiah, which originally formed a real unity, and expressed the ancient unity of religion and politics, have now been separated. A long process of religious development leads up to this. One factor in that development was the constant deferment of the restoration, the repeated experience of hope ending only in disappointment. A still stronger influence was the deepening understanding of the absolute nature of Yahweh, and the supremacy of the Law in the thought, feeling, and practice of Judaism. Together with this went the tendency to elevate the benefits of salvation to the sphere of the transcendental, which was a consequence of the dualistic view of the world. We must also note the tendency to rationalization in thought, which led to distinctions between the different areas of life: religion and politics no longer formed an inevitable unity. Men began to discuss seriously whether paying tribute to Caesar was compatible with the recognition of the lordship of God and the authority of the Law.[1]

It is obvious that, if account is taken of all this, we cannot lay down the general thesis that 'the person of the Messiah takes pride of place in Jewish eschatology'.[2] A careful distinction must be made between different circles and different periods.

An attempt has also been made recently to maintain that the idea of the Messiah played an important part in the cult of Judaism.[3] No cogent evidence can be adduced in support of this view.[4] The Messiah plays no part in the Jewish cult, except as a subject of prayer. The temple cult was, without qualification, the service of Yahweh and of Him alone. Prayer for the coming of the Messiah may, of course, have been fairly generally assumed to be included in the prayers in the Psalms for the restoration of Israel. In the synagogue the coming of the Messiah was included among all the other benefits of salvation for which prayer was offered. And of course no one will deny that the hope of, and belief in, the Messiah formed a generally accepted element in the Jewish faith.[5] The question is, how essential and central this

---

[1] Mark xii, 14, with parallels; cf. Moore, op. cit. II, p. 375.
[2] Riesenfeld, *Jésus transfiguré*, p. 54.   [3] Riesenfeld, op. cit., pp. 58ff.
[4] See Additional Note XIV.
[5] Rabbi Hillel's words, 'Israel has no Messiah (to come); they enjoyed him in the days of Hezekiah' (Sanhedrin 98b, 99a) are, as Moore says (*Judaism* II, p. 347 n. 2), 'solitary', and were refuted by other rabbis. Hillel did believe in a Messiah, even if he had already come. But this saying suggests that, for Hillel and his circle, the Messiah was not one of the central elements of the faith.

belief was. To which the answer may be given that it was not fundamental, and did not receive equal emphasis in every circle.

There was one milieu in which it was central and fundamental: certain apocalyptic circles. In the Apocalypse of Enoch and the circles which it represents, the figure of the Messiah is so prominent, that at times he seems to be put on equality with God Himself. Here we may justifiably say that we can hear 'the heartbeat of apocalyptic' in the sayings about the Messiah.[1] But, in the first place, apocalyptic ideas and the apocalyptic type of piety should not be treated as fully representative of Judaism. In the second place, we are here dealing, not with the traditional, national, political, this-worldly concept of the Messiah, but with the new, transcendental conception of the Son of Man, which had a quite different religious quality. It is for a Messiah of a new kind that the apocalyptist's heart beats. We must also note that in 2 Enoch the Messiah could be replaced by the advocate which the community has in the exalted Enoch himself, a conception of which there are also traces in 1 Enoch.

But both apocalyptic and its conception of the Messiah were suppressed in normative Judaism (see below, pp. 418f.), partly as a result of the reaction against Christianity. The only traces of the apocalyptic picture of the Messiah which have been left in the conceptions of the rabbis and of the more orthodox literature are certain individual features, and occasionally an increased emphasis on the superhuman, miraculous traits in the Messiah (see above, pp. 333ff.).

But these are the views of individual rabbis, rather than generally accepted doctrine. This is clear, for instance, from the form which the Messianic idea has assumed in modern Judaism.[2] The transcendental element is less prominent; and the national element is emphasized, together with the importance of the Messiah for the coming, universal recognition of Israel's God, the one true God; the lord and creator of the world. The unifying, all-dominant idea in religion is the Law of God, and observance of all its commands to the glory of God. Together with this goes the believer's acceptance of what the Law and the Prophets teach about God

---

[1] Küppers in *Intern. Kirchl. Zeitschrift* xxiii, 1933, p. 251. His supposed proofs of the central importance for Jewish piety and theology of the belief in the Messiah (ibid., pp. 234ff.) are in fact valid only for apocalyptic, and for the conception of the Son of Man.

[2] On the following passage, see Stern, *Die Vorschriften der Thora welche Israel in der Zerstreuung zu beobachten hat.* But cf. also Stauffer in *Z.T.K.* (N.F.), xii, 1931, pp. 165ff., with full references to literature.

and His relationship to mankind, the world, and Israel. Included among these truths of faith is the idea of the Messiah. We read in the twelfth of the thirteen fundamental principles ('*ikkārîm*) which Maimonides laid down: 'I believe with perfect faith in the coming of the Messiah; and, though he tarry, I will wait daily for his coming.'[1] Of this Messiah it is said in an official Jewish religious text-book:[2] 'The restoration of Israel as a state will take place, according to the revelation by the prophets, through a descendant of David, who received the promise that his successors should rule for ever in Israel . . . In his time Jerusalem and the temple will be raised again in unprecedented glory; and the Torah will have unlimited authority as the law and constitution of Israel. For on him the divine spirit of wisdom will rest; and by it he will elucidate all obscurities in the Torah, and turn all hearts to it. By the wisdom of the Messiah and the revival of prophetic judgement, not only will Israel be recalled to the Torah, but all mankind will be brought to acknowledge and honour the only God, who has been revealed in Israel, and to live in accordance with the spirit of the Torah, so that only wisdom, justice, and love will rule on earth.'[3] It is expressly stated that this is 'God's Kingdom on earth'.

Here all the transcendent, other-worldly elements in the conception of the Messiah and in eschatology have disappeared. It is not even clear whether the Messiah is an eternal individual, or the first of several descendants of David. Nor is it clear whether the resurrection and the coming of the Messiah will coincide in time, or new generations arise in the earthly kingdom of God. There seems also to be an irreconcilable opposition between belief in the Messiah as the restorer of Israel as a state, and the view that the restoration which has already taken place (the establishment of the new state of Israel) is the beginning of the fulfilment of the Old Testament prophecies.

In reading orthodox modern Jewish text-books of religion, one gets a strong impression that this thought of the Messiah is by no means central in that unified spiritual structure which the Law has become. Zionism is, therefore, a characteristic phenomenon: a kind of politico-religious 'Messianism' without a Messiah, thought out in terms of immanent political forces, but coloured

[1] Cf. Stern, op. cit., pp. 38f.
[2] See Stern, op. cit., part I 'Ueber die Anerkennung Gottes und seiner Thora', ch. I 'In unseren Vorstellungen und Gedanken', in the paragraph on 'die Zukunft Israels und der Menschheit'.
[3] Stern, op. cit., p. 34.

by a romantic, religous nationalism.[1] Modern, liberal, philosophical Judaism is a still more striking example. There the personal Messiah has usually become the idea of an immanent power, a symbol of the everlasting progress of the human spirit, or of a future perfection which is the goal of evolution.[2]

Thus the idea of the Messiah has varied in importance within Jewish piety. It began as a particular feature of the notion of the kingdom of God, but gradually came to be separated from it in a way which led to the thought of the interim kingdom. It has always preserved its this-worldly, national, and political character, even when associated with a universalistic conception of the kingdom of God on earth, as in modern, orthodox Judaism. It has never been the natural expression of the essentially religious side of the kingdom of God. For this reason, the relation of the two ideas varied at different times. Belief in the Messiah has been strongest in times of national, political, and religious oppression and distress. It is significant that in modern times the Messianic faith has flared up most violently in the mystical Chasidism of Poland, which arose in times of political, social, and economic distress for the Jews. It is also significant that Messianism acquires a strongly political stamp in that context: the Messiah we find there is the national and political deliverer.[3] In settled times the Messianic faith could easily decline to a place among those articles of belief which are taken for granted, and which have no special and immediate relevance for the believer. It has always been subordinate to the thought of the kingly rule of God.[4]

---

[1] References to important books on Zionism are given by Gillet, *Communion in the Messiah*, p. 161 n. 1.

[2] Cf. Stauffer, ibid., pp. 166ff. See further, Wiener in *J.L.* IV, cols. 138f. Wiener emphasizes that these modern conceptions are at variance with the genuine spirit of Judaism, in which he thinks that belief in the Messiah has always been fundamental.

[3] See Ysander, *Studien zum be'štschen Hasidismus*, pp. 38ff.

[4] Gillet (op. cit., pp. 100ff.) exaggerates the place of the Messiah in Judaism. A structural study of Jewish belief shows that the idea is not nearly so central as might appear from a collection of separate Jewish sayings about the Messiah drawn from different ages. The evidence presented by Gillet also shows that the thought of the Messiah has been relegated to the background in modern Judaism. What has survived is the hope of a future 'Messianic' age without a real, personal Messiah; and even this expectation is often expressed in terms of immanent evolution. Stauffer, too, seems to me to exaggerate the place of the Messiah in orthodox modern Judaism. Most of the evidence he adduces (ibid., pp. 174ff.) is derived from ancient (in part, pre-Christian) times, and is not necessarily valid for today. Note that Stern's *Vorschriften der Thora* is an authorized, orthodox text-book. Friediger (*Laerebog i den jødiske Religion*, pp. 92ff.) makes as little of the Messiah as Stern, perhaps even less: here, as always, the Messiah is an earthly figure, 'who will restore Israel to her former splendour and glory'. With this is associated the modern dream, that he 'will bring the peace which will unite mankind in *one* brotherly love'. We are not told how.

It was only in certain apocalyptic circles in later Judaism that the idea became central to the structure of belief and vitally relevant. But this was because it had been transmuted into an essentially different 'Messianic idea', that of the Son of Man, which we must now examine.

CHAPTER X

The Son of Man

1. The Meaning of the Phrase

THE phrase which Jesus uses most frequently to express His mission and sense of vocation is 'the Son of Man'.[1] It is obvious that the Greek expression is an Aramaism, a literal rendering of *bar 'enāš* or *bar nāš*, or, in the definite form, *bar 'enāšā'*, *bar nāšā'*.[2] The corresponding Hebrew expression is *ben 'āḏām* (in the definite form *ben hā'āḏām*). This means literally a 'son of man', a 'child of man'; and it is not a special but a normal expression in Aramaic and Hebrew, which in itself means no more than an individual of the human species, a human being.[3] In these languages, an individual member of a species is commonly denoted by prefixing 'son (of)' to the name of the species. *'Āḏām* alone indicates 'man' in the collective sense, the species mankind. To express the idea of an individual man, we must say *ben 'āḏām*, or in Aramaic *bar nāš*. The Aramaic expression should, therefore (on this there is now complete agreement), really be translated simply 'a man', 'a child of man', or, in the definite form, 'the man'; and it can be applied to any single individual of the species man.[4]

It has been maintained that Jesus did not apply the term to Himself, because it was (so it is assumed) no more than a common expression for any individual man.[5] But even if the expression

---

[1] Sjöberg (*Der Menschensohn*, pp. 40ff.) gives a survey of recent discussions of the term and the concept, with references to the literature; cf. Riesenfeld, *Jésus transfiguré*, pp. 307ff.

[2] Badham's tables, in his article in *T.T.* xlv, 1911, pp. 400ff., do not provide any evidence that the Greek expression in the Gospels represents an Aramaic *bar 'āḏām* = son of Adam. Cf. below, p. 348 n. 3.

[3] It does not mean 'man' in the general sense (= mankind), as in expressions like 'man must suffer', as Schmidt maintains in art. 'Son of Man' in *E.B.*

[4] Wellhausen, *Skizzen und Vorarbeiten* VI, pp. 5ff., 187ff.; *Einleitung in die drei ersten Evangelien*², pp. 123ff.; Dalman, *Words of Jesus*, pp. 234–41; and see now especially the thorough investigation of all the evidence, including the evidence from inscriptions, by Sjöberg in *Act.Or.*, xxi, 1950, pp. 57ff., 91ff. See also Bowman in *E.T.* lix, 1947/8, pp. 283ff.

[5] E.g., by Wellhausen in *Einleitung in die drei ersten Evangelien*², p. 307 n. 1, and Lietzmann in *Der Menschensohn. Ein Beitrag zur neutestamentlichen Theologie*. For the discussion of the subject, see Brun, *Jesu evangelium*², p. 550; E. Meyer, *Ursprung und Anfänge des Christentums* II, p. 335.

was familiar in Galilean Aramaic in the time of Christ, it seems, nevertheless, not to have been *the* common, everyday expression for 'a man'. It seems always to have been used with a certain emphasis.[1] The result of the discussion is that there is no valid linguistic ground for denying either that the expression was a definite Messianic designation in certain circles,[2] or that Jesus could have used it of Himself.[3] Thus the problem concerns the history of ideas, and is not merely a linguistic one.

It is clear that when Jesus calls Himself 'the Man', simpliciter, He gives to this expression, or there is already implicit in it, a specific meaning. 'The Man' (with a capital 'M') is not the same as any man. This is indicated in English by the retention of the traditional but incorrect translation, 'the Son of Man'.

By this term Jesus means to express something essential to His mission as God's representative and the mediator of the kingdom of God; He uses it to interpret His Messianic mission.[4] Thus, in

---

[1] Dalman (*Words of Jesus*, pp. 234ff., cf. 241ff., 256ff.) has argued (on the assumption that Targum Onkelos represents early Palestinian Aramaic) that *bar 'ĕnāšā'* 'did *not* properly belong to the common language of the Palestinian Jews as a term for "man"; it was characteristic rather of the elevated diction of poetry and prophecy' (op. cit., p. 256). To this Bowman objects (*E.T.* lix, 1947/8, p. 286, referring to Kahle, *The Cairo Geniza*, pp. 229ff.) that 'Onkelos is neither Palestinian nor early, but represents an artificial Babylonian dialect. That *Bar-Nash* could be used for "anyone" or "a man" in early Palestinian Aramaic is shown clearly in the early Geniza fragments of the Palestinian Pentateuch Targum, for in Gen. iv, 14, *Bar-Nash* is used for "anyone", while in Gen. ix, 5–6. *Bar-Nasha* (thrice) and *Bar-Nash* (twice) alike translate *Ha-Adam* man'.
Sjöberg (ibid.), too, has corrected Dalman on this point, but maintains that, even so, the expression seems to have been used with a certain emphasis.
[2] So Dalman (see previous note); Bousset, *Relig.*[2], p. 305 ([3], p. 266) n. 1. The evidence for this is the use of the expression in the Apocalypse of Enoch and in Dan. vii, as we shall see below.
[3] Bousset, *Relig.*[2], p. 307 n. 2; Dalman, *Words of Jesus*, pp. 250ff.; Héring, *Le royaume de Dieu et sa venue*, pp. 88ff.; Brun, *Jesu evangelium*[2], pp. 545ff.; W. Manson, *Jesus the Messiah*, pp. 113ff. Campbell (in *J.T.S.* xlviii, 1947, pp. 145ff.) holds that Jesus could not have applied the term to Himself as a Messianic designation, because He could not have taken the phrase or the conception from so 'stupid' a book as the Enoch Apocalypse, and because Jesus was not interested in apocalyptic. But the entire eschatological outlook of Jesus, and not least the conception of the two aeons and of Satan's dominion in the present aeon, show that He and His environment were both influenced by the view which apocalyptic represents. To become familiar with these conceptions, Jesus need not, of course, have read any book. The ideas were common property within certain milieux, which were the background of the conceptions which Jesus held. It is a question, not of literary influences, but of traditions and ideas which were in circulation. Campbell, on the other hand, holds that Jesus used the expression of Himself in the sense 'this man' (I), by analogy with the periphrasis 'Thy servant' (as in Ps. xix, 12, and elsewhere) for the first person. The presupposition underlying this view is that in the time of Jesus 'the Man' was not a generally understood eschatological designation of the Messiah. But Campbell has not succeeded in disposing of the testimony of the Enoch Apocalypse and other sources that this was so. Cf. below, p. 356 and n. 6. Parker (*J.B.L.* lx, 1941, pp. 151ff.) maintains that 'the Son of Man' is a prophetic title.
[4] Cf. Dalman, *Words of Jesus*, 256ff.; see below, pp. 445ff.

order to understand the teaching of Jesus, it is important to determine what He means by 'the Son of Man', the more so since the expression was not a customary Messianic designation in general use.[1]

It is clear that Jesus was not the originator of this expression, which He uses to express His part in the establishment of the kingdom of God.[2] Before His time it was used, in certain circles, in Jewish religious phraseology, to denote a person who in many ways corresponds to the Messiah. It may even be said to have been used, in some of these circles, as a designation of the Messiah. By Jesus' time it had already acquired a certain content; and when He used it, it suggested to His hearers a number of definite conceptions of the mission and message of the Man who applied it to Himself.[3]

It is not, however, probable that Jesus simply took the expression in the same sense as it had before Him; since Jesus and His message represent an advance on all who had previously proclaimed the kingdom of God. But even before Him the phrase must already have included essential elements of what Jesus wanted to say about Himself; otherwise He would not have adopted it, and allowed it almost completely to supersede the title of Messiah and other titles He might have applied to Himself. If, therefore, we would understand fully what Jesus means by calling Himself 'the Son of Man', we must first discover what the phrase stood for in the religious terminology of later Judaism.

2. The Son of Man in Daniel vii and the Older Sources of Daniel

Earlier generations of scholars, who were not fully aware of the late Jewish background of the Gospels, held for the most part that Jesus had taken the expression 'Son of Man' directly from the Old Testament, and, in particular, from Dan. vii, and that there it is already used as a Messianic designation. When it became known that conceptions of the Son of Man were also to be found in late Jewish writings, which were earlier than the time of Jesus, it was

[1] Dalman, op. cit., pp. 241ff.; see below, pp. 364ff.
[2] Völter (Die Menschensohnfrage) has maintained that Jesus Himself coined this Messianic title, taking up the phrase 'son of man' (ben 'ādām) applied to Ezekiel. Holzinger (in the Buddefestschrift, pp. 102ff.) has decisively refuted this hypothesis.
[3] Badham (in T.T. xlv, 1911) appears to hold that before Jesus the expression had no special meaning whatsoever, and that it was He who gave it one. This view, of course, is possible only if all the Son of Man passages in 1 Enoch are deleted as Christian interpolations, as is done by Messel in Der Menschensohn in den Bilderreden des Henoch; see Badham, ibid., pp. 443-7. Campbell argues, too (see above, p. 347 n. 3; cf. p. 356 n. 6), that these passages are Christian interpolations in 1 Enoch. See below, p. 354.

contended that the idea was of purely scribal origin, and based solely on the exegesis of Old Testament passages.[1] Apart from the vocative 'O son of man' (child of man, man), addressed to Ezekiel, it was chiefly the vision of the beasts in Dan. vii that was thought of.

But it is in itself highly improbable that what was extracted from a passage of scripture by theological and exegetical treatment could have been the sole ground of a conception so important, so manifold in its development, and so widely circulated as the Son of Man.[2] An analysis of the contents of Dan. vii provides a clear refutation of the view.

In its present form the vision of the beasts in Dan. vii comes from the time just before 165 B.C. The seer beholds four fabulous monsters coming up out of the sea. They ravage the earth, and exercise a reign of terror. The fourth is the worst of them. It has ten horns, in addition to which there grows up an eleventh, which plucks up three of the others, and which has 'eyes like a man's eyes, and a mouth which speaks great things'. Clearly the meaning is that the four beasts succeed and supplant each other, and that the fourth unites in itself all the power and cruelty of its predecessors. Then the seer beholds that 'thrones were placed, and an Ancient of Days took His seat; His raiment was white as snow, and the hair of His head was like wool; His throne was flames of fire, and its wheels were ablaze. A stream of fire flowed forth and went out from them; a thousand thousands served Him; ten thousand times ten thousand stood before Him. The court took its seat, and the books were opened.' Judgement was passed, and the beast (i.e., the fourth beast, which united in itself all the power of its predecessors) was killed and burned. 'And behold, with the clouds of heaven there came one like a man (literally, "a son of man"); and he came to the Ancient of Days, and he was presented to Him. And to him was given dominion, and glory, and kingdom—that all peoples, nations, and tongues should serve him; his dominion shall be an everlasting dominion, which shall not pass away, and his kingdom a kingdom which shall not be destroyed.' In what follows, the seer beholds the interpretation of this vision. The four beasts signify four kings, or, rather, four empires,[3] which will arise (and supplant each other) on the earth.

---

[1] Schürer, *Geschichte*[4] II, p. 614; E. Meyer, *Ursprung und Anfänge des Christentums* II, p. 545. Ström, *Vetekornet*, p. 136, seems to hold this out-of-date and untenable view.
[2] The idea is decisively refuted by Bousset, *Relig.*[2], pp. 304ff., [3], pp. 265ff.
[3] See Rowley, *Darius the Mede and the Four World Empires in the Book of Daniel*, pp. 161ff.

The fourth is the worst and the most ungodly of these kingdoms. 'It shall devour the whole earth, and trample it down, and crush it.' The ten horns mean that out of this kingdom ten kings shall arise; and after them another shall arise, who shall be different from the former ones; and he shall put down three kings. He shall speak words against the Most High, and shall wear out the saints (plural, i.e., Israel) of the Most High'. It is clear that this refers to the kings of the Macedonian kingdom in Syria, and especially to the persecutor and blasphemer, Antiochus IV.[1] But when his time is ended ('a time, two times, and a half a time'), 'the court shall take its seat, and his dominion shall be taken away from him . . . ; and the sovereignty, and the dominion, and the greatness of the kingdoms under heaven shall be given to the people of the saints of the Most High (i.e., the people which consists of those who are consecrated to the Most High); . . . and all (other) dominions shall serve and obey them'.

The interpretation which Daniel receives in the vision clearly means that, as the four beasts are pictorial symbols for the four world kingdoms, which will supplant each other (the neo-Babylonian, the Median, the Persian and the Syro-Macedonian,[2]) so the Son of Man figure is a symbol for 'the people of the saints of the Most High', namely God's people in Israel. It is explicitly emphasized that it is this *people* which will finally receive the dominion. The vision indicates that during the period of Israel's affliction, from the exile until the restoration, four tyrannous kingdoms will supplant each other in holding dominion over the earth. The last will be the worst; and its last king will distinguish himself by blasphemous speech against the true God, and by bloody oppression of His people (the religious persecution under Antiochus). But when the time decreed by God is at an end, the world empire of the people of God will be established, and dominion will be given to Israel.

Thus in the present form of Daniel's visions of the beasts, the Son of Man is a pictorial symbol of the people of Israel, not an individual figure, and not a personal Messiah of any kind.[3]

---

[1] See Baumgartner, *Das Buch Daniel*, cols. 12f.

[2] See Bentzen, *Daniel²*, pp., 25, 39, 6of., 65ff.; Rowley *Darius the Mede and the Four World Empires in the Book of Daniel*, pp. 67–160.

[3] Ström, *Veterkornet*, pp. 136ff., would deny this plain fact, and asserts that the Son of Man is an individual figure, who is 'identical with' the people of Isra . He argues on the assumption of an ancient 'collectivistic' idea, which has been deservedly criticized by Edsman (*S.T.K.* xxi, 1945, pp. 272ff.; cf. *Kyrkohistorisk årsskrift*, xliv, 1944, 356ff.). Dahl also holds this unreasonable view (*Das Volk Gottes*, p. 90), and

But it is also clear, as scholars have for long pointed out,[1] that these symbols (the monsters who come up from the sea in the last times, and the man who comes with the clouds of heaven) were not *invented* by the seer to represent his thoughts, and did not arise spontaneously in his imagination during his visionary experience. As so often, the seer is using traditional material. Conceptions which were already present in his mind come forward in the vision, and are used as pictures, and symbolically re-interpreted in terms of what he wants to say, or what has been given him to say. If the pictures had arisen instantaneously as the allegorical expression of the seer's thought, one would expect them not to include any features other than those which have a counterpart in the interpretation. But the descriptions of the animals and of the figure like a son of man include several features which are not included in the interpretation. Why do the beasts come up from the sea? Why are we told about the four winds which made the sea bring forth? We can understand why the people of God are represented by a human form, in contrast with the heathen powers; but why is it said that the Man comes with the clouds of heaven, without any interpretation of this point? Israel was a people of this world like other peoples. Other points might be added. We must therefore conclude that the seer of Daniel vii (or the tradition which he represents)[2] was already familiar with the conceptions of a 'Man' such as this, who would one day come with the clouds of heaven, and that it was natural for the seer to use him as a symbol for

[1] See Gunkel, *Schöpfung und Chaos*, pp. 323ff.; Volz, *Eschatologie*[2], p. 280; Gressmann, *Der Messias*, pp. 343ff., 365ff., etc.

[2] Several attempts have been made to distinguish those details for which the seer is responsible from those which he took over from tradition. See the references to the literature in Bentzen, *Daniel*. Hölscher (in *T.S.K.*, 1919, pp. 133ff.), Bentzen, and others have held that it is possible to trace an earlier, pre-Maccabean vision, which Daniel revised in the Maccabean period. The theme of the four empires is, of course, itself older than Daniel. This is clear from Dan. ii, which forms, with the rest of i–vi, a literary stratum which is older than Daniel. But vii is, in all essentials, a single, *literary* composition, which plainly alludes to Antiochus IV (see Ginsberg, *Studies in Daniel*). But, of course, no verdict on the age of the content and the themes is thereby implied.

speaks of an 'individual-collective duality', a 'primitive' conception which is quite inconceivable at a period like that of rabbinic Judaism when thought was, in fact, so rational. This method of removing contradictions between varying conceptions in the sources is an exaggeration of the modern insight into the ancient view of the relationship between the individual and the community, which has been expounded in relation to Israel by Pedersen (*Israel* I–II). In ancient times men were aware of the difference between the community and the individual person who represented it, and, in certain situations, was its symbolic embodiment, conveying power by sharing the life of its soul. Cf. above, pp. 50, 83f. Lagrange (*Le judaïsme avant Jésus-Christ*, p. 66) also retains the individual interpretation of the 'one like a son of man', and describes as 'rationalistic exegesis' the interpretation which is, in fact, the apocalyptist's own.

Israel.[1] It is difficult to say with certainty whether this figure lay before him as an element in a longer, connected narrative (a 'myth'), in which the monsters from the sea also played a part, or whether the picture in Dan. vii was composed by the seer or by his apocalyptic tradition from symbols and other individual features, partly borrowed and partly newly devised.

Thus we can conclude from Dan. vii that about 200 B.C. or earlier there was in Judaism a conception of a heavenly being in human form ('one like a man'),[2] who, at the turn of the age, the dawn of the eschatological era, would appear, and would receive from God delegated power and authority over all kingdoms and peoples. He seems also to play a part in the judgement of the world, which precedes the transfer of power to him, and which is plainly involved in his enthronement as lord of the world. It is stated in the vision that 'thrones (plural) were placed'; but afterwards only one (the Ancient of Days) is mentioned as taking his seat. Why, then, is there more than one throne?[3] Since the seer has reinterpreted the figure as a symbol of Israel in conflict with the beasts, he naturally cannot use what is presumably a traditional feature in the narrative, that the one in human form sits on one of the thrones to give judgement. In the vision it is God who assigns dominion to him; and, therefore, he must be presented before the Ancient of Days. But the retention of the plural, 'thrones', shows that, in the original conception, the one in human form took part in the judgement of the world. He was thought of as sharing God's throne, a divine being in human form.

It is clear that there is a connexion between the Son of Man and this figure which lies behind Dan. vii. The connexion appears in the clear allusion made by Jesus to Dan. vii, when He predicted, in the presence of His judges, that the Son of Man would come with the clouds of heaven.[4] In fact, the conception of the Son of Man was the traditional material, which was available to the seer

[1] See the clear demonstration, surveying the underlying, mythological material, in Baumgartner, *Das Buch Daniel*, cols. 14f.

[2] This expression implies not merely that he had a certain likeness to a man, but that he was wholly in human form, by contrast with other supernatural beings, who might be wholly or partly in animal form, such as the cherubs in Ezek. i, or the four living creatures (literally 'animals') in Rev. iv, 7ff. The Hebrew and Armaic k^e, like the Accadian *kîma*, expresses not only similarity, but also full identity; see Cook, *The Old Testament: a Reinterpretation*, p. 105; Engnell, *Divine Kingship*, p. 29 n. 2.

[3] Rabbi Akiba was aware of this problem, and suggested 'One for Him (i.e., God) and one for David (i.e., the Messiah)'. See Moore, *Judaism* II, p. 337; Lagrange, *Le messianisme chez les juifs*, pp. 224f.

[4] Mark xiii, 26; xiv, 62, and parallels.

of Dan. vii, and which he reinterpreted as a symbol of the people of Israel. It is because of the reinterpretation and the juxtaposition with the beasts that Daniel does not use the name 'Son of Man' of him, but speaks of 'one like a man'.

Thus we can add still another feature to the conception of the heavenly being on which Dan. vii is based, namely that he was called simply 'the Man'. He must have had a special characteristic, which distinguished him from all the other heavenly beings (angels and spirits) who surround God in heaven. He must have been such that there were reasonable grounds for calling him 'the Man', although he was divine and heavenly.

If, then, Daniel himself knew, and gave a symbolic interpretation of, an older conception of a heavenly Man, the conceptions of the Son of Man in Jewish apocalyptic and in the teaching of Jesus Himself do not go back only to a Messianic interpretation of Dan. vii. In Daniel the conception is used as a symbol; and only those features in the figure are included which are appropriate to the allegorical interpretation in terms of Israel's divine kingdom and world dominion.

The figure of the Son of Man reappears in other pre-Christian, Jewish sources. There it has a number of specific, organically connected features, which do not appear in Daniel, and which cannot have been derived from the picture there, even by the methods of rabbinic exegesis. The same is true of the sayings of Jesus about the Son of Man. We return to these features later.

Thus the conception of the Son of Man existed in Judaism independently of Dan. vii.[1] All the variant forms of it which occur, including Dan. vii, must be dependent on earlier conceptions, which were in circulation in some circles in later Judaism, and which Enoch presents directly, whereas Daniel gives a symbolic reinterpretation.[2]

3. The Sources

Apart from Dan. vii, the chief source for the Son of Man conception is the Similitudes in the Ethiopic Book of Enoch (1 En. xxxvii–lxxi).[3] Whatever view one may take of the literary origin

---

[1] Cf. Reitzenstein, *Das iranische Erlösungsmysterium*, pp. 120f.

[2] It would be remarkable if an interpretation of the 'one like a man' in Dan. vii, which, in relation to Daniel's own interpretation, would be wrong (taking the figure to be the Messiah, instead of the people of Israel), should indicate correctly the meaning which the conception had before Daniel interpreted it as a symbol for the people.

[3] It is probable that this complex includes sections which are secondary. It is generally agreed that these include the Noachic sections (vi–ix; xxxix, 1–2a; liv,

and composition of Enoch, it is generally accepted that the Similitudes form an independent complex of tradition, which had a separate, literary existence before being incorporated in 1 Enoch as we now have it.[1] Whether they are themselves a literary unit, or are composed of several sources,[2] is of no particular interest for our present subject. The teaching contained in them forms a unity, dominated by the same basic thought: the fate of the righteous and the ungodly, and the eschatological role of the Son of Man as judge of the world and ruler of the righteous.

It is now generally agreed that the Apocalypse of Enoch is a Jewish book.[3] Nor is there any real division of opinion on the Jewish origin of the Similitudes.[4] On the other hand, attempts have often been made, and are still made, to maintain that the passages which speak of the Son of Man are later Christian insertions in the text, or adaptations of it.[5] Lagrange accepts the hypothesis of two literary sources in the Similitudes, of which one speaks of 'the Elect One', and the other of the Son of Man; and he holds that the latter is of Christian origin.[6] Messel has maintained that the term 'the Son of Man' is usually a later insertion, or replaces another expression, and also that the expression 'the Elect One' was inserted later in several passages.[7] In the few

[1] See Sjöberg, op. cit., pp. 1ff.
[2] On theories of sources, see Beer, ibid.; Charles, *The Book of Enoch translated*[2], pp. 64f.; Sjöberg, op. cit., p. 24. Sjöberg gives a convincing refutation of them, op. cit., pp. 25ff.
[3] On the attempts of von Hoffmann, Weisse, and Philippi to treat the book as Christian, see Sjöberg, op. cit., pp. 3ff., where the decisive arguments against the theory are repeated with added force.
[4] Hilgenfeld's attempt to show that they are Christian (*Die jüdische Apokalyptik in ihrer geschichtlichen Entwickelung*, pp. 150ff.; and in *Z.W.T.* xxxv, 1892, pp. 445ff.) is for the most part abandoned, and has been decisively refuted, e.g., by Sjöberg, op. cit., pp. 6ff.
[5] This was first suggested by B. Bauer, and was fully and more precisely presented, with supporting arguments, by Drummond (*The Jewish Messiah*, pp. 17ff.), and later by Pfleiderer (*Das Urchristentum*, pp. 312ff.), Bousset (*Jesu Predigt in ihrem Gegensatz zum Judentum*, pp. 105ff.), Messel (see below), Badham, Campbell, and others. Bousset later gave up the theory (*Relig.*[2], pp. 13, 301ff.).
[6] *Le judaïsme avant Jésus-Christ*, pp. 224ff. Lagrange is decisively refuted by Sjöberg, op. cit., pp. 17ff.
[7] *Der Menschensohn in den Bilderreden des Henoch*. Messel holds that the expression 'the Elect One' is original only from xlvi onwards, and that all the Son of Man passages after xlviii, 2 are secondary. On the basis of exegetical arguments which he feels must be advanced against most of the passages (but which, in fact, represent an unduly logical, modern approach), Messel assumes that xlvi, 3 and xlviii, 3 must be textually unsound, because these passages cannot be accommodated to his collective interpretation.

7–lv, 2; lx; lxv–lxix, 25), which form a separate complex of tradition from the same Enochian circles, but were interpolated into the Similitudes at a later stage. xlii is probably also later. See the survey and discussion by Beer (*A.P.A.T.* II, pp. 224ff.), Charles (*A.P.O.T.* II, pp. 163ff.), and Sjöberg (*Der Menschensohn*, pp. 33ff.).

passages which survive,[1] he holds that 'the Elect One' has the same meaning as 'the elect (ones)', and denotes the people of Israel. He also thinks that 'the Son of Man' is a personification of Israel, as in Daniel vii.[2] But none of these theories can be held save on arbitrary grounds; and Sjöberg has decisively refuted all the objections to the authenticity of the passages and the integrity of the text.[3] Once it is clear that the conception of the Son of Man in Dan. vii had an earlier history on Jewish soil, there is no valid reason for suspecting the conceptions of the heavenly Son of Man in Enoch. To interpret this figure in Enoch as a symbol for the community of the chosen then becomes impossible.[4]

Different views have also been held about the date of the Similitudes.[5] The question is bound up with the interpretation of the kings and mighty ones of the earth, who oppress the righteous. Several hold that the reference is to Jewish rulers, and put the Similitudes in the later Maccabean period.[6] But the reference is really to heathen empires and kings;[7] and it is, therefore, most probable that the Similitudes originated in the Roman period;[8] but the latest part of the Maccabean period is not impossible.[9] There is no ground for coming down into the Christian period. The problem of more precise dating is, however, not so important for the history of the idea of the Son of Man; for, as has been said, it is certain that the author has put into writing older traditions from apocalyptic circles.[10]

The Apocalypse of Enoch is extant only in an Ethiopic text, which is a translation of a Greek version. In recent times some

---

[1] Messel admits that he can advance no objection to the substance or form of xlv, 3c. What then becomes of his whole hypothesis?

[2] T. W. Manson (*The Teaching of Jesus*[2], p. 228; cf. 'The Son of Man in Daniel, Enoch and the Gospels', *B.J.R.L.* xxxii, 2, 1950), also holds the collective interpretation of 'the Elect One'. Messel is obliged to admit that xlix, 3 also does not suit this interpretation (see above, n. 1), but consoles himself with the fact that it is a quotation from Isa. xi, 2. But when Enoch quotes Isa. xi, 2, it is because he believes that the thought accords with his own.

[3] Op. cit., pp. 14–24.

[4] Against the collective interpretation, see p. 354 n. 7, and nn. 1, 2 above cf. Sjöberg, op. cit., pp. 14ff.; Taylor, *Jesus and His Sacrifice*, pp. 24ff.

[5] See the introductions and references to the literature in Beer (*A.P.A.T.* II, pp. 231f.) and Charles (*A.P.O.T.* II, pp. 163ff.); cf. also Messel, *Der Menschensohn in den Bilderreden des Henoch*, pp. 78f.; Schürer, *Geschichte*[4] II, pp. 279f.; Sjöberg, op. cit., pp. 35ff.

[6] E.g. Dillmann, Charles, Beer, and Bertholet.

[7] See Messel, op. cit., pp. 79ff.; Sjöberg, op. cit., pp. 36ff.

[8] So Schürer, Messel, and Sjöberg.

[9] In lvi, 5, the enemy is the Parthians. This fits best the time shortly before 63 B.C.

[10] This is shown, for example, by the inconsistency between lxx and lxxi; see below, pp. 284ff.

portions of the Greek text have been found.[1] This Greek text is itself undoubtedly a translation of a Semitic original; but it is still disputed whether this was in Hebrew or Aramaic. Most probably it was in Hebrew.[2]

In addition to the Ethiopic Enoch, there is also a Slavonic Enoch, which presumably is earlier than the fall of Jerusalem in A.D. 70.[3]

Another important book is the Ezra Apocalypse (2 Esdras), written in Hebrew in the time of Domitian, but now known only in Latin, Syriac, Ethiopic, Arabic, and Armenian versions, which all go back to a lost Greek version. But the Ezra Apocalypse is only a new, slightly revised edition of an earlier Shealtiel Apocalypse, which was probably written shortly after the death of Nero, and before the destruction of Jerusalem.[4]

There is also the Syriac Apocalypse of Baruch (2 Baruch), which was also originally written in Hebrew, and is usually considered to be a little later than the Apocalypse of Ezra, but should rather be placed just after the Shealtiel Apocalypse, which it used as a source.[5]

These books, then, are the sources for our knowledge of Jewish conceptions of the Son of Man.[6] But it must be noted that in the

[1] The first part (i–xxxii, 6) was found in a parchment manuscript in the excavations at Achmim in Egypt in 1886-7. A number of fragments are known from the Byzantine writer Syncellus (ca. A.D. 800) and from a Vatican manuscript. These passages are printed in Swete's edition of the Septuagint. More recently, the ending of the Greek text has been found, and was published by Bonner (*The Last Chapters of Enoch in Greek*).

[2] See the survey of the evidence given by Beer (*A.P.A.T.* II, pp. 217ff.) and Charles in *A.P.O.T.* II, pp. 171ff. Charles maintains that it was originally in both languages: i–v; xxxvii–cvi in Hebrew; vi–xxxvi in Aramaic. The problem appears to be nearer a solution as a result of the discovery of the 'Ain Feshkha manuscripts. Among the scrolls there is one which contains *in Aramaic* the Lamech or Noah Apocalypse, which is mentioned in a Greek Christian list of apocryphal books (see Schürer, *Geschichte*[4] III, pp. 358f.) and which clearly has been worked into the Enoch Apocalypse (see above, p. 353 n. 3, on the Noachic sections). See Trever in *B.A.S.O.R.*, 115, Oct. 1949, pp. 8ff. This might suggest that the Enoch Apocalypse, too, was originally in Aramaic, at least in part. Nothing further can be said, of course, until the new text is fully deciphered and examined in detail.

[3] See Bonwetsch, *Die Bücher der Geheimnisse des Henoch. Das sogenannte slavische Henochbuch*, p. xviii.

[4] See Torrey in *Munera studiosa. Studies Presented to W.L.P. Hatch*, pp. 23ff.

[5] See the above-mentioned essay by Torrey. It is usually thought that it was the Apocalypse of Ezra that Baruch used; but Torrey's arguments that it was Shealtiel seem decisive.

[6] Campbell (in *J.T.S.*, xlviii, 1947, pp. 145ff.) tries to discount the value of 1 Enoch as evidence for Jewish ideas about the Son of Man, by pointing out that it is extant only in a late translation, which is full of errors, and in late manuscripts, which have a long and confused history behind them. These difficulties do exist; but careful and methodical criticism can discern the leading ideas in the milieu from which the Enoch translations come. Nor should the literary composition of the book (which seems to the modern mind so confused) be used as an argument against its value as evidence of the thought of the apocalyptists.

apocalypses of Shealtiel, Ezra, and Baruch we do not find the conception of the Son of Man in a pure and unalloyed form. What we do find is, in the main, the figure of the national Messiah, with the title of Messiah, but amplified by a number of supernatural features derived from the Son of Man. This may be seen in the Apocalypse of Ezra, for instance, where the Messiah is a mortal man of David's line, and his kingdom an interim kingdom before the new aeon,[1] but where, nevertheless, he is revealed in a supernatural manner, and displays features which belong to the conception of the king of paradise.

To these more important sources we may add the Targums. They interpret the expression 'son of man' in Ps. viii, 5 and cxliv, 3 (where it really means any human being) and in Ps. lxxx, 18 (where it means 'the man', indicating the people of Israel) of the Messiah.[2] There are also echoes of the idea of the Son of Man in the Jewish Sibylline Oracles.[3]

The rabbis, too, knew of the identification which we find in the Targums, as is shown, for instance, when they interpret the 'one like a man' in Dan. vii, 13 of the Messiah, or take Anani, the last descendant of David, in 1 Ch. iii, 24, as the 'Cloud Man', the one who comes with the clouds of heaven, the Messiah-Son-of-Man.[4] But neither in the Targums nor in the rabbis is there any question of more than a transference of individual features from the Son of Man to the national Messiah. The conception is not borrowed in its entirety.[5]

The Revelation of St. John is in accord with the late Jewish apocalypses on the question of the Son of Man. In recent times it has been clearly recognized that the materials which the seer uses as symbols for his thoughts (what he did not himself devise, and what was not unknown to him when it came to him in revelations concerning the imminent coming of Christ and the final distress and judgement), the symbolic pictures, were in the main derived from the apocalyptic tradition in later Judaism, upon which Daniel, Enoch, Shealtiel, Ezra, and Baruch also drew.[6] In all its essential features, John's portrayal of the eschatological

---

[1] Cf. W. Mundle in *Z.A.W.*, xlvii, 1929, pp. 226f.

[2] For traces of the Messianic interpretation of Ps. viii, 5f., see Strack-Billerbeck III, p. 682.

[3] Sib. V, 414; cf. III, 46–50, 652. Cf. Moore, *Judaism* II, pp. 335.

[4] Sources in Strack-Billerbeck I, pp. 67, 486, 856f.; cf. Moore, op. cit. II, pp. 335ff.

[5] See above, pp. 322, 332f., cf. 266f., 283.

[6] See Mosbech, *Johannes's Aabenbaring*, pp. vii ff.; *Fortolkningen af Johannes's Aabenbaring i Fortid og Nutid*, pp. 77ff.

world drama is in agreement with that of the Jewish apocalyptists, except that he gives it a Christian interpretation in the light of the revelation in Christ and faith in Him. The correspondence with the framework and the fundamental ideas of late Jewish apocalyptic is particularly striking in the great picture of the last judgement in Rev. xix, 11–xxi, 8.[1] With the exception of those features which arise from experience of Christ's victorious suffering, death, and resurrection, the part played by Christ corresponds exactly to that of the Son of Man in apocalyptic. It is true that John does not use the expression 'Son of Man'. But the connexion with the older tradition is plain enough, when he describes Christ as 'one like a son of man' (i, 13). The Revelation of St. John may, therefore, be safely used as a source for the late Jewish conception of the Son of Man, provided it is used with sufficient caution.

The Gospels must also be considered. From what Jesus (or, at times, the Evangelists) says about the Son of Man, conclusions can sometimes be drawn about the Jewish conceptions which form the background of their words. This is particularly true of the eschatological discourse in Mark xiii, where most scholars think that Mark is directly or indirectly dependent on a Jewish, or Jewish Christian, apocalypse, which in some measure expresses Jewish conceptions.

4. *The Eschatological Character of the Son of Man.*

The first thing to be said of the Son of Man is that he is an eschatological figure.[2] He has not yet appeared; but in the last times he will be revealed (see below, pp. 388ff.). The presupposition of the allegorical use which Daniel made of the figure is that the coming of the Son of Man means the end of the heathen human empires of this aeon, and the dawn of the kingdom of God. In the Similitudes of Enoch, the eschatological transformation is the sole theme, which is presented in constantly changing figures. With this transformation the Son of Man is associated.[3] Enoch speaks of the elect righteous ones, to whom the Son of Man will one day appear, who form the congregation which will then appear, when the sinners have been punished and extirpated from the earth.[4] These elect ones are those 'whose elect works hang

[1] See Moore, *Judaism* II, pp. 339ff.
[2] Cf. Sjöberg, *Der Menschensohn*, pp. 61ff.; cf. also his contribution to *28:e Svenska Läroverksläraremötet i Stockholm*, 1946, pp. 254ff.
[3] Sjöberg, *Der Menschensohn*, p. 61.
[4] 1 En. xxxviii, 1ff., etc.

upon the Lord of Spirits'. The reference is clearly to the eschatological Israel, which will appear purified and glorified in the new
aeon (see below, pp. 379f.). To them the Righteous One will
appear.

This eschatological activity is his true task. Before the world
was created, the Lord of Spirits also created, chose, and preserved
him in order that by him all who dwell on earth should one day
fall down before God, and worship, praise, and extol the Lord of
Spirits (1 En. xlviii, 5). God will be acknowledged as God; His
name will be hallowed throughout the world; to this end the Son
of Man is who he is.

He fulfils this purpose in two ways: by saving the righteous, and
by condemning and destroying the wicked, who oppose God's
purpose and oppress the righteous.[1]

1 Enoch often refers to the righteousness of the Son of Man (see
below, pp. 366, 377f.). In a number of passages it is clear that
this means that he wins for the righteous their right, and this is
synonymous with his saving them: his righteousness is his saving
work (pp. 378f.). The important point in this connexion, however, is that the reference is to the eschatological judgement and
salvation. His real work belongs to the last times. The most high
has kept him 'unto the end of the days'.

> The Most High regarded his (the fourth beast's) times—
> And lo! they were ended;
> And his ages—
> (and) they were fulfilled.

When the times are ended, the Son of Man's activity begins; he
inaugurates 'the Age which is not yet awake', at the time which is

> the consummation of that which is corruptible,
> And the beginning of that which is not corruptible,

at 'the consummation of the times'.[2] This is also implied by the
conception that the Son of Man, is still hidden and preserved,[3]
namely, to be used when his time comes. All Enoch's visions
about the Son of Man are concerned with this change from one
age to another. As we shall see, the Son of Man was present at
the beginning; and he will also play a leading part at the end.

---

[1] 1 En. xlviii, 2–10; xli, 9; similarly 2 Esdras xii, 32ff.
[2] 2 Esdras xii, 32; xi 36–45; xiv, 9; vii, 26ff., 31; 2 Bar. lxxiv, 2; lxxvi, 2.
[3] See below, pp. 386f.; and further, 1 En. xl, 5; xlviii, 3, 6; lxii, 7; 2 Esdras xii, 32; xiii, 26.

from the older eschatology are found elsewhere in the Apocalypse of Enoch (xc, 30, 33, 37; xci, 14).

6. *The Name and Titles of the Son of Man*

The expression 'the Man', or 'the Son of Man' (taking the Aramaic expression literally), as a designation of an eschatological deliverer, first occurs (apart from Dan. vii) in the Apocalypse of Enoch.[1] Besides the phrase 'Son of Man', and with the same sense, we find the expressions 'Son of a man'[2] and 'Son of the offspring of the mother of the living'.[3] In the Ethiopic New Testament, the last of these is the regular rendering of the term 'the Son of Man' as applied to Jesus. All three expressions[4] render ὁ υἱὸς τοῦ ἀνθρώπου, which is used by the Greek translator (of Enoch) to represent the phrase in the Semitic original, whether it was the Hebrew *ben 'āḏām* or the Aramaic *bar 'enāšā*'. As we have seen (p. 355), there is no reason to suppose that the expression was later interpolated into the Ethiopic version or into the Greek text from which it was translated. Nor is it an important point that the translator used three different expressions to render the same original.[5] In general, the translator does not follow a strict rule of uniformity in his rendering of particular words and phrases.[6] That he should also occasionally use the expression which he knew from his Ethiopic New Testament is so natural, that the reverse would be astonishing.[7]

[1] 1 En. xlvi, 1-6; xlviii, 2-7; lxii, 5-9, 14; lxiii, 11; lxix, 26-9; lxx, 1; lxxi, 17 (?). In lxxi, 14 the expression is not Messianic (see below, pp. 441 ff.). The Ethiopic expression is *walda sabe'*. *Sabe'* has the same generic or collective sense as the Hebrew *'āḏām*, and perhaps corresponds etymologically to the Hebrew *ṣābā'* = army (company of men); see Messel, *Der Menschensohn in den Bilderreden des Henoch*, p. 6 n.

[2] Ethiopic *walda be'esī* (lxii, 5; lxix 29a, b; lxxi, 14); *be'esī* is the normal word for an individual man.

[3] Ethiopic *walda 'egʷāla 'em(m)aḥeyaw* (lxii, 7, 9, 14; lxiii, 11; lxix, 26f.; lxx, 1; lxxi, 17).

[4] A few late manuscripts have, in addition, a fourth expression, *walda be'esīt*, 'the son of woman'; but Sjöberg has shown clearly that this is simply a textual error.

[5] Messel (op. cit., pp. 5 ff.) tries to show that elsewhere in 1 Enoch the Ethiopic translator always uses *sabe'* of 'man' in the generic sense, and *be'esī* of an individual man; and, since ἄνθρωπος in the Greek text has the generic sense, all the passages which now have *walda be'esī* must have been interpolated or 'corrected' later. But first, since Messel has to admit that there is at least one passage, and possibly two, where this rule does not apply (xciii, 11 and lxxxix, 1), the point is not proved. And second, we simply cannot assume that the translator realized that ἄνθρωπος in the (to him) unfamiliar phrase was really (i.e., in the Semitic original) intended generically. Probably the Greek translator, too, was not clear on this point. It is, therefore, not surprising that the Ethiopic translator now and then varies his rendering with *be'esī* instead of the customary *sabe'*.

[6] See Charles, *The Book of Enoch, translated*, p. 128; [2], p. lxv; Sjöberg, *Der Menschensohn*, pp. 42 ff.

[7] On the same grounds as those mentioned in n. 5 above, Messel, followed by Camp-

The question then arises, whether the expression 'the Son of Man' = 'the Man', in the Apocalypse of Enoch, is a definite and fixed term for the eschatological figure to whom it is applied.[1] Several scholars have held that this cannot be so. They maintain that the expression does not occur as a fixed term, which conveys its own meaning irrespective of its content. As a rule, it is preceded by a demonstrative adjective 'this' or 'that', thus referring back to the first occasion in the book where this 'human figure' was introduced; and thus it has its eschatological and Messianic sense only in the context of this vision, and means here, 'the aforementioned Son of Man'.[2] They hold that here, as elsewhere, this phrase was, in itself, simply a customary expression for 'man', and thus means in 1 Enoch simply, 'the man who was named in the first vision'. This last point, at all events, is incorrect.[3] 'The son of man' was not at that time an everyday expression in Aramaic, but an infrequent and dignified one, which indicated something specific in the person of whom it was used.

Concerning the use of the demonstrative adjective, it has been objected against the view just mentioned, that it is only the attempt of the Ethiopic translator to render the definite article in the Greek phrase which he is translating.[4] Ethiopic has no definite article; and elsewhere the translator often gives a slavishly literal rendering. He had no great skill as a Grecian; 'he has translated wrongly or inaccurately about a fifth of his Greek text'.[5] Sjöberg has carried out a very thorough investigation of this subject, and

---

[1] This is how the question must be formulated, and not whether the expression is a fixed 'Messianic' term, and also elsewhere an established name for the Messiah. Fundamentally, we are not here dealing with the Messiah in the old sense, and, therefore, not with a normal Messianic name.

[2] This is maintained, in particular, by Lietzmann (*Der Menschensohn. Ein Beitrag zur neutestamentlichen Theologie*, pp. 42ff.), before him by Eerdmans (in *T.T.*, xxviii, 1894, p. 153) and later by Wellhausen (*Skizzen und Vorarbeiten* VI, pp. 187ff.).

[3] See Dalman, *Words of Jesus*, pp. 234ff.; cf. also Fiebig, *Der Menschensohn. Jesu Selbstbezeichnung, mit besonderer Berücksichtigung des aramäischen Sprachgebrauchs für 'Mensch'.* See the discussion in Sjöberg, *Der Menschensohn*, pp. 41ff.

[4] First conjectured by N. Schmidt in *J.B.L.*, xv, 1896, pp. 36ff.; and later maintained by Charles (*The Book of Enoch, translated*, pp. 86f.) and by Staerk, *Soter* II, p. 73. A number of scholars have accepted the explanation without much further investigation.

[5] Beer in *A.P.A.T.* II, p. 220.

---

bell (*J.T.S.*, xlviii, 1947, p. 148), would regard all the passages which contain *walda 'eg^uāla 'em(m)aheyaw* as having been subsequently interpolated or modified (from an original 'the Elect One', or the like). But here, too, the point is not proved. Even if Messel were right in thinking that the translator always had definite linguistic reasons for distinguishing between the use of *sabe'* and that of *be'esī*, there remains a third possibility: a Christian alteration of *walda sabe'* in accordance with the customary usage in the Ethiopic New Testament.

has reached the conclusion that it may be true that the translator's 'this' sometimes represents the Greek definite article; but that there are also several instances where it is certain or highly probable that the Greek text itself had a 'this' before the expression, and thus referred back to the first mention of the said 'Son of Man'. This makes it probable that the Semitic original also had a corresponding demonstrative.[1] But Sjöberg also shows that this is not decisive. The question, 'Is the Son of Man a Messianic title?' is wrongly put. In apocalyptic the Son of Man is something different from the Messiah. The question is what the expression 'the Son of Man' means in 1 Enoch and within the apocalyptic circles which it represents. And here the fact is that although the expression is used in the majority of places where it occurs in 1 Enoch as a description, and not as a name or a title, and the accompanying 'this' refers back to Enoch's first vision of a 'being whose countenance had the appearance of a man', concerning whom he asks the angel who he is (xlvi, 1ff.), yet the reference is to a heavenly being who actually exists. This heavenly being is described as 'that Son of Man (whom thou knowest)', and sometimes simply as 'the Son of Man'. In an eschatological, apocalyptic context, this description was entirely explicit and comprehensible to Enoch's hearers and readers. 'That Son of Man' (the Son of Man whom you know) refers not only to an earlier mention of him in a writing or in a message, but to a heavenly Son of Man, who actually exists, and of whom the hearers know. 'The heavenly Man belonged to this (i.e., the apocalyptic) world of ideas; in the first place, the existence of such a heavenly "Man" was established. But he could also be referred to by the term "the Man"; and, in association with the apocalyptic world of ideas, the meaning of this term was immediately plain'.[2] Within the circles where these apocalyptic ideas were alive, if anyone mentioned 'the Son of Man', everyone knew to what and to whom he was referring.

This means that the expression 'the Son of Man' was a current

[1] Sjöberg, op. cit., pp. 45ff. If the original language of 1 Enoch was not Hebrew but Aramaic, it could perhaps also be maintained that even if the demonstrative had always been present in the original text, we should not be committed to the view of Lietzmann and those who agree with him. In biblical Aramaic, the demonstratives dēk and dāk, denâh and dâ' are in process of becoming definite articles (see, e.g., Ezra iv, 21; v, 8; and cf. Brockelmann, *Grundriss der vergleichenden Grammatik der semitischen Sprachen* II, p. 79 (§ 39 c). A reflection of this weakened use of the demonstrative may be seen in the New Testament, e.g., Mark xii, 7; Matt. xviii, 26–8, where ἐκεῖνος simply has the character of a definite article.

[2] Sjöberg, *Der Menschensohn*, p. 59.

and comprehensible designation of the eschatological, heavenly deliverer, in whom they believed, and for whom they waited; and this designation conveyed also certain essential things concerning his nature and being. It is characteristic of him that his appearance is human, and that he has certain human traits, although he belongs to another sphere, that of heaven. This is implied by the tradition underlying Daniel: 'one (in appearance) like a man' (see above, pp. 348ff.). The same expression, with the same implication, is also used in the Apocalypse of Ezra: 'as it were the form of a man' (xiii, 3). The lion, which in the allegorical picture-language of the apocalyptist means the Messiah, sets upon the eagle (i.e., the heathen world power, Rome) with the voice of a man (xi, 37), precisely because he *is* 'the Man'.

Equally common in the Apocalypse of Enoch is the name 'the Elect One', or 'My Elect One'.[1] By contrast with 'the Son of Man' (which raises a problem, and cannot be explained in terms of Old Testament teaching) the term 'the Elect One' is derived from Old Testament usage. 'Elect' or 'chosen' in the Old Testament indicates that the person in question stands in a specially close relationship to Yahweh, partly as the object of His particular care, love, guidance, and protection, partly as His chosen instrument to fulfil some task and to carry out His will. The application of this expression to the Son of Man depends, of course, upon the Messianic interpretation of a number of passages in the Old Testament, including some in Deutero-Isaiah. Like Deutero-Isaiah,[2] Enoch also calls Israel, or those in Israel who are appointed for salvation, 'the elect ones';[3] and the king in the kingdom of the saved ones is 'the Elect One' par excellence. The word 'elect' is used specially of the king as Yahweh's favourite and instrument. In the Old Testament, David is called the 'elect' (or 'chosen') of Yahweh. Deutero-Isaiah says of Yahweh's instrument, His anointed, Cyrus, His friend and His beloved, that he has been 'called', that is, chosen as an instrument of Yahweh's purpose of salvation. It is also explicitly said of the Servant of the Lord that he has been chosen by Yahweh.[4] But what is true of kings and other elect instruments and representatives of the Lord is, of course, also true of the Messiah. It is, therefore, understand-

---

[1] 1 En. xxxix, 6; xl, 5; xlv, 3f. (xlvi, 3; xlviii, 6); xlix, 2, 4; li, 3, 5; lii, 6, 9; liii, 6; lv, 4; lxi, (4), 5, 8, 10. On the text in lxi, 4, see below, p. 406 n. 1.
[2] Isa. xliii, 20; xlv, 4; xlviii, 12, 15; cf. lxv, 9, 15, 22.
[3] 1 En, liii, 6; lxii, 7, 8, 15, and many other passages.
[4] Isa. xlv, 1–4; xliv, 28; xlviii, 14; of Cyrus, xlii, 6; of the Servant, xlii, 1.

able that the Targum interprets Messianically both the passages which refer to the chosen Servant, and other passages which speak of Yahweh's chosen.[1] Thus it is overwhelmingly probable that the title 'the Elect One' was transferred from the Messiah to the Son of Man, who was himself regarded as the Messiah. On the other hand, there is no reason to suppose that it was particularly from the Servant of the Lord that this title was taken, although individual ideas and phrases from the Servant Songs have been transferred to the Son of Man.[2] And although the Messianic interpretation of certain passages in Deutero-Isaiah helped to give rise to the title 'the Elect One', that does not in any way show that the ideas which were associated with the Servant of the Lord were also applied to the Son of Man or the Messiah.[3] This is clear from the Targum's complete reinterpretation of Isa. liii in a nationalistic sense (see above, pp. 330ff.).

When the Son of Man is called 'the Elect One' it is, in the first instance, the normal Messianic sense that the expression conveys. He is the leader of all the other elect ones, those who will share in the Messianic salvation. He has a specially close relationship to the Lord of Spirits, is the object of His favour, is appointed by Him to a glorious heritage, and will carry out His eschatological purpose and work.

Besides 'the Elect One', 'the Righteous One' sometimes also occurs as a name for the Son of Man.[4] In one passage he is called 'the Elect One of righteousness and of faith', that is, 'the righteous

---

[1] E.g., Isa. xlii, 1; xli, 8f.; xliii, 10. See above, pp. 283, 328f.

[2] The only certain evidence of this is in 1 En. xlviii, 4, where the Son of Man is called 'the light of the Gentiles' (following Isa. xlii, 6, which actually refers to Cyrus, and Isa. xlix, 6). See Sjöberg, *Der Menschensohn*, pp. 122f. Sjöberg can hardly be right in his contention that this one passage proves that there is also a special connexion between 'chosen', or 'elect', as applied to the Servant, and 'the Elect One', as used of the Son of Man (op. cit., pp. 122f., 127f.). Even taken together with the expressions, 'the Elect One', 'the Righteous One', and 'the servant of God', these echoes (they are hardly more) of terms used by the prophet are not sufficient to show that the author of the Similitudes in Enoch identified the Servant in Deutero-Isaiah with the Son of Man, as North holds (*The Suffering Servant*, pp. 7f.).

[3] This in opposition to the altogether too hasty conclusion drawn by Staerk (*Soter* II, pp. 75, 77ff.) and by J. Jeremias from verbal similarities to similarities in thought. See further below, pp. 410ff., and above, pp. 325ff. Wherever there are echoes of Old Testament passages in references to the Son of Man, it is a question of the interpretation simply of individual passages as alluding to the Son of Man, and not of the entire figure of the Servant as alluding to the Son of Man, and of an application to him of the portrait of the Servant. For later Judaism and the rabbis, biblical interpretation is always the interpretation of individual passages, not of entire systems of ideas. This has been pointed out by Moore (*Judaism* I, p. 229), and rightly advanced by Sjöberg against the attempts of Jeremias and Staerk to discover a real influence from the Servant of the Lord on the Son of Man (*Der Menschensohn*, pp. 118ff.).

[4] 1 En. xxxviii, 2; cf. xxxix, 6; liii, 6.

and faithful Elect One'. The title alludes to the Son of Man's most conspicuous characteristic and task, as we shall see later.

The description of the Son of Man as 'God's' or 'My Servant' is also the result of fusion with the earlier Jewish picture of the Messiah.[1] This is true of the Apocalypse of Baruch, where he is once called 'My Servant Messiah'.[2] As has been observed above (pp. 294, 325), it was in all probability this expression which was in the original Hebrew text of the Apocalypse of Ezra, where the Latin translation has 'My Son the Messiah'. It is clear that this is derived from Old Testament usage. The king in general, and the Messiah in particular, is the Servant of Yahweh (see above, pp. 225, 293). It is probable that passages in Deutero-Isaiah about Yahweh's servant (both those referring to Israel and those referring to the Servant in the special sense), which made the expression something other than a Messianic title, are also reflected in its application to the Son of Man. But here again there is no real transfer to the Son of Man of the ideas embodied in the figure of the Servant of the Lord. The nature and the functions of the two figures are quite different (see below, pp. 410ff.).

We have also seen above that the Targums take the expression in a quite different sense from that of the author of the Servant Songs. They take it as a royal title, as, for example, when David, or even Nebuchadrezzar, is called Yahweh's servant: one who, at Yahweh's command, and equipped by Him, carries out His purpose and His work. In Isa. liii and other passages, the Targum thinks of the victory and triumph of the Messiah over heathen peoples and kings. The Ezra and Baruch Apocalypses use the expression in the same way. It indicates, above all, one who stands in a particularly close relationship to God, who is chosen by Him and enjoys His confidence, whom no earthly wisdom can acknowledge or discover until he is revealed, God's representative, who in his own time reveals himself, in glory, in conflict and victory, in judgement and punishment on the heathen and sinners, on the kings and mighty ones of the earth, and who thereby brings salvation and happiness to the elect believers. In one passage (2 Esdras vii, 29) the word 'servant' is used in connexion with a reference to the death of the Messiah at the end of the Millennium (see pp. 325f); but it is a purely formal repetition from the previous

[1] See pp. 263f., 327, and p. 67 n. 3.
[2] 2 Bar. lxx, 9. Charles in *A.P.O.T.* II suggests that the verse may be an interpolation.

verse, which speaks of the Servant revealing himself in triumph; and, moreover, it must be noted that in so far as the author associates any particular thought with the word, the emphasis in the context is on the fact that, at the end of the Millennium, when all life ceases on the earth for a period of seven days, there is a complete reversion to the state of chaos (the 'silence'), as before creation: all created things must die, even so exalted a being as God's chosen, equipped, and favoured servant, the Messiah. The thought which is actually associated with this word in the Servant Songs is not linked with it in the late Jewish use of it as a Messianic title.

As has been said (pp. 293f.), it is sometimes maintained that the expression 'Son of God' was used in later Judaism as a designation of the Messiah. It occurs in rabbinic and orthodox Jewish literature only in quotations of Old Testament passages which were interpreted Messianically. Although it was, in Israel, as elsewhere, an ancient term for the king, orthodox Judaism did not readily use it of the Messiah, clearly because it was felt that it was too much in conflict with the strong emphasis on the distance between God and man; and Judaism's Messiah was a man. It might therefore be supposed that the expression was used in less orthodox circles; and it has been held that the Son of Man, in particular, was also called the Son of God. This claim is based on the passages in the Apocalypse of Ezra where the Latin text has the words *filius meus*. But this interpretation, as we have seen (p. 294), is untenable.

It is astonishing that the title 'Son of God' is not applied to the heavenly Son of Man. For, if the view which we shall later examine is true, that the conception of the Son of Man originated in common oriental ideas about a heavenly, Primordial Man, the use of such a title would be only natural. The Persian Primordial Man is explicitly called the Son of God ('Ahura Mazda's Son'); and in other instances of this idea a corresponding title recurs.[1] When demoniacs address Jesus as 'Son of the Most High God',[2] it is most natural to assume that they are using a designation of the Son of Man which was known and current in some circles, at least. It is improbable that the unhappy demoniacs should have known a secret about Jesus, which He Himself had not, as yet, revealed to anyone. Nor is it probable, as some have maintained, that it was

[1] See below, p. 427, and Mowinckel in *N.T.T.*, xlv, 1944, pp. 211, 215, 225, with references to literature.
[2] Mark v, 7; Luke viii, 28; Matt. viii, 29.

the tradition within the Christian community which put into the mouths of the demoniacs this specifically Christian term for the Messiah, in place of some less definite expression which they actually used. The term 'the Most High God' is not specifically Christian; and although it was used in the Old Testament and in Judaism, we know that it was not originally Jewish, but was also applied to a particular divinity in Canaan, in Syria, and in Mesopotamia. We notice, too, that in Matthew the Christian expression 'Son of God' replaces 'Son of the Most High God' in Mark and Luke. The fact that the expression is first applied to Jesus by a man from the half-heathen territory east of Jordan, together with the fact that the entire conception of the Son of Man originated in non-Jewish circles (see below, section 19), supports the authenticity of the tradition that the demoniac from the Gergesene district called Jesus 'Son of the Most High God', and suggests that he was using one of the titles appropriate to the Son of Man.

The question and answer at the trial of Jesus show that the expression was not a customary, orthodox, Messianic title.[1] The High-priest asks, 'Are you the Messiah, the Son of the Blessed?' (Mark), or, 'the Messiah, the Son of God?' (Matthew); and Jesus answers, 'I am; and you will see the Son of Man sitting at the right hand of power'. In Luke, the connexion is even clearer. The members of the council first ask, 'Are you the Messiah?'; and Jesus answers with the word about the Son of Man: 'then they all said, "Are you the Son of God?"'.

Thus there are several indications that the Son of Man was also called the Son of God.[2]

What was the content of this expression? Since it refers to a heavenly being, there is no need to take it in an adoptionist sense, of a subsequent act of adoption by God. It expresses a closer relationship with God than can be claimed for any mere man, even the scion of David. This is confirmed by the fact that, as we have seen, the expression was clearly not looked upon with favour in orthodox Jewish circles. There is, therefore, no reason to doubt the accuracy of the tradition that Jesus was condemned for blasphemy. To claim to be the Messiah was, for Jewish thought, no blasphemy (as those who have doubted the tradition rightly say);

---

[1] Mark xiv, 62; Matt. xxvi, 63f.; Luke xxii, 67–70.

[2] This connexion is reflected in the last line of the Lukan genealogy of Jesus (where Adam is called 'the Son of God' (Luke iii, 38), by contrast with 'A, the son of B' etc. Adam, not having been begotten by man, but created by a direct, divine act, is 'son of God', by contrast with all other men, who are 'sons of men'.

but it was another thing for a man to claim to be that Son of Man, who was also 'the Son of the Most High God', or of 'the Blessed'.

As Son of God, the Son of Man possesses the power of God's authority. It is at the right hand of 'Power' that his opponents will meet the Son of Man. In the Son of God the demoniacs see the formidable vanquisher of the demons and Satan and the evil powers: 'the Holy One of God', before whom the demons tremble, has 'Come to destroy us'.[1] In the light of what 1 Enoch tells us about the Son of Man, we recognize that it is his divine nature, his glory, and his power, that are expressed in the title 'Son of God'. If we consider that title in the light of what the comparative study of religion can teach us about the origin of the Son of Man conception, we see that it also suggests that he came into being before all time. He is different from the rest of creation. The conception need not be thought of in mythological or physical terms: the expression does not presuppose procreation, or a mother. It implies that, before time and before creation, the Son of Man came into existence from the Most High God, proceeding from Him in some way, as a fulfilment in the world of phenomena of His thought, will, and purpose for the world which He was to create. 'For this reason hath he been chosen and hidden before Him, before the creation of the world', that an innumerable host of perfect, holy, and righteous persons should praise the name of the Lord of Spirits (1 En. xlviii, 5f.).

7. *The Pre-existence of the Son of Man*

By contrast with the earlier, earthly Messiah of David's line, the Son of Man is a pre-existent, heavenly being. It is as such that he first appears in the Apocalypse of Enoch.[2] Enoch is carried away

---

[1] Mark i, 24; cf. Matt. iv, 3, 6 = Luke iv, 3, 9; Matt. xxvii, 40–2, 54; Mark xv, 39.

[2] Strack-Billerbeck (II, p. 334) maintain that 1 Enoch speaks only of an ideal pre-existence, or that the Messiah is one of the righteous dead from ancient times. But there is not a single word in the text to suggest that 1 Enoch xl, 5; lxii, 7; xxxix, 6f.; lxx, 1 mean that a dead person of an earlier age will return as the Son of Man. Lagrange and Messel, among others, have denied the real pre-existence of the Son of Man, on the ground that the passages which require, or seem to require, this interpretation are Christian interpolations, or refer to the nation Israel (so Messel, in part). We have seen above (pp. 354f.) that these hypotheses are untenable. Moore, too, maintains that only an ideal pre-existence is involved here, since the passages about the Son of Man deal with future events, which are not yet real (*Judaism* II, pp. 343f.). This is also incorrect. Many of the sayings about the Son of Man are dogmatic pronouncements about his nature, and presuppose that he already exists. See the discussion, and the decisive arguments in support of real pre-existence, in Sjöberg, *Der Menschensohn*, pp. 83ff. Black (*E.T.*, lx, 1948/9, p. 14) is inclined to deny that the Son of Man was a pre-existent being before he was identified with Enoch-Metatron (Black interprets 1 En. lxxi thus). But 1 En. xlviii, 2f. is not the only evidence of the thought of pre-existence, as Black seems to suppose.

from the earth by a whirlwind, and set down at the end of the heavens; and there, in a vision, he sees the other world. He sees first the dwellings of the holy and the resting places of the righteous, with the angels and the holy ones in heaven. The passage continues,

> In that place mine eyes saw the Elect One of righteousness and of faith,
> And I saw his dwelling-place under the wings of the Lord of Spirits.

('The Lord of Spirits' is the usual term for God in 1 Enoch.)

> ... And all the righteous and the elect before him shall be
> †strong †as fiery lights,
> And their mouth shall be full of blessing,
> And their lips extol the name of the Lord of Spirits.
>
> (1 En. xxxix, 3-7)

> Yea, before the sun and the signs were created,
> Before the stars of the heaven were made
> His name was named before the Lord of Spirits.   (xlviii, 3)

The statement that his name was named and existed with God before the creation refers here not merely to an ideal pre-existence in the mind of God, but to a real pre-existence. A little further on in the same vision we read,

> And for this reason (that all should do homage to the Lord of Spirits) hath he been chosen and hidden before Him,
> Before the creation of the world and for evermore.
>
> (xlviii, 6)

And again,

> Because the Elect One standeth before the Lord of Spirits,
> And his glory is for ever and ever,
> And his might unto all generations.   (xlix, 2)

The person whom Enoch sees in his vision, and about whom he is told by the angel who guides him, is a heavenly being who really exists, and not merely a visionary figure of the future who does not yet exist.[1] Enoch is carried up to heaven, to the Son of Man, who already exists there (lxx,1). Thus, as early as the time of Enoch (long before Abraham, as Jesus said), the Son of Man *was*, and it

---

[1] So Sjöberg, *Der Menschensohn*, pp. 50f., 53, rightly.

was to him that Enoch was transported, when he left the earth.[1]
It is said that the Most High has hidden him from the beginning
(xlviii, 6; lxii, 7); and therefore he must have existed from the
beginning.

But this does not mean that the Son of Man has existed from all
eternity in the same way as the Lord of Spirits Himself. That his
name was named by God before the creation of the world means
that he really was created by God before the world's foundation
was laid. He is the first stage in the fulfilment of that purpose of
God for the world, which was framed at creation, and was given
its direction when the fall of the angels brought sin and evil among
men, when Beliar gained dominion over them. The Son of Man
is the first of God's creatures, before the sun, and the stars, and
the sure ordinances of the cosmos. His origin is linked with the
creation of the world itself,[2] a thought which was at one time more
prominent than it is in the Apocalypse of Enoch (see below, pp.
420ff., 427, 434ff.). But that it received more emphasis in other
circles in later Judaism than it does in 1 Enoch, may be deduced
from the implications of Paul's words about Christ, 'He is the
firstborn before (any) other creature; for in Him all things were
created in heaven and on earth, the visible, and the invisible,
angel-thrones, rulers, powers, or authorities (in the spirit world),
all were created through Him and for Him. He is before all things,
and in Him all things subsist' (Col. i, 15f.); 'through Him are all
things' (1 Cor. viii, 6). It is very probably that Paul is here applying to Christ ideas from the theology of the Son of Man and the
Primordial Man, when we recall that he also regards Christ as the
last Adam (1 Cor. xv, 45), a typical conception of the Son of Man
as the Primordial Man and the eschatological Man.[3]

[1] 1 En. lxx, 1; cf. 2 Esdras xiv, 9. The pre-existence of the Son of Man also appears
in 1 En. xxxix, 6ff.; xl, 5; xlvi, 1f.; xlviii, 2f., 6; lxii, 7. On the other hand, xlix, 2f.
speaks of his future status as an eschatological being, and as inaugurating the new
order of the world; see Sjöberg, op. cit., p. 93.

[2] This does not mean that he was thought of as co-operating in creation, but that
in the explicit emphasis on his existence before the creation (1 En. xlviii, 3, 5f.) there
is an unconscious echo of an older idea, that his genesis had something to do with the
genesis of the world itself. This is explained by the connexion between the idea of the
Son of Man and that of the Primordial Man. The thought is also echoed in the
Apocalypse of Baruch (2 Bar. xxix, 3f.; see von Gall, *Basileia*, pp. 425f.), where the two
monsters of the fifth day of creation (Behemoth and Leviathan) seem to have been
regarded as the opponents of the Son of Man at the last reckoning. The equation of
the creation and the conflict with the dragon is eschatologically re-interpreted and
applied to the Son of Man.

[3] Cf. Bousset, *Relig.*[2], pp. 301ff., 405ff.; Reitzenstein, *Poimandres*, pp. 81ff.; Lietzmann, *Die Briefe des Apostels Paulus* I, pp. 154f. In 1 Cor. xv, 45 Paul seems to be
actually quoting some apocryphal writing. It seems hardly likely that 'as it is written'

It is also as pre-existent that the Son of Man is called 'the
Elect One' (pp. 365f.). He is the one whom God has already
prepared to carry out His purpose of eschatological judgement
and salvation (cf. 1 En. xlvi, 3; xlviii, 6). It is as the Elect One
that Enoch first sees him in heaven, in his dwelling-place under
the wings of the Lord of Spirits (xxxix, 6f.), under His protection
and care. He is also already the Righteous One in his heavenly
pre-existence; and it is by that name that Enoch introduces him
in the opening words of the first Similitude (xxxviii, 2). From the
time of his creation he is as he ought to be (that is the fundamental
meaning of the Hebrew word for 'righteous'); and he is the one
who will one day cause all things in the new aeon to become what
they ought to be (see below, pp. 377f., 393ff.). He is endowed in
advance with all the qualities which are necessary for this purpose,
and therefore in his pre-existent state he already belongs to the
righteous ones above (see below, pp. 388ff.).

8. *The Divine Equipment of the Son of Man*

The paradox of 'the Man' is that, in spite of his name, he is
not only a pre-existent, heavenly being, but also a divine being.

'His face was full of graciousness, like one of the holy angels,'
says Enoch.

'And I asked the angel who went with me and showed me all
the hidden things, concerning that Son of Man, who he was, and
whence he was (and), why he went with the Head of Days? And
he answered and said unto me:

> This is the Son of Man who hath righteousness,
> With whom dwelleth righteousness,
> And who revealeth all the treasures of that which is hidden,
> Because the Lord of Spirits hath chosen him,
> And whose lot hath the pre-eminence before the Lord of
> Spirits in uprightness for ever.' (1 En. xlvi, 1–3)

The Son of Man, as it were, accompanies God. The Son of Man
and the Lord of Spirits are mentioned in association with each
other, even in that order (lxx, 1). The Son of Man will, in his
time, sit on a throne of glory like God's own (lv, 4). But God has
from the beginning granted him this and glorified him, bestowing
upon him the divine glory, God's *kābôd* (lxi, 8; lxii, 2; li, 3).

---

refers to Gen. ii, 7, and that the latter part of *v.* 45 is Paul's own exegetical conclusion
from the passage in Genesis.

But he is also subordinate to God. He was created; his name was named, that is, he came into existence in God's presence, if but for a time, before creation (p. 372). 'The Man' is a man of a quite special kind. From one point of view he is a man, created and subordinate to God, but a unique man, divinely endowed. It is in this sense that the Targum interprets the passage in Ps. viii, 5f. about the son of man, whom God has made but a little lower than God. Judaism was always concerned to avoid the usurpation of God's place by anyone; and this fundamental principle also underlies all the greatest sayings about the Son of Man. It is as the servant and representative of God, as the Elect One, who stands before the Lord of Spirits, that he possesses glory and might (1 En. xlix, 2).[1] It is God who names the name of the Son of Man, who sets him on His throne, who causes him to dwell among the righteous (1 En. xlv, 4; xlviii, 2; lxi, 8; lxii, 2), and who decides the day and the hour for judgement. He knows the secrets of wisdom, because God has given them to him (li, 3). He judges in the name of the Lord of Spirits (lv, 4; lxi, 9). The song of praise at his appearing is, in reality, addressed to God (xlviii, 5; lxi, 9ff.).

But the Son of Man is exalted as near to God as was possible in Judaism, and too near to accord with the outlook of earlier, orthodox Judaism.

First and foremost, he has the divine glory. This thought was not alien to early Israel. The author of Ps. viii is transported by the thought of God's unspeakable goodness in making earthborn, mortal man (the human race as a whole) 'almost a divine being' and crowning him with glory and honour (_kabôd_ and _hādār_). But he who is 'the Man' par excellence, the Son of Man, has this glory in a special degree, which the Old Testament could not think of attributing to any earthly man, save in poetic style, as in Ps. cx. At one time, as we have seen, it is even granted to the Son of Man to sit on the throne of God's glory.

The word 'glory' also alludes to the visible radiance which surrounds and shines forth from the appearance of the Son of Man. In the Old Testament and in later Judaism, the conception of brilliant light surrounding God, hiding him from human eyes, and, in a sense, representing Him,[2] is very common.[3] But the

[1] On the interpretation, see Sjöberg, _Der Menschensohn_, pp. 8of.
[2] Cf. Ezek. i, 4ff.; iii, 23; viii, 4 (cf. 2); xliii, 1–5.
[3] Exod. xvi, 10; xxiv, 16f.; xxxiii, 18ff.; xl, 34f.; Lev. ix, 23; Num. xiv. 10, 22; xvi, 19; 1 Kings viii, 11; Ezek. i, 28; iii, 12; x, 4, 18; xi, 22; Ps. lxxxv, 10; 2 Chron. vii, 1; and the previous note. References to literature in Gesenius-Buhl[16], s.v. _kabôd_. Cf. Mowinckel in _G.T.M.M.M._ I, on Exod. xvi, 7a.

divine glory is also, in general, the celestial nature, such as divine beings (*beńê 'elōhîm*) share. It includes the celestial, ethereal 'substance', which is the bodily clothing of those who are of divine origin, and also the aura, the angelic, awe-inspiring beauty and radiance, which in the literal sense shines out from them and surrounds them,[1] and the miraculous power with which they are filled, and which issues in glorious deeds which are worthy of praise. This is the glory which the Son of Man has.

What Enoch means by it is indicated in the words quoted above: 'and his face was full of graciousness, like one of the holy angels' (xlvi, 1). But the word also sums up all the inward and outward divine qualities with which the Son of Man is endowed. The idea recurs in Paul, when he speaks of Christ sharing the form of God (Phil. ii, 6; Col. i, 15). He is thinking, not so much of bodily form, as of the radiant glory and the qualities which it represents. The Son of Man is more than an angel; he is exalted high above them.[2] When he is revealed as judge of the world, the angels, too, must come before his throne (see below, p. 394). At his enthronement he is hailed with songs of praise by all the other heavenly beings (1 En. lxi, 1ff.).

But apart from this purely 'numinous'[3] endowment, the Son of Man is also furnished with a number of qualities and characteristics which belong to the sphere of personal life, namely moral qualities; and, as was customary in certain circles in Judaism, these are traced back to endowment with God's spirit.[4]

Ideas about the fruits of this endowment with the spirit are, naturally, strongly influenced by older biblical conceptions of the gifts of the spirit in the Messiah. We read,

> And in him dwells the spirit of wisdom,
> And the spirit which gives insight,
> And the spirit of understanding and of might,
> And the spirit of those who have fallen asleep in righteousness.
>
> (1 En. xlix, 3)

---

[1] This side of the idea of *kābōd* is represented in the later strata of the Old Testament, especially in the Priestly code, but was influenced by ancient oriental and Persian thought on the idea of the royal glory (*hwarena*). On this, see A. Christensen, *Die Iranier* (*Kulturgeschichte des alten Orients* III, 1, 2), pp. 229, 257, referring to Hertel, *Die arische Feuerlohe I*; Söderblom, *Gudstrons uppkomst*, pp. 256–84, passim; Widengren, *Hochgottglaube im alten Iran*, pp. 151ff., 176ff., 372ff.

[2] Werner (*Die Entstehung des christlichen Dogmas, problemgeschichtlich dargestellt*, pp. 303ff.) has maintained that the Son of Man is only one of the angels. Against this, see Sjöberg, *Der Menschensohn*, pp. 94f.

[3] To borrow the expression used by Otto in *The Idea of the Holy*.

[4] 1 En. xlix, 3; lxii, 2. For a heathen analogy, see von Gall, *Basileia*, p. 418 n. 4.

It is in accord with the whole Old Testament view of the working of the spirit that this endowment is thought of as a spirit of miraculous power. This power is thought of as directed chiefly against the enemies of the Son of Man (following Isa. xi, 1ff.). When he comes, everything which he sees trembles, and wherever his voice proceeds out of his mouth, those who hear his voice melt, as wax melts when it feels the fire. He destroys them without effort, by his bare word of command, which is likened to flames of fire.[1]

Particular emphasis is laid on the wisdom of the Son of Man (1 En. xlvi, 3; xlix, 1ff.; li, 3). It accords with a major interest of the apocalyptists, and also with the eschatological character of the Son of Man (pp. 358ff.), that special importance is attached to his insight into all the hidden mysteries of the ordering of the world, of the creation, and of the end time. He will reveal all the treasures of hidden things; all the secrets of wisdom will come forth from the thoughts of his mouth, for this has been given him by the Lord of Spirits. In 1 En. lii we read that all the hidden things of heaven, the ordering of the cosmos, the mountains and the metals, will serve the dominion of God's Anointed (the Son of Man), so that he may be strong and mighty on the earth. Admittedly, the metals and the mountains are interpreted allegorically, as in Dan. ii, of the kingdoms which will be superseded by the kingdom of the Son of Man. But this interpretation of the metal mountains 'in heaven' is somewhat forced and secondary; and it seems clear that the apocalyptist is reinterpreting an earlier, cosmic conception. The Son of Man has insight into the secrets of the cosmos and into the structure of the universe: doubtless that is the original sense. There are other indications that the Elect One has authority over the ordering of the cosmos, the secrets of the lightning and the thunder, of the winds, of the clouds and the dew, of the sun and the moon (as it is put in 1 En. xli, 3ff.). These occupy a central place among the heavenly secrets over which the Son of Man is Lord. Here, too, we can discern an original connexion between the Son of Man and the ordering of creation.

But of course wisdom is also taken to mean religious and moral insight. The Son of Man has the spirit of instruction, as 'the Messiah will teach us everything when he comes' (John iv, 25; see above, pp. 311, 321). He has the power to read all hearts, and to know everything; therefore he will judge hidden things, and no one will be able to lie to him (1 En. xlix, 4).

[1] 2 Esdras xiii, 3, 38; cf. 1 En. lxii, 2; and see Staerk, *Soter* II, p. 76.

Summing up, we may say that it is the spirit of righteousness which dwells in him. That is clearly the meaning of the remarkable saying quoted above, that 'in him dwells . . . the spirit of those who have fallen asleep in righteousness' (1 En. xlix, 3). Sometimes this has been taken to mean that the individual spirits of the departed 'enter into him to be preserved until the end'.[1]

But, as the context shows, the reference here is not to the individual, human spirits (in the plural) of the pious, thought of in psychological terms, but of the divine spirit (in the singular). The meaning can only be that the Son of Man is inspired by the same divine spirit of righteousness and piety which was active in the pious heroes, patriarchs, prophets, and sages of former times; and it may be that it is also suggested that it was from him, from his spirit, that these wise and righteous men derived their spiritual equipment.

But it cannot be denied that the expression is a striking one. It suggests that we have to do with a reinterpretation of an earlier conception, which the apocalyptist no longer understood, there is reason to suppose that it comes from that earlier conception of 'the Man', which gave rise to, and provided material for, the Son of Man idea in later Judaism, namely the conception of the Primordial Man (see below, section 19). In several parts of the east, including some Jewish centres, the Primordial Man was regarded as the Primordial Soul (or simply, 'the Soul', *anima generalis*), in whom all other souls have pre-existence, and to whom they return at death.[2] The expression in 1 En. xlix, 3 is a survival from this earlier phase of the idea of the Son of Man, which the apocalyptist reinterpreted as a means of expressing his endowment with the spirit of piety and righteousness.[3]

Righteousness is the supreme element in the equipment of the Son of Man, and the one to which the sources most frequently refer.[4] He is 'the Elect Righteous One', 'the One who has righteousness'. As in the Old Testament, the word embraces the

---

[1] See Murmelstein in *W.Z.K.M.*, xxxv, 1928, p. 266; Otto, *The Kingdom of God and the Son of Man*, p. 189. It is by no means clear to me what Beer actually means by his explanation (*A.P.A.T.* II p. 264 n.v.), 'The Messiah fulfils the eschatological hope of the pious who have fallen asleep'. Messel, (*Der Menschensohn in den Bilderreden des Henoch*, p. 39 n.) tries to dispose of the problem by a textual alteration. He can claim support for his suggestion from the parallel with Isa. xi, 2, which clearly inspired the passage. [2] See Murmelstein, ibid., pp. 261ff.

[3] Sjöberg's attempt (*Der Menschensohn*, pp. 98ff.) to explain the remarkable way in which the thought is formulated in 1 En. xlix, 3 in terms of Isa. xi, 2 is too literary, and takes insufficient account of the traditio-historical factor.

[4] 1 En. xxxviii, 2; xxxix, 5f.; xlvi, 3; xlix, 2; liii, 7; lxii, 2f., etc.

sum of religious and moral virtues and states, and could be rendered by 'perfection', considered as a virtue or a state. The Son of Man is the Righteous One because he is 'right', as he ought to be in order to carry out the tasks for which he was chosen (p. 373). But, from one point of view, he is also the Righteous One, because he is the first of the righteous ones (see below, pp. 380ff.), the representative, as it were, of the community of the pious and the saved. He is the perfect One, who expresses, and himself lives in and mediates to others, the state of perfection. He *mediates* it: in 1 Enoch 'righteousness' has the same double significance as in the Old Testment.[1] The word indicates not only a religious and moral quality, a virtue, but also those right conditions which exist where the righteous man rules;[2] and therefore it often denotes the ability to create right moral and religious conditions. When the thought of the opposite kind of conditions is present, the word 'righteousness' often simply means salvation. This is also true in 1 Enoch. The Son of Man is 'righteous', because he makes his people, the elect ones, righteous, that is to say, he saves them.[3] The righteousness of the Son of Man has a clear relationship to his eschatological task. In several passages, 'righteousness' simply means 'justification', or 'salvation'. The Son of Man is the mediator of that state which exists where righteousness prevails, the state of bliss and salvation. He is 'the Elect One of righteousness and of faith' (1 En. xxxix, 6), that is, the chosen one who faithfully fulfils the promises and the hope of salvation for the godly. In the words that follow,

> And righteousness shall prevail in his days,
> And the righteous and elect shall be without number before
> Him for ever and ever,

the thought is of the bliss of the redeemed. 'The secrets of righteousness' (1 En. xlix, 1; cf. xxxviii, 3) means the things which belong to the eschatological salvation.[4] They are 'the secrets of heaven', which have to do with the establishment of the kingdom, with judgement, and with salvation (1 En. xli, 1f.). 'The fountain of righteousness' is the fountain of life, from which the righteous drink in the other life (1 En. xlviii, 1). The 'number' or 'time of

[1] Cf. Leivestad, *Guds straffende rettferdighet*, pp. 8ff., 16ff.
[2] Cf. Isa. xxxii, 1ff.; and see Pedersen, *Israel* I–II, pp. 336ff., 358ff.; Leivestad, op. cit., pp. 16ff.
[3] 1 En. xxxviii, 3; xlvii, 4; xlviii, 1; xlix, 2; lviii, 5; lxii, 12; lxxi, 16; cf. T. Levi viii; 2 Tim. iv, 8.
[4] See Messel, *Der Menschensohn in den Bilderreden des Henoch*, p. 48.

righteousness' is the time when salvation will break forth (1 En. xlvii, 4). That the spirit of righteousness was poured upon him is shown first by the fact that

> The word of his mouth slays all the sinners,
> And all the unrighteous are destroyed from before his face.

(1 En. lxii, 2)

He is the Righteous One, because it is he who will gain for the oppressed righteous ones their right (1 En. liii, 7).

Thus, from his origin, the Son of Man is God's guarantee that 'righteousness' will one day be realized in the world.[1] It is said that he preserves the lot of the righteous (1 En. xlviii, 7). 'This he does by his very existence. Before the creation of the world, God prepared the coming deliverer. Therefore the coming deliverance is sure. The righteous will not lose their lot.'[2] But they still must wait. The Son of Man is still hidden (see below, pp. 385f.). But one day he will be revealed (pp. 388ff.). From the time of his origin he has all the equipment he needs to accomplish his task.

9. *The Heavenly Community: the King of Paradise*

The divine equipment of the Son of Man corresponds to his task. We often hear that he is still hidden and kept beside the Lord of Spirits till a fixed time comes. Then he will go into action. But the remarkable thing is that he is, in fact, already in action. He is the leader of a company of elect ones in heaven. He is associated with a heavenly community: the righteous, the elect, the holy.[3]

In 1 Enoch all these expressions denote the same person, and are used in more or less the same sense. In the oldest parts of the book, the visions of the ten weeks,[4] the meaning is, as often in the Old Testament, the whole of Israel as the chosen people.[5] The expressions are used more or less as a formula, as when we speak of 'the faithful'. Elsewhere in the book they are often applied to the community which exists here on earth.[6] But in the Similitudes it is used of those who, in virtue of a personal decision, have come into a right relationship with God, who are 'right' (righteous) in His eyes, and therefore 'chosen' from the mass of mankind to be

---

[1] See Sjöberg, *Der Menschensohn*, pp. 96f.   [2] Sjöberg, loc. cit.

[3] 1 En. xxxix, 4ff.; xl, 5; xli, 2; xlv, 3f.; xlvii, 1ff.; liii, 6; lxi, 12; lxx. See Staerk, *Soter* II, pp. 440ff.

[4] 1 En. xcii; xciii; xci, 12–17; see Beer in *A.P.A.T.* II, p. 230.

[5] See Schrenk, art. ἐκλεκτός in *T.W.B.N.T.* IV, pp. 188f.

[6] 1 En. x, 17; xci, 3; xciii, 2, 5, 10; cvii, 1; cf. Isa. lxi, 3; Jub. i, 16; vii, 34; xvi, 26; xxi, 24; xxii, 11; xxv, 3.

holy, that is, belong to God. Thus the expressions are in contrast
to sinners and wrongdoers.[1] The righteous are those who worship
the one true God, who observe the Law and who keep themselves
clear of the impurity of the heathen and sinners. But the words
also imply that they live in faith and in the hope of the restoration of Israel, of the coming of the kingdom of God, of the new
aeon, the last judgement, and the eschatological salvation in which
the righteous will share. Thus all the expressions denote the community of the godly, which has always existed on earth since the
days of the patriarchs,[2] and which exists within Israel, but is not
absolutely identical with the nation Israel. In 1 Enoch these expressions also imply that the righteous are chosen and sanctified
precisely that they may share in the eschatological salvation. Although the term 'the righteous' emphasizes their religious and
moral 'rightness', 'the elect' and 'the holy ones' suggest that they
are separated and sanctified for the coming salvation, and belong
to the world to come. They are at once an empirical and an
eschatological community. This usage corresponds with what we
find in the New Testament.[3]

But it is noteworthy that the eschatological community already
exists in heaven. In the passage where Enoch sees the dwelling of
the Elect One under the wings of the Lord of Spirits, he also sees
the dwellings of the righteous, and the resting places of the holy
ones (xxxix, 1ff.). There the righteous and the elect praise the
name of the Lord of Spirits without ceasing. This is meant as a
vision not of the future, but of something which already is. We
also hear of whom this community consists. They are the patriarchs and the righteous, who from ancient times dwell in that
place, all the godly from the past.[4] They are those who have
fallen asleep in righteousness, who have been of the same spirit as
the Son of Man (1 En. xlix, 3; see above, p. 377). Because their
souls (cf. 2 Bar. xxx, 2ff.) now belong to the heavenly community,
they, too, are called 'the holy ones',[5] a name which is used in the
Old Testament only of supernatural divine beings.[6] In 1 Enoch,
as we have seen, it has acquired a special, eschatological content.

---

[1] 1 En. v, 7; xli, 2; l, 1f. [2] Cf. Staerk, *Soter* II, p. 441, top.
[3] There, too, the term 'the elect' is predominantly eschatological; see Schrenk, op.
cit., pp. 191ff. The same is true of 'the saints' in the New Testament; see Asting, *Die
Heiligkeit im Urchristentum*, pp. 70f., 137ff., 153ff.
[4] Cf. Staerk, *Soter* II, p. 442 n. 2.
[5] 1 En. xxxviii, 4; xxxix, 4; xlvii, 2, 4; xlviii, 1, etc.
[6] In the Old Testament 'the holy ones' always means simply 'divine beings', even
in Ps. xvi, 3; see Deut. xxxiii, 3; Zech. xiv, 5; Pss. lxxxix, 6, 8; Job v, 1; xv, 15; Dan.

It is to this community in heaven that favoured individuals are carried away, while still alive, to be with the Son of Man, in the place of the elect and the righteous. So it befell Enoch, Ezra, and Baruch.[1] There they will remain till the times are fulfilled, preserved till the end of the times, when the Son of Man will appear.

The Son of Man is clearly regarded as king of this heavenly people.[2] This shows us a side of his character and status which the Enoch Apocalypse does not, as a rule, bring out so clearly.

In the Apocalypse of Ezra (2 Esdras xiii, 12, 39ff.) this conception of the Son of Man and his people appears in a form which indicates more clearly its original implication.[3] After the destruction of the hostile powers, of which we shall hear more below, the Son of Man gathers to himself a peaceable army, an innumerable host of those who have hitherto lived in a distant land, where no man has previously lived, and which can be reached only in a wonderful way, by travelling underground for the space of a year and a half. The apocalyptist's thought is that this tunnel is to be found in the Tigris-tunnel at Bylkalein, where the river goes underground for some distance,[4] at the narrow passages of the Euphrates, where,

---

[1] 1 En. lxx; 2 Esdras, xiv, 9; 2 Bar. lxxvi, 2.

[2] That the Son of Man represents the community, and draws it into his own destiny, his appearing, and his glorification, is not the same as the view that the Son of Man and the community are mystically identical, and that the Son of Man is at once individual and collective, as Dahl holds. Dahl's view is dependent on his interpretation of 1 En. xlix, 3 in terms of what he takes to be the ancient Israelite corporate view of the representative person. He does not allow for the fact that the factor under discussion must be understood in the light of the earlier stage of the Son of Man as Primordial Man and *anima generalis* (see above, p. 377). In fact, Dahl treats somewhat mechanically, and thus caricatures, the ancient view, which Pedersen has expounded in *Israel*. Representative unity and a corporate conception of the leader as the bearer of the whole, and of the individual as a type of the race, is not the same as literal and actual identity. The fact that in the cult a person represents the whole, or, in a symbolic sense, *is* the whole, means that there is an intimate community of destiny between them, that in the realm of the soul power may pass from one to the other, as, for instance, the king's blessing flows into the community. But many passages in the Old Testament show that the king and the people are distinguished from each other. Nor is there, in 1 Enoch, reference to anything more than 'close association', to use Dahl's own expression (*Das Volk Gottes*, p. 90). Even if primitive thought had at one time regarded the community and its representative as identical to the degree which Dahl holds, later Judaism had advanced far beyond that stage, and its thought was different and quite ratiocinative, as is clearly shown by the logical arguments of the rabbis. Dahl's view reappears, in extreme caricature, in Ström's *Vetekornet*, where it is the dominant point of view.

[3] Cf. Bousset, *Relig.*[2], p. 558, [3], p. 490.   [4] See Gressmann, *Der Messias*, p. 382.

---

viii, 13; cf. 1 En. lxi, 8. It is, of course, to them that Ps. lxxxii refers. Staerk's objection (*Soter* II, p. 439 n. 1) arises from the equation of 'holy' and 'morally worthy'; but see Ps. xvi, 3. The word 'holy' practically never has any ethical reference in the Old Testament. On the other hand, Staerk is entirely right in his contention that a heavenly community of righteous men cannot be derived solely from Old Testament ideas.

as was thought in antiquity, both Euphrates and Tigris emerged. He interprets the innumerable multitude as the vanished ten tribes, who had dwelt there from the time of their deportation until the last times. But originally this land had nothing to do with geography. When the innumerable multitude is said to be those who have been restored by the hand of God (i.e., the eschatological remnant), and to have dwelt hitherto in His holy territory, it is clear that the land was originally paradise, where the 'blessed' dwell, and that the apocalyptist has reinterpreted it here allegorically. It was through such a subterranean passage, which it took twelve double hours to traverse, that the ancient Babylonian hero Gilgamesh came to the garden of the gods in the other world. It is significant that in the Ezra Apocalypse the distant land is called 'the other land'.[1] It is also explicitly stated in 1 Enoch that it is all those who dwell in the garden of life who praise the Son of Man (lxi, 12) and thus that it is there that his throne is set up. Enoch is carried away to the heavenly paradise, where the patriarchs and the righteous have dwelt from time immemorial (lxx, 4). It is in the garden of righteousness that the tree of wisdom and all the other fragrant trees of paradise grow (xxxii, 3). Underlying this there is doubtless a mythical conception of the Son of Man as king of paradise, king from primordial times in the land of the gods, which is no longer here on earth. This explains why his people are those who have been translated, pious and righteous men, who, by a special divine favour, were transported to the other land, to paradise.

This underlying thought in the Ezra Apocalypse justifies us in interpreting a passage in the Testament of Levi xviii as originally alluding not to the earthly, political Messiah, but to the Son of Man. Of the Messiah from Levi it is said,

> In his priesthood shall sin come to an end,
> And the lawless shall cease to do evil . . .
> And he shall open the gates of paradise,
> And shall remove the threatening sword against Adam.
> And he shall give to the saints to eat from the tree of life,
> And the spirit of holiness shall be on them.
> And Beliar shall be bound by him,

---

[1] *'ereṣ 'aḥereṭ*; see Gunkel in *A.P.A.T.* II, p. 397, with references to the literature. The Latin text has *arzeret*; but, according to Schiller-Szinessy (*Journal of Philology*, 1870, pp. 113f.), this = *'ereṣ 'aḥeret* (Deut. xxix, 27) = *terra alia* (2 Esdras xiii, 40). Cf. Schürer, *Geschichte*⁴ II, p. 627 nn. 43 and 44.

And he shall give power to his children to tread upon the evil spirits.

(vv. 9–12)

The king who can destroy Beliar and the demonic powers and restore paradise is himself the king of paradise. The king of primordial time has also become the king of the end time. Here we get a glimpse of the fact that at one time the role of king of paradise belonged to the Son of Man. The land beyond, which he represents, is the paradise that is now lost, to which no earthly man can come. In that paradise the Son of Man was thought of (at least at one period and in certain circles) as ruling. It is a common feature in late Jewish eschatology that in the end time paradise, which has now been carried away to an unknown place in the other world, will return to men.[1] The Son of Man, who was at one time thought of as the king of primordial time, will also be the king of the end time in paradise; and traces of this thought recur in apocalyptic (see p. 382).

Thus there is a difference here from the earlier Messianic saying in Isa. xi, 1ff. In Isaiah, paradise in the literal sense and the future king are not linked together as two necessarily related factors; but features from the paradise myth are transferred to the state of bliss which the future king will bring, or, in other words, this bliss is described in pictures from the paradise myth, on the general assumption found in conceptions of the restoration, that it will be as it was in the beginning.[2] In the Isaiah passage it is the figure of the future king which has been, as it were, amplified by features from the paradise myth; but it is a constitutive element in the very idea of the Son of Man that he is king of paradise. As we shall see below (pp. 422ff.), this feature has striking parallels in the Iranian and Indian mythology of the primordial time and the end time.

10. *The Typical, Ideal Man*

It is a striking fact that the Son of Man is a pre-existent, heavenly being, but yet is called 'the Man'. But there are also certain features in his nature which are appropriate to his humanity. As we have seen, he is called 'the Righteous One'. In the Old Testament, righteousness is also a divine quality. But the word denotes first and foremost the most essential quality of man, when

---

[1] See above, p. 276, and Volz, *Eschatologie*[2], pp. 413ff.
[2] See above, pp. 142f., 143ff., passim, 182, 270, 275.

he is what he ought to be: the 'right' man, the ideally pious and moral person.[1] The Son of Man is also called 'the Elect One'; but this is used only of men who have been selected for some purpose by the deity. There is something distinctive about an 'elect' man; but he has been selected because he has all the ideal human qualities, which lead to his being chosen as representative of the others. The moral equipment of the Son of Man includes those qualities which constitute the 'right' man: wisdom, uprightness, piety, and the like (see above, pp. 375ff.); and he is closely connected with 'the elect ones', 'the upright ones', a community which consists of 'elect' men. He is the representative of this people, consisting of such men (pp. 379ff.).

This also sheds light on his name 'the Man', and on its content. The heavenly community is the elect kernel of the righteous and the elect in general, that is, of Israel, the people of God, the men who are what men ought to be. They form the heavenly earnest (already in existence) of the new, elect mankind, as it will one day exist in the state of perfection. At their head stands the Elect One, the Righteous One, as the representative and pattern of the righteous ones.

This shows that 'the Man' is also in a measure regarded as the typical or ideal man.[2] At first sight it seems to be a modern, European idea. Indeed, in an earlier generation, modern interpreters of the Gospels often put this modernizing construction on the term 'Son of Man' as used there. But, when rightly understood, it is seen to be connected with the thought of the ancient east. It must be taken in the light of what the ancient, eastern myths say about a divine Primordial Man, who was also the typical man, the ideal man, and the pattern for mankind. This connexion with the whole race of mankind, as its type and ideal representative, is also reflected in the Ethiopic rendering of the expression 'Son of Man' in the Gospels: *walda 'eg^uāla 'em(m)aheyaw*, 'the son of the offspring of the mother of the living' (see above, p. 362).

It is a natural consequence of the Jewish outlook that in apocalyptic the content of this ideal is conceived and presented in

---

[1] Cf. Pedersen, *Israel* I–II, pp. 336ff.

[2] This aspect of the Son of Man has been particularly emphasized by Brede Kristensen in *T.T.*, xlv, 1911, pp. 1ff. In modern times much has often been made of it, but without adequate knowledge of the religious background which gives the thought its true content and perspective. It is, therefore, with some justification dismissed by experts in the history of religion (see e.g., Bertholet in *R.G.G.*[1] IV, col. 297).

religious terms. The whole Jewish approach to life was religious. Therefore the Son of Man appears in the descriptions as the typical and ideal pious man, the typical sage, the typical righteous man, the one who in himself fulfils, and enables men to fulfil, the goal for which God created them, to be to the honour and praise of the Almighty (see pp. 372, 409f.). In Judaism generally, and in apocalyptic, the ideal is the righteous sage, the pious man. The Son of Man is the primordial sage, the primordial righteous man; that is, he is the ideal man, the pre-existent, heavenly ideal and pattern; and one day the pious will be exalted to be with him.

But this thought is not greatly emphasized. If we had not known from other sources that, at an earlier stage in the history of the idea, the Son of Man was held to be the pattern man, the prototype of humanity,[1] it would have been difficult to discern traces of the idea in later Jewish apocalyptic. It was not consciously present there, except as the conception of his perfect righteousness and wisdom, and his status as the first of the righteous.[2] Nothing explicit is said about the Son of Man as an ethical pattern, or of imitating and following the Son of Man. That is because *this* apocalyptic Son of Man has no earthly or human existence. He is a purely heavenly being, who has nothing to do with mankind before his parousia, when the end comes; and then it is as judge, and as conqueror of Satan and of the host of wickedness and of the kings and rulers of the world, that he appears. He does not humble himself and become like us, so that we may have the desire and the courage to be like him. He is not the Son of Man 'come in the flesh'. It remained for the future to show that realization of the ideal man.

11. *The Hidden Secret*

Before the creation of the world, the name of the Son of Man was named by the Lord of Spirits. This means that he was created, and since then has existed in heaven. At the end of time his name will again be named before the Lord of Spirits. That one of the ministering spirits in heaven, whose task is to remind the Lord of what must take place,[3] will mention his name before Him, and he will then be enthroned and appear in glory (see below, pp. 388ff.).

---

[1] See Mowinckel in *N.T.T.*, xlv, 1944, pp. 225f., cf. ibid., p. 195.
[2] Sjöberg (*Der Menschensohn*, pp. 195f.) goes too far when he denies that there are any traces of the idea in the Enochian Son of Man.
[3] On the high court official, whose task it is to remind the ruler of all important matters on the agenda of government, see Begrich in *Z.A.W.*, lviii, 1940-41, pp. 1ff.

In the meantime he is hidden and kept beside the Lord of Spirits, in his dwelling-place under the wings of the Lord of Spirits (1 En. xxxix, 7), from the beginning. We read that the Most High has preserved him 'in readiness for His power',[1] and revealed him to the elect.[2] God has appointed him for a special task (xli, 9) in His own time.

The whole question of the Son of Man, his nature, his pre-existence, and his coming, is a divine secret, which will be revealed only in its own time. 'Just as one can neither seek out nor know what is in the deep of the sea, even so can no one upon earth see my servant [rendered "Son" in *A.P.O.T.* II; cf. above, p. 360 n. 2.] ... but in the time of his day' (2 Esdras xiii, 52).

The thought of the divine secrets is central in apocalyptic.[3] This was what gave the apocalypses their value in the eyes of the pious, that they were revelations of the divine secrets, which God, had permitted elect individuals, like Enoch, Shealtiel, Ezra, Baruch, and other sages, to see. These men had had a glimpse of heaven itself, had seen the secrets and had them explained, and then had written them down in their 'hidden' (apocryphal) books, as necessary instruction for the other righteous and elect persons. The secrets include more than the last things and the signs of them, although the contemporary religious interest in them was chiefly directed to eschatology. The content of this word 'secrets' may be expressed in modern terms as embracing the whole of God's purpose for the world from creation to the end, including the structure and laws of the universe, which both bear witness to God's wisdom, might, and majesty (which certainly can and will fulfil His appointed end), and which also are the means He will use to attain His end, the new world. Insight into all these things strengthens faith, and is useful for those who want to be prepared when the signs begin to take place. Therefore the Most High has revealed them to His elect upon earth: he who reads must see to it that he discerns them.

The Son of Man is initiated into all these secrets. He is lord over all that is hidden (1 En. lxii, 6; see n., ad. loc., in *A.P.O.T.*

---

[1] The text has 'before His power', which is usually taken to mean 'in His presence', 'before His face'. But this periphrasis for 'Himself' seems very unusual; and it is, therefore, reasonable to interpret 'before' as 'in readiness for', 'for the use of'. Otto's interpretation of the expression as 'before his (i.e., the Son of Man's) power', before the power was bestowed on him at the end of days (*The Kingdom of God and the Son of Man*, pp. 161, 192, 217), can hardly be right. See also Sjöberg, *Der Menschensohn*, p. 90 n. 26.

[2] 1 En. xlvi, 7; cf. 2 Esdras xii, 32; xiii, 25f.; 1 En. xl, 5; xlviii, 6.

[3] See Sjöberg, op. cit., pp. 104ff.

II). When he sits upon his throne, all the secrets of wisdom will issue from his mouth (1 En. li, 3). He will reveal all the treasures of what is hidden (1 En. xlvi, 3). He also knows the secret ways of the angels (1 En. lxi, 9). There can be no doubt that Paul is using familiar ideas when he says of Christ, that in Him 'are all the treasures of wisdom and knowledge hidden' (Col. ii, 3). But the Son of Man is himself the greatest and most important of all these secrets. He is himself still hidden; but one day he will be revealed.

The central theme in the Similitudes of Enoch is that this secret, too, has now already been revealed to the elect.[1]

> And the wisdom of the Lord of Spirits hath revealed him to
> the holy and righteous;
> For he hath preserved the lot of the righteous,
> Because they have hated and despised this world of un-
> righteousness;
> And have hated all its works and ways in the name of the
> Lord of Spirits.   (1 En. xlviii, 7)

They will know that in him they have the guarantee that their hope will be fulfilled, and that they will not be deprived of their portion (see below, pp. 401ff.). Enoch's view of the secret of the hidden Messiah is similar to the teaching of the Fourth Gospel, the Epistle to the Hebrews, and primitive Christian theology in general, that it was by hope in Christ, who should one day come, that the godly ones of the old covenant lived their religious life and endured affliction.[2]

But it is only the righteous elect, the godly and disparaged community on earth (those for whom the apocalyptists wrote their books), that can fully discern this secret and use it aright. For there is also an illegitimate or distorted revelation of the heavenly secrets, which comes from the fallen angels, and has been misused by men for sin and idolatry.[3] The full secret and its meaning are hidden from sinners and unknown to them. 'The great privilege of the righteous is that they have learned to know these divine secrets, and thus to know the Son of Man also.'[4]

But when he is revealed to the sight of the whole world on the day of the Son of Man, then woe betide the sinners!

[1] 1 En. lxii, 7; xl, 5; lxix, 26; cf. 2 Esdras xii, 32; xiii, 25f.
[2] John viii, 56; Heb. xi; xiii, 26. Cf. Wernle, *Die Anfänge unserer Religion*[2], pp. 306f.
[3] See Sjöberg, *Der Menschensohn*, pp. 111ff.
[4] Op. cit., p. 115.

12. *The Epiphany of the Son of Man*

The most important point about the Son of Man is that he will come forth from the place where he is safely kept beside the Lord of Spirits, and appear in the sight of men. It is the epiphany or revelation of the Son of Man which absorbs the interest of the apocalyptists, which they behold in vision after vision, for which they long and pray. The message that it is at hand is what they proclaim to the righteous and elect ones who long for it.[1] When the time is at hand, 'the Righteous One shall appear before the eyes of the righteous'.[2] The change of the times is inaugurated when 'that Son of Man has appeared'. 'My servant the Messiah shall be revealed'; 'when all is accomplished that was to come to pass in those parts', 'after the signs have come, of which thou wast told before', 'the Messiah shall then begin to be revealed', 'the principate of My Messiah will be revealed'.

This certainly does not merely mean, as when reference is made to the appearance of the national Messiah, that he will come forth from earthly obscurity and show himself to be the Messiah by beginning to perform the Messianic works. The thought is of something more, of what is conveyed by the word *epiphany*: from his hidden state of pre-existence he will suddenly appear, and reveal himself to the longing righteous ones in his celestial splendour and glory, his $\delta \delta \xi a$, to which explicit reference is made in 2 Bar. xxx, 1.

As long as the Son of Man is hidden from men, he has the subordinate position of one who serves, 'standing before' the Lord of Spirits, as Enoch says (xlix, 2), like the others in the hosts of heaven. But his revelation in his full glory begins when he is invested with full, divine authority. The epiphany is thought of as an enthronement. His name is named before the Lord of Spirits (1 En. xlviii, 2); that is, in the heavenly council, he and the purpose for which he was appointed are remembered, as it was said of the kings of old that their name was named for lordship by the gods.[3] Then follows the real manifestation, when he is set on the throne.

> For that Son of Man has appeared,
> And has seated himself on the throne of his glory.
>
> (1 En. lxix, 29)

---

[1] See von Gall, *Basileia*, p. 423. This important point is not brought out by Staerk (*Soter* I, pp. 72ff.; II, pp. 438ff.).

[2] 1 En. xxxviii, 2; for the phrases which follow, see lxix, 29; 2 Esdras vii, 28; 2 Bar. xxix, 3; xxx, 1; lxxii, 2; xxxix, 7.   [3] See Sjöberg, *Der Menschensohn*, pp. 62f.

In reality it is God Himself who sets him on the throne of glory,[1] installing him as ruler. In two passages it seems that it is on God's own throne of glory (the glorious throne[2] which also bears witness to the glory of its occupant) that he is set.[3] This is not in itself inconceivable. Even in the Old Testament the king is thought of as sitting on Yahweh's throne.[4] But as a rule the reference is to the throne of the Son of Man, the thought being the same as that in the conception of the Son of Man underlying Dan. vii, where we hear of 'thrones', namely for 'the Ancient of Days' and for 'the Man'.[5] When he is enthroned, they kneel and pay him homage (1 En. xlviii, 5); and he is hailed with praise not only by 'all who dwell above in heaven' (lxi, 6ff), but also by all the living; 'and the kings and the mighty and all who possess the earth shall bless and glorify and extol him (i.e., the Son of Man) who rules over all, who was hidden'.[6]

This means that his enthronement is not only something which is visible in heaven. It is the great change of the ages, inaugurating the judgement and the new aeon. Therefore it is also a revelation to the whole world, a manifestation to all the kings, the mighty men, and the nations of the earth, a cosmic event. It is, in fact, the same thought that occurs in the Gospels: 'as the lightning comes from the east and shines as far as the west, so will be the coming of the Son of Man' (Matt. xxiv, 27; Luke xvii, 24). It is the thought of an epiphany and a parousia similar to that described in Dan. vii, or rather, in the myth of the Son of Man which Daniel used and applied to Israel. In the Gospels both Jesus and His opponents assume it as an article of current belief that the Son of Man 'will come with (or "on") the clouds of heaven'.[7] This was

---

[1] 1 En. lxi, 8; lxii, 2. In lxii, 3–5 also the context shows that God is thought of as the real agent. Other passages are indefinite, and say only that he sits on his throne of glory; 1 En. xlv, 3; li, 3; lv, 4; cf. Matt. xix, 28; xxv, 31.

[2] Adjectival genitive, Hebrew, *kissē' kābôd*, or *kissē' hak-kābôd*, or *kissē' kebôdô*. Sjöberg's discussion (op. cit., pp. 63ff.), whether the expression 'throne of glory' in 1 Enoch, as later in the rabbinic writings, is a fixed term for God's throne, seems a little too subtle. Passages like Jer. xiv, 21; xvii, 12 suggest that in earlier Judaism the expression brought to mind the throne of God: the presence or absence of the definite article in prophetic style ought not to be pressed, especially since, even in the Old Testament, the king's throne is thought of as ideally identical with that of Yahweh (see Ps. cx, 1; 1 Chron. xxviii, 5; xxix, 23; 2 Chron. ix, 8).

[3] 1 En. li, 3; lv, 4. The text of the latter passage is uncertain; the best MSS. read 'on the throne of glory'. See Sjöberg, op. cit., p. 65.

[4] See n. 2, above.

[5] See above, p. 352. Sjöberg (op. cit., p. 66 n. 24) refers to the parallel in 3 En. x, 1; xlviii, C 5, where Metatron (which is really a variant form of the idea of the Son of Man; see below, p. 439) does not sit on the throne of glory itself, but receives a throne which corresponds to it. [6] 1 En. lxii, 6f.; see also lxi, 7, and cf. lxix, 26.

[7] Matt. xxiv, 30; xxvi, 64; Rev. xiv, 14; cf. Mark xiii, 26; xiv, 62; Luke xxi, 27; xxii, 69.

also known to the Jewish apocalyptists. As the Apocalypse of Ezra puts it, 'this Man flew with the clouds of heaven' (xiii, 3). The rabbis, too, following Dan. vii, think of the Messiah as revealing himself on the clouds of heaven. They include among the names of the Messiah 'Anani', which they interpret as 'Cloudman'; and the Targum adopts the same interpretation of the masculine personal name in 1 Chron. iii, 24.[1]

Alongside this conception we also meet another striking thought, namely that the Son of Man will come from the sea. In the Apocalypse of Ezra it is combined with the thought of his coming with the clouds of heaven. 'I dreamed a dream by night: <and I beheld,> and lo! there arose a violent wind from the sea, and stirred all its waves. And I beheld, and lo! <the wind caused to come up out of the heart of the seas as it were the form of a man. And I beheld, and lo!> this man flew with the clouds of heaven.' Then follows a description of how everything at which this man looks trembles, and everything towards which he utters his voice melts like wax before the fire (2 Esdras xiii, 1ff.).

In the sequel the apocalyptist himself interprets this feature of the coming of the Son of Man from the sea: 'and I said, O Lord my Lord, show me this: wherefore I have seen the Man coming up from the heart of the sea. And he said unto me: Just as one can neither seek out nor know what is in the deep of the sea, even so can no one upon earth see my servant [*or those that are with him*], but in the time of his day' (2 Esdras xiii, 51f.; 'my servant' is here substituted for 'my Son', the rendering in *A.P.O.T.* II). Ezra does not mean that the Son of Man will really come from the sea. He takes it as a symbol, existing only in the vision, and present there only because it conveys a definite idea, which must be interpreted and applied. But the interpretation is forced; and it is certain that the apocalyptist did not himself invent this feature of the coming of the Son of Man from the sea: he took it from the apocalyptic tradition.

In the Apocalypse of Baruch we find an allegorical modification of the same conception. Baruch sees a cloud rise from the sea, full of white water and black water, which stream down upon the earth, alternating with each other twelve times. But from the summit of the cloud there came 'as it were the likeness of great lightning'. He is then given the interpretation that the alternating streams of white and black water denote the alternating periods

[1] Strack-Billerbeck I, pp. 67, 486, 956f. See above, p. 357.

in Israel's history: piety and prosperity, impiety and affliction. The great lightning is interpreted as the Messiah, who comes at last, and saves his people, and destroys their enemies (2 Bar. liii; lxxii f.). Here, too, the coming of the Son of Man with the cloud is combined with his coming from the sea: the cloud rises from the sea. Baruch is undoubtedly borrowing from the Apocalypse of Ezra and refashioning its symbolism.

That the idea of the coming of the Son of Man from the sea belongs to an earlier tradition is evident from the attempts made by the apocalyptists to interpret the idea. If Ezra had wanted to express only the fact that the Messiah was as unfathomable as the depths of the sea,[1] he could easily have found an image which would have expressed the thought better; or it could have been more easily derived from the coming of the Son of Man from heaven: for those who dwell on earth, the inside of heaven and its 'secrets' (see p. 386) are even more unfathomable than the sea. The forced interpretation shows that inherited, traditional conceptions are present.[2]

The teaching about the coming of the Son of Man from the sea did not preclude (for Ezra, or Baruch, or those circles which were familiar with it) belief in him as a heavenly being. They clearly take it for granted. They connect his coming from the sea with his being hidden until his epiphany, when he appears in an unexpected and surprising way; and they understand it as an allegorical symbol. It is not easy to say what the coming of the Son of Man from the sea originally meant. That a pre-existent eschatological being should descend from heaven presents no problem; but why should he come up from the sea? In the Old Testament, and, to some extent, in later Jewish tradition, the sea represents the chaotic, demonic principle in the universe, which is hostile to God. It is in accord with this that in Daniel the four monsters, which represent the world powers, come up from the sea. This purely traditional feature in the Son of Man, which the apocalyptists no longer understood, is probably derived from an earlier phase of the conception, from some variant of the idea of the Primordial Man, as is the feature that in him is the spirit of the righteous departed (see above, p. 377). Even in that earlier phase it may have been connected with the fact that he was hidden and inaccessible. Of Adam or Mana, one of the many Mandean

---

[1] So, e.g., Messel, *Der Menschensohn in den Bilderreden des Henoch*, pp. 73f., 77.
[2] So Gunkel, rightly, in *A.P.A.T.* II, p. 397, followed by most scholars since.

variants of the Primordial Man, it is said that he dwells 'in the sea' and comes up from it for his work of deliverance.[1] And of the Persian 'saviour' Saoshyant, to whom several features from the myth of the Primordial Man have been attached, it is said, in varying versions, that he came into existence from the seed of the prophet Zarathushtra, which was hidden in a holy lake, and that he was 'born from the waters of the lake of Kansaoya'.[2]

Eschatology, in both its national and its universalistic, other-worldly forms, spoke of omens which would precede the end; and here, too, there is mention of signs and wonders which precede the epiphany.[3] The Apocalypse of Baruch says, 'After the signs have come, of which thou wast told before, when . . . the time of My Messiah is come . . .' (2 Bar. lxxii, 2). The Apocalypse of Ezra describes these omens: ' . . . *And there shall come astonishment of mind upon the dwellers on earth: and they shall plan to war one against another, city against city, place against place, people against people, and kingdom against kingdom.* And it shall be when these things shall come to pass, and the signs shall happen which I showed thee before, then shall my servant be revealed whom thou didst see as a Man ascending' (i.e., from the sea) (2 Esdras xiii, 30f.; 'my servant' is here substituted for 'my Son', the rendering in *A.P.O.T.* II).

It is 'the day of the Elect One', 'the day of the Son of Man', which then comes.[4] Like the day of Yahweh, or like the day of a deity or a king (in the sense in which these phrases were used in ancient times), this expression denotes the day of his appearing and enthronement, the day when he is manifested in all his glory. It is in keeping with the eschatological character of the Son of Man that a day of this kind should await him. It is unlikely, therefore, that the idea is borrowed from the day of Yahweh; it belongs to the Son of Man conception. He was thought of as king of paradise (see pp. 382f.); and in his eschatological role he exercised kingly functions. Paul is certainly borrowing an element from the Son of Man theology, when he uses the expression 'the day of Jesus Christ' as a regular term for the eschatological day.[5]

But the words are also used with an extended meaning, denoting 'the days of the Son of Man', referring to the time which

[1] Reitzenstein, *Das iranische Erlösungsmysterium*, pp. 50, 51, 121f.
[2] See further, Mowinckel in *N.T.T.*, xlv, 1944, pp. 228ff.
[3] See von Gall, *Basileia*, p. 423.
[4] 1 En. lxi, 5; 2 Esdras xiii, 52; 2 Bar. lxii, 2; Luke xvii, 22, 26, 30; Matt. xxiv 37ff.
[5] 1 Cor. i, 8; v, 5; 2 Cor. i, 14; Phil. i, 6, 10; ii, 16; 1 Thess. v, 2f.; 2 Thess. i, 10; ii, 1.

will follow, the blessed new aeon, when the Son of Man will rule as king.

The Son of Man does not come alone. He 'shall be revealed, together with those who are with him' (2 Esdras vii, 28; xiii, 52). These are not necessarily identical with the heavenly community. 1 Enoch distinguishes clearly between a circle of angelic heavenly beings, and a host of elect, righteous ones, who are now in heaven, where they have their blessed abodes near those of the angels, and are with the Elect One.[1] It may well be that some of the blessed ones from the earth can appear together with the Son of Man, as when Moses and Elijah appeared together with Jesus on the mount of the Transfiguration. But when the Son of Man comes in his glory, he reveals himself together with the divine, heavenly beings.[2] This conclusion certainly follows from similar statements in the New Testament (which sound like echoes of traditional teaching), that he will come 'with all His saints', 'with the angels of His power'.[3]

13. *The Judge of the World*

When the Son of Man comes, he comes as judge, to effect the ultimate, eschatological judgement of the world. 'He shall sit on the throne of his glory.' Thereby he acquires a status similar to that of God Himself; and sometimes it is said that he will sit on God's (or 'My') throne of glory (see above, pp. 388f.). The thought was that he should be associated with God in judgement, a thought which lies behind the expressions in Dan. vii (see above, p. 352). There are other passages in apocalyptic, where God Himself is judge of the world.[4]

For 1 Enoch and the circles which it represents, the judgement is ultimately God's judgement.[5] It is said that God appears as judge; or He is described as a judge; but it is also said that the Son of Man comes with Him then (1 En. xlvi, 1; xlvii, 3; xlviii, 2).

Although it is explicitly stated that the Son of Man is installed as judge, God Himself is sometimes described as the real agent, and He more or less displaces the Son of Man (1 En. lxii, 10ff.; lxiii). But the prevailing conception is that God hands over His authority

---

[1] 1 En. xxxix, 4–7; see above, pp. 379ff.; and cf. Staerk, *Soter* II, pp. 441, 516ff.
[2] But contrast Staerk, *Soter* II, p. 516.
[3] 1 Thess. iii, 13; 2 Thess. i, 7; Matt. xxv, 31.
[4] Dan. vii; 2 Esdras vii, 26ff.; 1 En. xxxviii, 4; xlvi, 1; xlvii, 3; xlviii, 3, 7; l, 1ff.; liv, 5f.; lviii, 6ff.; lx, 2; xc, 20; cf. xxv, 3.
[5] Cf. Sjöberg, *Der Menschensohn*, pp. 8off.

as judge to the Son of Man, even if the latter is always thought of as acting by God's warrant and as His instrument.

The judgement of the Son of Man is universal and cosmic, a judgement on heaven and earth.[1] When the Messiah-Son-of-Man reveals himself, 'whatever will then befall (will befall) the whole earth' (2 Bar. xxix, 1). He will summon all the nations (2 Bar. lxxii, 2). Everything in the world will be brought low (2 Bar. lxxiii, 1). 'All who dwell on earth shall fall down and worship before him' (1 En. xlviii, 5).

> And the Lord of Spirits placed the Elect One on the throne of glory.
> And he shall judge all the works of the holy above in the heaven,
> And in the balance shall their deeds be weighed.
>
> (1 En. lxviii, 8)

He is also appointed as judge over all the angels (1 En. xli, 9). He will judge all the sinners and unrighteous, all kings, great men, and mighty ones, and all who dwell on earth (1 En. lxii, 2ff.). All judgement is given to the Son of Man (1 En. lxix, 27). When the mighty ones of the whole earth are presented before his judgement seat,

> he shall reprove them for their ungodliness,
> rebuke them for their unrighteousness,
> reproach them to their faces with their treacheries.
>
> (2 Esdras xii, 32)

A great host of people is brought before him, some of whom are glad, some sorrowful, some in bonds, some bringing others as an offering (2 Esdras xiii, 13, alluding to Isa. lxvi, 20); Jews and heathen, godly and ungodly will then be brought to judgement, including the Jews of the Dispersion, whom the heathen will bring as an offering to the true God.

As already mentioned, the angelic powers will also be brought to judgement.[2] Later Judaism was familiar with the notion that there existed wicked, fallen angels, the protector deities of the heathen empires, and those who lured men into sin. It is a leading

---

[1] 2 Bar. xxviii–xxx; lxix–lxxiv; 1 En. xlv–l; lxi–lxiv; lxix, 26ff.; 2 Esdras xii f.; John v, 22–27.

[2] 1 En. xli, 9; lv, 4; lxi, 8; cf. 3 En. xvi, 1; xlviii, C 8 (here transferred to Metatron). See Sjöberg, *Der Menschensohn*, pp. 67f. 'The holy above' (1 En lxi, 8) also denotes the angels; see above, p. 380 n. 6.

idea in the Apocalypse of Enoch, where it is explicitly stated that the kings and mighty ones 'shall have to behold Mine Elect One, how he sits on the throne of glory and judges Azazel (i.e., Satan), and all his associates, and all his hosts in the name of the Lord of Spirits'.[1] This feature, the destruction of Beliar and of the demonic powers, also appears in the Messiah ben Levi, where it is undoubtedly a borrowing from the Son of Man (cf. pp. 382f.). But also the good angels, 'the holy', must have their actions tested by the judgement of the Son of Man.[2]

Both in 1 Enoch and elsewhere it is the condemnation of the heathen, the mighty and godless ones of this world, which is in the foreground and is the object of most interest. The oppression of the godly by the ungodly is the background of the thought of judgement. Hope looks forward to the destruction of the present, evil, world rulers, to the liberation of the godly, to the redemption of Israel, and the coming of the new aeon. The judgement is regarded in a one-sided way, as a judgement of condemnation. Only occasionally does it appear that the godly will come for judgement, will be acquitted, and will obtain their right. That is why some come rejoicing before the throne of the Son of Man (2 Esdras xiii, 13), whose souls will be strengthened and who will go gladly to their innumerable dwellings (1 En. xlv, 3). But as a rule the justification or acquittal of the godly is taken for granted. For them, judgement is actually identical with the condemnation of the ungodly and the destruction of all evil powers. Therefore, they flock joyfully to the Son of Man to receive their reward (2 Esdras xiii, 13; see below, pp. 401ff.).

Where the idea of judgement occurs at all (see below, p. 396), it is thought of in forensic terms, as a real act of judgement, with accusation, conviction, and condemnation,[3] or acquittal.

> And he shall judge the secret things,
> And none shall be able to utter a lying word before him.

> And righteousness is judged before him,
> And no lying word is spoken before him.

He will convict the nations of their evil devices; for when the assize begins, the books are opened and judgement is passed

[1] 1 En. lv, 4. On the destruction of Satan, see below, pp. 397f.
[2] 1 En. lxi, 8f. See Sjöberg, op. cit., pp. 67f.
[3] 1 En. xlix, 4; lxii, 3; 2 Esdras xii, 32; xiii, 13, 37; Dan. vii, 9ff.; 1 En. lxi, 8. See above, p. 394 n. 1.

according to what is written in them. In another figure, which is used in Egyptian and Persian religion, the Elect One will weigh men's actions in the balance.[1]

The execution of judgement on the wicked also occupies a relatively large place in the description. The Son of Man shall first 'set them alive for judgement; and when he hath rebuked them he shall destroy them' (2 Esdras xii, 33).

> And all the kings and the mighty and the exalted ones
>   and those who rule the earth
> Shall fall down before him on their faces,
> And worship and set their hope upon that Son of Man,
> And petition him and supplicate for mercy at his hands . . .
> And the angels of punishment shall take them in charge,
> To execute vengeance on them because they have oppressed
> His (God's) children and His elect.
>   (1 En. lxii, 9–11; see *A.P.O.T.*, ad loc., for text of *v.* 11.)

> And he caused the sinners to pass away and be destroyed
>   from off the face of the earth,
> And those who have led the world astray.
> With chains shall they be bound,
> And in their assemblage-place of destruction shall they be
>   imprisoned,
> And all their works vanish from the face of the earth.
>   (1 En. lxix, 27f.)

The description of the destruction is particularly prominent in the many passages where the conception of a judicial process is not maintained.

In addition to this, we also find another and more mythological conception of the judgement as a victorious conflict and the destruction of the wicked. As we have seen above (pp. 378f, 384f.), judgement is really only another expression for the destruction of the enemy and the salvation of the godly, very much as it was in the earlier Jewish hope of restoration and eschatology (see above, pp. 176ff., 311ff.). In the prophets and the earlier future hope, the forensic conception of judgement as a judicial process in the proper sense occurs relatively infrequently and is intended metaphori-

---

[1] 1 En. xli, 1; lxi, 8; cf. Job xxxi, 6; Prov. xvi, 2; xxi, 2; xxiv, 12; Ps. lxii, 10; Dan. v, 27; Ps. Sol. v, 6. Cf. Brandt in *Jahrbücher für protestantische Theologie*, 1892, p. 431; Stade-Bertholet, *Biblische Theologie des Alten Testaments* II, p. 454, with references to the sources and to literature.

cally.[1] It is more characteristic of later Jewish eschatology (see above, p. 273). When the Son of Man appeared on the clouds of heaven, Ezra saw that 'there was gathered together from the four winds of heaven an innumerable multitude of men to make war against the Man that came up out of the sea' (2 Esdras xiii, 5f.). This is applied by the apocalyptist to the heathen nations who assemble to fight against Israel's Messiah. Elsewhere, too, it is said that no instruments of war will avail in the conflict with the Elect One (1 En. lii, 6ff.). The similarity to the older myth of the conflict of the nations (p. 140) is obvious.

But there is reason to believe that the original tradition spoke of an army of all the demons that heaven holds, 'the spiritual hosts of wickedness in the heavenly places'. This is, at all events, in agreement with what the Testament of Levi expects of the Messiah, the 'new priest':

And Beliar shall be bound by him,
And he shall give power to His children to tread upon
the evil spirits. (xviii, 12; cf. T. Dan v, 10)

It is by his miraculous power that the Son of Man destroys his adversaries:

And the word of his mouth slays all the sinners,
And all the unrighteous are destroyed from before his face.
(1 En. lxii, 2; cf. 2 Esdras xii, 33; xiii, 38)

Here, too, belong all the many passages in the apocalypses, which speak of the assault made by Satan or Beliar against God, His kingdom, and His saints, and of the destruction of Satan and his angels,[2] a destruction which is sometimes also connected with with the judgement.[3] The fact that the archangels Gabriel and Michael frequently appear as leaders in the conflict with Satan[4] is probably a modification in terms of Jewish nationalism of an earlier universalistic conception of the Son of Man as the leader of God's army in the conflict with Satan, such as we find in Rev. xix, 11, where the rider on the white horse, who overcomes Satan, is the same as the one whom the seer beheld appearing in the like-

---

[1] Cf. W. Cossmann, *Die Entwickelung des Gerichtsgedankens bei den alttestamentlichen Propheten*, a work which, however, does not give adequate treatment of the point mentioned above.

[2] 1 En. xvi, 1ff.; x, 16; liv, 4ff.; lv, 4; lxviii, 5; xc, 21ff.; T. Judah xxv, 3; cf. T. Dan v, 10. See von Gall, *Basileia*, pp. 294, 297, 299.

[3] 1 En. xvi, 1ff.; cf. 2 En. vii, 1ff.

[4] Dan. x, 13, 21; xii, 1; Rev. xii, 7ff.; Ass. Mos. x, 1f.

ness of a son of man,[1] the herald of the final judgement on the enemies of God.

Thus the judgement of the Son of Man is a judgement of cosmic dimensions. Alongside it, however, we find the conception (somewhat more limited by Jewish nationalism) of a judgement on Israel's earthly enemies and a reckoning with them. This is only to be expected, since the Son of Man was equated with the Jewish Messiah. Even the Apocalypse of Enoch, which includes the whole world and the cosmos in its purview, loves to assert that judgement will fall upon the kings and mighty ones of the earth, who have not acknowledged Israel's God (xlvi, 6), but have oppressed the righteous, and maltreated the children and the elect of the Lord of Spirits.

> And they shall be a spectacle for the righteous and for His
> elect:
> They shall rejoice over them,
> Because the wrath of the Lord of Spirits resteth upon them,
> And His sword is drunk with their blood. (1 En. lxii, 12)

Behind the Apocalypse of Ezra there is actual experience of the destruction of Jerusalem; and in it this nationalistic attitude is still more evident, though there, too, the universalistic background is clear enough.[2] 2 Bar. lxxii, 4–6 says quite explicitly, 'Every nation, which knows not Israel and has not trodden down the seed of Jacob, shall indeed be spared . . . But all those who have ruled over you, or have known you, shall be given up to the sword.'

Thus the Apocalypse of Baruch makes a distinction among the heathen. Those who have had no hand in the oppression of Israel shall survive. Elsewhere, the prevailing thought is that the world powers and the heathen will be utterly destroyed: they are all sinful, and instruments of the wicked demonic powers and of Satan's enmity against the Lord of Spirits. But occasionally we find traces of an earlier, more sober, national eschatology. In the Apocalypse of Enoch there is a short section[3] which tells how, when a change comes for the holy and elect, when, on the day of affliction, evil has been treasured up for sinners, when the righteous have been victorious over them in the name of the Lord of

---

[1] Rev. i, 13; xiv, 14; cf. the woman in heaven who gives birth to a male child (xii, 13).

[2] 2 Esdras xi, 32–45; xii, 32–4, xiii, 12ff., 35ff.; xi, 46.

[3] 1 En. l. On the authenticity of the chapter, see Sjöberg, *Der Menschensohn*, pp. 142f.

Spirits, then 'the others' will repent, and abstain from the works of their hands, because, though He is righteous in His judgement, He will have compassion on them, because His compassion is great. They will be saved by His name; but they will receive no honour from the Lord of Spirits. The reference here is clearly to the survivors of the defeated and destroyed heathen nations, and to their association with Israel as obedient vassals, a thought which is common in the earlier nationalistic eschatology (see p. 314). But this is not an essential feature in the thought of the Son of Man and his judgement.[1]

14. The Son of Man and the Resurrection

The prevailing thought in the eschatology of later Judaism is that the resurrection of the dead precedes the judgement.[2] This is so in 1 Enoch, where the resurrection follows the appearance and enthronement of the Son of Man.

> And he shall chose the righteous and holy from among them:
> For the day has drawn nigh that they should be saved.
> And the Elect One shall in those days sit on My throne . . .
> (1 En. li, 2f.)

This passage does not directly indicate who shall raise the dead. Within normative Judaism it is taken for granted that the resurrection is God's own work.[3] God is 'He who quickens the dead', as the Shemoneh Esreh puts it, although sometimes it is one of the archangels who gives the signal by a blast on the trumpet.[4] The Messiah of the earlier period has nothing to do with the resurrection.[5]

But there are occasional indications that the resurrection was connected with the Son of Man: it is he who is the intermediary at the resurrection, or who calls forth the dead.[6] 2 Bar. xxx, 1ff. runs: 'And it shall come to pass after these things, when the time of the advent of the Messiah is fulfilled, that He shall return in glory' (i.e., from heaven to earth). 'Then all who have fallen asleep in

---

[1] Cf. Sjöberg, op. cit., p. 143.

[2] See above, p. 273. In 2 Esdras vii, 32 the resurrection follows the Messianic kingdom. This is a logical consequence of the fact that there the kingdom has become a temporary kingdom, before the dawn of the new aeon. The Apocalypse of Baruch is less consistent, and, therefore, not clear (see xxix f.).

[3] See Bousset, Relig.², pp. 308ff., especially p. 315.

[4] 2 Esdras vi, 23; 1 Cor. xv, 52; 1 Thess. iv, 16.

[5] Bousset, op. cit., ibid.; cf. above, p. 397, on the archangels.

[6] See von Gall, Basileia, pp. 426f. The relevant passages are: 2 Bar. xxx; lxxii 2 Esdras xii, 33; 1 En. li, 1ff.; lxi, 4f.

hope of Him shall rise again.' (This must refer to the hope that he would raise them up.) Then the souls of the righteous shall rejoice, while the souls of the wicked shall 'waste away the more. For they shall know that their torment has come and their perdition has arrived.' The same thought occurs (but with a more collective emphasis) in connexion with the reference to the fate of the different nations at the judgement, when it is said that he will call forth all the nations for judgement, and will spare some but slay others. Similarly we find the explicit statement in 2 Esdras xiii, 33: 'At the first he shall set them alive for judgement; and when he hath rebuked them he shall destroy them.' If the reference were to those who were still alive on earth, it would be quite unnecessary to say that they would be set alive for judgement. 1 Enoch, too, says, as we have seen, that at the resurrection the Elect One will choose out the holy and elect among them, because the day of their redemption will then be at hand. This suggests that Enoch is echoing a tradition which originally said that the Son of Man summons forth the dead. So, too, when we read,

> And these measures shall reveal all the secrets of the
>   depths of the earth,
> And those who have been destroyed by the desert,
> And those who have been devoured by the beasts,
> And those who have been devoured by the fish of the sea,
> That they may return and stay themselves
> On the day of the Elect One. (1 En. lxi, 5)

Elsewhere, too, there are traces of this belief that the Son of Man has a connexion with the resurrection. The statement in a late Jewish writing[1] that the Messiah raises the dead is not derived from Old Testament ideas, or from the conception of the national Messiah. The same is true of the saying, which occurs once in the rabbinic literature, that at the resurrection the Messiah will raise Adam first.[2] Ideas from the conception of the Son of Man have survived in certain strata of the tradition, and have ultimately been connected with the Messiah. The same conception underlies the saying of Jesus that 'the hour is coming, and now is, when all who are in the graves will hear his voice' (i.e., the voice of the Son of Man; John v, 27–29).

But the thought that the Son of Man will raise the dead is over-

---

[1] See Strack-Billerbeck I, p. 524, and above, p. 319 and n. 3.
[2] See Strack-Billerbeck III, p. 10 and p. 337 above.

shadowed by the more theocentric view, that God himself will work the miracle; and we never find a clear and emphatic statement that the Son of Man will raise the dead. This is no doubt because we are here dealing with a thought associated with an earlier, pre-Jewish phase of the idea of the Son of Man (see below, pp. 420ff.), which was pushed into the background because in Jewish eyes it was too violent an invasion of God's own prerogatives.

15. *The Deliverance of the Godly*

For the godly (the elect, the holy, the righteous) the coming and judgement of the Son of Man mean salvation and deliverance.[1]

He shall be a staff to the righteous whereon to stay themselves and not fall,
And he shall be the light of the Gentiles,
And the hope of those who are troubled of heart . . .
He hath preserved the lot of the righteous,
Because they have hated and despised this world of unrighteousness,
And have hated all its works and ways in the name of the Lord of Spirits:
For in his name they are saved,
And according to his good pleasure hath it been in regard to their life.

And the righteous and elect shall be saved on that day,
And they shall never thenceforward see the face of the sinners and unrighteous.

And he shall choose the righteous and holy from among them (those who have been raised):
For the day has drawn nigh that they should be saved.

In 1 Enoch the deliverance of the pious is not described in very precise terms. That deliverance is primarily from the oppression and tyranny of the ungodly, heathen, world powers. Therefore the main emphasis is laid on the description of the judgement of these powers, and of the final destruction of them and of all the wicked cosmic powers (cf. above, p. 397). But deliverance also means that the godly, the elect, and the righteous, share in the blessedness which God has appointed for them. Therefore they

[1] 1 En. xlviii, 4ff.; lxii, 13; li, 2; lxi, 4f.; 2 Esdras xii, 34; xiii, 26, 29.

2D

greet with joy the enthronement of the Son of Man and his appearance to judge sinners.

> Then will I cause Mine Elect One to dwell among them (the
> elect) . . .
> For I have provided and satisfied with peace My righteous
> ones
> And have caused them to dwell before me:
> But for the sinners there is judgement impending with Me,
> So that I shall destroy them from the face of the earth.

The righteous will rise up to eternal life, and light, and blessedness. They will share in the divine wisdom, righteousness, and compassion.[1]

This is God's work; but it may also be regarded as the work of the Son of Man, not only because it accompanies his appearing and judgement, but because it is said that at the resurrection he will choose the righteous as his own (1 En. li, 2), and that they will stand before him (1 En. lii, 8).

On the other hand, nothing is said about the Son of Man delivering his own from sin. The deliverance is from the oppression of the ungodly. The godly have sinned, of course (all men fall into unwitting sin or sins of weakness), and need forgiveness.[2] But the Christian recognition of the complete bondage to sin, from which all men need to be delivered, and of 'justification' as a justification of sinners, is not the prevailing attitude in apocalyptic, although the general sinfulness of man is strongly emphasized.[3] In apocalyptic the Son of Man is the righteous judge of sinners, not their deliverer.

The deliverance of the righteous can, however, be regarded from a more nationalistic standpoint, or from one that is more individualistic and universalistic. Within the framework of a more nationalistic eschatology, it means that the Son of Man, like the Messiah of the earlier period, delivers Israel, and saves God's people who survive, who have been saved thoughout His borders, as the Most High says in 2 Esdras xii, 34. This salvation also means that the Son of Man gathers to himself all the dispersed, including the lost ten tribes, and leads them back to Israel's land (2 Esdras xiii, 12f., 39ff.). The aim of salvation may be regarded

---

[1] 1 En. lxix, 26f.; xlv, 4–6; xlviii, 2–4; li, 1f.; lviii, 3–6: lxi, 5; xxxix, 5; xlviii, 1; lviii, 4f.; cf. Sjöberg, *Der Menschensohn*, pp. 79f.
[2] 1 En. v, 6ff.; on the above, see Sjöberg, op. cit., pp. 79f.
[3] 2 Esdras iii, 4ff.; vii, 116ff.; viii, 34f.

as the restoration and glorification of Israel (2 Esdras x, 35ff., 50ff.), when the Son of Man appears and ends the world power and its ungodly kings (2 Esdras xi f.). The Apocalypse of Enoch also says that on that day the Israelites who have been carried away will come from the ends of the earth, and fall down and worship the Lord of Spirits.[1]

But it is characteristic of apocalyptic eschatology that this idea appears only once in 1 Enoch, and has no organic connexion with the thought of the book as a whole; and in the Apocalypse of Ezra the national kingdom of the Son of Man is regarded as an interim kingdom before the real restoration and the coming of the new aeon.[2]

The fundamental idea in apocalyptic is a different one. There the good and the wicked are not necessarily identical with Israel and the heathen. There are many sinners in Israel, too, who come mournfully before the Son of Man and are condemned. Ezra laments that the majority must be lost.[3] The Apocalypse of Enoch, too, recognizes that there are many sinners in Israel; it depends upon the decision and choice of the individual whether he belongs to the righteous or to the sinners. The ideas about deliverance are not framed in accordance with the narrow outlook of Jewish particularism; and the ideas about the saving work of the Son of Man are in accord with the universalistic, cosmic view of the nature and mission of the Son of Man. Salvation itself is thought of in cosmic terms. Accordingly we read of the Man who rose up from the depths of the sea, 'This is he whom the Most High is keeping many ages [(*and*) *through whom he will deliver his creation*]' (2 Esdras xiii, 26). '*The day shall come when the Most High is about to deliver those that are upon earth*' (2 Esdras xiii, 29).

16. *The Kingdom of the Son of Man*

Because the deliverance is connected with the appearing and judgement of the Son of Man, it can also be regarded as a participation in the kingdom of the Son of Man. His appearing was both his enthronement and the inauguration of his dominion (see above, pp. 388f).

In the first place, his kingdom is a world dominion.[4] He comes

---

[1] 1 En. lvii. On the authenticity of the chapter, see Sjöberg, *Der Menschensohn*, p. 144.
[2] See above, pp. 277, 321, 324, and below, p. 404.
[3] 2 Esdras iii, 4ff., and frequently. See Gunkel in *A.P.A.T.* II, pp. 337ff.
[4] 1 En. xlvi, 4–6; lii, 3f.; liii, 1; lxii, 2, 5ff.; lxi, 6ff.; 2 Bar. xxxix, 7f.

and takes his seat on his (or, sometimes, God's) throne of glory (see above, p. 389). He requires all the kings of the earth to praise and exalt him. All might must bow down before him, that he may be mighty and strong on the earth. 'All who dwell on the earth and sea and islands shall bring to him gifts and presents and tokens of homage.' 'And all who dwell above in the heaven received a command and power and one voice and one light like unto fire.

> And that One (with) their first words they blessed,
> And extolled and lauded with wisdom.'

His kingdom is also an everlasting kingdom.[1] He, who was created and chosen before the creation of the world, will also remain for ever before the Lord of Spirits.

> The Elect One standeth before the Lord of Spirits,
> And his glory is for ever and ever,
> And his might unto all generations.

As early as Daniel (which means the tradition before him) we hear that to the Son of Man, who came on the clouds of heaven, there was given 'dominion and glory and kingdom, that all peoples, nations, and tongues should serve him. His dominion is an everlasting dominion, which shall not pass away, and his kingdom a kingdom that shall not be destroyed' (Dan. vii, 14).

Where the fusion of the Son of Man and the Messiah has led to the thought of the interim kingdom, we find also that the dominion of the Son of Man is limited in time. This is so in 2 Esdras vii, 29ff.; xii, 34; and in 2 Bar. xxxix f. But there the Son of Man appears in the guise of the national, this-worldly Messiah. And when we read, 'And his principate will stand for ever, until the world of corruption is at an end, and until the times aforesaid are fulfilled' (2 Bar. xl, 3), the original thought of the everlasting dominion of the Son of Man is still perceptible in the blend of the two theological ideas.

The Son of Man has become a king, and sits upon his throne; and it was as king that the evangelists thought of Jesus, the Son of Man.[2]

On the location of the kingdom of the Son of Man, testimony varies, and there is an elusive vagueness. When it is stated that he will come with the clouds of heaven or from the sea, and that

---

[1] 1 En. xlviii, 6; xlix, 2; 2 Bar. xl, 3; lxxiii, 1; cf. T. Levi, xviii.
[2] Matt. xxv, 34; xvi, 28; xx, 21; Luke xxii, 29f.; cf. Matt. xix, 28f.

he will return,[1] it is assumed that it is to earth that he will come. Both the Ezra Apocalypse and the Baruch Apocalypse regard the interim kingdom (as they hold the Messianic kingdom to be) as a kingdom on this earth. But it is an 'earth' which is superterrestrial and ideally transfigured in a far greater measure than in the older, this-worldly eschatology. The blessed will enjoy an everlasting banquet on the flesh of the two great sea-monsters, Behemoth and Leviathan, which were created on the fifth day of creation, and preserved until that time to serve as food for those who survive (i.e., the remnant which is saved). 'The earth also shall yield its fruit ten thousandfold and on each (?) vine there shall be a thousand branches, and each branch shall produce a thousand clusters, and each cluster produce a thousand grapes, and each grape produce a cor of wine. And those who have hungered shall rejoice: moreover, also, they shall behold marvels every day. For winds shall go forth from before Me to bring every morning the fragrance of aromatic fruits, and at the close of the day clouds distilling the dew of health. And it shall come to pass at that self-same time that the treasury of manna shall again descend from on high, and they will eat of it in those years, because these are they who have come to the consummation of time' (2 Bar. xxix, 5 8).

1 Enoch, too, speaks of 'the dominion of His anointed' (on the earth), where the righteous shall dwell and the elect walk. But it is a transfigured earth, together with a transformed heaven:

And I will transform the heaven and make it an eternal bless-
ing and light:
And I will transform the earth and make it a blessing:
And I will cause Mine elect ones to dwell upon it:
But the sinners and evil-doers shall not set foot thereon.[2]

It is a world which has been created anew, an earth where stands the throne of God and of the Son of Man, and where the elect will live in blessedness. Immediately before the saying about the transformed heaven and earth, we read,

Then will I cause Mine Elect One to dwell among them;

but it is also said that the Elect One will stand before the Lord of Spirits, endowed with glory to all eternity. And conversely, it is also said that

---

[1] 2 Bar. xxx, 1. See von Gall, *Basileia*, p. 427. Kautzsch (in *A.P.A.T.* II, p. 423) supplies 'to heaven'; but this does not agree with what the context says about the interim kingdom.   [2] 1 En. xlv, 4f.; cf. lii, 4; li, 3–5; xlix, 2.

The elect shall begin to dwell with the Elect One[1] . . .
On the day of the Elect One.

But the dwelling of the Elect One is in heaven, with the Lord of Spirits.

Some light may be shed on this dual character of the kingdom of the Son of Man by another seemingly obscure passage: 'And after this the Righteous and Elect One shall cause the house of his congregation to appear: henceforth they shall no more be hindered in the name of the Lord of Spirits' (1 En. liii, 6). The reference is clearly to the heavenly community, which is with the Son of Man even now, before his parousia.[2] In the last times it will be revealed. The eschatological community of holy and righteous elect ones, which from one point of view is the remnant, those who have passed through the final afflictions, and have been saved from evil at the coming of the Son of Man, is also, from another point of view, identical with, and the 'earthly' realization and manifestation of, the heavenly community around the Son of Man. It is the eschatological *communio sanctorum*, the society of the holy, the new, distinctive, eschatological, people of God, consisting of both the elect in heaven and the elect on earth. The hindrances which have befallen the earthly community, have also befallen the heavenly community which is manifested: the two are one. Similar conceptions also appear in 2 Esdras vii, 28; xiii, 52; xiv, 9.

The obscurity in Enoch's view of the kingdom is inherent in the nature of the subject, in the superterrestrial logic of the kingdom. It follows from the fact that the writer is dealing with realities of faith, which do not belong to the empirical world: the absolute eschaton (to use Otto's expression), matters which cannot be expressed by earthly conceptions and thought-forms, that which is and yet is not, that which is at the same time present and remote, at once heavenly and earthly.[3]

Thus it is a new world of another kind which is made real when the kingdom of the Son of Man is revealed. 2 Esdras vii, 26 says

[1] 1 En. lxi, 4. The text has 'the elect shall begin to dwell with the elect' (see *A.P.O.T.* II, ad loc.), which does not make sense. The line must originally have ended with a singular. Elsewhere in the Ethiopic text there is confusion of the singular and plural forms of this expression.

[2] See above, p. 379ff. 'The synagogues which the Messiah restores' (so Beer, *A.P.A.T.* II, p. 266) cannot be the sense here. The reference is to eschatological realities, which, like the Son of Man himself, will one day appear. In xlvi, 8 'the houses of His (i.e., the Lord of Spirits) congregations' clearly refers to the dwellings of the pre-existent heavenly community 'the faithful who hang upon the name of the Lord of Spirits'. [3] With the above, cf. Dahl, *Das Volk Gottes*, pp. 85ff.

that the city that is now invisible shall appear, and the land which is now concealed shall be seen. God transforms heaven and earth (1 En. xlv, 4f.; cf. l, 4). Men, too, are transformed, and become as the angels in heaven (1 En. li, 4).

Behind all this lies the conception of paradise, which, according to later Jewish belief, would remain hidden with God until the end. As we read in 1 En. xlviii, 1,

> And in that place (i.e., where the throne of the Lord of
>   Spirits stands) I saw the fountain of righteousness
> Which was inexhaustible:
> And around it were many fountains of wisdom:
> And all the thirsty drank of them,
> And were filled with wisdom,
> And their dwellings were with the righteous and holy and
>   elect.

The reference here is to the fountain of paradise with the water of life. The invisible city and the hidden land are the heavenly Jerusalem and paradise, which are elsewhere mentioned together.[1] 2 Bar. xxix, 5ff. describes the fruitfulness of paradise. Alluding quite overtly to the paradise narrative and to the features from the paradise myth in Isa. ix, 1ff., the writer describes conditions in the new world, where

> asps and dragons shall come forth from their holes to submit
>   themselves to a little child.
> And women shall no longer have pain when they bear.
> (2 Bar. lxxiii, 6f.)

In T. Levi xviii, the connexion of the Messiah with paradise is clear:

> And he shall open the gates of paradise,
> And shall remove the threatening sword against Adam.
> And he shall give to the saints to eat from the tree of life.
> (vv. 10f.)

As we have already seen (pp. 382f.), the Messiah is also associated in another way with the conception of paradise.

The kingdom of the Son of Man is also a kingdom of peace

> And it shall come to pass, when he has
>   brought low everything that is in the world,

---

[1] 2 Bar. iv; Rev. xxii, 2; see Gunkel in *A.P.A.T.* II, p. 370.

And has sat down in peace for the age on the throne of
   his kingdom,
That joy shall then be revealed . . .   (2 Bar. lxxiii, 1)

All the world's martial power and skill in arms are destroyed before him.

And there shall be no iron for war,
Nor shall one clothe oneself with a breastplate.
Bronze shall be of no service,
And tin [shall be of no service and] shall not be esteemed.
And lead shall not be desired.
And all these things shall be [denied and] destroyed from
   the surface of the earth,
When the Elect One shall appear before the Lord of Spirits.
                       (1 En. lii, 8f.)

Where the elect have drunk of the fountain of righteousness and
wisdom, and have themselves become righteous and holy, like the
angels in heaven, they have become perfect, in accordance with
the will of the Most High. 1 En. xxxix, 5f. says that righteousness
will prevail in his days, and that it flows before them as water for
ever and ever. The righteous stay themselves upon him, and do
not fall (1 En. xlviii, 4).

Wisdom is poured out like water,
And glory faileth not before him for evermore . . .
And unrighteousness shall disappear as a shadow,
And have no continuance. (1 En. xlix, 1f.)

Sinners and transgressors are no more. Tyrants are overthrown;

And on the day of their affliction there shall be rest on
   the earth. (1 En. xlviii, 10)
And from henceforth there shall be nothing corruptible.
                       (1 En. lxix, 29)

For the Son of Man, who rules over them, is himself full of wisdom
and righteousness, of the spirit of might and understanding (1 En.
xlix, 3).

Salvation is then realized, and blessedness attained. But, as
1 Enoch sees it, the essence of the blessedness of the elect is the
personal fellowship they will have with the Son of Man in his
kingdom before God's face.

And the Lord of Spirits will abide over them,
And with that Son of Man shall they eat
And lie down and rise up for ever and ever. (1 En. lxii, 14)

Like him, they will be arrayed in the heavenly glory.

And the righteous and the elect shall have risen from
the earth,
And ceased to be of downcast countenance.
And they shall have been clothed with garments of glory,
And these shall be the garments of life from the Lord
of Spirits:
And your garments shall not grow old,
Nor your glory pass away before the Lord of Spirits.
(1 En. lxii, 15f.)

Arrayed in the heavenly festal attire, to share in an everlasting, joyous banquet with the Son of Man: this is the simple picture by means of which the apocalyptist tries to express the inexpressible.

But the ungodly, the mighty ones and the tyrants, may not set foot on this transformed earth (1 En. xlv, 5). In their affliction they cry for mercy, but are denied it.

'And we pass away from before His face on account of
our works,
And all our sins are reckoned up in righteousness . . .

Our souls are full of unrighteous gain, but it does not prevent us from descending from the midst thereof into the †burden† of Sheol.'

And after that their faces shall be filled with darkness
And shame before that Son of Man,
And they shall be driven from his presence,
And the sword shall abide before his face in their midst.
(1 En. lxiii, 9 11)

But the last aim which the Lord of Spirits appointed for the work of the Son of Man, when He called him by name, before the creation of the sun and the zodiac, and chose him, and hid him beside Himself, is that all who dwell on earth should fall down and worship and praise and extol and celebrate with song the name of the Lord of Spirits. When the Son of Man has taken his seat for judgement on his throne of glory, he will summon the whole

host of heaven, all the holy ones in the height, God's host, cherubim, seraphim, and ophannim,[1] all the angels of power, all the
angels of dominion, the elect ones, and all the other powers, those
on earth, and those over the water (i.e., the water above the vault
of heaven) and on that day they will unite with one voice to praise
and glorify, to extol and celebrate with song in the spirit of faith,
wisdom, patience, mercy, peace, and goodness, and all will say
with one voice 'Blessed is He, and may the name of the Lord of
Spirits be blessed for ever and ever' (1 En. xlviii, 5f.; lxi, 9ff.).

That God alone should have the glory for ever is the sum of the
mission of the Son of Man.

17. *Atoning Suffering and Death*

Finally, the question arises, did later Judaism have any doctrine
of the vicarious suffering and death of the Messiah; or, more correctly, was it also part of the character and work of the Son of
Man in pre-Christian Judaism to suffer and die for the salvation
of men? We have seen above (pp. 325ff.) that no such idea was
connected with the conception of the national Messiah. If it did
exist in the theology of later Judaism, it must have been in association with the idea of the Son of Man. What, then, is the position?

As Dalman and Klausner have maintained,[2] the answer must be
that in the entire apocalyptic literature there is not a single passage
which suggests that it is part of the vocation of the Son of Man that
he must suffer and die to atone for the sins of men, Only in the
Apocalypse of Ezra is there mention of the death of the Messiah;
and that, as we have seen (p. 285; cf. p. 277), is merely a relic of the
old conception of a wholly this-worldly, mortal Messiah, which is
occasionally adopted in later Jewish theology in order to bridge
the gulf between the this-worldly and the other-worldly eschatology by means of the idea of the Millennium. At the end of the
interim kingdom, the Messiah must die like all other men. There
is no mention of suffering or atonement. After seven days' silence,
such as there was before the creation, the Messiah and the rest of
the dead rise up again to everlasting glory.

Nevertheless J. Jeremias has revived the view that in later
Judaism there actually was a belief in the suffering and death of

---

[1] *'ôpannîm*, literally 'wheels', denotes a class of angels. The expression is derived
from Ezekiel's vision (i, 15). See Odeberg, *3 Enoch*, pp. 147ff., and Index, s.v.
"Ophannim'.
[2] See Dalman, *Der leidende und sterbende Messias*; Klausner, *Die messianischen Vorstellungen des jüdischen Volkes im Zeitalter der Tannaiten.*

the Son of Man.[1] The main argument for the hypothesis is that, in the Apocalypse of Enoch, the Son of Man is conceived and described after the pattern of the suffering Servant of the Lord in Deutero-Isaiah, and must therefore be thought in terms of the Servant in his exaltation, after enduring his atoning suffering and death.

The hypothesis has recently been exhaustively examined by Sjöberg, who has worked through all the arguments in support of it, point by point, and has shown that it is untenable.[2] Dalman and Klausner were right.

First, we must note that neither Jeremias nor the others who have adopted his views have seriously attempted to show that the thought that the Son of Man has actually suffered and died occurs in 1 Enoch, or that his heavenly glory is presented there as a reward for any atoning suffering.[3] The only passage to which they have been able to appeal is 1 En. xlvii, 4, where it is said the blood of the righteous has been required before the Lord of Spirits. But the context makes it certain that the singular, 'the righteous', is here, as in some other passages in 1 Enoch (xci, 10; xcii, 3f.), used generically or collectively for 'the righteous ones'.[4] The only positive argument advanced by Jeremias is that in 1 Enoch there are indications in the Son of Man of influence from the description of the Suffering Servant; but he is unable to show that the idea of suffering has left any trace whatsoever.

It is true that individual ideas and phrases in the Servant Songs can be shown to have influenced the sayings about the Son of Man. But, as both Moore and Sjöberg have pointed out,[5] the fact that the rabbis or the apocalyptists interpreted detached passages of Scripture as Messianic is no proof that they also understood the whole to which these passages belong as referring to the Messiah or the Son of Man, or that they actually applied the entire des-

---

[1] J. Jeremias in *Deutsche Theologie*, ii, 1929, pp. 106ff.; see above, p. 327 n. 1. Schniewind (*Das Evangelium nach Markus*, pp. 110f.) and Johansson (*Parakletoi*, pp. 113ff.) both support Jeremias. Sjöberg (*Der Menschensohn*, p. 116 n. 4) points out that Jeremias's main contention and all his arguments were presented by Billerbeck in *Nathanael*, 1905, pp. 89ff.; cf. Strack-Billerbeck I, p. 481; II p. 282 n. 1.

[2] See the article in *S.E.Å.* v, 1940, pp. 163ff., and *Der Menschensohn*, pp. 116ff.

[3] Neither the fact that the Son of Man is for the time being hidden (that is, with the Lord of Spirits in heaven; see above, pp. 385ff.), nor the possibility that he is thought of as identical with the exalted Enoch (see below, pp. 437ff.) has any bearing on his supposed suffering and death. See Sjöberg, *Der Menschensohn*, pp. 130ff. The question of the death of the Messiah-Son-of-Man in the Apocalypse of Ezra has already been considered above; cf. Sjöberg, op. cit., pp. 134ff.

[4] See Charles, *The Book of Enoch translated*[2], p. 90; Sjöberg, op. cit., pp. 128ff.

[5] See Moore, *Judaism* I, p. 229; Sjöberg, *Der Menschensohn*, p. 119.

cription to either of them. The way in which the Targum interprets Isa. liii of the Messiah is a valid proof of this point. The
actual description of the Servant in the Songs, his story, and the
thoughts about him are simply *not* applied to the Messiah in the
Targum. Even if it could be shown that Enoch's description of
the Son of Man contained, in thought and in phraseology, many
individual reminiscences of the sayings about the Servant of the
Lord, this would not prove that the Son of Man was regarded as
the exalted Servant of the Lord, or was, in general, conceived in
terms of that specific figure.[1]

In fact, the reminiscences of the Servant Songs and of Deutero-
Isaiah in the descriptions of the Son of Man are not nearly so
numerous or so obvious as Jeremias, Staerk, and others hold.[2]
Neither 'the Righteous One' nor 'the Elect One' is so distinctive
a designation of the Servant of the Lord that it must have been
derived from that source for the Son of Man in 1 Enoch.[3] Nor is
the title 'Servant of God', as applied to the Son of Man (see
above, pp. 367f.), sufficiently distinctive of the Servant of the Lord
to justify the view that it was derived from the latter. As we have
seen (p. 225), it is so familiar in the thought and phraseology of
the Old Testament, that it readily presents itself as a designation
of the Messiah or of one who had a task like that of the Son of Man.
But there is a characteristic difference between the two kinds of
service. The supreme elements in the Servant's service are his
message, his vicarious suffering and death, and the bringing back

[1] So, also, G. Kittel in *R.G.G.*[2] III, col. 2120; and Sjöberg, *Der Menschensohn*, pp.
133ff. The rabbinic passages about the Servant's anguish and suffering, which are
discussed above, pp. 294ff., have no bearing on the Son of Man, or on any atoning
suffering or death, but arise from the application of normal Jewish doctrines and
exegesis to the national Messiah.
[2] The passages on which Jeremias builds his case are dealt with, one by one, by
Sjöberg (op. cit., pp. 121ff.). Staerk mentions, as evidence of influence from the
Servant of the Fourth Song, the following passages: 1 En. xlv, 3ff.; xlvi, 4, 6; xlviii, 4;
xlix, 2, 4; liii, 4ff.; lxii, 1, 3ff., 9f.; lxiii, 11 (*Soter* I, pp. 82f.). What has been said above
in reply to Jeremias is sufficient comment on these arguments.
[3] See above, pp. 365f. The fact that the Servant is once called 'the Righteous One,
My Servant' (Isa. liii, 11; but contrast the rendering above, p. 199), and that the Son
of Man is occasionally called 'the Righteous One' (see above, p. 366) is really of no
importance. 'Righteousness' is too common a characteristic among the godly to be
used as evidence of literary or theological dependence. Moreover, there are two different shades of meaning. In the Servant, righteousness is primarily his innocence; in
the Son of Man, it refers primarily to his activity as judge and saviour (see above, pp.
378f.; and cf. Sjöberg, op. cit., p. 121). Nor does the designation 'the Elect One'
prove direct dependence on the Servant Songs and Deutero-Isaiah. The expression
is too commonly applied to those agents whom Yahweh has called (see above, pp.
365f.; and cf. Sjöberg, op. cit., pp. 122f.). In the Servant Songs, the Servant is the
only one who is 'chosen' or 'elected' to lead Israel back to Yahweh; in 1 Enoch, the
Son of Man is 'the Elect One' because he represents 'the elect' as a people.

of Israel to God, which he will thus bring to pass. The supreme elements in the Son of Man's service are not humiliation and suffering, nor any message, but the judgement of the world, and the destruction of the enemies of God, the righteous, and the elect.[1]

The statement that the Son of Man will be 'the light of the Gentiles' is really a quotation from the Servant Songs. But this does not involve any profound influence from the figure of the Servant and the ideas associated with it. At most it is a minor theme, subordinate to the leading idea. In the Similitudes and elsewhere in I Enoch, the thought of the possible conversion of other nations to the religion of Yahweh is quite overshadowed by the idea of judgement and of the destruction of unbelievers (see above, pp. 394ff.).

On the other hand, it is obvious that certain expressions and phrases from Deutero-Isaiah, and especially from the Servant Songs, recur in the descriptions of the glory of the Son of Man; and through this point of connexion some influence is actually present. I Enoch says of the Son of Man,

And this Son of Man whom thou hast seen
Shall †raise up† the kings and the mighty from their seats,
[And the strong from their thrones]
And shall loosen the girdles of the strong,[2]
And break the teeth of the sinners.
[And he shall put down the kings from their thrones and
  kingdoms]
Because they do not extol and praise Him,
Nor humbly acknowledge whence the kingdom was bestowed
  upon them.
And he shall put down the countenance of the strong,
And shall fill them with shame.

(1 En. xlvi, 4–9)

---

[1] Cf. Sjöberg, *Der Menschensohn*, p. 134.
[2] The text has 'reins'; so *A.P.O.T.* II. Beer and Sjöberg render *Zügel*. The line refers to the throwing off of the yoke of the strong from the godly. But the parallel line which follows suggests that there is a direct reference to the destruction of the power of the strong and of sinners. It may be that the Greek translator misunderstood a word in the original text, namely, *mûsār* (Job xii, 18) or *môsēr* (ibid., Targum and V) or *môsērâh*. In Job xii, 18 it is parallel to '*ēzôr*, and undoubtedly denotes the girdle of kings, as a symbol of rank and strength; cf. the phrase 'to gird with strength' (1 Sam. ii, 4, etc.) and the idea of the 'girdle of strength'. 'To loosen the girdle of kings' then means to deprive them of the symbol of their rank and strength, and so of their power, to dethrone them. See Mowinckel, *Die Sternnamen im Alten Testament*, p. 41.

He shall be a staff to the righteous whereon to stay
themselves and not fall,
And he shall be the light of the Gentiles,
And the hope of those who are troubled of heart.

(1 En. xlviii, 4)

Unquestionably there is here influence from the passages about
the Servant of the Lord and about Cyrus.[1] But the question is,
which 'servant of the Lord' underlies the picture of the Son of Man
in 1 Enoch? Is it the true Servant, who voluntarily sacrifices his
honour and his life for 'the many', or the transformed one,
nationalistic, victorious, and triumphant, as found in the interpretations of the Targum and of later Judaism in general?
   The answer clearly is the latter. It is the triumphant, Jewish
Messiah, who has here lent to the portrait of the Son of Man certain decorative details, which he himself borrowed unjustifiably
from the Servant of the Lord. There is not the slightest trace here
of the essential character of the Servant of the Lord. Nor is there
any trace of support for the assertion that 'the conception of the
suffering Messiah can be demonstrated in pre-Christian Jewish
theology' (Staerk). Staerk admits that if we ask more particularly
to what extent Jewish theology regarded the supposed sufferings
of the Messiah and the Son of Man as atoning and redemptive,
the only evidence is indirect, namely the occasional interpretation
of Isa. liii of the Messiah. But, as has just been pointed out, that
fact does not prove anything, directly or indirectly.
   It is from this that the application of the title, 'the Servant of
the Lord' to the Son of Man derives its meaning. In all the passages where we can give some account of the sense in which the
writer used it, it is used with the same meaning as in the Targum's
interpretation of Isa. liii: the supernatural hero, called, equipped,
and helped by God, who victoriously carries through God's plan,
judging and crushing the heathen, and triumphing over all the
kings and mighty men of the earth.[2]

[1] With the passages cited from 1 Enoch, cf. Isa. lii, 15; xlii, 6; xlix, 6. See Sjöberg,
op. cit., pp. 124ff.
[2] See above, p. 367. On this whole question, see Sjöberg's thorough investigation,
and his decisive criticism of the contention that the Servant of the Lord and the Son
of Man were identified in Judaism, and, in general, of the hypothesis of a suffering Son
of Man or Messiah in Judaism. Sjöberg's criticism is also a decisive refutation of
Johansson's revival of the hypothesis of Jeremias; see *Der Menschensohn*, pp. 116ff.
Engnell's assertion (in *S.E.Å.*, xii, 1947, p. 132 n. 47), 'Johansson is right on every
point, in spite of the polemic of E. Sjöberg', is a bare assertion, and is incapable of
disposing of Sjöberg's actual exegesis of the sources.

How alien the thought of a suffering and dying Son of Man was to Judaism, and even to those circles where the influence of apocalyptic was effective, is clear from the violent reaction of Peter and the other disciples to Jesus when He (the first to do so) announced this new message of the way of the cross (Matt. xvi, 21ff.).

18. *The Spread of the Idea of the Son of Man in Judaism*

How widespread were these ideas about the Son of Man in later Judaism? To a certain extent they stamped the Jewish Messianic conception as a whole, in so far as the supernatural, miraculous traits in the Messiah are much more prominent in later Judaism than in the earlier period, a fact which is connected with the idea of the Son of Man. When, for example, the more official, orthodox, rabbinic theology thinks of the Messiah as pre-existent, that is, in itself, inexplicable in terms of Jewish presuppositions (see p. 334); but it may fairly be assumed that the pronounced ideas about the pre-existence of the Son of Man also exercised an influence. We have also seen how these ideas left their mark on the national, this-worldly Messiah (pp. 334ff.).

Both the Ezra and Baruch Apocalypses think of the Messiah as an earthly being, and apply to him the Jewish national titles, 'the Servant of God' and 'the Anointed'. But, equally, they include the idea of his pre-existence in heaven, and of his coming with the clouds of heaven or from the sea.

Both the Ezra Apocalypse and the Testaments of the Twelve Patriarchs regard the Messiah as mortal. In T. Levi xviii it is quite clear that the Messiah is the founder of a Messianic dynasty, the first of a line of Messiahs, who replace each other in the natural succession of generations. But we also hear that he will open the doors of paradise, remove the cherub's sword which threatened Adam, give the holy ones to eat of the tree of life, bind Beliar, and give his children power to trample on the evil spirits. The individual expressions may be connected with figures and phrases in the Old Testament; but the whole description goes far beyond the ancient conception of the Messiah. The Messiah of earlier Judaism was never the king of paradise.[1]

[1] In accordance with the description of the Jewish Messiah given above, this point must be made in opposition to Gressmann (*Der Messias*, pp. 286ff.), Staerk, and other more recent students of the history of religions, who have followed Gressmann's attempt to make the earlier Jewish Messiah purely mythological. The oriental conception of the sacral king (and hence of the Messiah) is not derived from the Primordial Man and the king of paradise (see above, pp. 55, 81f.).

We have seen above (pp. 360ff.) that it was as Messiah, as the fulfilment of the promises of the ancient prophets to the fathers, that the Son of Man was conceived in later Judaism. Nevertheless, it must be said that the two types of Messianic expectation existed side by side. In some circles, men spoke of the Messiah, and, in the main, thought of him in terms of the earlier, national, political, this-worldly figure. In other circles, they spoke of the Son of Man, sometimes giving him the ancient Messianic titles, and attributing to him features from the ancient national idea of the Messiah, but otherwise putting the emphasis on his superterrestrial, universalistic, cosmic aspect, and on his connexion with the dawn of the new aeon, the judgement of the world, the establishment of the kingdom of the transcendent Son of Man, the salvation of the simple, and the return of paradise.

Thus it is clear that the Son of Man, as an eschatological figure, is linked with the new eschatology of later Judaism, with the teaching about the two aeons, the resurrection, the other-worldly kingdom of God, paradise, universalism, and individualism.

But the spread of ideas about the Son of Man does not necessarily coincide with the spread of the new eschatology. As a system, the latter had greater influence in Jewish religion than the teaching about the Son of Man. Dualism, the teaching about this aeon and the coming aeon, the other-worldly element in salvation, belief in the resurrection, and the thought of the transcendental paradise, left their impress on the national, this-worldly, politically orientated future hope. In the time of Jesus, no circles in Judaism were wholly uninfluenced by the new ideas. By comparison with this relatively extensive borrowing of dualism and other-worldly eschatology, the idea of the Son of Man counted for much less, although it belonged to the same system of ideas. The circles which spoke of the Son of Man instead of the Messiah, or thought of the Messiah more or less in the guise of the Son of Man, were few by comparison with the others, or, at least, counted for much less in the official outlook of Judaism.

The Son of Man does not appear in literature except in 1 Enoch, the Ezra Apocalypse (to a less extent), the Baruch Apocalypse, the Gospels, and other parts of the New Testament. Thus the idea was known in some (not all) apocalyptic circles, which cannot easily be more precisely defined, geographically, socially, or in relation to the official Jewish Church,[1] and in those circles from

[1] On the difficulty of precisely defining late Jewish literature, especially apocalyptic,

which Jesus and the original apostles came, that is, a Galilean milieu, which, because of its strongly eschatological and apocalyptic tendencies, had a certain connexion with other apocalyptic circles. It would undoubtedly be a mistake to assume that these circles formed a popular, or specially 'lay' milieu. It is certain that apocalyptic has one of its roots in the preoccupation of scholars with the prophetic tradition and the prophetic books, and in the professional 'wisdom' of the time. This is plain, not least, from the mass of learned material which is collected in 1 Enoch, astronomical, astrological, cosmological, meteorological, theological, etc.[1] Apocalyptic has another root in the pessimistic religiosity, with tendencies towards mysticism, existing in certain particularly learned circles, a religiosity which, with its spiritual experiences and its consciousness of inspiration, continues something of the old prophetic movement in new forms. But this mystical piety itself seems to have its home in intellectual scribal circles. Another testimony to the connexion between literary circles and the other-worldly, Messianic ideas appears in the Greek translation of the Old Testament, which in several passages seems to introduce into the text conceptions of the pre-existent, heavenly Messiah, and which also found him in the 'one like a man' in Daniel.[2]

On the other hand, the milieu of Jesus and the apostles undoubtedly had a more popular character. But it is significant that very few direct quotations from the apocryphal, apocalyptic literature occur in the New Testament. Nevertheless, in certain ideas a close kinship is apparent, particularly the dualistic, other-worldly eschatology and the conception of the Son of Man, which are prominent in the apocalyptic of a slightly earlier period, namely in 1 Enoch. But, at all events, the ideas in question were connected with each other, and were 'in the air' in that milieu as a result of the influence of living traditions. They belonged to the realm of its inherited religious ideas, and existed there in many varying forms

---

[1] See Hölscher, *Geschichte der israelitischen und jüdischen Religion*, pp. 187ff.; Jansen, *Die Henochgestalt*, pp. 9ff., 13ff. Davies (in *E.T.* lix, 1947/48, pp. 235ff.) gives very good reasons against the common view that apocalyptic represents a 'popular' milieu, by contrast with the learned one of rabbinism.

[2] See Bousset, *Relig.*[2], pp. 304f. Cf. G of Job, which introduces belief in the resurrection into its rendering of Job xiv, 14; Gerleman, *Studies in the Septuagint I, The Book of Job*, pp. 6of.

---

see Skat Hoffmeyer, *Den apokryfiske og pseudepigrafiske Literaturs Stilling til Partidannelserne i den palaestinensiske Senjødedom.* The recent discoveries of manuscripts seem to shed clearer light on the subject; see above, p. 356 n. 2, and p. 289 n. 4.

and in no ordered system, as religious ideas usually do exist in the mind of the public. The ordinary man neither knows nor inquires whence he derived them. In the time of Jesus, the theologians and those who had theological interests would try (as theologians always do) to find them in Scriptures; and if the question were put to them, they would answer that that was their source. The question, which is often raised, whether Jesus took the expression and the idea of the Son of Man from Dan. vii or from 1 Enoch is a fundamentally mistaken one.[1] He drew them from the milieu in which He grew up, and from which His earliest religious ideas were derived.

Another observation reveals something of the spread of these ideas in Judaism. Paul, the learned theologian, does not use the expression, 'the Son of Man'; but, on the other hand, it is quite clear that his own view of Christ corresponds in large measure with the picture of the Son of Man in 1 Enoch.[2]

From the above we may conclude that even before the time of the Maccabees (as Dan. vii shows), ideas about the Son of Man had found their way, together with the new other-worldly eschatology, into certain circles of learned and pious interpreters of the prophets and apocalyptists, and were so widely known that the author of the Similitudes in 1 Enoch (perhaps shortly before 63 B.C.[3]) could assume that the teaching about the Son of Man would be known and accepted among his readers. During that and the following period it was in still wider circulation, and formed part of the eschatological presuppositions in the circles from which Jesus came, and also in others, in Galilee and east of Jordan, which lay behind the origin of the Mandean sect,[4] for there, too, 'the Man' has an important part to play as a

---

[1] It is raised again, for example, in Taylor, *Jesus and His Sacrifice*.

[2] See Bousset, *Kyrios Christos*, pp. 158ff.; J. Weiss, *The History of Primitive Christianity* II, pp. 478ff.; cf. 603ff.; Staerk, *Soter* II, pp. 154ff.; Mowinckel in *N.T.T.* xlv, 1944, p. 205.

[3] See above, p. 355. It cannot be inferred from the idea of the Son of Man that the author is later than Daniel; for his use of it is independent of Daniel (*pace* Messel, *Der Menschensohn in den Bilderreden des Henoch*, pp. 78f.).

[4] On the Jewish and Transjordanian origin of the Mandeans, see Schou-Pedersen, *Bidrag til en analyse af de mandaeiske skrifter*, pp. 211ff. Cf. also Asting in *N.T.T.* xxxii, 1931, pp. 209ff. On Mandaism in general, see Bauer, art. 'Mandäer' in *R.G.G.*[2] IV; Brandt, *Die mandäische Religion, ihre Entwickelung und geschichtliche Bedeutung*, and *Die Mandäer ihre Religion und ihre Geschichte*; Lidzbarski, *Das Johannesbuch der Mandäer* I–II, and *Mandäische Liturgien*. Cf. also the bibliography given by Schou-Pedersen, and the articles by Schlier in *T.R.* (N.F.) v, 1933, pp. 1ff., 69ff., and by Baumgartner in *T.Z.* vi, 1950, pp. 401ff., and in the *H.U.C.A.* Jubilee Volume, Part I. (xxiii, 1950–51), pp. 41ff. Cf. also Rosenthal, *Die aramaistische Forschung seit Theodor Nöldeke's Veröffentlichungen*, pp. 238ff.

divine saviour.[1] Something of the same kind is also found in Manicheism.[2]

But it appears that this figure again became less prominent in what may be called the more orthodox and official Jewish theology. Compared with the Enoch Apocalypse, both the Ezra Apocalypse and the Baruch Apocalypse represent a more conservative attitude to the teaching about the national Messiah, and, as it seems, a reaction against the more sectarian outlook, as they held it to be, which was expressed in the Enoch Apocalypse. They, too, are based on the other-worldly eschatology; but they make every effort to combine with it the national inheritance of Judaism and the ancient future hope. The result is the compromise provided by chiliasm, the teaching about the Millennium. The Messiah has acquired a number of the characteristics of the Son of Man, but he has been reduced to the status of a temporary ruler, a transitional figure between the two aeons, before the real, new world, the resurrection, the last judgement, and the transformation of heaven and earth. Thus in spite of everything the earthly Messiah has triumphed over the Son of Man.

There are probably several reasons why the idea of the Son of Man had greater difficulty in gaining ground than the other-worldly eschatology, with which it was in fact connected. One very important reason probably was that the Son of Man conflicted in one essential point with a leading idea in Jewish eschatology, namely the thought of God himself as judge of the world, and, in general, the idea of the kingly rule of Yahweh. Yahweh Himself is the judge; and it is He himself, not the Messiah, who is the actual king of the end time. Jewish teaching deals with the kingly rule of *Yahweh* (the kingdom of God) not that of the Messiah or the Son of Man. We note that even where the idea of the Son of Man has gained ground, it is sometimes God Himself who is the judge (p. 393, pp. 169ff.). According to the Ezra Apocalypse, it is only when the kingdom of the Messiah is at an end, and the world has returned to chaos, that the resurrection comes. Then the Most High reveals Himself on the throne of judgement; and then comes the end (2 Esdras vii, 33). This is the usual conception in apocalyptic.

In the Christian era, official Jewish scribal learning once again

---

[1] See *N.T.T.* xlv, 1944, pp. 205ff.
[2] See *N.T.T.* xlv, 1944, pp. 209ff., with references to the literature; cf. below, p. 425 n. 3.

repudiated the thought of the Son of Man.[1] That is understandable. It thereby also repudiated Christianity, which proclaimed that the Son of Man had already been on the earth as Jesus of Nazareth, and that this Jesus would soon return on the clouds of heaven as the glorified Son of Man. We therefore find very few traces of the Son of Man in the theology of the synagogue. Dan. vii, and other passages, such as Ps. lxxx, 18, continued to be interpreted Messianically.[2] But that does not indicate how much or how little of the ideas about the Son of Man were present in the interpretation. Rabbinic theology, like the latest apocryphal writings,[3] has much to say about the godlike Primordial Man, the first Adam, the likeness of God.[4] But the rabbis were unaware that (as there is every reason to believe, and as we shall see below, pp. 422ff.) the Primordial Man had any connexion with the ideas about the Son of Man. Nor is there anything to suggest that they attributed to Adam, the Primordial Man, any eschatological role; and that is the essential feature of the Son of Man.

The last word of official, orthodox Judaism on the Son of Man is a complete rejection of the Christian belief in Jesus as the Son of Man. 'If a man says, "I am God", he is lying. If he says, "I shall go to heaven", he may say it, but he will not be able to do it.'[5]

19. *The Origin of the Conception of the Son of Man*

It ought to be obvious that the heavenly, pre-existent being, 'the Man', of divine, angelic character, preserved and hidden with God until the time of his epiphany, surrounded by a heavenly community of elect, righteous ones, the souls of the great departed, did not originally have any connexion with the Old Testament Messiah,[6] and cannot be explained either by Old Testament presuppositions[7] or by the royal ideology of the ancient east (see

---

[1] With what follows, cf. von Gall, *Basileia*, pp. 410ff.
[2] See the passages in Strack-Billerbeck I, p. 486
[3] 2 En. xxx, 10ff.; xxxi, 1–xxxii, 1; Life of Adam xii ff; Asc. Isa. xi.
[4] See Staerk, *Soter* II, pp. 7ff., and below, p. 426.
[5] Jer. Taanit ii, 1, 65b, 59.
[6] Cf. Staerk, *Soter* II, p. 471: 'the special character of the figure of the heavenly Man can . . . not be explained in terms of the Christology (*sic*) of the Old Testament'.
[7] Procksch (in *Christentum und Wissenschaft*, iii, 1927, pp. 425ff.) would derive the expression and the idea from the phrase addressed to Ezekiel, 'Thou Son of Man'. But there is no possible transition and no real connexion between this purely human, though rather dignified (see above, pp. 346f.), expression and the 'theological hypostatization of the image of God' which is expressed, as Procksch holds, by 'the Son of Man'. See above, p. 348 n. 2. Küppers, too, (in *Intern. Kirchl. Zeitschrift* xxiii, 1933, pp. 234ff.) claims to have shown that the figure of the transcendent Messiah-

above, pp. 32, 55). In fact, the difference is even greater than Staerk, for example, recognizes. For the Old Testament Messiah is never divine in the absolute, metaphysical sense like 'the Man', nor has he originally anything to do with paradise. He is not the king of paradise, as Gressmann, Staerk, and others have sought to maintain (see above, pp. 47, 81). Nor has the Old Testament Messiah anything to do with the doctrine of ages or of aeons. He will come in the midst of the historical process, called and equipped by the God of history. It was not until the later period of Judaism that this change of fate within history came to be regarded as a change from one age to another. The Messiah and the Son of Man have no common origin, not even in the royal ideology of the ancient east.[1]

If the origin of the idea of the Son of Man is a problem for those scholars such as Gressmann, Sellin, and Staerk who try to find as much as possible of the later eschatological and mythical figure of the Messiah or saviour already present in the ancient Messiah of earlier Judaism, it is still more of a problem for a sober historical approach, such as the preceding chapters have sought to adopt, in which the supernatural, divine, mythical element in the older conception of the Messiah is limited to those features which he has simply because he is an oriental royal figure, derived from the mythical, divine ideal of kingship in the ancient east. If, then, we would understand the origin of the ideas about 'the Man' in Jewish eschatology, we must seek possible parallels and sources in the environment of Judaism, in the world of eastern religion as a whole.[2]

---

[1] See above, p. 32. Bentzen goes too far in his concession to Engnell (*Det sakrale kongedømme*, pp. 116f., and *S.E.Å.* xii, 1947, pp. 36ff.).

[2] Staerk (*Soter* II, p. 2) is entirely right in thus limiting the field of inquiry.

Son-of-Man can be explained as a native development of Jewish religion. But that cannot be proved by artificial, theoretical speculations. Küppers's supposed evidence, that the heavenly Son of Man is not the result of ideas borrowed by Judaism from without, is without substance; and he contents himself with the contention that non-Jewish origin 'cannot be proved with certainty' (ibid., p. 245). Perhaps not; but what can be proved with mathematical certainty in the history of spiritual development? It is sufficient that the alien origin of the Son of Man can be shown to be highly probable, that it is the most likely explanation of the many which have been advanced, and that, in any event, the idea cannot be satisfactorily explained in terms of Jewish presuppositions. Black (*E.T.* lx, 1948/49, pp. 13ff.) admits the possibility that an earlier figure from Gnostic mysticism may have provided the background for the Jewish conception of the Son of Man, but holds that in Judaism the figure has lost all trace of its original character. Black inclines to the view that Isaiah (i.e., Deutero-Isaiah) as well as Daniel (i.e., Dan. vii) 'has been the inspiration of the Similitudes'. But echoes of individual expressions in Deutero-Isaiah do not suffice to show that the figure is inspired by him; these individual features may well be later accretions.

THE SON OF MAN

This problem has been the subject of much discussion since it was first raised fully a generation ago. Various mythical or divine oriental figures have been suggested; but thought has concentrated more and more on the widespread oriental conceptions of the divine, Primordial Man, 'the god Anthropos', a figure of varying importance in a number of Hellenistic religions and religio-philosophical systems. It may, in effect, be said that all attempts at explanation reckon with some variant of the divine, wise, Primordial Man.[1]

Conceptions of a more or less divine Primordial Man were widespread in the ancient east. Apparently there is a historical connexion between the varying figures of this type, which seem all to be derived, directly or indirectly, from Iranian or Indo-iranian myths.[2]

We must note, however, that an essential distinction must be made between the idea of the Primordial Man and that of the

[1] See the survey of theories in Staerk, *Soter* II, pp. 422ff., and in my article in *N.T.T.* xlv, 1944, pp. 190ff. To the scholars there mentioned may be added the names of Brede Kristensen (following the 'Babylonian' line; see *T.T.* xlv, 1911, pp. 1ff.), Sjöberg (*Der Menschensohn*, pp. 190ff.), and Arvedson, *Das Mysterium Christi. Eine Studie zu Mt 11, 25–30*, pp. 115ff. Reitzenstein held that a myth of the god Anthropos could be reconstructed (see *Poimandres*, pp. 81ff.); and he clearly demonstrated the connexion of the figure with Persian ideas about the Primordial Man (see *Das mandäisches Buch des Herrn der Grösse und die Evangelien-überlieferung*). The derivation from Persian conceptions is opposed by E. Meyer (*Ursprung und Anfänge des Christenumst* II, pp. 345ff.); but his attempt to explain the thought of Philo and Paul about the first Adam as free speculation based on Gen. i f. seems unduly rationalistic. Hommel (*E.T.* xi, 1899/1900, pp. 341ff.), Winckler (*Altorientalische Forschungen* III, pp. 296ff.), and Zimmern (*A.R.W.* ii, 1899, pp. 165ff.; *K.A.T.*[3], pp. 520ff.) attempt to derive it directly from the Adapa myth. Otto thinks that there is a connexion with the Persian conception of the fravashi: the Son of Man is the primordial fravashi (*The Kingdom of God and the Son of Man*, pp. 389ff.). Jansen thinks of a correspondence with the Babylonian Ea-Oannes (*Die Henochgestalt*, pp. 86ff.). In *Theologia Fennica* i–ii, 1939–40, p. 47, Yrjö Juotsi, says, 'The Son of Man is the most strongly spiritualized form of the entirely eschatological person, the great, heavenly redeemer and judge, who will appear in glory and power at the end of days'. If by this he means that the Son of Man has no original connexion with the Primordial Man (as his remark, op. cit., p. 46, might imply), then he is wrong. The sentence just quoted clearly provides no explanation of the origin of the figure; for we may go on to ask where we may find this 'entirely eschatological person', of which the Son of Man is said to be a spiritualization, and how it arose. At all events, it is not to be found in the Old Testament. I cannot appraise the grounds advanced by Juotsi for his contention, since I cannot read his Finnish book, *Ihmisen Poika*, of which he gives an account.

[2] Literature on the conception of the Primordial Man: Bousset, *Hauptprobleme der Gnosis*, pp. 16off.; Abegg, *Der Messiasglaube in Indien und Iran*; A. Christensen, *Les types du premier homme et du premier roi dans l'histoire légendaire des Iraniens*; Creed in *J.T.S.* xxvi, 1925, pp. 113ff.; J. Jeremias, art. ἄνθρωπος in *T.W.B.N.T.* I, pp. 365–367; C. H. Kraeling, *Anthropos and Son of Man*; Mowinckel in *N.T.T.* xli, 1940, pp. 26off., and xlv, 1944, pp. 189ff.; Reitzenstein, *Das iranische Erlösungsmysterium*; Schaeder, in part II of Reitzenstein-Schaeder, *Studien*; Troje, art. 'Urmensch' in *R.G.G.*[2] V; Scheftelowitz in *A.R.W.* xxviii, 1930; Nyberg, *Irans forntida religioner*, pp. 32f., 258ff., 338, 341ff., 437.

first created man.[1] The idea of the Primordial Man is really a cosmological idea, and arose from an attempt to explain the origin of the world or the cosmos. The Primordial Man is the cosmos itself, thought of in human form, the macrocosm conceived of in terms of the microcosm. From this cosmological Primordial Man the world is thought to have arisen in various ways: by the sacrifice or slaughter of the Primordial Man, and the building up of the cosmos from the various parts of his body, or by the emanation of the cosmos from him in one way or another. In northern Europe this conception is most familiar in the form which it had in Norse mythology, the story of the giant Ymir, killed by the Aesir, who made the earth from his body, the sea, the lakes, and the rivers from his blood, the vault of heaven from his skull, the clouds from his brains, and so on.[2] As a cosmogonic potency, the Primordial Man is also regarded as the Primordial Soul, from which all other souls proceed. This sometimes leads, in mythological thought, to his being regarded as ruler over unborn and departed souls. He may also be said to be incarnated in later heroes and saviours. Accordingly, in Iranian mythology the Primordial Man was also connected with eschatology. When the new world comes, it is the Primordial Man who returns; and the eschatological saviour Saoshyant is regarded as an incarnation, both of Zarathushtra, the founder of the religion, and of Gayomart, the Primordial Man.[3] In Indian religious speculation, the Primordial Man is connected with the teaching about ages (see above, pp. 263). At the beginning of each new age, it is the Primordial Man or god-Man (Purusha), who is incarnated in a new figure.

Distinct from this specific conception (of Indo-Iranian origin) of the Primordial Man are the conceptions of the first created man, the ancestor of mankind. The idea of a first man or man and wife is a natural one and practically universal, being derived from the conditions of tribal society, with its relationships and outlook, by which every association is thought of in terms of ancestry. The first man represents not the cosmos, but the human race. In both Babylonia and Israel, the idea of the first man was familiar. On the other hand, all the evidence suggests that neither the Babylonians nor the ancient Israelites originally knew anything about a myth of a real Primordial Man. Neither the Adam of the Bible

[1] Cf. Bousset, *Hauptprobleme der Gnosis*; and Mowinckel in *St. Th.* II, i, 1948/9, pp. 71ff.
[2] See Grønbech, *Nordiske myter og sagn*, pp. 23ff.
[3] See also Widengren, *Religionens värld*[2], pp. 364f., 389f.

nor the Babylonian sages of ancient times and founders of culture, like Adapa[1] or Oannes,[2] is the cosmological Primordial Man. In Ezek. xxviii and Job xv, 7f., the reference is really to the first Man, and not to the Primordial Man.[3] A description is given of one who is the prototype of glory and wisdom, living as the sum of creation, perfect in beauty, on the throne of God and the mount of God, etc. But in this description there is no suggestion of any cosmological significance, any more than there is in the account of Adam in Gen. i; ii f.[4]

But the two conceptions have many points of contact, and, on the whole, are akin to each other; and therefore they are likely to have influenced each other. Both are present in the thought of 'the first' and in that of 'the perfect', the idea of the golden age. That is why we often find, in the numerous variants of the oriental myth of the Primordial Man or Anthropos, many elements borrowed from myths and legends about the first man.[5] To this must be attributed the fact that the Primordial Man sometimes appears as king of paradise. This is a borrowing in particular from Babylonian conceptions of the first man, and of the wise culture-hero of primordial time; later it reveals the influence of the biblical conceptions of Adam and of paradise. Conversely, we note that ideas about the Primordial Man influence and transform the conception of the first man, as in the late Jewish and rabbinic legend about Adam,[6] where 'ādām ḳaḏmônî has all the marks of a cosmological figure.

The oriental, Hellenistic 'god Anthropos' is of mixed Iranian and 'Chaldean' origin. The varying ways in which the conceptions are combined represent different localities and different

---

[1] Cf. *N.T.T.* xlv, 1944, p. 213; Jansen, *Die Henochgestalt*, pp. 36f. Sumerian A-DA-AP = Accadian *amēlu* = man; see Langdon in *E.T.* xliii, 1931/32, p. 45. Adapa is *zêr amēlūti*; he represents the human race, not the cosmos.

[2] Cf. Jansen, *Die Henochgestalt*, pp. 105ff.

[3] Cf. Gunkel, *Schöpfung und Chaos*, pp. 148ff.; *Genesis*[4], pp. 33ff.

[4] See further my article in *St.Th.* II, i, 1948/49, pp. 71ff.

[5] Bousset, *Hauptprobleme*, pp. 220ff.

[6] See Staerk, *Soter* II, pp. 7ff.; cf. *Soter* I, pp. 158ff. See also the fuller evidence in Strack-Billerbeck I, pp. 705, 801f.; III, pp. 477–8; IV, pp. 105, 1120, and Index, s.v. 'Adam'. Cf. Murmelstein in *W.Z.K.M.* xxxv, 1928, pp. 242ff.; xxxvi, 1929, pp. 51ff.; Dupont-Sommer in *R.H.R.* cxix, 1939, pp. 182ff.; Guttmann in *E.J.* I, cols. 761ff.; Horodezky, ibid., cols. 776ff.; Mowinckel in *N.T.T.* xlv, 1944, pp. 196ff. This cosmological version of the story of Adam occurs in the apocalyptic work, *The Life of Adam and Eve*, for which see *A.P.A.T.* II, pp. 506ff.; *A.P.O.T.* II, pp. 123ff. On 'ādām ḳaḏmônî in later Jewish mysticism (the Kabbala), see Horodezky in *E.J.* I, cols. 783ff.; Ginzberg in *J.E.* I, pp. 181ff.; Serouya, *La Kabbale ses origines, sa psychologie, mystique, sa métaphysique*, pp. 351ff. The cosmogonic idea appears in the saying that the Holy One created the world and other creatures according to Adam's pattern (Serouya, op. cit., p. 351).

periods; and the figure appeared in many differing forms, which modified each other, so that they are not easy to distinguish.

In Iranian, Chaldean, and Indian religio-philosophical speculation, and in many of the Gnostic systems (both pre-Christian Jewish and Christian Gnostic) an important part was played by the Primordial Man, the divine Anthropos.[1] This is also true of Mandaism[2] and Manicheism.[3] In the Gnostic systems, the Primordial Man often appears as the Primordial Soul, which descends into matter, and in that way produces the visible world. Salvation is then the redemption of the Primordial Soul from matter, so that he is able to redeem the other souls by his plain teaching (the idea of 'the redeemed redeemer').

But in most of these varying forms it is an essential feature that the Primordial Man (Anthropos) is an eschatological figure, as well as belonging to primordial time. Even in those spiritualized Gnostic systems which have a strongly individualistic tendency, something of the eschatological role of the Primordial Man is still apparent.

Recent research has made it increasingly clear that the Jewish conception of 'the Man' or 'the Son of Man' is a Jewish variant of this oriental, cosmological, eschatological myth of Anthropos. This follows, not only from the correspondence in the main point (the dual role of a pre-existent, cosmological and eschatological being), but also from a number of striking correspondences in detail. All those features in the Son of Man, which cannot be explained naturally in terms of Old Testament conceptions, and which, in a measure, appear as incomprehensible, traditional elements with no apparent connexion with the nature and work of the Son of Man, are explained by what was narrated about the Primordial Man in some of the oriental accounts of that figure and of Anthropos: for instance, his coming from the sea (see above, pp. 390ff.), or his appearance as king of paradise (see above, pp. 382f.), his connexion with creation (which is not readily apparent

---

[1] Bousset, *Hauptprobleme der Gnosis* is of fundamental importance here; see also Creed's treatment of the Gnostic Primordial Man (*J.T.S.* xxvi, 1925, pp. 113ff.).

[2] On Mandaism, see above, p. 418 n. 4.

[3] Cf. Mowinckel in *N.T.T.* xlv, 1944, pp. 209ff.; Creed in *J.T.S.* xxvi, 1925, pp. 113ff.; Scheftelowitz in *A.R.W.* xxviii, 1930, pp. 212ff. (cf. above, p. 422 n. 2). On Manicheism, see Flügel, *Mani, seine Lehre und seine Schriften*; Lehmann in *Illustreret Religionshistorie*[1], pp. 381ff.; Kessler, *Mani* (cf. Nöldeke's review in *Z.D.M.G.* xliii, 1889, pp. 535ff.), and art. 'Mani, Manichäismus' in *P.R.E.*[3] xii, pp. 193ff.; Nyberg in *Illustreret Religionshistorie*[1], pp. 589ff., and in *S.T.K.* xi, 1935, pp. 27ff.; Schaeder, art. 'Manichäismus' in *R.G.G.*[2] IV, and *Urform und Fortbildung des manichäischen Systems*.

in the Jewish accounts; see above, p. 372), the thought that the souls of the departed are in him (see above, p. 377), and much else. Even the essential feature in the Son of Man (the fact that he is at once pre-existent from primordial time and an eschatological being) becomes clear when seen against the background of the myths about the Primordial Man or Anthropos.

Moreover, there is definite evidence that later Judaism was familiar with the conceptions of the Primordial Man. It is not inconceivable that the accounts of 'the first man' in Ezekiel and Job had already been influenced by them, as when (by contrast with Gen. i f.) he is said to have been created before the hills. It is certain that the late Jewish legend about Adam was influenced by the idea of the Primordial Man. There Adam is definitely a divine being, who came into existence before creation, as a cosmogonic principle (macrocosm), as the Primordial Soul,[1] as the original type of the godly, righteous fulfiller of the Law, and as the one who is reincarnated in the godly men of later times, etc.[2] Indirect testimony to Jewish speculations about the Primordial Man is provided (with an eschatological turn) by the Mandean figures of the Primordial Man and redeemer, Anosh or Enosh (the Man); for there can be little doubt that Mandaism goes back to a Jewish-Christian or Jewish sect.[3] Paul's ideas about the First and the Second Adam are also indirect evidence of corresponding ideas in Judaism.[4] Further evidence is provided by the many Jewish, or Jewish-Christian, Gnostic sects, where the Primordial Man Anthropos, Protanthropos, the Soul (Psyche), or Wisdom (Sophia), plays the part of a cosmogonic potency and of the redeemed redeemer.[5] Thus it is established that Judaism was familiar with many varying conceptions of the Primordial Man and the god Anthropos.

As we have seen, the Hellenistic and oriental Anthropos myths existed in numerous variant forms, known to us now only through fragments and religio-philosophical survivals which have undergone a measure of reinterpretation. If, then, in order to make a comparison with the Son of Man, we give an account of the most

[1] The thought of the Primordial Soul survives in the Kabbala; see Serouya, op. cit., pp. 355ff.

[2] See my survey in *N.T.T.* xlv, 1944, pp. 196ff.

[3] See Schou-Pedersen, *Bidrag til en analyse af de mandaeiske skrifter med henblik paa bestemmelsen af mandaeernes forhold til jødedom og kristendom*, résumé, and pp. 211ff.; cf. *N.T.T.* xlv, 1944, pp. 205ff., with fuller references to the literature.

[4] Cf. *N.T.T.* xlv, 1944, p. 205; and above, p. 372 and n. 3.

[5] See Bousset, *Hauptprobleme*, pp. 167 ff.; Mowinckel in *N.T.T.* xlv, 1944, pp. 200ff.

important features in the Anthropos myth, the result will to some extent be an abstraction, an artificial picture. There is certainly no ground for holding that the late Jewish conceptions of the Son of Man were directly borrowed from any simple development of the Anthropos myth. Many intersecting influences from many quarters were undoubtedly present; and Judaism took over much of the material in fragmentary, disintegrated form. But the essential point is that the figure of the Son of Man, as both a primordial and an eschatological saviour, is a form of the common oriental conceptions of Anthropos, which at some time made their way into Judaism, and were to some extent and in some circles equated with the Messiah. It is clear that this could not happen without important changes in the character of the Primordial Man taking place within Judaism. Both monotheism and the Messianic faith made this inevitable. But in establishing connexions in the history of religion, the essential point is not the larger or smaller number of differences. It is obvious that, in being adopted into and assimilated to another religion with a different total structure, any given conception will take on a very different appearance, and may even undergo radical transformation. But in determining affinity and common origin, the decisive factor is the number and character of the similarities which exist, in spite of the differences in the total structure into which the idea has been adopted and with which it has been fused.[1]

The following may be taken as the most important features in the figure of Anthropos. They recur with varying frequency in its different forms.[2]

1. He is a divine, heavenly, pre-existent being, who came into existence before all creation, the 'son' of the supreme god, or identified with one of the high gods. He has divine qualities and characteristics, and is endued with the divine radiance or glory.

2. He is called Man, the One like a man, Anthropos, the Primordial Man, Adam, Adamus, Adamanus, Anosh, Enosh, Mortal Immortality, etc.

3. He is in the closest relationship to creation. The cosmos and mankind came into existence through his death, his sacrifice, his voluntary descent, or his moral fall into the world of matter. He is, in fact, originally a cosmogonic idea, the mystical, speculative

[1] Reitzenstein rightly makes this point again and again in his works on the problem.
[2] For what follows, see *N.T.T.* xlv, 1944, pp. 225f., where the results of a survey of the evidence are summarized. References to the sources are given, ibid., pp. 196–223, and a fuller discussion, pp. 227–33

expression of the cosmos itself, the macrocosm regarded as a microcosm in human form.

4. He is often thought of as king of paradise, as ruler in the world beyond, the other land, which can be thought of as the place where departed or unborn souls are.

5. He is the Soul, the Primordial Soul, which includes all the individual souls, the *anima generalis*, to which, or into which, the souls of the dead return.

6. As Primordial Man he is also the typical man, the prototype and pattern, the ideal man, and is, therefore, sometimes called 'the right or righteous man'. He is thought of as the first, perfect, godly one, as *homo religiosus*, the first adherent and preacher of the true religion.

7. In particular, he is the typical sage, the wise man of primordial time, possessing all secrets, the source and mediator of all understanding. Among the Mandeans he is known as 'the Understanding of Life'.

8. His destiny is a type of the destiny of mankind and of the individual man or soul. His imprisonment in the material, and his redemption from it are the symbol and the realization of the imprisonment and redemption of the individual man. To put it in the naïve language of myth: there come to him in his kingdom of light the other 'perfect' and 'elect' ones, who, through his liberation and his work of redemption, have been helped to gain their freedom from matter and evil.

9. Sometimes it is said that the Most High God has created him for conflict with evil, darkness, and the devil, and to liberate the light from captivity to darkness. He belongs to the hidden world beyond; and therefore he is himself hidden, as it is said of the Mandean Adakas (the hidden Adam). But one day he appears, revealing himself in his bright glory, as the Mandean 'Envoy'.

10. Thereby he becomes a redeemer and saviour, partly because his own redemption is an act of creative symbolism, anticipating and having as its consequence the redemption of the other souls, and partly because he is regarded as the saviour who acts and intervenes. The understanding which he conveys is the means of redemption from matter and evil.

11. Both as the typical and ideal man and as redeemer, he is incarnated in the godly ones or 'helpers' of later times. It is his soul or spirit which is also in the other helpers and righteous ones, those of whom it is most natural to think when reference is made

to those who ascend to his world of light. He gathers to himself a people in the other world, the redeemed righteous ones, or, in the Mandean phrase, the righteous ones who have been translated.

12. As a cosmogonic potency, he is more frequently connected with the thought of recurring ages. He reappears at the beginning of the era of the new world. As redeemer he is, in particular, the helper of the godly in the catastrophe brought about by the destruction of the old world and the genesis of the new, or by the transition to the pure spiritual existence in the paradise of light. In most Gnostic systems he has thus acquired a certain element of the eschatological redeemer. In a religion with a clear eschatology, he must become not only a figure from primordial time, but an eschatological figure, indeed, *the* eschatological figure. His position in the Gnostic systems implies that in certain circles or sects in Persian religion (the only eschatological religion which can come into question), he played this part of the returning eschatological saviour. It is natural to think of the sect of Gayomartians, who manifestly made confession of Gayomart as helper in the conflict against the evil power.[1] Even in the official Zarathushtrian theology there are indications that the saviour of the end time has assimilated important features from the Primordial Man.[2] In the Gnostic systems his eschatological role is often considerably reduced in consequence of the strong spiritualizing and individualizing tendencies in Gnostic thought.

13. As a heavenly being, the Primordial Man reveals himself in the clouds.

14. In several contexts he is connected with the resurrection. Of both Gayomart and Adam it is explicitly stated that they will be the first to rise again.

For the purposes of comparison, we add a brief summary of the most important features in the figure of the Son of Man.[3]

1. He is divine by nature, arrayed in the glory of the deity, in appearance like the angels (pp. 373ff.). In some circles he may also have been called 'Son of the Most High God' (pp. 368ff.).

2. He is a heavenly being, who dwells on high with the Lord of Spirits, where the elect righteous ones have their dwellings (pp. 371, 379ff.).

3. He is not merely an apotheosized man, who has been taken

---

[1] See Bousset, *Hauptprobleme der Gnosis*, pp. 207f.; but see also Schaeder in Reitzenstein-Schaeder, *Studien*, p. 236; and cf. Mowinckel in *N.T.T.* xlv, 1944, p. 218.

[2] See *N.T.T.* xlv, 1944, pp. 214, 218.

[3] See *N.T.T.* xlv, 1944, pp. 194f.

up to heaven, like Enoch or Elijah, or who has become one with the deity in mystical cultic experiences, like the king-god of the ancient east. He has always belonged to the heavenly plane. He was pre-existent (pp. 370ff.).

4. In spite of this he is called 'the Man' (the Son of Man), the typical man, the prototype of mankind. Thus, he is a divine being in human form, a 'Man' with a divine nature (pp. 362ff., 373ff.).

5. It seems that he is in some way connected with creation. It is strongly emphasized that he came into existence before the creation of the world, and in order to fulfil God's purpose for creation; and he will in the end be lord over creation (pp. 370ff., 388ff.).

6. He is in some way connected with the conception of paradise, and was at one time thought of as king of paradise (pp. 381ff.).

7. The name 'the Man' seems to have implied that he was the ideal pattern of mankind (see above, para. 4.). He is called 'the Righteous One' and 'the Elect One', which seems to show that he was, or at one time had been, regarded as the prototype of the righteous, elect (pp. 383ff.).

8. As such, he is even now the head of a heavenly community of the departed of earlier times, the translated patriarchs and godly men, the righteous elect, who surround him in heaven, and have their dwellings with the Lord of Spirits (pp. 379ff.).

9. It seems, too, that at one stage, at least, of the history of the idea, there was a mystic connexion between the Son of Man and the spirits of the righteous departed, so that they were thought of as identical with him in some way (p. 377).

10. His most characteristic qualities are wisdom and understanding (pp. 375f.; cf. pp. 385ff.).

11. His connexion with the last times is much clearer than it was at first. He is an eschatological figure, and will be the instrument in the re-establishment of creation's original state of perfection, which is the content of eschatology (pp. 358f., 388ff.).

12. He is connected with the dualistic view of the world and of history, with the conception of this aeon and the coming aeon, and with the cosmic and universalistic eschatology (pp. 360ff., 388ff., 401f.), not with the national Messianic hope. He came into being, and has been chosen and preserved for the final conflict against Satan and the evil powers, over which he will be victorious (pp. 385f., 388ff., 397f.).

13. He is now hidden with the Lord of Spirits; but one day he

will be revealed, when 'the hour of his day' has come. Then he will take his seat on his, or God's, throne of glory (pp. 385ff.).

14. He will come with the clouds of heaven (pp. 357, 389f., 397); but it is also said that he will rise up from the sea (pp. 390f.).

15. He seems to have had some connexion with the resurrection (pp. 399f.).

16. He is judge of the world, who, at his coming, will judge the living and the dead (pp. 393ff.; cf. p. 400).

A comparison of the characteristic features in these two figures puts it beyond doubt that they are akin to each other, or, more precisely, that they have common roots. Anthropos and the Son of Man both go back to the myths about the Primordial Man. Since it is clear that the Son of Man cannot be explained in terms of earlier Jewish and Old Testament conceptions, and is different in character from the Old Testament Messiah, no other conclusion is possible. This is confirmed by the fact that the conception of the Son of Man includes several features, which are incomprehensible as long as we consider only its late Jewish form, but which are explained when seen as vestiges of the earlier connexion with the idea of the Primordial Man. We may instance facts such as the coming of the Son of Man from the sea, or his connexion with the souls of the godly departed, or the traces (admittedly very slight) of a connexion with creation, and so on.

But as indicated above, we certainly cannot point to any single one of the many variants of the Anthropos myth as the only source and the direct source of the idea of the Son of Man. Everything suggests that the Jews acquired their knowledge of these myths and conceptions from many quarters, in many varying forms, and at different periods.[1] We may instance the difference in character between the rabbinic legend about Adam and the Son of Man in 1 Enoch; and further evidence is provided by the ideas about Metatron, a variant of the Primordial Man (see below, p. 439). The figure of the Son of Man in later Judaism may be regarded as a new, specifically Jewish variant of a widespread, oriental, Hellenistic type, which readily combines in itself features from the 'god Anthropos' and the Primordial Man as found in the most diverse religions and systems, and which may also reflect the

---

[1] Cf. Mowinckel in *N.T.T.* xlv, 1944, pp. 192f.; Reitzenstein-Schaeder, *Studien*, p. 129. The character of the material makes it impossible to carry out a satisfactory investigation of the details. An attempt is made by C. H. Kraeling, *Anthropos and Son of Man*, pp. 74ff.; cf. Sjöberg, *Der Menschensohn*, p. 194 n. 11.

influence of other divine or mythical figures alongside features from the Old Testament and from genuine Jewish tradition.[1]

It is on other grounds natural enough to assume such influence (ultimately Iranian and Chaldean in origin) on later Judaism. It is a fact that it was affected in several ways from that quarter.[2] First and foremost, there was the principle of dualism itself, and the absolute eschatology, the conception of the definitive termination of the course of this world, and the replacement of it by something new of an essentially different kind. Of the numerous specific details, we may mention the cosmological chronology (the division of this aeon into a chronological system of ages), the termination of this aeon by a world conflagration, the seven archangels, which are connected both with the seven Babylonian planetary gods, and the seven Persian Amesha Spentas (holy powers), much of the narrative material in the legends about Ezra, Ahikar, and Tobit, and the story of Darius and the three pages in 1 Esdras, besides much else.

There is no question here of influences from purely Iranian religion and culture, but from that syncretistic fusion of Iranian, Mesopotamian, and Babylonian factors, which, adopting the terminology of the Hellenistic age, we call 'Chaldean', after the Chaldeans, the dominant people in the neo-Babylonian Empire, who were regarded in the circle of Hellenistic culture as representing the Babylonians.[3] The most prominent feature in Chaldean syncretism is Persian dualism, combined with Babylonian astronomy and astrology, with belief in fate, and with other elements of science and mythology. In the Hellenistic age it was regarded as the supreme wisdom, science, and revelation. It is the basis of Gnosticism, and undoubtedly left marked traces in later Judaism. Accordingly, in considering so un-Jewish a figure as the Son of Man, we must from the outset allow for influence from Iranian and Chaldean sources.

As Bousset has pointed out,[4] it is not difficult to discover the meet-

[1] It is, therefore, an oversimplification, when von Gall (*Basileia*, pp. 409ff.) would regard the Persian Gayomart myth as the only source of the idea of the Son of Man, or when Widengren (*Religionens värld²*, p. 363) says that 'the Jewish conception (of the Son of Man) is phenomenologically the Jewish counterpart of the Iranian Gayomart'.

[2] On what follows, see Bousset, *Relig.²*, pp. 555f., [3], pp. 482ff.

[3] See above, p. 264 n. 10. This Chaldean syncretism was the seed-bed of the pre-Christian oriental Gnosis and redeemer-religions, and so of the Anthropos myth in its developed Hellenistic form. On this Gnosis, see Jonas, *Gnosis und spätantiker Geist* I.   [4] Bousset, *Relig.²*, p. 548.

THE SON OF MAN

ing place of Judaism with the Iranian and Chaldean spirit and
religion. It was Babylonia, which, as early as the time of Ezra and
Nehemiah, was the most important spiritual centre of Judaism,
the home of the reforming movement, and later of theology and
the Talmud. Here, too, the Iranian and Iranian-Chaldean sects
spread, and were subject to influences from Babylonian and many
other sources. Here, to this very day, live the last survivors of that
syncretistic religion, the Mandeans.

It is not difficult to understand how the Jews could recognize
and approve of the conceptions of the eschatological Man, which
they found there, assimilate them to their own world of religious
ideas, and connect them with their thoughts of the Messiah. In
fact, the myths about the pre-existent, heavenly Man, included
much which could link them to Jewish ideas. In the Primordial
Man, who was like a god or an angel, it was not difficult to see
(or to read in) the earlier Jewish conceptions of paradise on the
mountain of God, and of Adam before the fall, created in the image
of God. Judaism had long awaited a saviour who was to come at
the end of the ages. The Messiah had come to be endowed with
mythical, superhuman features, derived from the myths about
paradise and primordial time, as we see in Isa. ix, 1ff., or in the
interpretation of Isaiah's Immanuel prophecy as a Messianic
prophecy, and the like. The future king was more and more
thought of as a divinely endowed superman, detached from the
realism of his original cultic and sacral setting, and regarded as
the one who would bring back the glory of paradise. Accordingly,
it was also natural to see him in the super-terrestrial king of paradise, 'the Man'. As Jewish theology began to ascribe to the most
important blessings of salvation (such as the Law) an ideal pre-
existence, and to regard the Messiah as one of these pre-existent
blessings of salvation,[1] so it became natural to find the Messiah in
the figure of a pre-existent saviour, which they found in so many
quarters among neighbouring peoples and religions.

We note, too, that the figure of the Son of Man left different
impressions in different Jewish circles. The apocalyptist in Daniel
found it suitable as a symbol for the people of Israel, whereas the
world powers were symbolized by monsters who came up from the
sea. This is connected with the fact that Daniel, like so many in

[1] See Strack-Billerbeck II, 324, 335, 353, 355, (340ff.), 528; III, pp. 12, 144, 145,
511, 579; IV, pp. 4, 443, 450, 985. See above, p. 334.

433

2F

other circles in Judaism, was not particularly interested in the idea of the Messiah, whom he never mentions. Other circles, from which the later, orthodox, rabbinic theology is derived, were reserved in their attitude to the conception of the Son of Man. It scarcely appears in the sayings of the rabbis, though it had influenced their ideas about the Messiah (see pp. 333ff.). But their attitude is connected, in part with their opposition to Christianity, in which the Son of Man was a central idea (see pp. 329f.). The older theology, which underlies the Targums, is not quite so negative. For example, it interprets 'the son of man', in several of the psalms (see p. 357), as the Messiah, undoubtedly under the influence of the ideas about the Son of Man. The full content of these ideas was accepted only in certain apocalyptic circles, which are represented especially by the Apocalypse of Enoch.

But this borrowing also involves a refashioning of the figure in accordance with the spiritual structure of Judaism itself.

This is shown above all by the identification of the Son of Man with the Messiah. This means that the Son of Man is associated with the thought of the election, the covenant, and the promises to the chosen people. 'The elect' in 1 Enoch are, admittedly, those who have been chosen, in virtue of their piety (righteousness), to share in the coming Kingdom of God. But the conviction is always present that they belong to Israel, the elect people. It is for the sake of the elect that 'the Elect One' exists. It is the kingdom for the true Israel that he will establish. The nationalistic note is quite clearly heard in the Apocalypse of Ezra. There 'the Son of Man' is used, not as a name or a title, but as a characterization. The author applies to him the Old Testament phrases, 'the servant of the Lord', or 'Messiah, the servant of the Lord'. The 'righteousness' of the Son of Man in 1 Enoch is affected by the Jewish view of righteousness as the ideal piety, which is expressed in perfect fulfilment of the Law of the Lord. The righteousness of the Son of Man is the perfection which enables him also to secure right and salvation for the elect, righteous ones (see above, pp. 378f., 401f.).

In late Judaism the Son of Man was God's instrument for bringing in 'the absolute eschaton' (as Otto puts it). But since this saviour is also the Messiah, he is inseparable from the realistic historical, future hope, according to which God's purpose for

Israel will be fulfilled on a new earth, and not in any impersonal world of pure spirituality and ethereal substance.

Naturally, the identification with the Messiah laid all the emphasis on the eschatological side of the nature and work of the Son of Man. In spite of his pre-existence, the Son of Man is in Judaism a purely eschatological being with a purely eschatological task.[1]

The negative consequence of this is that the cosmogonic foundation is almost completely removed. Only occasional traces of it appear; and their existence can be shown only by the methods of the scientific, comparative study of religion.[2] Of course, the Jewish belief in creation also exerted an influence. God alone is the almighty creator (from the time of Deutero-Isaiah this was a basic element in Jewish belief[3]); and He created the world by His will and by His almighty word, without any intermediary.

Another consequence is that the principle of monotheism is maintained. In late Judaism the Son of Man is not a 'second God' (δεύτερος θεός), as so often in Gnosticism. Although pre-existent, he was created by God according to His will and for His glory, like all angels, powers and holy ones. The object of the genesis of the Son of Man before all time is that all who dwell on earth may fall down and worship, praise, laud, and extol the name of the Lord of Spirits;[4] and he attains that object by his eschatological work.

But another consequence is that what was originally the essential characteristic has been removed. In late Judaism the Son of Man is not regarded as the Primordial Man.[5] It is only by the methods of the scientific, comparative study of religion that we can discern that he was formerly so regarded outside Judaism, and that we can show the feeble traces of this thought, which survive in certain individual sayings and phrases applied to him, the original meaning of which was no longer known in Judaism.[6]

It also follows that his peculiar role as redeemer, which he had acquired in Chaldean, Hellenistic, Gnostic systems, was not taken

---

[1] Cf. Bousset, *Hauptprobleme*, p. 219; C. H. Kraeling, *Anthropos and Son of Man*, pp. 149, 151; Otto, *The Kingdom of God and the Son of Man*, pp. 389f.; Mowinckel in *N.T.T.* xlv, 1944, p. 236; Sjöberg, *Der Menschensohn*, pp. 197f.

[2] See above, pp. 372, 376, 382, 391. To this extent Juotsi is right in his contention that in Judaism the Son of Man 'is a soteriological and not a cosmological idea' (*Theologia Fennica* i–ii, 1939–40, p. 46). But this implies nothing about the earlier or original character of the figure; cf. above, p. 422 n. 1.

[3] This, of course, does not mean that it was not found much earlier, e.g., in the Psalms.

[4] 1 En. xlviii, 3–7; cf. lxi, 9ff. See above, pp. 371, 409f.

[5] Cf. Sjöberg, *Der Menschensohn*, pp. 193f.   [6] See above, n. 2.

over in Judaism.[1] In these systems we meet many varying forms of the thought that this material and sinful world came into existence because the heavenly Man descended into matter and was fettered to it. Redemption takes place, in part because the redeemer himself is first redeemed, and in part because he wins his own freedom from matter, and then draws the souls of light with himself back to the eternal source of light. In Judaism all this has vanished from the figure of the Son of Man. We hear nothing about the fall of the Son of Man, or his conflict with darkness at the beginning, or about his death and resurrection, and the like. The redemption of the righteous does not consist in any mystic, cultic participation in the redemption of the redeemer; it is a result of his eschatological appearance for judgement and for the destruction of all the evil powers.

The apocalyptists have, in fact, nothing to tell about the life and work of the Son of Man in his pre-existence. All the emphasis is laid on his eschatological role. Before he assumes that role, he is hidden and preserved beside the Lord of Spirits. It is only then that he is revealed, coming in his glory with all his companions, and heralding the resurrection. In this way he brings to fulfilment the purpose for which he was created, chosen, and preserved by God.

Judaism, then, was unaware that the Son of Man was really the Primordial Man. What it had to say about the Primordial Man was connected with the biblical figure of Adam as he is presented in the rabbinic legend of Adam.[2] Instead, by identifying the Son of Man with the Messiah, Judaism made him the representative of the living, personal God, who created the world and who reveals Himself and is at work in the actual course of history. There emerged a Messianic figure both eternal and transcendental, and also historical and human, in an eschatology both historical and also supra-historical and absolute. It is, therefore, not without justification that Sjöberg claims that the difference between the Primordial Man and the Son of Man is greater than the similarity.[3]

In the Messiah-Son-of-Man, the continuation of revelation history into later Judaism provided a form for the longing and

[1] See Sjöberg, op. cit., pp. 194f.
[2] See Staerk, *Soter* II, pp. 7ff.; cf. I, p. 158; Murmelstein in *W.Z.K.M.* xxxv, 1928, and xxxvi, 1929; Strack-Billerbeck, Index, s.vv. 'Adam', 'Mensch, der erste'. Cf. also Bousset, *Relig.*[2], pp. 346ff.
[3] Sjöberg, *Der Menschensohn*, p. 193. Black (in *E.T.* lx, 1948/49, pp. 14f.) emphasizes, even more than Sjöberg, the complete transformation of the oriental figure, which took place in Judaism, see above, p. 420 n. 7.

hope cherished by God's people. This was the hope of a saviour
who could be more than a this-worldly, national, political Messiah,
and who could also bring the fulfilment of the demand for the
victory of justice over injustice, and the victory of the power of
God over the world power, which was the ethical and religious
core in the national hope of restoration and of a Messiah. It was
also the hope of a saviour, who could bring victory over the power
of sin and the devil, both in men and outside them, a mediator
who could bring the transcendent and holy God near to sinful,
suffering men, and bring the kingdom of God down to earth and
into the souls of men.

Jesus was God's answer to this divinely directed longing and
expectation.

20. *Is Enoch the Son of Man?*

Finally, we must append here a brief consideration of a question
which has often been raised in connexion with the late Jewish conceptions of the Son of Man. Was he regarded (at least, in some
Enochian circles) as an apotheosized man, or as a being who was
at some time incarnate as an ordinary human being? Several
scholars[1] have maintained that there is a special, mystical connexion between the Son of Man and the apocalyptic figure
Enoch, so that either Enoch is an earthly incarnation of the Son
of Man,[2] or the Son of Man is Enoch after his translation to
heaven. The reason for the detailed examination of the question
here is that Otto draws from it far-reaching conclusions concerning
Jesus' view of Himself as the Son of Man.

Appeal is made first and foremost to 1 En. lxxi, but also to certain passages about Enoch in 2 Enoch, 'which seem to identify
him with the heavenly Man'.[3]

[1] Dalman, *Words of Jesus*, p. 244; Beer, *A.P.A.T.* II, p. 277; Bousset, *Relig.*², pp.
406f.; Volz, *Eschatologie*², pp. 21, 25, 198; and especially Otto, *The Kingdom of God and
the Son of Man*, pp. 201ff.; most recently Jansen, *Die Henochgestalt*, pp. 124ff.; Johansson,
Parakletoi, p. 101; and, with detailed arguments, Sjöberg, *Der Menschensohn*, pp. 147ff.;
on the other side, Charles, *The Book of Enoch translated*¹, pp. 183f., and (with arguments
based on literary criticism) *The Book of Enoch translated*², pp. 142ff.; Staerk, *Soter* I, p. 74
(following Charles, op. cit.²); II, p. 68 n. 3, p. 125, and *Nachtrag*, p. 495 (accepting the
identity of Enoch and the Son of Man in 1 En. lxxi, 5ff., but holding that that chapter
is a later addition, and that the identity is not taught elsewhere in 1 Enoch); decidedly
against the identity, Mowinckel in *N.T.T.* xlv, 1944, pp. 57ff.; and similarly Dillmann,
Das Buch Henoch übersetzt und erklärt, p. 218.

[2] So Beer, *A.P.A.T.* II, p. 277; Arvedson, *Das Mysterium Christi. Eine Studie zu Mt
11, 25–30*, p. 117; Johansson, *Parakletoi*, pp. 101f.; and, to some extent, Odeberg, art.
'Ενώχ in *T.W.B.N.T.* II, pp. 554, 556. This seems to be Jansen's view in *Die Henochgestalt*, where he makes a distinction between the heavenly and the earthly Enoch;
but his observations on this point are not clear. [3] Staerk, *Soter* II, p. 447.

It is true, as Odeberg and Jansen have shown, that the figure of Enoch in later Judaism had assimilated a number of characteristics from a transcendent, heavenly being, the wise, heavenly scribe and possessor of the divine secrets, whom the Jews combined with the old story of Enoch who was taken up to heaven.[1] In the Enochian literature, Enoch has become the heavenly scribe and sage, who can reveal to those on earth the secrets of the world beyond and of the coming aeon. First, he is lifted up to heaven in visions, sees all the secrets,[2] and receives an explanation of them.[3] This is what he recorded in his 'hidden' (apocryphal) books to enlighten, comfort, and admonish the righteous and elect.[4] He has become the great apocalyptist above all others. Finally, he was translated to heaven bodily, while still alive,[5] and installed as 'scribe', 'the scribe of righteousness'.[6] In 2 Enoch we hear that he is brought before God's throne; and God says to him, 'Arise and stand before my face into eternity'; i.e., he is installed as God's Grand Vizier and is arrayed in heavenly glory, so that he becomes as one of 'the glorious ones', in no way differing from them in appearance (2 En. xxii, 1ff.). Indeed, he is given a place beside God's throne, together with Gabriel (xxiv, 1), and God reveals to him the most sublime secrets, which He has not even revealed to the angels (xxiv, 2; xxxiii, 4). He is made into a heavenly being.

Sjöberg is entirely right in his contention that this is the exaltation of one who has hitherto been an earthly man, not the return to heaven of one who has been incarnated.[7] It is also clear that an alien mythology has been transferred to Enoch. Among the Babylonians, the god Nabu was the heavenly scribe, who kept the books recording the deeds of men and the destiny which the gods had decided in their council.[8] In Egypt, the god Thoth had a similar function.[9]

But this conception of the heavenly scribe existed independently of its application to Enoch, and was undoubtedly combined at an

---

[1] Gen. v, 24. How far these conceptions had already been connected with Israelite ideas about Enoch, and how far we have to do with foreign (presumably Babylonian) conceptions, is a separate question, into which we need not enter here.
[2] On this idea, see above, pp. 386f. [3] 1 En. i, 2ff.; xxxvii; lxxii, 1ff., etc.
[4] 1 En. lxxxi, 1ff.; lxxxii, 1; lxxxiii, 10; xc, 20; xciii, 1; xcvii, 6; c, 6; ciii, 2; civ, 11f.; cvii, 1; cviii, 1, 7; 2 En. xxxviii, 5ff.
[5] Jub. iv, 23ff.; 1 En. lxx; 2 En. i–xxiii; 3 En. iii–xv; xlviii, C.
[6] 1 En. xii, 3f.; xv, 1; xcii, 1; cf. lxxxi, 1f.; lxxxix, 62, 71; xc, 17.
[7] Sjöberg, *Der Menschensohn*, pp. 171f. [8] See Zimmern in *K.A.T.*[3], pp. 400f., 403f.
[9] See Erman, *Die ägyptische Religion*[2], pp. 13f.; Steindorff-Seele, *When Egypt Ruled the East*, p. 137; Mowinckel in *Act.Or.* viii, 1930, pp. 30ff.

earlier period with another, namely that of Metatron,[1] 'the one who has the throne next after God'.[2] The conception of Metatron was known to the rabbis; but among them it was already of diminishing importance, being suppressed by Jewish orthodoxy, because it was felt to be too much in conflict with the basic dogma, monotheism.[3] But it plays an important part in the Enochian literature, and even more so in later Jewish mysticism (the Kabbala).[4] In 3 Enoch, Metatron is God's servant, 'whom I appointed prince and ruler over all the princes of My kingdoms and all the dwellers in heaven . . . And every angel and every prince who has a matter to lay before Me must go to him instead, and present his case to him. And every command that he gives in My name you shall observe and fulfil . . . I have appointed him over all the treasuries of the palaces of the highest heaven, and over all the stores of life that I have in the high heavens' (3 En. x, 3ff.). He has a throne which is a copy of 'the throne of glory', God's own throne (xlviii, C, 8f.). He is God's representative, and has God's authority. As 'Prince of the Presence' who stands immediately before God and represents Him, he is the highest heavenly being, the judge of those who dwell in heaven and on earth. He is a copy of God Himself, and is actually called 'the lesser Yahweh' (xii, 5). He rules over the stores of life, shares in God's omniscience, knows all secrets, and is aware of men's hidden thoughts. Metatron himself says, 'from the beginning the Holy One, blessed be He, revealed to me all the mysteries of the Law and all the secrets of wisdom . . . All the secrets of the universe and all the secrets of creation were revealed to me, as they are revealed to the creator of the world' (xi, 1). God says of him, 'Every secret did I reveal to him as a father' (xlviii, C, 7).[5]

This conception is clearly not Jewish in origin. It is also clear that Metatron's status corresponds in many ways to that of the Son of Man. Bousset recognized that this Metatron was ultimately a variant of the Primordial Man,[6] combined with the idea of the

---

[1] On Metatron, see Bousset, *Relig.*[2], pp. 296, 406f.; *Hauptprobleme der Gnosis*, pp. 199ff.; Odeberg, *3 Enoch*, pp. 79–146, and in *Kyrkohistorisk Årsskrift*, xxvii, 1927, pp. 1ff.
[2] On the probable etymology of this word, see Odeberg, *3 Enoch*, pp. 125ff.
[3] Targum of Pseudo-Jonathan on Gen. v, 24. Bab. Hagigah 15a; Leviticus Rabbah xxxiv 8; Bab. Sanhedrin 38b. Cf. Odeberg in *Kyrkohistorisk Årsskrift*, xxvii, 1927, p. 9.
[4] Cf. Odeberg, *3 Enoch*, pp. 111ff.; Serouya, *La Kabbale, ses origines, sa psychologie mystique, sa métaphysique*, p. 97. From the earlier period, Bowman (*E.T.* lix, 1947/48, p. 287) mentions Elisha ben Abuya, who, 'when he attained the Chariot vision saw Metatron, and said, "Are there perhaps two first principles?"'.
[5] On the above, see Odeberg, *Kyrkohistorisk Årsskrift* xxvii, 1927, pp. 2ff.
[6] See Bousset, *Hauptprobleme der Gnosis*, pp. 199ff.; Odeberg, ibid., pp. 4f.

heavenly scribe and Grand Vizier. In an oriental, royal court, the 'scribe' is more than a recorder; he is a high official, who is in a position to make his influence felt in the highest quarters. To him men turn when they seek a favour from the king himself. This is still more applicable to the heavenly scribe. The name and nature of his office show that he is God's agent and intermediary.[1] The Jewish mystics are, in a measure, aware that Metatron is the Primordial Man incarnate in Adam ('āḏām ḳaḏmônî).[2]

It is, however, peculiar to the Enochian literature that Enoch is identified with Metatron.[3] When Rabbi Ishmael asks Metatron the reason for his name and his exalted status, the answer is, 'Because I am Enoch, the son of Jared' (3 En. iv, 2). To explain Enoch's name of honour 'Aleph' ('lp), the Most High says, 'I seized him, and I took him, and I appointed him:[4] that is Enoch, the son of Jared, whose name is Metatron. I took him from among the children of men, and gave him a throne like My own throne' (xlviii, C, 1f.). It is uncertain whether any of these ideas about Metatron have left their mark on the figure of Enoch in 1 and 2 Enoch. At all events, these books do not apply the name Metatron to him. But it is clear that when Metatron is equated with Enoch, all the original ideas about the Primordial Man recede into the background. Enoch is then regarded as an ordinary, mortal man, who, as a reward for his piety, was taken up from earth and exalted to his position as Metatron and God's scribe.[5] Thus Enoch is made Metatron, a position which, in the view of the Enochian circle, did not exist before his translation. In this way, the exaltation of Enoch means a lowering of the idea of Metatron in the interests of monotheism.

The question then arises, whether 1 Enoch speaks only of the exaltation of Enoch to an elevated position in heaven, similar in many ways to that of the son of Man (which would be natural enough, *inter alia*, because the two conceptions have a common source in the idea of the Primordial Man), or whether it also teaches that Enoch is exalted to *become* the Son of Man and is made one with him. As we have seen, this latter view is the more widely accepted, and Sjöberg recently sought to present detailed exegetical support for it. But it can hardly be right.

[1] See Mowinckel in *N.T.T.* xlv, 1944, p. 65.   [2] See Odeberg, ibid.
[3] See the references above, p. 439 and n. 1; Sjöberg, *Der Menschensohn*, pp. 172ff.; Mowinckel in *N.T.T.* xlv, 1944, pp. 65ff.
[4] '*lp* is taken as an abbreviation of the three verbs, '*ªḥaztîw, lᵉḳaḥtîw*, and *pᵉḳaḏtîw*.
[5] On this point, Sjöberg is entirely right (*Der Menschensohn*, pp. 172ff.); cf. also Mowinckel in *N.T.T.* xlv, 1944, p. 66.

1 Enoch refers several times to Enoch's translation to heaven and his position as 'scribe' (see above, p. 438f.), an idea which is found elsewhere in apocalyptic (2 Esdras xiv, 9; 2 Bar. lxxvi, 2). Thus Enoch becomes one (the leading one) of the righteous elect, the patriarchs and the righteous who have been in that place from the beginning (1 En. lxx, 3f.). He has become the head of the heavenly community (pp. 379ff.). It is explicitly stated that this means that he is taken up to the Son of Man and the Lord of Spirits (lxx, 1). So too, in 2 Esdras xiv, 9: 'For thou shalt be taken up from (among) men, and henceforth thou shalt remain with my Servant[1] (i.e., the Messiah, the Son of Man), and with such as are like thee' (i.e., the heavenly community).

It is, in fact, this idea (of translation *to be with* the Son of Man, not *to be* the Son of Man) which also occurs in 1 En. lxxi. Whatever be the literary relationship between lxx and lxxi (whether it was the author of the Similitudes or a later writer who added lxxi as the conclusion to the Similitudes),[2] it is at least clear that lxxi originally formed a separate tradition, independent of lxx.[3] Both chapters deal with the same subject: Enoch's translation and exaltation.[4]

1 En. lxx describes it quite briefly. Enoch was lifted up on 'the chariots of the spirit', and set down between two quarters of heaven, the north and the west, where angels took cords to measure the place for the elect and righteous. There he saw the patriarchs and the righteous, who have dwelt in that place from time immemorial. Between north and west in heaven is paradise.[5] There can be no doubt that Enoch is already in heaven, where the dwellings of the righteous are. It is there that he is with the Son of Man and the Lord of Spirits. It is obvious that this is identical with his installation as heavenly scribe, presupposed elsewhere in 1 Enoch.

In lxxi, 1, we read:

And it came to pass after this that my spirit was translated
And it ascended into the heavens;

---

[1] *Filius meus* = '*abdî*; see above, p. 294. *A.P.O.T.* II has 'my Son'.

[2] That lxxi or lxxi, 5ff. is a later addition has been maintained by Beer (*A.P.A.T.* II, p. 228), Lagrange (*Le judaïsme avant Jésus-Christ*, p. 252), Staerk (*Soter* II, p. 68 n. 3), Messel (*Der Menschensohn in den Bilderreden des Henoch*, pp. 17f.), and others.

[3] This has also been maintained by Beer (*A.P.A.T.* II), Volz (*Eschatologie*[2], p. 25), and, at one time, by Charles (*The Book of Enoch translated*[1], pp. 143f.).

[4] Sjöberg (*Der Menschensohn*, pp. 16off.) tries to show that not only lxxi, 1–4 and lxxv, 5ff., but also the whole of lxx f. forms a unified, coherent account, describing in three stages Enoch's translation and exaltation. But he ends (cautiously and correctly) by stating that there is no conclusive evidence of such a unity. It is a possibility; in Sjöberg's view, the possibility for which there is most support.

[5] 1 En. xxxii, 2f.; cf. Beer, *A.P.A.T.* II, p. 229.

after which Enoch falls on his face before the Lord of Spirits, and is then led into His presence in the highest heaven. Thus there can be no doubt that 'after this' in *v.* 1 did not originally indicate any continuation of lxx, because in lxx Enoch is already in heaven. lxxi describes in greater detail what has already been briefly recounted in lxx. If, then, lxxi does have a different conception of the position to which Enoch has been raised, namely that he himself actually becomes the Son of Man, it is clear that this is a special conception within 1 Enoch,[1] which differs from the usual view in apocalyptic and 1 Enoch itself about the position of Enoch and his relationship to the Son of Man, namely that he was exalted to be *with* the Son of Man as the foremost among the righteous ones above.[2]

But this interpretation of lxxi is in itself improbable. The usual view is based in the main on *vv.* 14–17:

14. And He[3] came to me and greeted me with His voice and said unto me:
    'Thou art the Son of Man, thou who art born unto righteousness,
    And righteousness abides over thee,
    And the righteousness of the Head of Days forsakes thee not.'

15. And He said unto me:
    'He proclaims unto thee peace in the name of the world to come;
    For from hence has proceeded peace since the creation of the world
    And so shall it be unto thee for ever and for ever and for ever.

16. And all shall walk in thy ways since righteousness never forsaketh thee:
    With thee will be their dwelling-places, and with thee their heritages.
    And they shall not be separated from thee for ever and ever and ever.

---

[1] To that extent Bultmann (in *T.R.* (N.F.) ix, 1937, pp. 23f.) has some justification for his view that 1 En. lxxi is a scribal speculation by an individual apocalyptist—always assuming that the usual interpretation of the passage is sound.

[2] Lagrange, too, rightly maintains this point (*Le messianisme chez les juifs*, pp. 89, 96f.).

[3] A number of MSS. have 'that angel'. On the text, see Sjöberg, *Der Menschensohn*, p. 153. *A.P.O.T.* II has 'And he (i.e., the angel)'; but the speaker is undoubtedly the Lord of Spirits Himself. See Sjöberg, op. cit., pp. 155f. In *vv.* 14, 16 the third person is substituted in *A.P.O.T.* II for the second; but these emendations are discarded in the translation printed above.

17. And so there shall be length of days with that Son of Man,
   And the righteous shall have peace and an upright way
   In the name of the Lord of Spirits for ever and ever.'

If we disregard for the time being the introductory words in *v.*
14, it is clear that Enoch's position as guide and pattern of the
righteous is on a higher plane than elsewhere in 1 Enoch, and re-
sembles that in 2 Enoch. In fact it has certain features in common
with the position of Metatron and the Son of Man elsewhere in
apocalyptic.[1] He is the first of the righteous. They dwell with
him; and he watches over their heritage. He is the guide, in whose
righteous ways they will all walk.[2] But we may not conclude from
this that Enoch is here installed as Son of Man.[3] The conclusion
is affected by the interpretation of *vv.* 14 and 17, and by the extent
to which that interpretation can be reconciled with what we find
elsewhere in 1 Enoch. It is universally admitted that *v.* 14 can
also be translated:

'Thou art the son of man, who is born[4] unto righteousness',
that is, to walk righteously, and to gain salvation, the reward of
righteousness. If that is so, it is clear that 'son of man' is used not
in the technical sense, 'that Son of Man', but in the ordinary sense,
as a common noun, 'that man who' etc. It then follows that lxxi
conveys the same meaning as lxx: the exaltation of Enoch to a
conspicuous position in the presence of the Lord of Spirits, but not
his exaltation to be the Son of Man.

That is also the meaning of the concluding words in *v.* 17.[5] We
read there that the righteous will have everlasting life 'with that
Son of Man', and that they will 'have peace and an upright way
in the name of the Lord of Spirits'. Sjöberg rightly paraphrases
this, 'all the righteous, not only Enoch', thus including Enoch
among the righteous, who will be *with* the Son of Man.[6] It is

---

[1] Cf. Sjöberg, *Der Menschensohn*, p. 153. But it is an exaggeration to say that Enoch
here 'occupies the same central position in the heavenly world as the Son of Man does
elsewhere'. There is, for instance, no reference here to judgement or enthronement.
[2] The main question is not seriously affected by differences about the text of *v.* 16.
See Beer, *A.P.A.T.* II, ad. loc., and Sjöberg, *Der Menschensohn*, p. 153 n. 15.
[3] *Pace* Sjöberg, op. cit., p. 153.
[4] The verb in this relative clause is in the second person. But, in accordance with
normal linguistic usage, the clause may be taken either as a more precise definition of
the predicate 'son of man', or as a clause in apposition to the subject 'thou'. See
Sjöberg, op. cit., p. 152.
[5] I admit that Sjöberg (op. cit., p. 152) is right in his interpretation of *v.* 17, as against
my earlier view (*N.T.T.* xlv, 1944), which, as he rightly suggests (op. cit., p. 153 n. 14),
I had already begun to doubt (*N.T.T.* xlv, 1944, p. 194 n. 22).
[6] Has Sjöberg noticed the inconsistency between this paraphrase and the interpretation of the chapter which he maintains elsewhere?

exactly the same thought which is more briefly expressed in lxx, that Enoch was exalted to the Son of Man and the Lord of Spirits to be with them. It is certainly not by accident that in *v.* 17, where the expression 'Son of Man' occurs in the technical sense, of the pre-existent Messiah, the translator uses the usual technical expression, *walda sabe'*, whereas in *v.* 14 he uses *walda be'esī* (son of man). This suggests that in *v.* 14 the expression is not the technical one, but the ordinary common noun, 'that man who' . . .

The view that 1 En. lxxi describes the exaltation of Enoch to *be* the Son of Man is, in fact, also incompatible with the ideas about the Son of Man, which are found elsewhere in the book. 1 Enoch describes the Son of Man as existing before creation. The Similitudes begin with the translation of Enoch in a vision to heaven, where he sees the Son of Man as one who has existed from the beginning. It seems out of the question that the same author can have thought that Enoch later *became* the Son of Man, for that would mean that the Son of Man did not exist until Enoch was finally translated to heaven, as Metatron, according to Enochian speculation,[1] also came into being as Metraton in and through the exaltation of Enoch to that position. If the meaning of 1 En. lxxi was that in some mystical fashion Enoch was made identical with the already existing Son of Man (e.g., fused with him in some kind of corporeal *unio mystica*), surely that would have been stated or suggested. References to ecstatic, mystical experiences are not uncommon elsewhere in 1 Enoch;[2] in this very chapter (lxxi, 11) we have the account of an ecstatic experience of this kind, in which Enoch sees the Head of Days. But there is no suggestion in lxxi of a fusion with the Son of Man.[3] That Enoch should thus, in a realistic, metaphysical sense, become one with the Son of Man is inconceivable, not only for our mode of thought,[4] but also for any reasonable mode of thought, and particularly in 1 En. lxxi, where the Son of Man does not appear at all, either actively or passively, but where there is only a reference to an exaltation to that heaven where the Son of Man is, in order to be with him there.[5]

---

[1] But note, not in the original teaching about Metatron; see above, pp. 439f.
[2] 1 En. xiv, 8f., 24f.; xxxix, 3, 14; lii, 1; lx, 3; lxxi, 1, 11; lxxxi, 5.
[3] This is admitted by Sjöberg, *Der Menschensohn*, p. 187.
[4] As Sjöberg admits, *loc. cit.*
[5] The parallels which Sjöberg mentions (op. cit., pp. 187f.: the union of the dead Pharaoh with Osiris, or the reunion of a dead Persian with his fravashi) shed no light on the conception in 1 En. lxxi.

THE SON OF MAN

21. 'The Son of Man' as Used by Jesus

In the ideas about the Son of Man, Jesus found a form which He could use to express His consciousness of His nature and His vocation, His task at the coming of God's kingdom.

The discussion of the question during the past two generations has made it quite certain that Jesus actually used this title by preference in referring to Himself.[1] Indeed, it is clear that He even deliberately avoided other Messianic titles.

It is not our present purpose to examine the content which Jesus found in and brought to the expression. This book is intended only to lead up to the message of Jesus about the Son of Man, to show the presuppositions behind it and to present the development of the various factors, and the form in which they lay ready to be used, transformed, and fitted into a new unity by Him. But a few observations may be made in conclusion.

The matter may be summarily expressed thus: Jesus came to be, not the Messiah, but the Son of Man.[2] He wanted to be the Messiah only in so far as the idea of the Messiah had been modified by, and was compatible with, that of the Son of Man.

In spite of incidental influence from the Son of Man, the Jewish Messiah had remained a figure who belonged to the future history of this present world. As soon as it is admitted that he cannot find fulfilment in the natural world, he loses his meaning. He is incompatible with a kingly figure, whose kingdom is not of this world, and whose royal nature it is to bear witness to the truth and to be crucified for the sake of the truth. Therefore a crucified Messiah is a stumbling-block to the Jews. If this is to come to pass, an earthly Messiah is not enough.[3]

It is also worth noting that Jesus did not associate Himself with the popular ideas and expectations. The popular Messianic expectations were the national, political, and this-worldly ones, to which His disciples so often clung. As we have seen (p. 415ff.), the ideas which He took up were those of more esoteric circles, ideas which circulated in narrower, and for the most part literary and theological circles, though they may have been to some extent familiar to a wider public.

By using the title 'Son of Man' and some of the conceptions

---

[1] See Héring, *Le royaume de Dieu et sa venue d'après Jésus et Saint Paul*; Baldensperger's surveys of literature in *T.R.* iii, 1900, pp. 201ff., 243ff. A critical survey of the most recent research is given by McCown in *The Journal of Religion* xxviii, 1, January 1948, pp. 1ff.   [2] This is frankly admitted by Héring, op. cit., pp. 11ff.
[3] Again it is a pleasure to refer to Toynbee, *A Study of History I–VI*, pp. 522f., 529f.

which were then associated with it, Jesus may be said to have associated Himself with the varied history which had led up to the late Jewish idea of the Messiah, with its borrowings in form and content from Jewish and pagan sources. He laid all the emphasis on those aspects of that idea which were represented by the title 'the Son of Man'. In so doing He set His seal on that process of religious development, and acknowledged its validity as revelation history. He also hallowed those features in it which were of non-Jewish origin, and in fact attested that He was a saviour for both Jews and Gentiles, the fulfilment of the hope of all mankind, being 'Son of Man' in the more modern sense of the term, which is justified by the connexion with the idea of the Primordial Man. When Peter in his vision saw a sheet let down from heaven full of clean and unclean animals, it was said to him, 'What God has made clean, you must not call common'. This may be applied to the history of the idea of the Son of Man, and to the heathen elements associated with it, which found their way into the Messianic belief of the people of God, and later of the new people of God.

Something must also be added about the sense in which Jesus uses the phrase 'the Son of Man'. Both what has been said above, and also the use of the phrase in the Gospels, make it plain that what Jesus seeks to express by it is not, primarily, the idea, which most readily occurs to the modern mind, of His connexion with us men, of the earthly and human side of His nature. His use of the phrase proclaims boldly the original paradox, that He, who will one day come with the authority of God, is called 'the Man'. But with Him the order is reversed: He, who now goes about as an ordinary man, is also the one in whom the miraculous powers of the kingdom of God are at work; it is He who has power over the mighty, and is Lord of the Sabbath; and it is He who will one day be revealed as 'the Son of Man', with divine glory and authority.

This change of emphasis is important. It has been said that it is the union of majesty and humility that is expressed in His use of the phrase.[1] For Jesus, the fact that *He* is the Son of Man is a paradox, a mystery of the kingdom of heaven, a cross for faith. Even

[1] Cf. Brun, *Jesu evangelium*[2], pp. 555f. When the idea of humility appears in Jesus' use of the phrase, it can be explained in the light of His personal consciousness of what it meant to be the Son of Man. But the thought is connected with a nuance which the context sometimes gives to the expression in the Old Testament, e.g., Ps. viii (combination of dignity and insignificance), or when the Most High addresses Ezekiel as 'Thou man' (*ben 'ādām*); cf. Bowman in *E.T.* lix, 1947/8, pp. 283f., with references to rabbinic interpretation.

the disciples find it hard to understand that He, who has been their companion as a poor man, really is the one in whom the kingdom of God is already present, and through whom it is at work. They were amazed that 'God had given such authority to men' (Matt. ix, 8). It is still more amazing that the one who says that He is the Son of Man does not appear in glory, and that He is not immediately judge with God's authority, but the preacher and mediator of God's forgiving grace, the friend of sinners and tax-collectors, the good shepherd, who seeks the lost and opens for them the door to the kingdom of God and to paradise. 'The Son of Man came to seek and to save what was lost' (Luke xix, 10). The fact that in Jesus the Son of Man has already come, and goes about, yet is hidden, means not judgement but God's love and grace. This is the visible offer of salvation for sinners and for the oppressed.[1] 'The atmosphere about Him is different' from that in the usual ideas about the Son of Man.[2]

How Jesus reached this understanding of Himself is His own personal secret, which cannot be penetrated by any attempt at psychological explanation. Jesus understood and fulfilled the thought of the unknown Messiah on earth in a manner entirely different from its presentation in the Jewish legend (see above, pp. 305ff.).

That the earthly Jesus was Himself the Son of Man can be interpreted in two different ways. Jesus may have meant that He was the heavenly Son of Man, who had come down in a mysterious manner, and now walked the earth. Or He may have meant that he was an elect man, who would be exalted to be what the initiated said that the Son of Man was in heaven. On this latter view it might be said that the Son of Man did not yet really exist in heaven, except in the purpose and thought of God (the *logos*), but that when Jesus was exalted to heaven, He would be endued with all the divine nature and authority inherent in the idea of the Son of Man. Then the Son of Man would come into existence; and as such Jesus would come in the clouds of heaven, and enter upon His dominion.

The former of these interpretations appears in the Fourth Gospel (iii, 13; vi, 62), and is also in accord with Paul's thought of the pre-existence of Jesus with God in heaven.[3] It seems very likely

[1] Cf. Sjöberg, art. 'Jesus Kristus' in *S.B.U.* I.
[2] See Sjöberg, 'Människosonen i judendom och urkristendom' in *28:e Svenska Läroverksläraremöte i Stockholm*, p. 265.
[3] 2 Cor. viii, 9; Phil. ii, 6f. Cf. Brun, *Paulus's kristelige tanker*[2], pp. 82ff. The passages

that Paul's thought here is affected by familiarity with the theology about the Son of Man. In the Fourth Gospel there is also evidence which points to another possibility, namely the idea of the *logos* in the Prologue: Christ existed before the origin of the world as God's creating and saving 'word', 'thought', and 'purpose'. If we confine ourselves to the sayings of Jesus in the Synoptic Gospels, it is natural to incline to the other possibility, that the man Jesus was selected to be, and would be, exalted to become all that the old traditions recounted about the Son of Man. The Synoptic tradition contains nothing which suggests that Jesus attributed to Himself (either in general, or as Son of Man) a real pre-existence.[1] There the title refers to the earthly existence of Jesus and His eschatological status at His exaltation. There seems to be justification for the statement that on the lips of Jesus the title has 'an enigmatic ring' for His hearers.[2] His parting word to the Council, 'Hereafter you will see the Son of Man sitting at the right hand of Power, and coming in the clouds of heaven' (Matt. xxvi, 64; cf. Mark xiv, 62; Luke xxii, 69), is most naturally understood in its fully paradoxical sense: He who is now an earthly human being will be revealed as the Son of Man at God's right hand.

But there is another great and incomprehensible innovation in Jesus' view of Himself as the Son of Man. It is an original and essential element in His thought, that the Son of Man will be rejected, and will suffer and die before He comes in His glory with God's angels and sits down on the judgement seat. Among the most outstanding of the sayings of Jesus about the Son of Man are those which express this thought.[3] As we have seen (pp. 325f., 410ff.), there is nothing corresponding to this in the Jewish conceptions of the Messiah and the Son of Man. Even the idea of the Son of Man was an inadequate expression of the self-consciousness of Jesus. It still had about it something of the Jewish hope of an earthly future. In the idea of the suffering, death, and resurrection of the Son of Man, Jesus added to it a new element. This new element is understood in the light of God's love. The death of the

---

[1] Cf. Brun, *Jesu evangelium*[2], pp. 543f., 559.
[2] Brun, op. cit., p. 560.
[3] See Héring, *Le royaume de Dieu et sa venue d'après Jésus et Saint Paul*, pp. 98ff.

---

which speak of the 'sending' of Christ need not presuppose sending from one place (heaven) to another (earth), but may be instances of the customary Semitic expression for a special vocation; cf. von Dobschütz in *J.B.L.* xli, 1922, pp. 212ff.

Son of Man, who is also the Servant, creates a new possibility that 'the many' may be saved.[1]

There can be little doubt about the source from which Jesus derived this idea. It came from Scripture, from the suffering Servant of the Lord. In the predictions in the book of Isaiah, He found God's answer to the problem raised by the opposition and obduracy of His own people.

As we have seen, no one in Judaism had really connected the Servant with the Messiah, the mediator of the kingdom of God, and of the new relationship between God and men. When the Servant in Isa. liii was identified with the Messiah, the passage was reinterpreted in such a way as to reverse the sense, and the Servant vanished in the national, political Messiah (see above, pp. 330ff.). Jesus was the first to take this prophecy seriously in its real meaning, and apply it to Himself.[2]

The essential and decisive way in which Jesus transformed the idea of the Messiah was that He combined the thought of the suffering, dying, and exalted Servant of the Lord with that of the Son of Man, who will come again on the clouds of heaven. The Son of Man will be rejected, will suffer many things, will die, be buried, and rise again on the third day.

But even for Jesus Himself this thought can hardly have been originally included in the idea of the Son of Man. Through adversity and suffering God had to show Him that it was so. For Him, too, it was a new realization that 'according to the Scriptures' the Son of Man must suffer and die.

Thus this aspect of Jesus' use of the phrase has all the tension of paradox. The Son of Man, who, as originally conceived, is the pre-existent, heavenly one, endued with the spirit, *He* will be humiliated, and will suffer and die. The thought was unheard of, both among the adherents of the national Messianic ideal, and still more among those who gave allegiance to the idea of the Son of Man. The Jewish Messianic concept is thereby transformed, and lifted up to a wholly other plane. In fact, the Jewish Messiah,

[1] Cf. Sjöberg, op. cit.

[2] Ström's supposed evidence that the two ideas had been combined in Judaism before the time of Jesus (namely the textual variants in 2 Esdras xiii, 32; *filius meus* and 'My Servant'; see above, p. 294) is too easy and superficial: 'hence we may conclude that we have here a combination of the Son of Man in Dan. vii with the Ebed Jahve of Isa. liii' (*Vetekornet*, p. 140). 'Here': where? Are both the variants original? As has been observed above, the title 'My Servant' is too commonly applied to an agent of Yahweh to justify the conclusion that it points to the influence of Isa. liii. Unfortunately, Ström can also cite Dahl (*Das Volk Gottes*, p. 91), who is dependent here on G. Kittel (in *R.G.G.*[2] III).

as originally conceived, and as most of Jesus' contemporaries thought of him, was pushed aside and replaced by a new redeemer and mediator of salvation, 'the Man', who comes from God to suffer and die as God's Servant, in order to save men from the power of sin, Satan, and death. For Jesus, the Jewish Messianic idea was the temptation of Satan, which He had to reject.[1] The new conception of a saviour, which Jesus created, unites in itself the loftiest elements in both the Jewish and the 'Aryan' spirit, and fuses them in a true unity, which is realized in Jesus Himself.

In so far as the Son of Man (both originally and in the thought of Jesus) is an expression for the victorious Messiah, God's representative, who comes in His glory on the clouds of heaven, it may be said that it is only after His exaltation, when He comes in glory, that Jesus becomes the Son of Man. With some justification it has been said that during His earthly life He was a prospective Messiah; and therefore it might be said, with greater justification, that He was a prospective Son of Man. But according to the testimony of the Gospels, which we can have no valid grounds for doubting on this point, Jesus also applied the term 'Son of Man' to Himself as He was when He went about preaching, in every way a man among men.[2] Here, again, the tension of paradox is apparent. This aspect of the matter is particularly evident in Paul's Christology: the humiliation of the Son of Man began before His rejection and suffering. The heavenly Son of Man went about on earth as an earthly man; and although 'foxes have holes and the birds of the air have nests, the Son of Man has nowhere to lay His head'. Jesus, the poor man, the carpenter from the provincial town in half-heathen Galilee, He is the heavenly Son of Man, who once was on high in divine glory. This paradox, which is clearly brought out in Paul's thought of Him who was rich and became poor, who shared the divine glory but emptied Himself, who did not count equality with God a thing to be snatched at, but was born in the likeness of man (Phil. ii, 6f.)—this paradox must go back to a similar tension in the soul and the consciousness of Jesus Himself, which finds expression in the daring way in which He transforms and uses the concept of the Son of Man.

[1] Mark viii, 27–33, and parallels; cf. the Temptation narrative, Matt. iv, 1ff.; Luke iv, 1ff. See Héring, *Le royaume de Dieu et sa venue d'après Jésus et Saint Paul*, pp. 122ff.
[2] Mark ii, 10, 28 and parallels; Matt. xii, 32 = Luke xii, 10; Matt. viii, 20 = Luke ix, 58; Matt. xi, 18f. = Luke vii, 33f.; Matt. xiii, 37.

Additional Notes

NOTE I (p. 3 n. 2)

Cf. Emmet in *E.R.E.* VIII, p. 570: 'Much confusion is caused by the fact that the term "Messianic" is used in a much wider range of meaning than "Messiah".' Students of the history of religion, orientalists, and even some theologians (who ought to know better) have often applied the misleading term 'Messianic' to all kinds of half mythological conceptions of kings and kingship. Labat (*Royauté*, pp. 295ff.) uses the term 'the Messianic king' of the Babylonian conception of the king as bringer of prosperity and blessing, although he is aware that the Babylonians had no eschatology (op. cit., p. 299), and therefore no Messiah. Widengren lays emphasis on the conception of the king as saviour (*R.o.B.* ii, 1943, pp. 74ff.). Engnell, too, speaks of 'Messianism' in the ancient oriental royal ideology (*Divine Kingship*, pp. 12f., 43ff., 68, 93ff.). By this expression he means 'elaborate king ideology not "eschatological" messianism' (op. cit., p. 43 n. 3, cf. p. 176). Widengren (*R.o.B.* ii, 1943, pp. 74ff.) would lay more emphasis on the king's position as saviour, son, and deputy of the god, upholding and embodying the cosmic order. (This last point, at least, does not apply to Mesopotamian kingship, though it no doubt does to Egyptian. See above, pp. 28ff.). Engnell later explains what he means at greater length: 'The sacral or divine kingship is the recognized term for an institution at once religious and political . . . which implies that "by divine grace" the king embodies the god in his own person and plays the part of the god in the cult. But at the same time, and in a special way, he represents the community, the people in its entirety . . . On him depend victory, prosperity, rain and fertility, the integrity of nature and of human life, the natural order of the cosmos, which he maintains against the powers of chaos, above all through the part he plays in the cult. All these circumstances are reflected in the ideology which is associated with his person; and when that ideology is so developed that the king appears as an ideal figure with whom the hope of salvation is bound up, a stage has been reached to which the term "Messianism" must be applied—a term which thus need not imply any eschatological reference' (*Gamla Testamentet* I, pp. 141f.). Even apart from the fact that this account of the 'ideology' is distorted and incorrect (in Babylonia the king is not an incarnation of the god, nor

ADDITIONAL NOTES

does he uphold the cosmic order), no adequate reason has been adduced
to show that we *must* use the epithet 'Messianic' of this ideology.[1]
Riesenfeld (*Jésus transfiguré*, p. 154) adopts the same position. Reicke
(*S.E.Å.* xii, 1947, p. 279) at least puts the word between inverted
commas, when he tries to interpret Mark vii with reference to Matt.
x, 35f. in terms of this royal ideology. Bentzen, in his essay, 'Kan ordet
"Messiansk" anvendes om Salmernes kongeforestillinger?' (*S.E.Å.* xii,
1947, pp. 36ff.), takes up the question of terminology. He feels justified
in using 'Messianic' of oriental kingship, since the latter always involves
an aspect akin to eschatology, an aspect which is described in the
present work as 'the unrealized elements in the ideal of kingship'. But
a clear terminology is better than one which conceals important differences. Used in Bentzen's sense, the term 'Messianic' is misleading,
because it suggests the existence of a genuine Messianic hope, which is
realized in the empirical king and is already in existence before it is
applied to him. The word is more fittingly used of the Persian Saoshyant (cf. Abegg, *Der Messiasglaube in Indien und Iran*) or of the Mahdi
of Islam, who are really eschatological figures of the same phenomenological type, to some extent, as the Messiah. Against the misleading
terminology, see also Kennett, *Old Testament Essays*, p. 224.

NOTE II (p. 36 n. 1).

Bentzen in *S.E.Å.* xii, 1947, p. 43 (cf. *King and Messiah*, p. 17), referring to Pedersen, *Israel* III–IV, pp. 409ff.; cf. pp. 440ff. Pedersen,
however, is speaking not about the enthronement of the earthly king,
but about the enthronement of Yahweh and the recapitulation of the
events of primordial time (*urtidsgjerninger*), which takes place in the cult.
(I regret that when I wrote my remarks in *St.Th.* II, i, 1948/49, p. 80, I
did not check the passage in Pedersen's book to which Bentzen refers.)
Pedersen is right in saying that the earthly king, too, is 'renewed'
through the creative power of the cult; but this is a conception which
we ought not to press as Bentzen does when he makes it a precise dogma
which explains the origin of the royal ideology, and an important element in that ideology. Nor ought we to use it as a starting point in
trying to understand the 'consciousness of predestination' in Hammurabi and other kings. Pedersen rightly says that the accession of the
king is connected with the actual recreation of the world *today* through
the festival with its repeated experience of creation and genesis. It is a
contemporary event of recreation rather than an event of primordial
time. But with Hammurabi we are concerned not with primordial
time made contemporary in the cult, but with a rational idea of creation

[1] Engnell himself admits (alas!) that he is unable 'to distinguish between the cultic
[in the above sense] and the historical-eschatological Messiah' (*Pedersenfestskrift*, p. 89
n. 13).

ADDITIONAL NOTES

as having taken place at a certain point in linear time. It is not his own coming into existence, but the determination 'of his fate' which Hammurabi dates back to the time before creation.

NOTE III (p. 40 n. 1).

See Frankfort, *Kingship*, pp. 281ff.; cf. also Zimmern in *Z.D.M.G.* lxxvi, 1922, pp. 52f. The reason in each case is that Marduk himself was originally a local god of fertility and of the power of life, representing the ever-changing rhythm of the life of nature, before he became the supreme god, a change which was certainly associated with the new position of the city of Babylon as the centre of political power in the whole country, and as 'capital of the world'. It is unnecessary to enter here into the attempts of Engnell and Widengren to make almost all the great gods of the east into 'high gods' (for this conception see Lang, *The Making of Religion*[3] I–II; Söderblom, *Gudstrons uppkomst*, pp. 209ff. = *Das Werden des Gottesglaubens*, pp. 150ff.; van der Leeuw, *Religion in Essence and Manifestation*, pp. 159ff. with detailed references to literature), or to regard the various fertility gods as secondary hypostatizations (*Abspaltungen*) of a particular aspect of the high god (Engnell, *Divine Kingship*, pp. 6f., 18ff., 23ff.; G. Widengren, *Hochgottglaube im alten Iran*, pp. 5–93; *Religionens värld*[2], pp. 54ff.). A theory of this kind becomes possible only if we define the idea of a high god so loosely that it means nothing. As for the hypostatization of particular aspects of a divine being and of his activities, it is true that this kind of thing does sometimes happen in the realms of religion (see A. Bertholet, *Götterspaltung und Göttervereinigung*); but that does not justify us in using this phenomenon as a master key in the history of religion. Against the overrating of the high god notion (occasioned primarily by the works of W. Schmidt, *Ursprung der Gottesidee*, and *Ursprung und Werden der Religion*, works rich in material, but somewhat over-systematized), see, among others, Sverdrup in *Nordisk Tidsskrift*, 1935, pp. 18ff.; Meek in *The Review of Religion*, 1940, pp. 286ff.; Albright, *From the Stone Age to Christianity*[2], pp. 133ff. A sound criticism of the theory of 'hypostatizations' is given by Edsman in *S.T.K.* xxiii, 1947, pp. 327ff.

NOTE IV (p. 45 n. 9).

Frankfort, *Kingship*, p. 311. Engnell (*Divine Kingship*, pp. 28ff.) and Widengren (*R.o.B.* ii, 1943, pp. 6off.) would interpret such statements as evidence that the king '*is*' the tree of life, representing Tammuz in the cult, and represented by the sacred tree or pole. Thus the king would be 'identical' with Tammuz, so that, for example, he would in his own person experience the death and resurrection of the god. It is certain that 'the Tree' was sometimes regarded as a divine being. It symbolized the very power of life in nature. The vegetation deity may be called 'the Tree-god' or 'the god-Tree' (= Gilgamesh; see Mo-winckel in *Act.Or.* xv, 1936, pp. 141ff.). But there is no evidence in the sources that the king was identical with the tree of life. Engnell finds such evidence in the saying of a devoted subject: 'King Shulgi, the gracious lord, is a date palm, planted by a watercourse.' We should be equally justified in maintaining that the righteous man in Ps. i, who is 'like a tree planted by streams of water', must be identified with the tree of life and the god of fertility. (Engnell in fact makes this equation in *Pedersenfestskrift*, pp. 84ff. Against his use of conventional metaphors such as *šāṭûl*, see Frankfort, *Kingship*, p. 408 nn. 67, 69.) It is not even necessary to suppose that so natural a metaphor, *qua* meta-phor, was borrowed from the Tammuz ideology. In the cult it is the king who, in his role as priest endowed with power, plants the tree of life; he is 'the gardener' who tends it. He himself receives his power from the tree of life (cf. Gadd, *Ideas of Divine Rule in the Ancient East*, pp. 91f.); his royal mace may be regarded as one of its branches. When, for instance, in need and sickness the king is described as a withered bough or a dead tree, the reason is not that he was regarded, in actual life or in the cult, as identical with Tammuz, the dead god of vegetation, or that in the appropriate psalm of lamentation he was to play the part of Tammuz, but simply that ideas from the Tammuz mythology were used as natural metaphors and applied to the king: he is now as miser-able as Tammuz in his degradation. See also Frankfort, op. cit., p. 408 n. 67.

Note V (p. 51 n. 1).

Dürr (*Ursprung und Ausbau*, pp. 134ff.) had previously tried to connect the Suffering Servant of the Lord in Isa. liii with the penitential ritual for the Babylonian king at the New Year festival. From this ritual Engnell draws the conclusion that the king, being identical with the god, suffers, and dies, and rises again in the cult, and that even else-where in the festival ritual he appears as Marduk, suffering and dying. This is an incorrect interpretation of the ritual. As will be seen very clearly from Frankfort's analysis (op. cit., pp. 313ff.), the king does not represent Marduk in his suffering. On the contrary, he appears as the companion and human helper of Marduk's son Nabu or Ninurta, when the latter is 'searching' for Marduk and setting him free. The ceremony of humiliation on the fifth day of the festival is not intended as the ritual death of the king in place of the god, but as a penitential ceremony, which, at the same time, marks the turning point in the great drama (see above, pp. 41f.). The rising again begins with the purification and restitution of the king (who is the representative of the congregation and the link between gods and men), so that during the rest of the festival he may again effectually represent both parties.

ADDITIONAL NOTES

Labat's view of the suffering of the king in the festival is fundamentally sound when he says (*Royauté*, pp. 323ff.) that because he is 'the incarnation (embodiment would be a better term) of his people, he is also in his relation to the gods responsible for any anonymous or collective sin'. The material collected by Labat (ibid, pp. 324ff.) concerning the king's role in the cult in atoning, confessing sin, and interceding must also form the basis of our understanding of the ritual of humiliation at the New Year festival.

Engnell further urges that the Babylonian psalms of lamentation are concerned in the main with the king and do not refer to historical political calamities, but to his cultic 'suffering' as the dying god (*Divine Kingship*, pp. 45ff.). Widengren has sought to interpret Ps. lxxxviii as a particularly clear instance of the fact that this idea of the 'sojourn of the king in the realm of the dead' was an essential element in the cult and the royal ideology in Israel (*S.E.Å.* x, 1945, pp. 66ff.). The king is certainly the speaker in most Babylonian, as well as in a great many Israelite, psalms of lamentation. But, as we have seen, the presupposition of Engnell's and Widengren's interpretation (viz., that in the cult the king *is* the god) is false. This disposes of any possibility of interpreting the psalms of lamentation as an expression of the cultic suffering of the king-vegetation-god and of his sojourn in the realm of the dead. See now my *Offersang og sangoffer*, ch. VII, 6 (pp. 243ff.). We have therefore no valid ground for maintaining that the 'aspect of suffering' is an essential part of the royal ideology.

NOTE VI (p. 52 n. 1).

Engnell quotes a great many statements by earlier scholars about the identity of the king with the god in the vegetation drama at Ugarit (*Divine Kingship*, pp. 104ff.). These are, however, in the main, general hypotheses and possibilities relating to some text or other, unsupported by convincing evidence. Engnell's own interpretation of the identity of the king with the dying and rising vegetation god (as he puts it, 'this identity in its double aspect as referring to the high god and the vegetation deity'; cf. op. cit., pp. 8off.) in texts other than the Karit Epic is to be found in *Divine Kingship*, pp. 110ff. Here, too, we find much that is hypothetical, suggesting that the identity has in fact been presupposed and read into the texts. The text V AB (op. cit., pp. 110ff.) speaks of the enthronement of the deity himself after the 'resurrection'; we hear nothing about the king. The same is true of II AB (op. cit., pp. 114ff.), and of I AB (op. cit., pp. 118ff.). Of course, Engnell's words, 'I feel convinced that the king is here the actor in the character of Ltpn 'il dp 'id' (p. 120) prove nothing. Nor does I AB (op. cit., pp. 121ff.) or IV AB (op. cit., pp. 124f.) say anything about the king and his role. Nor can I find in BH (op. cit., pp. 125ff.) any proof of the presence of the king. The sort of basis on which Engnell's interpretation rests is indicated by his remark, '*If I am on the right track* [i.e., in the previous interpretations] this text is of no little importance to us in our search for the divine king in the ritual of Ugarit' (op. cit., p. 125; italics mine). Beyond this 'if' we do not find much in the text or in Engnell's interpretation. In III AB, A (op. cit., pp. 127ff.) we still hear only of the god, even in the 'oracle' (op. cit., pp. 128f.). Possibly the god is represented by the king in the 'cultic marriage' in SS (op. cit., pp. 129ff.); but Engnell's 'proof' rests on his not very probable interpretation of '*il w'lmh* as a hendiadys (op. cit., p. 131). The undoubted merit of Engnell's interpretation of these texts is that they have shed new and clearer light on cultic ritual and cultic myth in Ugarit; but they say nothing directly about the royal ideology. Much the same is true of the Dan'il-Aqhat legend (op. cit., pp. 134ff.). Here we have to do with a demigod the deified founder of a dynasty (or a deity who has been made the human subject of a legend, like Gilgamesh). As the text now stands, Dan'il is a figure of the same type as Karit. As in the Karit Epic, therefore, we have here an indirect source for the royal ideology.

NOTE VII (p. 80 n. 1).

Widengren's arguments (*R.o.B.* ii, 1943, pp. 60ff., in agreement with Engnell, *Divine Kingship*, p. 28) for the view that in Israel the king was identified with the water of life and the tree of life are quite unconvincing. Consider the texts. In Isa. xi, 1 we have a metaphor which might arise in the imagination of a poet anywhere and at any time (cf. above, p. 161 n. 3 and Additional Note IV); and the prophet does not speak of the tree of life but of the tree or family of Jesse. Isa. xiv, 19 offers no analogy to the branch of the tree of life which withers and revives; on the contrary, the point in Isa. xiv, 19 is that when the branch is cast away it does *not* revive. In T. Judah xxiv, 4 (which is not found in the Armenian version, undoubtedly because it is a Christian interpolation) there is a metaphor for the Messiah derived from a Messianic interpretation of O. T. conceptions which originally had no Messianic content; the following verses 5f. reflect interpretations of Isa. xi, 1, combined possibly with Num. xxiv, 17, certainly with Ps. xlv, 7b. Here, too, the 'stem' that arises 'from your [i.e., Judah's] root' is a metaphor for the Messiah, as in Isa. xi, 1, and has nothing to do with the tree of life. That *ṣemaḥ*, 'the branch', in Zech. vi, 11–13 is a cultic, mythological idea, not Zechariah's own pun on and interpretation of the name Zerubbabel, remains to be proved; and that Jer. xxiii, 5 and xxxiii, 15 depend directly (in either the traditio-historical or literary sense) on Zech. vi, 11–13 seems to me to be obvious; see above, pp. 19f. and pp. 120, 164. It is possible, however, that the analogy of the sprouting symbol of fecundity and life (cf. the Adonis gardens, Isa. xvii, 10f.; see above, p. 82 n. 2) was present in the prophet's thought and helped to suggest his interpretation of Zerubbabel's name; see above, p. 164. In Isa. liii, 2 the metaphor is ultimately taken from the Tammuz rituals; but the Servant is no kingly figure, and proves nothing about the royal ideology. Against Engnell (and Hooke) see Frankfort, *Kingship*, p. 408 n. 67. Nor has Widengren proved that in Israel the king's consciousness of being 'called' took the special form of the sense that he was a *šālꟾaḥ*, one who is 'sent'; see above, p. 37. Isa. lxi, 1ff., does not speak about a king, but about a herald who brings the good tidings of the advent and enthronement of the king Yahweh. The Moses of the legends in Exodus–Numbers is 'sent', not as a king or chieftain, but as a prophet. It might perhaps be objected that the king is also a prophet; but this does not justify us in identifying the different conceptions and in concluding by formal logical deductions from them, e.g., that the king was also regarded as a *šālꟾaḥ*.

NOTE VIII (p. 85 n. 2).

The point is touched on by Hooke in *Myth and Ritual*, p. 84, and by T. H. Robinson, op. cit., p. 172ff., see pp. 183, 187; see also Johnson in *The Labyrinth*, pp. 73ff. Hvidberg (*Den israelitiske Religions Historie*, pp. 70, 111) holds that at least certain circles of a syncretistic character may have adopted the custom of weeping over the god, i.e., celebrating funerary ritual for his death; but he also admits that the thought of a dying Yahweh was so inconsistent with Israelite religion that the very idea cannot really have been adopted by it. The only passage which Hvidberg cites in support is Hos. x, 5; 'his [referring to the bull-deity] people shall mourn over him, his priests rejoice over him'—an allusion to death and resurrection (cf. Mowinckel in *G.T.M.M.M.*, ad. loc.). Here we have to do with a Yahweh who has in all essentials become like Baal. But it is also conceivable that, even in the baalized cult of Yahweh at Bethel, it was only the custom of weeping and rejoicing that was adopted, and not the idea of death which was originally associated with it, and that the 'weeping' was not looked upon as a rite of mourning over the god, but as one of penitence and supplication (weeping also formed part of the rites of penitence and humiliation; see Jer. iii, 21). At all events we may not draw conclusions from the wholly baalized cult of the bull-deity at Bethel about the conception of Yahweh in Jerusalem and the cult there, or about the conception held in those circles and that line of spiritual development of which the reforming prophets are the representatives.

To Haldar (*Associations* and *Studies in the Book of Nahum*) the theory of the dying and rising god seems so obvious, even in Jerusalem, that he uses it boldly as an exegetical master-key. There is, therefore, reason for considering his 'arguments'. In Mal. iii, 1 he assumes that the congregation is searching for the dead god, and accordingly the prophet here announces his return to the temple (*Associations*, pp. 128f.). The argument is that the situation presumably corresponds to the Accadian cultus, where the waiting cultic prophet precedes the god in the procession which mourns the death of the god. Thus the argument is that in both passages we hear of one person preceding another! In Amos v, 18ff., the reason why Yahweh abhors the festivals at Bethel, Gilgal, and Beersheba is supposed to be that Amos is thinking of the moment in the presumed cultic drama when Yahweh is in the underworld and the powers of chaos have occupied His temple and are now celebrating an impure cult there (*Studies in the Book of Nahum*, pp. 110, 156). The text itself suggests nothing of the kind. In Nahum i, 13 the figure of the yoke is used to express the oppression of Judah by the enemy (Assyria): the same figure (which occurs frequently in the Old Testament) is used in a Tammuz text, where his death is regarded as imprisonment in the underworld, and deliverance is metaphorically expressed by 'the yoke . . . shall be removed from thee'. Therefore Yahweh's people are here supposed to be dead in the underworld (op. cit., pp. 117f.). It is also assumed that Pss. lxxiv, lxxix, and xliv are descriptions of the misery which follows Yahweh's descent into the underworld (*The Notion of the Desert in Sumero-Accadian and West-Semitic Religions*, pp. 52ff.). But in the texts there is not a single word to suggest this. In fact they contradict it; for how can the congregation pray to Yahweh for help if He Himself is dead? In psalms of lamentation and prophetic sayings we often hear of Yahweh's 'rising', i.e., ending his inactivity and hastening to the aid of His distressed people. Haldar thinks that this shows that Yahweh is regarded as dead but is summoned to 'rise' from the dead, or that He announces that He is about to rise. He would also interpret Isa. xxxiii, 10; Ps. lxviii, 1, in this sense (op. cit., pp. 39ff.). But see Num. x, 35. Did Yahweh really rise from the dead whenever a new day's march began? In Ps. xliv, 24, the call to 'awake' is also taken to refer to death and resurrection, for 'sleeping' does often indicate the sleep of death (op. cit., pp. 53f.). But see 2 Kings xviii, 27, where the thought is certainly of sleep in the literal sense as a form of inactivity. In Ps. cvii, 16, we hear of Yahweh 'breaking the gates of brass and cutting the bars of iron asunder': according to Haldar this refers to Yahweh's 'leaving the underworld at the head of the cultic procession' (op. cit., p. 64.). But Ps. cvii is a psalm of thank-offering, in which the various classes of redeemed people (travellers who have lost their way in the wilderness but have been put on the right track, released prisoners, sick men who have been healed, mariners who have been brought safe to port) all come forward with their thank-offering and thank Yahweh for the deliverance which has been granted to them. For those in prison He has broken the gates of brass and the bars of iron. Finally we may note that by a quite arbitrary interpretation of Nahum i–ii, Haldar makes the context refer to Yahweh's breaking out of the realm of death and taking up the struggle against Chaos-Death, ascending the mountain of the gods, conquering the enemy, partaking of the cultic meal, and so on: *has-sōḵēḵ* in Nahum ii, 6 (which undoubtedly refers to the testudo of charging soldiers) is taken to indicate the cultic image of Yahweh, which is finally 'set up' after being carried in the festal procession (*Studies in the Book of Nahum*, pp. 51f.). According to Haldar this whole interpretation is justified by the fact that we hear of all these things in the cultic pattern of the Near East, which means that Haldar's explanation presupposes what has first to be proved, namely that the Jerusalem cult was derived from a pattern of this kind. Haldar's summary of his contentions in *Studies in the Book of Nahum*, pp. 153f. and *The Notion of the Desert in Sumero-Accadian and West-Semitic Religions*, pp. 5ff., 68ff., is devoid of textual and exegetical support.

Even the expression 'Yahweh lives' (*ḥay YHWH*), and the oath formula 'by the life of Yahweh' have been taken to show that it was thought that Yahweh was not always 'alive'. The former expression is used parallel to the formula of a wish, *bārûḵ YHWH* in Ps. xviii, 47; cf. cxliv, 1. It is quite probable that this goes back to a pre-Yahwistic original, which hailed the resurrected god as alive again. In Ps. xviii it is an expression of homage, which, as the context clearly shows, refers to the signs of active and vigorous intervention manifested by Yahweh in saving the king in war. Here no memory has survived of its background in the conception of a time when the god was not alive and active, performing miracles and saving life. In the oath formula, *ḥay* should certainly not be taken as an adjective, but as a substantive in the construct, whether the correct pronunciation is *ḥê*, or whether the *ḥay*, the old form of the construct, has survived in this fixed formula. The correct translation is 'by the life of Yahweh', as is shown by the analogous *bᵉḥê hāʿōlām* (Dan. xii, 7). The interpretation and translation, 'as sure as Yahweh lives', is a rationalistic modernism. The oath means that either by actually touching a sacred object or by mentioning its name a person is filled with the power of the deity or of the sacred object, so as to make his word true. In such expressions Yahweh's 'life' is synonymous with His 'soul'; cf. the oath by *ḥay YHWH wᵉḥê napšᵉḵâh* (1 Sam. xx, 3; xxv, 26; 2 Kings ii, 2). The expression has therefore nothing to do with any idea that Yahweh, or the deity, can be thought of as not being alive. When the Muslim swears 'by the beard of the prophet', he obviously does not mean, 'as sure as the prophet has a beard'; but, 'by mentioning the concrete manifestation of the holy power (the sign of the prophet's manhood) I fill my soul with this same power so as to make my word true, i.e., to keep and uphold it'. We may compare also the oath by the life of the king or Pharaoh, Gen. xlii, 15f.; 2 Sam. xv, 21.

ADDITIONAL NOTES

Note IX (p. 125 n. 1).

The literature dealing with the problem of the Jewish future hope and the nature and origin of eschatology is extensive. In contrast with all far-fetched notions of eschatology as already an essential feature in Mosaic religion (Sellin, *Der alttestamentliche Prophetismus*), we must always maintain, as the essential basis of the historical inquiry, a methodical and sober treatment of the sources, i.e., in this instance, primarily the prophetic books of the Old Testament. Naturally, such criticism of the sources must not take for granted any theory of the antiquity of eschatology; and it must never be forgotten that the prophetic books in their present form are collections of short utterances relating to their own time, assembled and arranged in larger sections (complexes of tradition), in accordance with the outlook of the Jewish community and its religious and cultic needs. It is therefore impossible to draw any conclusion whatever about the original character and essence of the future hope and of eschatology from the stereotyped arrangement (disaster followed by deliverance) or from the direct and abrupt transition from one subject to another in the extant collections and revisions of the earlier prophetic words. This is in opposition both to Gressmann and *die religionsgeschichtliche Schule* and also to the most recent tendency to overestimate the body of tradition as such, and the pessimism about the possibility of getting back to the *ipsissima verba* of the prophets (see Engnell, *Gamla Testamentet* I, pp. 30, 42; cf. Mowinckel, *Prophecy and Tradition*, pp. 84ff.). Still less can we follow Gressmann, the Pan-Babylonian school, and others and infer from such characteristics of the tradition the existence of a pre-Israelite eschatology common to the ancient East. The literary criticism, or rather, the tradition criticism of the prophetic books must go hand in hand with form-historical and stylistic analysis, which can help us (*inter alia*) to distinguish the original sayings from each other and also to distinguish between the earlier and the later prophetic style. Such criticism must, of course, be constantly combined with a comprehensive understanding of the main lines of the religious, political, and cultural history of Israel and of Judaism. In spite of all shades of difference between 'conservative' and 'radical' critics, there is a considerable measure of agreement about the results of such criticism. The majority of the genuine and unquestionable eschatological sayings are from the age of Judaism. Broadly speaking, what the prophets proclaimed was not eschatology, but an urgent message from God about the immediate future. I venture to refer the reader to *G.T.M.M.M.* III, where I have set out my view of the criticism of the prophetic books and of the message of the prophets; but I should now wish to maker greater reservations concerning Dr. Messel's view of the book of Ezekiel. Cf. also my discussion of the fundamental problems of tradition criticism in *Prophecy and Tradition*.

In spite of its one-sidedness and over-statement, Wellhausen's *Israelitische und jüdische Geschichte* is of fundamental importance for the modern view of the Israelite and Jewish future hope and eschatology; see pp. 109–47, 151–61, 206ff. The same basic view is given by Marti (*Geschichte der israelitischen Religion*[4], pp. 121ff., 180–92, 254–8), Smend (*Lehrbuch der alttestamentlichen Religionsgeschichte*[2], pp. 187ff., 230ff., 341–60, 367–75), Stade-Bertholet (*Biblische Theologie des Alten Testaments* I, pp. 212–17, 292ff., 302–10, 314ff.; II, pp. 135ff.), and, in general, by the older generation of critics. Gressmann's *Ursprung* sought to present a new view, which in one way was more traditional (eschatology older than the 'writing prophets' and including from the beginning both the eschatology of disaster and the eschatology of deliverance), and in another was more radical (eschatology in Israel borrowed from an ancient eschatology common to the east). The attempt has been made to exploit Gressmann's view, on the one hand in the direction of an extreme traditionalism (Sellin and others), and on the other hand by a strange combination of traditionalism with a Pan-Babylonian theory comprehending the whole history of religion (A. and J. Jeremias, Staerk, and others). My own view of the origin and nature of eschatology is set out in *Ps.St.* II, where, however, the chronology is not entirely clear. A more lucid outline is given in *G.T.M.M.M.* III (see the introduction to the prophetic books). Cf. also Hölscher, *Die Ursprünge der jüdischen Eschatologie*; and see Lindblom, *Profetismen i Israel*, pp. 509ff., 516–26, 565–82, who adopts substantially the same view. The outline given above in the text is no more than an outline, and does not enter into details or supporting arguments. Further reference may be made particularly to *Ps.St.* II, *G.T.M.M.M.* III, and the relevant paragraphs in Hölscher, *Geschichte der israelitischen und jüdischen Religion.*

NOTE X (p. 140 n. 1).

That the thought of Yahweh's kingship in Israel was in a special way associated with the epiphany festival (as shown by the present writer in *Ps.St.* II) has not been disproved by the objections of Eissfeldt (in *Z.A.W.* xlvi, 1928, pp. 81ff.), or of Caspari (in *Christentum und Wissenschaft*, iv, 1928, pp. 23ff.), or of Porteous (*The Kingship of God in Pre-exilic Hebrew Religion*). The thought cannot be explained in terms of a historical development from the ideas contained in the message of the prophets. It was the prophets who borrowed the thought from the prevailing cultic conceptions, with which they were fully familiar. The discoveries at Ugarit show that the thought of the god as king, and of his royal epiphany in the cult is older than Israel; cf. Kapelrud in *N.T.T.* xli, 1940, pp. 38ff. The conception of the god as king was general in the ancient east. Eissfeldt has rightly maintained this point, and also that this is the *general* background for the application to Yahweh of the title 'king'. But even in Israel the conception derived its particular and specific content from its connexion with the epiphany and enthronement festival; and since in Canaan this connexion goes back to pre-Israelite times, there is every reason to believe that in Israel it goes back to the time at which the festival was fully developed at the sanctuaries, above all at Jerusalem. There is, however, no ground for the distinction made by Buber (*Königtum Gottes*) between the universalistic, religious aspect of the conception and its nationalistic, political aspect; both are always present together. Nor is there any ground for attributing (for etymological reasons) to the Hebrew *melek*, as used of Yahweh, another meaning than that which it normally has in Hebrew, such as 'leader', 'counsellor', '*mitgehender Berater*', as Buber would do. In the Old Testament, the royal title as applied to Yahweh never refers to the nomadic, tribal God, but to the 'universal' God of the cultus, manifest, enthroned, and reigning, who *also* reveals Himself as king by His activity in history, the last point being specifically Israelite. There is, therefore, no justification for tracing the conception of Yahweh as *melek* back to the wilderness period, to the time of Moses, as Buber attempts to do. Buber cites Gideon's maintenance of the 'theocracy' in Judges viii, 22ff. But it is impossible to take a saying such as is put into the mouth of Gideon in Judges viii, 22ff., as an expression of a prevalent belief in the age of the Judges, as if we had there a faithful, documentary report of the incident. We must recognize that we are dealing with popular narratives, orally preserved for centuries; and naturally such details may be coloured by later developments. Gideon's rejection of human kingship in the interests of Yahweh's may be classed with Samuel's attitude in 1 Sam. vii; viii; x; and in contrast with this 'theocratic' view there is clearly another which is represented by the earlier tradition in 1 Sam. ix.

NOTE XI (p. 191 n. 1).

In *v.* 3, M.T. has 'Israel', which, however, is not found in one Hebrew MS. (Kennicott 96), and is also missing in several MSS. of G. For metrical reasons and because it is the *lectio facilior*, the word is not original. It cannot be denied that *yiśrā'ēl* in xlix, 3 disturbs the metre, even if it is maintained that regular metre is not always found in the prophets. That *some* of their oracles are in regular metrical form is indisputable; and it is clear that xlix, 1–6, consists in the main of symmetrical full lines (periods, bicola), each with two parallel half lines (members, cola), irrespective of whether we scan according to Sievers's system (full line = 3 + 3 feet) or Hölscher's (4 + 4, possibly truncated iambic feet; see *Buddefestschrift*, pp. 99f.). But, unlike the other full lines in the passage, *v.* 3 is asymmetrical in M.T. (Sievers: 3 + 4; Hölscher: 4 + 5, the final half line being very halting). The line may be read *wayyómer lí 'aḇdí 'attáh* / (*yiśrā'ēl*) *'ašér bĕḵā 'etpā'ér* (*ĕ* represents a shewa which has metrical value). It is plain that *yiśrā'ēl* here makes any metrical reading of the half line impossible. The Hebrew form of xlii, 1 presupposed by G clearly reveals the same defect.

hén 'aḇdí 'etmok-bô / *b'ḥírí rāṣĕtáh napší* is a regular, symmetrical, full line in the *māšāl* metre, with truncation of the unaccented syllable in the third foot in the first half line, and of the second foot in the second half line. The text presupposed by G: *hén ya'ᵃḳóḇ 'aḇdí 'etmok-bô* / *yiśrā'ēl b'ḥírí rāṣĕtáh napší* would be 5 + 5 (or, more correctly, 5 + 6, as *yiśrā'ēl* must have two ictus), a quite unparalleled form in Hebrew metre. To scan according to the system of Sievers (which is certainly wrong) would be no better: 4 + 4 or 3 + 4 as a parallel to 3 + 3 in v. 1b. Prätorius's defence on metrical grounds of the word *yiśrā'ēl* in xlix, 3 (*Z.A.W.* xxxvi, 1916, pp. 9f.) is worthless, since his scansion of the line conflicts both with the natural principles of rhythm (rhythm according to sense) and with Hebrew emphasis. The attempts of both Prätorius and Beer (in the *Baudissinfestschrift*, pp. 29ff.) to deal with the metre of the Servant Songs simply show that the unfortunate system of Sievers does not really help.

The decisive factor, however, is not the metrical considerations, but the textual evidence and conclusions. Although Kennicott 96 has in the main little textual value (cf. Bewer in *Jewish Studies* (*Kohut Memorial Volume*), pp. 86f.), it does not follow that all its readings are worthless. Each individual instance must be decided on its merits in accordance with the usual principles of textual criticism. It is indisputable that since the Servant Songs appear in a collection in which the expression 'the Servant of Yahweh' elsewhere often denotes Israel, and since the Servant in the special sense was by Jewish exegetes often identified with Israel (see above, p. 245 n. 5), it is much more likely that the word 'Israel' is an interpolation than that it originally stood in the text and was omitted. It is difficult to understand why the word should have been omitted from Kennicott 96, if it was present in its exemplar. Engnell (*B.J.R.L.* xxxi, 1, 1948, p. 19) tries to dismiss the fact that the word is missing in several MSS. of G, by asserting that G 'is tendentious on this point'. But, we may ask, in which direction? The tendency in G is precisely the reverse, as is shown unmistakably by the addition of 'Jacob' and 'Israel' in xlii, 1. G expresses the same tradition of interpretation as M.T. and Jewish exegesis, both of which more or less consistently try to identify 'the Servant' with 'My servant Israel' (cf. North, *The Suffering Servant*, pp. 8ff.); the existence of this tendency in M.T. is shown by xlii, 19–22, 'Israel' in xlix, 3; xlix, 8d; li, 16; lix, 21. When, nevertheless, 'Israel' does not occur at xlix, 3 in several MSS. of G, that is evidence that these MSS. represent a form of the text which is the genuine 'Septuagint', and which *here* is older than M.T. and the tradition which it represents, whereas other MSS. of G have been 'corrected' to agree with the tradition of M.T. Thus in both xlii, 1 and xlix, 3 the conclusions of textual criticism agree with those of metrical theory based on the natural rhythm of the text (cf. Mowinckel in *Bertholet-festschrift*, pp. 379ff.; *St. Th.* VII, i, 1953/54; *Pedersenfestskrift*, pp. 250ff.; *Z.A.W.* lxv, 1953, pp. 167ff.).

NOTE XII (p. 213 n. 1).

The most detailed discussion of the subject, refuting the collective interpretation, is given by Fischer in *Altestamentliche Abhandlungen* 6, and most recently by North, *The Suffering Servant* (see the summary, pp. 202ff.).

Those who collected and transmitted the Deutero-Isaianic sayings were the first to interpret the Servant as Israel, e.g., in the gloss 'Israel' in xlix, 3 (see Additional Note XI), and in the secondary (Trito-Isaianic) additions, xlii, 19–23; xlix, 8bα; li, 16. The same tradition is represented by G, e.g., in the glosses 'Israel' and 'Jacob' in xlii, 1 (see Additional Note XI), and in the Apocrypha (see North, *The Suffering Servant*, p. 8). It is very common in the medieval Jewish commentators (see North, op. cit., pp. 17ff.). We also find it in the Qumran Scrolls (see Ginsberg in *V.T.* iii, 1953, pp. 400ff.; Brownlee in *B.A.S.O.R.* 132, Dec. 1953, pp. 8ff.; 135, Oct. 1954, pp. 33ff.).

The starting point of the collective interpretation of the Servant is obviously the idea that it is made necessary because the Servant poems are included in the Deutero-Isaianic collection, where Israel is undoubtedly called 'the servant of Yahweh' (or 'My servant') in a number of passages. It may be confidently affirmed that if the poems had not been included in Isa. xl–lv, no one would have thought of interpreting them of Israel. But in fact this necessity is entirely illusory. It could be assumed to exist as long as it was taken for granted that the prophets were thinkers and authors who wrote connected, systematically arranged 'books', or delivered 'speeches' at length, so that the interpreter was obliged to take account of the 'context', i.e., the larger context provided by the 'book' of Deutero-Isaiah. But in the study of the prophets it has long been realized that no such context exists. The prophetic books are collections of individual sayings, which were originally quite independent, not connected with each other in content or by any literary bond. It is therefore a fundamental error to interpret in accordance with the 'context', which arises from the casual methods of arrangement (e.g., by 'catch-words') employed by the later collectors and custodians of tradition (see my *Prophecy and Tradition*, pp. 36–60, and my discussion with Bentzen in *D.T.T.* ix, 1946, pp. 142ff.). The 'context' in which Engnell (*B.J.R.L.* xxxi, 1, 1948, pp. 14ff., see above, p. 189 n. 2) puts Isa. xlii, 1–4 is an example of the kind of absurdity into which one can lapse by appealing to such 'contexts'. The real context is the internal logic and coherence of the individual saying. Even if the Servant poems come from Deutero-Isaiah, it is still possible that he may have applied the term 'the Servant of Yahweh' to the people in one saying, and to a definite individual person in others. It would be a mistake to feel that one passage *must* be interpreted in accordance with conceptions and expressions in another, if the former contained elements which were at variance with it. I cannot but regard it as a lapse from sound method when Eissfeldt (*Der Gottesknecht bei Deuterojesaja*; cf. also *E.T.* xliv, 1932/3, pp. 261ff.; *T.L.Z.* lxviii, 1943, cols. 273ff.), Wheeler Robinson (in *Werden und Wesen des Alten Testaments*, pp. 49ff.; cf. *The Cross of the Servant*), Pedersen (*Israel* III–IV, pp. 603f.), Nyberg (in *S.E.Å.* vii, 1942, pp. 5–82), Engnell (in *B.J.R.L.* xxxi, 1, 1948, pp. 3–42), and others allow their interpretation of the Servant to be determined by the fact that these passages have been transmitted together with other sayings in which the title 'servant' is applied to Israel. On this point Bentzen is much more reserved and cautious (cf. *King and Messiah*, pp. 52f.). It is plain that when 'servant' is applied as a title to Israel in Deutero-Isaiah it has a quite different content than when it is used of the special 'Servant of the Lord'. Used of Israel, it has the more passive sense of Yahweh's worshipper and chosen one, who is therefore the object of His covenant care, His love, and protection (cf. von Baudissin in *Buddefestschrift*, pp. 1ff.); whereas when used of the Servant, it denotes a special call to a definite and active task (see my *Der Knecht Jahwäs*, p. 3; Bentzen, *Introduction to the Old Testament*[2] II, pp. 110f.). Isa. xlii, 19 is not typical of Deutero-Isaiah's application of the word to Israel (against von Baudissin, op. cit., p. 5), for in that passage 'Trito-Isaiah' fuses the servant Israel and the special 'Servant' (see Mowinckel in *G.T.M.M.M.* III, pp. 213ff.). This in itself shows that to base the interpretation of the one servant figure on the other is methodologically unsound. We may take it as established that in Deutero-Isaiah (the Deutero-Isaianic collection of prophecies) there are to be found two distinct presentations of 'the servant of Yahweh'. This means that the Servant in the Servant poems must be interpreted in the light of these poems themselves, irrespective of any other meaning which the term may have in Deutero-Isaiah. It is therefore incorrect to say (as do Eissfeldt, Pedersen, Nyberg, Engnell, and others) that the conception of the servant in Deutero-Isaiah oscillates between the people and a representative person, who, in accordance with the ancient conception of the community *is* also the people. It is not a question of *one* servant figure with oscillating content, but of two different conceptions.

The idea that Deutero-Isaiah as transmitted provides a context lies behind the admittedly original form in which Lindblom seeks to revive the interpretation of the Servant as Israel (*The Servant Songs in Deutero-Isaiah*). The Servant is a symbolic or allegorical figure representing

465

Israel. In those poems in which the Servant speaks in the first person he is in fact the prophet; but the prophet also symbolically represents Israel. Lindblom holds that xlii, 5–9 is connected with xlii, 1–4 as an interpretation of the preceding 'allegory', and that lii, 12ff. provides the interpretation of liii. Lindblom's interpretation is ruled out by two considerations. In liii it is quite evident that it is Israel and not the heathen nations who are the object of the Servant's work; the 'we' in liii, 2ff. cannot, as Lindblom thinks, be identified with those who are referred to in lii, 12ff., for, in the nature of things, a prophetic vision is seen by an individual. Again, consideration of the form and content of xlii, 5f. show that it is quite independent of xlii, 1–4; and in my view it can be interpreted only of Cyrus (see above, p. 189 n.2). But above all there is nothing in the Songs to indicate that they are meant as allegories.

But the point may be made that the interpretation of the Servant as Israel is plainly stated in the text itself at xlix, 3; 'and He said to me, "My Servant art thou, Israel, by whom I will get myself glory". The authenticity of the word 'Israel' is discussed in Additional Note XI. To regard it as an interpretative gloss, like 'Jacob' in G of xlii, 1, is not simply a plausible device for disposing of an inconvenient piece of textual evidence; it is simply a text-critical solution which is at least as acceptable as the view that the word belonged to the original text. Indeed it would have been remarkable if a gloss of this kind had *not* found its way into the text at one point or another, when the Servant Songs were first incorporated in the collection of Deutero-Isaiah's sayings.

NOTE XIII (p. 281 n. 1).

This has been clearly recognized and proved by Bousset, *Relig.*[2], pp. 233ff., 264f., 279ff. Lagrange, too (*Le messianisme chez les juifs; Le judaïsme avant Jésus-Christ*, pp. 363–87), emphasizes that there are really two incompatible conceptions of the Messiah in later Judaism (e.g., *Le messianisme chez les juifs*, p. 261; *Le judaïsme avant Jésus-Christ*, p. 385). But the task he has set himself is too easy, because on the one hand he distinguishes too sharply between the two different types of eschatology (cf. above, p. 267 n. 2), and on the other he excludes all the passages about the Son of Man in 1 Enoch as Christian interpolations (against this view see Sjöberg, *Der Menschensohn*, pp. 14ff.). In this way also he is able to evade the religio-historical problem raised by the conception of a transcendental Messiah, and to try to derive both tendencies directly from an extension of Old Testament ideas. Thus in 1 Enoch both the term 'the Chosen One' and its content are supposed to be derived from Isaiah (i.e., Deutero-Isaiah), and the conception of the Son of Man to come directly from Dan. vii. The attempts recently made to conflate the two conceptions of the Messiah, e.g., by Bonsirven (*Le judaïsme palestinien au temps de Jésus-Christ*, chs. VIII and IX), Küppers (in *Int. Kirchl. Zeitschr.*, xxiii, 1933, pp. 193ff.; xxiv, 1934, pp. 47ff.; see above, p. 267 n. 2) and Riesenfeld (*Jésus transfiguré*, pp. 62ff.) do no service to scholarship. Of course later Judaism had no room for two separate Messiahs, one earthly and the other transcendental, though a similar idea does occur in the conception of a Messiah ben Joseph and a Messiah ben David (see above, pp. 290f.). But it is undeniable that the Messianic conceptions of certain circles produced the picture of a Messiah who is predominantly this-worldly, national, and political, whereas the views of other circles produced the picture of a predominantly transcendental, eternal, and universal Messiah. It is likewise a fact that these two complexes of ideas are *in part* represented by different names, 'Messiah' and 'Son of Man'. Finally, it is a fact that important features in the figure of the Son of Man are foreign, not Jewish, in origin. The recognition of this fact underlies the assertions made about two conceptions of the Messiah. It cannot be disposed of by saying, as Küppers does, that 'no comprehensive and systematic view' can be constructed out of the available sources. (op. cit., p. 251). Obviously not; it is precisely such an artificial systematization of complexes of ideas which are in part heterogeneous that we want to avoid by asserting: 1. that two such complexes do exist, each with its characteristic central idea; 2. that they overlap and are usually fused with each other; and 3. that nevertheless one or the other is usually dominant in the documents which bear witness to the fusion. Riesenfeld's position is not entirely clear; but he appears to maintain that there are not two different complexes, since one and the same central idea is always present, namely the transcendental, divine character of the Messiah; and he holds that all the elements which express this divinity (including that of the Son of Man) are derived from the oriental royal ideology and always belonged to the Messiah. To this we may reply: 1. the transcendent nature and characteristic features of the Son of Man cannot be derived from the royal ideology, but have a separate source in a distinct, primordial being (see above, pp. 420ff.), who is not identical in origin with the king, but wholly different in character (see above, p. 55); and 2. all that has been said above ought to have proved that the authentic Jewish Messiah, though undoubtedly derived from the oriental royal ideology (N.B., in its Israelite and Yahwistic form), always remained what he was at the first, a political, national, this-worldly figure with eschatological tendencies.

NOTE XIV (p. 341 n. 4).

Riesenfeld refers to Josephus, *Antt.* XV, 50–6; but the text says nothing to suggest that the anti-Herodian demonstrations in support of the young Hasmonean high priest Aristobulus were Messianic in character; nor was it as Messiah, but as High-priest, that Aristobulus performed his official duties. The fact that Ps. cxviii, 25f. was at this period interpreted of the Messiah (see Strack-Billerbeck I, pp. 849, 876; II, p. 256) proves only that the prayer that the Messiah would come was read into this festival psalm; and that the crowd hailed Jesus with these words shows only that they regarded Him as the coming Messiah, but not that the Messiah as such had a part in the temple cult. Nor is anything proved by the fact that the 'joy' was associated with the feast of Tabernacles, and that 2 Esdras vii, 28 expects that the Messiah, at his coming, will 'rejoice' those who are then alive. Riesenfeld's final argument is the wall paintings in the synagogue of Dura-Europos, where, among other themes, an enthroned Messiah is thought to appear. First, it must be observed that the interpretation of the enthroned figure in the topmost field above the Torah-niche on the west wall as an enthroned Messiah is very doubtful. du Mesnil du Buisson regards it as an apotheosized Moses (cf. the conception of the assumption of Moses); Grabar takes it as an enthroned David (see the survey in Parrot, *Archéologie mésopotamienne*, pp. 454f.); Sukenik as a representation of Pharaoh (in his Hebrew book, *The Synagogue of Dura-Europos and its Frescoes*, here quoted from the review by Rachel Wischnitzer in *J.B.L.* lxvi, 1947, pp. 482f.). Mrs. Wischnitzer rightly regards this last interpretation as very questionable. In her own book (*The Messianic Theme in the Paintings of the Dura Synagogue*, pp. 48ff.) she identifies the figure with David, probably rightly. She is probably also right in her view that the whole series of pictures is intended to give a presentation of the eschatological hope of Judaism, symbolized by persons and events from biblical history.

What is important for our present purpose is that there is no representation of the Messiah. Here, as so often, the use of the term 'Messianic' instead of 'eschatological' is misleading. Of course, no one would deny that the eschatological hope played a part in the cult of the synagogue, as an expression of faith and prayer. But if we are to speak of a connexion between the Messiah and the cult, we must mean something more than this (namely that the Messiah, in some form, was an object of worship, as Christ was in the primitive Church), or else we mean nothing at all. Even if the Messiah was represented in the decorations, this proves as little about any cultic role which he played (if such an expression means anything) as the pictures of Moses prove that he had a place in the cult of the synagogue. Connexion with the cult ('*rapports avec le culte*') is in Riesenfeld's discussion a meaningless phrase. In the Jewish cult the Messiah was neither worshipped nor believed to be present. On Riesenfeld's uncritical interpretations of the Dura pictures, see Kümmel's review in *Symbolae Biblicae Upsalienses* 11 (Supplement to *S.E.Å.* xiii, 1948), pp. 49ff.

List of Abbreviations

A.A.S.F. = *Annales Academiae Scientiarum Fennicae.*

Act. Or. = *Acta Orientalia.*

A.G.W.G. = *Abhandlungen der Gesellschaft der Wissenschaften zu Göttingen.*

A.f.O. = *Archiv für Orientforschung.*

A.J.S.L.L. = *American Journal of Semitic Languages and Literatures.*

A.N.E.T. = *Ancient Near Eastern Texts Relating to the Old Testament,* edited by J. B. Pritchard, Princeton, 1950.

A.N.V.A.O. = *Avhandlinger utgitt av Det Norske Videnskaps-Akademi i Oslo.*

A.O. = *Der alte Orient.*

A.O.T.B. = *Altorientalische Texte und Bilder zum Alten Testament,* edited by H. Gressmann, Tübingen, 1909, ²I–II, 1926 (= *A.O.T.*² and *A.O.B.*²).

A.P.A.T. = *Apokryphen und Pseudepigraphen des Alten Testaments* I–II, edited by E. Kautzsch, Tübingen, 1900.

A.P.O.T. = *The Apocrypha and Pseudepigrapha of the Old Testament* I–II, edited by R. H. Charles, Oxford, 1913.

A.R.W. = *Archiv für Religionswissenschaft.*

A.V. = Authorized Version of the Bible.

B.A.S.O.R. = *Bulletin of the American Schools of Oriental Research.*

Baudissinfestschrift. = *Abhandlungen zur semitischen Religionsgeschichte und Sprachwissenschaft. Festschrift für Baudissin zum 70. Geburtstage* (*B.Z.A.W.* 33), Giessen, 1918.

B.B.K. = *Berliner Beiträge zur Keilschriftforschung.*

Bertholetfestschrift. = *Festschrift Alfred Bertholet zum 80. Geburtstag gewidmet von Kollegen und Freunden,* Tübingen, 1950.

B.F.Ch.Th. = *Beiträge zur Förderung christlicher Theologie.*

*B.H.*³ = *Biblia Hebraica*³, edited by R. Kittel, Stuttgart, 1937.

B.J.R.L. = *Bulletin of the John Rylands Library.*

B.S.G.W. = *Berichte uber die Verhandlungen der Sächsischen Gesellschaft der Wissenschaften.*

Buddefestschrift. = *Beiträge zur alttestamentlichen Wissenschaft. Karl Budde zum 70. Geburtstag gewidmet* (*B.Z.A.W.* 34), Giessen, 1920.

B.W.A.N.T. = *Beiträge zur Wissenschaft vom Alten und Neuen Testament.*

B.W.A.T. = *Beiträge zur Wissenschaft vom Alten Testament.*

B.Z.A.W. = *Beihefte zur Zeitschrift für die alttestamentliche Wissenschaft.*

[*D.*]*T.T.* = *Theologisk Tidsskrift* (Danish).

LIST OF ABBREVIATIONS

D.T.T. = *Dansk Teologisk Tidsskrift.*

E.B. = *Encyclopaedia Biblica.*

E.H.Ph.R. = *Études d'Histoire et de Philosophie religieuses.*

Eissfeldtfestschrift. = *Festschrift Otto Eissfeldt zum 60. Geburtstage 1 September 1947 dargebracht von Freunden und Verehren,* Halle, 1947.

E.J. = *Encyclopaedia Judaica.*

E.R.E. = *Encyclopaedia of Religion and Ethics.*

E.T. = *Expository Times.*

Eucharisterion. = *Studien zur Religion und Literatur des Alten und Neuen Testaments, H. Gunkel zum 60. Geburtstage . . . dargebracht (F.R.L.A.N.T.* 36) I, Göttingen, 1923.

E.VV. = English Versions of the Bible (A.V. and R.V.).

Exp. = *Expositor.*

F.R.L.A.N.T. = *Forschungen zur Religion und Literatur des Alten und Neuen Testaments.*

F.u.F. = *Forschungen und Fortschritte.*

G = Greek text.

Gesenius-Buhl[16]. = W. Gesenius, *Hebräisches und aramäisches Handwörterbuch über das Alte Testament . . .*[16], bearbeitet von F. Buhl, Leipzig, 1915.

G.T.M.M.M. = *Det Gamle Testament,* oversatt av S. Michelet, S. Mowinckel og N. Messel, Oslo, I 1929, II 1935, III 1944.

H.A.T. = *Handbuch zum Alten Testament.*

H.D.B. = *Dictionary of the Bible,* edited by James Hastings, Edinburgh, 1898–1904.

H.K.A.T. = *Handkommentar zum Alten Testament.*

H.N.T. = *Handbuch zum Neuen Testament.*

H.S.A.T. = *Die Heilige Schrift des Alten Testaments,* edited by E. Kautzsch, [4] edited by A. Bertholet, Tübingen, 1922.

H.U.C.A. = *Hebrew Union College Annual.*

I.S.K.F. = *Instituttet for Sammenlignende Kulturforskning.*

J.A.O.S. = *Journal of the American Oriental Society.*

J.B.L. = *Journal of Biblical Literature.*

J.E. = *Jewish Encyclopaedia.*

J.L. = *Jüdisches Lexikon.*

J.M.E.O.S. = *Journal of the Manchester Egyptian and Oriental Society.*

J.N.E.S. = *Journal of Near Eastern Studies.*

J.R.A.S. = *Journal of the Royal Asiatic Society.*

J.T.S. = *Journal of Theological Studies.*

K.A.R. = *Keilschrifttexte aus Assur religiösen Inhalts,* edited by E. Ebeling, Leipzig, 1915–19.

K.A.T. = *Die Keilinschriften und das Alte Testament,* edited by E. Schrader, [3] edited by H. Zimmern and H. Winckler, Berlin, 1903.

K.A.T.Sl. = *Kommentar zum Alten Testament,* edited by E. Sellin.

K.B. = *Keilschriftliche Bibliothek.*

LIST OF ABBREVIATIONS

Kittelfestschrift. = *Alttestamentliche Studien Rudolf Kittel zum 60. Geburtstag dargebracht* (*B.W.A.T.* 13), Leipzig, 1913.

L.U.Å. = *Lunds universitets årsskrift.*

M.G.W.J. = *Monatshefte zur Geschichte und Wissenschaft des Judentums.*

M.T. = Massoretic Text.

N.G.W.G. = *Nachrichten der Gesellschaft der Wissenschaften zu Göttingen.*

N.K.Z. = *Neue Kirchliche Zeitschrift.*

N.T.T. = *Norsk Teologisk Tidsskrift.*

O.T.S. = *Oudtestamentische Studiën.*

Pedersenfestskrift. = *Studia Orientalia Ioanni Pedersen septuagenario a.d. VII id. nov. anno MCMLIII a collegis discipulis amicis dicata,* Copenhagen, 1953.

P.J.B. = *Palästinajahrbuch des Deutschen Evangelischen Instituts für Altertumswissenschaft des Heiligen Landes zu Jerusalem.*

P.R.E. = Hauck-Herzog, *Realencyclopädie fur protestantische Theologie und Kirche.*[3]

Ps.St. = S. Mowinckel, *Psalmenstudien* I–VI (*S.N.V.A.O.* II, 1921–24), Christiania, 1921–24.

R.G.G. = *Religion in Geschichte und Gegenwart,* Tübingen, 1903–13, [2]1927–1932.

R.H.Ph. = *Revue d'Histoire et de Philosophie religieuses.*

R.H.R. = *Revue de l'Histoire des Religions.*

R.o.B. = *Religion och Bibel. Nathan Söderblom-Sällskapets Årsbok.*

R.T.Ph. = *Revue de Théologie et de Philosophie.*

R.V. = Revised Version of the Bible.

S = Syriac Text.

S.A.T.A. = *Schriften des Alten Testaments in Auswahl.*

S.B.U. = *Svenskt bibliskt uppslagsverk.*

S.E.Å. = *Svensk exegetisk årsbok.*

S.J.T. = *Scottish Journal of Theology.*

S.N.V.A.O. = *Skrifter utgitt av Det Norske Videnskaps-Akademi i Oslo.*

S.T.K. = *Svensk teologisk kvartalskrift.*

Strack-Billerbeck. = H. Strack and P. Billerbeck, *Kommentar zum Neuen Testament aus Talmud und Midrasch* I–IV, Munich, 1924–28.

St.Th. = *Studia theologica cura ordinum theologorum Scandinavicorum edita.*

T.L.Z. = *Theologische Literaturzeitung.*

T.R. = *Theologische Rundschau.*

T.S.K. = *Theologische Studien und Kritiken*

T.T. = *Teologisch Tijdschrift.*

T.W.B.N.T. = *Theologisches Wörterbuch zum Neuen Testament.*

T.Z. = *Theologische Zeitschrift.*

U.U.Å. = *Uppsala universitets årsbok.*

V = Vulgate Text.

V.A.B. = *Vorderasiatische Bibliothek.*

V.T. = *Vetus Testamentum.*

471

LIST OF ABBREVIATIONS

W.B.N.T. =W. Bauer, *Griechisch-deutsches Wörterbuch zu den Schriften des Neuen Testaments und der übrigen urchristlichen Literatur*[4], Berlin, 1952.

W.Z.K.M. = *Wiener Zeitschrift zur Kunde des Morgenlandes.*

Z.A. = *Zeitschrift für Assyriologie und Verwandte Gebiete.*

Z.A.W. = *Zeitschrift für die alttestamentliche Wissenschaft.*

Z.D.M.G. = *Zeitschrift der Deutschen Morgenländischen Gesellschaft.*

Z.I.I. = *Zeitschrift für Indologie und Iranistik.*

Z.N.W. = *Zeitschrift für die neutestamentliche Wissenschaft.*

Z.S.T. = *Zeitschrift für systematische Theologie.*

Z.T.K. = *Zeitschrift für Theologie und Kirche.*

Z.W.T. = *Zeitschrift für wissenschaftliche Theologie.*

Bibliography

Aalen, S., *Die Begriffe 'Licht' und 'Finsternis' im Alten Testament, im Spätjudentum und im Rabbinismus* (*S.N.V.A.O.* II, 1951, No. 1), Oslo 1951.

Abegg, E., *Der Messiasglaube in Indien und Iran*, Berlin, 1928.

Albright, W. F., *Archaeology and the Religion of Israel*, Baltimore, 1942.

From the Stone Age to Christianity, Baltimore, 1940, [2]1946.

'New Canaanite Historical and Mythological Data', *B.A.S.O.R.* 63, Oct. 1936, pp. 23ff.

'The Oracles of Balaam', *J.B.L.* lxiii, 1944, pp. 207ff.

'On the Date of the Scrolls from 'Ain Feshkha and the Nash Papyrus', *B.A.S.O.R.* 115, Oct. 1949, pp. 10ff.

Alt, A., *Der Gott der Väter* (*B.W.A.N.T.* III, 12), Stuttgart, 1929) = *Kleine Schriften* I, pp. 1ff.).

'Israel's Gaue unter Salomo', *Kittelfestschrift*, pp. 1ff. (=*Kleine Schriften* II, pp. 76ff.).

'Die Staatenbildung der Israeliten in Palästina', *Reformationsprogramm der Univ. Leipzig*, Leipzig, 1930 (=*Kleine Schriften* II, pp. 1ff.).

'Neues aus der Pharaonenzeit Palästinas', *P.J.B.* xxxii, 1936, pp. 8ff.

'Das Königtum in den Reichen Israel und Juda', *V.T.* i, 1951, pp. 2ff. (=*Kleine Schriften* II, pp. 116ff.).

Aptowitzer, V., *Parteipolitik der Hasmonäerzeit im rabbinischen und pseudepigraphischen Schrifttum*, Vienna, 1927.

Arvedson, T., *Das Mysterium Christi. Eine Studie zu Mt 11, 25–30*, Uppsala, 1937.

Asting, R., *Die Heiligkeit im Urchristentum* (*F.R.L.A.N.T.* 46), Göttingen, 1930.

'Den mandaeiske religion og urkristendommen', *N.T.T.* xxxii, 1931, pp. 209ff.

Badham, F. P., 'The Title "Son of Man"', *T.T.* xlv, 1911, pp. 395–448.

Baldensperger, G., 'Die neueste Forschung über den Menschensohn', *T.R.* iii, 1900, pp. 201–10, 243–55.

Balla, E., 'Das Problem des Leides in der israelitisch-jüdischen Religion', *Eucharisterion* I, pp. 14ff.

Barnes, W. E., 'Cyrus the "Servant of Jehovah" Isa. xlii, 1–4 (7)', *J.T.S.* xxxii, 1931, pp. 32–9.

BIBLIOGRAPHY

Barth, C., *Die Errettung vom Tode in den individuellen Klage- und Dankliedern des Alten Testamentes*, Basel, 1947.

von Baudissin, W. W., *Adonis und Esmun*, Leipzig, 1911.

'Zur Entwicklung des Gebrauchs von 'ebed im religiösen Sinne', *Buddefestschrift*, pp. 1ff.

Bauer, H., 'Die Gottheiten von Ras Shamra', *Z.A.W.* li, 1933, pp. 81ff.; liii, 1935, pp. 54ff.

Bauer, W., *Griechisch-deutsches Wörterbuch zu den Schriften des Neuen Testaments und der übrigen Urchristlichen Literatur,*[4] Berlin, 1952. Cited as *W.B.N.T.*[4]

art. 'Mandäer', *R.G.G.*[2]

Baumgartner, W., *Das Buch Daniel*, reprinted from *Christliche Welt*, 1925, Nos. 31/32-37/39.

'Ras Schamra und das Alte Testament', *T.R.* (N.F.) xii, 1940, pp. 163ff.; xiii, 1941, pp. 1ff., 85ff., 157ff.

'Das Nachleben der Adonisgärten auf Sardinien und im übrigen Mittelmeergebiet', *Schweiz. Archiv für Völkerkunde* xliii, 1946, pp. 122ff.

'Ugaritische Probleme und ihre Tragweite für das alte Testament', *T.Z.* iii, 1947, pp. 81ff.

'Die palästinische Handschriftenfund', *T.R.* (N.F.) xvii, 1948/9, pp. 329-46; xix, 1951, pp. 97-154.

'Der heutige Stand der Mandäerfrage', *T.Z.* vi, 1950, pp. 401ff.

'Zur Mandäerfrage', *H.U.C.A.* Jubilee Volume, Part I (xxiii, 1950/51), pp. 41ff.

Beasley-Murray, G. R., 'The Two Messiahs in the Testaments of the Twelve Patriarchs', *J.T.S.* xlviii, 1947, pp. 1ff.

Beer, G., *Steinverehrung bei den Israeliten*, Berlin-Leipzig, 1921.

'Das Buch Henoch', *A.P.A.T.* II, pp. 217-310

'Die Gedichte vom Knechte Jahwes in Jes 40-55. Ein textkritischer und metrischer Wiederherstellungsversuch', *Baudissinfestschrift*, pp. 29-46.

Begrich, J., *Studien zu Deuterojesaja* (*B.W.A.N.T.* IV, 25), Stuttgart, 1938.

'Sopher und Mazkir', *Z.A.W.* lviii, 1940/41, pp. 1-29.

Bentzen, A., *Studier over det zadokidiske Praesteskabs Historie*, Copenhagen, 1931.

Daniel (*H.A.T.*), Tübingen, 1937, [2]1952.

Jesaja fortolket I-II Copenhagen, 1943/44.

Det sakrale kongedømme, Copenhagen, 1945.

Messias—Moses redivivus—Menschensohn, Zürich, 1948. Eng. Trans., *King and Messiah*, London, 1954.

Introduction to the Old Testament I-II, Copenhagen, 1948/9,[2] 1952.

'Quelques remarques sur le mouvement messianique parmi les juifs aux environs de l'an 520 avant J.-C.', *R.H.Ph.R.* x, 1930, pp. 493-503.

BIBLIOGRAPHY

'Priesterschaft und Laien in der jüdischen Gemeinde des fünften Jahrhunderts', *A.f.O.* vi, 1930/31, pp. 280–6.

'"De stille i Landet"', [*D.*]*T.T.* v, 1932, pp. 196–204.

'On the Idea of "the Old" and "the New" in Deutero-Isaiah', *St.Th.* I, 1947, pp. 183–7.

'Der Tod des Beters in den Psalmen. Randbemerkungen zur Diskussion zwischen Mowinckel und Widengren', *Eissfeldtfestschrift*, p. 57–60.

'Kan ordet "Messiansk" anvendes om Salmernes kongeforestillinger?', *S.E.Å.* xii, 1947, pp. 36–50.

'The Cultic Use of the Story of the Ark in Samuel', *J.B.L.* xlvii, 1948, pp. 37–53.

Berry, G. R., 'Messianic Predictions', *J.B.L.* xlv, 1926, pp. 232ff.

Bertholdt, L., *Christologia Judaeorum Jesu apostolorumque aetate*, Erlangen, 1811.

Bertholet, A. *Kulturgeschichte Israels*, Göttingen, 1919. Eng. Trans., *A History of Hebrew Civilization*, London, 1926, by E. K. Dallas.

Götterspaltung und Göttervereinigung, Tübingen, 1933.

Hesekiel, mit einem Beitrag von Kurt Galling (*H.A.T.*), Tübingen, 1936.

'Menschensohn im Alten Testament', *R.G.G.*[1] IV, cols. 296f.

'Hesekielprobleme', *F.u.F.* xiii, 1936, pp. 4ff.

Beth, J., 'El und Neter', *Z.A.W.* xxxvi, 1916, pp. 129ff.

'Noch einiges zum ägyptischen Neter', *Z.A.W.* xxxviii, 1919–20, pp. 87ff.

Bewer, J., 'The Text-critical Value of the Hebrew MS. Ken. 96 of Isaiah xlix, 3', *Jewish Studies in Memory of George A. Kohut*, pp. 86ff.

Bickerman, E. J., 'The Date of the Twelve Patriarchs', *J.B.L.* lxix, 1950, pp. 245ff.

Bieneck, J., *Sohn Gottes als Christusbezeichnung bei den Synoptikern*, Zürich, 1951.

Billerbeck, P., See under Strack-Billerbeck in the List of Abbreviations.

'Hat die alte Synagoge einen präexistenten Messias gekannt?', *Nathanael*, 1905, pp. 89ff.

Birkeland, H., *Die Feinde des Individuums in der Israelitischen Psalmenliteratur*, Oslo, 1933.

Zum Hebräischen Traditionswesen (*A.N.V.A.O.* II, 1938), Oslo, 1938.

'Oppstandelsetroen i Det Gamle Testament', *S.E.Å.* xiii, 1948, pp. 22ff.

'The Belief in the Resurrection in the Old Testament', *St.Th.* III, i, 1949/50, pp. 6off.

Birnbaum, S. A., 'The Date of the Isaiah Scroll', *B.A.S.O.R.* 113, Feb. 1949, pp. 33ff.

'The Dates of the Cave Scrolls', *B.A.S.O.R.* 115, Oct. 1949, pp. 2off.

BIBLIOGRAPHY

Black, M., 'The "Son of Man" in the Old Biblical Literature', *E.T.* lx, 1948/49, pp. 11–15.

'The Messiah in the Testament of Levi xviii', *E.T.* lx, 1948/49, pp. 321f.

de Boer, P. A. H., *Het Koningschap in Oud-Israel*, Amsterdam, 1938.

Böhl, F. M. Th., *De "Knecht des Heeren" in Jesaja*, 1927.

Nieuwjaarsfest en Koningdag in Babylonien en in Israel, Leiden, 1927.

Böklen, E., *Die Verwandtschaft der jüdisch-christlichen mit der parsischen Eschatologie*, Göttingen, 1902.

Boll, F. and Bezold, C., *Sternglaube und Sterndeutung*,[4] edited by W. Gundel, Leipzig and Berlin, 1939.

Bonner, C., *The Last Chapters of Enoch in Greek* (*Studies and Documents*, edited by K. and S. Lake, 8) London, 1937.

Bonsirven, J., *Le judaïsme palestinien au temps de Jésus-Christ* I–II, Paris, 1924.

Bonwetsch, G. N., *Die Bücher der Geheimnisse des Henoch. Das sogenannte slavische Henochbuch*, Leipzig, 1922.

Bousset, W., *Jesu Predigt in ihrem Gegensatz zum Judentum*, Göttingen, 1892.

Der Antichrist, Göttingen, 1905.

Hauptprobleme der Gnosis (*F.R.L.A.N.T.* 10), Göttingen, 1907.

Die Religion des Judentums im neutestamentlichen Zeitalter, Berlin, 1906, [2]1909, [3]revised by H. Gressmann, 1926. Cited as *Relig.*

Kyrios Christos. Geschichte des Christusglaubens von den Anfängen des Christentums bis Irenaeus (*F.R.L.A.N.T.* 21), Göttingen, 1913.

'Die Testamente der zwölf Patriarchen', *Z.N.W.* i, 1900, pp. 141–75, 187–209.

'Der verborgene Heilige', *A.R.W.* xxi, 1922, pp. 1ff.

Bowman, J., 'The Background of the Term "Son of Man"', *E.T.* lix, 1947/48, pp. 283–8.

Brandt, W., *Die mandäische Religion, ihre Entwicklung und geschichtliche Bedeutung*, Leipzig, 1889.

Die Mandäer, ihre Religion und ihre Geschichte (*Verh. d. kgl. Akad. v. Wetensch. te Amsterdam* Afdel. Letterk. N.R. XVI, 3), Amsterdam, 1915.

'Das Schicksal der Seele nach dem Tode nach mandäischen und persischen Vorstellungen', *Jahrbücher für protestantische Theologie*, 1892, pp. 405–38, 575–603.

Briem, E., *Babyloniska myter och sagor*, Stockholm, 1927.

På trons tröskel, Stockholm, 1948.

Brownlee, W. H., 'The Jerusalem Habakkuk Scroll', *B.A.S.O.R.* 112, Dec. 1948, pp. 8ff.

'The Servant of the Lord in the Qumran Scrolls. I', *B.A.S.O.R.* 132, Dec. 1953, pp. 8ff.; 'II', ibid., 135, Oct. 1954, pp. 33ff.

Brun, L., *Jesu Evangelium*[2], Oslo, 1926.

Paulus's kristelige tanker[2], Oslo, 1929.

Buber, M., *Königtum Gottes*, Berlin, 1932.

Buda, J., 'Semah Jahweh. Investigationes ad christologiam Iesianam spectantes', *Biblica* xx, 1939, pp, 1off.

Budde, K., *Die sogenannten Ebed-Jahwe-Lieder und die Bedeutung des Knechtes Jahwes in Jes. 40–55: Ein Minoritätsvotum*, Giessen, 1900. Published in English as 'The so-called "Ebed-Jahweh-Songs" and the Meaning of the Term "Servant of Yahweh" in Isaiah Chaps. 40–55', *The American Journal of Theology*, 1899, pp. 499–540.

Geschichte der althebräischen Literatur[2], Leipzig, 1909.

Jesajas Erleben: Eine gemeinverständliche Auslegung der Denkschrift des Propheten (Kap. 6, 1–9, 6), Gotha, 1928.

'Das nomadische Ideal im alten Israel', *Preussische Jahrbücher* lxxxv, 1896.

'Das Buch Jesaja Kap. 40–66', *H.S.A.T.*[4] I, pp. 653ff.

'Das Immanuelzeichen und Ahazbegegnung. Jesaja 7.' *J.B.L.* lii, 1933, pp. 22ff.

Review of Eissfeldt's *Der Gottesknecht bei Deuterojesaja* in *T.L.Z.* viii, 1933, cols. 323ff.

Buhl, F., *De messianske Forjaettelser i det gamle Testamente*, Copenhagen, 1894.

Psalmerne oversatte og fortolkede, Copenhagen, 1900, [2]1918. Cited as *Psalmerne*.

Det israelitiske Folks Historie[6], Copenhagen, 1922, [7]1936, edited by J. Jacobsen. ,

von Bulmerincq, A., 'Die Immanuelweissagung (Jes. 7) im Lichte der neueren Forschung,' *Acta et Commentarii Universitatis Tartuensis*, 1935, pp. 1ff.

Bultmann, R., 'Reich Gottes und Menschensohn', *T.R.* (N.F.) ix, 1937, pp. 1ff.

Burrows, M., *What Mean These Stones?* New Haven, 1941.

'The Discipline Manual of the Judaean Covenanters', *O.T.S.* VIII, 1950, pp. 156–92.

Campbell, J. Y., 'The Origin and Meaning of the Term Son of Man', *J.T.S.* xlviii, 1947, pp. 145ff.

Canney, M. A., 'The Magic of Kings', *J.M.E.O.S.* xvii, 1932, pp. 41ff.

Cannon, W. W., 'Isaiah 61 [1–3] an Ebed-Jahweh Poem', *Z.A.W.* xlvii, 1929, pp. 284–8.

Caspari, W., *Lieder und Gottessprüche der Rückwanderer (Jesaja 40–50)* (*B.Z.A.W.* 65), Giessen, 1934.

'Der Herr ist König', *Christentum und Wissenschaft* iv, 1928, pp. 23ff.

'Erwarten Amos und Hosea den Messias?' *N.K.Z.* xli, 1930, pp. 812ff.

Charles, R. H., *The Greek Versions of the Testaments of the Twelve*

BIBLIOGRAPHY

Patriarchs, edited from nine MSS. together with the Variants of the Armenian and Slavonic Versions and some Hebrew Fragments, Oxford, 1908.

The Book of Enoch, translated, Oxford, 1893, ²1912.

See also List of Abbreviations under *A.P.O.T.*

Cheyne, T. K., *Introduction to the Book of Isaiah*, London, 1895.

Christensen, A., *Die Iranier* in *Kulturgeschichte des Alten Orients* III, 1, 2 (*Handbuch der klassischen Altertumswissenschaft*), Munich, 1933.

Les types du premier homme et du premier roi dans l'histoire légendaire des Iraniens (*Archives d'Études Orientales* 14), Stockholm, 1917.

Clemen, C., 'Die Himmelfahrt Moses', *A.P.A.T.* II, pp. 311ff.

Conteneau, G., *La civilisation d'Assur et de Babylone*, Paris, 1937.

Cook, S. A., *The Old Testament: a Reinterpretation*, Cambridge, 1936.

The Religion of Ancient Palestine in the Light of Archaeology, London, 1930.

Coppens, J., *Nieuw licht over de Ebed-Yahweh-Liedern*, Bruges, 1950.

La Prophétie de la 'Almah (*Analecta Lovaniensia Biblica et Orientalia.* Series II, Fasc. 35), Gembloux, 1952.

Cornill, C. H., 'Die neueste Litteratur über Jes 40–66', *T.R.* iii, 1900, pp. 409ff.

Cossmann, W., *Die Entwicklung des Gerichtsgedankens bei den alttestmentlichen Propheten* (*B.Z.A.W.* 29), Giessen, 1915.

Cowley, A. E., *The Samaritan Liturgy* I–II, Oxford, 1909.

Creed, J. M., 'The Heavenly Man', *J.T.S.* xxvi, 1925, pp. 113ff.

Crook, Margaret B., 'A Suggested Occasion for Isaiah 9, 2–7 and 11, 1–9', *J.B.L.* lxviii, 1949, pp. 213ff.

Dahl, N. A., *Das Volk Gottes: eine Untersuchung zum Kirchenbewusstsein des Urchristentums* (*S.N.V.A.O.* II, 1941), Oslo, 1941.

Dalman, G., *Der leidende und sterbende Messias der Synagoge im ersten nachchristlichen Jahrhundert*, Berlin, 1888.

Die Worte Jesu I, Leipzig, 1898, ²1930. Eng. Trans. of first edition, *The Words of Jesus Considered in the Light of Post-Biblical Jewish Writings and the Aramaic* (Authorised English Version by D. M. Kay), Edinburgh, 1902.

Arbeit und Sitte in Palästina VI, Gütersloh, 1939.

Danell, G. A., *Studies in the Name Israel in the Old Testament*, Uppsala, 1946.

Davies, W. D., 'The Jewish Background of the Teaching of Jesus: Apocalyptic and Pharisaism', *E.T.* lix, 1947/48, pp. 233ff.

Delitzsch, Franz, *Messianische Weissagungen*, Leipzig, 1890, ²1899.

Dietze, K., *Manasse. Eine chronologische Untersuchung zu Jesaja*, 9, 1–6, offprint from *Festschrift des Bremer Gymnasiums*, n.d., place of publication not indicated. Cited as *Manasse*.

Dillmann, A., *Das Buch Henoch, übersetzt und erklärt*, Leipzig, 1851.

Dix, G. H., 'The Messiah ben Joseph', *J.T.S.* xxvii, 1926, pp. 130ff.

BIBLIOGRAPHY

von Dobschütz, E., 'Zeit und Raum im Denken des Urchristentums', *J.B.L.* xli, 1922, pp. 212ff.

Dossin, G., 'Les archives épistolaires du palais de Mari', *Syria* xix, 1938, 105–26.

Driver, G. R., 'Some Hebrew Roots and Their Meanings', *J.T.S.* xxiii, 1922, pp. 69ff.

Driver, S. R. and Neubauer, A., *The Fifty-third Chapter of Isaiah according to the Jewish Interpreters* I. Texts edited by Ad. Neubauer, II. Translations by S. R. Driver and Ad. Neubauer, Oxford and London, 1876–7.

Drummond, S., *The Jewish Messiah. A Critical History of the Messianic Ideas of the Jews from the Rise of the Maccabees to the Closing of the Talmud*, London, 1877.

Duhm, B., *Die Theologie der Propheten als Grundlage für die innere Entwicklungsgeschichte der israelitischen Religion*, Bonn, 1875.

Das Buch Jesaia übersetzt und erklärt (H.K.A.T.), Göttingen, [2]1902.

Dupont-Sommer, A., 'Adam "Père du Monde" dans la Sagesse de Salomon', *R.H.R.* cxix, 1939, pp. 182ff.

Dürr, L., *Ursprung und Ausbau der israelitisch-jüdischen Heilandserwartung*, Berlin, 1925. Cited as *Ursprung und Ausbau*.

Psalm 110 im Lichte der neueren altorientalischen Forschung, Münster, 1929.

'Reichsgründungsfeiern im Alten Orient', *Theologie und Glaube* xx, 1928, pp. 305ff.

'Die Ascensio Domini in der alttestamentlichen Liturgie', *Liturgisches Leben* vii, 1935, pp. 128ff.

Ebeling, E., *Der akkadische Mythus vom Pestgotte Era (B.B.K. II, 1)*, Berlin, 1925.

Edsman, C. M., Review of Å. Ström, *Vetekornet* in *Kyrkohistorisk Årsskrift* xliv, 1944, pp. 356ff.

'Evangeliskt och katoliskt om Corpus Christi, kyrkan och den enskilda', *S.T.K.* xxi, 1945, pp. 272ff.

'Allmän religionshistoria', *S.T.K.* xxiii, 1947, pp. 327ff.

Eerdmans, B. D., 'De oorsprong van de uitdrukking "Zoon des Menschen" als evangelische Messiastitel', *T.T.* xxviii, 1894, pp. 153ff.

Eissfeldt, O., *Ba'al Zaphon, Zeus Kasios und der Durchzug der Israeliten durchs Meer*, Halle, 1932.

Der Gottesknecht bei Deuterojeasaja (Jes. 40–55) im Lichte der israelitischen Anschauung von Gemeinschaft und Individuum, Halle, 1933. Eng. Trans., 'The Ebed-Jahwe in Isaiah xl–lv in the Light of the Israelite Conceptions of the Community and the Individual, the Ideal and the Real', *E.T.* xliv, 1932/33, pp. 261ff.

El im ugaritischen Pantheon (B.S.G.W. xcviii, 4), Berlin, 1951.

'Jahwe als König', *Z.A.W.* xlvi, 1928, pp. 81ff.

BIBLIOGRAPHY

'Neue Forschungen zum Ebed-Jahwe Problem', *T.L.Z.* lxviii, 1943, cols. 273ff.

'Mythus und Sage in den Ras-Schamra-Texten', *Beiträge zur Arabistik, Semitistik und Islamwissenschaft* (R. Hartmann und H. Scheel), Leipzig, 1944, pp. 267ff.

'Ein gescheiterter Versuch der Wiedervereinigung Israels', *La Nouvelle Clio*, iii, 1951, pp. 110ff.

Eisler, R., 'Das akkadische šīlu = "Gebieter" in Gen. 49, 10', *M.G.W.J.* lxix, 1925, pp. 444ff.

Eitrem, S., 'Apoteose' (review of H. P. L'Orange, *Apotheosis in Ancient Portraiture*), *Samtiden*, 1948, pp. 72ff.

Elliger, K., *Deuterojesaja in seinem Verhältnis zu Tritojesaja* (*B.W.A.N.T.* IV, 11), Stuttgart, 1933.

Elmgren, H., *Philon av Alexandria med särskild hänsyn till hans eskatologiska föreställningar*, Stockholm, 1939.

Emmet, C. W., art. 'Messiah', *E.R.E.* VIII, pp. 570ff.

Engnell, I., *Studies in Divine Kingship in the Ancient Near East*, Uppsala, 1943. Cited as *Divine Kingship*.

Gamla testamentet. En traditionshistorisk inledning I, Stockholm, 1945. Cited as *Gamla testamentet* I.

'The Text II K from Ras Shamra', *Horae Soederblomianae* I, 1944, pp. 1ff.

'Till frågan om Ebed-Jahve-sångerna', *S.E.Å.* x, 1945, pp. 31ff. Eng. Trans. (revised), 'The 'Ebed Yahweh Songs and the Suffering Messiah in "Deutero-Isaiah"', *B.J.R.L.* xxxi, 1, 1948. (cited according to pagination of reprint).

'Profetia och tradition. Några synpunkter på ett gammaltestamentligt centralproblem', *S.E.Å.* xii, 1947, pp. 110ff.

Eppel, R., *Le piétisme juif dans les Testaments des douze Patriarches* (*E.H.Ph.R.* 22), Strasbourg, 1930.

Erman, A., *Die ägyptische Religion*², Berlin, 1909.

Die Literatur der Aegypter, Leipzig, 1923. Eng. Trans., *The Literature of the Ancient Egyptians: Poems, Narratives, and Manuals of Instruction, from the Third and Second Millenia B.C.* Translated into English by Aylward M. Blackman, London, 1927.

Euler, K. F., *Die Verkündigung vom leidenden Gottesknecht aus Jes. 53 in der griechischen Bibel* (*B.W.A.N.T.* IV, 14), Stuttgart, 1934.

'Königtum und Götterwelt in den altaramäischen Inschriften Nordsyriens. Eine Untersuchung zur Formsprache der altaramäischen Inschriften und des Alten Testaments', *Z.A.W.* lvi, 1938, pp. 272ff.

'Die Bedeutung von *spr* in der Sudschin-Inschrift', *Z.A.W.* lv, 1937, pp. 289ff.

Fahlgren, K. H., 'hā'almā. En undersökning till Jes. 7', *S.E.Å.* iv, 1939, pp. 13ff.

BIBLIOGRAPHY

Falkenstein, A., 'Eine Hymne auf Susin von Ur', *Die Welt des Orients* 2, Dec., 1947, pp. 43ff.

Farley, F. A., 'Jeremiah and "The Suffering Servant of Jehovah" in Deutero-Isaiah', *E.T.* xxxviii, 1926/27, pp. 521ff.

Fiebig, P., *Der Menschensohn. Jesu Selbstbezeichnung mit besonderer Berücksichtigung des aramäischen Sprachgebrauchs für "Mensch"*, Tübingen-Leipzig, 1901.

Fischer, J., *Isaias 40–55 und die Perikopen vom Gottesknecht* (= *Alttestamentliche Abhandlungen* vi, 4–5), Münster, 1916.

Wer ist der Ebed in den Perikopen Is. 42, 1–7; 49, 1–9a; 50, 4–9; 52, 13–53, 12? (= *Alttestamentliche Abhandlungen* vii, 5), Münster, 1922.

Flügel, G., *Mani, seine Lehre und seine Schriften*, Leipzig, 1862.

de Fraine, J., *L'aspect religieux de la royauté israélite. L'institution monarchique dans l'Ancien Testament et dans les textes mésopotamiens* (*Analecta Biblica* 3), Rome, 1954. Cited as *L'aspect religieux*.

Frankfort, H., *Kingship and the Gods. A Study of Ancient Near Eastern Religion as the Integration of Society and Nature*, Chicago, 1948. Cited as *Kingship*.

The Problem of Similarity in Ancient Near Eastern Religions, Oxford, 1951.

Frazer, J. G., *Lectures on the Early History of the Kingship*, London, 1905.

The Golden Bough: a Study in Magic and Religion I–XII, London, 1911–1915.

Folklore in the Old Testament I–III, London, 1918.

Fridrichsen, A., *Hagios-Qadoš* (*S.N.V.A.O.* II, 1916, No. 3), Christiania, 1916.

Friediger, M., *Laerebog i den jødiske Religion*, Copenhagen, 1922.

Gadd, C. J., *Ideas of Divine Rule in the Ancient East*, London, 1948.

von Gall, A., Βασιλεία τοῦ Θεοῦ. *Eine religionsgeschichtliche Studie zur vorkirklichen Eschatologie*, Heidelberg, 1926. Cited as *Basileia*.

Galling, K., *Die Erwählungstraditionen Israels* (*B.Z.A.W.* 48), Giessen, 1928.

Gemser, B., 'Der Stern aus Jacob (Num. 24, 17)', *Z.A.W.* xliii, 1925, pp. 301f.

van Gennep, A., *Les rites de passage*, Paris, 1909.

Gerleman, G., *Studies in the Septuagint I. Book of Job* (*L.U.Å.* I, 43, 2), Lund, 1946.

Gillet, L., *Communion in the Messiah. Studies in the Relationship between Judaism and Christianity*, London and Redhill, 1942.

Ginsberg, H. L., *The Legend of King Keret* (*B.A.S.O.R.* Supplementary Studies 2–3), New Haven, 1946.

Studies in Daniel, New York, 1948.

'The North Canaanite Myth of Anath and Aqhat', *B.A.S.O.R.* 97, Feb. 1945, pp. 3ff.; 98, April 1945, pp. 15ff.

'The Oldest Interpretation of the Suffering Servant', *V.T.* iii, 1953, pp. 400ff.

BIBLIOGRAPHY

Ginzberg, L., *Eine unbekannte jüdische Sekte* I, New York, 1922.
art. 'Adam Kadmon', *J.E.* I, pp. 181ff.

Götze, A., *Kleinasien* in *Kulturgeschichte des Alten Orients* III, 1 (*Handbuch der klassischen Altertumswissenschaft*), Munich, 1933.

Graham, W. C., *The Prophets and Israel's Culture*, Chicago, 1934.
'Isaiah's Part in the Syro-Ephraimitic Crisis', *A.J.S.L.L.* l, 1934, pp. 201ff.

Gressmann, H., *Der Ursprung der israelitisch-jüdischen Eschatologie* (*F.R.L.A.N.T.* 6), Göttingen, 1905. Cited as *Ursprung*.
Das Weihnachtsevangelium, Göttingen, 1914.
Der Messias (*F.R.L.A.N.T.* 43), Göttingen, 1929.
'Die literarische Analyse Deuterojesajas', *Z.A.W.* xxxiv, 1914, pp. 254ff.
'Babylonische Mysterien', *Z.A.W.* xlii, 1924, p. 156.
'Messias und Erlöser', *Geisteskultur* xxxiii, 1924, pp. 97ff.
See also List of Abbreviations under *A.O.T.B.*

Grønbech, V., 'Primitiv Religion', *Illustreret Religionshistorie*[2], pp. 11ff.

Gunkel, H., *Schöpfung und Chaos in Urzeit und Endzeit. Eine religionsgeschichtliche Untersuchung über Gen 1 und Ap Joh. 12*[2], Göttingen, 1922.
Genesis übersetzt und erklärt[4] (*H.K.A.T.*), Göttingen, 1917.
Ein Vorläufer Jesu, Berne, 1921.
Die Psalmen übersetzt und erklärt (*H.K.A.T.*), Gottingen, 1926.
Einleitung in die Psalmen. Die Gattungen der religiösen Lyrik Israels . . . zu ende geführt von Joachim Begrich (*H.K.A.T.*), Göttingen, 1933. Cited as *Einleitung*.
'Die Königspsalmen', *Preussische Jahrbücher* clviii, 1914, pp. 42ff.
Review of N. Messel, *Die Einheitlichkeit der jüdischen Eschatologie*, *N.T.T.* xvii, 1916, pp. 196ff.

Güterbock, H., 'Die historische Tradition und ihre literarische Gestaltung bei Babyloniern und Hethitern bis 1200', *Z.A.* (N.F.) viii, 1934, pp. 2ff.

Guttmann, M., art. 'Adam in Talmud und Midrasch', *E.J.* I, cols. 761ff.

Gyllenberg, R., *Herrens Tjänare* (reprinted from *Teologisk Tidskrift*), Borgå, 1923.
'Till julevangeliets exeges', *S.E.Å.* v, 1940, pp. 83ff.

Haldar, A., *Associations of Cult Prophets among the Ancient Semites*, Uppsala, 1945. Cited as *Associations*.
Studies in the Book of Nahum (*U.U.Å.* 1946: 7). Uppsala and Leipzig, 1946.
The Notion of the Desert in Sumero-Accadian and West-Semitic Religions (*U.U.Å.*, 1950: 3), Uppsala and Leipzig, 1950.

Haller, M., 'Die Kyros-Lieder Deuterojesajas', *Eucharisterion* I, pp. 261ff.

BIBLIOGRAPHY

Hammershaimb, E., *Amos fortolket*, Copenhagen, 1946.
'Immanueltegnet', *D.T.T.* viii, 1946, pp. 223ff. Eng. Trans., 'The Immanuel Sign', *St.Th.* III, ii, 1949/51, pp. 124ff.

Hebert, A. G., 'The Pattern of Messianic Hope,' *Church Quarterly Review* cxlii, 1946, pp. 1ff.

Hehn, J., 'Zum Problem des Geistes im alten Orient und im Alten Testament', *Z.A.W.* xliii, 1925, pp. 210ff.

Hempel, J., 'Vom irrenden Glauben', *Z.S.T.* vii, 1929, pp. 631ff.
'Beobachtungen an der "syrischen" Jesajarolle vom Toten Meer (DSIa)', *Z.D.M.G.* ci, 1951, pp. 138ff.
art. 'Salbung', *R.G.G.*[2] IV.

Henneke, E., *Neutestamentliche Apokryphen*, Tübingen and Leipzig, 1904.

Héring, J., *Le royaume de Dieu et sa venue d'après Jésus et Saint Paul* (*E.H.Ph.R.* 35), Paris, 1937.
'Messie juif et messie chrétien', *R.H.Ph.R.* xviii, 1938, pp. 419ff.

Herntrich, V., *Ezechielprobleme* (*B.Z.A.W.* 61), Giessen, 1932.

Hertzberg, H. W., 'Die Entwicklung des Begriffes mišpāṭ im A.T.', *Z.A.W.* xl, 1922, pp. 256ff.; xli, 1923, pp. 16ff.

Hilgenfeld, A., *Die jüdische Apokalyptik in ihrer geschichtlichen Entwickelung*, Jena, 1857.
'Der Menschensohn-Messias', *Z.W.T.* xxxv, 1892, pp. 445ff.

Hocart, A. M., *Kingship*, London, 1927.

Hoffmeyer, S., *Den apokryfiske Literaturs Stilling til Partidannelserne i den palaestinensiske Senjødedom*, Copenhagen, 1918.

Hollmann, G., *Welche Religion hatten die Juden als Jesus auftrat?* Tübingen, 1910.

Hölscher, G., *Die Profeten. Untersuchungen zur Religionsgeschichte Israels*, Leipzig, 1914.
Geschichte der israelitischen und jüdischen Religion, Giessen, 1922.
Hesekiel, der Dichter und das Buch (*B.Z.A.W.* 39), Giessen, 1924.
Die Ursprünge der jüdischen Eschatologie, Giessen, 1925.
'Die Entstehung des Buches Daniel', *T.S.K.* xcii, 1919, pp. 113ff.
'Zur Frage nach Alter und Herkunft der sogen. Damaskusschrift', *Z.N.W.* xxviii, 1929, pp. 21ff.
Review of H. Gressmann, *Der Messias*, *Deutsche Literaturzeitung* 13, IX, 1930, cols, 1729ff.

Hommel, F., 'The Apocalyptic Origin of the Expression "Son of Man"', *E.T.* xi, 1899/1900, pp. 341ff.

Honeyman, A. M., 'The Evidence for Regnal Names among the Hebrews', *J.B.L.* lxvii, 1948, pp. 13ff.

Hooke, S. H., (ed.) *Myth and Ritual. Essays on the Myth and Ritual of the Hebrews in Relation to the Culture Pattern of the Ancient East*, London, 1933.
(ed.) *The Labyrinth. Further Studies in the Relation between Myth and Ritual in the Ancient World*, London, 1935.

The Origins of Early Semitic Ritual, London, 1938.
'The Mixture of Cults in Relation to the History of Hebrew Religion', *J.M.E.O.S.* xvi, 1931, pp. 23ff.
Horodezky, S., art. 'Adam in der Kabbala', *E.J.* I, cols. 776ff.
art. 'Adam Ḳadmon', *E.J.* I, cols. 783ff.
Horst, F., *Nahum bis Maleachi* in Robinson-Horst, *Die Zwölf Kleinen Propheten* (*H.A.T.*), Tübingen, 1938.
Humbert, P., *La " Teroṵa": analyse d'un rite biblique*, Neuchâtel, 1946.
'La relation de Genèse 1 et du Psaume 104 avec la liturgie du Nouvel-An israëlite', *R.H.Ph.R.* xv, 1935, pp. 1ff.
Huntress, E., '"Son of God" in Jewish Writings prior to the Christian Era', *J.B.L.* liv, 1935, pp. 117ff.
Hvidberg, F. F., *Menigheden af den nye Pagt*, Copenhagen, 1928.
Graad og Latter i det Gamle Testamente: en Studie i kanaanaeisk-israelitisk Religion, Copenhagen, 1938.
Den israelitiske Religions Historie, Copenhagen, 1944.
Hylander, I., *Der literarische Samuel-Saul-Komplex (1 Sam. 1–15) traditionsgeschichtlich untersucht*, Uppsala and Leipzig, 1932.
Jahnow, H., *Das hebräische Leichenlied im Rahmen der Völkerdichtung* (*B.Z.A.W.* 36), Giessen, 1923.
James, E. O., *Christian Myth and Ritual*, London, 1933.
The Old Testament in the Light of Anthropology, London, 1935.
James, M. R., *The Apocryphal New Testament, being the Apocryphal Gospels, Acts, Epistles, and Apocalypses, with Other Narratives and Fragments, newly translated*, Oxford, 1924. Cited as *The Apocryphal New Testament*.
Jansen, H. L., *Die Henochgestalt. Eine vergleichende religionsgeschichtliche Untersuchung*, Oslo, 1939. Cited as *Die Henochgestalt*.
Jastrow, M., *Die Religion Babyloniens und Assyriens* I–II, Giessen, 1905–12.
Jaussen, A., *Coutumes des Arabes au pays de Moab*, Paris, 1908.
Jenni, E., *Das Wort ʿōlām im Alten Testament*, Berlin, 1953 (= *Z.A.W.* lxiv, 1952, pp. 197ff.; lxv, 1953, pp. 1ff.)
Jensen, P., *Assyrisch-babylonische Mythen und Epen* (*K.B.* VI, 1.) Berlin, 1900.
Jeremias, A., *Handbuch der altorientalischen Geisteskultur*, Leipzig, 1913, [2]1929. Cited as *Handbuch*.
Das Alte Testament im Lichte des Alten Orients, Leipzig, [3]1916, [4]1930. Eng. Trans., *The Old Testament in the Light of the Ancient East*.
Manual of Biblical Archaeology I–II, Translated from the Second German edition, Revised and Enlarged by the Author, by C. L. Beaumont, edited by C. H. W. Johns, London, 1911.
Jeremias, Christliebe, *Die Vergöttlichung der babylonisch-assyrischen Könige* (*A.O.* xix, 3/4), Leipzig, 1919.
Jeremias, J., 'Erlöser und Erlösung', *Deutsche Theologie* ii, 1929, pp. 106ff.

BIBLIOGRAPHY

'Zum Problem der Deutung von Jes. 53', *Aux sources de la tradition chrétienne* (Volume in honour of M. Goguel), Neuchâtel, 1950, pp. 113ff.

art. ἄνθρωπος, *T.W.B.N.T.* I, pp. 365ff.

art. Ἠλ(ε)ίας, *T.W.B.N.T.* II, pp. 930ff.

art. Μωυσῆς, *T.W.B.N.T.* IV, pp. 852ff.

Johansson, N., *Parakletoi: Vorstellungen von Fürsprechern für die Menschen vor Gott in der alttestamentlichen Religion, im Spätjudentum und Urchristentum*, Lund, 1940. Cited as *Parakletoi*.

Johnson, A. R., *The One and the Many in the Israelite Conception of God*, Cardiff, 1942.

The Cultic Prophet in Ancient Israel, Cardiff, 1944.

'The Rôle of the King in the Jerusalem Cultus', *The Labyrinth* (ed. S. H. Hooke,), pp. 113ff.

Jonas, H., *Gnosis und spätantiker Geist*. I: *Die mythologische Gnosis*, Göttingen, 1934.

Juotsi, Y., 'Der Menschensohn', *Theologia Fennica*, i–ii, Helsinki, 1939–40, pp. 45ff. (summary of the author's Finnish work, *Ihmisen Poika*, Helsinki, 1936.)

Kahle, P., *The Cairo Geniza*, London, 1947.

Kapelrud, A. S., *Baal in the Ras Shamra Texts*, Copenhagen, 1952.

'Jahves tronstigningsfest og funnene i Ras Sjamra', *N.T.T.* xli, 1940, pp. 38ff.

Kees, H., 'Kultlegende und Urgeschichte. Grundsätzliche Bemerkungen zum Horusmythus von Edfu', *N.G.W.G.* Phil. Hist. Kl., 1930, pp. 345ff.

Keller, C. A., *Das Wort OTH als "Offenbarungszeichen Gottes". Eine philologisch-theologische Begriffsuntersuchung zum Alten Testament*, Basel, 1946.

Kennett, R. H., *Old Testament Essays*, Cambridge, 1928.

Kessler, K., *Mani, Forschungen über die manichäische Religion* I, Berlin, 1889.

art. 'Mani, Manichäismus', *P.R.E.*[3] xii, pp. 193ff.

Kissane, E. J., *The Book of Isaiah* I–II, Dublin, 1943.

Kittel, G., art. 'Menschensohn', *R.G.G.*[2] III, cols. 2118ff.

Kittel, R., *Die hellenistische Mysterienreligion und das Alte Testament* (*B.W.A.N.T.* ii, 7), Stuttgart, 1924.

Gedanken und Gestalten in Israel, Leipzig, 1925. Eng. Trans., *Great Men and Movements in Israel*, New York, 1929.

Klausner, J., *Die messianischen Vorstellungen des jüdischen Volkes im Zeitalter der Tannaiten*, Cracow, 1903.

Klostermann, E., *Das Lukasevangelium* (*H.N.T.*), Tübingen, 1919, [2]1929.

Knudtzon, J., *Die El-Amarnatafeln* (*V.A.B.* II), Leipzig, 1915.

Koch, R., 'Der Gottesgeist und der Messias', *Biblica* xxvii, 1946, pp. 241ff.

BIBLIOGRAPHY

Kraeling, C. H., *Anthropos and Son of Man* (*Columbia University Oriental Studies* 25), New York, 1927.

Kraeling, E. G., 'The Real Religion of Ancient Israel', *J.B.L.* xlvii, 1928, pp. 133ff.

'The Immanuel Prophecy', *J.B.L.* l, 1931, pp. 277ff.

Kramer, S. N., *Sumerian Mythology*, Philadelphia, 1944.

'The Oldest Catalogue: a Sumerian List of Literary Compositions Compiled about 2000 B.C.', *B.A.S.O.R.* 88, Dec. 1942, pp. 10ff.

Kristensen, W. Brede, *Livet fra döden*, Oslo, 1926.

'De term "Zoon des Menschen"', *T.T.* xlv, 1911, pp. 1ff..

Kümmel, W. G., Review of Riesenfeld, *Jésus transfiguré, Symbolae Biblicae Upsalienses* 11, Supplement to *S.E.Å.* xiii, 1948, pp. 49ff.

Küppers, W., 'Das Messiasbild der spätjüdischen Apokalyptik', *Intern. Kirchl. Zeitschrift* xxiii, 1933, pp. 193ff.; xxiv, 1934, pp. 47ff.

Kugler, F. X., *Im Bannkreis Babels*, Münster, 1910.

Labat, R., *Le caractère religieux de la royauté-assyro-babylonienne* (Études d'Assyriologie II), Paris, 1939. Cited as *Royauté*.

Lagrange, M.-J., *Le messianisme chez les juifs*, Paris, 1909.

Le judaïsme avant Jésus-Christ, Paris, 1931.

Lang, A., *The Making of Religion*[3] I–II, London, 1898.

Langdon, S., The Sumero-Babylonian Origin of the Legend of Adam', *E.T.* xliii, 1931/32, p. 45.

'A Sumerian Hymn to Ishtar and the Deified Ishme-Dagan', *J.R.A.S.* 1931, pp. 367ff.; cf. ibid., pp. 421ff.

de Langhe, R., *Het Ugarietisch Keretgedicht, Legende, Mythus of Mysterienspel?*, Louvain, 1946.

Latte, K., art. 'Soter', *R.G.G.*[2] III, cols. 171ff.

Lauha, A., *Zaphon: Der Norden und die Nordvölker im Alten Testament* (*A.A.S.F.*, B. XLIX, 2), Helsinki, 1943.

'Några randanmärkningar till diskussionen om kungaideologin i Gamla Testamentet', *S.E.Å.* xii, 1947, pp. 183ff.

van der Leeuw, G., *Phänomenologie der Religion*, Tübingen, 1933. Eng. Trans., *Religion in Essence and Manifestation: A Study in Phenomenology* (by J. E. Turner), London, 1938.

de Leeuw, V., *De Koninklijke Verklaring van de Ebed-Jahweh-Zangen* (*Analecta Lovaniensia Biblica et Orientalia*. Series II, Fasc. 33), Gembloux, 1952.

Lehmann, E. (ed), *Illustreret Religionshistorie*[1], Copenhagen and Christiania, 1924 (see also, Pedersen, J.).

art. 'Manikeismen', in the above.

art. 'Die Perser', in Chantepie de la Saussaye, *Lehrbuch der Religionsgeschichte*[4] (edited by A. Bertholet and E. Lehmann, Tübingen, 1925) II, pp. 199ff.

Leivestad, R., *Guds straffende rettferdighet* (Supplement to *N.T.T.*), Oslo, 1946.

BIBLIOGRAPHY

Christ the Conqueror. Ideas of Conflict and Victory in the New Testament, London, 1954.

Lévy-Bruhl, L., *Les fonctions mentales dans les sociétés inférieures*, Paris, 1910. Eng. Trans. *How Natives Think* (by L. A. Clare), London, 1926.

Lidzbarski, M., *Handbuch der nordsemitischen Epigraphik* I–II, Weimar, 1898.

Das Johannesbuch der Mandäer, Giessen, 1915.

Mandäische Liturgien (*A.G.W.G.* (N.F.) xvii, 1), Göttingen, 1920.

Lietzmann, H., *Der Menschensohn. Ein Beitrag zur neutestamentlichen Theologie*, Freiburg im Breisgau, 1896.

Die Briefe des Apostels Paulus (*H.N.T.*), Tübingen, 1913.

Lindblom, J., *Senjudiskt fromhetslif enligt Salomos psaltare*, Uppsala, 1909.

Profetismen i Israel, Stockholm, 1934.

The Servant Songs in Deutero-Isaiah. A New Attempt to Solve an Old Problem (*L.U.Å.* (N.F.), Section 1, vol. xlvii, 5), Lund, 1951.

Linder, S., *Studier till Gamla Testamentets föreställningar om Anden*, Uppsala, The Hague, and Leipzig, 1926.

Lindhagen, C., *The Servant Motif in the Old Testament. A Preliminary Study to the 'Ebed-Yahweh Problem' in Deutero-Isaiah*, Uppsala, 1950.

'De tre sista decenniernas Ebed Jahve-forskning', *S.T.K.* viii, 1932, pp. 35off.

Lods, A., 'La divinisation du roi dans l'Orient méditerranéen et ses répercussions dans l'ancien Israël', *R.H.Ph.R.* x, 1930, pp. 209ff.

'Le rôle des oracles dans la nomination des rois, des prêtres et des magistrats chez les Israëlites, les Egyptiens et les Grecs', *Mémoires de l'Institut Français du Caire* lxvi (*Mélanges Maspero* I), 1934, pp. 91ff.

Lofthouse, W. F., 'Some Reflections on the Servant Songs', *J.T.S.* xlviii, 1947, pp. 169ff.

L'Orange, H. P., *Fra antikk til middelalder. Fra legeme til symbol*, Oslo, 1944.

Apotheosis in Ancient Portraiture (*I.S.K.F.*, B 44), Oslo, 1947.

Keiseren på himmeltronen, Bergen, 1949.

Manson, T. W., *The Teaching of Jesus*[2], Cambridge, 1943.

'Miscellanea Apocalyptica III: Test. XII Patr.: Levi viii', *J.T.S.* xlviii, 1947, pp. 59ff.

'The Son of Man in Daniel, Enoch and the Gospels', *B.J.R.L.* xxxii, 2, 1950.

Manson, W., *Jesus the Messiah. The Synoptic Tradition of the Revelation of God in Christ: with Special Reference to Form-Criticism*, London, 1943.

The Epistle to the Hebrews, an Historical and Theological Reconsideration, London, 1951.

Marmorstein, A., 'Zur Erklärung von Jes. 53', *Z.A.W.* xliv, 1926, pp. 26off.

Marti, K., *Geschichte der israelitischen Religion*[4], Strassburg, 1903.

BIBLIOGRAPHY

May, H. G., 'A Key to the Interpretation of Zechariah's Visions', *J.B.L.* lvii, 1938, pp. 173ff.

McCown, C. C., *The Ladder of Progress in Palestine*, New York and London, 1943.

'Jesus, Son of Man', *The Journal of Religion* xxviii, 1, 1948, pp. 1ff.

Meek, T. J., 'Primitive Monotheism and the Religion of Moses', *The Review of Religion* iv, 1940, pp. 286ff.

Meissner, B., *Babylonien und Assyrien* I–II, Heidelberg, 1920–5.

Merx, A., *Der Messias oder Ta'eb der Samaritaner* (*B.Z.A.W.* 17), Giessen, 1909.

Messel, N., *Die Einheitlichkeit der jüdischen Eschatologie* (*B.Z.A.W.* 30), Giessen, 1915.

Der Menschensohn in den Bilderreden des Henoch (*B.Z.A.W.* 35), Giessen 1922.

Ezechielfragen (*S.N.V.A.O.* II, 1945, No. 1), Oslo, 1945.

'Salomos Salmer. Oversattelse og indledning', *N.T.T.* viii, 1907, pp. 297ff.

'Messiasideen og den 17de Salomo-salme', *N.T.T.* x, 1909, pp. 1ff.

'Den angivelige jödiske laere om Messias's ukjente herkomst.' *N.T.T.* xxi, 1920, pp. 67ff.

See also under *G.T.M.M.M.* in the List of Abbreviations.

Meyer, E., *Die Israeliten und ihre Nachbarstämme*, Halle, 1906.

Ursprung und Anfänge des Christentums I–III, Stuttgart and Berlin, 1921–3.

'Die Mosesagen und die Lewiten', *Ber. Berl. Akad. Wiss.*, 1905, pp. 651ff.

Meyer, R., *Der Prophet aus Galiläa. Studien zum Jesusbild der drei ersten Evangelien*, Leipzig, 1940.

Michelet, S., *Fra Mose til profeterne*, Christiania, 1915.

See also under *G.T.M.M.M.* in the List of Abbreviations.

Moe, M., 'Det mythiske taenkesaet', *Samlede Skrifter* (= *I.S.K.F.* B, 1–6) II, pp. 265ff.

Montgomery, J. A., 'The Hebrew Divine Name and the Personal Pronoun Hū'', *J.B.L.* lxiii, 1944, pp. 161ff.

Moore, G. F., *Judaism in the First Centuries of the Christian Era the Age o, the Tannaim* I–III, Cambridge, Mass., 1927–30. Cited as *Judaism*.

Morgenstern, J., 'A Chapter in the History of the High-Priesthood', *A.J.S.L.L.* lv, 1938, pp. 1ff., 183ff.

'The Mythological Background of Psalm 82', *H.U.C.A.* xiv, 1939, pp. 29ff.

'Psalm 48', *H.U.C.A.* xvi, 1941, pp. 1ff.

'Deutero-Isaiah's Terminology for "Universal God"', *J.B.L.* lxii, 1943, pp. 269ff.

Mosbech, H., *Fortolkningen af Johannes's Aaabenbaring i Fortid og Nutid*, Copenhagen, 1934.

BIBLIOGRAPHY

Johannes's Aabenbaring, Copenhagen, 1943.

Sproglig Fortolkning til Johannes's Aabenbaring, Copenhagen, 1944.

Mowinckel, S., *Kongesalmerne i Det gamle Testamente*, Christiania, 1916.

Statholderen Nehemia. Studier til den jödiske menigheds historie og litteratur, Christiania, 1916.

Der Knecht Jahwäs (Supplement to *N.T.T.*), Christiania, 1921.

Psalmenstudien II. Das Thronbesteigungsfest Jahwäs und der Ursprung der Eschatologie (S.N.V.A.O. II, 1921, No. 6), Christiania, 1922. Cited as *Ps.St.* II.

Psalmenstudien III. Kultusprophetie und prophetische Psalmen (S.N.V.A.O. II, 1922, No. 1), Christiania, 1923. Cited as *Ps.St.* III.

Diktet om Ijöb og hans tre venner, Christiania, 1924.

Profeten Jesaja. En bibelstudiebok. Oslo, 1925.

Jesajadisiplene. Profetien fra Jesaja til Jeremia, Oslo, 1926.

Die Sternnamen im Alten Testament (Offprint from *N.T.T.*), Oslo, 1928.

The Two Sources of the Predeuteronomic Primeval History (JE) in Gen. 1–11 (A.N.V.A.O. II, 1937, No. 2), Oslo, 1937.

Det Gamle Testament som Guds ord, Oslo, 1938.

Die Erkenntnis Gottes bei den alttestamentlichen Propheten (Supplement to *N.T.T.*), Oslo, 1942. Cited as *Erkenntnis Gottes.*

Zur frage nach dokumentarischen Quellen in Josua 13–19 (A.N.V.A.O. II, 1946, No. 1), Oslo, 1946.

Prophecy and Tradition. The Prophetic Books in the Light of the Study of the Growth and History of the Tradition (A.N.V.A.O. II, 1946, No. 3), Oslo, 1946.

Religion og kultus, Oslo, 1950. German Trans., *Religion und Kultus*, Göttingen, 1953.

Offersang og sangoffer, Oslo, 1951.

'Om nebiisme og profeti', *N.T.T.* x, 1909, pp. 185ff., 330ff.

'Die vorderasiatischen Königs- und Fürsteninschriften, eine stilistische Studie', *Eucharisterion* I, pp. 278ff.

'Stilformer og motiver i profeten Jeremias diktning', *Edda* xxvi, 1926, pp. 223ff.

'"Die letzten Worte Davids" II Sam. 23, 1–7', *Z.A.W.* xlv, 1927, pp. 30ff.

'Tuhot und Säkwi. Eine Studie zur Astrologie des A.T.' *Act. Or.* viii, 1930, pp. 30ff.

'Wann wurde der Jahwäkultus in Jerusalem offiziell bildlos?', *Act. Or.* viii, 1930, pp. 257ff. (See also *R.H.Ph.R.* ix, 1929, pp. 197ff.

'Die Komposition des deuterojesajanischen Buches', *Z.A.W.* xlix, 1931, pp. 87ff., 242ff.

'Die Chronologie der israelitischen und jüdischen Könige', *Act. Or.* x, 1932, pp. 161ff.

'Die Vorstellungen des Spätjudentums vom Heiligen Geiste als Fürsprecher', *Z.N.W.* xxxii, 1933, pp. 37ff.

BIBLIOGRAPHY

'Hat es ein israelitisches Nationalepos gegeben?', *Z.A.W.* liii, 1935, pp. 130ff.

'Wer war Gilgameš?', *Act. Or.* xv, 1936, pp. 141ff. (also xvi, 1937, pp. 241ff.

Review of Eissfeldt's *Der Gottesknecht bei Deuterojesaja*, *A.f.O.* xi, 1936/37, pp. 81f.

'Neue Forschungen zu Deuterojesaja, Tritojesaja und dem Ebed-Jahwä-Problem', *Act. Or.* xvi, 1938, pp. 1ff.

Review of Hvidberg's *Graad og Latter i det Gamle Testamente*, *N.T.T.* xl, 1939, pp. 16ff.

'Henokskikkelsen i senjødisk apokalyptikk. Opposisjonsinnlegg ved doktordisputasen om Ludin Jansen's *Die Henochgestalt*', *N.T.T.* xli, 1940, pp. 26off.

'Immanuelprofetien i Jes. 7', *N.T.T.* xlii, 1941, pp. 129ff.

'Til uttrycket "Jahves tjener"', *N.T.T.* xliii, 1942, pp. 24ff.

'Oppkomsten av profetlitteraturen', *N.T.T.* xliii, 1942, pp. 65ff.

'Komposisjonen av Jesajaboken kap. 1–39', *N.T.T.* xliv, 1943, pp. 163ff.

Review of Engnell's *Studies in Divine Kingship in the Ancient Near East*, *N.T.T.* xlv, 1944.

'Henok og Menneskesønnen', *N.T.T.* xlv, 1944, pp. 57ff.

'Opphavet til den senjødiske forestilling om Menneskesønnen', *N.T.T.* xlv, 1944, pp. 189ff.

'Selvstendige enkeltutsagn eller større taleenheter hos Deutero-jesaja', *D.T.T.* ix, 1946, pp. 142ff.

'Natanforjettelsen 2 Sam. kap. 7', *S.E.Å.* xii, 1947, pp. 220ff.

'Urmensch und "Königsideologie"', *St.Th.* II, i, 1948/49, pp. 71ff.

'Den senjødiske salmediktning', *N.T.T.* li, 1950, pp. 1ff.

'The Hebrew Equivalent of Taxo in Ass. Mos. ix', *Supplements to Vetus Testamentum* (Copenhagen Congress Volume), Leiden, 1953, pp. 88ff.

art. 'Drama, religionsgeschichtlich', *R.G.G.*[2] I, cols. 2000ff.

See also under *G.T M.M.M.* in List of Abbreviations.

Müller, W. E., *Die Vorstellung vom Rest im Alten Testament*, Leipzig, 1939.

Munch, P. A., *The Expression bajjôm hāhū'* (*A.N.V.A.O.* II, 1936, No. 2), Oslo, 1936.

Munck, J., *Petrus und Paulus in der Johannesapokalypse* (*Det laerde Selskabs Skrifter*, Aarhus. Teologiske Skrifter 1), Copenhagen, 1950.

Mundle, W., 'Das religiöse Problem des IV Esrabuches', *Z.A.W.* xlvii, 1929, pp. 222ff.

Murmelstein, B., 'Adam, ein Beitrag zur Messiaslehre', *W.Z.K.M.* xxxv, 1928, pp. 242ff.; xxxvi, 1929, pp. 51ff.

Musil, A., *Arabia Petraea* I–III, Vienna, 1907–8.

Neiman, D., 'A Canaanite Cult Object in the Old Testament', *J.B.L.* lxvii, 1948, pp. 55ff.

BIBLIOGRAPHY

Nikolainen, A. T., *Der Auferstehungsglauben in der Bibel und ihrer Umwelt* (*A.A.S.F.* B, XLIX, 3), Helsinki, 1944.

Nöldeke, T., Review of Kessler's *Mani*, *Z.D.M.G.* xliii, 1889, pp. 535ff.

Norden, E., *Die Geburt des Kindes* (*Studien der Bibliothek Warburg*), Leipzig, 1924.

North, C. R., *The Suffering Servant in Deutero-Isaiah: an Historical and Critical Study*, London, 1948. Cited as *The Suffering Servant*.

'The Old Testament Estimate of the Monarchy', *A.J.S.L.L.* xlviii, 1931, pp. 1ff.

'The Religious Aspects of Hebrew Kingship', *Z.A.W.* l, 1932, pp. 8ff.

'The Suffering Servant: Current Scandinavian Discussions', *S.J.T.* iii, 1950, pp. 363ff.

Noth, M., *Die israelitischen Personennamen im Rahmen der gemeinsemitischen Namengebung* (*B.W.A.N.T.* III, 10), Stuttgart, 1928.

Das System der zwölf Stämme Israels (*B.W.A.N.T.* IV, 1), Stuttgart, 1930.

Überlieferungsgeschichtliche Studien. I Die sammelnden und bearbeitenden Geschichtswerke im Alten Testament (*Schriften der Königsberger Gelehrten Gesellschaft*, Geisteswissenschaftliche Klasse, XVIII, 2.), Halle, 1943.

'Die Historisierung des Mythus im Alten Testament', *Christentum und Wissenschaft* iv, 1928, pp. 265ff., 301ff.

Nötscher, F., 'Gen. 49, 10', *Z.A.W.* xlvii, 1929, pp. 323f.; xlviii, 1930, p. 80.

Nyberg, H. S., *Irans forntida religioner*, Stockholm, 1937.

Hebreisk grammatik, Uppsala, 1952.

'Forskningar rörande manikeismen', *S.T.K.* xi, 1935, pp. 27ff.

'Smärtornas man. En studie till Jes. 52, 13–53,12', *S.E.Å.* vii, 1942, pp. 5ff.

Nyström, S., *Beduinentum und Jahwismus. Eine soziologisch-religionsgeschichtliche Untersuchung zum Alten Testament.* Lund, 1946.

Odeberg, H., *3 Enoch or the Hebrew Book of Enoch, edited and translated with Introduction, Commentary and Critical Notes*, Cambridge, 1928.

'Föreställningarna om Metatron i äldre judisk mystik', *Kyrkohistorisk Årsskrift* xxvii, 1927, pp. 1ff.

art. '*Ενώχ*, *T.W.B.N.T.* II, pp. 553ff.

Oppenheim, L., 'Assyriological Gleanings IV', *B.A.S.O.R.* 107, Oct. 1947, pp. 7ff.

Otto, R., *The Idea of the Holy. An Inquiry into the Non-rational Factor in the Idea of the Divine and its Relation to the Rational* (Eng. Trans., by J. W. Harvey, of *Das Heilige*[9]), London, 1923.

The Kingdom of God and the Son of Man. A Study in the History of Religion (Eng. Trans., by F. V. Filson and B. L. Woolf, of *Reich Gottes und Menschensohn*), London, 1938.

BIBLIOGRAPHY

Pallis, S. A., *The Babylonian Akîtu Festival* (*Det Kgl. Danske Videns-kabernes Selskab*. Historisk-filologiske Meddelelser XII, 1.) Copenhagen, 1926.

Pap, L. I., *Das israelitische Neujahrsfest*, Kampen, 1933.

Parker, P., 'The Meaning of "Son of Man"', *J.B.L.* lx, 1941, pp. 151ff.

Parrot, A., *Archéologie mésopotamienne. I. Les étapes*, Paris, 1946.

Paton, L. B., 'The Problem of Suffering in the Pre-exilic Prophets', *J.B.L.* xlv, 1926, pp. 111ff.

Peake, A. S., *The Servant of Yahweh and Other Lectures*, Manchester, 1931.

Pedersen, J., *Der Eid bei den Semiten in seinem Verhältnis zu Verwandten Erscheinungen sowie die Stellung des Eides im Islam* (*Studien zur Geschichte und Kultur des islamischen Orients* 3), Strassburg, 1914.

Israel I–II. *Sjaeleliv og Samfundsliv*[2], Copenhagen, 1934. Eng. Trans. of 1st edition, *Israel Its Life and Culture* I–II, London and Copenhagen, 1926.

Israel III–IV. *Hellighed og Guddomelighed*, Copenhagen, 1934. Eng. Trans., *Israel Its Life and Culture* III–IV, London and Copenhagen, 1940.

(ed.) *Illustreret Religionshistorie*[2], Copenhagen, 1948.

'Zur Erklärung der eschatologischen Visionen Henochs', *Islamica* ii, pp. 416ff.

'Die Krt-Legende', *Berytus* v, 1941, pp. 63ff.

'Islam, dens Tilblivelse og Udvikling" *Illustreret Religionshistorie*[1] (see Lehmann, E.).

'Kanaʿanaeisk Religion', *Illustreret Religionshistorie*[2].

Pfleiderer, O., *Das Urchristentum*, Berlin, 1887.

Pidoux, G., *Le Dieu qui vient* (*Cahiers Théologiques* 17), Neuchatel, 1947.

Porteous, N. W., *The Kingship of God in Pre-exilic Hebrew Religion* (*Lectiones in Vetere Testamento et in rebus Judaicis* 3), London, 1938.

Prätorius, F., 'Bemerkungen zu den Gedichten vom Knechte Jahwes', *Z.A.W.* xxxvi, 1916, pp. 8ff.

Preisker, H., art. 'Antichrist', *R.G.G.*[2] I, cols., 375ff.

Procksch, O., *Genesis übersetzt und erklärt*[3] (*K.A.T.Sl.*), Leipzig, 1925.

'Der Menschensohn als Gottessohn', *Christentum und Wissenschaft* iii, 1927, pp. 425ff., 473ff.

'Fürst und Priester bei Hesekiel', *Z.A.W.* lviii, 1940–1, pp. 99ff.

Puukko, A. F., 'Är den gammaltestamentliga forskningen på villovägar?' *Teologisk Tidskrift* (Helsinki) lii, 1947.

von Rad, G., 'Erwägungen zu den Königspsalmen', *Z.A.W.* lvii, 1940–1, pp. 216ff.

'Das jüdäische Königsritual', *T.L.Z.* lxxii, 1947, cols. 211ff.

Ratschow, C. H., *Werden und Wirken, eine Untersuchung des Wortes hajah als Beitrag zur Wirklichkeitserfassung des Alten Testaments* (*B.Z.A.W.* 70), Berlin, 1941.

'Epikrise zum Psalm 47', *Z.A.W.* lii, 1935, pp. 171ff.

BIBLIOGRAPHY

Ravn, O., 'Sumerisk og babylonsk-assyrisk Religion', *Illustreret Religionshistorie*[2], pp. 131ff.

Reicke, B., 'Mik. 7 såsom "messiansk" text, med särskild hänsyn till Matt. 10: 35f. och Luk. 12:53', *S.E.Å.* xii, 1947, pp. 279ff.

Reitzenstein, R., *Poimandres*, Leipzig, 1904.

Das mandäische Buch des Herrn der Grösse und die Evangelienüberlieferung, Heidelberg, 1919.

Das iranische Erlösungsmysterium, Bonn, 1921.

and Schaeder, H. H., *Studien zum antiken Synkretismus aus Iran und Griechenland (Studien der Bibliothek Warburg)*, Leipzig, 1926. Cited as *Studien*.

Riesenfeld, H., *Jésus transfiguré*, Copenhagen, 1947.

The Resurrection in Ezekiel XXXVII and in the Dura-Europos Paintings (U.U.Å. 1948, 11), Uppsala and Leipzig, 1948.

Rignell, L. G., *Die Nachtgesichte des Sacharja. Eine exegetische Studie*, Lund, 1950.

Robinson, H. W., *The Cross of the Servant*, London, 1926.

'The Hebrew Conception of Corporate Personality', *Werden und Wesen des Alten Testaments (B.Z.A.W.* 66), Giessen, 1936, pp. 49ff.

Robinson, T. H., 'Hebrew Myths', *Myth and Ritual* (ed. S. H. Hooke), pp. 172ff.

Rosenthal, F., *Die aramaistische Forschung seit Theodor Nöldekes Veröffentlichungen*, Leiden, 1939.

Rost, L., *Israel bei den Propheten (B.W.A.N.T.* IV, 19), Stuttgart, 1937.

'Sinaibund und Davidsbund', *T.L.Z.* lxxii, 1947, cols. 129ff.

Rowley, H. H., *Darius the Mede and the Four World Empires in the Book of Daniel*, Cardiff, 1935.

The Relevance of Apocalyptic. A Study of Jewish and Christian Apocalypses from Daniel to Revelation[2], London and Redhill, 1947.

The Biblical Doctrine of Election, London, 1950.

The Servant of the Lord and Other Essays on the Old Testament, London, 1952.

The Zadokite Gragments and the Dead Sea Scrolls, Oxford, 1952.

'The Figure of "Taxo" in the Assumption of Moses', *J.B.L.* lxiv, 1945, pp. 141ff.

'The Book of Ezekiel in Modern Study', *B.J.R.L.* xxxvi, 1, 1953, pp. 146ff.

Rudolph, W., 'Aus der alttestamentlichen Forschung', *Monatsschrift für Pastoraltheologie*, 1924, pp. 162ff.

'Der exilische Messias. Ein Beitrag zur Ebed-Jahwe-Frage', *Z.A.W.* xliii, 1925, pp. 90ff.

'Die Ebed-Jahwe-Lieder als geschichtliche Wirklichkeit', *Z.A.W.* xlvi, 1928, pp. 156ff.

de la Saussaye, Chantepie, *Lehrbuch der Religionsgeschichte*[4] I–II (ed. A. Bertholet and E. Lehmann), Tübingen, 1925.

BIBLIOGRAPHY

Schaeder, H. H., *Urform und Fortbildung des manichäischen Systems* (*Vorträge der Bibliothek Warburg*), Leipzig, 1924–5.
art. 'Manichäismus', *R.G.G.*[2] IV.
See also Reitzenstein, H.

Scheftelowitz, J., 'Der göttliche Urmensch in der manichäischen Religion', *A.R.W.* xxviii, 1930, pp. 212ff.

Schiller-Szinessy, S. M., Letter cited by W. A. W(right) in a note on the Arzereth of 4 Esdras XIII 45, *Journal of Philology*, 1870, pp. 113ff.

Schlier, H., 'Zur Mandäerfrage', *T.R.* (N.F.) v, 1933, pp. 1ff., 69ff.

Schmidt, H., *Der Mythus vom wiederkehrenden König im Alten Testament*, Giessen, 1925.

Die Thronfahrt Jahwes am Fest der Jahreswende im alten Israel, Tübingen, 1927.

'Kerubenthron und Lade', *Eucharisterion* I, pp. 120ff.

Schmidt, N., 'Was bar nashah a Messianic Title?' *J.B.L.* xv, 1896, pp. 36ff.
art. 'Son of Man', *E.B.*, cols. 4705ff.

Schmidt, W., *Ursprung der Gottesidee* I, Münster, 1912, [2]1926.
Handbuch der vergleichenden Religionsgeschichte. Ursprung und Werden der Religion, Münster, 1930. Eng. Trans., *The Origin and Growth of Religion: Facts and Theories* (by H. J. Rose), London, 1931.

Schnabel, P., *Berossos und die babylonisch-hellenistische Literatur*, Leipzig and Berlin, 1923. Cited as *Berossos*.

Schniewind, J., *Das Evangelium nach Markus* (*Das Neue Testament deutsch*), Göttingen, 1937.

Schoeps, H. J., 'Symmachusstudien III', *Biblica* xxix, 1948, pp. 31ff.

Schofield, J. N., *The Religious Background of the Bible*, London, 1944.

Schou-Pedersen, V., *Bildrag til en analyse af de mandaeiske skrifter med henblik paa bestemmelsen af mandaeernes forhold til jødedom og kristendom*, Aarhus, 1940.

Schrenk, T., art. ἐκλεκτός *T.W.B.N.T.* IV, pp. 186ff.

Schroeder, O., 'Miscellen', *Z.A.W.* xxxiv, 1914, pp. 69ff.

Schubert-Christaller, E., *Der Gottesdienst der Synagoge*, Giessen, 1927.

Schürer, E., *Geschichte des jüdischen Volkes im Zeitalter Jesu Christi*[4] I–III, Leipzig, 1901–9. Cited as *Geschichte*[4].

Seidelin, P., 'Der Ebed-Jahwe und die Messiasgestalt im Jesajatargum', *Z.N.W.* xxxv, 1936, pp. 194ff.

Sellin, E., *Der alttestamentliche Prophetismus*, Leipzig, 1912.
Das Zwölfprophetenbuch (*K.A.T.Sl.*), Erlangen, 1922.
Mose und seine Bedeutung für die israelitisch-jüdische Religionsgeschichte, Leipzig and Erlangen, 1922.
'Tritojesaja, Deuterojesaja und das Gottesknechtproblem', *N.K.Z.* xli, 1930, pp. 73ff., 145ff.

BIBLIOGRAPHY

'Die Lösung des deuterojesajanischen Gottesknechtsrätsels', *Z.A.W.* lv, 1937, pp. 177ff.

'Zu dem Judaspruch im Jakobsegen Gen. 49, 9–12 und im Mosesegen Deut. 33, 7', *Z.A.W.* lix, 1944, pp. 57ff.

Serouya, H., *La Kabbale, ses origines, sa psychologie mystique, sa métaphysique*, Paris, 1947.

Silver, A. H., *A History of Messianic Speculations in Israel from the First to the Seventeenth Centuries*, New York, 1927.

Simchowitsch, J. N., art. 'Messianische Bewegungen', *J.L.* IV, cols. 131ff.

Sjöberg, E., *Gott und die Sünder im palästinischen Judentum nach dem Zeugnis der Tannaiten und der apokryphisch-pseudepigraphischen Literatur* (*B.W.A.N.T.* IV, 27), Stuttgart, 1939. Cited as *Gott und die Sünder*.

Der Menschensohn im äthiopischen Henochbuch (*Acta reg. societatis humaniorum litterarum Lundensis* XLI), Lund, 1946. Cited as *Der Menschensohn*,

'Känner 1. Henok och 4. Ezra tanken på den lidande Människosonen?' *S.E.Å.* v, 1940, pp. 163ff.

'Frågan om den lidande Människosonen i 1. Henok', *S.E.Å.* vii, 1942, pp. 141ff.

'Människosonen i judendom och urkristendom', 28:*e Svenksa Läroverksläraremöte i Stockholm*, 1946, pp. 254ff.

'De förexilska profeternas förkunnelse. Några synpunkter', *S.E.Å.* xiv, 1949, pp. 7ff.

'בן אדם und בר אנש im Hebräischen und Aramäischen', *Act. Or.* xxi, 1950, pp. 57ff., 91ff.

art. 'Jesus Kristus', *S.B.U.* I, cols. 1037ff.

Skemp, A. E., 'Immanuel and the Suffering Servant of Yahweh', *E.T.* xliv, 1932/3, pp. 94f.

Smend, R., *Lehrbuch der alttestamentlichen Religionsgeschichte*[2], Freiburg im Breisgau, 1899.

Smith, H., Ναζωραῖος κληθήσεται, *J.T.S.* xxviii, 1927, p. 60.

Smith, S., *Isaiah, Chapters XL–LV: Literary Criticism and History*, London, 1944.

Smith, W. R., *Lectures on the Religion of the Semites: The Fundamental Institutions*[3], with an Introduction and Additional Notes by Stanley A. Cook, London, 1927.

Snaith, N. H., *The Jewish New Year Festival, Its Origins and Development*, London, 1947.

'The Servant of the Lord in Deutero-Isaiah', *Studies in Old Testament Prophecy Presented to Professor T. H. Robinson* (ed. H. H. Rowley), Edinburgh, 1950.

Review of A. R. Johnson's *The One and the Many in the Israelite Conception of God*, *J.T.S.* xliv, 1943, pp. 81ff.

BIBLIOGRAPHY

Söderblom, N., *Das Werden des Gottesglaubens. Untersuchungen über die Anfängen der Religion*, Deutsche Bearbeitung herausgegeben von Rudolph Stube, Leipzig, 1916.

Stade, B., and Bertholet, A., *Biblische Theologie des Alten Testaments* I–II, Tübingen, 1905–11.

Staerk, W., Soter. *Die biblische Erlösererwartung als religionsgeschichtliches Problem. Eine biblisch-theologische Untersuchung. 1. Teil: Der biblische Christus* (*B.F.Ch.Th.* II, 31), Gütersloh, 1933. Cited as *Soter I*.
Die Erlösererwartung in den östlichen Religionen. Untersuchungen zu den Ausdrucksformen der biblischen Christologie (*Soter* 2), Stuttgart and Berlin, 1938. Cited as *Soter II*.
'Zum Ebed-Jahwe-Problem', *Z.A.W.* xliv, 1926, pp. 242ff.
'Zur Exegese von Jes. 53 im Diasporajudentum', *Z.N.W.* xxxv, 1936, p. 308.

Stamm, J. J., *Erlösen und Vergeben und im Alten Testament. Eine begriffsgeschichtliche Untersuchung*, Berne, 1940.
Das Leiden des Unschuldigen in Babylon und Israel, Zürich, 1946.
'Die kulturellen Leistungen der Sumerer', *T.Z.* ii, 1946, pp. 1ff.
'La prophétie d'Emmanuel', *R.T.Ph.* (N.S.) xxxii, 1944, pp. 97ff.

Stauffer, E., 'Die Messiasfrage im Judentum und Christentum', *Z.T.K.* (N.F.) xii, 1931, pp. 165ff.

Steindorff, G. and Seele, K. C., *When Egypt Ruled the East*, Chicago, 1942.

Stern, L., *Die Vorschriften der Thora welche Israel in der Zerstreuung zu beobachten hat. Ein Lehrbuch für Schule und Familie*, Frankfurt, 1929.

Stevenson, W. B., 'The Interpretation of Isaiah XLI 8–20 and LI 1–8', *Exp.*, 8th Series, vi, 1913, pp. 209ff.

Strack, H. L. and Billerbeck, P., *Kommentar zum Neuen Testament aus Talmud und Midrasch* I–IV, Munich, 1922–8. Cited as Strack-Billerbeck.

Streck, M., *Assurbanipal* I–III (*V.A.B.* VIII), Leipzig, 1916.

Ström, Å. V., *Vetekornet. Studier over individ och kollektiv i Nya Testamentet med särskild hänsyn till Johannesevangeliets teologi. Joh. 12: 20–33*, Uppsala, 1944. Cited as *Vetekornet*.

Stummer, F., 'Ein akkadisches Segensgebet für den König', *A.f.O.* iv, 1927, pp. 19ff.

Sverdrup, G., 'De höieste religiöse forestillinger hos primitive folk', *Nordisk Tidskrift*, 1935, pp. 18ff.

Taylor, V., *Jesus and His Sacrifice. A Study of the Passion-sayings in the Gospels*, London, 1937.

Thureau-Dangin, P., *Die sumerischen und akkadischen Königsinschriften* *V.A.B.* I), Leipzig, 1907.

Torrey, C. C., *Pseudo-Ezekiel and the Original Prophecy*, New Haven, 1930.
'"Taxo" in the Assumption of Moses', *J.B.L.* lxii, 1943, pp. 1ff.
'"Taxo" Once More', *J.B.L.* lxiv, 1945, pp. 395ff.

BIBLIOGRAPHY

'A Twice-buried Apocalypse', *Munera studiosa. Studies Presented to W. L. P. Hatch*, Cambridge, Mass., 1946, pp. 23ff.

'The Messiah Son of Ephraim', *J.B.L.* lxvi, 1947, pp. 253ff.

Toynbee, A. J., *A Study of History*. Abridgement of Volumes I–IV by D. C. Somervell, London, 1946.

Trever, J. C., 'A Palaeographic Study of the Jerusalem Scrolls', *B.A.S.O.R.* 113, Feb. 1949, pp. 6ff.

'Identification of the Aramaic Fourth Scroll from 'Ain Feshka', *B.A.S.O.R.* 115, Oct. 1949, pp. 8ff.

Troje, L., art. 'Urmensch', *R.G.G.*[2] V.

Ungnad, A., *Die Religion der Babylonier und Assyrer*, Jena, 1912.

Usener, H., 'Milch und Honig', *Rheinisches Museum für Philologie* (N.F.), lvii, pp. 177ff.

Violet, B., *Die Ezraapokalypse*, Leipzig, 1910.

Volz, P., *Das Neujahrsfest Jahwes*, Tübingen, 1912.

Die biblischen Altertümer, Stuttgart, 1914.

Der Prophet Jeremia übersetzt und erklärt (*K.A.T.Sl.*), Leipzig, 1922, [2]1928.

Jesaja II übersetzt und erklärt (*K.A.T.Sl.*), Leipzig, 1932.

Die Eschatologie der jüdischen Gemeinde im neutestamentlichen Zeitalter[2], Tübingen, 1934. Cited as *Eschatologie*[2].

'Jesaja 53', *Buddefestschrift*, pp. 180ff.

Vriezen, T. C., *Onderzoek naar de paradiesvorstelling bij de oude semietischen volken*, Wageningen, 1937.

Wagner, M., 'Der Menschensohn', *N.K.Z.* xxxvi, 1935, pp. 245ff.

Waterman, L., 'The Martyred Servant Motif of Is. 53', *J.B.L.* lvi, 1937, pp. 27ff.

Weber, F., *Jüdische Theologie auf Grund des Talmud und verwandter Schriften*[2] herausgegeben von Fr. Delitzsch und G. Schnedermann, Leipzig, 1897. Cited as *Jüd. Theol.*[2]

Weiss, J., *Das Urchristentum*, Göttingen, 1917, Eng. Trans., *The History of Primitive Christianity* I–II (ed. F. C. Grant), London 1937.

Wellhausen, J., *Reste arabischen Heidentums gesammelt und erläutert* (= *Skizzen und Vorarbeiten* III)[2], Berlin, 1897.

Skizzen und Vorarbeiten VI, Berlin, 1899.

Einleitung in die drei ersten Evangelien, Berlin, 1905, [2]1911.

Israelitische und jüdische Geschichte, Berlin, [6]1907, [7]1914.

Werner, M., *Die Entstehung des christlichen Dogmas, problemgeschichtlich dargestellt*, Berne and Leipzig, 1941.

Wernle, P., *Die Anfänge unserer Religion*[2], Tübingen and Leipzig, 1904.

Widengren, G., *Hochgottglaube im Alten Iran* (*U.U.Å.*, 1938: 6), Uppsala and Leipzig, 1938.

Psalm 110 och det sakrala kungadömet i Israel (*U.U.Å.*, 1941: 7, 1), Uppsala and Leipzig, 1941.

2K

BIBLIOGRAPHY

Religionens värld. Religionsfenomenologiska studier och översikter, Stockholm, 1945, [2]1953.

'Det sakrala kungadömet bland öst- och västsemiter', *R.o.B.* ii, 1943, pp. 49ff.

'Konungens vistelse i dödsriket. En studie till Psalm 88', *S.E.Å.* x, 1945, pp. 66ff.

'Till det sakrala kungadömets historia i Israel', *Horae Soederblomianiae* I (*Mélanges Johs. Pedersen*), iii, Stockholm, 1947.

Wiedemann, A., *Die Unterhaltungsliteratur der alten Aegypter* (*A.O.* iii, 4), Leipzig, 1902.

Wiener, M., art. 'Messias', *J.L.* IV, cols. 134ff.

Winckler, H., *Geschichte Israels in Einzeldarstellungen*, Leipzig, 1895.

Himmels- und Weltenbild der Babylonier (*A.O.* iii, 2/3), Leipzig, 1903.

Altorientalische Forschungen III, Leipzig, 1905.

See also under *K.A.T.*[3] in List of Abbreviations.

Wischnitzer, R., *The Messianic Theme in the Paintings of the Dura Synagogue*, Chicago, 1948.

Review of E. L. Sukenik's *The Synagogue of Dura-Europos and Its Frescoes*, *J.B.L.* lxvi, 1947, pp. 482ff.

Witzel, M., *Tammuz-Liturgien und Verwandtes*, Rome, 1935.

Wolff, H. W., *Jesaja 53 im Urchristentum. Die Geschichte der Prophetie "Siehe es siegt mein Knecht" bis zu Justin*, Bethel, 1942, [2]Berlin, 1950.

'Herrschaft Jahwes und Messiasgestalt im Alten Testament', *Z.A.W.* liv, 1936, pp. 168ff.

Young, E. J., 'Of whom Speaketh the Prophet This?', *Westminster Theological Journal* xi, 1948/49, pp. 133ff.

'The Immanuel Prophecy Isaiah 7: 14–16', *Westminster Theological Journal xv*, 1952/53, pp. 97–124; xvi, 1953/54, pp. 23–50.

Ysander, T., *Studien zum be'štschen Hasidismus* (*U.U.Å.* 1933, Theologie 2), Uppsala and Leipzig, 1933.

Zimmern, H., *Zum babylonischen Neujahrsfest* I–II (*B.S.G.W.* lviii, 3; lxx, 8), Leipzig, 1906 and 1918.

Zum Streit um die "Christusmythe", Berlin, 1910.

Die Vergöttlichung des Königs Lipit-Ištars (*B.S.G.W.* lxviii, 5), Leipzig, 1916.

'Lebensbrot und Lebenswasser im Babylonischen und in der Bibel', *A.R.W.* ii, 1899, pp. 165ff.

'Babylonische Vorstufen der vorderasiatischen Mysterienreligionen', *Z.D.M.G.* lxxvi, 1932, pp. 36ff.

See also under *K.A.T.*[3] in the List of Abbreviations.

I Reference Index

(a) OLD TESTAMENT

REFERENCE INDEX

REFERENCE INDEX

REFERENCE INDEX

REFERENCE INDEX

(c) NEW TESTAMENT

REFERENCE INDEX

REFERENCE INDEX

(d) RABBINIC PASSAGES

II Index of Authors

INDEX OF AUTHORS

III General Index

(See also Table of Contents)

Aaron, Messiah from, 289, 292, 315
Abimelech, 59
Abodat hak-kodesh, 335
Abraham, 163, 202, 216, 328, 371
absolution, 41, 221
Accadian, 13, 48, 352, 424
  cultus, 458
Achmim, 356
Adad, 46
Adakas, 428
Adam, 320, 337, 346, 369, 382, 391, 400,
  407, 415, 420, 423f., 426ff., 433, 436,
  440
  the second, 372, 426
Adamanus, 427
Adamus, 427
Adapa, 422, 424
Adonis, 52, 236f.
Adonis gardens, 82, 457
adoption, 37, 78, 162, 294, 369
aeons: see 'ages'
Aesir, 423
Africa, 31
ages, doctrine of, 127, 130, 144, 263ff.,
  271ff., 277ff., 295, 321, 324, 326, 340,
  347, 359, 416, 419, 421, 430, 432
Agur, 171
Ahab, 60
Ahasuerus, 220
Ahaz, 61, 72, 110ff.
Ahikar, 432
Ahura Mazda, 368
'Ain Feshkha: see 'Dead Sea Scrolls'
Akiba, 285, 313, 352
Aleph, 440
Alexander, 150
Alexandria, 185
Aleyan-Baal, 52, 54, 105, 236f.
allegory, 465f.
Amalek, 13
Amarna Letters, 5, 48, 109
Amesha Spentas, 432
Ammon, 13
Amos, 18, 130, 132, 134, 458
Anani, 335, 357, 390
Anath, 53, 114f., 185
Anathyahu, 115
ancestor, 31f., 45, 59, 69f., 215ff.
  deified, 45, 75, 86

ancestor worship, 51, 54
Ancient of Days, 313, 349, 352, 389
angel, of God, Yahweh, 95, 298
angels, 77, 122, 264, 272f., 321, 353, 364,
  371ff., 387, 393ff., 407f., 410, 435,
  438f., 441, 448
anointing, 4ff., 63ff., 74, 78, 89, 95, 96f.,
  101
Anosh, 426f.
Anthropos, 422, 424ff.
Antichrist, 272f., 313
Antiochus IV, 350f.
Anu, 35
apocalyptic, 265ff., 282, 295, 320, 325f.,
  335, 338, 342, 345, 352ff., 361, 364,
  376, 383, 385ff., 388, 390f., 393ff.,
  402f., 410, 411, 415ff., 434, 436ff.
Aram: see 'Syria'
Aramaic, Aramean, 13, 61, 92, 117, 161,
  346ff., 364
Aristobulus, 468
ark, 26, 82ff., 86, 144
Armilus, 290, 313, 326
Asa, 88
Ashur (city), 42
Ashur (god), 38, 42, 94
Ashurbanipal, 35f., 46
Ashurnasirpal, 62
Asia Minor, 23, 51
Assyria, Assyrian(s), 5, 23, 34, 39, 41f.,
  51, 62, 70, 75, 83, 93f., 110, 115, 119,
  127, 130f., 136., 176, 266, 458
atonement, 205f., 209ff., 232, 234ff.,
  242ff., 249, 319, 327ff., 410ff., 455
  Day of, 224
  rites of, 39, 84, 209f., 221ff.
Atum, 31
Augustus, 164
Azazel, 395

Baal, 53f., 62, 64, 103, 108, 112, 457
Baba, 35
Babylon, Babylonia, Babylonian(s), 4,
  10, 14, 23ff., 34ff., 52, 54ff., 61, 67,
  74, 76, 78, 81f., 86, 88, 93f., 112, 127,
  130f., 135f., 139ff., 143, 148, 150f.,
  160f., 164, 178, 221ff., 230, 233, 236f.,
  243, 262, 264, 276, 313, 350, 422ff.,
  432f., 438, 451, 453, 454f.

GENERAL INDEX

521

GENERAL INDEX